THE ENGLISH
RELIGIOUS LYRIC
IN THE
MIDDLE AGES

The author Rosemary Woolf is Fellow of Somerville College, Oxford, and Tutor in English Language and Medieval Literature

THE ENGLISH
RELIGIOUS LYRIC
IN THE
MIDDLE AGES

Rosemary Woolf

OXFORD
AT THE CLARENDON PRESS
1968

Oxford University Press, Ely House, London W. 1

GLASGOW NEW YORK TORONTO MELBOURNE WELLINGTON
CAPE TOWN SALISBURY IBADAN NAIROBI LUSAKA ADDIS ABABA
BOMBAY CALCUTTA MADRAS KARACHI LAHORE DACCA
KUALA LUMPUR HONG KONG TOKYO

PRINTED IN GREAT BRITAIN

Preface

IT has become customary to divide the English lyrics of the Middle Ages into three groups, according to their origin in the thirteenth, fourteenth, or fifteenth century. In terms of style and content, however, only one dividing line is discernible: it occurs in the last few decades of the fourteenth century. The term 'dividing line' may be misleading. Rather than a line there is a divide of forty or fifty years: lyrics written on either side of this divide are clearly distinguishable in style. But in the divide itself lyrics, in varying proportions, repeat or recall the old style or show the beginnings of the new.

In the chapter headings of this book I have for brevity's sake described the earlier group of lyrics as belonging to the thirteenth and fourteenth centuries and the later group to the fifteenth. But many lyrics cannot be dated exactly, and, even when they can, I have disposed them between the parts according to style, not date. Therefore, whilst many of the lyrics in the large late fourteenth-century collections, such as John of Grimestone's preaching-book and the Vernon Manuscript, are discussed in the first part of the book, some are reserved to the second. By a similar licence a few lyrics composed in the early sixteenth century are included under the fifteenth century.

For quotations I have referred to the best and most readily available editions, occasionally emending or suggesting an emendation when a reading was so corrupt that the sense of the passage was lost. When ever practicable I have compared the texts of the quotations with the manuscripts, and as a result some mistakes have been corrected: they were usually in spelling, only very rarely did they affect the sense. I have throughout normalized the spellings *u*, *v*, and *w*; where editors had retained manuscript abbreviations, I have expanded them; and where they had retained medieval punctuation, I have modernized it.

In the manuscripts the lyrics are not given titles. Modern editors either follow the manuscripts in this or invent titles, but these are usually insufficiently distinctive or are in other ways inadequate. The lyrics in this work are therefore referred to by their first line, except that in the few instances where they have already become known by their refrain (e.g. *Quia amore langueo* or 'Wofully araid'), this form of title is continued.

The chief debt of any writer on the medieval English lyric must be to the work of the late Carleton Brown and Professor R. H. Robbins.

The Index of Middle English Verse laid the foundations for this study. Its one deficiency for the student of literary history, namely that it ended abruptly at 1500, has recently been corrected by the *Supplement to the Index of Middle English Verse*: unfortunately this work appeared too late for me to do more than include occasional footnote and index references to it.

I am very grateful to the librarians at the following who allowed me to study the manuscripts in their collections: Balliol College, Oxford; Emmanuel College, Cambridge; Lambeth Palace Library; the Pepys Library; Magdalen College, Cambridge; St. John's College, Cambridge; and Trinity College, Cambridge. I would also like to thank the librarians of the National Library of Scotland and the National Library of Wales for providing me with photostats and microfilms; and most especially I am indebted to the libraries with the main collections of manuscripts containing lyrics, the Bodleian, the British Museum, and Cambridge University. The Library of the Warburg Institute holds books relevant to this study that are not to be found anywhere else in England: it has been of great benefit to me to have been allowed to work there.

I am very grateful to the Trustees of the British Museum and to the Curators of the Bodleian Library for photographs of manuscript illuminations, and for permission to use them as illustrations in this work, and to the Victoria and Albert Museum for permission to print the poem here appearing on pp. 410–11. I am also grateful to the Editor of the *Review of English Studies* for permission to use in Chapter II material that first appeared in an article in his journal.

To friends and colleagues I owe very considerable debts: I have benefited from Professor E. J. Dobson's comments on the editorial handling of the texts of Middle English lyrics; Mrs. Clunies Ross checked footnote references and quotations in several chapters of this work; Miss Labowsky revised and amended my translations from the Latin; Professor Klibansky helped me over some problems of presentation of references; Miss Trickett read and commented upon a first draft of the work; and in the early stages of the work I profited from discussion of general issues with Miss Lucy Brown; Professor J. A. W. Bennett and Professor Helen Gardner gave me very helpful and valuable advice about the organization of the material. To all these, to others who gave me information or help more passingly, and to those from whom I have learned in a more general way I am deeply grateful.

Contents

INDEXES

List of Plates

Abbreviations

A.H.	*Analecta hymnica*, ed. G. M. Dreves and C. Blume (Leipzig, 1886–1922).
Archiv	*Archiv für das Studium der neueren Sprachen und Literatur.*
A.V.	Authorized Version.
Brown XIII	*English Lyrics of the Thirteenth Century*, ed. Carleton Brown (Oxford, 1950).
Brown XIV	*Religious Lyrics of the Fourteenth Century*, ed. Carleton Brown, 2nd edn. revised by G. V. Smithers (Oxford, 1957).
Brown XV	*Religious Lyrics of the Fifteenth Century*, ed. Carleton Brown (Oxford, 1939).
C.U.L.	Cambridge University Library.
Carols	*The Early English Carols*, ed. R. L. Greene (Oxford, 1935).
E.E.T.S.	Early English Text Society.
E.S.	Extra Series.
Index	Carleton Brown and R. H. Robbins, *The Index of Middle English Verse* (New York, 1943).
J.E.G.Ph.	*Journal of English and Germanic Philology.*
M.E.D.	*Middle English Dictionary.*
M.L.R.	*Modern Language Review.*
M.P.	*Modern Philology.*
O.E.D.	*Old English Dictionary.*
P.G.	*Patrologiae cursus completus*, series graeca, ed. J.-P. Migne.
P.L.	*Patrologiae cursus completus*, series latina, ed. J.-P. Migne.
P.M.L.A.	*Publications of the Modern Language Association of America.*
R.E.S.	*Review of English Studies.*
R.V.	Revised Version
S.A.T.F.	Société des anciens textes français.
Sonet	Jean Sonet, *Répertoire d'incipits de prières en ancien français* (Geneva, 1956).
S.T.C.	*Short Title Catalogue of English Books, 1475–1640*, ed. A. W. Pollard and G. R. Redgrave (London, 1926).
S.T.S.	Scottish Text Society.
Suppl.	R. H. Robbins and John Cutler, *Supplement to the Index of Middle English Verse* (Lexington, 1965).
Walther	Hans Walther, *Initia carminum ac versuum Medii Aevi posterioris Latinorum* (Göttingen, 1959).
Warburg Journal	*Journal of the Warburg and Courtauld Institutes.*

I

Introduction

AMONG the commonest and most attractive forms in medieval English literature are the short, religious, meditative poems. These poems have by recent convention been described as lyrics, though the term 'lyric' was not known to their authors: the manuscripts in a random way refer to them as meditations, treatises, or prayers. The classifying of medieval poetry according to classical genres, though often convenient, can be misleading. With these poems it is dangerous, for they possess very few of the qualities that the term 'lyric' may lead the reader to expect. In English criticism the word 'lyric' has descended from the sixteenth century, gathering associations on its way.[1] It now suggests a poem short, delightful, and melodious, and with a sweetness and light-heartedness that distinguish it from more serious and reflective poems. This description does not fit the medieval religious lyrics. Many of these are long, few were set to music, and all of them are devotionally and didactically serious.

The explanation of this lack of fitness is not the simple one that these generalizations apply to love lyrics only, for the religious lyric is not usually an autonomous genre. Like other forms of religious literature, it is normally an offshoot of a well-established secular form, which it adapts and exploits for its own purposes. Medieval French literature provides a clear illustration of this kind of development. In twelfth-century France, as is well known, there developed a flourishing tradition

---

[1] The term lyric was first used in England by the Elizabethan critics. Puttenham defined a lyric poet as one who wrote 'songs or ballads of pleasure, to be song with the voice, and to the harpe' or other musical instruments ('Of Poets and Poesie', *Elizabethan Critical Essays*, ed. G. Gregory Smith, Oxford, 1937, vol. ii, 26). Puttenham cites Horace and Catullus as examples. Francis Meres in *Palladis Tamia* quotes Spenser, Daniel, and Drayton as examples of English lyric poets (Smith, op. cit. 319). The lyric was thus recognized as a genre through the authority of classical literature, and was applied to English poetry through imitation. In later usage musical accompaniment was no longer considered essential to the form though its influence remained in a stress on melodiousness. The illustrative quotations in the *O.E.D.* (s.v. lyric) show that by the nineteenth century the word had acquired fresh associations, e.g. Ruskin's description, 'Lyric Poetry is the expression by the poet of his own feelings'. As will be seen (pp. 6–9), the latter definition is perhaps even more insidiously misleading when applied to the Middle English religious lyric than is the emphasis on musical qualities.

of secular lyric: the poems were short, elegant, designed for singing, and expressed personal, or feignedly personal, adoration of a mistress. In imitation of these, a body of poems was composed addressed to the Virgin, in similar metres and style. Singing contests were held for poets who wrote in honour of the Virgin, just as for poets who praised their mistresses. Therefore in the discussion of French religious poetry the qualities of secular lyric are pressingly relevant.

The best qualities of the Middle English religious lyric, however, derive from the fact that it did not arise from this kind of literary-historical situation. For until the end of the fourteenth century there was no substantial body of love poetry in England that had the prestige of being the literature of the Court, and could dominate the religious lyric in both its inception and development. The reason why love poetry was sparse was that English was a depressed vernacular, regarded as inferior not only to Latin, as were all vernaculars, but also to French, which was the language of the Court and of many of the aristocracy.[1] Lacking a suitable social environment a courtly English lyric could not flourish, and the religious lyric by this good fortune was able to develop untrammelled by the conventions and style of a secular form. After the strong emergence of secular love poetry at the end of the fourteenth century the English religious lyric no longer had this complete freedom. In the fifteenth century the influence of the secular lyric can be seen in the sudden copiousness of poems to the Virgin (they had been comparatively rare before), and here and there in the diction and rhetorical forms of poetry on the Passion and on death. But by this time the genre of the meditative poem was so well established that it could not be radically changed by the love lyrics that began to exist side by side with it.

The English religious lyric did not spring from the intention of putting secular conventions to the service of religion: it grew directly and unself-consciously from a Latin devotional movement, the authors using the vocabulary and verse-forms conveniently at hand. With the exception of a small group, chiefly the Harley Lyrics, they have no characteristic metres.[2] They share most of their verse-forms, couplets, quatrains, tail-rhyme stanzas, and rhyme royal, with the rest of Middle English poetry, with the mystery plays, the romances, the *Cursor mundi*, *Troilus and Criseyde*, Lydgate's *Fall of Princes*, etc. Whereas in France the distinctive lyric form, the ballade, was used by writers such as Deschamps for religious subject-matter, in England it was used by Chaucer and his

[1] In general, it is not easy to make rigid classifications of speakers of English and speakers of Anglo-Norman. For discussions of the subject see D. Legge, 'Anglo-Norman and the Historian', *History*, xxvi (1941), 163–75, and R. M. Wilson, 'English and French in England, 1100–1300', ibid. xxviii (1943), 37–60.

[2] H. J. Chaytor, *The Troubadours and England* (Cambridge, 1923), 98–135.

successors solely for secular themes. In terms of metrical structure there is therefore no difference between the lyric and narrative or dramatic works.

It follows from this that the Middle English religious lyric is not distinctively melodious. Though some of the poems have metrical grace, this is an accidental virtue and not one essential to the form.[1] Indeed, amongst the thirteenth- and fourteenth-century lyrics there occur many short and slightly clumsy verses, for which the metrical form seems to have been chosen, not to enhance the meaning by shapeliness and aural beauty, but simply because verse would make the content easier to memorize than would prose. Other poems, particularly of the later period, show greater technical accomplishment, but the metrical delicacy and lightness of the lyric genre is a beauty at which they rarely aim.

It is also clear from the lyric metres that the poems were not sung. There are a few exceptions: a small group of poems at the end of the thirteenth century were given polyphonic settings,[2] and in the early sixteenth century some slightly earlier lyrics were set to music and included in the Tudor song books.[3] The Harley Lyrics are not accompanied by music in the manuscript, but they are in stanza forms that in France were set to music, and therefore the possibility remains that they were intended to be sung. But these, about thirty poems in all, form only a minute proportion of the body of religious lyrics, and in various fashions they represent byways in the history of the form.[4]

Like so much medieval literature the religious lyrics have to be defined in terms of content not of form. When approached this way the lyrics can immediately be recognized as meditative poems, for their sources are invariably Latin works that are overtly and unmistakably meditations. The appropriateness of this description can also be seen in the fact that it excludes only a very small number of the poems normally called lyrics, and all of those excluded are poetically inconsiderable. They are largely versifications of the Pater Noster and Creed, confessions of sins,[5] Levation prayers, and other ejaculatory and simple, extra-liturgical

---

[1] There are difficulties in the way of measuring metrical skill, in particular those connected with pronunciation and bad texts. Textual variants indicate that between one manuscript text and another there has intervened transmission through one or more faulty memories. Lines that now seem rhythmically lame may show only the impoverishment that a poem often undergoes when transmitted orally. Cf. Notes on the Texts by E. J. Dobson accompanying a record of some Middle English lyrics [Argo, (Z) RG (5) 443].

[2] F. Ll. Harrison, *Music in Medieval Britain* (London, 1958), 153–5.

[3] John Stevens, *Music and Poetry in the Early Tudor Court* (London, 1961).

[4] The carols are not included in these generalizations; for a discussion of them see Appendix D.

[5] See Appendix B, p. 337.

prayers:[1] meditative poems may be in the form of a prayer, but the prayer is then founded in the meditation.

The term 'meditative poem', however, requires circumscription, for otherwise it would cover works, such as *The Pricke of Conscience*[2] or *A Stanzaic Life of Christ*,[3] which are shown by common sense to be different from the lyrics. The distinction between works of this kind and the meditative lyrics lies in the structure, for the lyrics are never purely narrative; though in the later lyrics there is often a sequence of action, there is always a single and static situation, consisting of the relationship between two people. A few lyrics are dramatic: Christ and Mary speak to one another, or the Body argues with the Soul. But more often they are, as it were, one-half of a dialogue, in which the meditator addresses Christ or Christ addresses the meditator. Sometimes, and less effectively, the speaker is a preacher who personally exhorts the meditator. The last category may seem to come close to a treatise or homily. But the speaker of this kind of lyric never gives the impression of being alone with his material or of addressing a public audience. There is no dispassionate arrangement of material, and displays of sermon rhetoric are rare.

In a preliminary discussion of medieval meditative lyrics it is helpful to compare them with the English meditative poetry of the seventeenth century.[4] There are sufficient basic similarities between the two to make this comparison relevant and, at least initially, fruitful. Not only do the medieval and Metaphysical lyrics have the same subject-matter and make use of the same liturgical or traditional commonplaces, but also they both have their roots in the meditative theories and treatises of their respective periods, in the seventeenth century in the *Spiritual Exercises* of St. Ignatius, and in the Middle Ages in the many Latin meditations that were the ancestors of the *Spiritual Exercises*. Though the comparison will reveal more differences than similarities, yet, on account of the fundamental likeness, the differences have an intelligible relationship and can therefore prove as illuminating as the similarities.

An immediately obvious and apparently very simple difference between the two is that we know the names of the Metaphysical poets, whereas for the medieval writers we know only what kinds of men they were by profession.[5] At first sight this may seem a chance and superficial

---

[1] For an account of these see R. H. Robbins, 'Popular Prayers in Middle English Verse', *M.P.* xxxvi (1939), 337–50, and 'Private Prayers in Middle English Verse', *Studies in Philology*, xxxvi (1939), 466–75.

[2] *The Pricke of Conscience*, ed. Richard Morris, Philological Society, 1863.

[3] E.E.T.S. 166.

[4] English seventeenth-century meditative poetry is discussed by Louis Martz, *The Poetry of Meditation* (New Haven, 1954). Cf. also *The Meditative Poem*, ed. Martz (New York, 1963).

[5] A more detailed account is given in Appendix B.

distinction, one that amounts to no more than that we are better in-
formed about the later period than about the earlier. For the seventeenth
century, however, this information is important because the individuality
of the poets is reflected in the style of their work. If the religious poems
of Donne, Herbert, and Crashaw were jumbled together in one volume,
the critic, by the very process of describing and evaluating them, would
sort them out again: poets usually have a personal manner of thought and
expression. It is therefore valuable to read a poet as a whole, for one
acquires thereby an appropriate response to this individuality, and
develops a conception of what to look out for and what to expect that
will enhance the appreciation of an individual poem. For unexpectedness that is total and unruly is merely foreign and bewildering. We gain
the greatest pleasure from a poem when familiarity with a mode of
thought and expression provides the framework within which variations
delightfully occur, both astonishing and fulfilling expectation. Therefore whenever poetry shows the impress of an individual mind, anonymity will often be an obstacle to the appreciation of it.

There is, however, a distinction between naturally anonymous and
accidentally anonymous poetry, and most medieval lyrics can be called
genuinely anonymous, for they were written by self-effacing poets, who
did not obtrude peculiarities of style and thought between the subject-
matter and the audience. Therefore when, in the earlier period, the
name of the author of a single poem is known, as is that of Thomas of
Hales, there is no temptation to attribute other poems to him because
there would be no profit.[1] In the later period, poets of a markedly distinctive style, such as Dunbar, were least recognizably themselves when
they wrote meditative poetry, as though the form they had adopted
demanded this abstinence from idiosyncratic style.

In the Middle Ages the writers of religious lyrics were not thought of
as men with keener powers of observation and with greater sensibility
than others, only as more learned and more articulate. The worth of
a poem was guaranteed, not by the dignity of the author, but by the
dignity of the source that he used.[2] Since this attitude is reflected in the
style and feeling, it must also become ours, even though it is counter to
modern literary preconceptions. For, whereas in studying later poetry
we justifiably search for an author with a distinctive cast of mind and
sensibility, in treating the medieval lyric we must consider a way of

---

[1] Knowledge of authorship is equally unimportant for other medieval literature such
as mystery plays and romances. The suggestion, for instance, that *Sir Orfeo* and the
Lai le freine may be by the same author arouses neither curiosity nor excitement. By
contrast, it is very tempting to read *The Pearl* and *Sir Gawain and the Green Knight*
in the light of one another, so that here knowledge of authorship would be very
valuable.

[2] See Appendix B.

thought and a particular emotional bias that was not peculiar to one man, but that for centuries characterized medieval devotion. The authors of the medieval lyrics are often no more than translators: frequently a short passage of Latin prose will be turned into a neat English verse. And even those who write most freely must be seen as skilled craftsmen transmitting a tradition. Of course, all religious poets have their subject-matter provided, but the medieval poets differ from the Metaphysicals in that they not only borrow the subject-matter and the techniques of display from a meditative tradition, but they also borrow with the subject-matter the emotion appropriate to it. Their personal moods and emotions are therefore not revealed in their poetry, for they are not concerned with the question of how they feel individually, but only with what kind of response their subject should properly arouse in Everyman. Therefore, in order to gain that familiarity with a way of thinking and self-expression which is necessary for the best enjoyment of poetry, it is often necessary to look behind the medieval poets to Latin devotional literature, and thus to acquire familiarity with a way of thought that the poets express without self-intrusion.

This abnegation of individuality is one of the most important differences between the medieval and the seventeenth-century religious lyric. The writers of both draw upon the contemporary methods of meditation of their respective periods, meditation on the Passion and, to a lesser extent, meditation on death. But, whereas the seventeenth-century poets show the poet meditating, the medieval writers provide versified meditations which others may use: in the one the meditator is the poet; in the other the meditator is the reader. The aim of Metaphysical religious poetry is to provide an example. According to Walton, Herbert said of *The Temple*: 'If he [Nicholas Ferrar] *can think it may turn to the advantage of any dejected poor Soul, let it be made publick.*'[1] The advantage would be the consolation of the example set by another man. For instance, the only medieval poems that have a sense of sin as their subject are the didactic verses in which the 'I' character confesses to the seven deadly sins.[2] These poems sprang from the penitential literature of the period, and are intended for the Christian organizing his thoughts before going to confession. Each sin is therefore confessed with equal emphasis —and therefore without regard to individual personality—and the expression of the sense of sin and of penitence are both muted, in order that nobody may find the one or the other beyond his emotional range. By contrast Herbert's 'The Pulley' expresses an individual awareness of the nature of rebellion, and it will be read most appropriately not by somebody in a comparable state of rebellion, but by somebody in a

---

[1] 'The Life of Mr. George Herbert', *Lives* by Isaac Walton (Oxford, 1940), 314.

[2] e.g. 'Swete ihesu crist, to þe, / copable wrecche ich ȝelde me', Brown xiv, 87.

relaxed and reflective mood, who at some future time will draw comfort from the memory of Herbert's rebellion and of its resolution. One of the few parallels to this in English medieval poetry is a poem of Audelay that has the refrain '*Passio Christi conforta me*', where the reader will not identify himself with the speaker, but will learn from the example of Audelay's faith, which is undiminished by the miseries of extreme old age and of approaching death.[1]

This distinction is an important one because it does not affect content alone but also tone and style. The seventeenth-century author, far from effacing himself, is, as it were, conscious of being watched: indeed both the poetic and the religious purpose require that the reader should watch him carefully. From this fact follows, for instance, the kind of dramatic openings that has been so much commented upon: 'I Struck the board, and cry'd, No more',[2] or 'Batter my heart, three person'd God'.[3] Such openings excite attention, but, were the reader's identification of himself with the speaker required, they would prove an initial stumbling block, in that they produce an immediate effect of distancing poet from reader. The openings of Donne's 'Holy Sonnets' are all of this kind, and they may be contrasted with those of *La Corona*, where the sonnets are in the medieval sense more meditative, in that they could be used as meditations. In these the first lines, though dramatic, are also quiet, as, for instance, the invocation of St. Joseph, '*With his kinde mother who partakes thy woe, | Joseph turne backe*'.[4] A contrast may also be made with the medieval lyric, which often begins in the following way: 'Wanne ich þenche þinges þre | Ne mai [ich] nevre bliþe be'[5] (a short lyric on the fear of death), or 'Wenne hic soe on rode idon, | ihesus mi leman'.[6] From one point of view these openings are dramatic, for there is no leisurely or decorative approach to the subject: the poet gains immediate attention by beginning at the heart of the matter. But there is nothing here abrupt or strange that might lead the reader to recoil in admiration rather than to approach in sympathy.

The effect of the awareness of being watched, does not, of course, touch only the openings, but also the whole poem in both tone and style. At its worst we may feel in the tone of some seventeenth-century poetry a kind of stridency, as though the poet were self-consciously striking attitudes. There is, no doubt, another cause for this in the difference of religious mood which followed the Reformation, and a parallel change took place between the art of the Middle Ages and that of the

---

[1] E.E.T.S. 184, 211–12.
[2] *The Works of George Herbert*, ed. F. E. Hutchinson (Oxford, 1941), 153.
[3] *The Divine Poems*, ed. Helen Gardner (Oxford, 1952), 11.
[4] Ibid., 3.
[5] Brown XIII, 12.   [6] Ibid. 35.

Counter-Reformation. But some of the later exaggeration is already to be found in fifteenth-century poetry, where the effect suggests that the author felt that unless every emotion was heightened to the point of hysteria, and every gesture or action made melodramatically compelling, the reader might remain unmoved. However, in the fifteenth century this change of sensibility could affect only the characters in the poem—most notably the Virgin—and in the lyric the poet was not as yet one of these, and there is therefore no feeling that the poet, in order to convey his devotion, must strike an attitude. The self-effacement of the medieval poet imposed limitations, as we shall see, but there was an advantage in the fact that the emotion expressed in the lyric was not controlled by the poet's own emotion or sensibility, but by the measure of what reason had shown to be appropriate, for this gave to the poetry a modest dignity and serenity, and, curiously enough from the modern point of view, a strong effect of sincerity, though not of course sincerity in the Romantic sense of spontaneity and autobiographical fidelity.[1] The sincerity resides, not in the poet's faithfulness to his own experience, but in his faithful transmission of well-tried religious devotion, and in a particular propriety of style to subject-matter.

Since it is the poet who meditates, it is fitting in the seventeenth century that a poem should be highly wrought and imaginatively inventive, but when it is the reader who meditates, any technical or imaginative flourish is likely to intrude between the reader and the meditation. In most of the medieval lyrics there is therefore no attempt at elevation: the prescriptions of rhetorical treatises for the amplifying or adorning of a subject are not normally followed by the authors of the lyrics, and when they are used it seems to be because they are inescapable and not because any rhetorical graces are intended. Moreover, there can, perhaps, never have been a poetry which was more exclusively written in the language of the common people—at least until the fifteenth century, when the religious lyric was caught by the fashion for aureate diction. At that period a different criterion of stylistic propriety was used, and the style sought for became one sufficiently dignified to suggest the magnitude of the subject. The result is that in some fifteenth-century poetry there is an artificiality and straining for effect that may be called stylistic insincerity. But in the earlier period the test of stylistic

---

[1] The concept of sincerity as a criterion of poetry has recently been discussed by: David Perkins, *Wordsworth and the Poetry of Sincerity* (Oxford, 1964); P. M. Ball, 'Sincerity: The Rise and Fall of a Critical Term', *M.L.R.* lix (1964), 1–11; W. Jackson, 'Sincerity: a Postscript on Antecedents and Correlatives', ibid. lxi (1966), 355–6. It is interesting that what Mr. Perkins enumerated as possible signs of spontaneity, 'a colloquial diction, an informal syntax, a natural or psychologically probable movement of thought' (op. cit. 41), are often signs of the meditative technique, the aim being, not to suggest spontaneity, but to achieve the kind of utterance which the meditator can make his own.

propriety would seem to have been the appropriateness of the style to Everyman, who is the speaker, and to the emotions, which are the two basic passions by which man is moved, fear and love. From this kind of propriety sprang the unstudied freshness and the stylistic sincerity which are amongst the most pleasing qualities of the early lyric. Inevitably there is a reverse and less attractive side to these qualities. Simplicity may easily turn into lack of poise—the plain inadequacy of a minor poet writing without a firm literary tradition behind him; and nearly always we miss the confident tone of the poet speaking in his own voice and with perfect mastery of his medium. However, as we shall see later, the state of the language in the thirteenth century was so exactly suited to the exigencies of the meditative theory, that it becomes impossible to distinguish between limitations of style that were intentionally adopted and those which were the inevitable result of historical conditions. This point may again be illustrated from the poems on penitence. The fact that the language of the thirteenth century was not the medium of either theological discussion or of much courtly literature limited its resources for moral or psychological reflection. But the medieval authors intended only to show the 'I' speaker examining his conscience for the sins which he shares with everyone, and for which there is a plain and objective solution in the sacrament of penance. By contrast, in the seventeenth century the language was far richer and more subtle, and the penitential poems, in accordance with the Ignatian tradition, describe a searching of the conscience that is far more personal, complex, and introspective.

The chief source of difference between medieval and seventeenth-century poetry, however, lies very precisely in the different meditative theories of the two periods. The Ignatian method required the exercise of the three faculties, memory, reason, and will. But the medieval method did not require all three faculties to be used, and, indeed, to make easy the emotional response of love, it largely excluded the activity of the reason, for love is not the natural end of intellectual exploration. Logical argument in verse was well within the range of medieval vernacular poets, as we can see from debate poetry or *The Pearl*. Its absence from the lyric—with the exception of the Body and Soul poems—must therefore be deliberate and follow from the meditative theory which saw love alone as the fruit of meditation. The exclusion of the intellect from religious poetry prevents an equal emphasis upon the Divinity and Humanity of Christ and therefore leads to the exclusion of paradox arousing wonderment. In this point medieval poetry on the Passion is quite different from *The Dream of the Rood* on the one hand or the poetry of Donne and Herbert on the other. Though, as we said before, *La Corona* is in one way more meditative in the medieval sense than

Donne's other religious sonnets, yet it is highly un-medieval in its progression by means of paradox. The sonnet on the Crucifixion, for
instance, contains in its central core a major paradox and a play on
words:

> In both affections many to him ran,
> But Oh! the worst are most, they will and can,
> Alas, and do, unto the immaculate,
> Whose creature Fate is, now prescribe a Fate,
> Measuring selfe-lifes infinity to'a span,
> Nay to an inch. Loe, where condemned hee
> Beares his owne crosse, with paine, yet by and by
> When it beares him, he must beare more and die.[1]

By its literary devices the sonnet compels the reader to remember,
and momentarily to understand imaginatively, that the man who is
suffering is God: paradox and riddling style force the intellect to understand. In the case of most medieval lyrics, however, a reader who did not
know of the divinity of Christ would not learn of it from them. The
following stanzas from a late thirteenth-century poem are typical of this
style of meditation:

> Of iesu crist hi synge,
> þat is so fayr and fre,
> swetest of alle þynge;
> hys oþwe hic oȝe wel boe,
> wl fer he me soþte,
> myd hard he me boþte
> wyþ wnde to and þree,
> wel sore he was yswnge
> and for me myd spere istunge,
> ynayled to þe tree.
>
> Wan hic my-self stond
> and myd herte ysee,
> yþerled fetd and onde
> wyt grete neyles þree—
> blody was hys eved,
> of hym nas nout byleved
> þet of pyne were vre—
> wel oþte myn herte,
> al for hys luve smerte,
> syc and sory be.[2]

Not only are there no paradoxes here, but also in this poem, as in so
many others, Christ is never referred to as God or by any other divine
title, nor is any activity ascribed to Him which is proper to the Godhead.

---

[1] *The Divine Poems*, 4. [2] Brown XIII, 63, pp. 120–1.

Moreover, even in the poetry of Richard Rolle, which is more subtle and less simply emotional than the main body of religious lyrics, titles of divinity are used only in non-paradoxical contexts. One poem, for instance, begins, 'Ihesu, god sone, Lord of mageste, / Send wil to my hert anly to covayte þe',[1] but in the description of the Crucifixion that follows, Christ is referred to as King but not as God. With this may be contrasted the references to Christ as God in paradoxical contexts in *The Dream of the Rood*: 'Genamon hie þær ælmihtigne God',[2] or 'Ongunnon him þa moldern wyrcan . . . gesetton hie ðæron sigora Wealdend'.[3] Such methods lead to amazement and a sense of glory and magnificence. The medieval method, as we can see from the above quotation, induces compassion, tenderness, and love. Exceptionally, in this point, we find the medieval lyric conforming more closely to later definitions of the lyric than does much seventeenth-century religious poetry. The insistence on one simple emotion, movingly expressed, is more 'lyrical' than the complex and ingenious thought of many Metaphysical lyrics.

From the fact that the medieval lyric makes very little use of intellectual ideas there follows the further point that it is very bare of imagery. To the modern reader this may at first sight seem strange, for since the nineteenth century we have come to think of imagery as being primarily emotive, and we should therefore suppose it to be particularly appropriate to a poetry of affective meditation. But to the medieval poet the chief function of imagery was to convey a truth, not to the heart or imagination, but to the intellect, and there is therefore little room for it in a poetry designed only to touch the emotions. From the modern point of view there would seem to be a further purpose for it in poetry that aims to present a scene vividly to the imagination. But metaphors or similes that convey how people looked or moved are always rare in medieval poetry. There are a few in Chaucer's work, such as the famous simile of the condemned man in *The Man of Law's Tale* or of the *meynee* of Jack Straw in *The Nun's Priest's Tale*, which are now much praised, but perhaps more because they conform to modern taste and theory than because they are exceptionally brilliant examples of Chaucer's narrative style.[4] But, apart from a few stock comparisons in the romances, imagery thus used is not a normal part of medieval narrative.

Moreover, only images that make the scene more living to the eye would have been appropriate in meditative poetry. For medieval medita-

---

[1] Brown xiv, 83, p. 99.

[2] l. 60b, ed. B. Dickens and A. S. C. Ross (London, 1945), p. 28. 'There they seized hold of almighty God.'

[3] ll. 65b–67a, ed. cit. 29–30. 'They made a tomb . . . and laid therein the Lord of victories.'

[4] There is a more subtle and 'modern' use of imagery in other works of Chaucer, such as *The Merchant's Tale*.

tion is concerned with only one of the five senses, that of sight, unlike some forms of Ignatian meditation which sought the aid of all five senses to bring a scene to life. Much medieval poetry is surprisingly unsensuous: even a poet's description of his mistress is merely visual and intellectual by later standards,[1] and in the religious poetry the rare passages that are sensuous in tone derive straight from the Song of Songs. Therefore imagery designed to convey what is apprehended of the physical world through the senses of hearing, taste, or touch, would be out of keeping with both meditative and poetic convention. A simple comparison may be made with a poem—now well known, for it is sung as a Christmas carol—by Christina Rossetti. It begins as follows:

> In the bleak mid-winter
>   Frosty wind made moan,
> Earth stood hard as iron,
>   Water like a stone;
> Snow had fallen, snow on snow,
>   Snow on snow,
> In that bleak mid-winter
>   Long ago.[2]

The treatment of the Nativity in this poem undoubtedly has its roots in the Middle Ages, but in this verse alone, in its emphasis on the sound of the wind, the hardness of the ground, and the hardness and coldness of the frozen water, it is conveying simple sensuous experience in a way quite foreign to medieval poetry.

Imagery is therefore usually found only in those medieval lyrics that are farthest from the lyric norm, in that they make use at least of implicit —and sometimes of explicit—argument; in these the imagery is traditional and its function is logical persuasion. Thus in the poems on the subject of the debate between the Body and the Soul the image of a horse and rider is used to persuade the reader of the need for the reason to control the flesh; or in the poems addressed to the Virgin the image of the sun passing through glass is used to assuage disbelief in the doctrine of *virginitas in partu*. Such images have obviously been invented for their logical rather than for their imaginative appropriateness. This method of using imagery is peculiar to the Middle Ages, in that whilst in later periods imagery might be chosen primarily for its logical force, an imaginative congruence was required as well; otherwise, as in Metaphysical poetry, the disparity was deliberately exploited. But medieval

---

[1] This point could be illustrated by innumerable examples, e.g. the contrast between the imagery in 'Mosti ryden by Rybbesdale' (*Harley Lyrics*, ed. G. L. Brook, Manchester, 1948, 37–39), in which there is only one sensuous simile (l. 76, 'eyþer side soft ase sylk'), and in Ben Jonson's 'Her Triumph' (vol. viii, ed. C. H. Herford and Percy and Evelyn Simpson, Oxford, 1947, 134–5), where the last stanza is strikingly sensuous.

[2] *Poetical Works* (London, 1904), 246.

poetry is austere in its elimination of subordinate associations and in its precise adherence to intellectual resemblances. It is only in fifteenth-century poetry that there is found some new awareness of the potentialities of imagery. A well-known example is the lyric beginning, 'I Syng of a myden þat is makeles',[1] in which the dew has ceased to be that which fell on Gideon's fleece—a much-used type—and has become, with less logical appropriateness but with greater evocative power, the dew which in the natural world falls on flower and grass.

The fact that the exercise of the intellect is excluded from these poems contributes to their genuine anonymity, for people are more distinguished from one another by the way they think than by the way they feel. Perhaps, even if medieval meditative theory had not precluded the use of the intelligence, the function of the poems as popular meditations might have determined and limited its activity, for otherwise the poems would have borne too personal a stamp for others to identify themselves with the speaker.

Since the Middle English lyrics are a genuinely anonymous form of poetry and since they served the purpose of a simple but organized form of meditation, they would have been valued, not for their authorship, nor primarily for their poetic merit, but for their value as meditations. There is, of course, an overlap here, for the lyrics, like nearly all other forms of medieval literature, aim to persuade, and their persuasiveness depends upon the effective use of literary techniques: a meditation on the Passion, which is successful in that it stimulates and makes articulate a pity for Christ in His sufferings, will also have some of the qualities of a good poem. But some poems escape this overlap: there are verses —particularly late ones—which were popular because they put into rhyme particular devotions, such as that of the Instruments of the Passion, and many of these devotions had no literary potentialities. It follows from this that a history of the religious lyric that seeks to be comprehensive must become in part a history of medieval meditation and devotion. Indeed a history of the religious lyric and a history of popular meditation in England in the Middle Ages would be distinguished, not by their material, but by their emphasis and by the kind of question implicitly asked. In a literary history the questions will not be the spiritual worth of a devotion, nor how yet another cause of the Reformation might be sought in it, but whether the devotion was potentially a good subject for a poem, with the intention of casting light thereby on a good poem, and of distinguishing amongst mediocre poems those which are merely inept from those which are circumscribed by the nature of the subject-matter. But even here there is not a radical distinction between the religious and the literary approaches. It was a change in religious temper

[1] Brown xv, 81.

that led to an emphasis on formalized devotions in the fifteenth century, and thus to a kind of subject insusceptible to poetic treatment. Moreover, excesses in devotion, such as the cult of the swooning Virgin, which were condemned alike by Anglican and Counter-Reformation writers, often tended also to produce bad poetry. Indeed, nearly all the virtues and the weaknesses of the religious lyric can be explained in terms of the spirituality from which they sprang.

That medieval meditative poetry is poetry of an unusual kind can be seen in the fact that later censures of religious poetry, when applied to it, fly wide of the mark. Dr. Johnson's well-known arguments[1] have no relevance, because the poetic ornament is unostentatious, and its purpose is, not to adorn the unadornable or elevate the exalted, but to persuade the average Christian to ponder and feel what he already believes. For the same reason the lyric remains untouched by T. S. Eliot's comments on the limitations of religious poetry: 'The religious poet is not a poet who is treating the whole subject matter of poetry in a religious spirit, but a poet who is dealing with a confined part of this subject matter: who is leaving out what men consider their major passions, and thereby confessing his ignorance of them.'[2] Commenting upon this, Professor Gardner has said: 'We cannot help missing the image of the natural man in the poet's image of the spiritual man.'[3] But in a sense it is the 'natural man' with all his passions who is the protagonist of the religious lyric. The lyrics are not illustrations of the spiritual man at prayer, but of the natural man, with his love of his family, his fear of death, and his attachment to his possessions, being persuaded and coaxed by the imaginative resources of poetry into a religious disposition.

Finally, the lyrics can be seen to evade the dilemma which Professor Gardner, taking Marvell's 'The Coronet' as her starting point, presents as follows:

In all poetry which attempts to represent the intercourse between an individual soul and its Maker there is a conflict between the ostensible emotion—adoring love, absorbed in the contemplation of its object, or penitence, overwhelmed by the sense of personal unworthiness—and the artist's actual absorption in the creation of his poem and his satisfaction in achieving perfect expression.[4]

This sense of a poet delighted by his own creation, communicated so strongly, for instance, by the work of Chaucer, is quite absent from the

---

[1] 'Life of Waller', *Lives of the English Poets*, ed. G. B. Hill (Oxford, 1905), i. 291–2.
[2] 'Religion and Literature', *Essays Ancient and Modern* (London, 1936), 97; quoted in John Donne, *The Divine Poems*, ed. H. Gardner, xv.
[3] Op. cit. xvi.
[4] Op. cit. xv–xvi.

Middle English religious lyrics. They give the impression that the author never looked at them with a satisfaction in poetic achievement, but fixed his mind on the one hand on his subject-matter, and on the other on the ordinary layman who would use the poem. Yet from this unself-conscious, 'unpoetical' approach, poetry often sprang.

Thirteenth- and Fourteenth-Century Lyrics

II

Lyrics on the Passion

WHEN considering the modes of thought in religious poetry, Dr. Johnson classified them according to methods of prayer: 'The employments of pious meditation are Faith, Thanksgiving, Repentance, and Supplication.'[1] These modes, however, are rare in the medieval English lyric, occurring chiefly in the poems addressed to the Virgin, which make a self-contained group with a distinctive ancestry. The main subjects of the medieval religious lyric are those central to medieval meditation, the Passion, and the Last Things, especially death, with the emotions proper to them, love and fear. In order that the reader of the poems may feel these emotions personally and keenly, he is persuaded by the lyric to imagine himself in a scene which will provoke them, and which is described often in minute visual detail. The reader is to imagine that he is present at the Nativity and overhears the Virgin comforting her Child, or that he is present at the Crucifixion and that Christ on the Cross appeals to him personally for compassion, or that he is present at the Entombment, and hears the lamentation of the Virgin; or he is to imagine that a corpse addresses him from its grave, or that he spies upon and overhears a dispute between a dead body and its former soul, or that he sees three knights suddenly meeting with their dead selves. Though some of the lyrics are reflective and recollect ruminatingly the scene, most of them are very immediate, and give the effect of being a key speech detached from a whole dramatic scene in which the reader actually takes part. Sometimes the visual outlines of the scene are fully described within the poem, sometimes they have in part to be supplied from the meditative tradition outside the poem. Quite a number of lyrics were later incorporated into the mystery plays:[2] not because the plays were lyrical, but because the lyrics were dramatic. The Crucifixion play, for instance, publicly enacted what could also proceed privately within a man's imagination and memory. In the fifteenth century the lyrics were often accompanied by illuminations in the

---

[1] *Lives of the Poets*, i. 292.
[2] Most of these are enumerated in G. C. Taylor, 'The English Corpus Christi Play and the Middle English Lyric', *M.P.* v (1907), 1–38.

manuscripts, which provided the visual image—perhaps of a Crucifixion or a skeleton—thus impoverishing the poem, since it would lack visual description, but making less demand upon the concentration of the reader, who would be spared the effort of imagining the scene for himself. Some of the lyrics are set in dialogue form, Christ speaking and man replying, but far more often only half, as it were, of this dialogue is made explicit: either Christ describes His sufferings in such a way as to stir pity and love in the reader-meditator, or the meditator, addressing Christ directly, lovingly and sadly describes His sufferings. Occasionally, and less effectively, the lyric is set in the third person, and a preacher, acting as intermediary, describes the pains of the Passion and instructs the meditator how he should feel.

The dominant theme of the lyrics is the Passion. For the early period the most important collection of lyrics on the Passion occurs in John of Grimestone's preaching-book.[1] This manuscript, compiled about 1375, belongs to a common type of preaching-manual: topics are arranged in alphabetical order, and useful material is set out in compressed or note form under each heading. The normal language is, of course, Latin, and the medium prose. John of Grimestone's book is exceptional in the number of English verses it includes, and unique in its treatment of the Passion. About a hundred topics are covered in its hundred and fifty pages, but, by a striking numerical disproportion, nineteen of these are devoted to the Passion,[2] and they consist chiefly of a series of English verses, about twenty-five poems in all. Whilst some of these occur for the first time, most of them are versions or adaptations of lyrics which had been in circulation in religious manuscripts for more than a hundred years. In order to understand these short lyrics, which had more than a century of popularity, it is necessary to know something of the religious doctrine and meditative theory from which they sprang.

Three late thirteenth- or early fourteenth-century manuscripts contain a verse—apparently a translation from the Latin—which lists the symptoms of meditation on the Passion:

> Loverd þi passion,
> Who þe þenchet arist þaron,
> teres hit tollet,
> and eyen hit bollet,
> nebbes hit wetet,
> ant hertes hit swetet.[3]

---

[1] The collection has never been printed as a whole, but the best are in Brown XIV, 62–76. The manuscript is traditionally, but inaccurately, referred to as a commonplace book: it is, however, an alphabetical preaching-book, distinguished only from many comparable works by the high proportion of vernacular verse that it contains. Preaching-books are discussed by H. G. Pfander, 'The Mediaeval Friars and some Alphabetical Reference-Books for Sermons', *Medium Aevum*, iii (1934), 19–29.   [2] ff. 117ʳ–26ʳ.

[3] Brown XIII, 56 B. *Tollet*: draws forth; *bollet*: makes swollen; *nebbes*: faces.

In other words, meditation on the Passion brings tears to the eye and sweetness to the heart: the meditator grieves and loves. This idea is the cornerstone of the Middle English Passion lyrics and of the Latin tradition of meditation lying behind them, a tradition that first flourished in the twelfth century. The dogma providing its intellectual foundation is that man's proper response to Christ's work in the Redemption is a response of love. There is here a radically different stress from that of the well-known text, 'If ye love me, keep my commandments': the point of a meditation is distinct from that of an exhortation to avoid the seven deadly sins or to practise the seven works of mercy. The new emotional emphasis of the twelfth century can be seen in a variety of ways, but perhaps most fundamentally in the doctrine of the Redemption itself, where there developed a new sense of a personal relationship between God and man. The Fathers of the Western Church had defined the doctrine of the Redemption in terms of outwitting or defeating the Devil:[1] in the drama of the Redemption, therefore, God and the Devil played the two chief parts and man had a subordinate role. He was reconciled to God, but as a result of an issue between God and the Devil: thus there were no immediate personal and emotional implications for him in the Incarnation and Passion. This doctrine can be seen very clearly reflected in the iconography of the Crucifixion up to the eleventh century. In this Christ stands firm and alive upon the Cross, kingly, heroic, and triumphant: His feet are supported by a suppedaneum and His head is adorned by a royal crown. The scene is a self-sufficient expression of a dogmatic truth, complete within itself, and demanding no specific response from those who look at it.

By contrast, in medieval theology the arrangement of parts in the Redemption was reversed: the stress then fell principally upon the restoration of man to God, and only secondarily upon the defeat of the Devil consequent upon this. A theological stress upon Christ's death and Passion first occurred in Anselm's *Cur Deus Homo*, a work which put its emphasis upon Christ's death as a supererogatory offering, which only He, as perfect man, was able to make.[2] In the work of later theologians emphasis on the Passion was intensified, but in a different way. St. Thomas Aquinas, who rejected Anselm's view that God could not have saved man by any other means, nevertheless gave as his first reason for God's choice of the method of the Passion His wish to demonstrate His love to man.[3] Peter Abelard's heretical doctrine that the sole

[1] See 'Doctrinal Influences on *The Dream of the Rood*', *Medium Aevum*, xxvii (1958), 142–3.

[2] *P.L.* 158, 359–432. See J. Rivière, *Le dogme de la Rédemption au début du moyen âge* (Paris, 1934).

[3] *Summa Theologica*, Pt. III, qu. xlvi, art. 3. For this quotation, and for similar

efficacy of the Redemption lay in Christ's revelation of His love to man, thereby stimulating and winning man's love in return,[1] was thus given a place in orthodox theology, by being accepted, not as the method of the Redemption, but as the motive for the particular form for it which God chose. As a meditative observation, rather than as a part of a rigorous theological scheme, it had already been a favourite comment of St. Bernard,[2] and similarly used it became a commonplace of medieval preaching.[3]

The new soteriological doctrine is also reflected by a change in iconography: indeed, in England the new spirit was expressed in art before it was formalized in doctrine. In a Crucifixion, for instance, from a late tenth-century psalter, perhaps from Ramsey Abbey, Christ hangs dead from the Cross, a little red blood streams clearly from the five wounds, whilst the Virgin and St. John stand in a state of dejection, delicately and poignantly conveyed by the swift, fine, jagged edges of the drapery.[4] In the Weingarten Crucifixion, fifty years later, the expression of suffering is much stronger:[5] pain is suggested, not only by the drapery, but also by the manner in which the figure of Christ sags from the arms, with the body twisted in an emphatic S-bend, and by the coarse, jagged, rough-hewn wood of the Cross. This kind of representation is different from that of the earlier period, not only because it has turned a scene of triumph into one of sorrow, but also because it has an emotional design upon the beholder, an intention to stir him to a compassionate involvement in the scene. It aims at the same kind of persuasiveness as later the lyrics were to do.

In accordance with the new theological emphasis upon the Passion there developed a corresponding emphasis upon the value of man's natural feelings, that is upon what St. Bernard, who was the great exponent of a theory of the emotions, described as carnal love in order to distinguish it from spiritual love.[6] In kind this love is no different from the love which a man gives to anybody who is dear to him, and its object is not the Godhead but Christ in His humanity. According to St. Bernard, the value of this kind of love is shown by the very fact that God became man in order to gain it. In other words, natural human feeling does not

---

passages from Hugh of St. Victor and Bonaventura, see 'The theme of Christ the lover-knight in Medieval English literature', *R.E.S.*, N.S. xiii (1962), 2.

[1] *Commentariorum super S. Pauli Epistolam ad Romanos Libri Quinque*, *P.L.* 178, 836.

[2] See E. Gilson, *The Mystical Theology of St. Bernard* (trans. A. H. C. Downes, London, 1940), p. 78 and footnote 102.

[3] e.g. in the *Fasciculus Morum*, where the *exemplum* of the lover-knight (see pp. 45–56) is preceded by the following statement: *Christus passus est et sanguinem eius fudit pro nobis ut nos ad eius amorem et caritatem celerius alliceret*, MS. Rawl. C. 670, f. 42ᵛ.

[4] MS. Harley 2904, M. Rickert, *Painting in Britain: the Middle Ages* (London, 1954), pl. 30.

[5] Rickert, op. cit., pl. 43.   [6] Gilson, op. cit. 78–81.

have to be suppressed in order that a man may love God, but encouraged
and ordered in a fresh direction. These two important and complementary conceptions, the first stressing God's display of, and demand
for, love in the work of the Redemption, and the second the potential
value of man's natural feelings, both contributed to the development of
the religious lyric.

The combined effect of these was that the devotional content and
tone of the lyrics, when they first appeared, rested on a secure foundation
of theological reasoning that protected them from emotional excesses.
They gained from the harmonious synthesis of reason and emotion in the
twelfth and thirteenth centuries, a synthesis seen in the work of many of
the great writers of this period, in which logical argument passes easily
into devotion, and devotion into logical argument, thereby ensuring that
the first was not usually arid, nor the second exaggerated or indecorous.
Decorum is a quality more easily remembered when absent than when
present, and it is possible therefore to take for granted the combination
of seriousness, intensity, and moderation in the early meditative lyrics.
That they possess decorum as a positive quality, however, becomes quite
clear when they are contrasted with the later meditative lyrics, which,
as we shall later see, lost this virtue when they lost their foundation in
reason.

The more important point for the beginnings of the meditative lyric,
however, is the relationship between the Bernardine emphasis on natural
feeling and the qualities of English in the thirteenth century, for here
there was a unique and fortunate coincidence between religious theory
and literary potentialities. The recognition and praise of ordinary human
emotion meant in literary terms that the language used to express it had
no need to be different from that of everyday life. Indeed, since the point
of the meditative poetry was to enable the ordinary layman, who was
without any particular holiness or knowledge of the discipline of contemplation, to visualize Christ in His humanity, and to love Him with
the love that he would give to his family, friends, benefactors, or to anyone who had helped him or saved his life, obviously the more familiar
and colloquial the language the more successful would be the poem.
The dignity of style that later periods would have thought suitable for
religious subject-matter, and any associations of learning or grandeur
that might suggest that God should be loved with a particularly elevated
love, would impair and perhaps destroy the meditation.[1] But only the
vocabulary and rhythms of common speech were available to writers

---

[1] For a very interesting account of the traditional arguments for the propriety of a
lowly style to religious subject-matter see Erich Auerbach, *Literary Language and its
Public in Late Latin Antiquity and in the Middle Ages*, trans. Ralph Manheim (London,
1965).

of the thirteenth century. The lowly status of English ensured that expressions of love should recall neither theological analyses, nor the magnificent passions of romantic lovers, but only the ordinary affection and tenderness of everyday experience. English was obviously at this time very limited as a medium for writing: subjects which required nobility or complexity of expression were ordinarily beyond its range. But, by a fortunate coincidence, what the language was admirably suited to express was exactly what the writers of the meditative lyrics required of it.

Yet a further literary advantage of the theory of carnal love was that all human relationships could be a source of appropriate imagery. The quality of the relationship between God and man did not need to be expressed in symbols, such as the fire and song of Richard Rolle, but could be conveyed in more homely and understandable terms. Three of the four kinds of love defined by the author of the *Ancrene Wisse*[1] provide imagery for the lyrics: in these Christ often pleads explicitly in the role of husband (lover), mother, or friend, and man speaks as the opposite person in these relationships. But, even when these are not used as deliberate, persuasive images, they are present implicitly in the style of the poems, which catches the colloquial tone and simplicity appropriate to a relationship which is intimate, and between people, perhaps of different age and sex, but not of different rank. The world of the lyric is not public or ceremonial: the tone suggests a private world, the affection, quarrels, reconciliations, and forgiveness which form the staple of the relationship between members of a family or friends.

This simplicity and familiarity are made possible by the fact that, as we said before, the object of the affection is not the Godhead, but Christ in His humanity. Nowadays crucifixes, reproductions of medieval and Renaissance paintings, Christmas cribs and Christmas cards, are so much taken for granted, that it may not easily be remembered that recollection and commemoration of Biblical scenes had scarcely any part in the liturgy or spirituality of the Church in its first thousand years. The value of a loving meditation upon Christ's human life was first propounded by St. Bernard of Clairvaux and St. William of St. Thierry, the two great founders of Cistercian spirituality: in their work it was formally recognized as an initial step on the ladder of mystical ascent. This kind of devotion was then completely new, for a preoccupation with Christ's human experience was quite alien to the orthodox minds of the early Church, concerned rather with the glory of the Divinity; and, whilst in answer to heresies they stressed Christ's human and divine natures equally, it was the divine that touched their imaginations and inspired their speculation. In the systems of meditation of Augustine and Gregory

---

[1] Ed. J. Tolkien, E.E.T.S. 249, 200–2.

the Great—which' have been so well expounded by Dom Cuthbert Butler[1]—the devout mind is shown to soar instantly on a Platonic upward flight, rather than to begin its contemplation cautiously on the natural level of human feeling. Nor was mystical experience an important element in the life of religious dedication. The spiritual purpose of the Benedictine monasteries was a dutiful obedience to God's will in the solemn performance of the liturgy and monastic offices, rather than individual piety and mystical exploration; and the services themselves were austerely free of emotional stimulus except of the most serene and doctrinal kind. Even the festivals of Christmas and Easter were commemorations of great dogmatic truths rather than of plain historical events: Christmas was the occasion for corporate recollection of the Word made flesh, not for personal meditation on the babe lying in a manger. Holy Week did not end in a day of mourning followed by a day of rejoicing; on the contrary, Good Friday was scarcely emphasized, and on Easter Sunday Christ's triumph over sin and death, through His doctrinally indivisible Crucifixion and Resurrection, was celebrated in one feast.

There can, of course, be found traces of historical commemoration in the Early Church: in the services at Jerusalem, for instance, which the pilgrim Etheria described in her account of the Holy Land, where on Good Friday the crowd assembled at Calvary and wept as they listened to the gospel narratives of the Crucifixion;[2] or, nearer at hand, in the cult of relics, such as those of the True Cross or the boards of Christ's crib that were placed in S. Maria Maggiore; or in some of the verses of the Gregorian Antiphonary that dramatically draw attention to the Biblical scene.[3] But though during the first thousand years the two great festivals of Christmas and Easter gradually acquired some historical emphasis, there was still no sentimental concern for the Christ-Child and no intense stress upon the sufferings of Christ in the Passion. It is not until the eleventh century that a new sensitivity to the sufferings of Christ can be discovered in religious thinking. Traces of it can be found in the work of Peter Damian,[4] and more amply in the work of John of Fécamp, or in England in the letter of instruction written by Goscelin,[5] in which he taught two forms of devotion to the Passion, both of which were to become exceedingly popular in the later Middle Ages, a devotion

[1] *Western Mysticism* (London, 1951).

[2] Éthérie, *Journal de voyage*, ed. with trans. H. Pétré (Paris, 1948), 236–8.

[3] *Liber Responsalis, P.L.* 78, 734, *Quem vidistis, Pastores, dicite*, etc., a text anticipating the later famous Christmas trope.

[4] e.g. *Opusculum quadragesimum tertium*, ch. v, *P.L.* 145, 683.

[5] C. H. Talbot, 'The liber confortatorius of Goscelin of Saint Bertin', *Studia Anselmia*, xxxvii (1955), 1–117; it is discussed by A. Wilmart, 'Ève et Goscelin (ii)', *Revue Bénédictine*, l (1938), 42–83; see also A. Wilmart, 'La Légende de Ste Édith par le moine Goscelin', *Analecta Bollandiana*, lvi (1938), 1–101.

to the Five Wounds, and an association of the seven monastic hours with seven stages of the Passion.

These are a few of the many anticipations of the kind of meditation upon the life of Christ, and in particular His Passion, that was first fully expounded and taught by the Cistercians. Both St. Bernard and St. William of St. Thierry stress in their instruction the value of a carnal love of Christ as a first stage in contemplation, a love which is to be stimulated by a devout concentration upon His life. The most important and best-known exposition of this doctrine occurs in St. Bernard's twentieth sermon on the Song of Songs.[1] In this sermon St. Bernard analyses the carnal love that man should give to Christ, and describes how those who are stirred by this kind of love are moved by the stories of Christ's life, and experience a deep compassion for His sufferings. This is the manner of meditation for those who cannot yet bear the full blaze of Christ's divinity, and must rest beneath the shadow of His flesh. The same point is made by St. William of St. Thierry in the tenth of the meditations he composed for those whom he called beginners in prayer:[2] those, he says, who are as yet infants in the Church, unable to partake of solid food, may feed on milk, that is meditate upon the Nativity and Passion, whilst they are still unable to gaze on the brightness of God's majesty. In his famous *Epistola aurea* to the Carthusians of Monte Dei,[3] St. William urges the monks, who were dedicated by their Carthusian vocation to a life of asceticism and contemplation, to spend at least one hour of the day in reflection upon the Passion, and defines this exercise as a spiritual partaking of the Eucharist.

This theory underwent a further development when it became modified to suit the needs of laymen. The extreme stage of this development can be seen in the comments of some of the fourteenth-century English mystical writers, Walter Hilton[4] and the author of *The Cloud of Unknowing*.[5] Though repeatedly recommended by Hilton, meditation on the Passion is not an integral part of his contemplative theory, whilst in *The Cloud* it is not even considered a part of the contemplative life, but, with the seven works of mercy, makes up the duty of the active life. In other words, meditation on the Passion ceases to be considered a first step in contemplation—this view would, of course, have been quite inconsistent with the negative mysticism of *The Cloud of Unknowing*—and becomes a devotional exercise complete in itself. The fact that this

---

[1] *P.L.* 183, 867–72; Gilson, op. cit. 78–80. A very ample account of St. Bernard's theory is given by J.-Ch. Didier, 'La Dévotion à l'humanité du Christ dans la spiritualité de saint Bernard', *La Vie spirituelle*, xxiv, xxv (Aug.–Sept. 1930).

[2] *Meditativae orationes*, ed. M. M. Davy (Paris, Liège, 1934), 210–21.

[3] *P.L.* 184, 307–54.

[4] *The Scale of Perfection*, ed. E. Underhill (London, 1948), 79–81 and *passim*.

[5] Ed. Phyllis Hodgson, E.E.T.S. 218, 47–48.

form of meditation does not logically fit in a comprehensive system of thought in the fourteenth-century mystical writers, as it had done in the work of St. Bernard, suggests that they commend it, not on theoretical grounds, but empirically as a common devotional practice of their time.

If meditation on the Passion was to be practised by those who had no particular intellectual or religious training, it was obviously necessary to do more than prescribe it: the uninstructed must not only be told to meditate, but also given a meditation. In Aelred's *Letter to his Sister*,[1] in the *Meditations of the Monk of Farne*,[2] in the very full and very popular *Meditationes vitae Christi*,[3] and in many other works, this kind of meditation is provided. Though most of these were at first intended for contemplatives, often women, the frequency with which some of them were translated into the vernacular shows that they later reached a wider audience. In the thirteenth century, however, it would be exceptional for a layman to possess a manuscript, other than a book of hours—even this would be still quite rare—and most people would therefore need to be verbally instructed and to be given a meditation that could be memorized. The early Passion lyrics would appropriately serve this purpose, and, indeed, most of the manuscripts containing them obviously belong to the preachers rather than the taught.[4] *Accidia*, in the person of a slothful layman, confesses in *Piers Plowman*:

> But I can rymes of Robyn Hood and Randolf erle of Chestre,
> Ac neither of owre lorde ne of owre lady the leste that evere was made.[5]

Here a knowledge of religious lyrics seems to be classed with a knowledge of the Pater Noster, the performance of penances, and the practice of the seven works of mercy.

The religious lyrics can thus be seen to spring from the doctrine of the great Cistercians, but the immediate sources were a number of Latin works, written in the preceding centuries, which were thought to be by St. Bernard himself, St. Anselm, and—with less appropriateness —by St. Augustine. In these certain themes recur, and passages thought to be particularly fine were borrowed from one meditation for another,

---

[1] *P.L.* 32, 1451–74. The second part, which includes the meditative section, has been translated by G. Webb and A. Walker (Mowbray's Fleur de Lys Series, 1957).

[2] Ed. Hugh Farmer, *Studia Anselmia*, xli (1957), 141–245; trans. with an introduction by Hugh Farmer (London, 1961).

[3] Bonaventura, *Opera omnia* ed. A. C. Peltier, xii (Paris, 1868), 509–630. The Quaracchi edition does not include the text (For authorship see below p. 183, n.1). The most recent and best translation, though taken from an Italian translation of the *Meditationes*, is that of Isa Ragusa and Rosalie Green (Princeton, 1961), and it is to this that all references will be made.

[4] For an account of the manuscripts see Appendix A.

[5] B Text V, 402–3, ed. W. W. Skeat (Oxford, 1924), 166.

and in fact became the common property of meditative writers, often being quoted out of context as independent passages. It was these passages that writers first translated into English, but in the earliest verses difficulties in attaining a satisfactory style and structure can be seen.

Lacking a native lyric tradition the authors at first produced verse clumsy in style and inhibitedly careful in its adherence to the content of the Latin original. These first attempts at an English meditative lyric have in common a mnemonic brevity and a bare listing of detail to provide the main points of an image for the visual imagination. In them can be seen most blatantly one of the chief characteristics of medieval poetry and art: its complete explicitness. This kind of poetry may seem at first sight attenuated to those who prefer the obliquely stated and half-concealed, and would have the emotional response less clearly delimited by the writer; but at its best it has the classical qualities of clear precision, harmonious control, lightness, and emotional balance: lucidity is quite different from *naïveté* and superficiality. At its worst, however, explicitness may produce a specious air of completeness and a thin enumeration of detail, and some of the earliest lyrics do not quite escape this.

The second difficulty, that of meditative structure, was particularly pressing, in that some of the finest passages of meditative detail in the Latin devotional sources were not set directly in a meditative form. There are three possible structures. Of these the least effective is that of a preacher's address to the meditator: this comes near to being merely narrative, but is distinct because the reader is personally addressed. The other two forms make up the two parts of a dialogue: either the meditator directly addresses Christ or Christ speaks to the meditator. But two of the Latin passages, which were adapted over and over again in the early lyrics, did not take any of these three forms, but, like much earlier contemplative writing, were addressed to God.

One was the passage beginning *Candet nudatum pectus* from the sixth of the *Meditationes* of St. Augustine,[1] recently identified as the work of John of Fécamp.[2] In its original context this passage was a prayer to God the Father (*Aspice, mitissime Conditor . . .*) to look on the sufferings of Christ and thereby to show mercy. In the English verse translations, this setting, irrelevant to the meditative purpose, was omitted;[3] but in the earliest version, which was copied at least eight times[4] from 1240 to

---

[1] *P.L.* 40, 906.

[2] J. Leclercq and J.-P. Bonnes, *Un Maître de la vie spirituelle au xiᵉ siècle, Jean de Fécamp* (Paris, 1946), 44 and footnote 1.

[3] There is one exception, 'þu þad madist alle þinc' (Brown XIII, 33). It is an appeal of Christ on the Cross to the Father, the author having taken the prayer to be the words of Christ.

[4] Six are enumerated in *Index*, 4088, to which must be added two other early manuscripts, Digby 45, 25ʳ, and Rawl. C. 317, 103ᵛ. I am very indebted to Dr. Hunt for this

1375 (John of Grimestone's preaching-book), it was not replaced by anything else:

> Wit was his nakede brest and red of blod his side,
> Bloc was his faire neb, his wnden depe an wide,
> starke waren his armes hi-spred op-on þe rode;
> In fif steden an his bodi stremes hurne of blode.[1]

The vocative address to God has gone and so have the present tenses, and as a result the immediacy of description has been lost. At the same time the translator has kept narrowly close to the content of the Latin, whilst at the same time inevitably not retaining its force, which derived from the deliberately unemotive listing of the signs of suffering in a series of three word phrases.[2]

It was not long, however, before this passage was translated with greater stylistic freedom and new powers of adaptive technique. In MS. Digby 55 (*c.* 1270) there occurs the following version:

> Wyt is þi nachede brest   and blodi is þi side,
> Starke weren þine armes   þat strekede weren so wyde.
> Falu es thi faire ler   and dummes þi sithe,
> Drie es þin ende body   on rode so ytycthe.
> Þine þedes hongen colde   al so þe marbre ston,
> Þine thirlede fet   þe rede blod byron.[3]

In the earliest version there had only been one hint of emotion, the adjective *faire*, but in this verse emotive adjectives are emphatically placed in the two middle lines, 'Falu es thi *faire* ler' and 'Drie es þin *ende* body', and the emotion suggested here is reinforced by the rhetorical use of *so*, 'on rode so ytycthe' and 'þat strekede weren so wyde'. The compassion conveyed by the style is appropriate to the change in structure, for this is a personal meditation, and the meditator is given here not only the details of a visual image but also a personal lament: the present tense and the direct address both bring home to him that in his imagination he is standing at the foot of the Cross, present in the historical

---

information. The text of Digby 45 is close to that in Bodley 42 (Brown XIV, 1 B): the differences are insignificant, except that it has the better reading *bloc* at the beginning of l. 2 (cf. Durham Cathedral A. III, 12, *bleye* and Adv. 18. 7. 21, 117ʳ *bleike*). The Rawl. text is linked to the latter (Brown XIV, p. 241) by the reading *lires* in l. 2.

[1] Brown XIV, 1 B. In l. 2. MS. *blod* is emended to *bloc*. Neb: face; *starke*: rigid; *hurne*: ran.

[2] Candet nudatum pectus. Rubet cruentum latus. Tensa arent viscera. Decora languent lumina. Regia pallent ora. Procera rigent brachia. Crura dependent marmorea. Et rigat terebratos pedes beati sanguinis unda. Brown XIV, p. 241.

[3] S. Harrison Thomson, 'The Date of the Early English Translation of the *Candet nudatum pectus*', *Medium Aevum*, iv (1935), 104 (this article is useful in establishing the thirteenth-century date of some of the manuscripts: the latter is noted in the second edition of Brown XIV, revised by G. Smithers, Oxford, 1957). In the copying of Middle English lyrics tenses were often confused: *weren* in l. 2 should surely be emended to *aren*. Falu: pale; *ler*: cheek; *drie*: lifeless; *þedes*: thighs; *þirlede*: pierced.

scene, and able to take part in it. This was the basic exercise in simple Cistercian meditation, which had begun with Aelred's *Letter to his Sister*: in this he directs her to imagine herself present in all the great episodes of Christ's life, and at the Crucifixion she is told to stand, not with the women, 'quae longe stant', but 'cum matre virgine et discipulo virgine accede ad crucem, et perfusum pallore vultum cominus intuere'.[1] This exercise recurs over and over again in Latin meditative prose and verse of the thirteenth and fourteenth centuries. With this short English verse it appears in English literature for the first time.

There is yet one further adaptation of the *Candet nudatum pectus* that is worth discussing. It is preserved in John of Grimestone's preaching-book, which contains both the old stilted version and the following much freer one:

> Bare was þat quite brest and red þe blodi side,
> þe bodi stark als þu wel sest, þe armes spred out wyde;
> þe lippes pale and reuli þat er weren brith and rede,
> þe eyne þat weren loveli nou ben dimme and dede;
> þe faire lemes bowed and bent hangend on þe rode,
> þe feet ben þirled an torent and stremen al on blode.[2]

Here the structure is the slightly less effective one of sermon address, but the listener is by implication exhorted to the same kind of meditation ('als þu wel sest'). The need for compassion is especially emphasized by the style: the degree of suffering is driven home by pairs of almost synonymous adjectives, *bowed and bent*, *þirled an torent*, and the pathos of Christ's agony is conveyed by the contrasts of the two middle lines. The succinctness of the Latin, verb, objectively descriptive adjective, noun, has here quite vanished, and, whilst the freedom adopted by the translator has perhaps led to a slight slackness in style, it is nevertheless quite an agreeable attempt at meditative verse: it may, of course, have been written a century or more before the date of John of Grimestone's preaching-book.

The other much-copied Latin commonplace is that beginning *Respice in faciem Christi tui*. The original context for this is now not known, but in slightly varying versions it is quoted by Richard Rolle and Ludolf the Carthusian (who attributes it to St. Bernard), and it is copied independently in MS. Digby 55 (where it follows the version of the

---

[1] *P.L.* 32, 1470 (where the treatise is printed as an appendix to the works of St. Augustine, under the title *De vita eremitica*) '. . . with the virgin mother and the virgin disciple go to the Cross and, together with them, gaze on His face suffused with pallor'. Cf. J. Leclercq, 'Les méditations d'un moine au xiie siècle', *Revue Mabillon*, xxxiv (1944), 1–19, where the monk accompanies Christ everywhere from the Nativity to the Crucifixion.

[2] MS. Adv. 18.7.21, 120^r. *Reuli*: pitiful; *þirled an torent*: pierced and torn.

Candet quoted above), and in John of Grimestone's preaching-book.[1]
The opening words are a quotation from Psalm lxxxiii. 10, and, as the
word *tuus* indicates, they are addressed to God. It is probable that it was
in this way that the passage was first used, but to turn the *respice* into
an injunction of a preacher was a very simple transformation to make,
and it is quite likely that, when the Latin was quoted independently in
devotional manuscripts, it was understood in this sense without any
verbal alterations whatsoever. With the exception of the related complaints, 'Man and wyman, loket to me'[2] and 'Alle þat gos and rydys
loket opon me'[3] (which we will discuss later), the English poems based
on this passage are in the form of sermon address. The earliest, 'Loke
man to iesu crist',[4] occurs in MS. Bodley 42, dated about 1260, and
also containing a version of the *Candet*. It is, however, too inferior to
quote: irregularities in the rhyme scheme suggest considerable errors
in transmission, but even so it is fair to assume that the original text
was unfeeling and unconfident.

The longer version of MSS. St. John's 15 and Harley 913[5] (despite
some padding in the latter) is much more successful:

> Loke to þi loverd, man, þar hanget he a rode,
> and wep hyf þo mist terres al of blode.
> Vor loke hu his heved biis mid þornes bi-wnde,
> and to his neb so bispet and to þe spere-wnde.
> Falwet his feyre luer, and desewet his sicte,
> drowepet his hendi bodi þat on rode biis itiht.
> Blickied his brest nacked and bledet hiis side,
> stiviet hiis arms þat istreid beð so wide.
> Loke to þe nailes on honde and on fote,
> hu þe stremes hurned of þat swete blod.
> Bigin at his molde and loke to his to,
> ne saltu no wit vinde bute anguisse and wo.[6]

This is the first poem to mention tears, which, from the time of St.
Bernard onwards, were considered the outward sign of the fitting inward
response to the Passion. The grounds for weeping are stylistically
evoked: by the emphatic placing of the verb at the beginning of the

[1] The Latin text from this manuscript is printed in Brown XIV, p. 242, where the
references to Richard Rolle and Ludolf the Carthusian will also be found. The correct
inference from the copying of the Latin alone in MS. Digby 55 and John of Grimestone's preaching-book is much more probably that the compilers knew an English
translation than that they did not.

[2] Brown XIV, 4.

[3] M. R. James, *A Descriptive Catalogue of the Manuscripts of Lambeth Palace Library*
(Cambridge, 1932), 760.

[4] Brown XIV, 2 A.

[5] A. Heuser, *Die Kildare-Gedichte* (Bonner Beiträge zur Anglistik, xiv), 128.

[6] MS. St. John's Coll. Camb. 15, Brown XIV, 2 B. *Falwet*: grows pale; *luer*: cheek;
desewet: grows dim; *blickied*: glows white; *hurned*: run; *molde*: head.

clause (a device borrowed from the *Candet*), by the use of loving epithets, *his hendi bodi*, *swete blod*, etc., and by the urgency of the repeated injunction, *loke, beholde*, etc. In the version of MS. Harley 913 there is a final couplet in which the relationship of love between Christ and the meditator is stressed by the phrase *þi swete lemman*:[1] the meditator is exhorted to look at his sweet lover, in whose body there is no place whole and free from suffering. In the use of this word and in the many loving epithets can be seen devices of style characteristic of the Harley lyrics and the poetry of Richard Rolle. They have been used here with skill to soften the austere compression of the style of the original Latin.

Another poem set in the form of sermon address and similarly based on a well-liked Latin passage is that beginning, 'Man, folwe seintt Bernardes trace':

> Man, folwe seintt Bernardes trace
> And loke in ihesu cristes face,
> How hee lut hys heved to þe
> Swetlike for to kessen þe,
> And sprat hise armes on þe tre,
> Senful man, to klippen þe.
> In sygne of love ys open his syde;
> Hiis feet y-nayled wid þe tabyde.
> Al his bodi is don on rode,
> Senful man, for þyne goode.[2]

It expresses neatly and movingly in allegorical form the doctrine of Christ's demonstration of love in the Passion. The earliest occurrence of the Latin text on which it is based is the thirty-second of the *Sermones ad fratres in eremo*,[3] though with some verbal differences which make it more austere in tone. In a more elaborate and emotive version it is presented in the tenth of the meditations attributed to Anselm.[4] Like the *Respice* it is a floating commonplace, one which was in due course attributed to St. Bernard, who had come to be thought of as a writer of meditations as well as an exponent of meditative theory. St. Bonaventura, who quotes the passage in the *De perfectione vitae ad sorores*, begins, like the English verse, with an authoritative reference to St. Bernard, 'Vide, inquit Bernardus . . .'.[5]

This passage was as popular in English devotional writing as it was

---

[1] l. 15. ed. cit. 128.

[2] Brown XIII, 69. *Lut*: bows; *klippen*: embrace.

[3] *P.L.* 40, 1293. The ascription of the sermons to St. Augustine is without foundation: they are a mixed collection, some, for instance, being by Caesarius of Arles; others cannot be earlier than the twelfth century.

[4] *P.L.* 158, 761–2. The meditation is of unknown authorship.

[5] *Decem Opuscula*, ed. PP. Collegii S. Bonaventurae (Quaracchi, 1949), 297. The attribution to St. Bernard is also found in MS. Trinity 323 (Brown XIII, p. 194).

in Latin: it was, for instance, echoed by the author of the *Ancrene Wisse*[1] and paraphrased in one of the poems of Richard Rolle.[2] Though the English verse, rather surprisingly, survives in only one manuscript, the Latin original is copied in two important lyric manuscripts, MS. Trinity 323[3] and John of Grimestone's preaching-book.[4] The correct inference from this may be that the compilers knew an English version rather than that they did not.

The occurrence of this verse in three languages, the three versions side by side in the manuscript,[5] whilst no doubt originally intended for the benefit of various audiences, nowadays draws attention to the meditative superiority of the English. The concision of the Latin drives home the ingenuity of the interpretation; the French is more immediate and direct, in that the past participles of the first half of the line have been replaced by active verbs; the English, however, not only has the active verbs, but also heightens the tone of personal and loving relationship by the insertion of the single adverb *swetlike*, and by the repetition of the phrase *senful man*, which recalls the traditional antithesis between the love of Christ and the unworthiness of man. The mystical kiss of love from the Song of Songs has by the simplicity of the English become transformed into an expression of personal tenderness: a series of clever parallels have lost the force of wit and have become instead a touching interpretation of Christ's pose in the Crucifixion as the familiar gestures of love.

The most complicated and perhaps the most successful of the very early Passion poems is that beginning 'Wenne hic soe on rode idon', which survives in seven related versions:

> Wenne hic soe on rode idon
> ihesus mi leman,
> and bi him stonde
> maria and iohan,
> his herte duepe i-stunge,
> his bodi wiþ scurge i-sswenge,
> for þe luve of man,
> hiþe hi mai wepen
> and selte teres leten,
> ief hic of luve chan.[6]

No Latin original for this is known, though it has various manuscript

---

[1] E.E.T.S. 249, 205. The Latin is copied as part of a prose paragraph at the very end of MS. Cott. Nero A. xiv, E.E.T.S. 225, xxii.

[2] *Ego Dormio, English Writings of Richard Rolle*, ed. H. E. Allen (Oxford, 1931), 68. A Latin rhymed version from MS. Arundel 248 is printed in Brown XIII, p. 219.

[3] f. 83ᵛ, adjoining a text of 'Wenne hic soe on rode idon'.

[4] MS. Adv. 18. 7. 21, 117ʳ.

[5] All three are printed in Brown XIII, 69.

[6] Brown XIII, 35, A. *Hiþe*: freely. 1. 6, *wiþ*, MS. *þis*; l. 10, *luve*, MS. *sunne* (cf. 35 B).

ascriptions: in St. John's 15, for instance, it is described as 'verba Sancti Augustini et Sancti Bernardi'. There is, however, nothing in the verse to suggest that it is a paraphrase of one of the great Latin common-places. After the meditative opening of the first line there is an outline description of the Crucifixion (a point we appreciate nowadays, when we are less used to constructing a whole picture from an assembly of individual details), but the source could well be one of the paintings of the Passion, which by the second half of the thirteenth century were becoming quite common in churches. There then follow two lines which, by contrast, have the precision of the *Respice* imitations, and indeed may well have been borrowed from one of them, whilst the final lines are a general statement about the propriety of tears. The placing of this at the end of the verse, instead of at the beginning, as in the *Respice*, is especi-ally effective, for the initial reference to Christ as *mi leman*, and the later emphasis on the fact that the sufferings were *for þe luve of man*, culmin-ate in the personal emotional statement. The poem therefore contains a movement of thought and a consequent attempt at construction which were necessarily absent from the static content of the other verses. In its construction and combination of Passion description with expressions of feeling, it seems an anticipation in miniature of the long, moving Passion laments of MS. Harley 2253, which we shall later describe.

The value of the meditative form in these short poems can very clearly be seen if a verse is compared with them, which at first sight seems to be of the same kind, and indeed is included with them in John of Grimestone's preaching-book:

> Man, siker helpe hast þu and prest:
> þe moder þe sone sewt hire brest,
> þe sone his fader his blodi side
> and alle his wondis depe an wyde.
> þer may ben non werningge
> þer love is of so gret sewingge.[1]

The ultimate source of this verse is the *De laudibus B. Mariae Virginis* of Arnold of Bonneval,[2] but it probably derives more immediately from 'Le triple exercise' of Stephen, the early thirteenth-century abbot of the Cistercian monastery of Sawley in Yorkshire,[3] where the form is also that of a vocative address to man. But, despite the direct sermon address of the hearer, suggesting the meditative tradition, this theme is unmeditative, in that it consists of a self-contained scene which does

---

[1] Adv. 18. 7. 21, 117ʳ, ll. 5–6, 'Love so powerfully demonstrated cannot be denied.' A text from MS. Harley 7322 is printed in E.E.T.S. 15, 264.

[2] *P.L.* 189, 1726.

[3] A. Wilmart, 'Le triple exercise d'Étienne de Sallai', *Revue d'ascétique et de mys-tique*, xi (1930), 355–74.

not involve the beholder. The subject is the perpetual intercession in heaven on man's behalf, wherein Christ to plead His sufferings shows His wounds to the Father, and the Blessed Virgin in the classical gesture of maternal appeal shows her breasts to Christ.[1] This theme of intercession has affinities with the Last Judgement,[2] and indeed in the representation of the latter in *Queen Mary's Psalter* the traditional interceding Virgin makes the same maternal gesture.[3] It is therefore the judge (Christ in the Last Judgement and God the Father in the *Scala salutis*) who is seated frontally and faces outwards, and the figures, who express their love for man, face inwards towards Him, and it is He who cannot deny their demonstration of love; and so the demand for compassion necessarily does not extend from the subject to the beholder or listener, but remains self-contained. The meditator is therefore excluded and can only admire the dogmatic truth thus pictorially expressed. It may well be for this reason that the English verse remains so stilted and unmoving, for it was most probably not composed before the fourteenth century when meditative verse was normally much more poised and effective.

The setting of the meditations so far described has either been that of sermon address—the preacher exhorts his hearer to gaze at Christ on the Cross and stresses the details of suffering there plainly to be seen —or that of first-person monologue, in which the meditator in his imagination stands at the foot of the Cross, grieving over the signs of pain and redemption. Of these two forms the second was the more pleasing, for its tone was the tender melancholy of a man expressing compassion for a beloved by describing to him the signs of suffering that he sees. By contrast, in the preacher's address there was a distinctly hortatory colouring. There was, however, a third form, equally popular and equally interchangeable with the others, in which Christ Himself appeals to man: the meditator still stands in the presence of Christ, but he is silent as Christ speaks to him. The tone of these complaints varies between the didactically reproachful and the loving, but there is in them always the effect gained from direct communication, which was necessarily lacking in the sermon form in which the preacher intervenes between Christ and the meditator.

This intimate directness can especially be seen in a short dialogue,

[1] The classical origins of this gesture are discussed by E. Panofsky, 'Imago pietatis', *Festschrift für Max J. Friedländer* (Leipzig, 1927), footnote 75, p. 302.

[2] In the fifteenth-century *Speculum humanae salvationis*, the representation of the Last Judgement is preceded by that of the *Scala salutis*: the accompanying types are Antipater showing his wounds to Julius Caesar (a story deriving from Peter Comestor and ultimately from Josephus), and Esther pleading before Ahasuerus. Ed. J. Lutz and P. Perdrizet, Mulhouse, 1907–9, ii, pls. 77–78.

[3] Ed. G. Warner (London, 1912), pl. 297. For the iconography see M. Meiss, 'An Early Altarpiece from the Cathedral of Florence', *Bulletin of the Metropolitan Museum of Art*, xii (1954), 302–17.

combining the complaint with the personal meditation. It adjoins the
Respice verse in MS. Digby 55:

> Swete leman y deye for þi love;
> yf y deye for þe
> wy ne wiltu lonþen me þin ore.
> þi love bindes me sore,
> Thenc wat y tholie lef for þe,
> Bylef þine sinnes and toren the to me.
>
> Wen ihc ave al don mine folie
> thanne wily Jesu merci þe crie.
> þin ore, þin ore mi swete leman,
> sore me reues that y ave misdon.[1]

In this, love, reproach, and contrition are touchingly combined. Though
at first sight the colloquial simplicity may suggest that this dialogue is
quite uncontrived, there is in fact in it a delicately ironic treatment of
the conventional plea for mercy. In the first speech Christ, like the
traditional lover, asks for *ore*, as though He were in the professedly
inferior position of the courtly lover. In man's reply, however, this is
reversed, as he pleads emphatically, 'þin ore, þin ore mi swete leman',
and in this exclamation the term *ore* seems to embrace both the mercy
shown by God to sinners and the mercy shown by the granting of love
to a beloved.

This verse, however, is exceptional, not only in being a dialogue, but
also in its sweet and very personal tone. For the origins of the complaint
form encouraged it to be personal but not intimate. These origins were
various sentences in the Old Testament, which by established tradition
in gloss and liturgy were interpreted as the speech of Christ: 'O vos
omnes qui transitis per viam, attendite et videte si est dolor sicut dolor
meus' (Lamentations i. 12); 'Popule meus, quid feci tibi?' (Micah
vi. 3); 'Quid est quod debui ultra facere . . .' (Isaiah v. 4). These texts
have in common that they address a plural audience, that they were used
in the Easter liturgy, and that from an early date they had provided the
authority and structure for a complaint of Christ at the Last Judgement.
The earliest known example of this kind of complaint, that of St. Ephraem in his *De Judicio et Compunctione*, illustrates well the main characteristics of the form:

. . . Propter vos flagellatus sum, propter vos virgis caesus sum, propter vos
crucifixus sum, exaltatus in ligno . . . Quid amplius his mihi fuit agendum,
quod non egerim, ut salvemini?[2]

---

[1] Thomson, loc. cit. 105. l. 3, *lonþen* for *lenden*?

[2] *Opera Omnia, Graece, Syriace, Latine*, ii, ed. S. E. Assemani (Rome, 1743), 51. 'For
you I was scourged, for you beaten with rods, for you I was crucified and raised upon

The descriptions of sufferings in a Last Judgement complaint were necessarily in the past tense, but the text from Lamentations would have facilitated—if indeed any help were needed—the transposition of the preterites into the present tense. The more difficult transition was from the plural to the singular, that is the appropriate change of tone for a speech addressed to a single meditator rather than to the assembled congregation of the Last Judgement. With the exception of the English verses which paraphrase the *Improperia*, this was generally achieved by supporting the simple grammatical change from plural to singular with a modification in tone which suggested the singling out of an individual: the meditator is not addressed as though the scene were a private meeting between lovers, but he seems to be isolated from a crowd and, though standing amongst many, to be the special object of the impassioned or reproachful plea.

The element of reproach remained especially strong, and many of the early complaints of Christ are unmoving, partly because they lack the sweetness and gentleness of the other forms, and partly because the reproach depended upon a paradoxical antithesis between Christ's charity and man's sinfulness. But the pointed expression of paradoxes requires a poise and precision that were normally beyond the capacity of English writers at least until the middle of the fourteenth century, and which, in comparison with those of seventeenth-century poetry, were beyond the range of English literature throughout the Middle Ages. This point may be illustrated from the various translations of a short Latin verse by Philip the Chancellor (of the University of Paris) at the beginning of the thirteenth century, which was copied many times, often being attributed to St. Bernard:

> Homo, vide, quae pro te patior,
> Si est dolor sicut, quo crucior,
> Ad te clamo, qui pro te morior,
> Vide poenas, quibus afficior,
> Vide clavos, quibus confodior,
> Cum sit tantus dolor exterior,
> Interior planctus est gravior,
> Tam ingratum dum te experior.[1]

Though in this there is insistence on the gazing at the signs of suffering, and the third line in its succinctness powerfully and movingly brings

the Cross ... What else ought I to have done, and did not do, that you might be saved?' This passage is quoted at greater length by A. S. Cook in his edition of the *Crist* (Boston, 1900), 210. His notes to *Crist*, 1379–1498, contain other useful quotations and references.

[1] *A.H.* xxi. 10. 'O man, see what I undergo for you, see whether there is any pain such as that which torments me; I, who am dying for your sake, now call to you. See the pangs which I suffer, see the nails by which I am pierced. But though my external suffering is great, yet even heavier is my inward grief when I find you so unkind.'

Christ and the meditator into the closest possible relationship, yet all this
is subordinated to the final, didactic paradox.

One of the earliest surviving English translations occur in the much-
copied Franciscan preaching-book, the *Fasciculus morum*.[1] In this Latin
work, which incorporates a number of English verses, the Latin of
Philip the Chancellor is first quoted and then there follows the English
verse, which inevitably misses the tight logic and theological precision[2]
of the original:

> Byholde, mon, what I dree,
> whech is my payne, whech is my woo,
> to the I clepe now I shal dye,
> Byse the wel for I mot go.
> Byholde þe nayles þat ben witoute
> How þey me þorlet to þys tre,
> Of all my pyne have I no doute
> But ȝif unkynde I fynde the.[3]

The only point of the Latin original that this preserves without impoverishment is the emphasis on looking. Otherwise the important echo
of Lamentations in line 2, the poignant compression of line 3, and the
paradoxical unexpectedness of lines 6–7, which is emphasized by chias-
mus, have all vanished in the translation. The verse is no longer the neat
and elegant expression of a scholastic commonplace, and although the
translator's aim has evidently been to keep close to the Latin, he has
in fact only succeeded in translating every other line. The force of the
Latin depends upon the tautness of its syntax, and the translator has
lost this without introducing any characteristic English virtues.

It would be tedious to enumerate and compare all the other translations of this verse.[4] But at least three of them are more successful, in that
to a greater or lesser extent they preserve the sense of the original, and
in that they compensate for what has been lost by adding emotive detail
from the native meditative tradition. One of these occurs in the Kildare
Manuscript,[5] another in John of Grimestone's preaching-book.[6] The

---

[1] This work, to which frequent reference will have to be made, is unfortunately
unprinted. It is described by A. G. Little, *Studies in English Franciscan History* (Manchester, 1917), 139–57. Its date and manuscripts are discussed by F. Foster. 'A Note
on the *Fasciculus morum*', *Franciscan Studies*, viii (1948), 202–4.

[2] It was for these qualities that St. Bonaventura quoted the verse in his answer to
the *quaestio*, 'Utrum dolor fuerit intensior in parte rationali animae Christi, an in parte
sensuali', *Sententiarum lib.* iii, Dist. xvi, art. ii, qu. 3, *Opera Omnia*, iii (Quaracchi,
1887), 359.

[3] MS. Rawl. C. 670, 45ᵛ.

[4] *Index*, 495, 1902, 2502, 3109, 3826, 3827. To the manuscripts listed in the *Index*
must be added MS. Digby 45, 21ᵛ–22ʳ. I owe the latter reference to Dr. Hunt.

[5] *Die Kildare-Gedichte*, 129.

[6] Brown xiv, 70. In his notes to this poem Brown refers to an Anglo-Norman version
in MS. Phillipps 8336 (now BM. Add. MS. 46919), but this poem (*inc.* 'Vous ke me
veez en la croiz morir') is not related to the *Homo vide*. There is, however, a French

best, however, is the version which accompanies the poems of Richard
Rolle in the Cambridge Manuscript:

> Unkynde man, gif kepe til me
> and loke what payne I suffer for þe.
> Synful man on þe I cry,
> alanly for þi lufe I dy.
> Behalde, þe blode fra me downe rennes,
> noght for my gylt bot for þi synnes.
> My hende, my fete, with nayles er fest;
> syns and vayns al to-brest;
> þe blode owt of my hert-rote,
> loke, it falles downe to my fote.
> Of al þe payne þat I suffer sare,
> with-in my hert it greves me mare
> þe unkyndenes þat I fynd in þe,
> þat for þi lufe þus hynged on tre.[1]

This version does not attempt to reproduce the brevity and concision
of the Latin: it introduces further signs of suffering, and adds touches of
the dramatic and pathetic. In particular it deals skilfully with the line
'Ad te clamo, qui pro te morior', translating it in its context by a simple
statement of love, '. . . alanly for þi lufe I dy', and then reverting to it in
the very last line of the poem, so that it forms the climax of the whole.

It is clear that the best English versions of the *Homo vide* are more
like in feeling to other vernacular meditative verses than to their source.
They are feeble only so long as they attempt to reproduce the logical
tightness and paradox of the Latin. Paradox and antithesis are more
likely to generate astonishment than love, and it may be for this reason
only that vernacular writers avoided them. But it is also possible that
they were aware of the limitations of the language they used. There is,
for instance, a moving and favourite passage in Latin meditations,
beginning, 'Quid commisisti dulcissime puer . . .'.[2] This passage seems

version, *inc.* 'Ha. hons et fame, voy que sueffre pur toy', which was often copied (Sonet
727). The eight-stanza text from MS. B.N. 12483 is printed by A. Långfors in *Notices
et extraits des manuscrits de la bibliothèque nationale*, xxxix (1909), 535–7; of this expanded
version stanzas 1, 2, and 5 are based on the *Homo vide*. The same text is copied on the
last page of MS. Douce 252, a manuscript described by K. Chesney, 'A Fifteenth
Century Miscellany', *Studies Presented to M. K. Pope* (Manchester, 1939), 61–70: this
poem, however, is omitted from the list of contents.

[1] Brown xiv, 77. Cf. Brown xv, 104 and note. There is no reason to believe that this
translation is by Richard Rolle. The group of poems in the Cambridge MS., of which
Brown xiv, 77 and 78 are the first two, are preceded by a general *incipit*, 'Hic incipiunt
cantus compassionis Christi . . .', but concluded by an *explicit* attributing the preceding verse to Rolle. There is thus a discrepancy between the *incipit* and the *explicit* (not
all the poems in the group are *cantus compassionis Christi*), and whilst there is uncertainty
about some poems in this section, it seems clear that the first two at least are governed
solely by the *incipit* (see also Appendix D).

[2] *Orationes*, 2, attributed to Anselm, *P.L.* 158, 861, and the *Meditationes* attributed to

to have been quite as much a *locus classicus* of meditative literature as
was the *Candet nudatum pectus*, and it was a very touching first-person
meditation. But it consists of a moving series of contrasts between
Christ's innocent sufferings and man's unscathed guiltiness, which
would not have gone smoothly into English verse. That this omission
was not merely accidental is suggested also by the treatment of the
Popule meus theme, though here the question of meditative effectiveness
might also have had influence.

The *Improperia*, or Good Friday reproaches, consists almost solely
of a series of ingenious antitheses. But, although its use was not confined
to the liturgy—it is quoted, for instance, in the *Soliloquies* of St. Bonaventura, where it is immediately preceded by the *Homo vide*[1]—it was
translated into English only twice. The first translation is that of Friar
William Herebert at the beginning of the fourteenth century, and is
exceptional in forming part of a set of liturgical paraphrases. The other
is in John of Grimestone's preaching-book, where it was presumably
intended for popular and devotional purposes. Neither is satisfying: the
earlier is stilted and the second diffuse, as can be seen from a comparison
of the following verses:

> Of the ston ich dronk to þe;
> And þou wyth galle drincst to me.[2]

> Heilsum water i sente þe
> out of þe harde ston;
> and eysil and galle þu sentist me,
> oþer ȝef þu me non.[3]

The second is the more disappointing, in that the first has the limited
aim of being a literal translation of a liturgical text, whereas in the second
we might have expected some meditative expansion. One would not, of
course, look for the invention or even the borrowing of paradoxes that
characterize the style of Herbert's 'The Sacrifice'. However, Herbert's
poem is not only more witty but also more moving, and one of the
reasons for its greater emotiveness is that he has reversed the order in
each antithesis, so that it is the statement of suffering that comes first,

Augustine, ch. 7, *P.L.* 40, 906. The first words were reproduced in the opening line of
a short lyric on the Passion (in an *exemplum* context) in MS. Lambeth 78, 264ᵛ, 'Swete
Ihesu what was thy gylt . . .' and in the second stanza of a hitherto unnoticed poem in
Dives et Pauper, 'Whan I þinke on cristes blod', MS. Douce 295, 143ʳ; it is a translation
of the Latin hymn, 'Reminiscens beati sanguinis', *A.H.* viii, 11. In the fifteenth-century
manuscript, MS. C.U.L. Kk. i. 6, 148ᵛ, in a series of translations said to be taken from
Augustine, Anselm, and Bernard, there occurs a fairly close prose translation, beginning
'O swete child, þe swetest þat ever was, what amysse dede ye, þat ye were so vylensly
juged . . .'.

[1] *Decem Opuscula*, 79–80.

[2] Brown xiv, 15. *Dronk, drincst*: gave, give drink.   [3] Ibid. 72.

the ironic contrast second. The whole poem thus becomes a consistent narrative of the Passion, whilst the Middle English poems remain a series of disjointed contrasts. This kind of simple but important re-arrangement would have been within the powers of a Middle English writer, but the difficulty of expressing paradoxes in English perhaps inhibited the construction of an independent poem.

It is valuable to make a contrast between these inadequate translations of the *Improperia* and a poem, 'Ihesus doþ him bymene', from a late four-teenth-century manuscript. This poem, which ironically relates the appearance of Christ in the Passion to the fashionable dress and habits of a dandy, shows a quite striking ability to control paradoxical anti-theses. The source of the poem is a very popular passage, which is quoted in the most important preaching books, the *Fasciculus morum*,[1] the *Legenda aurea*,[2] the *Summa praedicantium*, and (in English) in Mirk's *Festial*,[3] where it is, as elsewhere, attributed to St. Bernard. The passage in the *Summa praedicantium* may be considered close to the source of the Middle English lyric:

> Tu es homo, et habes sertum de floribus: et ego Deus, et habeo spineam coronam . . . Tu chirothecas habes in manibus et ego clavos. Tu tripudias cum pedibus: et ego laboravi. Tu in choreis brachia extendis in modum Crucis ad vanum gaudium: et ego in Cruce ad opprobrium. Tu habes latus apertum in signum vanae gloriae: et ego latus habui effossum ad poenam.[4]

In this passage each contrast is starkly stated and the tone is impersonal. In the English poem, though there are many amplifications, they do not diminish the tautness of the schematic contrasts, so ingeniously parallel and so ironically unlike, and at the same time they intensify the feeling, bringing to life the description of both the suffering Christ and the fastidious vanity of the dandy:

> Þyn hondes streite gloved,
> white and clene kept;
> Myne wiþ nailes þorled,
> on rode and eke my feet.

. . . . . .

---

[1] MS. Rawl. C. 670, 48ʳ.

[2] Trans. William Caxton, ed. F. S. Ellis (Temple Classics, 1900), i. 72. The passage in the *Legenda aurea* was imitated in the *Stanzaic Life of Christ*, 5921–48, E.E.T.S. 166, 200–1. A French version appears in the Dominican manuscript already referred to, MS. B.N. 12483; it is printed by E. Järnström and A. Långfors, *Recueil de chansons pieuses du xiiiᵉ siècle*, ii, Annales academiae scientiarum fennicae, Ser. B, xx (1929), 188–9. [3] E.E.T.S., E.S. 96, 113.

[4] John Bromyard, *Summa praedicantium*, ii (Venice, 1586), 180ʳ. 'You are a man and wear a wreath of flowers: and I am God and wear a crown of thorns. . . . You have gloves on your hands and I have nails through mine. You use your feet in dancing and I in toil. In the dance your arms are stretched out in the form of a cross in empty pleasure: and mine are stretched on the Cross in shame. Your side [i.e. the side of your gown] is slit to show your vanity: and my side is pierced for suffering.'

> opyne þou hast þi syde,
> spaiers longe and wide,
> for veyn glorie and pride,
> and þi longe knyf a-strout—
> þou ert of þe gai route:
> Myn wiþ spere sharpe
> y-stongen to þe herte;
> My body wiþ scourges smerte
> bi-swongen al aboute.[1]

The satiric touches (for instance the word *gay*, recalling Chaucer's Absolon) gain from a tradition of social satire well established in homiletic prose and verse from the beginning of the fourteenth century.[2] Though again in this poem the description of suffering comes second, as it does in the translations of the *Improperia*, there is here no effect of disjointedness, because the scenes in both are static, the dancing worldling as against Christ on the Cross; whereas in the *Improperia* only the second was consistent, the first element of the antithesis being drawn far and wide from Old Testament history.

For writers whose intention was to arouse a loving compassion for Christ in His sufferings, the *O vos omnes* text was potentially a better source than the *Improperia*, or even than the *Homo vide*, which, though it might attract by its epigrammatic enumeration of Christ's pains, was not potentially a source of pathos, being rather the neatly turned expression of a scholastic commonplace: but the difficulty with the *O vos omnes*, was that it had no literary completeness in itself, being rather an introductory summing-up. As an introduction, however, it was laden with meaning, for the text was a key authority for the theologians of the thirteenth century in their solution of the *quaestio*, 'Utrum in Christo fuerit acerbissimus dolor'.[3] Both St. Bonaventura in his *Commentary on the Sentences*[4] and St. Thomas Aquinas in the *Summa Theologica*[5] begin their exposition of the unique acuteness of Christ's suffering with the quotation of this text. St. Bonaventura develops the text by arguing that Christ's sufferings were unparalleled in three ways: in *causa*, for He suffered neither for His own sins nor on behalf of His friends, but for His enemies; in the *modus patiendi*, for He suffered in all parts of the body and for a longer time than one killed outright; and in the *conditio patientis*, for on account of the perfect constitution of His body

---

[1] Brown XIV, 126, pp. 225–6. *Spaiers*: slits in a gown; *a-strout*: sticking out; *bi-swongen*: beaten.

[2] Examples and references are given by G. R. Owst, *Literature and Pulpit in Medieval England* (Oxford, 1961), 404–11.

[3] 'Whether Christ suffered the highest possible degree of pain.'

[4] *Sententiarum lib.* III. xvi. i, 2, ed. cit. III. 348.

[5] *Summa Theologica*, III. xlvi. 6.

His sensitivity, both physical and mental, was more acute than that of any other person. St. Thomas gives four reasons for the uniqueness of Christ's sufferings, adding to the points of St. Bonaventura some further amplification and intellectual subtleties.

The earliest of the extant English verses on this theme, that in the late thirteenth-century manuscript, MS. Lambeth 557—of which a later variant appears in MS. New College 88—appropriately combines an *O vos omnes* opening with detail deriving from the *Respice* text:

> Alle þat gos and rydys loket opon me,
> If evere seye ye pynyn man also men pynen me.
> Loke man to my back hou yt ys ybeten,
> Loke to my sydyn wat blod it havyn iletyn.
> Loke doune to myne fet þat nayled been on rode,
> Loke to myn hevyd þat rennyn al on blode.
> To clensyn þe of synne opon þe rode tre
> I suffrede al þus pyne, man, for love of þe.
> Gyf þou me þat soule þat ys so dere ybouyhte
> Of all þat I þole ne ys me þen nouyhte.[1]

The meaning of the *O vos omnes* is here limited to that which is most readily moving and appropriate, namely that Christ suffered in all parts of the body, and the *Respice* passage then provides a traditional demonstration of this. The argument about the *conditio patientis* is necessarily neglected, for it would be too philosophical for a short meditative lyric, whilst the argument concerning the *causa* is introduced obliquely and given a devotional turn, for in this particular point it is shown that it is within the meditator's power to diminish the sufferings of Christ. However, despite the theoretical merits of this lyric, the clumsiness of metre weakens the effect.

Other paraphrases of the *O vos omnes*, however, make less attempt to develop the potentialities of the theme. The following brief verse from the *Fasciculus morum* is typical of several in its poetical unambitiousness:

> A, ȝe men, þat by me wenden,
> Abydes a while and loke on me,
> ȝef ȝe fynden in any ende
> Suche sorow as here ȝe se on me.[2]

[1] M. R. James, *Catalogue*, 760. The New College text is printed in Brown XIV, 4. Its opening lines, 'Man and wyman, loket to me, / u michel pine ich þolede for þe', lack the precise verbal reference to the *O vos omnes*, and its four concluding lines are independent. This is probably an example of an original poem so altered in transcription that it is difficult to decide whether in the extant texts we have one poem or two. The *Index* at no. 2042 refers for comparison to 3109 and 3827, but these are versions of the *Homo vide*.

[2] MS. Rawl. C. 670, 45ᵛ. *Index* 2596. Similar verses occur in MS. Harley 7322 (E.E.T.S. 15, 261) and in John of Grimestone's preaching-book (Brown XIV, 74). A version more ambitious in style and metre is found in MS. Rawl. poet. 175 (Brown XIV, 46), but it is trite and dull.

But the context of this—it follows a description of the raising of the Cross—makes plain that verses of this kind cannot be judged as though they had been designed as independent poems; instead it should be recognized that they are a mnemonic summing-up of a meditative theme, and that their force would depend upon the emotive quality of the meditation or sermon in which they were embodied.

All the *O vos omnes* verses compare poorly with the speeches set in this form in the mystery plays. In the York Passion sequence, for instance, the soldiers comment brutally in short alternate lines on the horrific difficulties of nailing Christ's body to the Cross; and after this episode, emphasizing with grotesque exaggeration the agony of Christ and the sadistic callousness of His executioners, and written in a harsh colloquial style, the dignity and serenity of the stylized *O vos omnes* speech makes a most impressive dramatic contrast in style, and in content is a most moving epitome and transformation of the preceding dramatic action.[1] This episode is obviously another way of making the meditative tradition popular, for Christ's speech is not addressed to characters technically within the play, but to the audience-bystanders in the street, who are thus drawn in their own person into the action, and who take part in a representation of it, instead of performing the more difficult exercise of holding the whole scene in their imaginations.

This comparison with the mystery plays suggests that the complaints of Christ, in which the hearer imagines himself amongst the crowd at the Crucifixion, grow in power when put in context, particularly a dramatic one, whilst in isolation they seem to contract and grow thin. There is, however, a group of complaints which are far more moving—even when brief and dependent upon narrative context—and in these the imagined public setting is replaced by a more private one.

In all the short verse complaints so far described the speaker has been Christ on the Cross, and the meditator has been required to imagine himself present in the Crucifixion scene. Either by ironic contrasts which move to compunction, or descriptions of suffering which move to compassion, Christ makes His appeal directly to the meditator; and the plea for love is driven home by the visual image held by the meditator in his imagination. There is, however, a group of fairly early complaints, in which a persuasive image is substituted for an historical meditation.[2] The meditator is not to imagine himself at the foot of the Cross, but must rather imagine how he would feel if Christ were a knight and lover, and he a prisoner, whom Christ had come to release from his enemies in order to win his love. The lyric complaints of Christ the lover neces-

---

[1] Ed. Lucy Toulmin Smith (Oxford, 1885), 357.
[2] Most of the material in the following section has been published in *R.E.S.*, N.S. xiii (1962), 1–16.

sarily contain no visualization, but what they lose by this they gain by
the illuminating quality of the metaphor, no longer merely implicit in
the simplicity and intimacy of the style, but worked out explicitly with
learning and emotional force.

Like some of the *O vos omnes* complaints the appeals or reproaches of
Christ the lover-knight often do not make a complete and self-sufficient
poem: knowledge of an enclosing story is pre-supposed. They are technically *exemplum* verses: a moment in the story, crucial both literally
and allegorically, is mnemonically expressed in verse. But the longer and
better complaints are too poetically developed to be described merely as
mnemonic verse. Their literary quality can be better illuminated by a
comparison with the original Breton lay, in which (it is thought) a lyric
expressed the emotional reaction of the main character to a specific
situation, the situation itself being explained in narrative form. It may
be assumed that the lyric would be moving, but not fully intelligible if
extracted from the story in which it was embedded. This is undoubtedly
true of the complaints of the lover-knight. The modern reader is thus
at a disadvantage in his reading of this group of religious lyrics, for
either they are short mnemonic verses dependent upon an existing
response to a story outside them, or else they are longer and more elaborate, but contain allusions and details that will seem inexplicable or
irrelevant to those who do not know one or more of the many versions
of the story.

The story itself has a dual ancestry that is reflected in differences of
emphasis in its various versions and thereafter in the related lyrics.
One source is the nuptial imagery of the Old Testament: Hosea ii.
1-20 and Ezekiel xvi, for instance, develop at length the allegory of
Israel as an ungrateful bride, who, despite her husband's generosity, has
become a harlot, and yet, it is said, God will forgive her and take her
back. In most of the Old Testament passages the way to reconciliation
led through the punishment and humiliation of the faithless wife, but,
as the theme developed in Christian times, the means of reconciliation
inevitably became the Passion. At this point the allegory became modified by a different allegorical tradition. A common metaphor for the
Passion in patristic times was that of a battle and by a convenient merg-
ing of the metaphors Christ is then imagined as a husband, who fights
to win back his faithless wife from her lover or abductor, the Devil.
Though this combination is found already in the Biblical exegesis of St.
Augustine,[1] it did not become a commonplace in religious writing until
it acquired a literary analogue in medieval romance; and with the help of
this analogue it ceased to be merely dogmatically apt and became also
emotionally persuasive.

[1] Ibid. xiii. 3.

Until twelfth-century French romance fighting and love had been distinct poetic themes. But in Arthurian romance a knight might by brave endurance and heroic encounters save the lady whom he loved from treacherous capture, hoping thereby to gain her favour, or he might joust brilliantly in front of her with the ambition of winning her love by his prowess. Fighting thus became a display of love and also an appeal for it.[1] Within this literary tradition Christ the warrior-bridegroom became transformed into a medieval knight and lover, and the emphasis shifted from the pattern of the action, which symbolized the Redemption, to the emotional content which fitted so well with the principles of affective meditation.

The earliest occurrence of the *exemplum* is the famous and beautiful version in the *Ancrene Wisse*. The earliest related lyrics, however, belong to the end of the thirteenth century. In both forms Christ the lover-knight was a popular theme. The dual ancestry of the story, however, leads to two kinds of presentation. The one that was less relevant to the meditative lyric was that which kept close to the Biblical and patristic origins by describing the heroine as faithless. In the *conte* of Nicholas Bozon, *Du roy ki avait une amye*, for instance, the lady willingly allows a traitor to carry her off from the king who loves her.[2] The narration of the story, however, as that of a faithless wife was awkward in literary terms, for in the conventional patterns of characterization of medieval literature there was no room for the wronged but forgiving husband. The Cistercian, Isaac of Stella, quotes in a sermon one of the key texts for this theme from Jeremiah iii, 'Fornicata es cum amatoribus multis, et tamen revertere ad me, dicit dominus', adding that whilst the Gospel allows separation for adultery, yet after a thousand adulteries God still calls back the soul;[3] and the author of the *Ancrene Wisse* likewise quotes the text from Jeremiah in his section on love, and translates it with added touches of affection: 'ȝet, he ȝeiȝeð al dei, þu þet havest se un-wreaste idon, biturn þe and cum aȝein; welcume schalt tu beo me.'[4] But for such extravagant charity there was most certainly no literary ana-

---

[1] Cf. *Ancrene Wisse*, E.E.T.S. 249, 199. '[Jesu] . . . schawde þurh cnihtschipe þet he wes luve wurðe as weren sumhwile cnihtes iwunet to donne.'

[2] A. Jubinal, *Nouveau recueil de contes, dits, fabliaux*, ii (Paris, 1842), 309–15. The poem has also been printed by T. Wright at the end of Peter Langtoft's *Chronicle*, ii (Rolls Series, 1868), 426–36.

[3] *Sermo*, xl, *In die Paschae*, P.L. 194, 1824. 'But thou hast played the harlot with many lovers; yet return again to me, saith the Lord' (Jer. iii. 1, A.V.). An interesting use of this text occurs in the *Lamentatio in passionem Christi* (P.L. 184, 770), where the context is the traditional one of the transformation of the harlot of the Old Testament into the spotless bride of the New. Christ humbled Himself, it is said '. . . certe ut de hac paupercula meretrice exhiberet sponsam non habentem maculam neque rugam. Ipsa sponsa est anima humana, quae fornicata est cum diis multis, quia cum amatoribus suis, sub omni ligno frondoso prosternebatur meretrix'.

[4] E.E.T.S. 249, 201.

logue; on the contrary the subject of the husband with an unfaithful wife usually belonged only to satire and fabliau burlesque. One fourteenth-century sermon in fact, with an explicitness of analogy that nowadays, at least, seems to lead to an unbecoming similitude, compares Christ to a cuckold. The passage in which this occurs is interesting, in that it contains a trivial English verse of secular origin, which has been transformed into a complaint of Christ by its context:

Cokewold, relictus ab uxore sua propria iam uti poterit post pascha illa amorosa cantilena:

> Ich ave a love untrewe
> þat myn herte wo,
> þat makes me of reufol hewe,
> late to bedde go.
> Sore me may rewe
> þat evere hi lovede hire so.

Nam infidelis amica est inconstans anima que relabitur ad peccatum post pascha pro qua dominus totus pallidus ivit ad lectum quando corpus eius laceratum positum fuit in sepulcro.[1]

The sermon adds that the foregoing words are spoken by Christ at His entombment. All these passages reflect the medieval transition from the corporate Israel to the individual guilty soul, and the moral commonplace that sin is a spiritual adultery. In less eccentric verse, Christ seems to speak only once as a deceived and mourning husband, and then it is only a touch, though a moving one, in a longer poem:

> þou þu wil nouth loven me,
> Siþen i þe my love schewe,
> Nedes i mot loven þe,
> Ne be þu nevere so untrewe.[2]

The theme of Christ's redemption of faithless Israel was therefore most commonly transformed, from the twelfth century onwards, in a manner according better with the new theology and devotion and the new literary tastes, and, although in narrative form relics of its former history remained, fundamentally it changed from the story of a husband reclaiming in his charity a lapsed and fickle wife to that of a king or knight fighting to save a lady and to win her love.

In nearly all versions of this frequently told *exemplum*[3] the knight,

---

[1] MS. C.U.L. Ii. 3. 8, 83ᵛ–94ʳ. In l. 4 *late* is emended from *lato*. 'For the unfaithful mistress is the inconstant soul which after falls back into sin, for whom the Lord, all pale, went to His bed when His wounded body was placed in the sepulchre.'

[2] Brown XIV, 76.

[3] The following are some of the most important versions: two early French sermons (for these see W. Gaffney, 'The Allegory of the Christ-Knight in *Piers Plowman*', *P.M.L.A.* xlvi (1931), 155–68; the *Gesta Romanorum*, E.E.T.S., E.S. xxxiii. 23–26;

before setting off to battle, either makes it a condition or, more romantic-ally, pleads that the lady should remember him. In the *Ancrene Wisse* he makes a long speech which includes the following: 'Nu þenne biseche ich þe for þe luve þet ich cuðe þe, þet tu luvie me lanhure efter þe ilke dede dead, hwen þu naldest, lives.'[1] In the version of the fifteenth-century vernacular treatise, *Dives et Pauper*, the knight at the point of death sends home with his blood-covered shirt a letter to his wife, of which the contents are given in verse:

> Beholde myn woundes and have hem in þine þouȝte
> For alle the good þat ben þine with myn blod I have hem bouȝte.[2]

It is obvious that in the relation of this *exemplum*, which, when effec-tively told would put the knight's request dramatically in the first person, there was the form and content of an appeal, and that this appeal could with an added note of reproach quite easily become a complaint. Since an *exemplum* self-evidently teaches by the exemplary method, the lady in it is invariably distressed and moved by the knight's death and obediently treasures his shirt or armour in memory of him. In the lyric form, however, the lady has obviously to be pleaded with. On the alle-gorical plane the individual intent upon his own pleasure is indifferent to Christ, and on the literal level, within the conventions of romantic love, the lady is *unkind*. *Unkind*, which was to become a keyword of the late fourteenth-century complaints—one poem even has the refrain, 'Whi art þou to þi freend unkinde'[3]—was already sometimes used in the earlier period. It has the evocativeness peculiar to negative adjectives, in that it suggests emotionally the qualities of the positive, whilst at the same time stating their rejection. It was a word used with specific meaning of a lady's behaviour. Whilst in the extreme forms of the courtly love convention a lady, such as Guinevere, for instance, in the *Chevalier de la charrette*, might lack completely in gratitude and generosity to her lover and still be above reproach, it was commonly thought that the unbounded loyalty of a lover entitled him to a reciprocal courtesy and consideration in his mistress, and that the lady without these would show a churlishness particularly unfitting in one of gentle birth: after relating the death of the knight, the author of the *Ancrene Wisse* asks, with the confidence of a rhetorical question: 'Nere þeos ilke leafdi of uveles cunnes cunde, ȝef ha over alle þing ne luvede him her efter?'[4]

Northern Homily Collection, Archiv, lvii (1877), 274–5; Henryson, 'The Bludy Serk', *Poems*, ed. H. Harvey Wood, Edinburgh 1933, 173–6.

[1] E.E.T.S. 249, 199. *Lanhure*: at least.

[2] MS. Douce 295, 142ᵛ. *Dives et Pauper* survives in five manuscripts and was printed by Pynson and Wynkyn de Worde. A description of it is given by H. G. Pfander, '*Dives et Pauper*', *The Library*, 4th ser. xiv (1934), 299–312.

[3] E.E.T.S. 15, 191–8.   [4] E.E.T.S. 249, 199.

The accusation of unkindness was, however, not restricted to lover-knight complaints: one version of the *Homo vide* begins: 'Unkynde man', and a mid-fourteenth-century complaint, 'Man, þus on rode I hyng for þe', contains the lines:

> Man full dere I have þe boght;
> How es it so þou lufes me noght?
> Unkyndely dose þou þare.[1]

Such usages clearly imply not a callous mistress but an intimate relationship of affection, in which one side has been lacking in a proper responsiveness and compassion. In the lover-knight lyrics, however, unkindness has additional overtones, for it is the quality that replaces the faithlessness of the lady in earlier versions.

A lyric included under the rubric 'Cantus compassionis Christi' in the 'Rolle-ian' manuscript MS. C.U.L. Dd. 5. 64, III, illustrates well the relationship of the lover-knight complaint to the *exemplum*:

> Lo! lemman swete, now may þou se
> þat I have lost my lyf for þe.
>   What myght I do þe mare?
> For-þi I pray þe speciali
> þat þou forsake ill company
>   þat woundes me so sare;
>
> And take myne armes pryvely
> And do þam in þi tresory,
>   In what stede sa þou dwelles,
> And, swete lemman, forget þow noght
> þat I þi lufe sa dere have boght,
>   And I aske þe noght elles.[2]

The first verse, with its quotation of *quid ultra debui facere*, is in typical complaint style, the only apparent eccentricity being that it would seem to be an address from the dead rather than from the dying Christ; but we should not press this distinction too closely (nor, incidentally, elsewhere be critical of the fairly frequent confusion of tenses), since, through the influence of the invariable representation in art of the dead Christ on the Cross, it must have been this image which came to mind in response to the injunction, 'see', 'behold', etc. The second stanza of this poem, however, makes it plain that the whole is in form equivalent to the letter of the dying knight in *Dives et Pauper*, for the climax and main point of the *exemplum* was always the treasuring of the blood-stained shirt or armour of the knight—allegorically the memory of the Passion—and it is this point that is made here. The injunction to

---

[1] Brown XIV, 47, p. 60.
[2] Brown XIV, 78. *Tresory*: a room or receptacle for valuable objects.

'forsake ill company' (the rival suitors of the *exemplum*) and to place the armour in a treasure chamber (*camera* or *camera secreta* in the *exemplum*) also indicates the close dependence of the poem on its narrative original. In emotional effectiveness the poem, unlike an *exemplum* verse, is self-sufficient, but its details may appear random if a narrative context is not pre-supposed.

A very interesting *exemplum* verse occurs in the *Fasciculus morum*, embedded in a long story, said to be about Aeneas.[1] In its first part it is close to the *exemplum* in *Dives et Pauper*; in both, the heroine is poor and is raised up through the courtesy of the hero to his own position; and in both, the hero sends a letter of which the Latin version (quoted in both) is as follows: 'Cerne cicatrices veteris vestigia pugne,/ Quesivi proprio sanguine quicquid habes.' The English version of this in the *Fasciculus morum*, however, is not a literal translation of the Latin, as was the verse we have already quoted from *Dives et Pauper*, but introduces a new idea which makes it more truly a complaint:

> Beholde myne woundes how sore I am dyȝth,
> Ffor all þe wele þat þu hast I wan hit in fyȝt.
> I am sore woundet, behold on my skyn,
> Leve lyf, for my love, let me comen in.[2]

In its context this verse is spoken by Aeneas, who, returning to his beloved after a battle fought on her behalf and being most severely wounded, finds that she *tanquam ingrata* has locked her doors and refuses to open them to him. The source of this episode appears to be two Biblical texts which, in the exposition of the allegory, Christ uses as he knocks on the door: 'Ecce sto ad ostium et pulso' (Rev. iii. 20) and 'Aperi mihi, soror mea, amica mea' (Cant. v. 2), and obviously the loving appeal of the last line of the English verse, which makes it so much more touching than the analogue in *Dives et Pauper*, derives from the Canticles text.

The same setting for a complaint, that of Christ's return to his beloved's door after the battle of the Crucifixion, appears to be used in a short verse in John of Grimestone's preaching-book:

> I am iesu, þat cum to fith
> With-outen seld and spere,
> Elles wer þi det i-dith
> Ȝif mi fithting ne were.
> Siþen i am comen and have þe broth
> A blisful bote of bale,
> Undo þin herte, tel me þi þouth,
> þi sennes grete an smale.[3]

---

[1] For the whole *exemplum* and further comments see *R.E.S.*, N.S. xiii. 7–9.
[2] MS. Rawl. C. 670, 42ᵛ.   [3] Brown XIV, 63.

Its brisk didacticism, however, makes it an unpleasing poem, and the injunction *undo*, unaccompanied by pleas or endearments, sounds at worst minatory and at best like practical advice. It should perhaps only be judged as a convenient versification of various sermon themes. A verse of similar style and quality is quoted in the context of a Latin sermon in a fifteenth-century manuscript, MS. Bodley 649:

> For þe I wax al *blo*dy open þe rode,
> to wasche in þi hert y scheedde *mi* blod.
> Amend þe betymes and seese of þi synne,
> Undo þe dore of þin hert and let me inne.[1]

There is only one poem extant on the *ecce sto* theme that is more than a sermon verse, being in itself a complete and exceptionally moving complaint: curiously enough, it is both the earliest and the best of the lover-knight complaints. It occurs with Latin sermon notes on the Passion in the late thirteenth-century manuscript, Lambeth 557:

> Allas, allas, wel yvel y sped,
> For synne Jesu from me ys fled,
>   þat lyvely fere.
> At my dore he standeth at one
> And kallys, undo, wit reuful mone
>   On þis manere:
>
> Undo, my lef, my dowve dere,
> Undo, wy stond [y] stekyn out here?
>   Iyk am þi make.
> Lo my heved and myne lockys
> Ar al bywevyd wyt blody dropys
>   For þyne sake.[2]

This appeal can be usefully compared with an eleventh-century Latin poem based on the same episode in the Song of Songs, *Quis est iste qui pulsat ad ostium*.[3] In the Latin poem, as in its source, the lady eagerly

---

[1] Brown, *Register* I, 24. L. 1. *blody*, MS. *rody*; l. 2, MS. *an blody scheedde to wasche in þi hert*.

[2] James, *Catalogue* 760. The poem is printed from John of Grimestone's preaching-book in Brown xiv, 68, but with the stanzas in the reverse order, and with an addition in different metre. Though the Lambeth text is the earlier by nearly a hundred years, it does not invariably present the better reading: *At one* (l. 4) should probably be emended to *alone*; ll. 10–11 seem to be corrupt in both texts, for Lambeth lacks a true rhyme, whilst in Adv. 18. 7. 21, the detail of the blood-stained body in l. 5 is almost certainly not original since the source is Cant. v. 2. It may be conjectured that the lines originally read: 'Lo mi lokkes and ek myn heved / Ar al wyt blody dropys bywevyd.'

[3] Peter Dronke, *Medieval Latin and the Rise of the European Love-Lyric*, i (Oxford, 1965), 269–71, points out that in the manuscript this poem is entitled 'Rhythmus de b[eata] Maria virg[ine]'. But it is very difficult to reconcile verse 2, 'Ego sum summi regis filius . . .' with this interpretation. It seems quite likely the medieval copyist provided an inappropriate title.

arises to answer her lover's knocking, only to find that he has fled. But
in the English poem the flight—by implication the exclusion of Christ
from the heart—has already taken place, and now, like the knight of the
Fasciculus morum, Christ 'tanquam gratissimus et fidelissimus pulsare
non desistit et clamare . . .'. In the Latin the tone of Christ's address
is also quite different:

> Ego sum summi regis filius,
> primus et novissimus;
> qui de caelis in has veni tenebras,
> liberare captivorum animas:
> passus mortem et multas iniurias.[1]

The Latin is much more dogmatic and impersonal, the English more
tender and lovingly reproachful. In the Latin the speaker is God the
Son, who once suffered death on earth to free the souls of those made
captive by the Devil. But in the English it is Christ the lover-knight
who speaks, come directly to His beloved with the signs of His sufferings
still upon Him (the dew upon the head of the lover of the Song of
Songs has become drops of blood), and He has suffered, not to save
mankind, but for His beloved alone, 'for þyne sake'. Both poems are
fine, but in the English the consistent tone of loving appeal and loving
reproach makes it perhaps the best of the thirteenth-century Passion
lyrics.

The lover-knight's complaints are, as we said earlier, more successful
than those in the *O vos omnes* form, for, whether the meeting takes place
in an unspecified place, or whether it is allegorically at the door of the
heart, the effect is always of a private and secluded encounter; and a
personal tone of loving affection is always appropriate in a way that it
could not be in an address to passers-by. The personal tone, in which the
medieval lyric excelled, was especially fitting to the theme of a perfect
knight returning home to an ungrateful lady. But there is a strain in some
of them which must be finally identified, and that is the element of
paradox, which in its exploitation of wit might seem closer to the
Improperia than to a lover's appeal to his lady.

The battle image was strikingly appropriate to the old doctrine of the
Redemption, partly so because the result of the Crucifixion was the
result normally peculiar to battle, namely an enemy defeated; and so long
as art represented Christ on the Cross as a hero triumphant, the description of the scene in terms of fighting had emotional congruity. But once

---

[1] *The Oxford Book of Medieval Latin Verse*, ed. F. J. E. Raby (Oxford, 1959), 158.
'I am the son of the most high king, the first and the last, who came from heaven into
this dark place in order to set free the souls of those made captive: I suffered death
and many wrongs.'

the moment of the Crucifixion chosen for representation was the time when Christ hung dead and blood-stained from the Cross, the discrepancy between the humiliated and suffering figure and the victorious knight became clear. In some versions of the lover-knight theme this discrepancy was not evaded but exploited, being developed into a series of paradoxes and conceits. This treatment is remarkable, in that it appears in English verse at a much earlier date than the period in which intellectual ingenuity was commonly put at the service of Passion poetry. But it shares with fifteenth-century style a common characteristic: the elements of shock and surprise do not, as in seventeenth-century poetry, derive from the invention of a startling and hitherto unthought-of term of comparison, but from the choosing of some ancient and well-established similitude, and then pressing every possible detail of it into the comparison.

The conceits in the Christ-knight literature depend upon an unstated question: if Christ on the Cross is likened to a knight in battle or tournament, in what manner then was he armed? A temperate paradoxical answer to this is that of the verse already quoted, 'I am Iesu, þat cum to fith / wiþouten seld and spere',[1] but more often, and particularly in sermon narratives, it is answered at length and with ingenuity. It may well be that St. Paul's allegory of the 'armour of God' had some influence upon the minutely detailed descriptions of Christ's arming, and it may be noted that an allegory of knightly armour in terms of the virtues was very popular in the Middle Ages; it was copied amongst the short prose works of Richard Rolle, and as part of the treatise-compilation, *The Pore Caitiff*:[2] in this, for instance, the horse is the body, the saddle *mansuetude*, the spurs fear and love.[3] This habit of allegorizing armour fitted well, of course, with the favourite set passages in romance, in which the arming of a knight was described. The earliest extensive allegory of this kind is the Anglo-Norman poem of Nicholas Bozon, *Du roy ki avait une amye*,[4] of which two texts survive in the important Phillipps Manuscript,[5] one of them copied in a group which includes a prose passage entitled *Modus armandi milites ad torneamentum* and the *Ordre de chevalerie* by Hue de Tabarie. This grouping reflects the obvious point that only those familiar with the technical terms of the

---

[1] Brown xiv, 63.

[2] *The Pore Caitiff* was an exceptionally popular compilation of the late fourteenth century. It is discussed by M. Deanesly, *The Lollard Bible* (Cambridge, 1920), 346–7, and by Sister Mary Teresa Brady, 'The Pore Caitif', *Traditio*, x (1954), 529–48.

[3] *Yorkshire Writers*, ed. C. Horstman, ii (London, 1896), 421–7.

[4] Jubinal, *Nouveau recueil*, ii. 309–15.

[5] A description of the manuscript is given by P. Meyer, 'Notice et extraits du ms. 8336 de la bibliothèque de Sir Thomas Phillipps à Cheltenham', *Romania*, xiii (1884), 497–541. The manuscript is now B.M. Add. MS. 46919.

romance convention would appreciate a witty extension of these. Bozon's allegory, however, is not only remote from meditative style through ostentatious technicality, but also in its application, for it refers primarily to the Incarnation, not the Crucifixion: in it the divine assumption of a human body in the womb of the Blessed Virgin is imagined as a knight's arming with the assistance of a maiden: his *aketoun*, for instance, is his white skin, his *chauces de fere* are his nerves, his *plates* are his bones.

However, whilst many descriptions remain as technical as this, in them it is not usually Christ's human flesh which is His armour, but rather the outward signs of His sufferings and the instruments of the Crucifixion. In a Latin allegory of the fourteenth century, for instance, the corselet is the wound-covered body, the helmet the crown of thorns, the gloves and spurs the nails in hands and feet, and the horse the Cross.[1] In this passage, of course, the technical words are in Latin, but in a similar allegory in the vernacular *Northern Homily Cycle* it is necessary to understand such words as *haburgon, basenet*, and *brases*,[2] which might well puzzle those unfamiliar with the terminology of the literature of chivalry. In passages such as these the sense of the allegory is that Christ suffered for man's sake, but, through the technicality of the vocabulary and the ingenuity of the relationships, it has little emotive effect.

There is, however, a complaint in MS. Harley 2316, beginning 'Men rent me on rode', which movingly incorporates the image of the Cross as a knight's horse:

> Biheld mi side,
> Mi wndes sprede so wide,
> Restles i ride.
> lok up on me! put fro ʒe pride.
>
> Mi palefrey is of tre,
> wiht nayles naylede þurh me.
> Ne is more sorwe to se—
> certes noon more no may be.[3]

The image here has been emptied of wit: it has neither the startlingly grim appropriateness of Christ's body covered with a multitude of wounds as a shirt of mail, nor the ironic poignancy of the lance, carried not point outwards, but driven inwards to Christ's heart; moreover, the paradoxical potentialities are not emphasized through its appearance in a series of similar images. Isolated from a witty list and remote from

---

[1] *R.E.S.* xiii. 12.   [2] Loc. cit. 12–13.
[3] Brown xiv, 51.

technical terms the comparison conveys sober pathos rather than the intellectual excitement of a conceit. The tone of the image has changed from triumph to melancholy, and strangely enough it seems more decorous as part of a lament than as part of a chivalric panoply.

This seems to be the only occasion on which the image of Christ's armour is used in a complaint, perhaps on account of inherent problems. Apart from the danger that ingenuity and technical vocabulary would intrude between the meditator and the meditation, there is in the poems discussed so far the further difficulty that the paradoxical parallels are embarrassingly ironic, in a way that they are not in the translations of the *Improperia* or 'Ihesus doþ him bymene'. In the latter the contrast is between the appearance of Christ in His sufferings and the habits and actions of man: man is therefore the object of the irony. But in the allegory of the armour the irony is directed straight at Christ Himself, though of course from Him it rebounds on man in the form of reproach. Self-directed irony, however, is likely to seem harsh and unmoving, and in this context the latent grotesqueness makes it the more inconvenient. The achievement of 'Men rent me on rode' lies in the manipulation of the image against its natural tendencies: the exploitation of the latter can best be seen outside the lyric in the Towneley Play of the Crucifixion, where the ironic contrasts become the jibes of the executioners as they nail Christ to the Cross. In this, the securing of Christ to the Cross, which is then raised and jolted into its socket, is likened to the raising of a king to his horse in preparation for a tournament:

> Sir, commys heder and have done,
> And wyn apon youre palfray sone,
>   ffor he [is] redy bowne.
> If ye be bond till hym, be not wrothe,
> ffor be ye secure we were full lothe
>   On any wyse that ye fell downe.[1]

The possible implications of the horse image have here been extended by laying an emphasis on the actual mounting, which then corresponds with the traditional amplification of the Passion story, according to which Christ was bound to the Cross as it lay on the ground, for the increase of His sufferings. There is no doubt that when the image is not purely intellectual it can be more readily developed towards horror than towards pathos.

There is, however, one other adaptation of the image in the lyrics that is pleasantly successful. It occurs in three verses of the rather long and disorganized lyric, 'Fadur and sone and holi gost'.[2] This poem is not a complaint, but a personal meditation in which the meditator puts on

[1] E.E.T.S. E.S. 72, 261.   [2] Brown XIV, 125.

the armour of Christ; but this armour is not the virtues described in Ephesians, but Christ's armour in the Crucifixion:

> At þe y mot myn armes borwe,
> Mi sheld shal be þe swerd of sorwe,
>   marie þat stong to þe herte;
> þe holi cros my baner biforn,
> myn helm þi garlond of sharpe þorn,
>   mi swerd þi scourges smerte.

> Mi plates shullen þi nailes be,
> myn acotoun þat spere tre,
>   þat stong þi swete syde.
> Now y am armed þus wel,
> nel y him [the Devil] fle nevere a del,
>   tyde what bi-tyde![1]

Some of the details of this allegory are unsatisfactory: to make a shield a sword (even though a metaphorical one) seems a random paradox, and there is a similar visual irrelevance between a jerkin and a spear. However, these discrepancies should not be pressed: when lyrics survive in more than one manuscript, a comparison of texts often suggests that such oddities are not original, and it is unfortunate that only one manuscript of this poem survives. The general allegory, however, which shows how the Christian defends himself from temptation by meditation on the Passion (a devotional remedy often recommended in religious treatises), works very satisfactorily indeed: it gives an ingenious and agreeable twist to an image that was devotionally unpromising.

There is also a small group of poems, related to the verses on the theme of Christ the lover-knight, but distinct from them in regard to both literary and meditative treatment. All the Passion poems so far discussed have had in common a brevity of form: many were only six or eight lines in length and few were more than twenty; they would thus be easy to memorize. They were also plain in style, thereby sometimes catching an unpretentious dignity, though at other times seeming merely weak or naïve. Their verse forms were commonly those of the short couplet or sometimes fairly easily manageable stanzas, largely those derived from the Latin. In content or manner of presentation there is nothing that could dismay or perplex an audience ignorant of other literature, except that the verses on the lover-knight theme would seem more apt to those who had at least a slight knowledge of romance conventions. Though it has been argued that the common people in the Middle Ages enjoyed only tales of rebellious folk-heroes, such as Robin Hood, this theory seems to impose an unnecessarily rigid differentiation between

[1] Brown XIV, 125, p. 223.

kinds of audiences, for romances such as *King Horn* seem fitted to please a hearer of any social class. That the majority of people in the Middle Ages knew nothing of stories of knights fighting to save their ladies—if only by hearsay—seems most improbable. The tastes of different audiences is more likely to have been reflected in the contrast between a simple and an elaborate style than in basic differences of plot.

However, as well as the lover-knight verses, short, in simple metres, and requiring at most a familiarity with the common outline story of romances, there were also a few poems which, though drawing on the same common traditions of theology and devotion, present them in a more literary and sophisticated way, and seem designed to please people with a literary taste formed by the style and artificial conventions of romances and secular lyrics. Though most of these poems survive in the great monastic literary miscellany, MS. Harley 2253, there is a probability that they were primarily intended for the devotional reading of ladies who also enjoyed romances, such as the one described in one of the secular Harley lyrics, 'wiþ lefly rede lippes lele, / romaunz forte rede'.[1] Thomas of Hales's 'Love Ron', which loosely belongs to the group which we are discussing, is said explicitly to have been written *ad instanciam cuiusdam puellae*, and the maiden is instructed to *sing*[2] it to herself and to learn it by heart. The poem is therefore not of the kind that would disappear with the departure of the reciter and his manuscript, unless it had been memorized, but would exist in a copy to be owned by the intended audience. The maiden is told to *untrende* [unroll] it: in other words, the poet intended it to be copied on a small parchment roll. One or two rolls of this kind still survive, and one would expect only an infinitesimal proportion to do so, on account of their smallness and fragility. Thomas's detailed directions are valuable in indicating that poems similar in kind may also have been copied on rolls.[3]

---

[1] *The Harley Lyrics*, ed. G. L. Brook (Manchester, 1948), 38. This edition does not fully supersede that of Karl Böddeker, *Altenglische Dichtungen des MS. Harley 2253* (Berlin, 1878).

[2] The word *sing* does not necessarily indicate a musical setting, cf. *O.E.D.* s.v. *sing* 2. Here it may have the meaning 'to read aloud'. The Latin *cantus* (used in the rubric) may similarly refer simply to a poem.

[3] Rolls have been discussed by R. H. Robbins, 'The "Arma Christi" Rolls', *M.L.R.* xxxiv (1939), 415–21, who shows that later illuminated rolls, such as William Billyng's, were not privately owned, but hung up in churches. The association of rolls with the 'Love-Ron' has been investigated by Betty Hill, 'The "Luue-Ron" and Thomas de Hales', *M.L.R.* lix (1964), 321–30, who argues that the early Franciscans used rolls rather than manuscripts for their early preaching material. It is not necessary to suppose that there was a uniform purpose for all rolls. Some friars may have carried small rolls about with them, but that referred to in the 'Love-Ron' is clearly in the possession of the maiden not in that of its Franciscan author. A roll now preserved in the Public Record Office (Chancery Miscellanea C/47/34/16) contains various Latin prayers and French devotional poems (the contents are described by Samuel Bentley, *Excerpta historica*, London, 1831, 405–13). This roll seems to have survived because its owner

The greater artifice of the Harley religious poems is most immediately seen in the comparative complexity of their metres. The native English simplicity of metres used for the short meditative lyrics is in extreme contrast to the work of the troubadours and trouvères, which was invariably in complicated and cleverly contrived stanza forms that seem to aim at pleasing the ear by the unexpected recurrence of a rhyme or by some other display of technical ingenuity. Though English poets never followed the French in their extremes of metrical cleverness, the authors of the Harley religious lyrics imitated some of the less extravagant trouvère stanza forms, adopting the metres of secular love poetry for their work, just as contemporary religious poets in the north of France had done.[1] The poems are thus manifestly works of craftsmanship in a self-conscious manner absent from the short poems; the poem 'Nu yh se blostme sprynge' ('When y se blosmes springe')[2] ends with an acknowledgement that a poem has been made:

> Iesu, lefman swete,
> Ih sende þe þis songe,

lines which can be compared with the common French convention, of which the following lines from the last stanza of a religious poem are an example:

> Dame, en lermes et en plours
> Ceste chançon vous present.[3]

But it is noticeable that these English poems are not merely a beautiful object in honour of Christ (or the Virgin), as are the French poems, which show the marks of the singing contests of the Puys, but, being rooted in the meditative tradition, they still remain something that can be used appropriately by a person other than the author.

Only one of these poems explicitly uses the theme of the lover-knight, but by content all are related to it in the sense that they derive from one of the traditions lying behind the lover-knight image, that of Christ as the lover of the individual soul. The main source for this idea was the medieval interpretations of the Song of Songs. Whereas the Fathers, such as Origen, had taken the Bride primarily to signify the Church, and only secondarily the individual Christian, medieval commentators, in accordance with the spiritual trend, which we have already noticed, reversed

---

was imprisoned, and perhaps executed, in the Tower. Rolls would be the only inexpensive and manageable way of producing a copy of a few short texts, but they would be extremely fragile and unlikely to survive. It is possible that poems of the kind of the Harley Lyrics circulated in this form and are now lost, or that some were far more widely known than their preservation in one, or at most two, manuscripts suggests.

[1] H. J. Chaytor, *The Troubadours and England* (Cambridge, 1923), 98–160.

[2] Brown XIII, 63; *Harley Lyrics*, 54–55.

[3] E. Järnström, *Recueil de chansons pieuses du xiii siècle*, i, Annales academiae scientiarum fennicae, Ser. B, iii (1910), 53.

this order.[1] Commentaries of this kind are too numerous for any one to be singled out, except perhaps for St. Bernard's *Sermons on the Song of Songs*, which were widely read in the Middle Ages, and which express the idea superbly. The intermediary, however, between Biblical gloss and literary development was the *De arrha animae* of the twelfth-century theologian, Hugh of St. Victor, who, in an imaginary dialogue between man and his soul, exploited the idea rhetorically and homiletically. The point of the dialogue is to expound the supreme love-worthiness of Christ through His immeasurable gift of the whole creation and through His personal amiability:

Sponsum habes, sed nescis. Pulcherrimus est omnium, sed faciem ejus non vidisti. . . . Noluit adhuc seipsum tibi praesentare, sed munera misit, arrham dedit, pignus amoris, signum dilectionis. Si cognoscere illum posses, si speciem illius videres, non amplius de tua pulchritudine ambigeres. Scires enim quod tam pulcher, tam formosus, tam elegans, tam unicus in tuo aspectu captus non esset, si eum singularis decor et ultra caeteros admirandus non traheret.[2]

Just as the author of the *Ancrene Wisse* seems to have been the first to develop the literary potentialities of the *exemplum* of the Christ-knight, so also he seems to have been the first to do the same in the vernacular for Christ the wooer:

Nam ich þinge feherest, nam ich kinge richest, nam ich hest icunnet, nam ich weolie wisest, nam ich monne hendest, nam ich þinge freoest?[3]

In the passage in which these lines occur Christ has been transformed into a courtly lover and pleads His merits with rhetorical dignity. The normal rule of courtly love, that a lady should choose the worthiest of her suitors, the most virtuous and nobly born, provided a secular convention into which Hugh's idea might be appropriately fitted. Indeed, though Christ demonstrates His love-worthiness in a manner too blunt for it to be compared with the circumlocutions of humility in the model speeches of Andreas Capellanus,[4] yet the actual standards it implies may well be compared with the artificial conventions of courtly love

---

[1] C. Chavasse, *The Bride of Christ* (London, 1940), though tendentious, is useful in tracing this development.

[2] *P.L.* 176, 954. 'You have a bridegroom, but you do not know him. He is the fairest of all, but you have not seen his face. . . . He has not wished yet to show himself to you, but he has sent you gifts; he has given you a betrothal-gift, a pledge of love, a sign of his affection. If you could know him, if you could see him, you would no longer doubt your own beauty; for you would know that no-one so fair, so handsome, so graceful, so peerless, could have been captivated by your looks, had he not been attracted by comeliness, eminent and admirable beyond the rest.'

[3] E.E.T.S. 249, 202–3.

[4] The *De arte honeste amandi* can now most conveniently be read in the translation of J. J. Parry, *The Art of Courtly Love* (New York, 1959).

esteemed by Eleanor of Aquitaine, and to some unanalysable extent, brought by her to England in the twelfth century. The recurrent question of the love-debate concerning what suitor had the most rightful claim to a lady's love, and the fictitious submission of issues of love to the justice of a mock court of law, provided a writer of literary inventiveness with a perfect background of associations for depicting Christ's pre-eminent claim to deserve man's love.

The idea of the Christ-bridegroom nowadays suggests a rare mystical experience peculiar to the saints, and this usage is common too in the Middle Ages: in the writings of the German and Italian women saints of the twelfth and thirteenth centuries it occurs frequently, both as a symbol of an otherwise inexpressible relationship, and also in records of visions in which Christ appeared and spoke in a manner befitting a tender and courteous lover. In the English literary tradition, however, the idea is bare of mystical symbolism, and becomes a simple moral and doctrinal allegory. It is only in the *Ancrene Wisse* and the 'Love Ron' that the idea is even associated with a vow of virginity. Like the lover-knight theme it is a persuasive image: that is to say, image and significance are not inseparable, as they are in the mystical tradition; rather, what could be stated in non-metaphorical language is by careful choice stated in metaphorical terms for their greater imaginative potency. There is, however, a difference between them, in that the image of the lover-knight is designed to illuminate what Christ has done for man in such a way that the hearer cannot fail to give the proper response, whereas the image of Christ the lover is primarily intended to manipulate the emotion itself. For this reason the poems are mainly first-person meditations and not appeals from Christ.

At first sight the subject of Christ the lover would seem to have offered quite exceptionally appropriate material for a complaint. The wooing speech in the *Ancrene Wisse*, for instance, could quite easily be turned into a complaint by a modification of it in the manner of the *Improperia*. However, until the late fourteenth century, when such complaints, with a didactic emphasis, became a favourite and finely used form, they do not occur in Middle English literature. It is interesting, however, to notice in passing that there is one thirteenth-century example of this form in Anglo-Norman. This is a short poem from MS. Lambeth 522, in which Christ as a lover appeals to and reproaches man, first enumerating the pains of the Passion and then asserting His dignity as a lover. The tone of the stanzas is that of a complaint, though this is modified by the brisk rhetorical challenge of the refrain, which is so different in tone from that of later refrains, such as *quid ultra debui facere*.

> Por tei fu a mort juge,
> Des Jeus a la croiz mene,

Entre larruns crucifiez
E mains e piez de clous fichez.
Si poez trover nul amant,
Ke por vus face autretant,
Lessez moi e amez lui;
En joie vivez ambedui.

.　　.　　.　　.　　.

Roi sui puissant e amiable,
Beaus e franc e charitable.
Si a moi volez fei tenir,
Au cel te frai a moi venir.
Si poez trover nul amant,
Ke por vus face autretant,
Lessez moi e amez lui;
En joie vivez ambedui.[1]

The only Middle English lyric of the earlier period that is close to the complaint form is the 'Love Ron', for in this, which is set in the first person, the preacher, as it were, acts as a paranymph for the divine bridegroom. The praise of Christ as the supreme exemplar of all qualities desirable in a lover goes back, as we have seen, to the *De arrha animae*. This tradition, begun in English by the author of the *Ancrene Wisse*, was continued in the early thirteenth-century prose treatise, *Þe Wohunge of ure Laverd*.[2] A large part of *Þe Wohunge* consists of an exposition of how Christ excels in the qualities of beauty, riches, generosity, wisdom, bravery, noble birth, and gentleness, the whole being expressed in an intense tone of personal loving. In the 'Love Ron' Christ is also praised for his beauty, nobility, wisdom, and riches, but pre-eminently for His eternity. The poet is here following a tradition of spirituality—Platonic in its ancestry—which, unlike much medieval didactic literature, admitted the beauty of all created things, but held them less than perfect on account of their transitoriness, though this very combination of the beautiful with the transient could incite the soul to search for the eternal. This attitude has been called romantic by Debruyne, who says of St. Bernard's theory: 'L'attitude fondamentale de Saint Bernard semble donc métaphysiquement et mystiquement romantique: la perception de la beauté sensible remplit l'âme d'une immense mélancolie et l'incite à s'en détourner en quête de l'immuable.'[3] As an example of the contrast between temporal beauty and eternity Debruyne quotes a passage from Gilbert of Hoyland's

---

[1] R. Reinsch, 'Mittheilungen aus einer franz. Handschrift des Lambeth Palace zu London', *Archiv*, lxiii (1880), 95.

[2] E.E.T.S. 241, 20–38.

[3] *Études d'esthétique médiévale*, iii (Bruges, 1946), 39, and op. cit. ii. 194–202 for a discussion of feminine beauty.

continuation of St. Bernard's *Sermons on the Song of Songs*, where he is explaining that one of the qualities of perfect beauty must be eternity:

> Quod si coelestia corpora attenderis: solem, lunam, et stellas: haec quidem pulchra sunt . . . sed de iis scriptum est: 'Ipsi peribunt, tu autem permanes'.[1]

By drawing on this tradition Thomas of Hales does not have to deny the value of worldly things, the beautiful ladies of the world of romance or the famous heroes, but is able to make them a logical springboard to the love of Christ. Thus he can use the *ubi sunt* formula evocatively, and he movingly introduces the awareness of transience:

> þeos þeines þat her weren bolde
> beoþ aglyden so wyndes bles
> Under molde hi liggeþ colde,
> and faleweþ so doþ medewe gres.[2]

Later he makes the implicit sense of regret quite plain:

> Hit is of heom al so hit nere,
> of heom me haveþ wunder itold.
> Nere hit reuþe for to heren
> hu hi were wiþ pyne aquold.[3]

The poet, having thus awakened a sense of loss and a longing for permanence, skilfully introduces Christ as the most noble of all possible lovers, and, in traditional terms, describes heaven as a place beyond the laws of change. The poem is filled with gentle emotion and mild didacticism, both delightfully controlled by a cool and persuasive argument which is carefully developed. It is one of the small number of outstanding poems amongst the Middle English lyrics.

With the 'Love Ron' may be compared an Anglo-Norman poem, 'Mon queor me dist que doi amer', in which the 'wooing' arguments are put in the form of a first-person monologue. Where Christ in the *Ancrene Wisse* says 'wultu . . .', the speaker in the poem says 'si ieo desire . . .'. The values of the world are enumerated and rejected for their deceptiveness and transience:

> Si ieo desire estre honurable,
> Honur de ceste secle n'est que fable
> Ffaus et faint et deceivable;
> Pur ceo sui en langour.
> Ieo querrai ioie plus estable
> Ou ficherai m'amour.[4]

---

[1] Op. cit. iii. 48. 'Now if you look at the celestial bodies, the sun, the moon, and the stars: they are indeed beautiful, but of them it is written: "They shall perish but thou remainest".'

[2] Brown XIII, 43, p. 68. *þeines*: brave men; *aglyden*: pass; *bles*: gust of wind; *molde*: earth; *faleweþ*: fade.

[3] Ed. cit., p. 70. 1st line: it is of them as though they had never been; *aquold*: put to death.   [4] Chaytor, op. cit. 157–8. He also refers to troubadour analogues.

The poem, however, is unexciting, and mention of it here serves only to throw into relief the excellence of the 'Love Ron'.

Both these poems are argumentative, but in the remaining lyrics on the theme of Christ the lover the speaker is already persuaded. They are in the form of love poems, in which the praises of the beloved are sung. They are not, however, religious love poems that fit into any well-established secular genre. It is of course the lover, not his mistress, who complains of love in the medieval lyric: poems which express the woman's point of view are usually either *chansons de mal mariee* or the love songs of young girls. Possibly the comparative scarcity of Middle English secular lyrics in the thirteenth and early fourteenth centuries, and, within these numerical confines, the fluidity of the form, may have encouraged this religious hybrid genre. The identification of the individual Christian with a woman in love, however, reinforces the point made previously, that these poems belong to the large body of vernacular devotional literature composed for pious women of noble birth or for women in religious orders.

In metre and subordinate conventions, however, the poems are close to French literary traditions, and in particular to the secular lyrics also copied in MS. Harley 2253. Two of the poems, 'Somer is comen and winter gon' and 'When y se blosmes springe', like some of the love lyrics in the same manuscript and like many trouvère songs, begin by setting the thought of love against a background of the beauty and natural joyfulness of spring-time:

> When y se blosmes springe
>   ant here foules song,
> A swete love-longynge
>   myn herte þourhout stong,
> al for a love newe,
> þat is so swete ant trewe,
>   þat gladieþ al my song;
> ich wot al myd iwisse
> my ioie ant eke my blisse
>   on him is al ylong.[1]

In this verse the identity of the lover is at first concealed, as often in the French secular convention. But he is *swete ant trewe* (adjectives recalling the 'Love Ron'), and the initial description of the freshness and beauty of spring is intended to recall the fairness of Christ, just as in 'Alysoun' it reminds the poet of his mistress. The implication here of the beauty of Christ (a theme that in other poems is explicit) does not reflect purely secular standards, but has authority in Latin meditations. In these the text from the Psalms, 'speciosus forma prae filiis hominum', is often

---

[1] *Harley Lyrics*, 54.

used with reference to Christ, and gained additional evocative power as an epitome of the bridegroom's beauty in the Song of Songs. Christ's beauty was held to be a sign of the perfection of His humanity. But in order to express in English the idea of Christ's beauty that characterized the Church's nuptial tradition, the authors of the religious lyrics had inevitably to draw upon the phraseology which was becoming current in romances and secular lyrics. In this poem Christ is *swete ant trewe* and (in the last verse) *milde ant swete*. In a narrative poem of the Crucifixion, 'On leome is in þis world ilist',[1] the word *swete* occurs yet more often, 'hisse two swete honden', 'is swete softe side', 'his swete wunden', and in the same poem Christ's face is *scene* and His body is described in the common pair of romance epithets 'feir and gent'.

After its opening stanza, 'When y se blosmes springe' turns into a Passion meditation. In this it departs from secular models, whose substance was normally a continued enumeration of the lady's graces, but remains firmly in the tradition of Christ the lover. Memory of the Passion had been linked to the theme of Christ the lover from its beginning: in the *De arrha animae* Hugh of St. Victor gives two supreme reasons why Christ deserves the soul's entire love, the first that He created all the world for the soul, the second that He redeemed the soul by a most painful death. In *Þe Wohunge of ure Laverd*, the Passion is emphasized above all:

> Ah over alle oðre þinges makes te luvewurði to me þa harde [atele] hurtes,
> þa schomeliche wohes þæt tu þoledes for me, þi bittre pine and passiun.
> þi derve deað o rode telles riht in al mi luve, calenges al mi heorte.[2]

In 'When y se blosmes springe' the poet's musing on love in springtime leads him to recollect his meditations on the Passion, in which he has stood at the foot of the Cross and seen Christ's pain with his own eyes. In the descriptions of suffering there is an implicit contrast between Christ's former beauty, symbolized by the fairness of spring, and His disfigurement on the Cross. In Latin devotional works this contrast was often stated plainly, and the text, already quoted, Psalm xliv. 3, was put in pointed contrast to Isaiah liii. 2, 'Non est species ei neque decor'. The oblique presentation of the contrast in this poem makes it, however, the more poignant in effect. 'When y se blosmes springe' blends a spring love song and a meditation on the Passion sweetly and agreeably together. Another poem, 'Somer is comen and winter gon',[3] that also makes use of the spring opening is less successful in its transitions, although a strong and overt attempt to link the two themes has been

---

[1] Brown XIII, 24.

[2] E.E.T.S. 241, 27. *Atele*: cruel; *wohes*: wrongs; *derve*: grievous; *telles riht*: be of great value; *calenges*: claims.

[3] Brown XIII, 54.

made by reference to the image of the Christ-knight. The poet feigns that in spring he is passionately preoccupied with the thought of a *child*—a favourite word in ballads and romances for a knight—who has sought him over hill and dale to release him from imprisonment. But, though the narrative is consistent, the tone is not. The poem in fact shows vigorous inventiveness rather than consistency, and seems a medley of exceptionally striking details: the spring opening, the lover-knight's adventure, the dramatic, colloquial speech of the executioners, the description of the mourning Virgin, and the unusual and powerful simile of Christ's body torn to pieces like that of a hunted deer. There is also a change in feeling, in that the spring love song is not resumed in the last stanza, as it is in 'When y se blosmes springe', and instead the poem adopts the harsh warning style of a sermon:

> Grone he may and wepen ay,
> þe man þat deiet wit-oute lay
> alone.[1]

The same progress from love to fear occurs in the wooing speech of Christ in the *Ancrene Wisse*,[2] and is equally disturbing there. The startling inversion of the Bernardine theory of the movement upwards from fear to love may perhaps score a rhetorical moral point, but poetically it must necessarily be unsatisfying.

The most moving of the Harley Passion lyrics is that beginning 'I syke when y singe'.[3] There is no spring opening in this, but the emphasis on sighing at the beginning, and on care and languishing (and, in one manuscript, on restless sleep)[4] at the end, indicates its affiliations with secular love-song. More importantly the secular influence can be seen in its organization, for technically the poem is not a Passion meditation but a poem about the poet's feelings when he meditates on the Passion. In this poem the formal echoes of the secular lyric are deftly blended with the tone of elegiac love-longing that colours the whole. It is the emotional tone, characteristic of this group of Passion lyrics, that distinguishes them from the short Passion lament. In the short verses there was sometimes no expression at all of love or grief, as, for instance, in the earliest versions of the *Candet*, which derive an unexpected power from this austerity; again, they may be indicated by a single loving epithet, often the more moving for being unique; and an explicit declaration of sorrow, when it does occur, as in 'Wenne hic soe on rode idon', is delayed until the end. A sustained tone of lament, however, as long as it is discreetly and delicately expressed, can be very moving.

---

[1] Brown XIII, p. 111. *Lay*: religion.
[2] E.E.T.S. 249, 204.
[3] *Harley Lyrics*, 22.
[4] Brown XIII, 64, ll. 51–52.

In his expression of this the author of 'I syke when y singe' seems especially to have been influenced by *Þe Wohunge of ure Laverd*, or texts related to it in style:

A þat luvelike bodi þat henges swa rewli, swa blodi and swa kalde. A hu schal I nu live for nu deies mi lef for me up o þe deore rode.[1]

This quotation from *Þe Wohunge*, though short, illustrates the chief characteristics of its style: the adjective from secular love poetry in *luvelike bodi*, the direct exclamation of anguish, and the emphatic triple use of *swa*. The same feeling is expressed, though more gently, in the following stanza from 'I syke when y singe':

> Þe naylis beit al to longe,
> þe smyt his al to sleye,
> þue bledis al to longe,
> þe tre his al to heye.
> þe stonis waxin wete—
> allas! ihesu mi swete,
> feu frendis hafdis ney(e),
> but sin Ion mur(n)ind
> and mari wepind,
> þat al þi sorwe seye.[2]

In this passage the emphatic use of *to* or *swa*—the former to suggest by litotes the pain of the narrator—is particularly moving. Exclamations of grief are rare, but in an earlier stanza the parenthesis 'hu soldi singe mor' is perfectly placed to suggest a climax of deep grief.

In contrast to the two poems with spring openings, in which compassion is mingled with delight, this poem is uninterruptedly sad. But the sadness is restrained, and its emotionalism can be clearly distinguished from the more profound and ecstatic feeling in the poetry attributed to Richard Rolle and from the hysterical extravagance of some later treatments of the Passion.

---

[1] E.E.T.S. 241, 34.

[2] Brown XIII, p. 123. For this stanza the readings of MS. Digby 2 seem preferable to those of MS. Harley 2253. *Smyt*: smith; *Sleye*: skilful. The mention of the smith probably derives from apocryphal legend, though it does not accord with the usual story of the smith who refused to make the nails. In *The Holkham Bible Picture Book* the smith is shown feigning illness, whilst his wife forges the nails, *Holkham Bible Picture Book*, ed. W. O. Hassall (London, 1954), f. 31ʳ and notes 131-2.

III

Lyrics on Death

THE Middle English verses on death are structurally very similar to those on the Passion, though there is a considerable difference in the proportions between the various kinds. Inevitably those set in the third person are the commonest, though there are quite a number in which the meditator reflects on death or in which he is directly addressed by the dead. Whilst some of the lyrics are discursive, most of them also resemble the Passion lyric in that the aim is to fix the mind of the meditator on a meditative object, which here cannot be the moment of death itself, since this scarcely exists in time and may be imperceptible, but is rather some moment in the process of dying and burial: the appearance of the dying man, the poverty of the winding-sheet and the grave, or the repulsiveness of the decaying body. Just as meditation on the Passion stirred the response of love, so meditation on these aspects of death provoked the response of fear. However, that fear should be the emotion generated in these poems as a proper response to death requires some comment from both the literary and the doctrinal points of view, for neither the propriety of fear to a semi-lyric form nor the propriety of fear as a Christian response to death is self-evidently right.

It is obvious that one of the aims of the Passion lyric was to prevent the emotional distancing that is the normal effect of transforming experience into poetry. Careful craftsmanship in the choice of material and vocabulary makes an emotion seem more poignant but less immediate than in everyday life. The meditative structure of the Passion lyric and the direct language prevent a sense of poetical remoteness. Love, however, is usually a pleasurable emotion, whether poetically transmuted or not: the method of the Passion lyric therefore does not raise any particular aesthetic problem. But this is clearly not true of fear, for this emotion, unless given poetic transformation, is repellent to all, and people shun situations that will provoke it. The writer of the Passion lyric could therefore expect an imaginative co-operation from the reader, whilst the writer of the death lyric would have to expect an evasive, self-protecting response. The latter was compelled to get under his reader's guard by some kind of art, and so the death lyric from its very beginnings shows far more poise and contrivance than does the Passion lyric. This was perhaps made possible by the fact that it benefited from a living tradition behind it in Anglo-Saxon and to some extent in Anglo-Norman literature, but it was demanded by the subject-matter. The result is a paradox: in that the death lyric stirs an emotion which the audience does not want to feel, it could more properly be called sermon than poetry, but in that it uses the skill and artfulness of poetry to win its reluctant hearers' attention, it has in its technique more of the obvious qualities of poetry than has the early Passion lyric. Nowadays, when we are spectators rather than participants in the meditative scheme, or at most but half involved, there is an undoubted pleasure in seeing how a short verse will suddenly compel the imagination to focus on what it would normally exclude and forget.

The sermon affiliations of death lyrics are very clearly shown in the fact that, unlike most of the Passion lyrics, they are not complete experiences in themselves. In the kind of fear prompted by the death lyrics there is no value unless it issues in action: the foundation of the death lyric is the Biblical text, 'Memorare novissima tua et in eternum non peccabis'.[1] Whereas love, when it has issued in action, remains love, fear, when it has issued effectively in action, rightly ceases to be fear. Fear is thus a transitional emotion.

The homiletic nature of the death lyric is also seen in the limited range of emotion it expresses. The Passion lyric too is dominated by one simple but strong emotion that controls the whole. But this exclusiveness to the point of intense simplicity is agreeable and moving. It will not constrict the average sensibility, which is not likely to bring to the subject thought or emotion more subtle or profound than that contained within the lyric: on the contrary, without the guidance of the lyric, meditation on the Passion may well elude the average Christian altogether. In this there is, perhaps, no difference between the reactions of a medieval audience and those of a twentieth-century reader. The same, however, is not true of the death lyric, for death is a subject to which everybody brings a powerful and instinctive emotion, and nowadays also an imaginative awareness, partly formed by the classical reflections on death that became a part of English literature during the Renaissance.

The thought of transience and of its arch-example, death, can stimulate a variety of responses. Death can, for instance, be imagined, not as a state to be feared, but as a peaceful sleep, a longed-for harbour after the weariness and uncertainties of life. This classical idea, so familiar from Renaissance literature,[2] is found only exceptionally in the English

---

[1] Ecclesiasticus vii. 40. 'Remember your end and you will never sin.'
[2] F. P. Weber, *Aspects of Death and Correlated Aspects of Life* (London, 1922), 227–54; Samuel Chew, *The Pilgrimage of Life* (New Haven and London, 1962), 250–2.

medieval lyric, and then only at the very end of the period. It occurs
occasionally as a minor theme in late moralizing lyrics: in the lines
'Thynk þat ded is opynly / Ende off werdes wo',[1] for instance, and, in the
form of a classical metaphor, it is expressed in a single clumsy stanza,
written by an early sixteenth-century hand in the margin of a thirteenth-
century manuscript of Gregory's *Decretals*:

> Howe cometh al ye That ben y-brought
>   In bondes,—full of bitter besynesse
> of erthly luste, abydynge in your thought?
>   Here ys the reste of all your besynesse,
>   Here ys the porte of peese, and resstfulnese
> to them that stondeth In stormes of dys[e]se,
>   only refuge to wreches In dystrese,
> and all comforte of myschefe and mys[e]se.[2]

Although this verse is included in Carleton Brown's fifteenth-century
volume, in literary terms it belongs with medieval poetry for style rather
than content: it shows a characteristic fault of medieval style at its worst,
that is a fragmentary appearance resulting from the expression of a
single, isolated thought in a verse lacking epigrammatic poise and polish.
But in date and content this stanza belongs to the Renaissance. Such a
view of death, which sees it as a release from care rather than as a gateway to heaven or hell, could obviously not form part of Christian didactic literature[3]—unless, of course, presented as a temptation, as is so
skilfully and movingly done in Despair's temptation of the Red Cross
Knight.

However, even if death is to be feared, it is still possible to consider
it and to treat it in literature in a number of different ways. Of these one
of the best known is the *Carpe diem* or *Carpe florem* theme, whether
developed independently or subsumed into love poetry. In its first form
it occurs in one of the most famous of medieval Latin secular songs, the
Gaudeamus, with its exhortation to enjoyment combined with the traditional, didactic invitation to visit the tomb:

> Gaudeamus igitur,
> Juvenes dum sumus;
> Post molestam senectutem
> Nos habebit tumulus.
> Ubi sunt, qui ante nos
> In mundo vixere?

---

[1] 'Thynk man, qware-off thou art wrought', Brown xv, 163, p. 258.

[2] Brown xv, 164.

[3] In the homiletic tradition this idea, if mentioned at all, was mentioned to be
rebutted. In the *Summa praedicantium*, for instance, the story is told of the man who
laughed at the approach of death, but out of pleasure at returning to his own country,
not from relief at leaving a troublesome world (s.v. *Mors*, ed. cit. ii. 60ᵃ⁻ᵇ).

Abeas ad tumulos,
Si vis hos videre.
Vita nostra brevis est
Breve finietur:
Venit mors velociter
Neminem veretur.[1]

This attitude to death has its ancestry in debased Epicureanism, and there is a famous and early example of it in Petronius's description of the handing round of a silver skeleton at the gluttonous and grotesquely opulent Feast of Trimalchio in the *Satyricon*;[2] there are traces of it too in the dancing skeletons engraved on some Roman gems and drinking cups.[3] But a macabre reminder of death could in general hardly serve effectively as an injunction to renewed dissipation for those brought up in a deeply rooted Christian society. No doubt for all Christians, as for St. Paul, the Epicurean attitude of 'Let us eat and drink; for to-morrow we die' had lost its force in face of the Resurrection. The Latin song derives its power from the bravado with which it parodies and reverses the sentiments of Christian didacticism: it fits with the ironic tone of Goliardic poetry, and is far removed from the earnestness of the Middle English lyric.

The *Carpe diem* theme, however, was perhaps ignored in medieval love poetry, not primarily through didacticism, but through the influence of the courtly love code, by which such an unadorned and pungent argument would certainly have seemed indecorous. Though this theme was made use of by Petrarch, and later by Ronsard,[4] it does not seem to occur in English literature until nearly the beginning of the seventeenth century: even Shakespeare, according to Leishman, does not employ it in his sonnets. It is interesting, incidentally, to notice that

[1] Weber, op. cit. 54–55. 'Let us therefore make merry whilst we are young for after burdensome old age the grave will enclose us. Where are they who lived before us in the world? If you wish to see them go to the graveyard. Our life is short and will quickly be ended. Death comes speedily and shows respect to no man.' With this Weber compares 'Scribere proposui de contemptu mundano' (E. du Méril, *Poésies populaires latines du moyen âge* (Paris, 1847), 125–7), which contains the lines, 'Ubi sunt qui ante nos in hoc mundo fuere? / Venies ad tumulos, si eos vis videre'. The last two lines of the second stanza quoted above also occur in this poem.

[2] *Petronii Cena Trimalchionis*, ed. Helmut Schmeck (Heidelberg, 1964), 8–9. Commenting on the silver larva Trimalchio says:

eheu nos miseros, quam totus homuncio nil est!
sic erimus cuncti, postquam nos auferet Orcus.
ergo vivamus, dum licet esse bene.

Cf. Weber, op. cit. 29–32.

[3] Weber, op. cit. 35–41.

[4] J. Leishman, *Shakespeare's Sonnets* (London, 1961), 95–101. E. Dubruck, *The Theme of Death in French Poetry of the Middle Ages and the Renaissance* (The Hague, 1964), 116–17.

whilst Boccaccio's Criseida responds to Pandaro's *Carpe diem* advice
with the words 'tu di' vero',[1] and then repeats it to herself in her first
monologue,[2] Chaucer's Criseyde ignores Pandarus's warning of crow's
feet beneath the eyes,[3] reproaching him instantly with lack of faith,[4]
and, whilst she reasons prudently in her monologue, she does not consider this cogent but pagan argument. There could be no better evidence
for the medieval attitude to the *Carpe diem* theme than Chaucer's very
delicate modification of his source at this point. That writers of the
Middle English lyric should have eschewed the *Carpe diem* theme is not
surprising: it became in itself a convention, but was not one that could
blend with theirs. But there are other attitudes to transience and death,
which seem not so much arguments appropriate to an occasion as a common part of human feeling, and therefore their exclusion, at least nowadays, seems an unwelcome limitation of human sensibility. For instance,
whilst sermons logically reiterate that to the Christian the transience of
an object is a sign of its worthlessness, human feeling, and in particular
the poetic imagination, finds that, on the contrary, transience confers
on things a poignant beauty and vitality. This opposition between the
homiletic and the poetic is, as we shall see, particularly clear in the
treatment of the *Ubi sunt* form, of which the potential nostalgia in English is nearly always constrained by the moralizing content of the context, provided nearly always by the Body and Soul debate or the visit to
the tomb. There is, for instance, nothing in English comparable to
Villon's well-known *Ballade des dames du temps jadis*. Indeed the only
time that the evocativeness is allowed to break through fully is in the
'Love Ron':

> Hwer is paris and heleyne
>   þat weren so bryht and feyre on bleo,
> Amadas and dideyne,
>   tristram, yseude and alle þeo,
> Ector, wiþ his scharpe meyne,
>   and cesar, riche of wordes feo.
> Heo beoþ i-glyden ut of þe reyne
>   so þe schef is of þe cleo.[5]

—and here the insidious nostalgia is exploited by the transference of
the saddened longing from the world to Christ.[6]

[1] Pt. II, stanza 55, *Tutte le opere di Giovanni Boccaccio*, ed. Vittore Branca, ii (1964),
56.

[2] Pt. II, stanza 71, ed. cit. 61.

[3] Bk. ii, l. 403. *Works*, ed. Robinson, 473. Chaucer has amplified Pandarus's speech
with the help of the *Ars amatoria*, iii. 59–80.

[4] Bk. ii, ll. 408 ff. *Works*, p. 474.

[5] Brown XIII, 43, p. 70. *Bleo*: appearance; *scharpe meyne*: keen strength; *wordes
feo*: worldly possessions; *cleo*: hill-side.

[6] For a more detailed discussion of this poem see above pp. 61–62.

It is clear even from the briefest consideration of the potentialities of
death as a subject for lyric poetry that the medieval treatment is so limited
that it cramps the sensibility. Nevertheless, within its homiletic confines
the English death lyric is extremely powerful; and, as with the meditative
poetry on the Passion, it gains its strength from the force of the doctrinal
and spiritual traditions lying behind it, and from the appropriateness to
them of the literary potentialities of the period.

The exclusive and didactic emphasis upon the fear of death had its
roots as firmly grounded in doctrine as had the loving meditation on the
Passion. The value of fear had been recurrently analysed by the Fathers,[1]
and their theory of it seems to have arisen from the need to synthesize
two texts, Christ's own exhortation in Matthew x. 28, '. . . sed potius
timete eum qui potest et animam et corpus perdere in gehennam',[2] and
the statement from I John iv. 18, 'Perfecta caritas foras mittit timorem'.[3]
They therefore distinguished between two kinds of fear, the one *timor
servilis*, by which a man would refrain from evil actions through fear of
punishment in hell, the other *timor filialis* or *castus*, by which a man,
already loving God, might fear through sin to lose Him. The second is
compatible with love of God in this world, the first not. This distinction
was maintained in the Middle Ages. It is, for instance, amply set out in
St. Thomas's analysis of fear,[4] and appears most importantly in the
Sentences of Peter Lombard, at the point where he discusses fear as one
of the Seven Gifts of the Holy Ghost:

Timor autem servilis est, ut ait August. super psal. 127, cum per timorem
gehennae continet se homo a peccato, quo praesentiam judicis et poenas
metuit, et timore facit quidquid boni facit, non timore amittendi aeternum
bonum quod non amat, sed timore patiendi malum quod formidat. Non
timet ne perdat amplexus pulcherrimi Sponsi, sed timet ne mittatur in
gehennam.[5]

What, however, distinguishes the medieval treatment of servile fear
from that of the Fathers is the place that it finds, not in theological
treatises, but in the work of mystical and affective writers. In this it is
often made the beginning of the soul's return to God: St. Bernard, followed by many others, such as St. Catherine of Siena, describes how

---

[1] An historical discussion is provided by A. W. Hunzinger, *Das Furchtmotiv in der
katholischen Busslehre* (Naumburg, 1906).

[2] 'But rather fear Him which is able to destroy both soul and body in hell.' (A.V.)

[3] 'Perfect love casteth out fear.' (A.V.)

[4] *De dono timoris, Summa theologica* II. ii. 19.

[5] Lib. III, dist. xxxiv, *P.L.* 192, 823–7. 'Fear is servile, as Augustine says on Ps.
cxxvii, when a man refrains from sin through fear of hell, when he fears the presence of
the judge and the punishments, and he does out of fear any good that he does, not fear
of losing the eternal good which he does not love, but fear of suffering the punishment
of which he is afraid. He does not fear that he may lose the embrace of the most beautiful
bridegroom, but he fears lest he be sent to hell.' Cf. *P.G.* 49, 153 ff. and *P.L.* 38, 882.

the sinful soul's path to divine union leads from servile fear through cupidity to love.[1] It is not surprising that, as with meditation on Christ in His humanity, this first and lowly step in the upward turning of the soul became detached from the pattern of ascent, and was presented to the non-contemplative layman as a self-sufficient meditative exercise.

In the earlier theological tradition the object of servile fear was said to be hell, and from this there arose the horrific and detailed descriptions of the torments of hell, which are commonplaces of sermon literature.[2] A clear example of this in early Middle English literature is *Sawles Warde*, where the allegorical outline of Wit's household being moved, first through fear of hell and then through cupidity for heaven, derives directly from Hugh of St. Victor's treatise *De anima*, but where the detailed content of Fearlac's speech has its ancestry in the Anglo-Saxon sermon.[3] It is interesting to see how a learned work has supplied the theory and how the native tradition has provided most of the meditative, visual description. Examples of such descriptions of hell, designed to stimulate servile fear, could be multiplied from English sermon literature, but they are rare in the lyric,[4] perhaps because of the inherent unsuitability of the subject-matter, perhaps because the fear they invoke is less immediate and intimate than that of death. People have to be taught to fear hell, they naturally fear death. This truth—so obvious from experience—was in the Middle Ages supported by the authority of Aristotle. St. Thomas, in his analysis of fear, quotes from the *Ethics*, iii. 6, 'Inter omnia terribilissimum est mors'.[5] But, though fear of death is a natural emotion, of which the potential effectiveness would be obvious to homilists and spiritual writers, its propriety must be explained in terms of theological doctrine. At first sight it may seem a contradiction in terms that the Christian should fear death: and, indeed, in the consolatory literature of the patristic period the faith of the Christian in the Resurrection is emphasized in contrast to the hopelessness of the pagan:[6] but the reference is, of course, to the death of others, not to one's own. But, whilst the Resurrection was an answer also to man's

---

[1] Gilson, op. cit., pp. 78, 96, and 101, footnote 131.

[2] In the meditative passages in the work of St. Bernard fear is aroused by descriptions of hell, e.g. in the sixteenth of the *Sermons on the Song of Songs*, P.L. 183, 852; cf. *Sermones de diversis*, xlii, *P.L.* 183, 664.

[3] Ed. R. M. Wilson, *Leeds School of English Language Texts and Monographs*, iii. In the *De anima* the messenger's name is *timor mortis*: the English adaptor perhaps omitted the reference to death in order that his long description of hell might be more appropriate to the speaker.

[4] The few there are enumerate the traditional list of the pains of hell, e.g. 'Unsely gost' (E.E.T.S. 49, 147–55), and an unprinted mnemonic list, 'Fyre and colde and tereshating [shedding]' from MS. Merton 248. Some early death lyrics, such as 'þene latemeste dai' (Brown XIII, 29), have the torments of hell as a subordinate theme.

[5] *Sum. theol.* I, 2, xlii, 2. 'That which inspires the greatest fear is death.'

[6] C. Favez, *La Consolation latine chrétienne* (Paris, 1937), 127–9.

instinctive horror of ceasing to be, and in religious terms an answer to the second death (the death of the soul), it did not alter the fact that death was unnatural, and that the most intense demonstration of the immediate consequence of the Fall was that the body was no longer subject to the soul. According to a classical tag, 'Lex non poena mors',[1] it is the way of the world which can be faced only by acceptance and resignation. But, according to St. Augustine, death is 'a sharp, unnatural experience', and a direct penalty for the Fall. He makes, however, a distinction between the death of the good and that of the bad, for, as a result of the Redemption, 'the first breach of nature' is 'good to the good, and bad to the bad';[2] '. . . by God's ineffable mercy the punishment of sin is become the instrument of virtue, and the pain due to the sinner's guilt is the just man's merit'.[3] This doctrine was often repeated in the Middle Ages. A convenient statement of it, combined with a meditative injunction, may be found in the *De disciplina claustrali* of Peter of Celle, in Chapter 23, *de meditatione mortis*, where he describes death as a debt to be paid, but one which for the good is eclipsed by the rewards that will follow:

Non ergo expavescat solvere debitum mortis, qui expectat soluto debito dotes tantae remunerationis. Debitum tamen est, quod omnibus et ab omnibus debetur et solvitur.

There follows from this the injunction, 'Depinge mortem ante oculos tuos, quam horrenda facies . . .'.[4] Paradoxically, man has to be made to fear death in order that he may become the kind of man who need not fear death. The average Christian must fear it, for, not being like the martyr who has conquered its terrors, he is only freed from the fear by the unmeritorious method of not thinking about it. Few people, except in time of danger, fear death regularly in any pressing sense. St. Thomas stated this, again quoting Aristotle, 'Quae valde longe sunt, non timentur: sciunt enim omnes, quod morientur; sed quia non prope est, nihil curant'.[5] The response of everybody is epitomized in the words of Partridge in *Tom Jones*: 'I know all human flesh must die; but yet a man may live many years for all that.'

The aim of the death lyric was to dispel this comforting remoteness by emphasizing both the uncertainty and the inevitability of death, and

---

[1] Weber, op. cit. 10. 'Death is the law of nature not a punishment.'

[2] Bk. xiii, ch. 2. *De civitate dei*, trans. John Healey (London, 1945), II, 2.

[3] Bk. xiii, ch. 4, ed. cit. 3.

[4] *P.L.* 202, 1131–2. 'The man, who, when his debt is paid expects to be rewarded with a great gift, shall not fear to pay the death which he owes. This is a debt that is owed by all and is payed by all and is everybody's share . . . represent death before your eyes and see how horrifying is his face.'

[5] I. 2, xlii. 2. 'Things that are very far off do not cause fear; all men know that they must die, but, because death is not near, they pay no heed to it.'

most frequently by, as it were, looking through a magnifying-glass at all the minutiae of death, so that time or aversion might not make its image blurred to the imagination. But this examination of the details of death can not only frighten the meditator into virtue, but also persuade him into a lesser estimation of the objects of his cupidity, for self-aggrandizement and reliance upon material splendour or prosperity seem insecurely based when measured against the eventual squalor and decay of the body in the grave. Explicit warnings to the proud make this subsidiary, didactic intention quite plain: in the *Fasciculus morum* death is discussed under the heading of humility;[1] in a later vernacular treatise, the *Disce mori*, meditation on death is recommended as a remedy against the sin of covetousness.[2]

Though there are traces of didacticism and irony in the Passion lyric —the latter springing from the disproportion between God's love and man's sinfulness—it is only in the death lyric that they are common and arise naturally from the subject-matter. This awareness of the moral implications of a remembrance of death is not peculiar to Christianity, and it can be developed in a manner which is satiric rather than penitential. A famous and early example of this kind of treatment is Lucian's *Dialogues of the Dead*: in it the vices and worldly pursuits of contemporary society are discussed within the framework of a conversation amongst the shades in Hades, so that their folly and pointlessness becomes plain; and, whilst the speakers are said to be mere shades, they are also little collections of bones and skulls, and by this means, in a manner common also in later preaching literature, the levelling power of death can be shown, and the uselessness of pride in beauty, in fine clothing, in physical strength, etc.:

Menippus Where are all the beauties, Hermes? Show me round; I am a new-comer.

---

[1] MS. Rawl. C. 670, 20ᵛ–21ᵛ.

[2] MS. Laud Misc. 99, 55ᵛ. The passage, containing many of the traditional themes of death that will later be described, is as follows: Ayenst this synne of covetise the best remedie is to a man to thenke besili on his deth, for as seith Seint Jerome, lightli he forsakith all thing that ofte thenkith he shal deye, and Seint Austyn biddeth a man consider what he shal be here aftir: Consider the sepulchres riche and povere, and what thei that lye in hem were somtyme and what now profited to hem their richesses and the vanyte of the world þat thei hunted so besily. Now is nought seen of theim but asshes. Loke than if ther be difference betwix a king and a knave, the faire and the foule, the stronge and the weyke, whiche and thei might speke wold say to you thees wordes: 'O ye unhappi wrecches to what entent renne ye so beseli to gete the richesses and vanite of the world? Whereto fille ye you wit covetise and vices? Considere ye our bones, so that at the hardest your covetise and miserie fere you therby. Suche as ye be, suche were we, and suche as we be, suche shal ye be.' Ymagine the richeste and mightiest of the world and now is he passed; alle his frendes, richesses, worshippes, and all other vanite or pompe of the world have left him naked, and nothing bereth wit him but synne or merit of his werkes.

Hermes I am busy, Menippus. But look over there to your right, and you will see Hyacinth, Narcissus, Nireus, Achilles, Tyro, Helen, Leda,—all the beauties of old.

Me. I can see only bones, and bare skulls; most of them are exactly alike.

Her. Those bones, of which you seem to think so lightly, have been the theme of admiring poets.

Me. Well, but show me Helen; I shall never be able to make her out by myself.

Her. This skull is Helen.[1]

There is, of course, no question of there being any influence from Lucian's *Dialogues* on medieval literature. Though the reference to Lucian, is often made in modern works on death in medieval literature[2] and art, it is useful only in showing how excellent a standard of measurement the fact of death provides for the satirist. It was, however, natural that English medieval literature, in which there was a strong semi-homiletic, semi-satiric vein, should make use of this inherent possibility. Amongst the lyric poetry the most striking example, the Dance of Death, is of the later period, but, though in the earlier centuries, which we are at the moment considering, purely satiric poems do not exist, the meditative often merges into the satiric.

The theory of the salutary value of servile fear is, in comparison with the doctrine of the value of love, of so ancient an origin that it is far more difficult to trace the meditative passages formed by it, which in turn provided the sources for the medieval lyric. The new stress on the value of fear in the spiritual writers of the twelfth century admittedly led to Latin treatises, which both enjoined the fear of death and provided appropriate meditative thoughts: of these the two most famous were the *De contemptu mundi* of Innocent III and the *Meditationes piissimae de cognitione humanae conditionis* long attributed to St. Bernard, but now known to be by William of Tournai. These works circulated widely in England (they survive in a large number of manuscripts), and they provided the sources for some of the lyrics, and perhaps in some sense the authority for them all. But these Latin works themselves have sources, and individual themes in them can be traced back, for instance, to the *De xii abusivis saeculi* of the eighth century, to some of the earliest sermons in the pseudo-Augustinian collection, the *Sermones ad fratres in eremo*, and further still, back to the work of St. Ephraem of Syria. The long and sometimes indistinct ancestry of various death themes is relevant to the lyric, for some of these themes had already passed into English literature in the late Anglo-Saxon period—into the

---

[1] *The Works of Lucian of Samosata*, trans. H. W. Fowler and F. G. Fowler, i (Oxford, 1905), 137.

[2] Weber, op. cit. 62–63.

sermons in the Vercelli Manuscript and the pseudo-Wulfstan collection, and into the poem on the Body and Soul debate—and from these directly into early Middle English literature. With the early lyrics it is therefore often not possible to tell whether the immediate source lies in the native vernacular tradition or in the international learned Latin tradition. This question, however, is of historical rather than literary importance, for there was no direct stylistic influence from Old English literature. The early lyrics are as remote from the rhetoric of the Old English sermon or the patterned style and rhythms of the Old English Body and Soul poem, as they are from any Latin original. For, though some death themes continued after the Norman Conquest unaltered in content, the vernacular in which they were expressed no longer retained the same range of associations: the metre was no longer that borrowed from courtly poetry, and the language had none of the dignified leisure of poetic diction. Had the subject-matter of the poetry been classical reflection on death, this change would also have been an impoverishment. The medieval death themes, however, like the meditation on the Passion, did not require nobility of language, but, on the contrary, their reference to ordinary, unheightened experience was best expressed by quick, exact, colloquial language: therefore the unique diminution of the vernacular in England made it a perfect medium for this kind of poetry. The immediate, uncomplex effect of the poetry was not in danger of being modified by an unintended learned or courtly air, for the vocabulary, since it was rarely used for literary or learned work or for courtly conversation, could have no overtones except those of everyday communication, and the style naturally remained close to the popular proverbial sayings which the poems so often quote: 'Al to late, al to late, / Wanne þe bere ys ate gate'[1] or 'Man may longe lyves wenen, / ac offte hym legeþt se wrench'.[2]

Therefore, although some of the early death lyrics, such for instance as 'þene latemeste dai' may borrow some of their content from native predecessors and also echo them verbally, they are quite different in effect from Anglo-Saxon literature, for no poetic diction, rhetorical inflation, or any sophisticated literary art softens, or adds grandeur to, the horror of death or the reproach accorded to a sinful life. There is a grim lack of pretentiousness, for the style is not one which could

---

[1] Brown XIII, 71. Cf. *Proverbs of Hendyng* (H. Varnhagen, 'Zu mittelenglischen Gedichten', *Anglia*, iv, 1881, p. 191, from MS. Camb. Gg. 1. 1), 'Al to late, al to late,/ Wan þe deth is at the ʒate'; *Pricke of Conscience*, iii. 2000–1, 'For when þe dede es at þe yhate, / þan es he warned over late'.

[2] Brown XIII, 10 B. *Hym legeþt se wrench*: he is deceived. Cf. *Proverbs of Alfred*, ll. 153–6, ed. E. Borgström (Lund, 1908), 7; *Proverbs of Hendyng* (from MS. Digby 86, *Anglia*, iv. 200), 47. The first stanza of XIII, 10 B is quoted in the *Ayenbite of Inwyt*, E.E.T.S. 23, 129–30.

potentially be used for a magnificent subject, and there is no elevation
of tone which might suggest remoteness from daily life. The language
has not the dignity or subtlety that would come from a long ancestry of
literary use, but has instead the immediate effect of everyday speech.
This makes it particularly suitable for brief, vivid, hortatory poetry,
though perhaps less suitable for the longer, more reflective poems, where
the absence of shades of meaning and the comparative smallness of
vocabulary can lead to monotony in tone and feeling.

There are a number of brief verses, written in quick-moving, metrically free, two-stressed couplets, which illustrate well the excellence of
these early meditative and mnemonic poems. The extremely popular
verse, 'If man him biðocte', which was copied and orally repeated consistently from the thirteenth to the fifteenth century, is a typical example:

> If man him biðocte
> inderlike and ofte
> þu arde is te fore
> fro bedde te flore,
> up reuful is te flitte
> fro flore te pitte,
> fro pitte te pine
> ðat nevre sal fine,
> i pene non sinne
> sulde his herte winne.[1]

The simplicity of the diction, combined with the alliteration and the
repetition of key-words from one couplet to another, drive home the
pattern of descent from bed to floor to grave to hell. Verses of this kind
have a 'catchiness' both poetically and morally effective, whereby they
haunt the memory and readily recur to it, even when there is no
conscious wish to retain them. The structure is the common meditative
one, an emotive description followed by the appropriate moral reflection,
and the content is traditional, the recollection of the death-bed, the
corpse laid on the floor, the grave dug in the ground, and hell, thought
of as lying at the centre of the earth. But, whilst the content is traditional
and grimly realistic, the arrangement into stages of a falling journey
to hell has an intellectual and ironic crispness. Whether this ingenuity
was the author's own cannot be told and scarcely matters. No exact
source has been identified, though there is a strong probability that
somewhere there are some lines of Latin prose, which describe clearly
but less pungently a similar pattern of descent.

In some manuscripts this verse is followed by a text of the most popular of all Middle English death lyrics, that on the Signs of Death. Its
popularity is partly accounted for by the fact that it was included in the

---

[1] Brown XIII, 13. L. 10 *Winne*, MS. *winnen*.

section on death in the *Fasciculus morum*, but the very high number of manuscripts containing it, and the large number of variant versions, show clearly the intrinsic value of the text to the Middle Ages. Nowadays the subject is chiefly familiar from the description of the death of Falstaff, whose feet were 'cold as any stone' and whose 'nose was as sharp as a pen'. It is not known where Shakespeare derived these details: it is not inconceivable that some Middle English version circulated orally, but, since the Signs were still part of received medical knowledge, he could have come across them in some less popular source. For instance, a short work containing them, entitled *The Boke of Knowledge, whether a sycke person beynge in perylle shall lyve, or dye*, was printed in 1535.[1] In this work the Signs appear in a purely medical context, and it was in this way that they originated in the *Prognosticon* of Hippocrates. At the beginning of this work Hippocrates describes with precision the symptoms by which a physician, when he first sees his patient, may know whether he will live or die: 'Nose sharp, eyes hollow, temples sunken, the ears cold and contracted with their lobes turned outwards, the skin about the face hard and parched, and the colour of the face as a whole being yellow or black . . .';[2] and, scattered through the *Prognosticon* and also the *Aphorisms*, these details are repeated and increased. The works of Hippocrates, translated and commented upon by Galen, were preserved, studied, and esteemed in Benedictine monasteries abroad from the time of Cassiodorus, and they appear in English manuscripts from the twelfth century onwards. A diagnosis of approaching death, which included the Signs, was often copied in Anglo-Latin medical manuscripts of the Middle Ages, and there are even a number of similar Middle English medical texts.[3] But in the twelfth century the Signs of Death were detached from their medical context and incorporated also into death literature. To the Middle Ages this would almost certainly not have seemed a substantial rerooting of the subject: there would be no reason why symptoms, scientifically observed by a physician, should not also serve as a moral warning. That the medical and the didactic were not unrelated can be seen in the fact that medical manuscripts quite often contain texts of one or two of the death lyrics.[4] However, no doubt often the medical origin of the Signs was forgotten or not known. Some manuscripts of the *Fasciculus morum* ascribe a Latin version to St.

---

[1] Marjorie Walters, 'The Literary Background of Francis Bacon's Essay "Of Death"', *M.L.R.* xxxv (1940), 7, quotes two other examples. Cf. also *Henry V*, ed. J. H. Walter (London 1954), note to II, iii. 14–17.

[2] Ed. W. H. S. Jones (Loeb Classical Library, 1959), ii. 8–9.

[3] The Signs, for instance, occur in the Latin medical manuscript, Sloane 1313, 29ᵛ, and amongst the vernacular medical notes printed by T. Wright and J. O. Halliwell, *Reliquiae antiquae*, i (London, 1841), 54.

[4] MS. Sloane 1313, for instance, contains an *exemplum* verse about a dying sinner on f. 134 ʳ⁻ᵛ (*Index*, 2307).

Jerome,[1] probably by analogy with the attribution to him of the Fifteen Signs of the Last Judgement. In other words, they are thought of as a solemn and prophetic warning from which the Christian should appropriately take fright.

The Signs of Death first appear in a didactic context in the twelfth-century Worcester Fragments, but, though it is not impossible that this adaptation was first made by the vernacular writer, it remains more probable that it first occurred in some Latin treatise now lost or unidentified. In the Worcester Fragments, which are the remains of a Body and Soul poem, The Signs form part of a prelude, describing the painfulness of dying and the loneliness and humiliation of the corpse. The Signs are as follows:

> Him deaveð þa aeren, him dimmeð (þa) eigen
> Him scerpeð þe neose, him scrinckeþ þa lippen,
> Him scorteð (þe) tunge, him trukeð his iwit,
> Him teoreð his miht, him coldeð his (fet).[2]

The Worcester Fragments were known to some of the writers of the early Middle English death lyric. They directly influenced 'þene latemeste dai' (as we shall discuss later), they perhaps contributed to the tradition of describing the preparations for burial which lies behind 'If man him biþocte', and finally they may have provided the source for the earliest lyric version of the Signs. There is not here any obvious, intermediary Latin source: the Signs do not, for instance, occur in the *De contemptu mundi* or in the *Meditationes*, though versions are often found adjoining these works in manuscripts, and works based upon them, such as *The Prick of Conscience*,[3] often amplify their original by including the theme. A description of the Signs was also a commonplace of medieval preaching on death.

Alongside the Middle English verses there occur Latin and also Anglo-Norman couplet versions,[4] but these may well derive from the English rather than vice versa, since there is no evidence of their having a circulation independent of the native tradition. Certainly the Latin and Anglo-Norman versions are inferior, lacking the quality of the vernacular couplets, which have a colloquial laconicism that makes them

---

[1] Brown XIII, p. 220. Some of the manuscripts that I have examined, such as MS. Rawl. C. 670, 20ᵛ, do not contain this ascription.

[2] *Die Fragmente der Reden der Seele an den Leichnam*, ed. R. Buchholz (Erlangen, 1889), 1. Ll. 3–4, His tongue ceases, his senses fail, his strength droops.

[3] Bk. i, ll. 812–27, ed. Morris, 23.

[4] A French and Latin version are printed by P. Meyer, 'Mélanges de poésie anglo-normande', *Romania*, iv (1875), 384. R. W. Hunt, 'The Collections of a Monk of Bardney: A Dismembered Rawlinson Manuscript', *Medieval and Renaissance Studies*, v (1961), 28, notes a ten-line version in MS. Rawl. C. 504, where it follows the *Meditationes piissimae*. The *Fasciculus morum* also contains a Latin version (Brown XIII, p. 220).

particularly forceful as moral verse. The Latin and Anglo-Norman also show far less variety—there are only minor verbal differences between the versions—whilst, despite the restriction imposed by rhyme in the brief two-stress couplet, the English reinvigorates the unchanging form by fresh detail, or by combinations which often constitute almost a new poem. Many groups of verses, however, are related as variants of one original which has been handed on orally—this is true of the largest group, that of the *Fasciculus morum*, MS. Harley 7322, and MS. Trinity 43—but others are independent and by no means stale treatments of the theme. The version of the *Fasciculus morum*, with its stark combination in each line of noun plus verb, is perhaps the most effective:

> When þe hede quakyth
> And þe lyppis blakyth
> And þe nose sharpyth
> And þe senow starkyth
> And þe brest pantyth
> And þe breþe wantyth
> And þe teþe ratelyȝt
> And þe þrote roteleþ[1]

. . . . . .

A slightly later and quite unrelated version of the theme occurs in MS. Arundel 507:

> When þe hee biginnis til turne
> And þe fote biginnis to spurne,
> And þe bak makes þe bowe,
> And þe mouthe makes þe mowe:
> þerby may þu see sone
> þat he sall go to þe dome.[2]

Here the leisure of the slightly longer line has enabled the poet to describe the distorted mouth and eye from Hippocrates and the bent back from a different list (that of the Signs of Old Age), in a way that catches the imagination by a cynical sprightliness, and to use a rhyme scheme which completely escapes the pairs of verbs necessarily recurring in the shorter-lined versions. An effective, though more learned, version of the Signs is found in some fifteenth-century manuscripts. In it the moral, instead of being reserved to the end, in accordance with the usual meditative structure, is interspersed between the Signs, the latter being the list from the *Fasciculus morum*:

---

[1] MS. Rawl. C. 670, 148ᵛ, Brown XIII, p. 222. *Blakyth*: grow pale; *ratelyȝt*: chatter; *roteleþ*: makes a rattling noise. This version occurs in the four Bodleian manuscripts which I have examined. The entry at *Index* 4035 is therefore misleading.

[2] C. Horstman, *Yorkshire Writers*, i (London, 1895), 156.

When thy hede quakyth:	Memento.
Then thy lyppys blakyth:	Confessio.
When thy noose sharpyth:	Contricio.
Then thy lymmys starkyth:	Satisfaccio.
When thy brest pantyth:	Nosce teipsum.
Than thy wynde wantyth:	Miserere.
When thy nyen hollyth:	Libera me domine.
Then deth folowyth:	Veni ad judicium.[1]

There is here a striking counterpoint between the static English description and the developing warning and prayer of the Latin. The use of significant phrases from Latin liturgical prayer is characteristic of some fifteenth-century poetry, and here it has given new force to what was by that time a well-worn theme.

Though the Signs of Death are still effective through their grim accumulation of disagreeable detail, their full power is probably lost in a period that no longer appreciates the medieval much-used rhetorical formula of the catalogue. The catalogue of feminine beauty, for instance, may nowadays seem a list of dismembered parts, which never become imaginatively integrated: nowadays the impressionistic is often more evocative than the meticulously precise. But this type of catalogue could not have been so popular in the Middle Ages, if the very form had weakened its effect.

Another effective little Middle English verse, which has the sting and force of an epigram, is 'Wen þe turuf is þi tuur'. This too has its ancestry in the literary no-man's land of the twelfth century, when the metre used was still the alliterative line with its length and leisure, but when the style already showed the ironic edge and colloquial directness that are characteristic of the death lyrics in the Middle Ages. The subject of the poem is the smallness and poverty of the grave contrasted with the splendour enjoyed by the dead man when he was alive:

> Wen þe turuf is þi tuur,
> and þi put is þi bour,
> þi wel and þi wite þrote
> ssulen wormes to note.
> Wat helpit þe þenne
> al þe worilde wnne?[2]

The theme itself is an ancient one, and can be found in the homilies of the Eastern Church, where most of the death themes begin. St. John Chrysostom, for instance, in a passage whose point is the despising of worldly glory, thus commented upon the death of a rich man: 'He has

---

[1] M. R. James, *Catalogue of the Manuscripts in Queens' College, Cambridge* (Cambridge, 1905), 15. Cf. *Cambridge Middle English Lyrics*, ed. H. A. Person (Seattle, 1953), 16–19.

[2] Brown XIII, 30. *Put*: grave; *wel*: skin, *note*: benefit.

departed to the grave which has seized all, and is buried within the space of three cubits.'[1] This emphasis on the physical smallness of the grave, which was to be a commonplace of medieval death literature, occurs in an early and striking form in England in the account of the death of William the Conqueror in the Anglo-Saxon Chronicle, where the style is obviously influenced by sermon rhetoric:

Eala hu leas and hu unwrest is þysses middaneardes wela. Se þe wæs ærur rice cyng and maniges landes hlaford, he næfde þa ealles landes buton seofon fot mæl; and se þe wæs hwilon gescrid mid golde and mid gimmum he læg þa oferwrogen mid moldan.[2]

A grimmer, less nostalgic, and more ingenious expression of the same idea had already occurred in Vercelli Homily ix, where the grave is briefly described as one of the five images of hell,[3] and its shallowness is emphasized by the harshly quaint description of the roof of the dead man's house lying above his chest: an ironic idea, which was to be repeated over and over again,[4] and probably stimulated further elaborations of the theme in twelfth-century poetry.

The idea of the smallness of the grave, ironically expressed, recurs almost as a refrain in the Worcester Fragments,[5] but the outstanding example of it is the twelfth-century poem now known as 'The Grave'. This poem has a cleverness, which is neither typically Anglo-Saxon nor typically medieval: it plays with the conceit of the grave as a house, exploiting with ironic wit the discords that arise from this basic metaphor. The oddity of the grave, thought of as a house, is stressed: the walls are disproportionately low, there are no doors, and the roof lies immediately above its inhabitant's chest; and the older idea of the loneliness of the corpse is here expanded into the idea that no friends will call upon the dead to ask him how he likes his new home:

> Dureleas is þæt hus   and dearc hit is wiðinnen,
> Ðær þu bist feste bidytt   and dæð hefð þa cæge.
>
> .   .   .   .   .   .

---

[1] *P.G.* 55, 511–12. See also 'Das Grab und seine Länge', *Kleinere Schriften von Reinhold Köhler*, ed. J. Bolte, ii (Berlin, 1900), 24–27.

[2] Ed. J. Earle and C. Plummer (Oxford, 1952), i. 219. 'Alas, how false and untrustworthy is the prosperity of this world. He, who had been a powerful king and ruler over wide lands, of all this land is now left with but seven feet; and he who was formerly clothed in gold and jewels now lies covered only with earth.'

[3] 'Ðonne is ðaere feorðan helle onlicnes byrȝen nemned; forþan þæs huses hrof bið gehnreged þe him on-ufan ðam breostum siteð.' *Der Vercelli-Codex cxvii*, ed. Max Förster (Halle, 1913), 92. The four other images are: pain, old age, death, torment.

[4] It appears, for instance, in the Worcester Fragments C, 31, and 'þene latemeste dai', 30. Later occurrences are too numerous to be listed.

[5] 'Die Fragmente der Reden der Seele an den Leichnam', ed. Buchholz, A 35–36, C 29–31, etc.

Nefst ðu nenne freond 　　þe þe wylle faren to,
Ðæt efre wule lokien 　　hu þe þæt hus þe likie.[1]

No thirteenth-century lyric treats the theme with such elaborate and
grimly inventive ingenuity, but the idea of the roof lying upon the breast,
chin, or nose remained a favourite commonplace, and with it variations
such as that of 'þene latemeste dai', where the dead man's house is said
to be constructed with a spade.[2] There is at play here the same kind of
wit as we have already seen in descriptions of the armour of Christ,
but here, at least from the modern point of view, it is well suited to the
theme.

'Wen þe turuf is þi tuur' is a very neat and pointed example of this kind
of wit, with the incongruity of the image made sharp by the simplicity
of the syntax, and with the yoking together of the nouns, by alliteration
in the first line and by the assonance of plosive consonants in the second,
as though these devices echoed a similarity of meaning. In its manuscript, MS. Trinity 323, this poem is preceded by a Latin couplet
version, but it does not follow that the copyist was right in taking the
English to be the translation rather than vice versa. Certainly the English
is the more ironically effective with its alliteration, and with the phrase
wormes to note (cf. Old English *wyrmum to hroðre*) for the Latin *cibus
vermium*.

A comparably ironic treatment of a similar subject occurs in the very
popular 'Erþe toc of erþe',[3] which is a punning elaboration of the well-
known Genesis-based text, 'Memento homo quod cinis es et in cinerem
reverteris', frequently quoted in Latin death literature and in the
liturgy of Ash Wednesday at the imposition of the ashes.[4] There are
also long, non-epigrammatic versions of these lines, and parallels of these
longer texts are found in Latin and Anglo-Norman. This is, therefore,
a text whose literary development cannot be unravelled to the point of
proof. It seems likely, however, firstly that it is the Latin and Anglo-
Norman versions that are the translations,[5] and that the vernacular is
their original; and secondly that it is the riddling epigram that has been
expanded into the clear and inclusive but diffuse texts, rather than that
these have been condensed into an epigram.[6] The verse itself is as
follows:

---

[1] Ed. A. Schröer, *Anglia*, v (1882), 289–90.

[2] 'Nu sal þin halle wid spade ben wrout', Brown XIII, 29, l. 25, p. 47.

[3] Brown XIII, 73; E.E.T.S. 141, 1.

[4] 'Remember man that you are dust and to dust you shall return', *Sarum Missal*,
ed. J. Wickham Legg (Oxford, 1916), p. 51, footnote 5.

[5] Nearly all the material (or references to it) is assembled in E.E.T.S. 141.

[6] The arguments for the theory that the Latin is a translation from the English are
set out in E.E.T.S. 141, xxix–xxxiii. Against the possibility that the present verse was
the opening of a longer poem, the copyist having forgotten the rest (see E.E.T.S. 141,

Erþe toc of erþe, erþe wyþ woh,
Erþe oþer erþe to þe erþe droh,
Erþe leyde erþe in erþene þroh—
Þo hevede erþe of erþe erþe ynoh.[1]

In estimating the quality of these lines it is important to remember that
the Middle Ages held a view of puns quite different from that of later
centuries. Nowadays puns imply confusion and they are therefore used
only when the intention is jesting or at least unserious. But in the Middle
Ages puns implied synthesis, for they were thought of as a rhetorical
means of revealing underlying correspondences. Ambiguities of meaning
were not random, nor similarities of sound comic coincidences, but
both were linguistic indications of the intricate unity of the divine plan.
Puns were therefore used for the most august subject-matter, particularly
when a paradoxical treatment was appropriate, as for the Incarnation:
the play on the similarity of sound in *virgo*: *virga* (rod, i.e. of Jesse) or
the idea of the Infant Christ as *Verbum infans*, the Word that could not
speak, are commonplaces of Latin religious poetry.[2] The subject-matter
of 'Erþe toc of erþe', the end of man and of his riches in the grave,
through the paradoxical clash between two standards of judgement, is
admirably suited to punning expression, and the total effect is of a harsh
and uneasily obscure riddle. Not everyone would agree on the meaning
of the first two lines, but the following is a possible interpretation of the
whole: Man, whose body is made of earth, is born in sin; in his lifetime
he accumulates riches for himself; in death he is laid in an earth-grave,
and then has he his fill of earth. This bare history of man is satirically
hidden behind the word *erþe*, which is substituted for every noun except
woh, and it is particularly effective, in that most Middle English lyrics
decline in tension on account of their moralizing conclusions, whereas
this begins quietly and enigmatically, and increases in force until the
last line, which is bluntly clear in meaning and gives a savagely ironic
summing up of the end of the avaricious man.

Not all the short early death lyrics, however, have the qualities of
those so far described. Though John of Grimestone's preaching-book
provided a possible starting-point for an appreciation of the Passion
lyric, it does not do so for the death lyric: with the exception of a four-
quatrain version of 'Erþe toc of erþe',[3] its death section is made up of
rather undistinguished verses, and a similarly mediocre collection is to

xv), is the undeniable effect of completeness given by the verse. If the related opening
of the long text from MS. Harley 913 (op. cit. 1–4) had survived alone, it would not
have given this impression of literary self-sufficiency.

[1] Brown XIII, 73. *Woh*: sin; *þroh*: pit.
[2] An excellent discussion of puns in Latin literature is given by W. J. Ong, 'Wit and
Mystery: a Revaluation in Mediaeval Latin Hymnody', *Speculum*, xxii (1947), 310–41.
[3] f. 87ᵛ. *Index*, 703.

be found in the *Fasciculus morum*. Many of the early verses, such as the following, can be dismissed as purely mnemonic:

> Wanne ich þenche þinges þre
> ne mai [i] nevre bliþe be:
> þat on is ich sal awe,
> þat oþer is ich ne wot wilk day.
> þat þridde is mi meste kare,
> i ne woth nevre wuder i sal fare.[1]

This is the rendering of a Latin aphorism whose roots extend back on the one hand to Cicero and on the other to the *Vitae patrum*.[2] A Latin verse form, 'Sunt tria vere, quae faciunt me semper dolere', is copied frequently in English manuscripts,[3] whilst the English version was exceptionally popular, being even incorporated (rather inappropriately) in the story of The Three Caskets in the English translation of the *Gesta Romanorum*.[4] The verse is mnemonic, in that the intention is not to arouse emotion but to enumerate three points to be memorized. In this it is like some of the penitential poems on the seven deadly sins: the appropriate emotion has to be generated from outside the poem. Moreover, in contrast to the terseness of the Latin analogue, which has an epigrammatic conciseness, this verse is faint and flaccid. Many other mnemonics are no more than rhyming tags. The *Fasciculus morum*, for instance, contains a pedestrian translation of 'Memorare novissima tua': 'Have mynde on þyn ende / And ever fro synne þu myth wende',[5] and John of Grimestone's book thus paraphrases the traditional formula, *Nosce teipsum*:

---

[1] Brown XIII, 12.

[2] Two of the three sorrowful things appear in the *Meditatio* vii of Anselm, 'Nihil certius morte, nihil hora mortis incertius'. A. Wilmart, *Auteurs spirituels et textes dévots du moyen âge latin* (Paris, 1932), 179, points out parallels or anticipations of this in the *Policraticus* of John of Salisbury (ii. 27, ed. Webb, i. 159), and long before this in the *De senectute* (xx. 74). The idea of three items, however, and the nature of the third, seems to have been suggested by a passage in the *Vitae patrum*:

> Dixit abbas Helias: Ego tres res timeo.
> unam quando egressura est anima mea de corpore,
> aliam quando occursurus sum Deo,
> tertiam quando adversum me proferenda est sententia. . . .
>
> (*P.L.* 73, 861)

Cf. R. Köhler, 'Mich wundert, dass ich fröhlich bin', *Kleinere Schriften*, ed. J. Bolte, iii (Berlin, 1900), 421–52, who also quotes many vernacular German parallels; this article is usefully summarized by R. Kozaky, *Geschichte der Totentänze*, ii (Budapest, 1936), 157–8.

[3] Walther 18886. Cf. p. 349, footnote 1. For this verse and references to other Latin analogues see Brown XIII, pp. 172–3. A different version from MS. Rawl. C. 510 is printed by Hunt, loc. cit. 34.

[4] E.E.T.S., E.S. 33, 304. It is attributed to a saint in the *Vitae patrum*.

[5] MS. Rawl. C. 670, 21ᵛ. *Ende*, MS. *endyng*.

þu man þat wilt knowen þiself loke quat þu hast þouth,
þenk of þi maneres quat þei ben, quat dedes þu hast wrouth,
þer saltu knowen best þiself and hym þat þe hat bouth.[1]

These three lines are even less self-sufficient than 'Wanne ich þenche
þinges þre', for not only do they lack emotional and persuasive content,
but also their meaning requires explanation. The idea of knowing oneself
has a long and varying philosophical history, which is not relevant to this
verse. But there is a subsidiary strain in the history of its significance,
extending from classical times to the Middle Ages, namely that of
knowing oneself mortal, through which it became a two-word summary of
all death themes. It is thus quoted in the *Dialogues of the Dead*, where
Menippus uses the phrase in his ironic comments on the follies of the
dead,[2] and Seneca and Juvenal also used the injunction *Nosce teipsum*
in this way; in the Museo delle Terme at Rome there is the mosaic figure
of a skeleton (originally belonging to a tomb on the Appian Way), accompanied by these words.[3] In the Middle Ages currency was given to this
usage by the opening of the popular source of death themes, the *Meditationes piissimae*, which begins 'Multi multa sciunt, et se ipsos nesciunt'.[4]
In later lyrics, such as 'In a Pistel þat poul wrouȝt'[5] from the Vernon
Manuscript and 'Mannys soule is sotyl and queynt'[6] from Digby 102,
this idea is set out with didactic amplitude:

> Knowe þi-self, þat þou schalt dye,
>   But what tyme þou nost never whenne;
> Wiþ a twynklyng of an eiȝe,
>   Everi day þou hiȝest þe henne.
> þi fleschly foode þe wormes wol fye—
>   Uche cristen mon ouȝte þis to kenne.[7]

But for the audience of John of Grimestone's lines this kind of thought
must have been supplied outside this seemingly vague and obscurely
didactic verse, and most probably in a sermon. The lines are in fact
no more than a jolt to the memory: information and persuasiveness have
already been communicated and are merely recalled through a brief

---

[1] f. 29ʳ, s.v. *de cupiditate. Index*, 3678.
[2] Trans. Fowler, 110.   [3] Weber, op. cit. 738–9.
[4] *P.L.* 184, 485. 'Many men know many things and do not know themselves.' A
work of similar kind is Helinand's *De cognitione sui* (*P.L.* 212, 721–35), where the Del-
phic, '*gnothi seauton*, id est: Nosce teipsum', leads to a lengthy treatment of the themes
of death. Cf. the quotation from Caesarius in Appendix H, p. 402 below, and Worcester Fragments, C 27–28 (ed. Buchholz, 4), 'þu wurpe [cn]eow ofer cneow. Ne icneowe
þu þe sulfen, / þet þu scoldest mid wurmen [wu]nien in eorþan' (the pun at so early
a date is very striking).
[5] Brown XIV, 100.   [6] E.E.T.S. 124, 27–31.
[7] Brown XIV, p. 141. *Fleschly foode*: the *M.E.D.* queries the meaning of this phrase;
the sense of the whole line is 'worms shall feed upon your flesh for their nourishment'.

mnemonic. From the modern point of view such verses are merely historical curiosities, which perhaps serve to throw into relief the qualities of the more successful lyrics.

In a more interesting variety of this kind of verse the context to be supplied is of a narrative kind. There are three early verses (two of them from John of Grimestone's preaching-book) that are warnings spoken by a corpse within his grave to a passer-by. Structurally they are of the same kind as the complaints of Christ, in which the meditator stands in his imagination at the foot of the Cross and hears Christ speak to him; but in these the meditator imagines that he stands by a grave and hears the warning voice from within. The verses are as follows:

> þu wreche gost wid mud ydet,
> þync on me her in þys pet!
> A man y was and mannes fere:
> Swylc schalt þu ben as ic am here.[1]

> Wat so þu art þat gost her be me
> Witstand and behold and wel beþenk þe
> þat swich as þu art i was wone to be
> And swich as i am nou saltu sone be.[2]

> Her sal I dwellen, loken under ston,
> Her sal I dwellen, ioy is her non.
> Her sal I dwellen wermes to fede,
> Her sal I dwellen domes to abide.[3]

Though structurally these verses are like Crucifixion complaints, in terms of meditation and literary effect they resemble the verses on the Christ-knight theme, for they are *exemplum* verses that depend for their power on the story that encloses them. This story has an ancient and complicated history,[4] in which the sermon injunction to visit the tomb ('loken under ston') met a tradition of classical epitaph in which the dead spoke to the living as exemplary mirrors of their future state, 'Swylc schalt þu ben as ic am here'. Both these traditions continued to flourish independently and profusely in the Middle Ages: the visit to the tomb is an invariable item in sermons and preaching-books, whilst the warning from the dead is one of the commonest forms of medieval

---

[1] Rolf Kaiser, *Medieval English* (Berlin, 1958), 294. *Wid mud ydet*: proudly adorned. The preceding rubric in the manuscript reads: 'De illis qui transeunt per cimiterium et nolunt orare pro defunctis' (B.M. Add. MS. 11579, 26ᵛ). The copyist has evidently put the verse into a wrong *exemplum* context.

[2] Owst, *Preaching in Medieval England*, 344.

[3] MS. Adv. 18. 7. 21, 87ᵛ. *Suppl.* 1210. 5; Robbins perhaps too readily assumes that the English is a translation from the accompanying Latin and not vice versa.

[4] For a detailed account see Appendix H.

epitaph. They combined, however, in an *exemplum* that became attached to the names of various historical personages, who were said in their pride and riches to have visited their father's grave and learnt from the decaying corpse humility and repentance. But, as with the Christ-knight *exemplum*, the hero of the present verses is the reader. It is he who, in his imagination, visits the grave and hears the warning from the dead.

This tradition does not merely provide the source for the three simple and unambitious verses of warning from the tomb, it also gives life to them. For the verses are not meant to be read in isolation: they are not self-sufficient, any more than is the short complaint of Christ, which obviously presupposes further knowledge of the Crucifixion. Traditional phrases, such as 'wyrmes to fede' or 'Swylc schalt þu ben as ic am here' would come trailing associations of fear and horror. The verses are thus mnemonic, but not in the sense that 'Wanne ich þenche þinges þre' is mnemonic. They are not an aid to remembering facts but to recalling emotions, and they gather force within the meditative framework. Mediocre in themselves, they may today tend to slide over the mind. But to anybody who made them part of a genuine meditation, the hints of putrefaction and the interlocking of the dead and the living would by no means be empty of emotional power.

The warning from the tomb is horrific, implying as it does the state of the decaying corpse, but the form in which this subject was explicitly and most terrifyingly emphasized was the Body and Soul debate. At first sight it may seem strange that a debate form can be included even roughly under the heading of meditative poetry, and particularly that it should in fact provide the most striking examples of death meditation until the end of the fourteenth century. This debate, however, could be used in three ways: firstly, and most frequently, to demonstrate that all pride and prosperity must end in the grave, in which the body will rot, whilst the soul is tormented in hell; secondly, in a more remote and learned way, to express in fictional form the philosophical relationship between body and soul; thirdly, to demonstrate vividly and allegorically the conflict during life between the senses and the reason. The first, therefore, is almost purely meditative, and it is only the other two which yield the intellectual pleasure that is normally expected from the debate form, with its classical ancestry and scholastic associations.[1] Amongst English Body and Soul poems, it is only in the very latest, 'Als i lay in a winteris nyt',[2] that there is an interest in intellectual argument

---

[1] For the history of the debate form see H. Walther, 'Das Streitgedicht in der lateinischen Literatur des Mittelalters' in *Quellen und Untersuchungen zur lateinischen Philologie des Mittelalters*, v. 2 (Munich, 1920), and, for the Body and Soul debate in particular, pp. 63–88.

[2] 'þe desputisoun bitwen þe bodi and þe soule', ed. W. Linow, *Erlanger Beiträge zur englischen Philologie*, i (1889).

as well as in the themes of the grave. Of the rest, 'In a þestri stude'[1] is a meditative dialogue, and the others—two short verses[2] and 'Þene latemeste dai'[3]—belong to the earlier tradition, in which the form consisted only of a monologue spoken by the soul.

The fact that so much meditative material is found in the Body and Soul debate, even when, as in 'Als i lay in a winteris nyt' or the popular, widely diffused Latin debate 'Noctis sub silentio', there is intellectual content as well, is explained by the history of the form, the development of a monologue into a debate under the literary pressures of the twelfth century.

Like the injunction to visit the tomb,[4] the speech of the soul to its former body is already found in the writings of Ephraem. In these there occur a number of passages in which the soul, as it passes from the body on its death-bed, either reproaches or praises the body for its previous conduct.[5] This dramatic fiction in due course became associated with the scene in the *Visio Pauli*, in which the souls of a righteous man and of an evil-doer are seen by St. Paul to leave their bodies, and where the emphasis is chiefly upon the blessedness of the saved soul welcomed into heaven and the terror of the damned dragged off to hell.[6] Though this scene continued to be depicted,[7] there arose a variation, found for instance in some Anglo-Saxon sermons[8] and in the Anglo-Norman *Li Vers del jüïse*,[9] wherein the setting is transposed from the moment of death to the Day of Judgement; and here, in association with the traditional treatment of the Last Judgement, the soul in its speech to the body lays particular stress on an enumeration of the body's sins, and especially on its failure to perform the corporal works of mercy. In this form the

---

[1] *The Latin Poems commonly attributed to Walter Mapes*, ed. T. Wright, Camden Society, 1841, 346–9.

[2] Brown XIII, 38 and 20.   [3] Brown XIII, 29.

[4] For the injunction to visit the tomb in the work of Ephraem see below, p. 401.

[5] In Canon lxix of the *Necrosima*, for instance, a good soul bids farewell to its body at death (*Opera omnia*, Graece, Syriace, Latine, iii, ed. S. E. Assemani, Rome, 1743, 325). This passage is quoted by Louise Dudley, *The Egyptian Elements in the Legend of the Body and Soul*, Bryn Mawr College Monographs, viii (1911), 104.

[6] *The Apocryphal New Testament*, trans. M. R. James (Oxford, 1953), 531–3. For an account of this work see T. Silverstein, *Viso sancti Pauli*, Studies and Documents, ed. Kirsopp and Silva Lake, iv, 1935. A Latin sermon that may well have been the intermediary between the *Visio Pauli* and various vernacular versions of the Body and Soul theme is discussed and printed by T. Batiouchkof, 'Le Débat de l'âme et du corps', *Romania*, xx (1891), 1–55, 513–80.

[7] For a useful display of related sermons on this theme, set out in parallel columns, see J. Zupitza, 'Zu "Seele und Leib" ', *Archiv*, 91 (1893), 369–404, and L. Dudley, 'An Early Homily on the "Body and Soul" Theme', *J.E.G. Ph.* viii (1909), 225–53.

[8] *Die Vercelli-Homilien*, ed. Max Förster (Bibliothek der angelsächsischen Prosa, xii, 1932), no. iv, pp. 85–99; Wulfstan, *Sammlung der ihm zugeschriebenen Homilien* (Berlin, 1883), no. xxix, p. 138.

[9] Ed. H. von Feilitzen (Uppsala, 1883). See below, p. 94, for the use of this setting in 'þene latemeste dai'.

Body and Soul theme offered a dramatic way of bringing home the eventual fate of man, the terrors of the Last Judgement, the pains of hell and
the joys of heaven.

However, when in didactic literature death rather than hell came to
be chiefly emphasized as the object of servile fear, it was natural that
there should be a change in the content—though not the moral purpose
—of the Body and Soul theme, and at this point an ancient legend became
useful, the superstition that the soul as part of its punishment was compelled to revisit its body after death.

This fiction provides the framework for a number of Body and Soul
passages in sermons,[1] and also for the Old English Body and Soul poem,[2]
but later poems, though some of them are at least indirectly related to it,
are free from this slightly esoteric superstition, and describe only how
the soul makes a farewell return to the body shortly after death, usually
addressing the body whilst it is still lying on the bier. In the two later
Middle English debates, 'In a þestri stude' and 'Als i lay in a winteris
nyt' (works influenced by two important Anglo-Latin debates of the
twelfth century, 'Noctis sub silentio'[3] and 'Nuper huiuscemodi visionem
somnii',[4] the fantastic nature of the subject-matter is made acceptable
by the enclosing of the scene within a dream-vision or within the convention of overhearing in a secret place. This kind of setting suggests
that it was not merely some of the content of the speeches that was to be
visualized, but also the speakers themselves—that the meditator was
intended to hold the scene in his imagination, just as he would, for
instance, with a dialogue between Christ on the Cross and the Blessed
Virgin. There is, however, a difference, in that the meditator on the
Passion would be able to fill out a bare reference by the memory of some
visual representation, whereas death themes were not portrayed in art
until nearly the end of the fourteenth century. The only poem to give
sufficient detail for the scene to be fully visualized is the 'Nuper huiuscemodi visionem somnii'. The dream here is not set in the first person but
related as that of a bishop:

---

[1] R. Willard, 'The Address of the Soul to the Body', *P.M.L.A.* 50 (1935), 957–83.

[2] *Soul and Body*, i, ll. 9–11, *Vercelli Book*, ed. G. P. Krapp (New York, 1932), 55.

[3] *Latin Poems attributed to Walter Mapes*, 95–106. This poem, often called the *Visio
Fulberti*, was exceedingly popular: it survives in more than a hundred western Euro-
pean manuscripts (Walther, *Das Streitgedicht*, 211–14) and it was later printed (E. Ph.
Goldschmidt, *Medieval Texts and their first Appearance in Print*, London, 1943, 33–34).
A fifteenth-century English translation is discussed below, pp. 326–8; an Anglo-Norman
translation was made by Nicholas Bozon, *Débat de l'âme et du corps*, ed. Ch. de Roche
(Basel, 1908).

[4] Ed. E. K. Heningham (Wisconsin, 1937). Though this poem survives in only one
manuscript, the French translation, 'Un samedi par minuit' (ed. W. Linow, *Erlanger
Beiträge*, i), was copied both in England and France, and was translated into German,
Norwegian, and Spanish (see G. Kleinert, *Über den Streit zwischen Leib und Seele*,
Halle, 1880, 57–76).

Viderat per somnium
    corpus viri mortuum,
Idque in marmoreo
    positum sarcofago,
Erat et ceruleo
    velatum sudario.
Viditque assistere
    haut procul a corpore
Viri eius animam
    in infantis formulam.[1]

However, already by the thirteenth century some people might have
been able to supply for themselves a visual image for the soul, because by
then there were paintings of the Last Judgement, in which, according
to traditional iconography, souls—stated by philosophers to be invisible
—were symbolically shown as small, naked, sexless figures: 'In infantis
formulam' as the Latin poem describes it. For the corpse, which was
usually said to be lying on a bier, there would be no need for an iconographic parallel: for this, as for all death themes which deal with the old,
the sick, and the dead, most people must have been able painfully to
draw on their own experience. It is probable that most writers presumed
this kind of background visual knowledge.[2]

There is one short thirteenth-century verse in which the scene is
entirely presupposed, for it consists solely of a short address to the body:
indeed it is only from knowledge of other Body and Soul poems that we
can with certainty infer that this is a reproach spoken by the soul:

Nu þu unseli bodi up-on bere list
Were bet þine robin of fau and of gris?
Suic day havit i-comin þu changedest hem þris,
þad makiit þe Hevin herþe þad þu on list,
þat rotihin sal so dot þe lif þad honkit on þe ris.
þu ete þine mete y-makit in confis,
þu lettis þe pore stondin þrute in forist and in is,
þu noldist not þe biþenchen forte ben wis,
For-þi havistu for-lorin þe Ioye of parais.[3]

In all probability this is an *exemplum* verse like the warnings from the
tomb. It is therefore designed to form the emotional and moral climax

---

[1] Ed. Heningham, 54. 'As he slept he saw the body of a dead man, lying in a marble
sepulchre and wrapped in a blue shroud; and he saw also the man's soul standing close
by the body in the shape of a little child.' Cf. 'Un samedi par minuit', ll. 1–8.

[2] For a fifteenth-century illustration of the theme see pl. 3 (*b*).

[3] Brown XIII, 38. *Unseli*: wretched; *robin*: garments; *of fau and of gris*: of variegated
and grey fur (a phrase of romance origin, cf. *Sir Orfeo*, 241, and 'Un samedi par minuit',
l. 37, 'E les vaiers et les gris'); *ris*: branch; *confis*, MS. *consis*, see *M.E.D.*, s.v. *confit*:
sauce; *forist*: frost.

of a narrative, in which the setting, both pictorial and didactic, will have been amply described. Against such a background it would lose its present fragmentary effect. Its very brevity and incompleteness, however, have power. One *ubi sunt* question, especially when it contains an evocative touch of romance phraseology, is not necessarily less effective than a whole series (as is usual in the longer poems); whilst the unmistakable force of the fourth line arises from the compression that leads to an ironic elision of ideas. In the poem as it stands there is a sardonic quality suggesting a contempt for a body too despicable to receive an address elevated by rhetoric and amplitude. This effect is probably accidental, but for the modern reader inescapable.

The other short poem, 'Nou is mon hol and soint', is more self-sufficient but less striking. The first part consists of a brisk and effective description of the preparations for burial, 'Me prikit him in on vul clohit / and legget him by þe wout';[1] but this is followed by a dull address of the soul, scarcely more than a list of the common sins of omission. The last two long lines, however, contain a traditionally stinging climax, though slightly clumsily expressed:

> þu salt in horþe wonien and wormes [þe] to-chewe
> And of alle ben lot þat her þe we[re] lewe.[2]

In the Anglo-Saxon homiletic tradition the meeting of Body and Soul was presented as an episode in a long sermon that often contained other themes of death. If these two verses belong to *exempla*, then they would normally have been used in the same way as their native predecessors. But in the twelfth century a development took place in the Body and Soul tradition—a development perhaps even more important than the transformation of monologue into dialogue—whereby the theme, instead of being a short and isolated anecdote, became a large and flexible framework, with all the traditional death themes accumulated into the reproach of the soul. This transition was of very great literary importance, firstly, because through it separate themes became organized into a dramatic whole, and, secondly, because the tone inevitably changed, for what before had been a rhetorical and objective description of a preacher became, when spoken by the soul, entirely filled with a personal vindictiveness and horror.

The beginnings of this development may be seen in the Old English Body and Soul poem, which incorporates some very detailed description

---

[1] Brown XIII, 20, ll. 7–8, p. 31. *Prikit*: fastens; *Wout*: cellar (?), outhouse (?) (the meaning of *wout*, literally an arched space, is not certain: the sense is plainly that the body is disrespectfully put well out of the way until buried).

[2] Ibid. *-chewe*, MS. *chewen*; *horþe*: earth; *And of alle ben lot* . . .: and be hated by all whom you had loved.

of decay in the tomb,[1] of a kind that had before only occurred independently of the Body and Soul form in homiletic narrative. But it was in the twelfth century that this development became fully established. Three poems written in that period, the two Latin ones already referred to, 'Noctis sub silentio' and 'Nuper huiuscemodi visionem somnii', and the vernacular Worcester Fragments, contain all, or a high proportion of, the following themes: the *ubi sunt* formula, the signs of corruption, the humiliations of burial, the greed and faithlessness of executors or heirs, the smallness of the grave, and the gnawing of worms. The first of the thirteenth-century lyrics to be influenced by this tradition was 'Þene latemeste dai': verbal echoes prove its dependence upon the Worcester Fragments,[2] and an affiliation with the Latin poems is likely, though not equally demonstrable. In setting 'Þene latemeste dai' by-passes the known twelfth-century tradition, for the soul's complaint is spoken on the Day of Judgement, 'þe sorie soule atte dom makit hire mon', as in late Old English sermons;[3] but in themes it is the direct descendant of the three twelfth-century poems. According to these themes the poem falls roughly into five (unequal) parts. The first is the description of the preparations for burial. In the actual description it here perhaps lacks the force of the laconic straightforwardness of the analogous lines in the Worcester Fragments:

> þonne biþ þe [fei]ge iflut to þen flore
> he biþ eastward istreiht he biþ sone stif
> he [col]deþ also clei hit is him ikunde.[4]

But in the harsh, ironic playfulness with which it manipulates the image of the grave as a house, it is superior to its twelfth-century source:

> þin hus is sone ibuld þer þu salt wonien inne,
> Boþe þe wirst and þe rouf sal liggen uppon þin chinne;
> þenne sulen woremes woniin þe wid-innen,
> Ne salt þu þe nout weriin wid neppe ne wid pinne.[5]

The fantasy of the last line is especially witty and macabre. The poem then continues:

> Nu sal firrotien þine teit and þine tunke
> And al þat is wid-innen þe—þi liverre and þi longe
> And þi þrote-bolle wid þat þu soncke—
> And þu salt ben in putte ful faste bi-þronge.

---

[1] *Soul and Body*, I, ll. 108–25. There had been occasional touches of this in earlier sermons, such as 'Modo es esca vermium et putredo ac pulvis', Dudley, 'An Early Homily', *J.E.G. Ph.* viii. 230. But in this Latin sermon and its imitations, touches such as this are strongly subordinated to the moral or eschatological themes.

[2] E. K. Heningham, 'Old English Precursors of *The Worcester Fragments*', *P.M.L.A.* lv (1940), 291–307. [3] See above, p. 90.

[4] B 29–31, ed. Buchholz, 2. [5] Brown XIII, p. 47. *Wirst*: ceiling; *neppe*: brooch.

This is a version of the theme which may be called the Signs of Decomposition, for in it the symptoms of decay are enumerated in the same
way as the symptoms of dying are enumerated in the Signs of Death.
This theme does not occur in the extant Worcester Fragments, though
it may well have formed part of the complete poem. In its origins going
back to the works of Ephraem, it first appears in the context of the Body
and Soul convention in the Old English poem:

> Bið þæt heafod tohliden,   handa tolidoðe,
> geaglas toginene,   goman toslitene,
> sina beoð asocene,   swyra becowen,
> fingras tohrorene. . . .[1]

In the twelfth century this theme was very strikingly expressed in
'Nuper huiuscemodi visionem somnii', though the passage is too lengthy
and repulsive for quotation.[2] It is an obvious danger that such descriptions may induce a perverse fascination rather than profitable fear, but
in 'þene latemeste dai', at least, the speed and succinctness of the lines
prevents this. The list-like effect also imposes a much needed formality
on the repugnant material, though for the modern reader the disuniting
effect of this kind of series may seem to have a horrible appropriateness.
The author of 'þene latemeste dai' shows a typically English discretion
in his treatment of this material, and his brisk quatrain may to his advantage be contrasted with the over-amplified passage in the Latin poem,
and with the *lauda* of Jacopone da Todi, in which the signs of corruption
provide the whole subject for a dialogue between living and dead.[3]

In 'þene latemeste dai' the signs of corruption are followed by a
series of verses in the *ubi sunt* form:

> Wer beit nou þine frend, faire þat þe biheten,
> Ofte þe igretten bi weis and bi streiten?
> Nu heo wollet, wrecche, þe alle forleten,
> for nulle hore never on nou, hore *þonkis*, þe imeten.
>
> Wer boit þine ponewes love þat þe weren?
> Of þine riche weden nou þu ard al scere;
> Bo þu inne þin putte wormis ifere—
> Hit boit sone of þe so þu never nerre.[4]

---

[1] *Soul and Body*, i, ll. 108–11. 'The head is split open, the hands have dropped off,
the jaws gape, the palate is split, the nerves dried up, the neck is gnawed through and
the fingers rotted away.'

[2] Ed. Heningham, 64–65. The Signs of Corruption sometimes appear outside the
Body and Soul debate, for instance, in *Sermones ad fratres in eremo*, 48, *P.L.* 40. The
passage in the latter is quoted by B. P. Kurtz, *Gifer the Worm* (California, 1929), 257,
as a possible source of the Old English poem. But some of the *Sermones* belong to the
twelfth century or later, and no. 48 is probably one of these.

[3] *Laude*, xxv, ed. S. Caramella (Bari, 1930), 51–53.

[4] Brown XIII, p. 47. *Hore þonkis* (MS. *stonkis*): of their own will; *ponewes*: money; *þu
ard al scere*: you are completely shorn (the reference to sheep-shearing is probably more
alive in the original than it is in the translation).

The association of the *ubi sunt* questions with the themes of the grave is of ancient origin,[1] the disturbing answer to these rhetorical questions being the injunction to visit the tomb.[2] The propriety of so brutal a reply can be best understood if it is emphasized that these questions, though commonly called *ubi sunt*, should in the context of the themes of death more correctly be described as being in the *quid profuit* tradition. Though the questions may often appear stylistically identical in form,[3] they have a dual ancestry, one strain going back to Baruch iii. 16, 'Ubi sunt principes gentium', and the other to Wisdom v. 8, 'Quid nobis profuit superbia'.[4] In the genuine *ubi sunt* form the verbs are governed by kinds of people or by proper names, usually of an evocative kind, whilst in the *quid profuit* form they are governed by nouns indicating various kinds of possessions, or by abstract nouns such as 'pride' or 'vain-glory'. In 'þene latemeste dai' the things that have vanished are friends, riches, fine clothing, food, and drink. Such a list is in itself didactically tendentious and could not arouse the nostalgic romanticism of a question such as, 'Hwer is paris and heleyne / þat weren so bryht and feyre on bleo'.[5] The context of the grave, therefore, does no more than intensify the contempt for the world already inherent in the subject-matter. But when these questions are spoken by the soul to the body and not by a preacher there is a turn of the screw: any inclination that the reader may have to interpret the form as a great commonplace about the sad inevitability of transience is totally eradicated by the soul's tone of grim and personal ferocity.

After the *quid profuit* passage, 'þene latemeste dai' continues with a list of sins committed by the body, a brief statement of the pains to be suffered by the soul in hell, 'I sal biveren in vours and chiverren in ise',[6] and finally a description of the terrors of the Last Judgement and of the horrifying appearance of the Devil. At a point in this narrative that is not clearly indicated the speaker ceases to be the soul and becomes once more the preacher who introduced the poem. The style itself becomes gradually more objectively rhetorical and more plainly didactic, so that the last

---

[1] For examples see J. E. Cross, '*Ubi sunt* passages in Old English—sources and relationships', *Vetenskaps-Societetens i Lund Årsbok*, 1956, pp. 33, 37, footnote 51, etc. In a Body and Soul context they appear in Vercelli iv, *Die Vercelli-Homilien*, ed. Förster, 98.

[2] J. E. Cross, '*The Dry Bones Speak*', *J.E.G. Ph.* lvi (1957), 434–5.

[3] *Ubi sunt* is commonly used where *quid profuit* would be more appropriate. A notable exception is the passage in Helinand's *Vers de la mort* beginning 'Que vaut biautez'; see below, p. 111, footnote 1.

[4] 'Where are the princes of the nations'; 'What has pride profited us'; E. Gilson, 'De la bible a François Villon', *Les idées et les lettres* (Paris, 1955), 1–38, notes these texts as sources for the *ubi sunt* but does not distinguish them.

[5] Brown XIII, 43, ll. 65–66, p. 70.

[6] Brown XIII, 29 A, l. 71, p. 48. The description of the pains of hell in the text of MS. Cott. Cal. A ix (xiii, 29 B) is longer.

two unadornedly homiletic stanzas do not come as a sudden contrast to the rest. As we shall see, all the long Body and Soul poems have a conclusion of this kind, and its purpose is self-evidently didactic, not literary.

But whereas 'þene latemeste dai' also begins in a bluntly didactic way, the other two poems open in a distinctively literary style. The Body and Soul dialogue which precedes it in MS. Digby 86, 'In a þestri stude',[1] has a *chanson d'aventure* opening, in which the poet in a secluded place overhears the speakers. A beginning of this kind had already been used in English literature in *The Owl and the Nightingale*, but this may well be the first time that it was used for a didactic work. The artifice of the opening is matched by the fastidiousness with which the author treats the traditional themes. There is, for instance, no detailed enumeration of the signs of corruption: the theme is reduced to one brief line of lament by the body, 'Wormes shule eten myn herte ant my whyte syde'; and similarly the *ubi sunt* questions are not hammered home with heavy repetition, but are expressed briefly and lightly, as in 'Body, wher aren þy solers, thi castles, ant þy toures?'. The controlled manipulation of the themes is reflected in the shapely design by which stanzas are allotted alternately to the speakers: a design which the debate form inherited from its classical origins, though in vernacular debate poetry, at least, a more ragged and naturalistic arrangement was very often preferred. This sense of design in the poem unfortunately does not extend to the end. It is abandoned when the soul gives a description of the Seven Signs of the Last Judgement, signs which by their violent unnaturalness were intended to foretell and symbolize the horror of the Judgement: trees sweat blood, the ocean rises out of its place, the earth burns, etc.[2] Though the Signs nowadays may seem extraordinary, they should also be awe-inspiring in effect and therefore a style with touches of epic magnificence would be needed to express them adequately in poetry. But the description of them here is mechanical, and this theme (normally a preacher's warning) does not gain from being embodied in the reproaches of the Soul. The poem continues with a few verses of prophecy of the Judgement itself, and then wanders away in what is certainly a later addition:[3] in it the tone changes

---

[1] E. Stengel, *Codex manu scriptus Digby 86* (Halle, 1871), 93–96. In this manuscript the two poems have been deliberately joined together, the last lines of 'In a þestri stude' being omitted to allow the sense to run on. A pointing hand in the margin, however, emphasises the beginning of 'þene latemeste dai'. There is no recent edition of the poem: quotations here are taken from the text of MS. Harley 2253, Böddeker, *Altenglische Dichtungen*, 235–43.

[2] W. Heist, *The Fifteen Signs before Doomsday* (East Lansing, 1952), gives a full account of the origin of this theme and of its treatment in Old and Middle English literature.

[3] The conclusion in MS. Trinity 323 is substantially the same as that in MS. Harley 2253. The original ending may have been at l. 194, 'ant rotieþ endeles', ed. cit. 242.

to a more colloquial one, and the metrical pattern is disturbed. Death lyrics often gained accretions of other death themes, and on grounds of style and metre it is clear that the concluding moralizations do not belong here. The poem tails away in a series of didactic and sometimes colloquial comments, nearly all of them commonplaces, often of a proverbial kind, such as 'When the flor is at thy rug, the rof ys at thy neose . . .'.[1] The first part of the poem, however, is much more accomplished, though possibly the themes of death require a gaunter and heavier treatment than one finds in these well-turned stanzas.

Although the first half of 'In a þestri stude' consists of dialogue, it is no more a debate than is the single address form of 'þene latemeste dai', for the body's speeches are all of agreement. The dialogue form has been achieved simply by transforming some of the reproaches of the soul into laments of the body. The only vernacular poem that is properly a debate is 'Als i lay in a winteris nyt'.[2] This is by far the most brilliant of medieval Body and Soul poems in any language: indeed, for ingenuity and intellectual vivacity it compares better with Marvell's 'Dialogue between the Soul and Body' than with even the best of medieval debates, 'Noctis sub silentio' or 'Un samedi par minuit'. It is not, of course, that the author's thought or imagery is original in the way that Marvell's is. Though one had read all seventeenth-century metaphysical poetry, Marvell's image of the soul enmeshed, as it were, in an anatomical diagram[3] would astonish and please by its wit and inventiveness, whilst, on the contrary, familiarity with 'Noctis sub silentio' and 'Nuper huiuscemodi visionem somnii' in particular, and with medieval death literature in general, shows that there is scarcely anything in 'Als i lay in a winteris nyt' that is not in substance found elsewhere; but the poet not only borrows the ironic devices of some of the earlier debates, but also manipulates straight meditative material with a new ironic deftness, and exploits consistently the paradoxes and incongruities inherent in the fiction of the Body and Soul theme.

The Body and Soul form belongs to that kind of debate in which neither side is completely right or completely wrong, and in which arguments have been selected for the opponents according to their immediate polemical efficacy rather than as stages in the coherent presentation of a philosophic truth. In order to maintain an even balance, intellectual ideas have to be manipulated for a literary end.

---

[1] Cf. Brown XIII, 71, ll. 20–21.

[2] Ed. Linow, *Erlanger Beiträge*, 1; *Latin Poems of Walter Mapes*, 334–46.

[3] *Poems and Letters*, ed. H. M. Margoliouth, i (Oxford, 1952), 20–21. In some emblems the soul as a young child peeps out through the cage-like skeleton of the ribs, e.g. Francis Quarles, *Emblemes*, v, no. 8; cf. Samuel Chew, *The Pilgrimage of Life* (New Haven, 1962), p. 250, note 3, and fig. 147.

The Soul and Body, for instance, do not share a common definition of the word 'body'. The Soul, as in previous Body and Soul literature, uses 'body' in the sense in which St. Paul used it, when he opposed it morally to spirit: the term, thus used, is neither philosophically nor psychologically precise, but it is a convenient one to cover everything in human nature that is not turned towards God: to it, therefore, can be attributed, not only the three carnal sins, gluttony, lust, and sloth, but also the other four—apparently spiritual—deadly sins. In so far as the Soul in the debate is philosophically coherent, it holds the dualist view, inherited from Plato and from Epicurean philosophers, that the soul is a noble substance, made captive in the body. Though this idea might seem too suspiciously Manichean to form part of orthodox Christianity, it was retained by spiritual writers of the Middle Ages, for it accorded well with the Pauline use of the word 'body'. The Body in its rejoinder evades this accusation by relying on the more strictly philosophical view that the body without the soul would have been incapable of good or evil: without the soul it would at best have been an animal (there is probably here an implied reference to the doctrine of the plurality of forms)[1]; it is, indeed, implied that it was taught evil by the soul. Such ingenious and endless recriminations, which fly wide of the mark, are of course an ironic sign of damnation: in a fourteenth-century debate where the dead man is not damned a reconciliation of body and soul is brought about by an angel.[2] But through the irony of the participants' distortion of the truth a whole truth is emphatically presented to the reader.

The dexterity of the poet lies in his treatment and combination of the three possible elements in the Body and Soul debate, which we have already enumerated, meditative material, moral conflict, and philosophical relationship. The following verses give an excellent example of the first:

> Nouȝ mouwe þe wilde bestes renne
>   And lien under linde and lef,
> And foules flie bi feld and fenne,
>   Siþin þi false herte clef.
> þine eiȝene are blinde and connen nouȝt kenne,
>   þi mouth is dumb, þin ere is def;
> And nouȝ so lodly þouȝ list grenne
>   Fro þe comeþ a wikke wef.

---

[1] For the philosophical background see A. Pegis, *St. Thomas and the Problem of the Soul in the Thirteenth Century* (Toronto, 1934). St. Thomas's Aristotelian definition of the soul as the form of the body, and his rejection of the doctrine of the plurality of forms, denied to the Body and Soul convention the philosophical foundation provided by the Franciscan school of philosophers.

[2] See Appendix I.

Ne nis no levedi, briȝt on ble,
> þat wel weren iwoned of þe to lete,
þat wolde lye a niȝth bi þe,
> For nouȝth þat men miȝte hem bihete.
þouȝ art unsemly for to se,
> Uncomli for to cussen suwete;
þouȝ ne havest frend þat ne wolde fle,
> Come þouȝ stertlinde in þe strete.[1]

In these two stanzas the thought in the first four lines may be original: certainly the contrast between the knight's former prey, now safe from him and alive, and his own decaying body is very effective. The next stanza contains two variations of the traditional and recurrent idea, that of human abhorrence of a decaying body. The former friends who shun a corpse are often mentioned in Body and Soul literature, but there is a macabre twist in the description of how they would flee should they meet the corpse swaggering[2] down the street. The revulsion which would be felt by women had been stressed in the Latin poem:

> Modo non est aliqua
> > meretrix tam publica,
> Que eam contingere
> > vellet nedum pectere.[3]

Though the basic idea is the same, the difference in tone is characteristic of the two poets. The author of the Anglo-Latin poem prefers the heaviest emphasis possible, and therefore emphasizes how not even a common prostitute would touch the hair of the corpse: in the Middle English poem the prostitute has become a 'levedi, briȝt on ble', and this slight verbal allusion to the world of romance conveys the same idea with greater lightness of touch but more pointed shock.

Mingled with the Soul's description of the retribution now suffered by the Body is a retrospective account of the moral conflict between body and soul during life (a theme never used in isolation in England, as it was, for instance, by Jacopone da Todi in one of his *laude*).[4] Its aim is to bring into the open the issue between natural inclination for comfort and prosperity and its rejection by conscience or reason, a conflict which might otherwise pass muffled and unheeded in the thoughts of the unreflective, self-indulgent person. In 'Als i lay in a

---

[1] Ed. Linow, 41.

[2] *O.E.D.* s.v. *startling*. In the Middle Ages the word is elsewhere used to denote the prancing of horses; the usage here seems, therefore, to be ironically metaphorical.

[3] ll. 959–62, ed. Heningham, 64. 'There is now no prostitute, however cheap, who would wish to touch [your hair], let alone comb it.'

[4] No. 3, ed. Caramella, 6–8.

winteris nyt' the Soul describes how the Body, urged on by the world, the flesh, and the Devil, resisted its virtuous suggestions:

> ʒwan i bad þe erliche to rise,
> Nim on me, þi soule, kep,
> þouʒ seidest, þou miʒtest a none wise
> Forgon the murie morwe slep.[1]

Whilst the effect is not quite as strong as when this kind of debate is imagined to take place during life, for then both sides speak, and it is an immediate not a remembered argument, yet it is ingeniously included here, and the self-indulgent tone of the Body's reported reply is subtly and ironically caught. This strain in the debate is close to the type of psychological allegory found in the *Roman de la rose*, where personifications such as *Dangier* and *Bel Accueil* thwart each other's intentions.

However, the moral relationship between body and soul is yet more emphasized than the psychological. The philosophical basis for this we have already discussed, for it was relevant to the whole design of the poem and to the ironic tensions that run through it. It is, however, worth noticing in particular the two main images through which it is expressed. One is that of horse and rider: the Body, as horse, took the bit between its teeth and bolted; and the Soul, as rider, failed to control it. Previous writers have shown that this image can be traced back to Platonic philosophers and to the Fathers.[2] The more interesting image, however, in that it is more philosophically subtle and has more literary reverberations, is that of Soul and Body as husband and wife or as a pair of lovers. This image reflects the philosophical tenet that the soul did not merely inhabit a body but had a natural aptitude and desire to do so. The image therefore expressed at once the philosophical point of the soul's desire for the body and the moral point of the enormity of the soul (man) being ruled by the body (woman):[3] 'For love þi wille i folewede al / And to min oune deth I drouʒ'. Behind this image lies the list of deceitful women so popular in sermon tradition, and above all their archetype, Eve: for it is implied that the body tempts and deceives the soul ('And madest me an houve of glas'), and that the soul for love of the body ('And al mi love on þe i kest'), like Adam, succumbs. The

---

[1] Ed. Linow, 51.

[2] M. U. Vogel, *Some Aspects of the Horse and Rider Analogy in the Debate between the Body and the Soul* (Washington, 1948).

[3] This inversion of the natural order had been expressed in *Nuper huiuscemodi visionem somnii* by the equally pointed, but poetically less interesting, image of mistress and servant, 'Debuissem domina / esse, et tu famula' (ll. 439–40). Cf. the following passage from some unpublished meditations in the fifteenth-century MS., C.U.L. Kk. i. 6: '. . . for þat the soule sholde have daunted þe flesshe and have holde her undyrfote and made here obedyent to here, as the servaunte to þe lady, but ayens ordor of reson she hath put here above here, the lady undyr here servaunt . . .' (f. 156ᵛ). Later (f. 157ʳ) the soul is said to be in hell 'for þe inordinate love she had to that caytif careyne'.

parallel with Adam and Eve had already been developed by Hildebert of Lavardin in his *De Querimonia carnis et animæ*, where he describes how the body, being the weaker, like Eve, is tempted first.[1] But the Middle English poet weaves it more skilfully into his work, and draws evocatively upon the well-established literary tradition of noble men whose downfall is brought about by faithless and domineering women.

The poem ends with a description of how the soul is dragged off to hell in a mock hunting scene. This is a set piece, placed in the same position and serving the same purpose as the description of the Devil in 'þene latemeste dai' and of the Seven Signs of the Last Judgement in 'In a þestri stude'. Whilst the poet still shows his technical skill in this part, it inevitably lacks the poise and subtlety of the debate. But the debate itself is probably the cleverest passage in all Middle English lyrics, and gives pleasure to the intellect in a way quite exceptional in medieval meditative poetry.

In terms of meditative structure the Body and Soul debate is of the kind where the reader is present in the scene only as silent spectator, and, indeed, in the last two he is at one further remove, for there is already a spectator within the poem, though his function is largely exemplary: he is the model onlooker, with whom the reader should identify himself. There are three other poems, reflective monologues, which are exemplary in a different way: they are dramatic monologues, and the reader, as it were, listens, but is not addressed. All are laments of an old man, a figure who in the literature of death was thought of as a herald and warning of the grave. This association is seen very clearly in some *exempla*. There is, for instance, the recurrent story, told at length by Gower, in the *Confessio amantis*, of the Trump of Death:[2] in this story an exact parallel is made between the aged man, by whom the king is reminded of death, and the trumpet-call, which signals to his brother that the king has ordered his execution. There is also the version of the Faust story in which a man sells his soul to the Devil, but on condition that the Devil shall give him three warnings of his approaching death: the Devil keeps his bargain by warning him in the shape of an old man, so his unthinking victim pays no attention and does not repent.[3]

Far earlier than these stories, however, there was a list of the Signs of Old Age, similar to the Signs of Death and the Signs of Decomposition in shape, but earlier in date. This is a tradition of ancient origin: Horace, in his *Ars poetica*, gives a description of the Four Ages of Man, listing amongst these the *incommoda* of old age,[4] but the characteristics here

[1] *P.L.* 171, 998.

[2] Ed. G. C. Macaulay, i (E.E.T.S. e.s. 81), 90–96.

[3] The version from the *Speculum laicorum* is printed by T. Wright, *Latin Stories* (Percy Society, viii, 1843), no. 33. Cf. *Summa praedicantium*, s.v. *Mors*, ed. cit. ii. 54ʳ.

[4] ll. 16)–74.

enumerated are mental ones, querulousness, timidity, etc. There is, however, a brief list of physical signs in a letter of Jerome to Furia;[1] and such a list as this was much amplified in the *De duodecem abusivis sæculi*,[2] a work written by an anonymous Irish monk of the seventh century, but which throughout the Middle Ages carried the authoritative name of St. Cyprian or, occasionally, of St. Augustine. It was an extremely popular work, as can be deduced from its fairly frequent entry in the catalogues of medieval libraries,[3] and the opening, which summarizes the Twelve Abuses in epigrammatic form, was versified over and over again in English throughout the period.[4] The second of the Twelve Abuses is *si sine religione senex esse inveniatur*, and this contains the list of signs, 'Dum oculi caligant, auris graviter audit, capilli fluunt, etc.'[5] From the late Anglo-Saxon period onwards this description was detached from its context and included in sermons as a warning of the end of pride in the incapacities and humiliations of old age. It is thus used in Vercelli Homily ix[6] and in pseudo-Wulfstan xxx.[7] In the fourteenth century it was similarly included in John Bromyard's *Summa prædicantium* under the heading of *Mors*.[8] Meanwhile, however, the Signs had been put authoritatively into a mortality context in the *De contemptu mundi*, and Innocent III concludes his chapter on old age with words actually borrowed from the visit to the tomb, '. . . quod sumus iste fuit, erimus quandoque quod hic est'.[9] In this chapter, however, another tradition has met with that of the *De duodecem abusivis*, that is the tradition of the Elegies of Maximian,[10] and through this the list of signs has been extended.[11]

[1] *Epistola*, 54, *P.L.* 22, 557: 'Jam incanuit caput, tremunt genua, dentes cadunt: et fronte ob senium rugis arata, vicina est mors in foribus'.

[2] Ed. S. Hellman, *Pseudo-Cyprianus de xii abusivis saeculi* (Leipzig, 1909).

[3] R. M. Wilson, 'The Contents of the Medieval Library', in F. Wormald and C. E. Wright, *The English Library Before 1700* (London, 1958), 90.

[4] R. H. Robbins, *Historical Poems of the xiv^{th} and xv^{th} Centuries* (New York, 1959), nos. 55 and 56, and notes pp. 326–8.

[5] Ed. Hellman, 34. 'When his eyes grow dim, his hearing fails, and his hair grows thin . . .'.   [6] Förster, *Der Vercelli-Codex cxxvii*, 91.

[7] Ed. Napier, 147–8.   [8] Ed. cit. ii. 53^v.

[9] 'What we are he was, and we too shall be what he is', Bk. I, ch. x, 'De incommodo senectutis', ed. Michele Maccarone (under the title, *De miseria humane conditionis*), Lugano, 1955, p. 16. I continue to use the familiar title, although Maccarone (pp. xxxii–xxxv) shows it to be not original. The Signs of Old Age occur also in the *Cursor mundi* (applied to Joseph), E.E.T.S. 57, 211–12, *The Pricke of Conscience*, i. 766–801 (closely followed by the Signs of Death, i. 816–29), and in a fifteenth-century imitation of the Merchant's Tale, the *Prohemy of a Marriage* (once attributed to Lydgate), Percy Society, ii. 27.

[10] *Poetae latini minores*, iv, ed. E. Baehrens (Leipzig, 1872), 313–48. See R. Ellis, 'On the Elegies of Maximianus', *American Journal of Philology*, v (1884), 1–15; G. Kittredge, 'Chaucer and Maximianus'; ibid. ix (1888), 84–85; G. R. Coffman, 'Old Age from Horace to Chaucer', *Speculum*, ix (1934), 249–77.

[11] Scattered through the first elegy are the *primitia mortis*, loss of sight, hearing, and

These elegies, however, also reinforced the potential ambiguity in the treatment of old age. The figure of the old man could be seen as a moral warning to all of the closeness of death; but it could also serve as a type for the satirical treatment of the characteristic, or supposedly characteristic, vices of old age. Elegies 2 to 5 contributed to the second style: in them the contrast between the enjoyments of youth and the weakness of old age is reduced to one instance, that of impotence, and they consist therefore of the narration of a series of successful love adventures in youth and of an obscene and ineffective sexual relationship in old age. But, despite the preponderance of eroticism and cynicism in the elegies, the first provided a very effective picture of the humiliating miseries of old age, which fitted well with the Christian didactic conception, and the aptness of this interpretation was made pointed by the last, which describes the levelling power of death. The companion pieces of these elegies in medieval manuscripts (works such as the *Disticha* of Cato) show that they were valued primarily for their morality, and that their meaning had, therefore, presumably been illuminated for medieval readers by the didactic tradition of the sufferings of old age. For vernacular writers on the subject the first elegy served as a model in three ways. Firstly, it provided the form, that of a reflective, dramatic monologue: there is no parallel to this in the earlier Middle English lyric, for normally all first-person speeches are addressed to someone, either the reader or a character in the poem, or else it is intended that the reader should identify himself with the speaker, so that the thought of the poem becomes his own; the superficial resemblance to verses such as 'Wanne ich þenche þinges þre' or to penitential lyrics is therefore misleading. Secondly, it provided the dominating theme of the poems, brought out by the series of contrasts between youth and age, which drive home the fearfulness of the latter. Finally, the elegies as a whole provide the foundation for the suggestion in the poems—one which it is difficult to pinpoint in any particular place—that an old man is not only a mortality warning but also in himself ludicrous and contemptible.

Despite their common source and form, there is considerable difference of tone between the three poems. 'Heʒe loverd, þou here my bone' is more serious, penitential, and exemplary. The substance of the poem is encased in a prayer, and one long stanza consists of a confession of the seven deadly sins. Though comparatively small space is given to it, the contrast made between the old man's former popularity and pride and his present helplessness and repulsiveness is effectively done:

smell, rheum of the eyes, cough, and back bent double. The latter detail (*statura curvatur*) was included in Innocent III's list of the signs of death, and became a common detail in vernacular versions of the theme.

Whil ich wes in wille wolde,
In uch a bour among þe bolde
    yholde wiþ þe heste;
Nou y may no fynger folde,
Lutel loved ant lasse ytolde,
    y-leved wiþ þe leste.
A goute me haþ ygreyþed so,
ant oþer eveles monye mo,
    y not whet bote is beste.
þat er wes wilde ase þe ro,
nou y swyke, y mei nout so,
    hit siweþ me so faste.[1]

The second poem, 'Le Regret de Maximian'—it is, exceptionally, given a title in the manuscript—is longer and excessively disordered in thought, but nevertheless powerful. It opens didactically with a narrative of 'Maximian', who had been the most beautiful man 'wiþ-houten apselon', but who in his old age regretted his 'wilde lore'. This plain didacticism is continued in the apprehension of death expressed in the first stanza of the monologue:

To wepen and to wone,
To makien muchele mone,
Al me hit deþ for nede.
An ende ounder þe stone
Wiþ flesse and eken wiþ bone
Wormes shulen we fede.[2]

But as the poem continues it becomes subordinated to a passionate lament. Whereas the speaker of 'Heʒe loverd' provides a model for imitation, 'Maximian' provides an example of rebellion. The final stanza, in which 'Maximian' thinks how he would treat his mockers, if he were young again and could get them by the hair of the head in some secret corner, provides the poem with a fierce sting in its tail. In this poem dramatic effectiveness and moral warning combine less tamely than they do in 'Heʒe loverd'.

In some ways the third of the poems on old age, 'Elde makiþ me geld',[3] is the least didactic of them. In content it is far less soberly decorous, emphasizing, as Maximian had done, the frustration of impotence, and openly describing some of the more disagreeable physical symptoms of senility. In style it is one of the few Middle

---

[1] Brown xiv, 6, p. 4. *In wille wolde*: in command of my pleasures; *fynger folde*: clasp ('The line probably means that the poet is too old for love', Brook, *Harley Lyrics*, p. 81); *lasse ytolde*: esteemed even less; *yleved*: considered; *ygreyþed*: afflicted; *hit siweþ*: it (the gout) pursues.

[2] Inc. 'Herkneþ to mi ron', Brown xiii, 51, p. 93.

[3] *Die Kildare-Gedichte*, 170–1.

English lyrics of the early period in which vocabulary is allowed to dominate the sense. Two stanzas show the relish for comic verbal effects which one finds later in Dunbar:

> I grunt, i grone, i grenne, i gruche,
> I nese, i nappe, i nifle, i nuche,
> and al þis wilneþ eld.[1]

But the lack of didacticism is seen above all in the figure of the old man, for, unlike his counterparts in the other poems, he is himself quite unaware of the moral implications of old age, and therefore gives no warning: at most he expresses the inevitability of his wretchedness. The poem shows the exuberance and fertility of satiric invention, characteristic of the poems in the Kildare Manuscript, and through these the picture of the wretchedness of old age gains in force. In the manuscript it is followed by a version of 'Erþe toc of erþe', and it seems most likely that to the medieval reader it would by implication have carried the same warning of the end of worldly prosperity, despite the absence of explicit didacticism.

All the poems so far discussed have in common the point that their organization is literary: that is, the framework and structure of the poems are provided by a meditative image, and the moralizations arise aptly and inevitably therefrom. Another group of poems from this earlier period, however, may be called sermons in design. It is not meant by this that they have the fixed rhetorical structure prescribed for sermons in medieval *Artes praedicandi*—though it has been argued that all of them conform either nearly or completely to this model[2]—but that their organization is homiletic: the subject is not a debate between body and soul or a warning from the tomb, but a moral, such as that riches end in the grave, and previous death themes therefore become subordinate elements in a framework of pure didactic statement. In these poems themes, such as the complaint of the soul, revert to their earlier function of being minor illustrative episodes in discursive moralization.[3] It may well be questioned, therefore, whether it is merely difference of length that divides the homiletic lyrics from long didactic poems such as *The Pricke of Conscience*. Certainly they have in common a homiletic design, and sometimes a particular indebtedness to specific Latin treatises: the death section of *The Pricke of Conscience* is based on the *De contemptu mundi* and three of this group of lyrics[4] on

---

[1] Op. cit. 171. *Nese*: sneeze; *nifle*: snivel.

[2] H. Pfander, *The Popular Sermon of the Medieval Friar in England* (New York, 1937).

[3] 'þeos holy gostes myhte', for instance, gives one stanza out of fifty-nine to a complaint of the soul (E.E.T.S. 49, 83); it is associated with the Last Judgement.

[4] *Die Kildare-Gedichte*, 89–96; E.E.T.S. 117, 511–22; ibid. 443–8.

parts of the *Meditationes piissimae*. There are, however, other important differences: in *The Pricke of Conscience* the monotonous couplets and prosaic style contribute to the effect of versified treatise, whereas the lyrics at their worst attempt, and at their best achieve, vigour and variety of style, whilst their metres, like those of the laments for old age, are fairly elaborate stanza forms borrowed from French secular poetry.

Though the discursive poem has an initial disadvantage through its lack of framework, it was not inevitable that it should be tediously didactic. An agreeable example of the kind is 'Swet Iesus, hend and fre' from the Kildare Manuscript, and probably by Friar Michael, who names himself in the verse colophon of another poem in the same manuscript. The metre of the poem is by medieval English standards an unusually complicated stanza form, with only two rhymes for ten lines and also two lines rhyming internally. Such an elaborate verse form necessarily accelerates or impedes the force of a poem: here it is used with such poise that the long passage of rebuke to the rich is turned into a spirited and unhalting attack, and the handling of traditional death themes is enlivened by an easy vigour of expression and a picturesque turn of phrase, as when the poet says to the rich man 'þe pover chest ssal be þi nest', or:

> Riche man beþenche þe,
> Tak gode hede, wat þou be!
> þou ne art bot a brotil tre
> Of schorte seven fote,
> Ischrid wiþ ute wiþ gold and fe—
> þe ax is at þe rote;
> þe fent unfre halt al to gle
> þis tre adun to rote.
> So mote ich þe, ich rede þe: fle,
> And do þi sowle is bote.[1]

This poem, which is explicitly a warning to the proud, is less indiscriminately inclusive than weaker ones such as 'þeos holi gostes myhte': nevertheless, the effect of strong, coherent thought is achieved, less by a clear design than by the power of the style, which sweeps the reader on without giving him time to criticize the degree of order in the thought. In this poem, as in so many, it would be possible to alter the sequence of the stanzas without deranging the thought. This, of course, is true of many Middle English lyrics, and in many poems, where variant texts survive, we can see that it has actually happened.

The other death poem in this manuscript, 'þe grace of godde and holi chirche',[2] is one of the three that are related to the *Meditationes*

---

[1] *Die Kildare-Gedichte*, 82.   [2] Ibid. 89–96.

piissimae. In Chapters II and III of this work there is a detailed description of the humiliating aspects of birth and bodily life, the corruption of the grave, and, in an *ubi sunt* passage, of the futility of worldly values. In England the *Meditationes* was copied into innumerable manuscripts, and the *ubi sunt* passage was copied separately as a favourite set piece; a translation was printed by Wynkyn de Worde, and new editions continued to be produced in the seventeenth century.[1] The Kildare poem is the best of the three lyrics based on it. In 'þe grace of godde and holi chirche' the material of the original is made less repulsive and more stinging by the colloquial speech and swing of the verse, and it is also sometimes enlivened by a curious fantasy of imagination. The elaboration of a detail, probably derived from the *De contemptu mundi*, 'Vivus generavit pediculos et lumbricos',[2] into a comic image of the human body as a hunting-ground shows the same kind of exuberant satiric inventiveness as is found also in the *Land of Cokaygne*[3]:

> Man of þi schuldres and of þi side
> þou miȝte hunti luse and flee;
> Of such a park ine hold no pride,
> þe dere nis nauȝte þat þou miȝte sle.[4]

It is tempting to suppose that these two, 'þe grace of Godde' and the *Land of Cokaygne*, are by the same author, and that his work also includes 'Swet Iesus, hend and fre', and possibly other poems in the Kildare Manuscript. They show sufficient imagination and verbal skill for the general rule about the natural anonymity of the Middle English lyric not to apply to them.

The better-known poem, called in one manuscript 'Les diz de seint Bernard',[5] has none of the force or individuality of the Kildare poem. The repulsiveness of the original is here not made poetically bearable by the astringency of the style, but simply by weakening omission. The material is in fact related in a fairly dogged but unconfident manner until the author reaches the *ubi sunt* passage, when, suddenly assured like a man at last on his home ground, he firmly and thoughtfully expands the epigrammatic style of the original into the well-known and striking stanzas:

> Where ben heo þat biforen us weren,
> þat houndes ladden and haukes beeren

---

[1] *S.T.C.* 1916–21.

[2] Bk. i, ch. 8, ed. Maccarrone, 14. 'Alive he bred lice and stomach-worms.'

[3] *Die Kildare-Gedichte*, 145–50; R. H. Robbins, *Historical Poems of the xiv*[th] *and xv*[th] *Centuries*, 48.

[4] *Die Kildare-Gedichte*, 89. L.3. *Ine* does not make sense, but a syllable is metrically necessary here. That it is part of a verb, *inhold* (recorded later), does not seem very probable.

[5] E.E.T.S. 117, 757–61.

And hedden feld and wode;
þis Riche ladys in heore bour,
þat wereden gold in heore tressour,
    Wiþ heore brihte rode?

þei eeten and dronken and maden hem glad,
In Ioye was al heore lif I-lad,
    Men knelede hem biforen:
þei beren hem here so stout and hiȝe,
Ac in twynklyng of an eiȝe
    Heore soules were forloren.[1]

It is astonishing how the poet is able to amplify the brief phrase *amatores mundi* of his original into the familiar figures of the romance world, with its very phraseology, and yet to exclude all sense of regret or loss. The marmoreal severity of tone can be especially appreciated if this poem is compared with a free paraphrase of the *Meditationes* into Anglo-Norman, 'Mult est cil fous, ke trop se fie', which is of roughly the same date.[2] In this the morally useless, but poetically delightful, melancholy, which is likely to spring from an *ubi sunt* list of kings, knights, ladies, etc., is firmly controlled by the answer to each question, 'En la terre gisent pouriz . . .'. But there is an undertone of regret, which becomes explicit in the lament for the noble ladies who are dead:

Alas, les dames e les puceles,
Ke furent tant bones e beles,
Come est dolur de regreter
Lor mort, dont le mal est amer.
Qu'est devenu lur vis rovent,
Lor cors, ke tant fu bel e gent,
Les oilz rianz, li duz parler,
Le col tresblanc, le bien chanter,
Le char, ke tant fu blanche e tendre?
Alas, ore n'est fors poudre e cendre.[3]

It is perhaps too easy for a poet to extract this kind of nostalgia from the *ubi sunt* form for this writer to be especially praised for it, whilst the

---

[1] Ibid. 521.

[2] R. Reinsch, 'Mittheilungen aus einer franz. Hs. des Lambeth Palace zu London', *Archiv*, lxiii (1880), 59–61.

[3] ll. 63–72, *Archiv*, lxiii, 59. The first part of 'Amur et pour ad Deu mis' (H. J. Chaytor, *Poem on the Day of Judgment*, Cambridge Anglo-Norman Texts, 1924), is also a free paraphrase of the *ubi sunt* passage from *Meditationes*; as a separate piece, this poem occurs in only one manuscript, but it survives also as part of a longer poem, 'Chekun deyt estre amee', ll. 331–510 (P. Meyer, 'Notice du MS. Rawlinson Poetry 241', *Romania*, xxix (1900), 14–17), and this longer poem was incorporated in William of Waddington's *Le manuel des pechiez* (ed. F. J. Furnivall, Roxburghe Club, 1862, 426–34), though not in the text used by Robert Manning, unless he deliberately omitted it in his translation.

strong, unsentimental version of the English probably required more skill. But to the modern taste the English stanzas perhaps seem too formidably austere to be congenial. But their merit was appreciated in the Middle Ages and, like their Latin original, they were sometimes detached from their context and copied separately.[1]

This English *ubi sunt* passage is briefly echoed in the last of the three poems related to the *Meditationes*, 'þe Mon þat is of wommon I-bore', which is the weakest of the group. Structurally it falls into two halves, the first dealing with the common sermon theme of the three messengers of death, disasters, illness, and old age,[2] and the second following the pattern of thought in the *Meditationes*. In this part the *ubi sunt* passage is followed by a meditation on death conducted with the familiar ironies:

> þe halle-Roof is cast ful lowe,
> þer beoþ none Chaumbres wyde;
> Me may reche þe helewowe
> And þe wal on uche a syde.[3]

This poem is an example of the kind of moderately competent verse that occasionally springs vigorously to life with the aid of the meditative tradition; and even in the duller parts the familiar content is sufficiently clearly expressed for the warning to come truly home.

It may be suspected that behind these sermon-style verses there lies the Anglo-Norman tradition of moralizing poetry, which was already well established a century before the Middle English analogues. These Anglo-Norman poems of the twelfth century were probably themselves written in imitation of the new didactic literature of France. The most famous of the Anglo-Norman poems is *Le Sermon* of Guischard de Beaulieu,[4] in which, throughout nearly 2,000 long lines, moral themes are interspersed with a disconnected history of man's Fall and Redemption in a bewildering and repetitive way. Elsewhere, generalized moral reflection was combined with a satiric attack on contemporary corruption, particularly amongst the clergy: the anonymous *Roman des romans*[5] is an example of this genre, which in Latin included the *De contemptu mundi* of Bernard of Cluny[6] and in French the *Bibles* of Hugues de Berzé[7] and of Guiot de Provins.[8]

---

[1] Brown XIII, 48. For a discussion of the textual relationships see J. E. Cross, '*The Sayings of St. Bernard* and *Ubi sount qui ante nos fuerunt*', *R.E.S.*, N.S. ix (1958), 1–7.

[2] S. Chew, *The Pilgrimage of Life*, 235–6.

[3] E.E.T.S. 117, p. 447. *Helewowe*: end-wall.

[4] Ed. A. Gabrielson (Uppsala and Leipzig, 1909); see also D. Legge, *Anglo-Norman in the Cloisters* (Edinburgh, 1950), 31–35.

[5] *Deux poèmes moraux anglo-français*, ed. F. J. Tanquerey (Paris, 1922).

[6] Ed. H. C. Hoskier (London, 1929).

[7] Ed. Félix Lecoy (Paris, 1938).

[8] *Les Œuvres de Guiot de Provins, poète lyrique et satirique*, ed. J. Orr (Manchester, 1915).

Anglo-Norman didactic verse is not of a very high quality: indeed, by comparison with it the Middle English verses have a lack of garrulity and a sense of direction that make them far less discouraging to read. There are, however, a number of important French poems of the twelfth and thirteenth centuries which are far superior, and which were evidently read in England, for they survive partly in manuscripts of English origin: Hélinand's *Vers de la mort*,[1] *Le romans de carité*, and the *Miserere* of the 'Renclus de Moiliens',[2] *Le poëme moral*,[3] etc. Even these can be shapeless, lacking in precision and variety, the metrical form being a misleading inducement to length rather than an aid to compression and sharpness. But at their best, as in *Le Vers de la mort* of Helinand, French didactic poems show the thought of a powerful and ranging mind, shaped into verse of extreme technical skill. They excel in vigorous and often magnificent passages on the omnipotence of death: the fine description, e.g. of Death's ravages in *Le Vers de la mort*,[4] or, in the *Miserere*, of Death's game of dice against those marked out to die, with his recurrent exclamation of *hasard* as he makes the winning throw.[5]

French poetry, however, lacks the detailed meditative description of death, and there is nothing in it comparable to the short, incisive verses which are particularly characteristic of Middle English. It would therefore be neither fair nor accurate to suggest that French poetry was superior: it is rather that the qualities of the French and English poetry on death are of different kinds. Nevertheless, the reading of contemporary French poetry helps to define what is missing in the Middle English: for, if one stands back from the appreciation of individual poems and from the consideration of the meditative tradition from which they sprang, then it is the absence of any grandeur of generalization that one regrets. This style is never found in the main current of the Middle English lyric, whether in the earlier or the later period, but it is interesting to see that it does occur in the eccentric and striking group of refrain lyrics, copied in the Vernon Manuscript at the end of the fourteenth century. Amongst them are three poems on transience and death, those with the refrains 'And sum tyme þenk on ȝuster-day',[6] 'For uche mon ouȝte him-self to knowe',[7] and 'þis world fareþ as a Fantasy'.[8] Though

---

[1] Ed. F. Wulff and E. Walberg, S.A.T.F., 1905. A passage from this was copied in an early Cistercian manuscript (now at Maidstone); see C. Brown in *M.L.R.* xxi (1926), 4–6, who at that time did not identify the extract. The *Vers de la mort* contains a very fine passage beginning, 'Que vaut biautez, que vaut richece', based on the *quid profuit* theme: for the influence of this on two stanzas in the English Dance of Death see below, p. 351.

[2] Ed. A. G. van Hamel (Paris, 1885).
[3] Ed. A. Bayot (Brussels and Liège, 1929).
[4] Ed. cit. 28–31.   [5] Ed. cit. 256–7.
[6] Brown xiv, 101.   [7] Ibid. 100.
[8] Ibid. 106.

these poems draw upon the common stock of meditative death themes, such as the taking warning from the spectacle of the old or from a corpse laid on a bier, such details are subordinate elements in a pattern of abstract reflection or argument, and are never developed visually. From a reading of these poems it is evident immediately how the vitality of the death lyric derived from the abundance of closely visualized description. For, by contrast to the poems in the main meditative tradition, the Vernon lyrics, like most of the French, have a sober greyness that repels responsive excitement. But they show the capacity to match a great generalization with an equal elevation of style, and at the same time to supply some imaginative twist, which gives to the familiar commonplace the force of the unexpected. The following lines provide a simple example:

> Arthur and Ector þat we dredde,
> Deth haþ leid hem wonderly lowe.[1]

But they appear most consistently in the finest of the three poems, 'þis world fareþ as a Fantasy'. This poem is based on Ecclesiastes,[2] sometimes translating verses from it almost word for word, sometimes depending upon it only for the sustained tone of resignation, scepticism, and impatience with worldly pursuits. The most dignified statements of transience come straight from Ecclesiastes:

> Kunredes come, and kunredes gon,
> As Ioyneþ generacions.[3]

and:

> Dyeþ mon, and beestes dye,
> And al is on Ocasion:[4]

but the poet supplies for himself many of the illustrations of the furious but vain activities of men:

> For þus men stumble and sere heore witte,
> And meveþ maters mony and fele;
> Summe leeveþ on him, sum leveþ on hit,
> As children leorneþ for to spele.
> But non seoþ non þat a-bit,
> Whon stilly deþ wol on hym stele.[5]

Nor should dignified translations of Biblical texts be underrated. With

---

[1] Brown XIV, p. 142.
[2] G. Sitwell, 'A Fourteenth-Century English poem on *Ecclesiastes*', *Dominican Studies*, iii (1950), 285–90.
[3] ll. 25–26, Brown XIV, p. 161. Eccl. i. 4.
[4] ll. 49–50, ibid. Eccl. iii. 19.
[5] ll. 73–78, Brown XIV, p. 162.

the exception of works as remarkable as *The Pearl*, Middle English poems are usually at their weakest, not their strongest, when versifying the Vulgate.

It is particularly interesting that the poet should base his work on Ecclesiastes, as others had done on the *Meditationes piissimae*; for whilst in general it is fair to assume that medieval poets chose their sources according to some external aim rather than according to personal taste, there is here, surely, an exception. For the Vernon lyrics are altogether an exception, in some ways reminding one more of Old English elegiac poetry—which also drew on similar Biblical sources—than of the contemporary lyric. They make, however, a slightly strange mixture, for in them noble generalizations, which would lead to feelings of regret and melancholy acceptance of the way of the world, are combined sharply with plain didactic lessons. It is a combination which could not satisfactorily provide a model for the lyric in general, but without the Vernon lyrics the medieval death lyric would certainly exhibit a far narrower range.

IV

Lyrics on the Virgin and her Joys

WITH the poems addressed to Christ the lover may be compared some of the poems in praise of the Blessed Virgin. These fall roughly into three groups: those that praise the Virgin and implore her mercy, and that in doing so partly draw on the metres and conventions of secular poetry; those that are semi-liturgical celebrations of the Virgin's five joys; and finally those poems—mainly lullabies—in which the Virgin is associated with the Christ-Child. The first and third groups are astonishingly sparse, though we shall have to seek two different causes for the paucity of the two different kinds: the cause of the first is probably literary, of the second doctrinal.

Up to the end of the fourteenth century there are no more than eight poems extant which praise the Virgin in semi-secular style, and not only are they so few in quantity but they are also very narrowly diffused. Of the eight, six survive only in one manuscript each, and the other two only in two. This is a situation comparable to that of the poems on the theme of Christ the lover, but very different from that of the lyrics on the Passion and on death, which are too numerous to be conveniently counted, and are mostly extant in anything from five to twenty manuscripts. This could be explained in terms of audience, and we might argue that these are poems intended for people of literary taste, who were yet speakers of the vernacular. But it is perhaps more illuminating to explain it in terms of literary tradition, though the two explanations are, of course, but facets of a single situation.

In England in the thirteenth century, there was, as we have repeatedly observed, a perfect coincidence between the traditions of meditative piety and the potentialities of literary expression. But to this felicitous coincidence the devotion to the Blessed Virgin was an important exception. By the thirteenth century England had had quite a long history of Marian piety, and in fact this country had been one of the chief originators in western Europe of many of its forms: thus by the time of the earliest lyrics devotion to Mary was firmly established in many learned, liturgical, and public ways. But for its expression in vernacular literature there was lacking an adequate language and secular models.

Therefore, whilst the large bulk of religious poetry in France chiefly consists of poems to the Virgin, England before the revival of secular love literature at the end of the fourteenth century has comparatively few.[1] Most Middle English Marian poems are either carols—a semi-liturgical form which did not develop before the end of the fourteenth century—or aureate praises in the style characteristic of fifteenth-century secular poetry.

In some ways the history of devotion to Mary is similar in outline to that of meditation on the Passion. It is well known that the theological assertion of the unique pre-eminence of the Blessed Virgin was made at the Third Council of Ephesus, when the traditional but disputed description of her as *Theotokos* was proclaimed orthodox. Though a consequence of this decree was the glorification of the Virgin, its intention was primarily to refute the Christological heresy of the Nestorians, who were accused in their theology of dividing the Person of Christ. In order to emphasize the one Person, though with two natures, it became common amongst opponents of Nestorianism to attribute to Christ, referred to by a divine title, some quality of His humanity. Of the startling paradoxes which sprang from this method of description there was none perhaps more dazzling than that of the Blessed Virgin's title of Mother of God. Indeed, all the later extravagant praise of the Virgin may be seen to be only literary efforts to rival and amplify the dignity which had so early been accorded to her.

In the work of the Latin Fathers the singular rank of Mary is expressed in the common theme of Mary as the second Eve, an extension of the Pauline idea of Christ as the second Adam. Sermons, treatises, exegesis, hymns, all record over and over again this basic idea, with its many possible amplifications:[2] 'By the woman folly, by the Virgin wisdom' (Ambrose); 'Eve by her disobedience merited punishment, Mary by obeying obtained glory' (Augustine); 'The first man, by persuasion of a virgin, fell, the Second Man, with consent of a Virgin, triumphed . . . An evil angel of old seduced Eve, a good angel likewise encouraged Mary . . . Eve perished by a word; to the Word likewise did Mary commit herself' (Augustine); 'Death by Eve, life by Mary' (Jerome), and in a hymn ascribed to Venantius Fortunatus, with a common conceit:

> Sumens illud Ave
> Gabrielis ore,

---

[1] It is interesting to notice that Anglo-Norman poems in praise of the Virgin are far more numerous in proportion to the total quantity of Anglo-Norman verse surviving.

[2] The subject is usefully discussed by Thomas Livius, *The Blessed Virgin in the Fathers of the First Six Centuries* (London, 1893), 35–59: it is from here that the quotations following above are taken. See also M. M. Desmarais, *S. Albert le Grand docteur de la médiation mariale* (Paris, Ottawa, 1935), 115–22.

Funda nos in pace
Mutans nomen Evae.[1]

Although the Western Fathers accepted the unique relationship of Mary to Christ in His work of redemption, it was obviously not a uniqueness which would fascinate and dominate the imagination so long as liturgical feasts remained commemorations of dogmatic truths rather than of historical events. But in the East there was, as with the Passion, a different tradition and emphasis. The hymns of St. Ephraem, for instance, are filled with extravagant praise of the magnificence of the Blessed Virgin, combined with a dramatic treatment of the interchange at the Annunciation and a tender meditation upon the mutual love of Mother and Child.[2] From the East too came the apocryphal histories of Mary, which soon became current in the West. The scarcity of information about Mary in the gospels made her a particularly suitable subject for the collector of apocryphal legends, and there arose on the one hand the history of Mary's parents, Joachim and Anna,[3] and of her upbringing in the Temple, and on the other hand that of her Assumption, which, whether or not its substance be true, is presented in the gospel of the Pseudo-Matthew, etc., with the fantastic and magical prolification of miracles that so sharply distinguishes the apocryphal books from those of the canon.[4] Perhaps through the influence of these apocryphal narratives there were also established in the East feasts which celebrated the Virgin alone, her Conception and her Nativity, feasts which in the early Middle Ages were adopted in the West.

Devotion to the Blessed Virgin had already appeared in England in the late Anglo-Saxon period: the *Regularis concordia*, for instance, prescribes a mass *de sancta Maria* for every Saturday[5] (the day already singled out for special commemoration of the Virgin),[6] some eleventh-century manuscripts contain an office of the Virgin,[7] and the feast of the Conception was celebrated at Winchester and other places.[8] Though

---

[1] *A.H.* li. 140. 'Take up that "Ave" from the mouth of Gabriel, and, reversing the name of Eva, establish us in peace.' This conceit was to be especially popular in the Middle Ages, see A. Salzer, *Die Sinnbilder und Beiworte Mariens in der deutschen Literatur und lateinischen Hymnenpoesie des Mittelalters* (Linz, 1893), 476–87, and below, p. 130.

[2] Yrjö Hirn, *The Sacred Shrine* (London, 1958), 260–1; Wellesz, op. cit. 358.

[3] See below, pp. 293–7.

[4] For the texts (in translation) see M. R. James, *The Apocryphal New Testament* (Oxford, 1953), 38 ff. and 201 ff.

[5] *Regularis concordia*, ed. and trans. Dom T. Symons (London, 1953), p. 20 and footnote 4.

[6] On this see L. Gougaud, *Devotional and Ascetic Practices in the Middle Ages* (trans. G. C. Bateman, London, 1927), 66–74.

[7] *Facsimiles of Horae de Beata Maria Virgine*, ed. E. S. Dewick, Henry Bradshaw Society, xxi (1902).

[8] S. J. P. van Dijk, 'The Origin of the Latin Feast of the Conception of the B.V.M.', *Dublin Review*, 228 (1954), 251–67; E. Bishop, 'On the Origins of the Feast of the Conception of the Blessed Virgin Mary', *Liturgica Historica* (Oxford, 1918), 238–59.

Anglo-Saxon monastic customs did not survive the Norman Conquest uninterrupted—there is, for instance, no mass for the Virgin in Lanfranc's *Constitutions*, perhaps a deliberate omission—nevertheless, in various ways England in the twelfth century was remarkable for its encouragement of Marian devotion. The feast of the Conception was reintroduced and encouraged by a miracle story of English origin, in which the celebration of the feast was divinely ordered.[1] The chief apologists of the doctrine of the Immaculate Conception, such as Eadmer, the disciple of Anselm, were also English,[2] and, whilst opposition to this dogma, such as that of St. Bernard in his letter to the Canons of Lyons,[3] rested solely on a care for exact theology—the inevitable transmission of original sin and the inescapable need of all for Christ's redemption—and was not intended as a derogation of Mary, the supporters of the doctrine, at least before Duns Scotus, seem to have been moved primarily by a desire to find a further means of glorifying the Blessed Virgin. The earliest collections of miracle stories of the Virgin, which were so outstandingly popular throughout the Middle Ages, were made in England in the twelfth century, and from here spread to the rest of western Europe.[4] The subject of the Virgin and Child also became common in English iconography of the thirteenth century: the newly built lady-chapels would normally contain statues of this kind—none survive, but they are frequently alluded to in contemporary documents—and it was also a fairly frequent subject of wall-paintings and carving, the latter sometimes occupying the dominating position of the tympanum.[5]

The extent to which celebration of the Virgin became part of the devotions of the religious can be seen from the *Ancrene Wisse*, where the anchoresses are instructed to say the Office for the Virgin, a meditative prayer on the five joys, and an anthem.[6] It was no doubt also for religious women that the *God Ureisun* in MS. Cotton Nero A. xiv was written,[7] a unique example of passionate praise and prayer at a startlingly early date. But devotion to the Virgin was made compulsory for everybody at the Lateran Council of 1215, when the Ave Maria was added to the

---

[1] R. W. Southern, 'The English Origins of the "Miracles of the Virgin" ', *Mediaeval and Renaissance Studies*, iv (1958), 194–8.

[2] *Tractatus de conceptione B. Mariae*, *P.L.* 159, 302–24. Cf. A. W. Burridge, 'L'Immaculée Conception dans la théologie de l'Angleterre médiévale', *Revue d'histoire ecclésiastique*, xxxii (1936), 570–97. Another English defender of the doctrine was Osbert of Clare, see the *Letters of Osbert of Clare*, ed. E. W. Williamson (Oxford, 1929).

[3] *Epist.* 174, *P.L.* 182, 332–6.

[4] Southern, loc. cit. 177.

[5] M. D. Anderson, *The Imagery of British Churches* (London, 1955), 140; G. Zarnecki, 'The Coronation of the Virgin on a Capital from Reading Abbey', *Journal of the Warburg and Courtauld Institutes*, xiii (1950), 1–12.

[6] E.E.T.S. 249, 22–26.

[7] Brown XIII, 3.

Pater Noster and Creed, as part of the basic minimum of doctrine and prayer which every layman must learn. There are, in fact, a number of rhymed translations of the Ave of no poetic merit whatsoever. They belong in kind with the versifications of the Pater Noster and Creed, and usually these three are copied together in manuscripts.[1]

The underlying idea of the new devotion to Mary expressed in the Ave Maria[2] was that she, whose relationship to Christ was both intimate and unique, should have a share in the praise which the religious orders constantly offered to God, praise fittingly due to the *Mater Dei* and mother of redeemed mankind. By the twelfth century there had merged with this devotion, founded on strict theology, a more emotional idea of Mary as a particular source of mercy, who was on the one hand the supreme intercessor with Christ, and on the other a tender and benevolent *interventrix* in the affairs of the world. The most beautiful and careful description of Mary as the refuge of sinners occurs in St. Bernard's famous sermon for the Nativity of the Virgin:

Totis ergo medullis cordium, totis praecordiorum affectibus, et votis omnibus Mariam hanc veneremur; quia sic est voluntas ejus, qui totum nos habere voluit per Mariam. Haec, inquam, voluntas ejus est, sed pro nobis. In omnibus siquidem et per omnia providens miseris, trepidationem nostram solatur, fidem excitat, spem roborat, diffidentiam abigit, erigit pusillanimitatem . . . Sed forsitan et in ipso majestatem vereare divinam, quod licet factus sit homo, manserit tamen Deus. Advocatum habere vis ad ipsum? Ad Mariam recurre. Pura siquidem humanitas in Maria, non modo pura ab omni contaminatione, sed et pura singularitate naturae. Nec dubius dixerim, exaudietur et ipsa pro reverentia sua. Exaudiet utique Matrem Filius, et exaudiet Filium Pater. Filioli, haec peccatorum scala, haec mea maxima fiducia est, haec tota ratio spei meae.[3]

From this way of thought it followed that, whilst the formal confession of guilt, as in the *Confiteor*, was made primarily to God, prayers of

---

[1] e.g. MS. Camb. Gg. iv. 32, 12ʳ⁻ᵛ. As explained in the Introduction (p. 3) and in Appendix B (p. 377), these stand outside the meditative tradition.

[2] The Ave Maria at this date ended with '. . . benedictus fructus ventris tui'. The petition, now concluding it, was a later addition.

[3] *P.L.* 183, 441. 'Let us therefore venerate Mary in the very marrow of our hearts, with all the feelings in our breasts, and with all our devotion; for this is the will of Him who has ordained that we should have all through Mary. This, I say, is His will, but it is for our sake. In all things and in all ways she provides for us in our wretchedness: she soothes our agitation, she stirs our faith, she strengthens our hope, she dispels our mistrust, and gives strength to us in our faintheartedness. . . . But perhaps you also fear the divine majesty in Him, for, though it was permitted that He should become man, yet He remained God. Do you want an advocate to plead with Him? Then turn to Mary. For Mary's human nature is pure, pure not only from all defilement, but pure also in that she had but one nature. I tell you certainly that she will be heard because of the reverence due to her. The Son hears the prayer of His mother, and the Father hears the prayer of His Son. My little children, this is the sinners' ladder, this is the firm ground of my confidence, this is the whole reason of my hope.'

penitence and remorse were more appropriately addressed to the Virgin. The finest examples of such prayers are numbers l–lii in the collection of prayers attributed to Anselm, these being composed by him, as Wilmart has shown.[1] They exhibit most movingly the perfect pattern of prayer to the Virgin, not disassociating her from Christ, nor failing to emphasize that the ground of her mercy is that she is the mother of the merciful Redeemer.[2]

Amongst the English lyrics there are comparatively few prayers of penitence, but of these, apart from the poems that are translations of the *Confiteor* or models of self-examination, in that they progress steadily through the seven deadly sins, nearly all are addressed to Mary.[3] It is clear that in the new devotional temper an appeal to Mary was a sign of sincere remorse, for, once the idea of a hierarchy of appeal had been accepted, a direct and immediate invocation of Christ might suggest a presumptuous unawareness of one's own sinfulness rather than a theologically correct recourse to the only and ultimate source of forgiveness. This idea of a proper fear, preventing a direct plea to Christ, underlies all the Marian penitential lyrics, and is stated explicitly in the last verse of a poem to the Virgin, which we shall later discuss more fully:

> Ihesu, seinte marie sone, þu i-her þin moder bone!
> to þe ne dar i clepien noht, to hire ich make min mone.[4]

The mercy of the Blessed Virgin is especially implored for the hour of death and at the Last Judgement. Impetus was probably given to the former by the many miracle stories in which the Virgin, to reward some particular devotion to her, appeared to a dying man to comfort and reassure him; and this idea became so popular that, by the fifteenth century, the appearance of the Virgin at the hour of death was promised to all who had persistently performed some Marian devotion. In origin, however, the custom of invoking the Virgin's aid at death is of learned and semi-liturgical origin. In Anselm's much used *Admonitio morienti* the sick man is directed to say the following prayer:

> Maria, mater gratiae, mater misericordiae, tu nos ab hoste protege, et hora mortis suscipe: per tuum ergo, Virgo, Filium, per Patrem, et Spiritum sanctum, praesens adsis ad obitum meum, quia imminet exitus.[5]

---

[1] *P.L.* 158, 948–59; Wilmart, op. cit. 480.

[2] With this moderate and doctrinally based conception of the role of Mary may be contrasted more extravagant ideas, such as that embodied in the recurrent *exemplum*, in which the Virgin protects her faithful by extending her cloak between them and the arm of an angry Christ, who, like Apollo, is about to launch His arrows against the earth (for this *exemplum* see P. Perdrizet, *La vierge de miséricorde*, Paris, 1908, 113–24).

[3] F. Patterson, *The Medieval Penitential Lyric* (New York, 1911), 7, 13, 19, 62.

[4] Brown XIII, 55, p. 113.

[5] *P.L.* 158, 687. 'Mary, mother of grace and mother of mercy, protect us from

A translation of the first half of this forms part of one of the very few simple and popular prayers to the Blessed Virgin; it is quoted in the *Fasciculus morum*:

> Mary moder of grace we cryen to þe,
> Moder of mercy and of pyte.
> Wyte us fro þe fendes fondyng,
> And helpe us at oure last endyng.
> And to þy sone oure pes þu mak
> þat he on us no wreche take.
> Alle þe halewen þat aren in heven
> To ʒow I crye wit mylde stevene,
> Helpe þat Cryst my gult forʒeve,
> And I wol him serve whyl þat I leve.[1]

From the point of view of sources and content this verse falls into two parts. The first four lines are a translation of the prayer from the *Admonitio morienti*, padded out to scan, and this derivation is made explicit by the fact that the opening words of the Latin are quoted immediately before the English. The second part is fitted to the *exemplum* in which the verse occurs: it is the common story—used to make understandable the invocation of Mary and the saints—of the man who, having offended the king, so that he dare not appear in his presence, goes first to the queen to ask her to intercede on his behalf, then to the king's knights, and then to the lower members of the royal household. The verse itself has no literary pretensions: it is written in plain rhyming couplets, easy to memorize, there is no influence whatsoever from French poetry, and the only signs of liturgical style are the phrases *moder of grace* and *moder of mercy and of pyte*, which are direct translations of the Latin original. Like the similar verse, 'Maidin and moder þat bar þe hevene-kinge',[2] these lines should probably be classified with the versifications of the Ave rather than with the Marian poetry we are about to discuss. This literary impression is confirmed by the fact that 'Maidin and moder' is copied in a manuscript together with versifications of the Pater Noster and Ave.[3]

The two penitential poems, however, which may properly be called lyrics are 'Hayl mari! / hic am sori'[4] and '[I]Blessed beo þu, lavedi, ful of hovene Blisse'.[5] Both poems are metrically elaborate: '[I]Blessed beo þu' is written in mono-rhyming quatrains with long lines diversified by

---

the enemy, and receive us in the hour of our death: therefore, O Virgin, through your Son, and through the Father and the Holy Spirit, be present at my dying for my departure is at hand.'

[1] MS. Rawl. C. 670, 15ᵛ; printed from MS. Caius Camb. 71 by R. H. Robbins, 'Popular Prayers in Middle English Verse', *M.P.* xxxvi (1939), 345.

[2] Brown XIII, 68.
[3] MS. Cott. Cleo. B. vi. 204ᵛ.
[4] Brown XIII, 65.
[5] Ibid. 55.

alliteration, whilst 'Hayl mari' is in a light but complicated stanza form where the stanzas are verbally interlinked, a device borrowed from the French. They are thus technically quite distinct from the short popular verses, which did not aim at any kind of literary adornment. They also differ from didactically penitential poems, such as 'Levedi sainte marie, moder and meide'[1] (a work influenced by the *Poema morale*), for the content is not an enumeration of sins committed, in confessional style, but a prayer for help, in which is established a sense of love for and dependence upon the Blessed Virgin. Both poems are touching in their treatment of the relationship between the sinner and the Virgin, and the dignity which is maintained, despite the admission of helplessness, no doubt springs from the implicit courtly or feudal analogy. There is a sense of a well-ordered, hierarchic world, in which the speaker may use a style both formal and private, a style which gives a strong impression of the kind of objective sincerity we have already discussed.

'[I]Blessed beo þu, lavedi' is the more generalized of the two, and its tone can best be illustrated by quotation:

> Iblessed beo þu, lavedi, so fair and so briht,
> al min hope is uppon þe, bi dai and bi nicht.
> Helpe þruh þin milde mod, for þel þu mist,
> þat ich nevere for feondes sake fur-go þin eche liht.
>
> .   .   .   .
>
> Bricht and scene quen of storre, so me liht and lere,
> in þis false fikele þorld so me led and steore,
> þat ich at min ende-dai ne habbe non feond to fere.
> ihesu, mit ti spete blod þu bohtest me ful deore.[2]

In this poem two ideas are beautifully brought into relationship: on the one hand, the glory and sweetness of the Virgin, conveyed by eulogistic titles, *moder of mildernisse* or *quen of hovene*, and adjectives such as *fair*, *hende*, *scene*, *briht*, that recur with refrain-like effect; on the other hand, the sinfulness of the speaker and the perilousness of the world, expressed in phrases such as *þis false fikele þorld* or in exclamations such as *þel ofte ich sike and sorþe make*. The two ideas are very finely brought together in the penultimate stanza quoted above. The final stanza is plainer and more didactic, ending the poem on a penitential and unpoetical note.

In contrast to their use in this poem, terms of praise are rare in 'Hayl mari', and the sinner's situation is presented, not in a general and reflective way, but in precise and dramatic terms. As we shall see, the dramatic force of the poem springs from the depiction of analogous scenes in common *exempla*. The two situations for which the Virgin's help was especially invoked in the Middle Ages were the day of death

---

[1] Brown XIII, 2.   [2] Ibid. p. 112.

and the Last Judgement. In 'Hayl mari' the first of these is described as follows:

> at min endin-day
> þe warlais þai wil be her
> fort[o] take þair pray.
>
> To take þar pray,
> alse hi her say,
> þai er redi boyt nite and day;
> so strange er þai
> þat we ne may
> agaynis þaim stond, so way la way!
> but-gif þu help us, mitteful may,
> wit þi sunes grace.
> wan þu comes þai flet a-wai,
> dar þai not se þi face.[1]

The idea of the fiends hovering around the bed of a dying man, waiting to seize his soul, is an ancient one that extends back to the Body and Soul passages in the Apocalypse of Paul: its inherently dramatic quality can be best appreciated from the vigorous illustrations of the subject in the fifteenth-century block books of the *Ars moriendi*.[2] Accounts of the Virgin putting devils to flight occur in the miracle stories of the Virgin, such as the one in which a dying monk sees this drama taking place in his room.[3]

In the stanza quoted above, the theme of the devils lying in wait for the soul at death is extended by that of the Devil ever ready to trap the sinner during his lifetime, and of the Virgin's championship of the sinner in this battle. In this very common subject there are signs of a popular mythology. In correct theological terms it is obvious that the Virgin could only protect the individual from sin, as so many prayers implore, by interceding with God that He should through the infusion of His grace strengthen the soul against temptation. But the learned tradition of the Virgin as the pre-eminent enemy of the Devil gave the opportunity for a more striking though fantastic manner of representing her power. Her dominion over the Devil, based upon the traditional exegetic application to the Virgin of Genesis iii. 15, *ipsa tibi conteret caput tuum*, became constantly exemplified in miracle stories in

---

[1] Brown XIII, pp. 124–5. *Warlais*: devils; *mitteful may*: mighty maiden; *flet a-wai*: vanish.

[2] Émile Mâle, *L'art religieux de la fin du moyen âge en France* (Paris, 1949), 382–7.

[3] A. Poncelet, 'Index miraculorum B.V.M.', *Analecta Bollandiana*, xxi (1902), 1478. A. Mussafia, 'Studien zu den mittelalterlichen Marienlegenden', ii, *Sitzungsberichte der kaiserlichen Akademie der Wissenschaften*, cxv (Vienna, 1888), no. 25, p. 51; H. L. D. Ward, *Catalogue of Romances in the British Museum*, ii (London, 1893), 617–18.

which the Virgin physically intervened in the unending warfare, and by skill or cunning overcame man's enemy. The earliest and most popular of the Miracles of the Virgin, the story of Theophilus, illustrates this well: in this legend, which may be called the Faust story with a happy ending, the Virgin seizes from the Devil the document in which Theophilus has signed away his soul.[1] These miracle stories had the purpose of driving home the efficacy of prayer to the Virgin, and, whilst theologically this confidence in the Virgin rested on the kind of argument used by St. Bernard, in the popular imagination it must have seemed to rest on the spectacular demonstrations of her power in the much-told miracle stories.[2] Her instant response to the plea of the apparently undeserving was, as it were, a dramatic expression of St. Bernard's magnificent exclamation, 'Let him who has ever had his prayer rejected refuse to pray to Mary'.

Miracle stories also recorded instances of the Virgin's protective intervention on behalf of the soul as it journeyed upwards to its judgement,[3] and during the *psychostasis*[4] the Virgin might help the sinner by putting some object, such as the hem of her robe or a rosary, into the scale so inadequately filled by good deeds. The culmination of this way of thought was the common supposition that the Virgin would continue to intercede even at the Last Judgement. The last four lines of the 'Hayl mari', though simple in style, are not weak in effect if the force of their subject-matter is thoroughly understood:

> wan we þenke hu we sal far
> wan he sal dem us alle;
> we sal haf ned þare
> a-pan mari to calle.[5]

There is also a visual element in these lines, for in the common iconography of the Last Judgement the Virgin kneels in intercession (as in the fifteenth-century wall-painting which still survives over the chancel arch of St. Thomas's in Salisbury),[6] or shows her breasts, as in the

---

[1] Poncelet, op. cit. 74; Ward, op. cit. 595–600. The story is told in both the *Northern Homily Cycle* and the *Southern English Legendary*, and also in an independent version (*Index*, 25, 1883, and 3266).

[2] Apart from the collections of Miracles of the Virgin (for which see Ward, op. cit. 586–740), miracles occur also in early preaching-books such as the *Liber exemplorum* (ed. A. G. Little, British Society of Franciscan Studies, i, 1908) and the *Speculum laicorum* (ed. J. Th. Welter, Paris, 1914).

[3] Mussafia v, *Sitzungsberichte*, cxxxix, 8, 64–70; Jean Mielot, *Miracles de Notre Dame*, xvii, ed. G. F. Warner (Roxburghe Club, 1885), 13–14; cf. also p. xv.

[4] For the psychostasis in art see M. P. Perry, 'On the Psychostasis in Christian Art', *Burlington Magazine*, xxii (1912/13), 94–105, 208–18; W. H. Hildburge, 'An English Alabaster Carving of St. Michael Weighing a Soul', *Burlington Magazine*, lxxxix (1947), 129–31; cf. *Legenda aurea*, ed. cit. iv, 251–2; *Speculum laicorum*, ch. li, ed. Welter, 74.

[5] Brown XIII, p. 125.   [6] Anderson, op. cit., pl. 1.

illustration in the early fourteenth-century *Queen Mary's Psalter*[1] to which we have already referred. This (theologically unreasonable) consummation of the Virgin's mercy remained a popular theme throughout the Middle Ages, and it was one of the medieval iconographic forms that was condemned by Molanus, the Counter-Reformation commentator on traditional iconography:

> Neque tunc B.V. Maria genua flectet ante Iudicem, ostendens illi ubera ad rogandum pro peccatoribus: neque beatus Iohannes Baptista tunc etiam procumbet ad genua, ut intercedat pro hominibus, quemadmodum pictores depingunt formam iudicii. Sed et beata virgo, et beatus Ioannes tunc assidebunt supremo iudici, ut etiam iudicent mundum tamquam assessores. Tunc enim amplius misericordiae non erit locus, sicut nunc, sed solummodo iustitiae.[2]

Fortunately, from the literary point of view there is no need to be disquieted by this lack of conformity between the will of Christ and the will of the Virgin. Therefore in 'Hayl mari' the thought that the Virgin's mercy will above all be needed at the Last Judgement seems as natural and fitting as does the direct plea to Christ in the *Dies irae*. The sublime antitheses of the latter are, of course, not attempted in 'Hayl mari', but the recollection of the Blessed Virgin's help at the Last Judgement undoubtedly brings the poem to a quietly powerful and fitting conclusion.

Prayer to the Virgin to intercede with her Son, and to protect sinners from the Devil and hell, and particularly at the hour of death and the Last Judgement, are the recurrent themes of the early lyrics to the Virgin; but mingled with this, often predominating, though sometimes subordinated, is the praise of the Blessed Virgin. In English (unlike Latin with many works such as the *Viola*[3] of John of Howden), there are no poems which consist solely of praise, nor are there any which, like many French poems to the Virgin, reserve the prayer until the last stanza. Poems consisting almost solely of praise are either nearest to the French style, as in 'Nu skr[y]nketh rose' from MS. Harley 2253,[4] or nearest to the style of Latin hymns and sequences, as in William of Shoreham's 'Marye, mayde mylde and fre'.[5]

But, though praise of the Virgin may be traced on the one hand to the

---

[1] Ed. G. F. Warner (London, 1912), 297. See above, pp. 34–35.

[2] Johannes Molanus, *De historia SS. imaginum*, iv, 24 (Louvain, 1594), 194. 'The Blessed Virgin Mary will not then kneel before the Judge, showing her breasts to plead for sinners; nor will the Blessed John the Baptist likewise fall on his knees in order to intercede for men, in the manner that painters portray the scene of the Last Judgement. But both the Blessed Virgin and the blessed John will then be seated beside the supreme judge in order that they may judge the world as assessors. At that time there will be no farther room for mercy, as there is now, but only for justice.'

[3] *Poems of John of Hoveden*, ed. F. J. E. Raby (Surtees Society, cliv), 194–202.

[4] Brown XIV, 10.   [5] Ibid. 32.

liturgy and on the other to French love poetry, in various ways the two unite, and a traditional religious idea may be expressed in the vocabulary of secular conventions. This is particularly clear in the praise of the Virgin's beauty, which is one of the most recurrent themes of the lyric: 'For on þat is so feir ant brist', 'lavedi brit', 'Levedi milde, softe ond swete', 'bricht in bure and eke in halle', 'þat levedy gent and smal', 'so fair and so briht', 'so feire and so hende', etc. Since praise of the lady's beauty was one of the chief themes in trouvère verse, the Harley secular lyrics, which are modelled upon them, developed a conventional vocabulary of adjectives to describe feminine beauty, and this the Marian lyric drew upon. But the idea of the Virgin's beauty had authoritative foundation in the Song of Songs, whose reference to the Virgin had been established by many twelfth- and thirteenth-century commentators, and from it many of the antiphons in the Little Office of the Virgin derived; in particular, it provided the *locus classicus* of the idea of the Virgin's beauty: 'Tota pulchra es, amica mea, et macula non est in te' (iv. 7).[1] Other key texts were 'Et concupiscet rex decorem tuum' (Ps. xliv. 12),[2] which was applied to the Incarnation as well as the Assumption, and the description of Esther, 'Erat enim formosa valde' (Esther ii. 15).[3] It was, moreover, logical to infer the Virgin's beauty from that of her Son, and in the *Mariale*, the reply to the question 'Utrum [beatissima virgo] pulchritudinem corporalem habuerit', begins with this argument:

Respondendo dicimus, quod sicut Dominus noster Jesus Christus fuit *speciosus forma prae filiis hominum*, ita beatissima Virgo pulcherrima et speciosissima fuit inter filias hominum: et quod ipsa habuit summum et perfectissimum gradum in pulchritudine, qui esse potuit in mortali corpore secundum statum viae, operante natura.[4]

Furthermore, some of the traditional metaphors, such as rose, lily, violet, which are also commonplaces of French secular poetry, poetic- ally and deliberately suggest physical as well as spiritual beauty. In illuminated manuscripts, though the Virgin is not given the precise stylish costume of heroines of romances, being dressed in flowing robes,

---

[1] 'Thou art all fair, my love; there is no spot in thee.' (A.V.)

[2] 'So shall the king greatly desire thy beauty.' (A.V., Ps. xlv. 11).

[3] 'For she was exceedingly beautiful.' Esther was often considered a type of the Virgin; see Salzer, op. cit. 473–6, and below, pp. 284–5.

[4] *B. Alberti Magni opera omnia*, ed. A. Borgnet, xxxvii (1898), 38; quoted by Des- marais, op. cit. 30. 'We say in reply that just as our Lord Jesus Christ was beautiful in appearance above the sons of men, so the very Blessed Virgin was most lovely and beautiful amongst the daughters of men, and that she had the highest and most perfect degree of beauty possible in a mortal body, nature giving it to her always according to her age.'

yet in face and general outline she resembles them, whereas Christ remains distinguished by a Byzantine gravity.

Associated with the praise of the Virgin's beauty is that of her nobility, and especially her title of Queen, which had been attributed to her in patristic times, when her glory was especially celebrated.[1] This title, so popular in every form of Marian devotion, sums up all her virtue, beauty, and dignity. Until medieval art became more fully naturalistic, Mary, in representations of the Virgin and Child, is crowned: a fine example occurs at the end of the Lisle Psalter, where the Virgin also has the symbolical beasts of Ps. xc. 13, beneath her feet.[2] Already in the twelfth century St. Bernard had taken for his text for a sermon on the Assumption, '. . . Mulier amicta sole, et luna sub pedibus ejus et in capite ejus corona stellarum duodecim',[3] and this remained a most common application: John Bromyard, for instance, constructed his section on *Maria* as an allegory of the sun, moon, and twelve stars.[4] In the lyrics the title of *quene* is equally emphasized: 'Briht and scene quen of hovene', 'Edi beo þu, hevene quene', 'heie quen in parais'. Again the praise of the Virgin's rank is not incongruous with the French style.

In the earliest elaborate poems in praise of the Virgin, the two macaronic lyrics in MS. Trinity 323, 'Seinte mari, moder milde'[5] and 'For on þat is so feir ant brist',[6] there is no description which could not derive from Latin sources. Both the metre and the Latin lines show how closely the poems are related to Latin models. They would seem to be intended for the educated but not learned: the English lines carry sufficient of the meaning for the poems to be roughly understood even by someone who knew no Latin, and a modest familiarity with the phraseology of the liturgy would enable the whole to be easily understood. It should be added, however, that there is some evidence that the poems had the status of Latin hymns despite the admixture of English, for 'For on þat is so feir' is included with a group of Latin hymns in the learned manuscript, Rawl. C. 504.[7] Though sentences of prayer are interwoven in these poems, they are largely Marian eulogies, extolling her by her liturgical titles and by the enumeration of her noble qualities and great deeds. They are not, however, as solemn and objec-

---

[1] On the early iconographic expression of this see Carlo Bertelli, *La Madonna di santa Maria in Trastevere* (Rome, 1961), 47–59.

[2] E. Millar, *English Illuminated Manuscripts of the xiv^{th} and xv^{th} Centuries*, pl. 10.

[3] *In dominica infra octavam assumptionis B. V. Mariae sermo*, P.L. 183, 429–38. 'A woman clothed with the sun, and the moon under her feet, and upon her head a crown of twelve stars.' (Apoc. xii. 1, A.V.) This text did not as yet have particular reference to the Immaculate Conception.

[4] *Summa praedicantium*, ii (Venice, 1586), 8–11.

[5] Brown XIII, 16.   [6] Ibid. 17.

[7] R. W. Hunt, 'The Collections of a Monk of Bardney: A Dismembered Rawlinson Manuscript', *Mediaeval and Renaissance Studies*, v (1961), 34.

tive in tone as this description would suggest. Whilst eulogistic description occurs in both the Latin and English lines, the expressions of penitence and appeals for help are confined to the English, as for instance in the following:

> For on þat is so feir ant brist
> velud maris stella,
> bristore þen þe dai-is list,
> parens et puella,
> i crie þe grace of þe.
> levedi, prie þi sone for me
> tam pia,
> þat i mote come to þe,
> maria.[1]

There is therefore an agreeable and touching balance between the formal descriptions, which make the Virgin noble and remote, and the simple pleas in English, which suggest a direct and dignified intimacy. The preponderance of praise distinguishes these poems from the two penitential lyrics we discussed earlier, but they share with them some of the qualities we previously noticed and praised.

The poems, however, that chiefly show French influence are two in MS. Corpus 59, 'Edi beo þu, hevene quene'[2] and 'Moder milde, flur of alle',[3] and one in MS. Harley 2253, 'Nu skr[y]nketh rose'.[4] The first of these is one of the few English lyrics accompanied by musical notation, which is here a two-part polyphonic setting.[5] This setting may be interpreted as a corroboration of the sophisticated quality of the poem. Apart from the poise with which the traditional material is here used and the intensity of the love-language, the most interesting point is its use of the image of a feudal relationship:

> Nis non maide of þine heowe
> swo fair, so sschene, so rudi, spo bricht;
> spete levedi, of me þu reope
> And have merci of þin knicht.

---

[1] Brown XIII, p. 24.　　　　　　　　[2] Ibid. 60.
[3] Ibid. 61.　　　　　　　　　　　　　[4] Brown XIV. 10.
[5] On the few early examples of vernacular verse with polyphonic settings see F. Ll. Harrison, *Music in Medieval Britain* (London, 1958), 153–5, who connects 'the appearance of simple polyphony in the vernacular' in the early period, 1224–1300, with the activity of the friars. That the polyphonic setting is an indication of learned origin is borne out by the fact that the poem is preserved in a manuscript from Llanthony Priory. The passage from Gerald of Wales in which he describes the instinctive ability of Yorkshire people to sing in two parts (cf. Brown XIII, p. xv) should perhaps be quoted less often and less unreflectingly.

. . . . .
Levedi milde, softe and swote,
ic crie þe merci, ic am þi mon,
boþe to honde and to fote,
on alle þise þat ic kon.[1]

Despite the common generalization that French lyrics to the Virgin were modelled upon the secular, both in form and tone, the feudal image of the lady with her lover-servant does not occur frequently. Nevertheless, here and there lines such as the following occur: 'De fin cuer sanz repentir / La servirai ligement.'[2] Since the relationship between lover and mistress in the secular Harley lyrics is imagined informally (only in one of them is there a suggestion of chivalric service), the influence on 'Edi beo þu hevene quene' probably came directly from the French. The French convention may have seemed especially appropriate through the much-told miracle story on the *Marienbräutigam* theme:[3] a man devoted to the Virgin is nevertheless persuaded to abandon his religious vocation and to marry, but on his wedding day the Virgin appears to him in her beauty to recall him to her service. There is an explicit parallel here between the earthly and the heavenly bride, which nowadays may not seem quite decorous. None the less, in the religious lyric the chivalric metaphor is both moving and appropriate. Whereas in the secular lyric the image pleased by its artificiality and elegant unlikeness to reality, in the Marian poetry it has the unexpected power of a well-worn metaphor which is suddenly given a new and more fitting application.

A more unusual poem, harsher and less ornate, but making use of the same motif, is that from MS. Harley 2253, 'Nou skr[y]nketh rose and lylie flour', which combines two themes that merge into one another with adroitness and intricacy. The first is the contrast (which had been made in the 'Love Ron') between the permanence of heaven and the transience of the world:

Ne is no quene so stark ne stour,
ne no levedy so bryht in bour
þat ded ne shal by-glyde.[4]

and against the fading beauty of earthly ladies is set by implication the stable eternity of the Virgin: 'on a ledy myn hope is'. The second theme

---

[1] Brown XIII, p. 116.   [2] Järnström, op. cit. I. xv, p. 49.
[3] See, for instance, the *Liber de miraculis sanctae Dei genetricis Mariae*, ed. B. Pez (Vienna, 1731), reprinted with introduction and notes by T. F. Crane (Ithaca, London, 1925), 18–19 and notes p. 89; Gautier de Coincy, *Du clerc qui fame espousa et puis la lessa*, ed. E. v. Kraemer (Helsinki, 1950).
[4] Brown XIV, 10, p. 11. *Stark ne stour*: vigorous and strong; *ded . . . by-glyde*: die.

is that of the healing power of the Virgin. There is a close parallelism between this and various passages in the poetry of the trouvères, and once again there is a coincidence between secular and sacred: on the one hand the secular *topos* of love as a disease and the lady as a physician,[1] and on the other hand the religious metaphor, of ancient origin when applied to Christ, of sin as a disease and Christ the Redeemer as physician. In one of Anselm's prayers to the Virgin there is a striking passage which illustrates this idea:

Tibi, o genetrix vitae, o mater salutis, o templum pietatis et misericordiae tibi sese conatur praesentare miserabilis anima mea, morbis vitiorum languida, vulneribus facinorum scissa, ulceribus flagitiorum putrida, tibi nititur quantum moribunda valet supplicare, ut potentibus tuis meritis et piis tuis precibus digneris eam sanare ... Rogare enim te, domina, desidero, ut miserationis tuae respectu cures plagas et ulcera peccatorum meorum.[2]

The emphasis in the Harley poem, however, is different, in that it is the resemblance between sin and the physical ugliness of disease which moves Anselm, whereas the poet plays with the idea of the Virgin's healing medicine decoratively, with a touch of paradoxical style and perhaps of shrewd practicality:

> Betere is hire medycyn
> þen eny mede or eny wyn—
>   hire erbes smulleþ swete—
> from catenas in-to dyvelyn
> nis þer no leche so fyn
>   oure serewes to bete.
> Mon þat feleþ eni sor
>   ond his folie wol lete,
> wiþ-oute gold oþer eny tresor
> he mai be sound ant sete.[3]

In the poems so far described the Virgin has been praised in a manner which, though more reverent than that used with reference to a poet's mistress—her beauty, for instance, is not described with an undignified minuteness—yet in general terms resembles the secular style. There were, however, two traditional theological ways of praising the Blessed Virgin, which have no connexion with love poetry. The first of these is

---

[1] e.g. *Book of the Duchesse*, ll. 36–40, *Works*, ed. Robinson, p. 316.

[2] *P.L.* 158, 948–9. 'To you, O source of life and mother of health, O temple of pity and mercy, to you my wretched soul tries to come: it is weak from the diseases of sin, rent by the wounds of evil deeds, corrupt with the ulcers of shameful actions: as much as it is possible for one at the point of death, it endeavours to beseech you that you condescend to heal it by your powerful merits and your holy prayers. . . . O lady, I desire to ask you that you heal the wounds and ulcers of my sins with the glance of your compassion.'

[3] Brown XIV, p. 12. *From catenas in-to dyvelyn*: From Caithness to Dublin, i.e. anywhere in the world; *sete*: content.

by types, the enumerating of the Old Testament figures which fore-shadow her, the enclosed garden, Gideon's fleece, the burning bush, etc. Of these the most important was that of the second Eve fulfilling at the Annunciation God's prophecy 'ipsa conteret caput tuum'. In the famous *Biblia pauperum* the first picture, that of the Annunciation, is surrounded on one side by God addressing these words to the Serpent and on the other by Gideon's fleece.[1] The Virgin's role as the second Eve emphasized in the reversal of the name Eva in the angel's *Ave* was, as we have seen, the common theme of the Early Church, and it survived in a particularly conspicuous form in Latin hymns. Of all the types this is the only one used in the Marian lyrics so far discussed, for instance in 'For on þat is so feir':

> Al þe world it wes fur-lorn
> þoru *eva peccatrice*,
> to-forn þat ihesu was iborn
> *ex te genitrice*;
> þorou *ave*, e wende awei,
> þe þestri nist ant com þe dai
> *salutis*,
> þe welle springet out of þe
> *virtutis*.[2]

But the only poem which presents a triumphant procession of types, as in the sequences of Adam of St. Victor, is that beginning 'Marye, mayde mylde and fre',[3] written by William of Shoreham, the early fourteenth-century Augustinian canon and rector of Chart, who composed quite a number of didactic and religious poems: in this poem the Virgin is greeted as Noah's dove, the burning bush, Sarah, David's sling, Solomon's temple, Judith, Esther, etc. Whilst it is so liturgically formal that one would not expect to find its exact counterpart in poems of secular style, it is perhaps surprising not to find in them any allusion whatsoever to some of the more common types, such as the burning bush, as one does in Anglo-Norman and Northern French poetry.[4] There is evidence of complicated typological schemes in visual art by the end of the twelfth century,[5] and neither the explanation that typology was less commonly used in England than in France, nor the possibility that even fairly common types might have perplexed the audience of the lyrics seems convincing.

Allied to the neglect of typology is the omission of the paradoxes

---

[1] Ed. H. Cornell (Stockholm, 1925), pl. 1.
[2] Brown XIII, p. 25. Cf. ibid. 32, ll. 34–37.
[3] Brown XIV, 32.
[4] e.g. Järnström, op. cit. 1: the burning bush: xxix. 28–29 (p. 79); xxxi. 40 (p. 85); Gideon's fleece: xxiii. 29 (p. 66); cf. also *Romania*, xiii. 509–10, nos. 10, 11, etc.
[5] M. R. James, 'Pictor in carmine', *Archaeologia*, xciv (1951), 146.

which had been one of the commonest ways of praising the Virgin in the
work of poets who ingeniously explored all the brilliant and bewildering
contradictions logically deriving from the title *Mater Dei*. The earliest
and most recurrent of the paradoxes is that which is now best known
from Dante's famous line, 'Vergine madre, figlia del tuo figlio'.[1] The
idea has been traced back to the sermons of St. Augustine, for instance,
'. . . crearetur ex matre, quam creavit',[2] and perhaps the most famous
source for it was a verse from the hymn 'Quem terra, pontus, æthera',
by Venantius Fortunatus:

> O gloriosa femina
> excelsa super sidera,
> qui te creavit provide,
> lactas sacrato ubere.[3]

In the Middle Ages this idea was embodied in the liturgy by the use
of the foregoing hymn and of the eleventh-century antiphon, *Alma
redemptoris mater*, which contains the words: 'Tu quae genuisti / Natura
mirante tuum sanctum genitorem'.[4] Whilst the most popular of the
paradoxes was the *mater et filia* motif, another one used almost as
frequently, and also occurring in the liturgy, is that later so well
expressed by Donne, 'Immensity cloysterd in thy deare wombe'.[5]
In medieval Latin hymns and poems such paradoxes are innumerable:
in the thirteenth-century poem *De Maria virgine* by Walter Wimborne,
for instance, the style is developed with vigorous excitement:

> Virgo mirabilis novo prodigio
> Deum obpalliat sub carnis pallio,
> magnum abbrevians in parvo spatio,
> immensum metiens ventris in medio.
>
> Convertit genitor in matrem filiam,
> antiquus prosilit ad pueritiam,
> novam ingreditur rex regum regiam,
> nec venter virginis sentit injuriam.[6]

---

[1] *Paradiso*, xxxiii, l. 1. 'Virgin mother, daughter of your son.'

[2] 'That He should be created as the son of the mother whom He had created.' For
this reference and for an illuminating investigation of the theme see A. L. Mayer,
'Mater et filia', *Jahrbuch für Liturgiewissenschaft*, vii (1927), 60–82.

[3] *A.H.* ii. 27. 'O lady full of glory, elevated above the stars, at your holy breast
you suckle Him who created you in His providence.' A Middle English translation
occurs in the *Primer*, E.E.T.S. 105, 2.

[4] *The Sarum Missal*, ed. J. Wickham Legg (Oxford, 1916), 172; Raby, op. cit. 226.
'You, who, to the astonishment of nature, did give birth to your holy Father.'

[5] 'Annunciation', l. 14, *Divine Poems*, ed. Gardner, 2.

[6] *The Latin Poems Commonly Attributed to Walter Mapes*, ed. T. Wright, Camden
Society, 1841, 192. 'The Virgin—a new miracle and marvel—has clothed God in a robe
of flesh, contracting largeness into a small space and bounding immensity within her
womb. The Father transforms His daughter into His mother and the Ancient of Days

Similarly in French and Anglo-Norman poetry to the Virgin paradoxes of this kind are used fairly frequently: sometimes the style is treated with poetic inventiveness, as in the following French verse:

> Li fruiz planta l'arbre dont il issi
> Et dou ruissel descendi la fontainne,
> L'uevre l'ouvrier aleva et norri
> Et li solaus vint de la tresmontainne.[1]

But Anglo-Norman poetry does not show an equal freedom, though it rhymes the conventional paradoxes fairly frequently, and with a mediocre ease, as in the following:

> Douce dame, pie mere
> de ky nasqui vostre pere.[2]

In English, however, such paradoxes are extraordinarily rare: in 'Edi beo þu' there occurs an isolated example of the response from the Office of the Virgin, '. . . him þat hevenes myȝte not take, þou bare in þi wombe',[3] turned into verse:

> Seolcudliche ure loverd hit diȝte
> þat þu, maide wið-ute pere,
> þat al þis porld bicluppe ne miȝte,
> þu sscholdest of þin boseme bere.[4]

and in the poem on the five joys from Trinity 323, 'Seinte marie, levedi brist', the second is thus defined:

> Seinte marie, moder milde,
> þi fader bi-com to one childe.[5]

The only poem, however, which suggests intellectual pleasure in the exploration of a paradox is 'þou womman boute vere', by William Herebert, a friar whose work consists chiefly of translation from Latin hymns, and who was perhaps influenced by Anglo-Norman poetry. In the first half of this poem the *mater et filia* paradox with its implications is worked out through three stanzas:

springs forth in childhood. The King of Kings enters a new palace and the Virgin's womb suffers no hurt.' This poem from MS. Cott. Titus A. xx (Walther 10699) is a shorter version of that referred to by B. Smalley, *English Friars and Antiquity in the Early xivth Century*, 51, note 2, from MS. Laud misc. 368 (Walther 14232). Cf. also A. H. l, p. 630.

[1] Järnström, op. cit. I. xxiii. 17–20, p. 66.

[2] *Romania*, xiii. 513. Cf. the same manuscript, f. 53, 'Ave seinte Marie gloriouse mere / Virgine pretiose ki portastes tun pere . . .'. The same paradox appears in French poetry, e.g. Järnström, loc. cit. II. cxiii. 35–36, 'De roi es fille et mere, / Et si portas ton pere'.

[3] *The Prymer or Lay Folks' Prayer Book*, E.E.T.S. 105, 5.

[4] Brown XIII, p. 117.

[5] Ibid. 18, p. 28.

þou wommon boute vere
þyn oune vader bere.
  Gret wonder þys was
þat on wommon was moder
To vader and hyre broþer–
  So never oþer nas.

þou my suster and moder
And þy sone my broþer–
  Who shulde þoenne drede?
Who-so havet þe kyng to broder
And ek þe quene to moder
  Wel auhte vor to spede.

Dame, suster and moder,
Say þy sone my broþer,
  þat ys domes-mon,
þat vor þe þat hym bere,
To me boe debonere–
  My robe he haveth opon.[1]

These stanzas illustrate the difficulty that writers in the earlier period of the Middle English lyric had in expressing wit: their style is clumsy, blunting the pointedness of the idea. Compared with the fine compression and deceptive ease of Donne's line 'Thy Makers maker, and thy Fathers mother'[2] the unshaped diffuseness stands out: unlike the other poems, this one attempts wit, but fails. In particular, the second verse, lacking dignity of style, seems pertly confident when compared with the fifty-second prayer of Anselm,[3] who develops the same idea gradually, with diffidence and awe. It is difficult nowadays to estimate the value of this kind of paradox, for it is clear from passages such as that in the *Cur Deus homo*, where Anselm explains in terms of fantastic relationships why it was fitting that only the Second Person of the Trinity should become incarnate,[4] that people in the Middle Ages were far more sensitive to the absolute quality of the family hierarchy than we are, and therefore less likely to consider some inversion of it merely grotesque or quaint. Nevertheless, a paradox which becomes a commonplace is by definition enfeebled, since it has lost the force of the first shock of surprise, and, if the reader is not startled into some imaginative response to the incomprehensible sublimity of the Incarnation, then the statement may seem merely curious or dull: either a well-turned variation, as in the French quoted above, or perfect poise in expression is required to make the familiar startling. Since poise, as we have already said, was

[1] Brown XIV, 16, p. 19. *Boute vere*: peerless; *domes-man*: judge.
[2] 'Annunciation', l. 12, *Divine Poems*, 2.   [3] *P.L.* 158, 952–9.
[4] Bk. ii, ch. 9, *P.L.* 158, 407.

beyond the range of English in the earlier Middle Ages, the unwilling-ness to use paradoxes might be explained as the inspiration of literary good sense. But the absence of types as well as of paradoxes shows that a further, though obvious, comment is needed. The celebration of the Virgin's unique position does not accord well with meditation upon Christ in His humanity, and, in particular, types and paradoxes designed to draw attention to the glory of Christ's divinity would be out of place. The method of praising the Virgin that at the same time recalled the Godhead of Christ was therefore left almost unused, and the Virgin was praised solely in human terms, for her beauty, her nobility, and her mercy.

There was, however, a further way of eulogizing the Blessed Virgin, that of praising her through an enumeration of her five joys, one of the earliest of formalized meditative exercises, and probably the first to be embodied in the Middle English lyric. The poems so far discussed in this chapter have not been meditative. Admittedly, to a medieval audience they may well have offered greater visual precision than they do to the modern reader, for statues and paintings abounded, and people would rightly have felt that to make an association between the physical appearance of the Virgin in these and in the lyrics, was an appropriate way of under-standing the texts. But the intention of the poems is not to kindle a visual image, but to make something fitting to the honour of the Virgin. At most they may be said to have used one of the techniques of medita-tion, that of the analogical situation: the speaker imagines that he is a lover and that the Blessed Virgin is the mistress whom he adores. As we have seen, the poems are at their best when drawing upon the personal relationship and feeling proper to such a situation, and dullest when the poems are most public and objective.

The poems on the five joys, however, deal with potentially meditative subjects, and it is only a few of them that have no intention of dealing with them meditatively. In general they vary from the slightly to the predominantly meditative, and there is a corresponding variation in literary quality, the more meditative being also the most satisfactory as poetry. The differences in meditative emphasis arise in two ways. Firstly, according to liturgical ancestry: in one strain of the tradition the joy is rehearsed as a means of glorification of the Virgin, in the other it is described in more evocative detail and made the basis of a petition. Secondly, according to the subject: three of the joys are demonstrations of divine power, the Resurrection, the Ascension, and the Assumption, and should properly arouse a sense of glory and wonder rather than of compassion and love. It is interesting to notice that there are no inde-pendent poems on these subjects until the fifteenth century, when changes in spiritual tone and literary style made them more appropriate.

But the two more human joys, the Annunciation and the Nativity, fitted well with the emotional emphasis of the meditative tradition, and were therefore treated less mechanically in the poems on the five joys, and were also made the subject of separate poems. Indeed, it is in some ways only surprising that there are not more poems on these two subjects before the end of the fourteenth century.

The history of this private devotion has been traced by Wilmart,[1] who found much of the earliest evidence for it in England, although a reference to it in the work of Peter Damian shows that the custom was already known in eleventh-century Italy.[2] Amongst early texts in English manuscripts that have affinity with the meditation on the five joys are a prayer used by a nun at Shaftesbury, in which twenty-five *aves* are each linked to an episode in the life of Christ[3] and the antiphon *Gaude Dei genetrix*, consisting solely of salutation and praise.[4] In the fully developed form of the five joys, first found in England in the *Ancrene Wisse*,[5] the two elements of meditation upon the life of Christ and praise of the Virgin are combined in proportions that vary from text to text.

As the emphasis upon significant number suggests, the main texts are in the form of liturgical exercises. They divide, however, into two liturgical kinds: one is the genuine *gaude*, which salutes the Virgin in a manner comparable to the *ave*,[6] and celebrates her in direct address by enumerating the great and joyous events of her life: most of the many Latin hymns on the subject belong to this group. The other kind, which

[1] Op. cit. 326–36. See also G. G. Meersemann, *Der Hymnos Akathistos im Abendland*, ii (Freiburg, Switzerland, 1960), 29–43, and 190–213 for a valuable assembly of Latin texts.

[2] *P.L.* 145, 588. The text, *Gaude Dei genetrix*, here presented as part of a miracle story, appears some decades later in an eleventh-century English *horae*; see note 4 below.

[3] E. Beck, 'A Twelfth-Century Salutation of Our Lady', *Downside Review*, xlii (1924), 185–6.

[4] Meerseman, op. cit. 34–35 and 33–38, for a discussion of it in relation to its background in Greek hymnody, and particularly to the famous *Akathistos* hymn (for a brief, clear account of the latter see E. Wellesz, *Byzantine Music and Hymnography*, Oxford, 1961, 191–7). This antiphon was popularized by a miracle story that was one of the earliest and most invariable elements in the collections (see Southern, loc. cit. 183); cf. note 2 above.

[5] E.E.T.S. 249, 22–24. The devotion of the five joys seems to have continued to be practised by the religious until, in the fifteenth century, it reached many of the laity too, being one of the most recurrent items in books of hours. In the intervening period there are a few signs of both lay and religious use of a prose form: there is a *gaude* text in Anglo-Norman in a fourteenth-century book of hours (MS. Harley 1260) belonging to the Percy family (Wilmart, op. cit. 359), and another of a similar kind in MS. Digby 86 (cf. E. Stengel, *Codex manu scriptus Digby 86*, Halle, 1871, 6–7). Each is linked to the other and to the prayer in later *horae* by an initial rubric, which gives the devotion authority by relating how the Blessed Virgin sent it herself to Maurice bishop of Paris (Maurice de Sully), and adds the promise that the Virgin will appear five days before his death to anyone who repeats it five times daily. Cf. B.M. Add. MS. 46919, 27ᵛ.

[6] Meerseman, op. cit. ii. 33, points out that the Greek form of the angelic salutation χαῖρε was rendered in Latin by *gaude* as well as *ave*.

in Latin is found chiefly in prose prayers and meditations, consists of a greeting and description of the joy balanced by a petition, which in the purest forms is related symmetrically to the joy,[1] the transition being accomplished by phrases such as *per illud indicibile gaudium, pur cele ioie*, and *for þe ioie þat ever is newe*. Sometimes, however, this distinction between the *gaude* and the petitionary prayer was either casually or deliberately ignored. A very fine example of a hybrid form is the early thirteenth-century *Meditationes* of Stephen of Sawley,[2] in which all possible elements of the theme are combined, meditation on the event, *gaude* salutation, and petition.

In the early English lyric the three themes are also often intermingled, but usually in a more disordered and random way. The only early poem that is formally a *gaude* is the translation in MS. Trinity 323 of the well-known Latin hymn, 'Gaude virgo mater Christi, / quae per aurem concepisti', in the version that compresses two joys into each stanza.[3] The result of this compression is that the Latin seems austerely bare and the English preserves its content at the cost of every felicity of style. A curious and perhaps inexplicable detail of this poem is that it renders the repeated *gaude* by *glade us* (give joy to us), a variation that weakens the meaning of the poem.[4]

There are three later poems from the Vernon Manuscript in which a formal structure is also emphasized. In one, 'Have Ioye, Marie, Modur and Maide',[5] a *gaude* salutation is combined with a petition, the six-line stanza being divided into four and two. In the others, 'Marie Modur, wel þe bee'[6] and 'Heil beo þou, Marie: Mylde qwen of hevene!',[7] the structure is entirely petitionary. Therefore these poems again lack space for meditative expansion, although there is one stanza for each joy. The last of the four enumerated, 'Heil beo þou, Marie', is nevertheless agreeable, for the long line of its quatrains allows room for some sweetness of feeling in its eulogistic periphrases for the Virgin. She is 'Qween Corteis and hende', 'Corteis, feir and swete', and 'So Rose in Erber rede'. The poem also contains some distinct petitionary stanzas in which the speaker prays, for instance, for the Virgin's help at the day

---

[1] Often, and particularly in fifteenth-century books of hours, this was further developed into a liturgical exercise by the instruction to say a Pater Noster and Ave at the end of each joy.

[2] Wilmart, op. cit. 339–58.

[3] Brown XIII, 22. The Latin version here translated is that printed by F. J. Mone, *Lateinische Hymnen des Mittelalters* (Freiburg im Breisgau, 1853–5), ii. 162, not that in *A.H.* xxxi. 172, referred to by Brown in his note on p. 181.

[4] It may be that in the early *gaude* poems the absence of the verb 'rejoice' (not recorded in its intransitive sense before Chaucer [*O.E.D.* s.v. rejoice (verb) 5]) proved an obstacle to the translator.

[5] E.E.T.S. 98, 25–26.

[6] Ibid. 133–4.

[7] Ibid. 30–32.

of death, and three stanzas in which the ground of the petition is the compassion of the Virgin. These interrupt the series of the five joys and must be considered at least out of place. But, though this summary may give the impression of a hodge-podge of themes, the poem is in fact far more pleasing than the others so far mentioned, which are better organized, but dull. The poem is unified by a distinctive tone, that of a sustained and tender enthusiasm.

Of the remaining three early poems on the five joys the most unusual is 'Ase y me rod þis ender day',[1] from MS. Harley 2253. It is the purest example in English of a love song to the Virgin, influenced by French conventions, and yet, like the secular Harley lyrics, it has a sweetness and informality remote from the elaborate artifice of the originals:

> wiþ al mi lif y love þat may,
> he[o] is mi solas nyht and day,
> my ioie and eke my beste play
>   ant eke my lovelongynge;
> al þe betere me is þat day
>   þat ich of hire synge.[2]

The description of the five joys that follows the opening stanzas of love-longing is marred by the stylistic weakness of the transition, 'nou y may ȝef y wole / þe fif ioyes mynge'. But, though the style is weak, the thought is coherent, the point being that the joys are here enumerated as a celebration of the Virgin's greatness (in the same way as French poems so often described the saving of Theophilus).[3]

The use of the five joys in this way has the advantage that each stanza can be given solely to meditative description, since no space is taken up by salutation or description. Two other early poems, 'Seinte marie, levedi brist'[4] and 'Levedy, for þare blisse',[5] also have this advantage of spaciousness within the stanza. The first is in a twelve-line stanza, in which the petition is confined to the last three lines, whilst in the second there are only occasional touches of either *gaude* or petition, which perhaps weakens it in form, but again leaves space for a literary development of each joy. With the exception of 'Have Ioye, Marie' and 'Ase y me rod', the poems on the five joys cannot usefully be assessed as love poems to the Virgin: they stand or fall by the extent to which the joys become small but moving units of meditation. In examining the poems from this point of view we shall find that those most worth quoting are the ones in which the poet had most space, and which are nearer to meditation than to liturgical forms.

In terms of meditation the five joys fall into two groups: on the one

[1] Brown XIV, 11.   [2] Ibid. p. 13.
[3] Järnström, op. cit. I. ii. 35–40 (p. 23); vi. 38–44 (pp. 31–32); xli. 45–48 (p. 107), etc.
[4] Brown XIII, 18.   [5] Ibid. 41.

hand the Infancy group—the Annunciation, the Nativity, and sometimes the Epiphany; and on the other hand what might be called the
supernatural group—the Resurrection, the Ascension, and the Assumption. As we have said, the English style of tender meditation was
obviously more suited to the first group than to the second. Nevertheless, all the subjects are to some extent potentially meditative, in that
they would normally evoke a visual image, for they were amongst the
most common iconographic themes, and also they could all stir the
meditator by arousing in him a sympathetic joy. It was therefore
necessary to stress the intense emotion of the Virgin in the scenes
described.

The easiest way of conveying the Virgin's delight at the Resurrection
and of uniting her with the resurrected Christ in a relationship of love
was to use the pious fiction that Christ made the first of His Resurrection
appearances to His mother. In an Anglo-Norman poem on the five joys,
which is copied in all the great manuscripts of Anglo-Norman verse, the
fourth joy is thus described:

> Ma dame apres la passiun mult parfutes lee
> Quant vous veitis vostre fiz de mort releve,
> Entre vos deus braz le aviez embraze;
> Pur le duz amour de luy de mei eyez pite.[1]

The common sources for this idea in the earlier Middle Ages were the
Legenda aurea,[2] and the *Meditationes vitæ Christi*,[3] where a solemn and
loving reunion is beautifully related. Nevertheless, the absence of this
appearance in the gospels led to some hesitation in the use of the theme:
both Jacob of Voragine and Ludolf the Carthusian, in the *Vita Jesu
Christi*, point out that it is no more than a reasonable and fitting belief:

> Dignum namque erat, ut Matrem prae ceteris visitaret, et Resurrectione
> sua prius laetificaret, quae prae ceteris plus dilexit, ejus amoris desiderio
> plus afficiebatur, plus de ejus morte doluit, plus dolore afflicta ejus Resur-
> rectionem exspectavit.[4]

It was not until the Appearance to Mary had been given apparent
authority in the much-copied and highly esteemed *Revelations* of

---

[1] This poem, usually copied as part of 'Ave, sainte Marie, mere au Creatur' (Sonet
145), occurs in MSS. B.M. Add. 46919 (*olim* Phillips 8336), Digby 86, Lambeth 522,
etc. P. Meyer, 'Notice du MS. Bodley 57', *Romania*, xxxv (1906), 574, prints the first
three joys. The above quotation of the fourth is taken from MS. B.M. Add. 46919, 54ᵛ.
The same passage is repeated on f. 118ᵛ.

[2] *The Golden Legend*, i. 96.   [3] Trans. Ragusa and Green, 359–60.

[4] *Vita Jesu Christi*, ed. L. M. Rigollot (Paris, 1878), iv. 180–1. 'Truly it was fitting
that He should appear to His mother before all others, and first give joy to her by His
Resurrection: she who loved Him more than the others, who was filled with a greater
longing for His love, who grieved more deeply at His death, and, afflicted with sorrow,
more ardently awaited the Resurrection.' Pourrat, op. cit. ii, 485–8, gives a brief account
of this work.

St. Bridget[1] that it was fairly commonly represented in art, although it perhaps appears in England as early as the late twelfth-century Psalter of St. Louis.[2]

It is remarkable that none of the early English poems on the five joys refers overtly to this scene, though the poems that stress the Virgin's joyful demeanour on Easter morning may perhaps hint at it, or would certainly recall this scene to anybody who knew of it from another source. In general, however, English poets eschewed the apocryphal in their treatment of the joys (only Lydgate, who uses a great deal of legendary material in his poem on the fifteen joys, also describes this scene), and their discretion necessarily led to a description of the Resurrection that was impersonal and unmoving. Only the author of 'Seinte marie, levedi brist' writes feelingly on this subject, and his success springs from the simple but effective device of leading into the joy by a traditional description of the Virgin's earlier grief:

> Seinte marie, quene in londe,
> godes moder ant godes sonde,
> þat te sculde ben so wo
> iewes heden þi sone an honde—
> iudas sold im hem to honde—
> on þe rode heo gonnen him slo.
> þe þridde dai he ros to live;
> levedi, ofte were þou bliþe
> ac never so þou were þo.
> levedi, for þen ilke siþe
> þat tou were of þi sone bliþe,
> al mi sunnes þou do me fro.[3]

In contrast to the Resurrection, where the difficulty lay in the fact that it was only in legendary tradition that the Virgin and Christ were united in one scene, the Ascension presented no problem. The same poem, 'Seinte marie, levedi brist', describes it as follows:

> In muchele blisse þat tou were
> þo þinne swete sone ibere
> iseie him into hevene sten.[4]

[1] Bk. vi, ch. 94, *Revelationes sanctae Brigittae*, olim a Card. Turrecremata recognitae et a Consalvo Duranto notis illustratae, II (Rome, 1628), 162.

[2] B. Blumenkranz, *Juden und Judentum in der mittelalterlichen Kunst* (Stuttgart, 1963), 76–77: it remains a possibility, however, that the Appearance there represented is to Mary Magdalene, though this is also rare in early western iconography. For later English examples see Anderson, op. cit. 126 and pl. 14 (fifteenth-century Flemish glass at Fairford) and G. McN. Rushforth, *Medieval Christian Imagery* (Oxford, 1936), 255 (stained glass at Malvern). A list of continental representations dating from the fourteenth century onwards is given by Louis Réau, *Iconographie de l'art chrétien*, ii. 2 (Paris, 1957), 556. É. Mâle, *L'Art religieux du xiiie siècle en France*, 227, suggests that this subject was included in the carving of the Resurrection appearances at Notre-Dame.

[3] Brown XIII, p. 28. *Sonde*: messenger.   [4] Ibid.

A solid orthodox tradition enabled the poet to put his stress on the Virgin's delighted beholding of her Son's ascent into heaven. The belief that the Virgin was present at the Ascension was common in the patristic period,[1] and in Syrian art from the sixth century onwards she is shown present amongst the apostles.[2] In the early Middle Ages, when the iconographic convention of representing the ascending Christ only by His feet, as they disappear above,[3] was preferred to the forms where He strides up into the heavens or ascends sitting majestically surrounded by a mandorla and a host of worshipping angels,[4] the emphasis of the composition was necessarily not on Christ, but rather on the Virgin, as she stood in the middle of the apostles, sometimes standing slightly higher, and immediately beneath the ascending feet.[5] The stylization of the paintings requires that the Virgin shall appear as a solemn witness rather than a rejoicing mother, but both art and poems agree in stressing the act of seeing.

The only joy which was not Christocentric was the Assumption, and in terms of meditation it is therefore different, in that the meditator does not share the Virgin's rejoicing but himself rejoices for her. The actual ascent, of which the angels were imagined to say 'Quae est ista, quae progreditur quasi aurora consurgens, pulchra ut luna, electa ut sol, terribilis ut castrorum acies ordinata?'[6] (Cant. vi. 9), obviously required a splendour and dignity of treatment to be found only in Renaissance art. In art contemporary with the early lyrics it is the Coronation rather than the Ascent that is shown, and in the lyrics both Assumption and Coronation are mentioned most often in combination. In so far as the lyrics succeed in suggesting the emotional quality of the fifth joy, they achieve it in two ways. The one is by remembering the eternal reunion between Mother and Son:

[1] It was also believed that she was present at Pentecost, and in sets of the fifteen joys, such as the *Meditationes* of Stephen of Sawley (Wilmart, loc. cit. 354–6) or a Latin hymn from MS. Arundel 248 (*A.H.* xxxi. 185), the Coming of the Holy Ghost is the fourteenth joy.

[2] É. Mâle, *L'Art religieux du xiie siècle en France* (Paris, 1953), 89 and fig. 75.

[3] On this see M. Schapiro, 'The Image of the Disappearing Christ', *Gazette des beaux arts*, xxiii (1943), 135–52.

[4] For the iconography of the Ascension see Mâle, and Réau, op. cit., and for more detailed studies H. Schrade, 'Zur Ikonographie der Himmelfahrt Christi', *Vorträge der Bibliothek Warburg* (1927–8), 66–190, and H. Gutberlet, *Die Himmelfahrt Christi in der bildenden Kunst* (Strassburg, 1934).

[5] Examples of this type of composition may be seen in the late twelfth-century psalter, MS. Hunterian Mus. 229 (E. G. Millar, *English Illuminated Manuscripts from the xth to the xiiith Century*, Paris and Brussels, 1926, pl. 61); *Queen Mary's Psalter*, ed. cit., pl. 291; *Peterborough Psalter* (as one of the five joys), ed. M. R. James (Roxburghe Club, 1921), pl. 7. In the *Holkham Bible Picture Book*, (ed. W. O. Hassall, London, 1954), pl. 38, though the whole Christ is seen in the cloud above, the Virgin is prominent in the forefront of the apostles below.

[6] 'Who is she that comes forth like the rising dawn, beautiful as the moon, superb as the sun, and terrible as a well-ordered battle-line?'

> þe fifte ioie is feirest in wede
> þo þou in-to hevene trede
> to him þat was of þe iborn.[1]

The other is by an often implicit contrast between Mary's corporeal
Assumption and the reflections on the horror and indignity of decay in
the grave, which was so recurrent a theme of the death lyric. In 'Ase y
me rod þis ender day', for instance, there is stress on the reunion of soul
and body:

> þe fifte ioie of þat wymman,
> when hire body to hevene cam
> þe soule to þe body nam
> ase hit wes woned to bene.[2]

The point of these lines is undoubtedly the glorious exception to the
universal but unnatural severance of body and soul, the deeply horrific
separation which was so often and so pointedly stressed in the Body and
Soul poems.[3] Recognition of this kind of association does not, of course,
diminish the flatness of style in this poem, but a sentiment rooted in
powerful associations can better survive undistinguished expression
than a trivial one, and it is on account of the evocative force of the content that this verse, and indeed so much medieval poetry, successfully
touch the imagination and emotions.

The Annunciation and the Nativity are invariably the first two of the
early joys of the Virgin, and in the English tradition the Epiphany is
sometimes the third, the Ascension being then omitted: this group
occurs in 'Ase y me rod þis ender day', the Anglo-Norman poem already
quoted,[4] and in the passage inserted in one of the manuscripts of
the *Cursor mundi*.[5] There can be no doubt that a brief reference to the
Annunciation would often recall, not the bare narrative of Luke, but the
apocryphal stories of Mary's life, her upbringing in the Temple, her
vow of virginity, her humility, and her reading of Isaiah's prophetic
text at the moment that the angel appeared. The most relevant of the
associative material, however, is the traditional emphasis on Mary's
consent to the Incarnation. The most famous expression of this idea
is in the fourth sermon of St. Bernard on the text *Missus est*, where he
movingly and dramatically apostrophizes the Virgin not to refuse the
salvation of mankind:

Exspectamus et nos, o Domina, verbum miserationis, quos miserabiliter pre-
mit sententia damnationis. Et ecce offertur tibi pretium salutis nostrae; statim

---

[1] Brown XIII, 18, p. 29.

[2] Brown XIV, 11, p. 14.

[3] In the *Legenda aurea*, the necessity for the flesh of Christ's mother to be free from
the otherwise universal fate of 'putrefaction and worms' is cited as an argument for the
Assumption (*The Golden Legend*, iv. 244).

[4] See above, p. 138.   [5] Brown XIV, 31.

liberabimur si consentis . . . O Domina, responde verbum, quod terra, quod inferi, quod exspectant et superi. Ipse quoque omnium Rex et Dominus quantum concupivit decorem tuum, tantum desiderat et responsionis assensum: in qua nimirum proposuit salvare mundum.[1]

This dependence of salvation on the Virgin is expressed in an incomplete poem on the Annunciation in John of Grimestone's preaching-book:

> In blissid time were þu borne
> Oure saveour þu bere,
> Al þis werde it were forlorne
> Ne were þat þu ne were.[2]

In narrative form, however, the idea is expressed implicitly by emphasis upon the Virgin's acceptance of the angel's message. Whereas in the patristic tradition the stress was upon the Virgin's humble and prudent distrust of the angel—in contrast to Eve's self-indulgent consent to Satan's tempting—in the Middle Ages the stress was on the Virgin's instant and loving co-operation in the work of Redemption. In 'Seinte marie, levedi brist' the poet directly celebrates the Virgin's humility and obedience:

> Godes word ful wel þou cnewe;
> ful mildeliche þer-to þou bewe
> ant saidest so it mote be,—
> þi þonc was studevast ant trewe.[3]

But the convention of one joy to one stanza normally gives very little scope for conveying the dramatic importance of the scene, and it is only in an independent poem on the subject, such as the translation of the *Angelus ad virginem*,[4] that the importance of the Virgin's reply can be reflected in its length. This poem, 'Gabriel, fram evene-king',[5] survives with other Latin hymns and translations in a learned manuscript, MS. Arundel 248, and despite the fact that it follows the complicated stanza form of the original—it was set to the same music—the English is successful, and, though less dignified than the Latin, far more agreeably natural:

> Wan þe maiden understud
> and þangles wordes herde,
> mildeliche with milde mud
> to þangle hie andswerde:

---

[1] *P.L.* 183, 83. 'And we also, O queen, wretches oppressed by the sentence of damnation, await your word of compassion. And behold the price of our salvation is offered to you; if you agree to it we shall be immediately set free . . . O queen, speak the word for which earth, hell and heaven are waiting. The king himself also, He, the lord of all things, wishes for your assent as much as He desired your beauty: for truly by this word He intends to redeem the world.'

[2] f. 23[v]. *Index*, 1061.

[3] Brown XIII, 18, p. 27.

[4] *A.H.* viii. 51.

[5] Brown XIII, 44.

'hur lordes þeumaiden iwis
ics am, þat her a-boven is.
anenttis me,
fulfurthed be
þi sawe;
þat ics, sithen his wil is,
maiden, withhuten lawe
of moder, have þe blis.'[1]

In this stanza, in particular, the suggestion of humility and grateful joy is far more becoming than is the stiffer formality of the Latin.

The only other early and long Annunciation poem is 'Nu þis fules singet', written in honour of one of the Virgin's joys, as the initial rubric loosely indicates: *Exemplum de beata virgine et gaudiis eius*. It is unusual in that it paraphrases only the Virgin's question and not her consent, though the ballad-like style of the central narrative suggests that what is omitted is not therefore necessarily unimportant. In this poem there are touches of French conventions, though these are subordinated to the English informality of style and the English rhythms of the long-line quatrains:

Nu þis fules singet hand maket hure blisse
and þat gres up þringet and leved þe ris;
of on ic wille singen þat is makeles,
þe king of halle kinges to moder he hire ches.[2]

In its vivacity and lightness of tone the poem conveys personal delight, not, of course, that of the Virgin in her Son, but that of the speaker in the Virgin. It is a love poem to the Virgin, and, as in 'Ase y me rod', the joy is narrated to celebrate her glory.

The treatment of the Nativity in early poetry is at first sight surprising, for in the lyrics on the five joys the handling of it is extremely doctrinal and unmeditative, and no separate poems on the Nativity survive before those in John of Grimestone's preaching-book. The newness of the subject is perhaps there indicated in the fact that, although this is an alphabetical preaching-book, the poems are not copied under a heading of the Nativity, but are included in some preliminary material or under the heading of the Passion.[3] Yet by 1375, when these lyrics were copied, devotion to the Christ-Child had for a long time been an important element in medieval spirituality, and the Nativity had been the subject of many Latin meditations.[4]

The spiritual history of the Nativity runs parallel to that of the

---

[1] Brown XIII, pp. 75–76. For the musical setting see Harrison, op. cit. 155.
[2] Brown XIII, 31, p. 55.   [3] ff. 3ᵛ–6ʳ; 120ʳ⁻ᵛ.
[4] A useful history of the development of the devotion to the Christ-Child is given in the *Dictionnaire de la spiritualité* s.v. *Enfance de Jésus*, iv (Paris, 1959), 652–82.

Passion. The Fathers, as we have already said, were more concerned in their Christmas sermons with the doctrine of the Incarnation than with contemplation and delight in the Christ-Child, and, when pointedly aware of the historical baby, they were usually moved not by quasi-maternal tenderness, but by a deep sense of marvel, which expressed itself in paradoxes such as the much-repeated *Verbum infans*,[1] the Word that could not speak. But, as with the Passion and the cult of the Virgin, there were in the patristic period elements that were to influence the new devotion of the Middle Ages: there were, for instance, in the East, the hymns of St. Ephraem,[2] which show sensitivity to the charms of childhood and maternal love; in Rome, relics such as the boards pre-served from the sixth century onwards in S. Maria Maggiore, which were believed to be those of the manger;[3] and throughout the Church the detailed narratives of the Nativity in the apocryphal gospels, which, contrary to the doctrine that the Virgin gave birth to Christ without the pains of labour, described the work of the midwives and the washing of the Christ-Child, and also established for all time the picturesque presence of the ox and the ass.[4]

St. Bernard's devotion to Christ in His humanity included a love for the Christ-Child, and in his Christmas sermons there are many touching descriptions of the Nativity. In the thought of St. Bernard it is clear that meditation on the Christ-Child will find evidence of love in the divine acceptance of the limitations of childhood, and in the uncom-fortable and lowly circumstances of His birth,[5] revealed in a manner only less striking than in the Crucifixion. St. Bernard, therefore, whilst on the one hand moved like the Fathers by the glorious paradox of the Christ-Child, on the other likes to emphasize the possibility of love for the infant Christ—for no one can fear a baby[6]—and in a famous passage, which has been said to anticipate the Ignatian 'composition' of a scene, he recalls the particularly hard circumstances in which Christ chose to be born, the cold, the dark, the poor clothes, the manger.[7] He imagines too the Virgin's tender care for the Child, and the Child in return smiling

---

[1] e.g. Augustine, *Sermo* cxc, *In natale domini*, vii, *P.L.* 38, 1008, '. . . Infans enim dicitur, quod non possit fari, id est loqui. Ergo et infans et verbum est'.

[2] See p. 116, footnote 2.

[3] K. Young, *Officium pastorum* (Transactions of the Wisconsin Academy of Sciences, Arts and Letters, xvii, pt. i, 1912), 336–7.

[4] M. R. James, *The Apocryphal New Testament*, 46–47 and 74.

[5] *In Epiphania Domini*, i. 2, *P.L.* 183, 143, 'Quanto enim minorem se fecit in humani-tate, tanto majorem exhibuit in bonitate; et quanto pro me vilior, tanto mihi charior est'. Quoted by P. Pourrat, *La spiritualité chrétienne*, ii (Paris, 1951), 33, footnote 3, and see pp. 64–68 for an account of St. Bernard's devotion to the Christ-Child. See also J. C. Didier, 'La Dévotion à l'humanité du Christ dans la spiritualité de saint Bernard', *La vie spirituelle*, xxiv (1930), 7.

[6] *In nativitate*, i. 3, *P.L.* 183, 116. Cf. Pourrat, op. cit. 67.

[7] *In nativitate*, iii. 1–2, *P.L.* 183, 123. Cf. Didier, op. cit. 11.

up into His mother's face, a recurrent detail for which a source has been suggested in Virgil's 'messianic' eclogue, but which seems to have been a *topos* with various uses, such as the striking passage in Tertullian where the Holy Innocents smile at the slayer with his knife.[1]

It is, however, in Aelred's *Letter to his Sister*, as we said earlier, that there first occurs the kind of meditation in which the meditator actually imagines himself present in the scene. For this involvement the Nativity obviously gave more opportunity than the Crucifixion, for, whereas in the latter the meditator could only gaze on the Cross, in the Nativity he could take part, meekly helping the midwives, or reverently touching or holding the Christ-Child.[2] Amongst the many coincidences between medieval meditations and the visions of the mystics is the fact that all the great women saints of Germany and Italy, St. Gertrude, St. Mechthild, St. Angela of Foligno, etc., are said in their Lives to have been given the privilege of holding the Christ-Child.[3] Devotion to the Christ-Child was also one of the elements of Cistercian spirituality that particularly influenced St. Francis, and the Christmas crib, which so delighted him,[4] became through Franciscan influence a common property of churches throughout western Europe.

In Anglo-Latin poetry of the late twelfth and thirteenth centuries can be found both the 'witty' style and that of simple meditation. In the poem to the Virgin by Walter Wimborne, already mentioned, a large part consists of variations and statements of the well-known paradoxes and of doctrinal rhetoric, but it also contains a passage in which the author imagines himself remaining behind, after the Magi have gone, to watch the tender interchanges between Mother and Child:

> Magi revisere si velint patriam,
> vadant verumtamen per viam aliam;
> ego cum parvulo moram hic faciam,
> Joseph et virgini devotus serviam.
>
> .   .   .   .   .   .
>
> Ad sua redeant illi celeriter,
> Herodem fugiant, qui furit fortiter;
> ego remaneo visurus qualiter
> jocatur filius ad matrem dulciter.[5]

---

[1] *Apologeticus*, viii, *P.L.* 1, 313.

[2] 'Amplectere dulce illud praesepium. Vincat verecundiam amor, timorem depellat affectus, ut sacratissimis pedibus figas labia . . .', *P.L.* 32, 1466.

[3] *Dictionnaire de la spiritualité*, loc. cit. 662.

[4] Pourrat, op. cit. 253. For Bonaventura's description see Young, op. cit. II, 430.

[5] *Latin Poems attributed to Walter Mapes*, 196. 'If the wise men wish to return to their country they shall go by another way: But I tarry with the little child and devoutly serve Joseph and the Virgin. . . They quickly return to their own country, fleeing from Herod who rages furiously: but I remain in order to see how the child sweetly plays with His mother.' For the ascription to Walter Wimborne see p. 131, footnote 6

Slightly later, in the very fine poem, the *Philomena* by John Pecham, the Franciscan Archbishop of Canterbury, Prime, the first hour of the meditation, is devoted to the Nativity, and its treatment shows both the meditative convention and also the medieval feeling for poverty:

> Plorans ergo clamitat:
> dic, fons pietatis,
> Quis te pannis induit
> nostrae paupertatis?
> Tibi quis consuluit
> sic te dare gratis,
> Nisi zelus vehemens,
> ardor caritatis.
>
> . . . . .
>
> Felix, qui tunc temporis
> matri singulari
> Potuisset precibus
> ita famulari,
> Ut in die sineret
> semel osculari
> Suum dulcem parvulum
> eique iocari.
>
> O quam dulce balneum
> ei praeparassem,
> O quam libens umeris
> aquam adportassem,
> Præsto matri virgini
> semper ministrassem
> Pauperisque parvuli
> pannules lavassem.[1]

This meditation leads to a description of how the pious mind stirred by these reflections thirsts for poverty, plain food, and poor clothes.

It would have seemed a most reasonable guess that if the authors of Latin poetry chose, despite the difficulties of their linguistic medium,

above. For the meditative approach cf. the adaptation of the *Stabat mater* printed by H. T. Henry, 'The two Stabats', *American Catholic Quarterly Review*, xxviii (1903), 68–89, 291–309, in which the meditator pleads with the Virgin, 'Fac me parvum rapere'. For a parallel in the *laude* of Jacopone da Todi, see P. Hilarin Felder de Lucerne, 'La Madone dans les poésies de Jacopone de Todi', *Études franciscaines* xi (1904), 262–3.

[1] *A.H.* l. 604–5. 'Weeping she [the nightingale] repeatedly cries aloud: O fountain of mercy, tell me who clothed you in the rags of our poverty: What else but violent love and ardent charity thus counselled you to give yourself freely. Happy he who at that time could attend the incomparable mother entreating her to be allowed once in a day to kiss her sweet child and fondle Him. How pleasant a bath I would have prepared for Him, and how willingly would I have carried the water on my shoulders; I would always have been at hand ministering to the Virgin Mother and I would have washed the tiny rags of the baby born so poor.'

to suggest the poverty, helplessness, and sweetness of the Christ-Child
and the loving-kindness of His mother, that the vernacular poets of the
thirteenth century, writing in homely English, would also have provided meditations on the Nativity, deliberately exploiting its emotional
potentialities. For in women especially, but in men also, there was
obviously natural affection for a baby, which could, like other kinds of
love, be extended to include the Christ-Child; and in emotional associations the scene of a mother with her child in a cradle was more likely
to recall the familiar, and to thrive from this likeness, than any other
gospel incident. Yet, not only did writers ignore the subject, but also in
the poems on the five joys where the Nativity had to be described the
treatment is exceptionally formal and dogmatic: in 'Seinte marie,
levedi brist', as we have already seen, the joy is defined by a rare use of
paradox,[1] and the rest of the stanza is devoted to the Virgin's conquest
of the Devil; and in 'Levedy, for þare blisse' the joy is similarly expressed in a paradox, though a flaccid one, and the doctrinal point of the
painlessness of the birth is made:

> Moder, bliþe were þu þo
>   hwanne þu iseye heoven-king
> Of þe ibore wiþ-ute wo
>   þat scop þe and alle þing.[2]

It is the latter point that is emphasized again both in 'Have Ioye, Marie',
and in the insertion in the *Cursor mundi* with the much used analogy
of the sun shining through glass, 'Als sun schines thoru þe glas / Swa ert
þu, leved[i], wemles'.[3] From these typical examples it can be seen that
the subject of the second joy was usually taken as an opportunity to
reiterate the doctrine of the perpetual virginity of Mary rather than for
meditation on the Mother and Child.

The space of at least a hundred years between the beginning of
devotion to the Christ-Child and the appearance of this devotion in
vernacular poetry is very interesting evidence for the strength of the
Passion meditation with its roots in theology. The Passion meditation
deriving, as we have emphasized, from the doctrine of the Redemption
and its implications concerning the relationship of love between God and
man, transcended the pattern of the liturgical seasons: being the very
heart of theology and devotion it could self-evidently not be confined to
Good Friday. The Nativity, however, clearly remained a seasonal
celebration. Meditation upon Christ in His humanity is a recurrent
theme in the work of St. Bernard, but, whereas a Passion meditation may
arise at any point, the capital passages for his devotion to the Christ-
Child occur only in the sermons for the Nativity. Moreover, with the

---

[1] See above, p. 132.   [2] Brown XIII, p. 66.
[3] Brown XIV, p. 45.

exception of one meditation in the Anselmian collection, now identified as the work of Aelred,[1] the Latin meditative sources on which writers of the lyric drew are not concerned with the Nativity. The Nativity poems in John of Grimestone's preaching-book ought therefore, perhaps, to be seen as an example of the non-doctrinal spread of meditation, which was typical of the later period of medieval literature.

Surprise at the absence of devotional poetry on the Nativity does not involve an implicit expectation of a dominant cult of the Christ-Child of the kind which developed only in the spirituality of the Counter-Reformation.[2] For, whilst most Counter-Reformation devotions have their antecedents in the Middle Ages, there seems to have been a far greater difference in intensity between the Berullian emphasis on the Christ-Child and that of popular medieval devotion than there was, for instance, between the seventeenth-century cult of the Sacred Heart and that of the fifteenth century. The surprise is limited to the fact that a minor current of Latin devotion, which was particularly appropriate to expression in the English vernacular, was for a considerable time neglected, without even some turn of phrase or small detail to hint at its existence.

It seems likely that the new attention to the subject of the Nativity round about the middle of the fourteenth century was stimulated by the mystery plays, in which the Nativity became detached from its liturgical season, and in which the relevant human sentiments were thoroughly explored. Between early meditative poetry and visual representation there was a relationship of mutual influence and of common dependence upon Latin authority. With the subject of the Passion, art could supply details too numerous to set out in a brief meditative poem, and in realistic emphasis on pain it was even more emphatic. But medieval art far more quickly passed from stylization in its Passion scenes than it did in its Nativities, and, although the severely hierarchic representations of the Virgin and Child[3] do not seem to have continued after the early thirteenth century, Nativity scenes remained highly stylized: the Child, small, swathed, doll-like, lies in the background on the altar-manger, whilst in the forefront lies the Virgin gazing ahead or sideways towards the beholder; the Child is hardly recognizable as a child, and in purely naturalistic terms the Virgin is indifferent to Him. This is obviously congruous with the doctrinal emphasis of the lyrics, but, with its indifference to family tenderness, art here gave no impetus to this sentiment in literature. But, whilst in the

---

[1] *Meditatio* 15, *P.L.* 158, 785–6; Wilmart, op. cit. 196–7.

[2] On this see H. Bremond, *Histoire littéraire du sentiment religieux en France*, iii (Paris, 1921), 201–60.

[3] e.g. the Virgin enthroned from the Shaftesbury Psalter (MS. Lansdowne 383), Millar, op. cit., pl. 33.

mystery plays the Christ-Child must have been as visually uninteresting as He was in art—only the techniques of Renaissance painting could reproduce the idealized physical characteristics of babyhood—yet the attendants upon the Christ-Child, the Virgin who addresses Him with reverence and love (York), the midwives (Chester, Coventry), and the shepherds with their trivial gifts appropriate to a baby, all draw attention to a realistic scene of childhood, unlike the unevocative, doctrinally controlled designs of art.

Whilst meditations on the Passion could, at the cost of incompleteness but without indecorum, exclude recollection of the Divinity, whose glory and impassibility would have broken the mood of grief and suffering, the Nativity could not fittingly be treated in this limited way, and therefore both poetic and visual treatments of it usually in some way demonstrate the nature of the Child. In the later iconographic form, given currency by the *Revelations* of St. Bridget, the Christ-Child lies in the centre, physically babyish but surrounded by divine rays, and the Virgin kneels in reverence to Him, herself supplying the gravity inevitably missing in the Child.[1] Likewise, there is no lyric which does not include some divine title, some doctrinal reference, or, as most commonly, look forward to the Crucifixion. The Nativity in its poverty and lack of worldly comforts may already foreshadow the pain of Crucifixion, or the security of the Christ-Child cared for by its mother may instead point a contrast with the Cross.

All the early poems on the Nativity—there are seven of them—occur in John of Grimestone's preaching-book. Only one of them, 'In Bedlem is a child i-born', approximates to the form we have been chiefly discussing, that of an address to the Virgin, and it is rather a public narrative song, which in its last verse hortatorily urges prayer to the Virgin:

> Prei we alle þat precious þing,
> Of þraldom þat mad us fre—
> Wif, mayden, and moder so ying,
> Was nevere non but sche.[2]

Before this it proceeds in its quick-moving quatrains through the events from the Annunciation to the Massacre of the Innocents, and jumps then to a brief account of the Crucifixion. It is a straightforward narrative of no particular distinction, and perhaps deserves comment for no better reason than that it is grouped with the Nativity poems at the beginning of John of Grimestone's book. In its choice of incident this

[1] For varieties in the iconography of the Nativity, and especially for this form, see Henrik Cornell, *The Iconography of the Nativity of Christ*, Uppsala Universitets Årsskrift, 1924.

[2] Brown XIV, 57, p. 78.

poem has obvious affinities with the mystery cycles, and another poem in carol style belonging to this group,[1] 'Als i lay up-on a nith / I lokede up-on a stronde',[2] seems to be similarly related, in that its subject is the reaction of St. Joseph to Mary being with child. In contrast, however, to the comic treatment of St. Joseph's suspicions in the mystery plays, this poem stresses his trust in the virtue of Mary:

> I troste to hire goodnesse,
> Sche wolde no þing mis-do;
> I wot et wel i-wisse,
> For i have founden et so,
>
> Þat raþere a maiden sulde
> With-outen a man conceyve,
> Þan marie mis-don wolde
> And so Ioseph deceyve.[3]

In tone, therefore, the poem is serious, a little touching and a little dull. In meditative structure it is a dramatic dialogue between the meditator and St. Joseph, set within the *chanson d'aventure* convention. This framework, more familiar from secular poetry,[4] enables the poet to evade the sharp, personal immediacy of openings such as 'Wenne hic soe on rode idon', and yet still to retain the first-person narrative of a partici-pator in the scene described. In terms of strict meditation the formal fiction of the dream opening prevents an immediate identification of the 'I' of the poem with the reader, and this is probably the reason for its use in this early carol-style poem (and in many later carols), for the carol as a song is obviously public poetry, and the slight emotional distancing is decorous and appropriate in poetry not intended for private devotion.

The third poem in this group, also set within the *chanson d'aventure*

---

[1] I describe the three poems in this group, Brown XIV, 56, 57, and 58, as being in carol style. Only one of them, no. 56, is technically a carol in that it alone has a refrain. But the three are otherwise so alike, being identical in their quatrain form and very close in style, that it seems unreasonable to make a radical distinction between them. A refrain that is not part of the stanza form is anyway so detachable that it would be rash to infer much from its absence, or perhaps even from its presence (cf. R. H. Robbins, 'Middle English Carols as Processional Hymns', *Studies in Philology*, lvi, 1959, p. 576, footnote 71). For a general discussion of carol style see Appendix B.

[2] Brown XIV, 58.

[3] Ibid. p. 79. The dramatic exploration of St. Joseph's distrust of Mary has its origins in the work of the eastern Fathers and in Byzantine hymns; see A. S. Cook, 'A remote analogue to the miracle play', *J.E.G.Ph.* iv (1902), 421–51, and Wellesz, op. cit. 357. It was resumed in the mystery plays where the character of Joseph was partly assimilated to the aged cuckold of the fabliau tradition. In contrast to this, and perhaps as a deliberate counter to it, an unnaturalistic but doctrinally edifying interpretation of Matt. i. 19, appears in sermons and works such as the *Speculum humanae salvationis*, ch. vii, 12–50, ed. Lutz and Perdrizet, i. 16.

[4] Helen Sandison, *The Chanson d'Aventure in Middle English* (Bryn Mawr College Monographs, 1913).

convention, is 'Als i lay vp-on a nith / Alone in my longging'.[1] Unlike the other, the dreamer here does not take part in the scene but over-hears a dialogue cast in lullaby form:

> Als i lay up-on a nith
> Alone in my longging,
> Me þouthe i sau a wonder sith,
> A maiden child rokking.
>
> þe maiden wolde with-outen song
> Hire child o slepe bringge;
> þe child þouthte sche de[de] him wrong,
> And bad his moder sengge.[2]

The lullaby is in fact the predominant form of the Nativity poem, and it is able to draw directly on the homely and familiar, for both the form and the words, 'lull', 'lullay', 'lullaby', lowly and onomatopoeic in origin, seem only to have entered literature and the written language with the Nativity poems. There is, however, a difficulty here in that the medieval conception of a lullaby cannot be defined from outside the Nativity poems themselves, as traditional homely lullabies survive only from many centuries later.[3] The next two verses of 'Als i lay up-on a nith', however, make plain that the medieval definition was fuller than that now given in the *O.E.D.*, 'a soothing refrain':

> 'Sing nou, moder,' seide þat child,
> 'Wat me sal be-falle
> Here after wan i cum to eld—
> So don modres alle.
>
> Ich a moder treuly
> þat kan hire credel kepe
> Is wone to lullen lovely
> And singgen hire child o slepe.'[4]

The first stanza here quoted suggests that the subject-matter of a lullaby was often a prophecy of the baby's future (presumably a romantic promise of great and happy achievements). This characteristic of the lullaby is important, because in the religious adaptation it would fit so well with the traditional linking of the Nativity with the Crucifixion. It

[1] Brown xiv, 56.   [2] Ibid. pp. 70–71.

[3] I. and P. Opie, *Oxford Dictionary of Nursery Rhymes* (Oxford, 1951), 18–19, cite Brown xiv, 28 and 65, as the earliest lullabies in English. They refer, however, to a passage in Trevisa's translation of the *De proprietatibus rerum* of Bartholomew de Glanville, describing how nurses sing lullabies to their children. To this reference may be added the scene in the Coventry play of the Massacre of the Innocents, in which the mothers sing the carol lullaby, 'O sisters too' to their children (E.E.T.S. E.s. 87, 29 and 32); cf. below p. 386. F. E. Budd, *A Book of Lullabies 1300–1900* (London, 1930), has assembled an interesting collection of literary lullabies.

[4] Brown xiv, 56, p. 71. *Lovely*: lovingly.

was not, however, believed that the Virgin foreknew the Crucifixion, but that the Christ-Child in the omniscience of His Divinity was aware of all the future. In this poem, therefore, the Virgin can only relate Christ's story up to the time of the Adoration of the Shepherds, and it is the Child, by a poetic fiction able to speak, who relates the future to His mother, and thus Himself provides the material for His lullaby. The colloquial tenderness is to be seen more in the Virgin's speeches than in the Child's, which are severely didactic, though there is one quite charming interchange, when the Child replies to His mother, who has said that she would like to see her son a King:

> 'Do wey, moder,' seide þat swete,
> 'þerfor kam i nouth.'[1]

The full sweetness of the lullaby tradition, however, is most clearly seen in the lament of the Virgin beginning 'Ihesu, swete sone dere'.[2] Though sweet, it is not repellently sentimental: the Virgin's lament is exceptional in its tone of solemn, yet touching, grief, and the pathos in the first two verses is most discreetly developed:

> Ihesu, swete sone dere,
> In porful bed þu list nou here,
> And þat me grevet sore;
> For þi credel is als a bere,
> Ox and asse ben þi fere—
> Wepen may i þer fore.
>
> Ihesu, swete, be nout wroth,
> I have neither clut ne cloth
> þe inne for to folde;
> I ne have but a clut of a lappe,
> þerfore ley þi feet to my pappe,
> And kep þe fro þe colde.[3]

The subsequent two verses are more doctrinal, and, whilst the change of tone is not jarring, but on the contrary quite agreeably acerbic, it is possible that the first two verses originally formed an independent poem, for they are copied without the continuation in MS. Harley 7322.[4]

---

[1] Brown XIV, p. 74. *Do wey*: stop. The illustrations of this phrase in the *O.E.D.* s.v. *do*, 53, suggest that the tone of the phrase (invariably in the imperative) is often colloquial.

[2] Brown XIV, 75. For the argument that the first stanza of this poem as printed by Brown, 'Ler to loven, as i love þe', should be read as an independent poem see below, pp. 156–7.

[3] Ibid. p. 91. *Bere*: bier; *fere*: companions; *clut of a lappe*: a rag from a garment; the reading in MS. Harley 7322, 'For ich nabbe cloute ne lappe' (where *lappe* means 'a piece of cloth') probably gives better sense.   [4] E.E.T.S. 15, 225.

The poverty of the Christ-Child had once before been expressed in a fragment of English verse, based on an ingenious paradoxical passage attributed to St. Bernard:

> Of one stable was is halle
> is kenestol on occe stalle
> sente marie is burnes alle.[1]

The simplicity of the English perhaps obscures the intellectual ingenuity of the content, later to be made quite plain in Southwell's more poised version in 'New Prince, New Pompe':

> This stable is a Prince's courte,
> The cribb His chaire of State.[2]

But the treatment of poverty in 'Ihesu swete sone dere' is quite different, in that it is not wittily and paradoxically manipulated, but developed directly through actions of compassion which recall the content and tone of the *Meditationes* ascribed to Bonaventura, where it is related how the Virgin had nothing but her head-covering in which to wrap the Child when He was born, and how the ox and the ass, recognizing their Master, kept Him from the cold by their warm breath.[3] There is the same kind of idea here, though the intimacy of Mother and Child is emphasized by the Virgin herself warming the Child's feet by holding Him to her breast. The sentimentality of the description is made solemn by its symbolic anticipation of the Crucifixion: the mood of the poem is that of St. Francis's description of how Lady Poverty followed Christ everywhere in His life, even to the Cross, so that as He had nothing to cover Him when He was born, so He had nothing to cover Him when He died.[4] The two ideas are united in the poem, partly by the imperceptible movement by which the Virgin passes from description of present to that of future suffering, partly by the image 'For þi credel is als a bere', a simile recalling the common representation in art of the manger as an altar. Balance and antithesis between a hero's birth and death were a favourite device in the Middle Ages (for instance the marvellous birth and death of Arthur), and in the religious tradition many parallels between the circumstances of the Nativity and those of the Crucifixion were found, with typical medieval ingenuity. But in this

---

[1] Brown XIII, p. 192. *Burnes*: knights. The Latin fragment does not seem to come from St. Bernard and I have not been able to identify its source. The same Latin original appears to be paraphrased in *lauda* lxv, ll. 21–26, of Jacopone da Todi, ed. Caramella, 144. Cf. Owst, *Literature and the Pulpit*, 501–2.

[2] *Complete Poems*, ed. A. B. Grosart (London, 1872), 108.

[3] Trans. Ragusa and Green, 33–34.

[4] *Sacrum commercium, The Converse of Francis and his sons with Holy Poverty* (Temple Classics, 1904), 6–10, 44–48.

poem the adjoining of birth and death is not exploited to quicken intellectual understanding, but only to make an extension of grief, and in the last two verses the grave resignation of the Virgin, so unlike the later treatment of her, is particularly decorous and moving. If they are an addition, they are a felicitous one.

All the Nativity poems so far discussed have been concerned primarily with the Virgin, or in them at least she has shared the position of chief protagonist with the Christ-Child. The last three, however, like the Passion lyrics, concentrate on the relationship between the Christ-Child and the meditator, and in terms of meditative structure, therefore, they do not belong with Marian poetry, but rather with the Passion lyric: in John of Grimestone's book one is included with the preliminary lyrics to the Virgin, but the other two occur in the Passion section. It would have been possible here to follow the manuscript classification, but in feeling and content they are so closely related to the previous poems that they may all be fittingly examined in an epilogue to this chapter. Indeed the two lullabies spoken by the meditator cast light on the role of the Virgin in poems such as 'Ihesu, swete sone dere'. It is clear that in this, as in some of the later Crucifixion complaints of the Blessed Virgin—particularly those in the mystery plays—the grief of the Virgin is expressed partly in order that the audience may identify themselves with her: they are to feel the same compassion for the sufferings of Christ as did she. Elsewhere, therefore, the same thoughts and sentiment may be attributed to the meditator, and indeed the likeness between the two kinds of lullaby is so close that it is possible nowadays to disagree on whether the speaker is the Virgin or Everyman. In his *Index* Carleton Brown classified each of the two poems we are about to discuss[1] as 'A lullaby of the B.V.',[2] but expressions of sinfulness and penitence make them appropriate only to a meditator.

In these poems, in accordance with the kind of meditation expounded by Aelred, the speaker imagines himself present in the scene, singing a lullaby to the Christ-Child as he kneels by the manger, or perhaps, unhistorically, by a cradle, for in 'Als i lay' the Virgin rocks the Child. The lullaby in carol form, 'Lullay, lullay, litel child, / Þu þat were so sterne & wild',[3] is excellent in its expression of coherent doctrine modulated by variations in tone: the meditator, representing mankind, laments that he has lost his inheritance through the stealing of an apple, and recognizes that it is for this that the baby weeps, and that were it not for this weeping and the pains which the Child must endure, he would be damned. But interwoven with this doctrinal recognition of the

---

[1] Brown XIV, 65 and 59.   [2] Nos. 2023 and 2024.
[3] Brown XIV, 59. In his note to this poem, Brown describes it as being different from 'others of its type in that it is addressed to Christ by a penitent' (p. 265).

Christ-Child is the *lullay* motif, with the recurrent use of the word *litel*,
so sentimentally evocative:

> Lullay for wo, þu litel þing,
> þu litel barun, þu litel king;
> Mankindde is cause of þi murning,
> þat þu hast loved so ȝore.[1]

Through this combination, the poem, despite its lightness of metre,
expresses with poise a dignified penitence and sober tenderness.

The second and much finer meditator's lullaby, 'Lullay, lullay litel
child, child reste þe a þrowe',[2] is unusual in that it seems to be modelled
upon another lullaby expressing the themes of transience, 'Lollai,
lollai, litil child, whi wepistou so sore?'.[3] Both poems are in the same
stanza form, have the same refrain in the penultimate line, are highly
wrought, and in tone are at once harsh and sad. The earlier, according
to the evidence of the manuscripts, is the secular lullaby:[4] it is very
ingenious, in that in it the themes of death are skilfully adapted to a new
form. The child is told in his lullaby how in the world he is not 'a
pilgrim bot an uncuþe gist', how his foot is already set on Fortune's
wheel, and the speaker invites him when he is older to consider 'Whan
þou commist, whan þou art, and what ssal com of þe',[5] until in the end
'deth ssal com wiþ a blast ute of a wel dim horre'.[6] The fact, however,
that the poem is cast as a lullaby leads to a tone very different from that
of the death lyrics, for the content is not delivered as a well-merited
warning to the sinner, but as a sad statement to the child of man's
condition in the world. In its mingling of grim warning with melancholy
it anticipates the idiosyncratic style of some of the Vernon lyrics.

The meditator's lullaby is an equally accomplished poem, and in its
power and confidence equally stands out from the class of poems to

---

[1] Ibid. p. 80.

[2] Ibid. 65. Brown considered this a poem spoken by the Virgin and in this he is
followed by G. Kane, *Middle English Literature* (London, 1951), 143. But the aside
in l. 9, 'ȝef love were in myn herte', and the confession of guilt in the last verse make it
certain that the speaker cannot be the Blessed Virgin. Indeed, the whole tone, which is
set by a profoundly moved, but controlled, understanding of pain, transience, and sin,
would be inappropriate to the Virgin with her innocent and dedicated life.

[3] Brown xiv, 28.

[4] MS. Harley 913 probably preceded MS. Adv. 18. 7. 21 by at least fifty years,
and this order at first sight seems to be confirmed by the literary impression given by
the poems, namely that the Nativity lullaby was modelled upon the secular. It remains
possible, however, that the Nativity lullaby was composed earlier than the date
of the manuscript that preserves it, and the speculation that the poems are companion
pieces by the same author is attractive.

[5] The disagreeable implications of these questions recall the repulsive detail of the
De contemptu mundi of Innocent III, i, ii, iv, and viii, ed. Maccarrone, 8–15.

[6] l. 27, p. 36. *Wel dim horre*: a very dark corner. The meaning of *blast* (gust? clap?)
is uncertain: it seems too early for this to be a reference to death's trumpet (see below,
p. 354).

which it belongs. Its affinity to the secular lullaby is shown in its emphasis upon the general hardships of the 'weping dale' into which the Christ-Child is born, the cold, the hunger, and above all the poverty:

> Child, it is a weping dale þat þu art comen inne,
> þi pore clutes it proven wel, þi bed mad in þe binne;
> Cold and hunger þu must þolen as þu were geten in senne,
> And after dey3en on þe tre for love of al man-kenne.
>   Lullay, lullay litel child, no wonder þou þu care,
>   þu art comen amonges hem þat þi det3 sulen 3are.[1]

That the Christ-Child should suffer the hardships of the world has, of course, a peculiar irony and poignancy, and these general sufferings lead by a natural train of thought to the specific pains of the Passion, which seem already reflected in the Child's crying: 'Lullay, lullay, litel child, wel mauth þu cri3e, / For þan þi bodi is bleyk and blak, sone after sal ben dri3e.'[2] This poem, like its companion, excels in a new-found poise of style, so that great generalizations, that had earlier carried conviction through content rather than expression, in this poem are expressed in a style which conveys the impressiveness of the true, the perceptive, and the inevitable. The skill of the poem is particularly clear in the last two lines, with their deliberate superficial disjointedness:

> Lullay, lullay litel child, softe slep and faste,
> In sorwe endet everi love but þin at þe laste.[3]

The last of the Nativity poems to be discussed is a unique example of a complaint of the Christ-Child. It consists of a single stanza only:

> Ler to loven as y love þe;
> On al my limes þu mith i-se
> Hou sore þei quaken for colde;
> For þe i suffre michil wo.
> Love me, swete, an no-mo—
> To þe i take and holde.[4]

This stanza is usually thought to be the first verse of the Marian lullaby, 'Ihesu, swete sone dere', which would in that case become a dialogue. The evidence of the manuscripts is open to varying interpretations. In MS. Harley 7322 the verses appear to be linked together by a scrap of Latin narrative: 'Et Regina mater sua nichil habuit unde posset eum induere; ideo dixit sibi'.[5] But it is quite possible that the copyist did not

---

[1] Brown XIV, p. 83. *Binne*: manger; *care*: lament; *3are*: prepare.

[2] ll. 11–12, p. 83.   [3] Brown XIV, p. 84.

[4] Ibid. 75 (first stanza only).

[5] E.E.T.S. 15, 255. 'And the queen His mother had nothing with which she might clothe Him; and therefore she said to him' (*sibi* presumably used for *eo* here).

intend the *et* to have a strong connective force. In John of Grimestone's book 'Ler to loven' is transcribed separately in a second column, and—very significantly—it is preceded by the Latin tag, associated with Crucifixion complaints, 'Aspice mortalis, pro te data ostia talis', translated into French and English underneath, and it is followed by another complaint poem, 'Water and blod for þe i swete':[1] this position of the stanza is amended by a line of dots. Here it is obvious that the copyist understood this verse to be an independent complaint, whilst a reviser corrected what he took to be a mistake. It seems most likely that two distinct poems became associated or joined through the frequency of the dialogue form and the chance identity of metre. But the mingling of didacticism with pathos in the stanza, as in the meditator's lullabies, and a demand for love founded on suffering, as in the Crucifixion complaints, make it plain that this is an appeal from the Christ-Child to man. As the opening verse of a dialogue it loses much of its force, whereas as an address to man it is an excellent and interesting example of an appeal to the meditator from the Nativity scene, very comparable in style and tone with many Crucifixion complaints.

The restraint in all these poems in emphasizing the humanity of the Christ-Child is very marked: they reflect the caution of the preaching-books[2] which, when they provide material for the Nativity, do so doctrinally under the heading of the Three Comings, and without any enthusiasm for a childish or maternal scene. It is in accordance with this tradition that, as we have said before, John of Grimestone has no section for the Nativity. The maternity of the Blessed Virgin is therefore rarely stressed in the English lyric, and the supreme instance of it, her suckling of the Christ-Child, is mentioned only with reference to her intercession in heaven, although the descriptions in Latin poetry and prose and the lactation miracles might well have led to a meditative emphasis upon it.

The lyrics to the Virgin form a much less homogeneous group than do those on the Passion and death. Whereas the latter are direct off-shoots of one central tradition, the Marian lyrics spring from a number of miscellaneous influences. Unlike the other lyrics, for which there are scarcely any parallels in other languages, the lyrics to the Virgin are an offshoot of a western European tradition which, though it was part of English spirituality from an early date, did not become firmly rooted in English literature until the fifteenth century. In these lyrics there is a strong attempt to adapt the formal, ornate style of poetry in Latin and

---

[1] Brown XIV, 76.
[2] A convenient list of friars' preaching books is provided by H. G. Pfander, 'The Medieval Friars and Some Alphabetical Reference-Books for Sermons', *Medium Aevum*, iii (1934), 19–29.

other vernaculars to the English personal, meditative style, and to describe a personal and private relationship rather than to make a beautiful object. But there was here no simple literary-devotional situation, as for the Passion and death lyrics, and whilst the problems do not show themselves in lack of quality, they do in lack of quantity.

V

The Lyrics of Richard Rolle and the Mystical School

ALL the poetry so far discussed is unmystical. It may vary in the degree of literary formality, but the emotion expressed in it has no affinities with the fervour and elevation of the mystics; in kind it is the emotion familiar to every man and woman. Even in such works as Þe Wohunge of oure Laverd, which was probably intended for the same kind of religious audience as the *Ancrene Wisse*, the emotion expressed is ordinary emotion highly intensified, rather than the quite different kind of love described by Richard Rolle and his followers. The poetical antecedents of Rolle's mystical poetry do not lie in vernacular literature, but they may be found in some of the great Anglo-Latin mystical poetry of the twelfth century, the *Philomena* of John of Howden and the *Dulcis Iesu memoria*. It is only from Rolle's time onwards that there is a continuous tradition of devotional-mystical writing in English—whether in prose or verse—and there can be no doubt that it was the work of Rolle and the outstanding authority of his name that restored the prestige of English as a medium for contemplative writing: evidence for this can be seen in the fact that vernacular works of Rolle were in due course to appear in the devotional *collectiones* of monks, who had hitherto copied for themselves only Latin treatises, the works of St. Bernard, St. Bonaventura, etc.[1]

Rolle's works fall roughly into two kinds. Firstly, those that are records of and reflections upon his own mystical experience.[2] These, according to established tradition, were written in Latin (his contemporary, Julian of Norwich, was unique in writing in English, even though a woman: the visions of women mystics on the Continent were usually set down in Latin, normally by means of a cleric who acted as

[1] For references to monastic collections, containing works in the vernacular, see W. A. Pantin, 'English Monks before the Suppression of the Monasteries', *Dublin Review*, cci (1937), 250–70.
[2] The most recent account of Rolle as a mystic is that of D. Knowles, *The English Mystical Tradition* (London, 1961), 48–66.

their secretary). Secondly, the works intended for the instruction of women recluses. These, reviving the tradition begun by the *Ancrene Wisse*, were written in English.[1] The important distinction between the two is that, whilst the principle of the *Incendium amoris* and the *Melos amoris* is a faithful exposition of his own thought and experience, that of the *Ego dormio* and *The Form of Living* is a faithful adherence to the teaching appropriate to beginners in the spiritual life. Nevertheless Rolle's works of instruction were inevitably influenced by his thought as a contemplative, and the lyrics[2] too reflect this double current of the individualistic and the traditional.

In his own thought as a contemplative Rolle was scarcely concerned with meditation on the Passion; but, as an adviser to women in religious orders he taught meditation on the Passion according to the method that had become traditional.

Like the author of the *Cloud of Unknowing*[3] and Walter Hilton,[4] Rolle accepts meditation on the Passion as a grade in the Christian life. It is higher than the active life with the works of mercy and the basic assent of faith, but inferior to the life of mystical contemplation: in the thought of the writers on meditation it represents a midway stage on the ladder of the good life. It would seem that there is here the formulation of a theory designed to explain common practice. The harmonious scheme of St. Bernard, with its place for meditation on the Passion, cannot have convinced an exponent of the negative form of mysticism inherited from the Pseudo-Dionysius, and the fact, therefore, that the author of the *Cloud of Unknowing* praises it as yielding '. . . moche good, moche helpe, moche profite, and moche grace'[5] shows both how strong was the tradition, and at the same time how it could be detached from the theological roots whence it had originally sprung. Even in the thought of Rolle, Passion meditation was less integral than in that of St. Bernard. It is clear from a comparison of the *Incendium amoris* with the English Epistles that Rolle considered Passion meditation to be a

---

[1] Women would not normally know Latin (see the introduction to *The Chastising of God's Children*, ed. J. Bazire and E. Colledge, Oxford, 1957, 71).

[2] It is assumed in the following pages that the lyrics embodied in Rolle's prose works are by Rolle and that some of those in MS. C.U.L. Dd. v. 64 are there rightly ascribed to him. A fuller discussion of this is given in Appendix C.

[3] E.E.T.S. 218, 31–32, 47, and 54. The author distinguishes a kind of life that is partly that of Martha (with the works of mercy) and partly that of Mary (contemplation). The contemplation appropriate to the intermediate stage between the active and contemplative life is chiefly meditation on the Passion.

[4] *The Scale of Perfection*, ed. and trans. E. Underhill (London, 1948), 9, 79–81, and 358–60. Hilton recognizes meditation on the Passion as a grade of the contemplative life. For Hilton in general see Knowles, op. cit. 100–18, and Helen Gardner, 'Walter Hilton and the Mystical Tradition in England', *Essays and Studies*, xxii (1936), 103–27.

[5] E.E.T.S. 218, 39.

stage which the learner in contemplation made use of and then left behind: he therefore does not describe it in his own experience but recommends it to beginners. But to St. Bernard meditation on the Passion was, as it were, a gateway to contemplation of the Divinity, and was therefore never left behind, but constantly passed through on every mystical journey, and returned to for refreshment after the arduous experience of a more direct communion.

This difference between Rolle and St. Bernard, which may have been influenced by the popular practice of meditation on the Passion as an end in itself, is not, however, the only important one: the other is that Rolle and St. Bernard had quite different conceptions of love. St. Bernard's theory of love obviously had affinities with St. Augustine's, in that they both expound a love which has been called physical or natural, as against ecstatic, and both see no unbridgeable divide between true self-interest and the love of God. To St. Bernard, as we have already seen, love of oneself is an emotion which may be taught and guided to grow into the love of God: to St. Augustine the two were even closer, for God is the *summum bonum*, and the man who loves false objects is self-deceived concerning his own best interests, for, as the well-known quotation so perfectly expresses it, 'Thou has made us for Thyself, and our hearts are restless till they rest in Thee'. To the mystical school to which Rolle belongs, however, there can never be this tranquil relationship between love of God and man's natural desires, for love is violent, compelling, and unreasonable, and it does not make use of man's natural faculties, but possesses him by thwarting and overcoming them. A short passage from the translation of the *Philomena* on the *ecce sto* theme may be quoted as an illustration of the difference in tone:

> Kyng of love, strengest of alle,
> I here þe at my dore calle.
> þou fyndest it loke wiþ barres stronge,
> But brek hem up, stond not to longe.[1]

Here man cannot open the door himself, and love must break in by violence. In the Passion meditations of Rolle it is this kind of love that is described, and therefore, whilst they make use of many traditional details, the tone and style are quite different from those of popular meditative poetry and, originally at least, they were probably intended for a religious, not a lay, audience.

---

[1] E.E.T.S. 158, 22 (ll. 827–30). This is an exceptionally fine paraphrase translation of a twelfth-century Latin poem, the *Philomena* of John of Howden. The Latin text is edited by C. Blume (Leipzig, 1930). The value of the E.E.T.S. edition is diminished by the fact that the editor did not at that time recognize the English poem as a translation. Later, however, she made a comparison between the two: Charlotte d'Evelyn, 'Meditations on the Life and Passion of Christ', *Essays and Studies in Honor of Carleton Brown* (New York, 1940), 79–90.

Of this small group of mystical poems four are exclusively Passion meditations: 'My keyng þat water grette', from the *Ego dormio*; 'My trewest tresowre', one of the set of poems in MS. Dd. v. 64 attributed by the copyist to Rolle; and 'Ihesu þat hast me dere i-boght' and 'Crist makiþ to man a fair present', which both belong to the same 'school' of lyric writing, although there is no suggestion that either is by Rolle. The *Ego dormio* is a text written for an anchoress or nun: like Aelred, but unlike the author of the *Ancrene Wisse*, Rolle both advises meditation on the Passion and also provides a meditation. It may well be a sign of the strength of the previous lyric tradition that the meditation is in verse. Rolle advises the reader of his treatise 'Thynk oft on his passyon', and then follows the poem with the title *Meditacio de passione Christi*.[1] Like fifteenth-century Passion meditations, which we shall later be discussing, the poem does not confine itself to the Crucifixion, but traces the Passion sequence from the time of the scourging. For the Crucifixion itself Rolle borrows the description of the *Candet nudatum pectus*, but, despite such familiar details, the tone of the poem is quite unfamiliar. This is partly on account of the direct statements of mystical desire, 'þi face when may I see', 'Al my desyre þou ert', or—with the image of burning, characteristic of Rolle's writing—'Kyndel me fire within'. But there is a change of tone, not only in the expressions of love and in the petitions associated with the Passion meditation, but also in the description of the Passion itself. In this Rolle exploits the device of paradox, whereby in a description of Christ's human suffering He is ostentatiously given a title referring to His divinity, as in 'And nayled on þe rode tre, þe bryght aungels brede', or in a much finer passage:

> A wonder it es to se, wha sa understude,
> How God of mageste was dyand on þe rude.[2]

In the ordinary Passion meditation this kind of splendour would have daunted the familiar tenderness which the writer wished to evoke, for only ecstatic love is the fitting response to it. The magnitude of the object is then matched by the intensity and excitement of the meditator's feeling. This type of paradox is often repeated in the mystical poetry, for example, the brief statement 'Lyf was slayne' and its immediate derivation is probably the *Philomena*, in which such paradoxes abound, and it is noteworthy that the English poems succeed in achieving the same dignity—though necessarily not the same succinctness—as the Latin. There is admittedly nothing in Rolle's poems which has the monumental and complex quality of Langland's 'The lorde of lyf and of liȝte tho leyed his eyen togideres',[3] which shows the imaginative

---

[1] *English Writings of Richard Rolle*, ed. Hope Emily Allen (Oxford, 1931), 67–69.
[2] Ed. cit. 68.
[3] B Text xviii, 59, *Piers Plowman*, ed. Skeat, 524.

range of a great poet. Nevertheless, in Rolle's work the potential magnificence of the form is never obscured by feebleness of expression.

In contrast to this poem, 'My trewest tresowre' is more nearly a meditation in the non-ecstatic style.[1] Though each stanza in it begins with a periphrasis for Christ, 'My well of my wele', 'My dere-worthly derlyng', 'My salve of my sare', they do not with dazzling directness refer to Christ's divinity, but have rather the tone of loving endearments, which accentuate the painfulness of the detailed description of the Passion sequence. Emotive adverbs and phrases, 'sa saryful in syght' or 'sa dolefully', with their reference to personal sorrow, lead up to the description of Christ as a knight, 'My fender of my fose', whose shield at the time of evensong is unlaced from His body. In general, the feeling of this poem is not unlike that of some of the Harley lyrics, but the absence of secular adornments, and the crowded and emotional descriptions, almost over-emphasized by alliteration, give a much stronger effect of urgency and distress.

'Ihesu þat hast me dere i-boght' is a poem deriving from the vernacular translation of the *Philomena* of John of Howden. This is a long Latin poem, of which the author himself composed a French version for Eleanor, wife of Henry III, to whom he was chaplain,[2] but which was not translated into English until about a hundred years later. In this very fine work, which is sustained throughout its length with an inexhaustible vigour and power of variation, a meditation on the Passion is given form by two images: firstly by the allegory that it was the force of love that compelled Christ at every stage, and secondly by the invocation to love to wound the heart of the meditator by writing upon it the details of the Passion. Neither of these ideas, however, is used in the short poem we are discussing. Although the theme of the compelling power of love is, as we shall see, a fairly common one in the mystical lyrics, the constructor of 'Ihesu þat hast me dere i-boght' has avoided it, and in the verses he has borrowed, in which love is implored to write on the meditator's heart, he has substituted for love the name Ihesu, as in the following:

> Ihesu, write in my hert depe
> how þat þou began to wepe
> þo þy bak was to þe rode bent,
> With rogget nayll þy handes rent.[3]

This poem is obviously a short popularization of the original. The translation of the *Philomena*, 2,254 lines in length, would clearly be too unwieldy for the normal type of meditation: whereas it survives only

---

[1] Brown XIV, 79.
[2] L. W. Stone, 'Jean de Howden, poète anglo-normand du xiii⁰ siècle', *Romania*, lxix (1946–7), 496–519.   [3] Brown XIV, 91, p. 116.

in one manuscript, 'Ihesu þat hast me dere i-boght' survives in a large
number and remained popular into the fifteenth century. In some
manuscripts it is preceded by a rubric prescribing it as a devotional
exercise. There is no evidence that the compiler of the poem knew the
Latin original: his method was to take and shorten a consecutive passage
of Passion meditation, and then to append to this some of the striking
protestations of love from various other parts of the poem. There is
hardly a line that he has not transferred word for word from his source.
Nevertheless, the effect of the poem is not one of patchwork. If the
translation of the *Philomena* had not survived, it would have been impossible to detect the author's method of working. Indeed, the progress
of thought in the poem develops with far greater logical steadiness than
in many other lyrics. It is difficult, however, to praise the poem except in
terms of selection and organization: for, whilst all of it is fine and many
individual passages such as the following are moving,

> Whan I am lowe for þy love
> Þan am I moste at myn above,
> Fastynge is feest, murnynge is blis,
> For þy love povert is richesse.

this is the achievement of the translator of the *Philomena*, an excellent
poet, whose work is nowadays unfortunately far too little known.

Though the author of 'Ihesu þat hast me dere i-boght' simplifies his
poem by excluding from it the ideas of love writing upon the heart and
of the compelling power of love, both of these are in fact found recurrently in the mystical lyrics, and respectively form the dominating
themes of two poems, 'Ihesu, god sone' and 'My keyng þat water grette'.
The image of love writing a meditation of the Passion on the heart of the
meditator is a slightly conceited variation of the recurring mystical idea
of the wound of love, the spiritual wound that Rolle so often prayed to
be granted, particularly in his Passion meditations, 'In lufe þow
wownde my thoght', or 'Wounde my hert with-in'. The text on which it
was based, *amore langueo*, was one much quoted by the exponents of
ecstatic love, such as Richard of St. Victor. Though this text could be
taken to refer to the *languor* of love, 'I languysch for lufe', more often it
was taken to refer to the wound of love, the Latin rendering of the
Septuagint reading, *amore vulnerata sum*, being preferred to the Vulgate
text.[1] The wound of love was an experience often referred to by early
medieval mystics, though it did not receive a full technical definition
until the work of the Spanish mystics in the fifteenth century: however,
as Rousselot has so well pointed out, the use of this image is always a

---

[1] The Septuagint reading at Cant. ii. 5, was: '. . . ὅτι τετρωμένη ἀγάπης ἐγώ'.

certain sign of the ecstatic view of love, and the violence of its effect.[1] In literary usage, however, it is possible to trace the associations of this image rather more precisely.

In origins it is, of course, not an invention of the mystical writers, but rather the classical idea of Cupid shooting with his bow (in contrast, for instance, to the Old Testament, where arrows are symbols of God's anger). The classical theme passed as a commonplace into Provençal and French poetry, either in the form of brief references—of which there is an imitation in one of the secular Harley lyrics[2]—or as an extended narrative description of the kind occurring in the *Roman de la rose*.[3] In the shape of classical allusion it appears in 'Ihesu þat hast me dere i-boght':

> Lat now love his bow bende
> And love arowes to my hert send,
> þat hit mow percen to þe roote,
> For suche woundes shold be my bote.[4]

The image is already in the Latin ('Telum arcus Amoris iaciat'),[5] but the English translation manipulates it a little to make the likeness to the love-shot of Cupid more explicit. Commonly, however, in Passion poetry the allusion to Cupid's wound of love is more undefined, for the wound is said to be inflicted, not by a bow and arrow, but by the spear that pierced Christ's side. The development of this idea can be traced in religious thought. In the Song of Songs there was a second reference to the wound of love, this time applied to the bridegroom, not the bride: 'Vulnerasti cor meum, soror mea . . .' (iv. 9),[6] and inevitably this wound was associated both with that of *amore langueo* and with the wound in Christ's side, which, in that it touched His heart, was in itself a supreme symbol of Christ's love: the physical wound thus became an allegory of Christ's love for man. It was, however, possible to transfer this wound from Christ to man. The Pauline prayer to be crucified with Christ led quite easily to a full reversal, whereby the details of Christ's sufferings might be attributed to man as a symbol of his love for Christ. An example of this kind of reversal occurs in Gilbert of Hoyland's continuation St. Bernard's of *Sermons on the Song of Songs*: 'Talia in me utinam multiplicet [Christus] vulnera a planta pedis usque ad verticem,

---

[1] P. Rousselot, *Pour l'histoire du problème de l'amour au moyen âge* (Münster, 1908). The analysis of ecstatic love, pp. 56–87, is very illuminating.

[2] Brown XIII, 86, 'Ant love is to myn herte gon wiþ one spere so kene.' There is already a confusion here between the secular and religious traditions, for the spear is of Christian origin.

[3] Ed. E. Langlois, S.A.T.F. ii. (Paris, 1920), 47–51.

[4] Brown XIV, 91, p. 118.

[5] Verse 620, ed. cit. 51. 'Let the bow of Love shoot forth an arrow.'

[6] 'Thou hast wounded my heart, my sister . . .'. The A.V. has 'ravished'.

ut non sit in me sanitas. Mala enim sanitas, ubi vulnera vacant quae Christi pius infligit aspectus.'[1] This image could therefore be used very appropriately in Passion meditations as an expression of love for Christ in His Passion.

In a poem from the Cambridge Manuscript, 'Ihesu, god sone', the image is used very skilfully. The second stanza begins with a plea for the wound of love:

> Ihesu, þe mayden sone, þat wyth þi blode me boght,
> Thyrl my sawule wyth þi spere, þat mykel luf in men hase wroght.[2]

This plea is repeated in the fourth stanza, 'Wounde my hert with-in', and, with a variation in the fifth, 'Rote it in my hert, þe memor of þi pyne'. It is answered in the last section of the poem, in which there is a moving description of the Passion, made evocative by emotive epithets. Unless this relationship is understood, the last four stanzas may seem an ill-fitting appendage. Here, in the way that we have described before, the plea for ecstatic love is matched by an emotionally heightened description of the Passion.

The other theme, that of the compelling power of love, was also characteristic of writers on ecstatic love. Their view of love, that it was by its nature irresistibly violent, became transformed into an allegorical conceit, in which love was imagined to have overcome Christ Himself. This idea was first fully elaborated by Hugh of St. Victor in a short treatise much read in the Middle Ages, the *De laude caritatis*, of which it is the main theme:

> Sed fortassis facilius vincis Deum quam hominem, magis praevalere potes Deo quam homini, quia quo magis beatum, eo magis Deo est debitum a te superari. Hoc optime tu noveras, quae ut facilius vinceres, prius illum superabas; adhuc nos rebelles habuisti, quando illum tibi obedientem de sede paternae majestatis usque ad infirma nostrae mortalitatis suscipienda descendere coegisti. Adduxisti illum vinculis tuis alligatum, adduxisti illum sagittis tuis vulneratum. Amplius ut puderet hominem tibi resistere, cum te videret etiam in Deum triumphasse. Vulnerasti impassibilem, ligasti insuperabilem, traxisti incommutabilem, aeternum fecisti mortalem.[3]

---

[1] *P.L.* 184, 156. 'O that Christ would multiply such wounds in me, from the sole of my foot to the crown of my head, so that nothing in me would be healthy. For health is bad when the wounds are lacking that a devout gazing upon Christ inflicts.'

[2] Brown XIV, 83, p. 99. *Thyrl*: pierce.

[3] *P.L.* 176, 974–5. 'But perhaps it would be easier for you to conquer God than man, to prevail more strongly with God than with man, because the more blessed it is to be overcome the more God was bound to be so overcome. You knew this well and therefore, to have an easy victory, you conquered Him first; when in obedience to yourself you had made Him come down from the throne of His Father's glory to take on the weakness of our mortal state, you still had to deal with us, the rebels. You brought Him, bound with your chains and wounded by your arrows, so that man might be ashamed to resist you any longer when he saw that you had triumphed over God Himself. You

It can be seen from this that the idea of Christ's submission to the omnipotent force of love is a brilliant and paradoxical way of expressing the motive for Christ's sufferings and their extent. Its natural context is therefore a Passion meditation, and it is thus that it is used in the English mystical lyrics. It occurred, for instance, in the poem from the *Ego dormio* that we have already discussed, 'My keyng þat water grette':

> A wonder it es to se, wha sa understude,
> How God of mageste was dyand on þe rude.
> Bot suth þan es it sayde þat lufe ledes þe ryng;
> þat hym sa law hase layde bot lufe it was na thyng.[1]

The last two lines are to be found almost word for word in the last chapter of the *Incendium amoris*: '. . . sed verum dicitur quia amor preit in tripudio, et coream ducit. Quod Christum ita demissum posuit, nihil nisi amor fuit.'[2] The *O.E.D.* shows that by the end of the fourteenth century the phrase 'to lead (or rule) the ring' had acquired the meaning 'to be foremost', but the use of the expression in Latin suggests that in Rolle's time awareness of the metaphor had by no means been suppressed by common usage, and that, with love as the subject, there is an allusion to the God of love 'carolling', as he does in the *Roman de la rose*.[3] The last line, with its statement that it was nothing but love which laid Christ low, is a clear, if slightly clumsy, expression of the domination of love.[4]

In 'My keyng þat water grette' the idea of the omnipotent force of love is a subordinate image in a Passion meditation. It is in the very fine poem, 'Crist makiþ to man a fair present', that a Passion meditation is organized entirely within the framework of this paradox. This lyric, not by Rolle, though succeeding the *Form of Living* in two of its three manuscripts, is more than any other indebted to the tone and style of the *Philomena*. In the opening stanza, as in a large section of the *Philomena*, love is implored to explain the wild incomprehensibility of its actions:

> O Love, love, what hast þou ment?
> Me þinkeþ þat love to wraþþe is went.[5]

The poem then shifts to a direct address to Christ, in which is given a

---

wounded the Impassible, you bound the Invincible, you drew the Unchangeable, you made the Eternal mortal.'

[1] *English Works*, ed. Allen, 68.

[2] Ch. 42, ed. M. Deanesly (Manchester, 1915), 276. 'But it is truly said that love goes first in the dance and leads the ring. It was nothing but love that put Christ thus low.'

[3] Ed. cit. 51.

[4] F. M. Comper, *The Life and Lyrics of Richard Rolle* (London, 1928), 229, footnote 5, erroneously assumes the lines to mean that 'it was hate not love that nailed Christ upon the Cross'.

[5] Brown XIV, 90, p. 113.

saddened description of what love has done, 'þi loveliche hondis love
haþ to-rent', and:

> Þi mylde boones love haþ to-drawe,
> Þe naylis þi feet han al to-gnawe;
> Þe lord of love love haþ now slawe—
> Whane love is strong it haþ no lawe.[1]

In this the violent irrationality of love is most powerfully expressed.
In particular, the skilful syntactical inversion in line 3 and the poised
generalization of line 4 show a style that has risen to the magnificence
and complexity of its subject. After three less effective stanzas, the
poem returns to its initial theme of the questioning of love, and it is in
this passionate questioning that it most clearly catches the tone of the
Philomena, 'O Love, love, what hast þou ment?', 'Love, love, where
schalt þou wone?', 'Love, love, whi doist þou so?'. These apostrophes
may be compared in their vehemence with the opening of many stanzas
in the *Philomena*, such as 'Amor, audi: quis est, quem crucias?' (274) or
'Amor, adhuc audi, quem laceras' (312).[2] Likewise with the paradoxes of
the eighth stanza—

> Love haþ schewid his greet myȝt,
> For love haþ maad of day þe nyȝt;
> Love haþ slawe þe kyng of ryȝt,
> And love haþ endid þe strong fiȝt.

—it echoes the style of the innumerable paradoxes of the *Philomena*,
'Amatorem, Amor, cur proicis?' (271) or 'Vitam mori dum Amor
imperat . . .' (443).[3] The accomplishment of the English is, of course, by
no means diminished by this comparison, and, fine though the English
translation of the *Philomena* is, it might be thought that this short poem
surpasses it in its catching of the impassioned tone of the Latin.

It is interesting to notice that the idea of Christ dominated by love
did not remain restricted to the more sophisticated mystical poetry.
In John of Grimestone's preaching-book the idea is effectively worked
into the form of a complaint:

> Love me brouthe,
> And love me wrouthte,
> Man, to be þi fere.
> Love me fedde,
> And love me ledde,
> And love me lettet here.

---

[1] Ed. cit., p. 113.

[2] Ed. cit. 24 and 27. 'Hear me Love! Who is it whom you torment?'; 'Again, hear
me Love! Whom are you wounding?'.

[3] Ed. cit. 24 and 36. 'Why, Love, do you thrust from you your lover?'; 'While Love
commands Life to die . . .'.

Love me slou,
And love me drou,
And love me leyde on bere.
Love is my pes,
For love i ches,
Man to byȝen dere.

Ne dred þe nouth,
I have þe south,
Boþen day and nith,
to haven þe,
Wel is me,
I have þe wonnen in fith.[1]

The repetition of the word 'love' drives home the idea, though the verses lack the dignity of 'Crist makiþ to man'. The last verse, entirely mediocre in quality, inappropriately reduces the theme by confining it to the plea of a lover-knight. Two other short narrative verses in the same manuscript also make use of the idea: one a fairly perfunctory four lines, 'Love made crist in oure lady to lith',[2] and the other modelled upon it, but with *reuthe* instead of love as the compelling power:[3] this weakened substitution indicates how the original sublime and complex meaning had become lost in popular usage.

Besides the Passion poems there are also a small number of mystical poems that are mixed in content. They are held together by sustained intensity of tone rather than structure, and in them Passion meditation, praise of the beloved, and praise of Love itself are linked together: indeed, it is one of their characteristics that they are as much concerned with the idea of love itself as with the beloved. The two least interesting of these are from the Cambridge Manuscript, 'All vanitese forsake'[4] and 'Thy ioy be ilk a dele',[5] which could be called hortatory love songs, similar to the 'Love-Ron' in their juxtaposition of the vanity of the world with the joy of loving Christ. But in contrast to the sweet reasonableness of the 'Love-Ron', the plea in these poems proceeds solely by appeals to the emotions. They contain many passages that are typical of the best style of Rolle's writing, but there is nothing in them that is not done consistently better in other poems.

Of these others the finest are 'Luf es lyf þat lastes ay' and the lyric with which the *Ego dormio* concludes, 'My sange es in syhting'. 'Luf es lyf' falls into two parts, which on both literary and textual grounds we may assume to have been originally distinct. The first part consists of a discussion of the nature of love, where discursive and sometimes

---

[1] Brown XIV, 66.   [2] Ibid. p. 266.
[3] Inc. 'Reuthe made God on mayden to lithte', f. 119ʳ.
[4] *English Works*, 49–51.   [5] Brown XIV, 86.

homiletic comment is subordinated to a series of definitions, which produce, through taut parallelism, a strong emotional impact:

> Lufe es thoght wyth grete desyre, of a fayre lovyng;
> Lufe I lyken til a fyre, þat sloken may na thyng;
> Lufe us clenses of oure syn, lufe us bote sall bryng;
> Lufe þe keynges hert may wyn, lufe of ioy may syng.
>
> . . . . .
>
> Luf es a lyght byrthen, lufe gladdes ȝong and alde,
> Lufe es with-owten pyne, als lofers hase me talde,
> Lufe es a gastly wynne þat makes men bygge and balde,
> Of luf sal he na thyng tyne, þat hit in hert will halde.[1]

Behind verses such as these there lies a stylistic form common in French secular poetry, which may be illustrated by a famous example, that of the description of love in Reason's speech to the lover in Jean de Meung's continuation of *Le Roman de la rose*:

> Amour ce est pais haïneuse,
> Amour c'est haïne amoureuse;
> C'est leiautez la desleiaus,
> C'est la desleiautez leiaus
> C'est peeur toute asseuree,
> Esperaunce desesperee;
> C'est raison toute forsenanable,
> C'est forsenerie raisnable;
> C'est doux periz a sei neier;
> Griés fais legiers a paumeier;
> C'est Caribdis la perilleuse,
> Desagreable e gracieuse;
> C'est langueur toute santeïve,
> C'est santé toute maladive;
> C'est fain saoule en abondance;
> C'est couveiteuse soufisance.[2]

More immediately close to Rolle's work, however, are the English definitions of love preserved in MS. Digby 86:

> Love is þe softeste þing in herte mai slepe.
> Love is craft, love is goed wiþ kares to kepe.
> Love is les, love is lef, love is longinge.
> Love is fol, love is fast, love is frowringe.
> Love is sellich an þing, wose shal soþ singe.

---

[1] Brown XIV, 84, pp. 102 and 104. *Lovyng*: lover; *bote*: remedy; *gastly wynne*: joy for the spirit; *tyne*: lack.

[2] S.A.T.F. ii. 212–13. This passage with various other examples is referred to by P. Meyer, 'Mélanges de poésie anglo-normande, ix: Une définition de l'amour', *Romania*, iv (1875), 382–4.

> Love is wele, love is wo, love is gleddede
> Love is lif, love is deþ, love mai hous fede.[1]

The similarity of metre suggests that Rolle may have known the poem from which this quotation comes: certainly in style it could have formed a transition between the French manner and that of the mystical poetry. For the French style, with its many Latin analogues, insists primarily upon epigrammatic paradoxes: whereas the English is more concerned with the insistence upon the power of love, conveyed through the accumulation of definitions. In Rolle's poem there are no paradoxes ('Luf es a lyght byrthen' is a later variant, as the absence of internal rhyme shows),[2] and the substance of the poem is not in origin poetical, for it derives from the *Incendium amoris*.[3] But certainly it would not have been given this structural and stylistic form, had it not been for the precedents, remote perhaps, in French, and immediate in English literature.

In this poem there are altogether about twenty definitions of love: it is a fire, it is eternal, it is God's darling, it comforts, it purges of sin, etc. The ultimate sources are of various kinds: the symbol of fire, for instance, is characteristic of Rolle's mystical thought, whilst the idea that 'Lufe us reves þe nyght rest' suggests the conventions of secular poetry. There is, however, one definition in the poem which is particularly important, and which in a sense sums up all the rest. It is the line 'For luf es stalworth as þe dede, luf es hard as hell'. This is a translation of a text from the Song of Songs, 'Fortis est ut mors dilectio, dura ut infernus emulatio', which along with the other text, *amore langueo* (which we have already discussed), was frequently quoted by the great exponents of ecstatic love. In his *De iv gradibus violentae caritatis*, for instance, Richard of St. Victor uses this quotation in his analysis of the fourth (i.e. the highest) degree of love.[4] The *Glossa ordinaria* and other commentaries agreed in taking *aemulatio* to be synonymous with *amor*,[5] thus making it an imaginatively astounding definition of love. Rolle often quoted this text in his English epistles, and in 'Luf es lyf' it comes as a magnificent conclusion to a stanza, which in its first three lines was subdued and didactic in tone:

---

[1] Brown XIII, 53, p. 108. *Craft*: strength (?); *les*: false; *frowringe*: comfort; *sellich*: wonderful.

[2] The reading in MS. Lambeth 853, 'a birþun fyne' (E.E.T.S. 24, 25), preserves the rhyme.

[3] Brown XIII, p. 209, and XIV, p. 270.

[4] Ives, *Épitre à Séverin sur la charité*, Richard de Saint Victor, *Les quatre degrés de la violente charité*, ed. and trans. G. Dumeige (Paris, 1955), 149. The *De iv gradibus violentae caritatis* contains one of the most important expositions of the theory of ecstatic love.

[5] *P.L.* 113, 1165.

For nou lufe þow, I rede, cryste, as I þe tell,
And with aungels take þi stede—þat ioy loke þou noght sell.
In erth þow hate, I rede, all þat þi lufe may fell;
For luf es stalworth as þe dede, luf es hard as hell.[1]

The second part of 'Luf es lyf' begins at line 69 with the opening, 'I sygh and sob bath day and nyght for ane sa fayre of hew': the manuscript evidence suggests that this may originally have been a separate poem,[2] and this is confirmed by the fact that the first line has the ring of an introduction. There follow four verses of love-song for the Christknight, 'þat swete chylde', in general theme resembling some of the Harley lyrics, but more passionate and inwardly orientated. Thereafter praise of Christ the lover is intermingled with ecstatic praise of love itself. In style and tone this part of 'Luf es lyf' resembles the love song (Rolle actually calls it 'A sang of lufe') which concludes the *Ego dormio*, 'My sange es in syhtyng'.[3] This is a pure love song, in that it contains no Passion meditation, nor any didactic warning. Its theme is 'Nou wax I pale and wan for luf of my lemman'. In its compactness, coherence, and sustained intensity, it is perhaps the finest of Rolle's lyrics.

Both 'Luf es lyf' and 'My sange es in syhtyng' include verses expressing the devotion to the Holy Name,[4] and for these to be fully appreciated it is an advantage to know something of the history of this devotion; and this in turn leads naturally into a discussion of the small group of poems in English which have this as their subject.

This devotion, which had its roots in the Old and New Testaments,[5] was to some extent formalized before the end of the patristic period. In Christian thought the Name of Jesus acquired both the sanctity attributed to the divine name in the Old Testament, and the power, deriving from an identity with Himself, which Christ attributes to it in the New Testament. Thus the Name, Jesus, was not thought to be an arbitrary means of identification, but to signify almost in a sacramental manner the Saviour to whom it refers: it was therefore endowed with a high sanctity and with an efficacy deriving from that which it signified. Much of this can be seen in the earliest extended reference, the poem

---

[1] Brown XIV, p. 104. L. 3, 'I advise you to hate everything on earth that may destroy your love'.

[2] A text of the poem in southern dialect occurs in MS. Lambeth 853 (E.E.T.S. 24, 22–31) but with the poem, 'Ihesu god sone, lord of mageste' (Brown XIV, 83), inserted between ll. 68–69. It is a fair inference that three originally distinct poems have here been conflated.

[3] *English Works*, 70–72.

[4] Brown XIV, p. 106; *English Works*, 71.

[5] F. M. Lemoine, 'Le Nom de Jésus dans l'ancient testament', and C. Spicq, 'Le Nom de Jésus dans le nouveau testament', *La vie spirituelle*, lxxxvi (1952), 5–18 and 19–37.

of Paulinus of Nola, *De nomine Jesu*,[1] and in the much later passage from
a sermon of Peter Chrysologus, in which the powers of Christ, the
healing of the sick and the raising of the dead, are attributed to His
Name.[2] In the twelfth century, however, in accordance with the new
forms of spirituality, this idea acquired a fresh emphasis and its devotional implications were explored. The two most important texts of this
period were the fifteenth of St. Bernard's *Sermons on the Song of Songs*[3]
and the still well-known hymn, *Dulcis Iesu memoria*, long thought
to be also by St. Bernard, but shown by Wilmart to be of Yorkshire
Cistercian origin.[4] In both of these the Name is praised, not merely in
objective Biblical terms, but also in terms of the religious experience
of those who meditate upon it. It is honey in the mouth, melody in the
ears, the comforter of the distressed, the hope of the penitent, the
destroyer of vice, a light which heals and restores. Above all it is *dulcis*,
a word repeated over and over again. In medieval spirituality, in fact,
the devotion to the Holy Name becomes a form of devotion to Christ in
His humanity, but, unlike that of the usual meditation, its practice does
not involve a visual image. Its expression in literary terms demands a
use of rhetoric and metaphor which will evoke a sensation of love without the help of the visualization of the object, and therefore the poetry
on this subject, both Latin and English, is characterized by an incanta-
tory repetition of the Name of Jesus—at the beginning of each stanza
or even of each line—exotic and sensuous metaphors, often borrowed
from the Song of Songs, by eloquent variations upon one idea, and by
accumulation rather than by the steady development of a theme.

This devotion seems to have flourished especially in England. In the
twelfth century there were written, not only the *Dulcis Iesu memoria*,
which was to be repeatedly copied in manuscripts,[5] but also striking,
though short, passages in other works, as in *Meditatio* ii of Anselm[6]
(where the Name is lingered upon and praised as the refuge of the justly
fearful), and in the *Philomena* of John of Howden.[7] The devotion also
appeared early in vernacular poetry: the opening of the *Wohunge of oure
Laverd*[8] echoes successfully the *Dulcis Iesu memoria*, and this Latin

---

[1] *P.L.* 61, 740–2. This poem is referred to by A. Cabassut, 'La Dévotion au nom
de Jésus dans l'église d'occident', *La vie spirituelle*, lxxxvi, 46–69, who provides a useful
series of references to works on the subject of the Holy Name. See also M. Meertens,
De Godsvrucht in de Nederlanden, i (Louvain, 1930), 103–11.

[2] *P.L.* 52, 586.

[3] *P.L.* 183, 843–8.

[4] A. Wilmart, *Le 'Jubilus' dit se saint Bernard* (Rome, 1944).

[5] Ibid. 17–24, 29–32.

[6] *P.L.* 158, 724–5. Cabassut, loc. cit. notes that this prayer was copied in many
later books of hours.

[7] *A.H.* l. 29–31.

[8] E.E.T.S. 241, 20.

hymn was echoed again in two Anglo-Norman poems of the thirteenth century,[1] of which one forms part of the *Manuel des pechiez*, though Robert Manning did not include it in the *Handlyng Synne*. In these there first appears the typical English tendency to incorporate into poems on the Holy Name a passage of meditation on the Passion.

The two earliest English poems on the Holy Name are preserved in MS. Harley 2253. The less remarkable of these is that beginning 'Swete Ihesu, king of blisse', which seems to have begun as a short three-stanza poem (the text of MS. Digby 86),[2] and then to have become expanded into the text of the Harley manuscript.[3] The influence of the *Dulcis Iesu memoria* is seen in the opening of each of the fifteen stanzas with the words 'Swete Ihesu', and by turns of phrase in many individual lines, but, like a later poem in the Thornton Manuscript, 'Ihesu Criste, Saynte Marye sonne',[4] it is partly penitential. Whereas the Latin hymn is a poem of pure praise of Christ and His love, with one verse only set in the form of a prayer, the English in both its short and expanded forms is an expression of contrition and prayer for mercy. In other words, it develops one of the minor ideas of the hymn, that of Jesus as *spes penitentibus*, into the controlling idea of the work. It lacks entirely the sustained ecstatic expression which makes the *Dulcis Iesu memoria* so exceptionally fine a poem. The second lyric, 'Ihesu, swete is þe love of þee', is much more striking, and in some ways anticipates by several decades the ecstatic style of Richard Rolle's poetry. After its first two verses, which are again closely dependent upon the Latin, it progresses independently, preserving the spirit, though not the thought and expression, of the original. One of its themes, for instance, is one we have already discussed, that of Christ overpowered by Love: 'Ihesu, þi love was us so fre / þat it fro hevene brouȝte þee', an idea not found in the Latin. Again it has a kind of moving, simple directness, possible only in English:

> Iheus my god, ihesu my kyng,
> þou axist me noon oþir þing,
> But trewe love and herte ȝernyng,
> And love teeris with swete mornyng.[5]

It is, perhaps, not so accomplished or so filled with fine emotional rhetoric as the slightly later poetry of the 'school' of Rolle, and it is

---

[1] On these see H. E. Allen, 'The Mystical Lyrics of the *Manuel des pechiez*', *Romanic Review*, ix (1912), 154–93.

[2] Brown XIII, 50.

[3] *Harley Lyrics*, 51–52.

[4] F. A. Patterson, *The Middle English Penitential Lyric*, 53.

[5] Brown XIV, 89, p. 112 (from MS. Hunterian Mus. V. 8. 15). The Harley text, which is longer and in many of its readings inferior, is printed by Böddeker, *Altenglische Dichtungen*, 198–205.

occasionally feeble, as in the line 'I wole þee love and þat is riȝt': indeed, there is throughout a slight *naïveté* of expression, perhaps indicating the lack of literary precedent, but it is an agreeable early attempt at a poem of ecstatic love.

The devotion to the Holy Name did not receive its fullest expression in vernacular poetry until the work of the fourteenth-century mystics: it is a recurrent theme of the *Scale of Perfection* and a substantial element in the mystical thought of Rolle. Rolle in his *Comment on the Canticles* follows St. Bernard by turning the text, 'Oleum effusum nomen tuum', into a meditation on the Holy Name:

O nomen admirabile. O nomen delectabile. Hoc est nomen super omne nomen. Nomen altissimum, sine quo non operat quis salutem. Hoc est nomen suave et iocundum, humano cordi verum prebens solacium. Est autem Ihesus in mente mea cantus iubileus, in aure mea sonus celicus, in ore meo dulcor mellifluus. Unde non mirum si illud nomen diligam, quod michi in omni angustia prestat solamen. Nescio orare, nescio meditari nisi resonante nomine Ihesu. Non sapio gaudium quod non est Ihesu mixtum. Quocumque fuero, ubicumque sedero, quicquid egero, memoria nominis Ihesu a mente mea non recedit. Posui illud ut signaculum super cor meum, ut signaculum super brachium meum, quia fortis est ut mors dilectio.[1]

This exceptionally fine meditation, of which the above quotation is only a small part, was very popular: in a vernacular translation it circulated independently, and it also forms part of the didactic compilation, *The Pore Caitiff*.

The subject also recurs in Rolle's vernacular works, in the *Form of Living*, where he instructs that 'þis name Jhesu' should be rooted firmly in the heart,[2] and in *The Commandment*, where he says: '. . . forgete noght þis name Jhesu, bot thynk it in þi hert, nyght and day, as þi speciall and þi dere tresowre.'[3] Above all it is to be found in the fine

---

[1] Wilmart, op. cit. 275. The title derives from Cant. i. 2. Amongst the many Biblical texts that could be relevantly quoted by writers on the Holy Name this seems to have been the most popular. Ubertino of Casale, for instance, quotes it three times in his chapter on the Holy Name in the *Arbor vitae*, ii. 2 (edn. of Venice, 1485, fols. ii^v–vi). Rolle's *Oleum effusum* was later translated into the vernacular and survives in a number of manuscripts: it was also incorporated into *The Pore Caitiff*. The following is the translation of the above quotation from the text of MS. Harley 1022: 'A, þat wondurful name, A, þat delytabul name! þis is þo name þat es above al names, name alþer-heghest, with-outen qwilk na man hopes hele. þis name es swete and Ioyful, gyfand sothfast comforth unto mans hert. Sothle þo name of Ihesu es in my mynde Ioyus sang, in my nere hevenly sounde, in my mouth hunyful swetnes. Qwarfor na wondur if I luf þat name þe qwylk gyfs comforth to me in al angwys. I can noght pray, I can noght have mynde, bot sownand þo name of Ihesu; I savour noght Ioy þat with Ihesu es noght mengyd. Qwar-so I be, qwar-so I sit, qwat-so I do, þo mynd of þo name of Ihesu departes noght fra my mynde. I have set it as a takenyng opon my hert, als takenyng apon myn arme: ffor "luf es strange as dede".' C. Horstman, *Yorkshire Writers*, i (London, 1895), 186–7.

[2] *English Writings*, 108.

[3] Ed. cit. 81.

lyric from 'My sange es in syhtyng', where, as we have already seen, the theme of the Holy Name is combined with that of Christ the lover:

> Jhesu, þi lufe is fest, and me to lufe thynk best.
> My hert, when may it brest to come to þe, my rest?
> Jhesu, Jhesu, Jhesu, til þe it es þat I morne
> For my lyfe and my lyvyng. When may I hethen torne?
>
> Jhesu, my dere and mi drewry, delyte ert þou to syng.
> Jhesu, my myrth and melody, when will þow com, my keyng?
> Jhesu, my hele and mi hony, my whart and my comfortyng,
> Jhesu, I covayte for to dy when it es þi payng.[1]

In some medieval verses the authors would seem to be the mechanical servants of rhetorical forms, but here Rolle manipulates them in order to attain a higher degree of passionate intensity. This craftsmanship must be stressed, since a modern reader might easily attribute the obvious poetic superiority merely to a greater degree of personal feeling. There is, of course, no doubt that Rolle is in one sense a romantic poet, in that it is his own experience, passionately apprehended, that is the subject-matter of his poetry. His experience itself, however, has been moulded by the traditional thought of the Church and the traditional literary forms for expressing it; but these literary forms he was able to use exceptionally, since, as his prose style demonstrates even more clearly, he had an ear sensitive to the rhythms of language.

The influence of Rolle can be seen in several later poems on the Holy Name: 'Swete Ihesu, now wol I synge',[2] a long poem, preserved in many later fourteenth- and early fifteenth-century manuscripts, shows in many places the marks of Rolle's thought. It is in part a combination of the two poems already described, but there are many additions. It contains, for instance, Rolle's ideas of fire ('Love-sparkes send þou me') and of melody ('Teche me, lord, þi luf-songe'), and other ideas we have already noticed, such as the wound of love. In it, too, can be seen the tendency, already mentioned, for the Name of Jesus to recall the Passion. In a long passage the chief stages of the Passion are enumerated in direct address, each verse beginning 'Ihesu':

> Ihesu swete, þou hynged on tre,
> Noght for þi gylte bot al for me;
> With synnes I gilte, so wo is me,
> Swete Ihesu, forgyf it me.[3]

The lack of logical arrangement inherent in the kind made such a digression possible, and enables the incoherence to appear, at least to some

---

[1] Ed. cit. 71. *Brest*: break; *drewry*: beloved; *whart*: health.
[2] *Yorkshire Writers*, ii. 9–24.
[3] Op. cit. 13.

extent, deliberately contrived, and proper to the fervour and excited devotion of a lover.

The association of the Holy Name with expressions of penitence continued in poems of the late fourteenth century. One of these, 'Ihesu, þi name honourde myȝt be', is severely penitential in tone, but contains one verse that expresses touchingly the pure devotion to the Holy Name:

> Ihesu, my lufe and my lykynge,
>   for evere more blyste mot þou be.
> Mi lufely lorde, my dere darlynge,
>   ful were me [fayne] myght I þe se.
> Ihesu, my lorde, þou gar me synge
>   a lufely kynge is comen to me;
> My swete swetnes of alkyn thynge,
>   my hope and tryste is al in þe.[1]

The other poem from the Thornton Manuscript, 'Ihesu Criste, Saynte Marye sonne',[2] has been said to fall into two parts, one of penance, the other of devotion. But the transition from one to the other is not abrupt but gradual, so that it cannot be considered the combination of two originally distinct poems. In the second half there is the lingering upon the Name of Jesus, and the metaphorical variations of it, which always form the substance of this kind of poetry; and into it, too, there is incorporated, in weakened form, a verse from the lyric of the *Ego dormio*:

> Ihesu my Ioy and my lovynge,
> Ihesu my comforthe clere,
> Ihesu my godde, Ihesu my kynge,
> Ihesu with-owttene pere.
>
> .   .   .   .   .   .
>
> Ihesu my dere and my drewrye,
> Delyte þou arte to synge;
> Ihesu my myrthe and my melodye:
> In to thi lufe me brynge.[3]

Devotion to the Holy Name, even when blended with penitential themes or with meditation on the Passion, seems to have belonged chiefly to the contemplative, rather than to the active layman, or at least

---

[1] E.E.T.S. 15, 140. Brown xv, 144, prints this poem as a pendent to 'Ihū, Ihū, mercy I cry', which in both manuscripts precedes it. The *Index*, however, gives it a separate entry, and both Patterson, loc. cit. 54 and E.E.T.S. 15, 139–40, present it as an independent poem. The correctness of this is indicated by the style of the first line of this poem and by the finality of the last line of the preceding poem, 'Ihc̄, Amen, Maria, Amen'.

[2] *Yorkshire Writers*, i. 364–5; Patterson, op. cit. 53 and notes p. 190.

[3] Op. cit. 365. The second of these verses is a weakened version of two lines from the poem in the *Ego dormio*, quoted above, p. 176.

to the educated aspirant to contemplation, and not to those with little time for reflection. Nevertheless, like the idea of love's dominion over Christ, it also found expression in more popular poetry. An unpublished poem from John of Grimestone's preaching-book illustrates this:

> Ihesu God is becomen man,
> Ihesu mi love and my lemman.
> Ihesu to Marie cam
> Ihesu for to delivere man.
> Ihesu of Marie was born,
> Ihesu to saven þat was forlorn.
> Ihesu for senne wep allas,
> Ihesu for senne peined was.
> Ihesu mi love stedefast,
> Ihesu to rode was nailed fast.
> Ihesu is herte let undo
> Ihesu to bringen man him to,
> Ihesu wit blode and water cler.
> Ihesu wes man to bringen him ner.
> Ihesu þe devel overcam,
> Ihesu to blisse brouthte man.
> Ihesu sal cumen to demen us,
> Beseke we merci to swete Ihesus.
> Ihesu of senne delivered us alle.
> Ihesu þu bring us in to þin halle,
> Ihesu to wonen wit þe in blisse,
> Ihesu þeroffe þat we ne misse.[1]

To begin each line with the Name, Jesus, is a fairly common device of style in poems on the Holy Name. It occurs, for instance, in one of the verses we have just quoted from the Thornton poem, and in the fourteenth-century translation of the *Philomena* the substance of the passage on the Holy Name in the original is repeated, with the modification that nearly every line begins with the Name.[2] The use of anaphora in this simple Passion poem, however, is particularly striking, in that it is often unsyntactical, and its intrusion into the sentence effectively draws attention to its importance.

With the exception of the two poems from John of Grimestone's preaching-book discussed earlier, and some of the lesser poems on the Holy Name, the poems associated in this chapter form a quite distinct group, their distinctiveness being indicated by both manuscripts and style. They are preserved in manuscripts of contemplative works, and from their style it is clear that they could have no other useful place, for they could be of interest to the average person only in the modern

---

[1] f. 119ᵛ.
[2] E.E.T.S. 158, 28–29, Latin text ed. Blume, 29–31.

period, when they can be read as literature: in the fourteenth century they clearly served as meditative adorations for the religious. In terms of style the audience is still important, for, despite the intensity of personal feeling, the design is still controlled by their needs. In homeliness and comprehensibility they are far nearer to the ordinary English Passion lyric than, for instance, to the poems of St. John of the Cross. It is perhaps this combination of homeliness with rapture that makes these poems so especially moving and aesthetically satisfying.

Fifteenth-Century
Lyrics

VI

Lyrics on the Passion

POETRY on the Passion continued to be copious in the fifteenth century, but in tone, content, and length it changed considerably. The content ceased to be the isolated Crucifixion scene and the sources short passages from the *Meditationes* attributed to Anselm and Augustine: instead, it became the whole Passion narrative from the arrest to the burial, and the sources, whether directly or ultimately, were such works as the *Meditationes* ascribed to Bonaventura.[1] The poems therefore became much longer—the average length would be some hundred lines rather than, as earlier, about fifteen—and the more elaborate diction and stanza-forms of the fifteenth century were used to sustain this length. At the same time there was a change in tone from devotion to didacticism. A few devotional poems on the Passion were composed, but in general the expression and excitation of grief were reserved for the *planctus* of the Blessed Virgin, and the complaint of Christ, which now became the dominant form, went full circle in its history, returning to the tone of its original appearance in homiletic Judgement-Day complaints. The appeal ceases to be solely for love, and is at least equally concerned with moral reform.

The impression of didacticism is intensified by the decrease of visual meditative detail in the poems. Often the meditative picture is only alluded to in the text, and is supplied in detail by an accompanying illustration or by a rubric referring the meditator to a statue or painting in church. It is difficult now to disentangle the historical development here, and to know what initially was cause and what effect: whether it became customary to provide a meditative illustration because the poems themselves had become so bare of detail, or whether a custom of providing illustrations led to visual description becoming redundant within the poems. But, whatever the beginnings were, it seems clear that the ampler supply of devotional representations in churches, and

[1] This was an extremely popular work throughout western Europe. Forty-three of the 113 manuscripts of the Latin text, enumerated by P. C. Fischer, 'Die "Meditationes Vitae Christi" ', *Archivum Franciscanum Historicum*, xxv (1932), 3–35, are of English origin; cf. op. cit. 175–209 and 449–83 for details of vernacular translations and authorship. The diffusion and popularity of the English translation of this work is discussed by E. Zeeman, 'Nicholas Love—a Fifteenth-Century Translator', *R.E.S.*, N.S. vi (1955), 113–27.

in books of hours and other manuscripts, led during the course of the fifteenth century to an author's assuming that his readers would gain knowledge of a visual image, not from a literary description provided by himself, but from a statue or a painting, and that ideally an illumination would actually accompany the poem in the manuscript.

This development was odd because originally literary meditation and painting had been thought of as alternative ways of making the Passion comprehensible and moving to the average layman. One of the chief arguments in the defence of images in the fourteenth century was their efficacy in stirring the feelings of the beholder. Walter Hilton, for instance, in his treatise in the defence of images, writes: 'Inter que signa statuit ecclesia ymagines Domini nostri crucifixi . . . ut per inspeccionem ymaginum revocaretur ad memoriam passio Domini nostri Iesu Christi et aliorum sanctorum passiones, et sic ad compuccionem et devocionem mentes pigre et carnales excitarentur. . . .'[1] The use of the word 'carnal' here deliberately recalls St. Bernard's exposition of a 'carnal' love for Christ in His Passion. The patristic view of pictures as *libri laicorum*[2] has thus become transformed in the light of Bernardine doctrine, so that their function is now held to be the stirring of emotion rather than the imparting of knowledge. This theoretical defence of images, however, is also closely related to contemporary iconography, which in the Middle Ages became progressively more emotionally compelling in both subject-matter and style. In particular, the iconographic theme characteristic of the fifteenth century, the *imago pietatis*, is highly emotive, and the many lyrics that transpose this picture into words are usually affective; but it is a weakness of the fifteenth-century lyric, judged as a whole, that so often it only alludes to this form with the intention that the emotive effect should derive from a visual representation external to the poem.

The particular emotiveness of the *imago pietatis* derives from the fact that it is a picture in which the figure of the suffering Christ is isolated from the historical sequence of the Passion.[3] He stands in an

---

[1] This passage is quoted from J. Russell-Smith, 'Walter Hilton and a Tract in Defence of the Veneration of Images', *Dominican Studies*, vii (1954), 194; the treatise is unpublished. 'Amongst which signs the Church sets up images of Our Lord crucified . . . in order that the Passion of Our Lord Jesus Christ and also the martyrdoms of other saints may be recalled to the memory by the looking at these images; and thus slow and carnal minds may be stirred to compunction and devotion.' Further discussions of this defence of images and other works of the iconoclastic controversy will be found in G. R. Owst, *Literature and Pulpit in Medieval England*, 136–48, and A. Caiger-Smith, *English Medieval Mural Paintings* (Oxford, 1963), 102–17.

[2] A useful collection of texts illustrating this point from both the Fathers and medieval authorities has been made by L. Gougaud, 'Muta praedicatio', *Revue Bénédictine*, xlii (1930), 168–71.

[3] A fuller account of the *imago pietatis* and of its diffusion in England will be found in Appendix E.

attitude of pain, the wounds clearly marked upon His body, and the crown of thorns upon His head. Often a part of the Cross or some of the instruments of the Passion may be seen behind Him. Reference to historical time is deliberately evaded: Christ is shown oppressed by suffering, although the Crucifixion is past, as the wounds in hands, feet, and side bear witness. No historical or dogmatic purpose is served by this representation. The intention is entirely meditative, to confront the beholder with a timelessly suffering Christ and thus to arouse his compassion.

The association between the fifteenth-century Passion complaint and the *imago pietatis* may be initially illustrated from the following verse:

> [O] man unkynde
> Have thow in mynde
> My passion smerte.
> And thow schalt me ffynde
> To the ryght kynde,
> Lo here myn hert.[1]

A meditative image of the speaker is lacking in the manuscript from which this text is taken, but in three of its five occurrences this verse is accompanied by an illustration. The most interesting of its manuscripts is B.M. Add. MS. 37049, a devotional compilation of Carthusian origin, as important for the later lyric as John of Grimestone's preaching-book is for the earlier lyric. In this manuscript the verse is copied twice,[2] and on both occasions it is visually dominated by a full-length Man of Sorrows who points to His wounded side or heart. This verse was one of the rare lyrics to be printed: it occurs on the last page of the edition of 1534 (?) of *A devote treatyse for them that ben tymorouse and fearefull in conscience* by William Bonde,[3] a Syon monk: above the verse appears a woodcut of the *imago pietatis* with an indulgence attached to it. The verse is labelled *Vox Christi*. In both manuscript and printed volume the illustration is far more emotive than the verse: the one is affective on its own, the other is not.

There is, however, a hint of a meditative image in the last line, for the heart should be visualized. In the Carthusian Manuscript there is on the same pages as the verse either a heart or a heart-shaped shield with a device of the five wounds upon it.[4] In one of the other two manuscripts,

---

[1] MS. Tanner 407, 102ᵛ. A text from B.M. Add. MS. 37049 is printed by T. W. Ross, 'Five Fifteenth-Century "Emblem" Verses from Brit. Mus. Addit. MS. 37049', *Speculum*, xxxii (1957), 276. This article also contains a useful account of the manuscript. A longer version is printed in Brown xv, 108.

[2] ff. 20ʳ (the longer version) and 24ʳ.

[3] *S.T.C.* 3275; cf. *S.T.C.* 20972 (a volume of devotional treatises).

[4] Neither heart, however, is solely related to this poem: on f. 20ʳ the heart is accompanied by a six-line verse beginning, 'þies woundes smert / bere in þi hert'

MS. Tanner 407 (a commonplace book), the last word of the verse is omitted and instead a heart is sketchily outlined in red. This emphasis upon Christ's heart and its widespread depiction in fifteenth-century art derives from a devotion that was to lead directly into the later cult of the Sacred Heart. This theme is to some extent indistinguishable from that of the wound of love, and a parallel is often made between the love-wounded heart and the lance-wounded heart.[1] In this tradition Christ's wounded heart is a symbol and proof of His love. The wounded heart, however, may also be thought of as a resting-place, in which a man may hide enveloped in Christ's love.[2] The line 'Lo here my herte' may therefore simply mean 'Look on my heart, the proof of my love' or 'Here is my heart as a refuge for you'. There is, however, a third, more attractive though less certain, possibility. In works that range from the lives of the mystics to sermon *exempla* a fairly common theme is an exchange of hearts. This occurs, for instance, in the lives of the German women mystics, St. Luitgard and St. Mechtild,[3] and in a parallel, but weaker form, in an *exemplum* in which Christ lays open His heart to a reluctant penitent:[4] no doubt the symbolical meaning of this theme varies according to the context. It is possible, therefore, that in this verse Christ offers His heart to man as his beloved, and the heart thus becomes a visible symbol of enduring fidelity and passionate love.[5]

It would be possible to go further and to see this as an offer that has a second root in secular literature. The exchange of hearts can be secular as well as religious: it is now best known from the opening line of one of the poems in Sidney's *Arcadia*, 'My true love hath my hart and I have his';[6] but the lover's offer of his heart to his beloved is a recurring theme of the fifteenth-century courtly lyric, 'My harte ye

---

(F. M. Comper, *The Life and Lyrics of Richard Rolle*, 318), and on 24ʳ a statement in verse and prose of the number of drops of blood shed by Christ (Comper, op. cit. 318); for this theme see below, p. 204. For a reproduction of the former see pl. 1 and of the latter *Speculum*, xxxii, plates between pp. 280–1.

[1] e.g. Bonaventura, *Vitis mystica*, ch. iii, *Decem opuscula*, 415.

[2] This idea is adumbrated in the sixty-first chapter of St. Bernard's *Sermons on the Song of Songs* (*P.L.* 183, 1070–4), stimulated there as thereafter by Cant. ii. 13, '. . . et veni, columba mea, in foraminibus petrae', and was developed more emphatically by mystical writers such as Suso. An illuminating account of early references to the wounded heart in England is given by E. Colledge, *The Mediaeval Mystics of England* (London, 1962), 11–13.

[3] On the German mystics (and for the whole subject) see K. Richstaetter, S.J., *Illustrious Friends of the Sacred Heart of Jesus*, trans. M. E. Merriman (London, 1930); also J. Bainvel, *Devotion to the Sacred Heart*, trans. E. Leahy (London, 1924).

[4] *Speculum laicorum*, ed. J. Th. Welter (Paris, 1914), no. 136, pp. 30–31: 'Ipse [Christ] apprehendit manum suam, misit in latus suum et cor suum posuit in manu dicens: "Ecce ego ostendi cor meum et ostendas tu mihi cor tuum".'

[5] It is in this sense that Christ pleads for man's heart in the refrain of a carol complaint of Ryman, 'O synfull man, *geve me thyn hert*', *Archiv*, lxxxix (1892), 218–19.

[6] *The Poems*, ed. W. A. Ringler (Oxford, 1962), 75.

PLATE 1

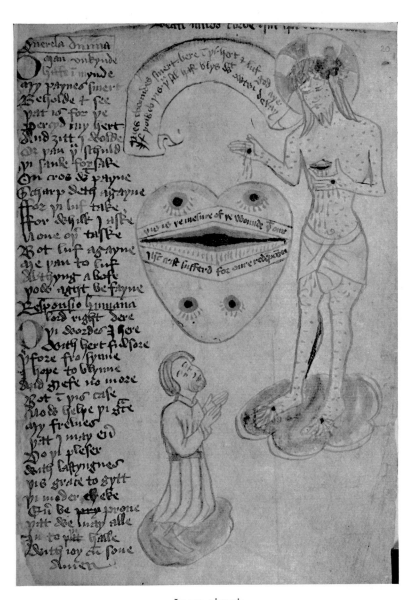

Imago pietatis
B. M. Add. MS. 37049

have to kepe'[1] or 'She hathe my harte and ever shall'.[2] A poem from MS.
Porkington 10 begins 'Have all my hert and be in peys',[3] a line which
thereafter becomes the refrain. There is a companion piece to this
poem, 'Trewlove trewe, on you I truste',[4] which according to the rubric
is 'Querimonia Cristi languentis pro amore'. If the rubric were ignored
it might well be read as a secular love poem, and the possibility must
remain open that the copyist may have misinterpreted it, whether
deliberately or unintentionally. The ambiguity is sharpest in the lines
that the two poems have in common:

> Therfor, have alle myne herte and beon yn pees,
> and þynke I love you soveranly—
> ffor þat I say hit is no lese—
> Wolde god ye wyste as wele as I.
>
> ffor wele I se, bothe day and nygth
> That trew love wyle me never cese.
> Have mercy on me, worthly wiygth,
> Have all my herte and be yn pese.[5]

It seems certain from the style that these lines began as a secular appeal
for love, but the central image 'Have alle mine herte' would be equally
appropriate in either a devotional or a secular context. Later in the
poems there are touches that suggest Christ the lover: the line, for
instance, 'A! dere herte, whan dyde I ylle' may echo the familiar
question, *quid ultra debui facere*, whilst the plea, 'Therfor, dere herte, loke
ye be trewe, / And love me wele withouten lese', being coloured with a
tinge of the didactic, is better interpreted as a divine command than as
a lover's plea for mercy. Certainly the feeling in this poem is quite
different from that of its secular companion: it reads well as a religious
adaptation of secular convention. Though it lacks meditative vitality, in
that the courtly style precludes the visualization of either the lover or his
heart, it has in compensation an idiosyncratic intensity which is not
quite that of either the devotional or the secular tradition.

An unusual feature of this poem is that the only solid link between
secular and sacred is the image of the lover's heart. More commonly the
fusion of the two is achieved through echoes of the style and imagery of
the Song of Songs. A very fine example of this kind of complaint is
'In a valey of þis restles mynde',[6] which has as its refrain the words
Quia amore langueo, a key text from the Song of Songs for the wound of
love. The poem begins in courtly fashion with a *chanson d'aventure*

---

[1] *Secular Lyrics of the xivth and xvth Centuries*, ed. R. H. Robbins (Oxford, 1952),
p. 128.

[2] Op. cit., p. 125. [3] Op. cit. 135.

[4] Brown XV, 110. [5] Ibid. p. 176.

[6] E.E.T.S. 15, 180–9.

setting, but the *chanson d'aventure* elements are allegorized: the poet in the valley of restlessness seeks over field and hill for a true love (the figurative use of valley to signify the world seems so well established that the inconsistency here is unobtrusive). He comes upon a lamenting figure, who is then described as follows:

> Upon þis hil y fond a tree;
> Undir þe tree a man sittynge,
> From heed to foot woundid was he,
> His herte blood y siȝ bledinge.

This is not quite an *imago pietatis*, but suggests very strongly the analogous iconographic theme of 'Christ in distress' (*Christus im Elend*), in which the wounded Christ is seated beneath the Cross. As von der Osten has stressed, this scene has no proper place in the historical sequence.[1] Like the *imago pietatis* it is a devotional image, realistic in its emphasis upon suffering, but symbolical in that it constructs its realism without reference to time or historical action. In the poem the setting is superficially a pastoral scene: the speaker of the complaint is seated beneath a tree on the top of a hill, but the poet obviously intends that the visual imagination should penetrate beneath this appearance to the Cross and Mount Calvary.

After the opening there follows an appeal for love, the thought and imagery of which are rooted in the Song of Songs. Mankind is the *spouse* and *wife* for whom Christ, the bridegroom-husband, has suffered, and whom he now seeks assiduously and patiently, however indifferent or faithless she may be. There is an unusual sensuousness of descriptive detail in this poem, deriving directly from the Song of Songs:

> Fair love, lete us go pleye!
> Applis ben ripe in my gardayne,
> I schal þee cloþe in a newe aray,
> þi mete schal be mylk, hony, and wiyn.[2]

But in the first part echoes of the Song of Songs are subordinated to an allusive description of the Passion, which draws rather upon the *Improperia* and the allegory of the lover-knight:

> My fair spouse, and my love briȝt,
> I saved hir fro betynge, and sche haþ me bet;
> I cloþid hir in grace and hevenli liȝt,
> þis bloodi scherte sche haþ on me sette,

---

[1] G. von der Osten, 'Job and Christ', *Warburg Journal*, xvi (1953), 153–8. A more detailed study by the same author, *Christus im Elend, ein niederdeutsches Andachtsbild* (1952), does not seem to be available in English libraries.

[2] Op. cit. 184.

> For longynge of love ȝit wolde y not lett;
>   Swete strokis axe þese; lo,
>   I have loved hir evere as y hir het,
> Quia amore langueo.[1]

The use of a variety of sources has led to some inconsistencies within
the poem, though one of these, the fluctuation between the ideas of
sister and *spouse*, derives directly from the Song of Songs itself. There
are, however, other inconsistencies. Christ at one point, for instance,
cannot move because love has nailed His feet together, whilst at another
He speeds before man to intercept her foe. In terms of relationship He
is sometimes the faithful and pleading lover to whom man is 'daungerus',
at another He is the maternal protector comforting man in his distress.
The latter, in fact, is developed into a detailed image, becoming an
allegory within an allegory:

> My love is in hir chaumbir: holde ȝoure pees,
>   Make ȝe no noise, but lete hir slepe:
> My babe, y wolde not were in disese,
>   I may not heere my dere child wepe.
>   With my pap y schal hir kepe.
> Ne merveille ȝe not þouȝ y tende hir to;
>   þis hole in my side had nevere be so depe,
> But quia amore langueo.[2]

The strangeness of the image of Christ as mother may become less
alienating if it is related to its devotional roots.[3] The ultimate source was
a series of Biblical texts, particularly Matthew xxiii. 37, and Isaiah xlix.
15 and lxvi. 12–13. Early exponents of the theme most commonly
quoted the first two of these. The author of the *Ancrene Wisse* makes the
text from Isaiah xlix the foundation of his comparison between Christ's
love for man and that of a mother for her child:

> þet he luveð us mare þen eani moder hire child, he hit seið him seolven
> þurh ysaie: Nunquid potest mater oblivisci filii uteri sui? Et si illa oblivi-
> scatur, ego non obliviscar tui. Mei moder, he seið, forȝeoten hire child? ant
> þah heo do, ich ne mei þe forȝeoten neaver.[4]

The text from Matthew is used in *Oratio* 65 of Anselm:

> Sed et tu, Jesu, bone Domine, nonne et tu mater? Annon es mater? Qui tan-
> quam gallina, quae congregat sub alas pullos suos. Vere, Domine et tu mater.

---

[1] Op. cit. 182.
[2] Op. cit. 186.
[3] For a history of the image see A. Cabassut, 'Une Dévotion médiévale peu connue,
la dévotion à "Jésus notre mère"', *Revue d'ascétique et de mystique*, xxv (1949),
234–45, and 'God is our Mother', *The Life of the Spirit*, ii, no. 15 (1945), 49–53.
[4] E.E.T.S. 249, 202.

Nam quod alii parturierunt et pepererunt, a te acceperunt. Tu prius propter illos, et quos pepererunt, parturiendo mortuus es, et moriendo peperisti.[1]

From the fundamental Biblical idea that God's love for man, in its protectiveness and intensity, resembles and yet exceeds that of a mother for her child there developed a tendency to express this by symbolic or allegorical variations related to the details of the Passion: the allegory of the blood-bath in the *Ancrene Wisse* is an early example of this.[2] The most elaborate exploration of the potentialities of this kind of imagery occurs in Chapter 60 of *The Revelations of Divine Love* by Julian of Norwich. Here, as in the *Oratio* of Anselm, the sufferings of the Cruci-fixion become the pains of labour and, with an unstated echo of Isaiah lxvi,[3] the sacraments become the milk with which Christ nourishes His children:

> The mother may give her child suck of her milk, but our precious Mother, Jesus, He may feed us with Himself, and doeth it, full courteously and full tenderly, with the Blessed Sacrament. . . . The Mother may lay the child tenderly to her breast, but our tender Mother, Jesus, He may homely lead us into His blessed breast, by His sweet open side, and shew therein part of the Godhead and the joys of heaven. . . .[4]

Julian's use of language is more sensitive and discrete than that of the author of *Quia amore langueo*, and by subtly dividing her allegory into two parts she evades the sharp juxtaposition found in the poem, which forces the implication that a man may feed from Christ's side as a baby from its mother's breast. In this too many layers of allegory have been elided with slightly distasteful effect. But, whilst the comparison with the *Revelations* enables one to define the defect in this stanza, it also (with the other quotations) reveals the emotional potentialities of the image which the author of the poem has succeeded in conveying, despite some lapse. Against this background the image no longer stands out obtru-sively as though it were an original and grotesque invention.

Within the structure of the poem the image of Christ as mother is a metaphor used by Christ the lover: this relationship is indicated very skilfully by the transition from 'My love' in the first line of the stanza to 'My babe' in the third, and by the return to the lover's refrain in the

---

[1] *P.L.* 158, 981–2. 'But Jesus, good Lord, surely you too are our mother? Or is it not true that you are our mother who are as a hen that gathereth her chickens under her wings. Truly, O Lord, you also are a mother. For what others have given birth to and brought forth, they received from you. You first died on account of those who gave birth, bringing them forth, and giving birth you died.'

[2] Ed. cit. 24.

[3] 'Quia haec dicit Dominus: Ecce ego declinabo super eam quasi fluvium pacis et quasi torrentem inundantem gloriam gentium, quam sugetis; ad ubera portabimini, et super genua blandientur vobis. Quomodo, si cui mater blandiatur, ita ego consolabor vos . . .', Isa. lxvi. 12–13.

[4] Ed. Grace Warrack (London, 1945), 150.

last line. But even if this structural justification were not noticed or seemed insufficient, this image, together with the other inconsistencies earlier mentioned, would remain acceptable, even appropriate. This untroubled acceptance of conflicting images, whether organized paratactically or as image within image, depends firstly upon their logical relationship to the implicit, non-allegorical meaning of the poem, that is Christ's demonstration of love in the Passion; and secondly upon the sustained intensity of tone, which convinces the reader that the incongruities are not lapses in craftsmanship but a fine poetical expression of the complexity and variety of love: everything is fittingly subsumed to the dominating allegory of Christ as lover.

A curious example of Christ pleading as a lover occurs in a late complaint, modelled upon a secular song, 'Come over the borne, Besse', in which the speaker becomes Christ and Bess mankind.[1] The policy of allegorizing secular verses was an ancient one, belonging chiefly to the sermon tradition. Like the use of *exempla* it had the advantage for the preacher of catching his audience's attention, and in addition it would provide an inescapable religious reference for a secular song that they were likely to hear or sing in daily life. A well-known example of this in French literature was the song of the *Bele Aaliz*,[2] which was allegorized in various ways: in a sermon once attributed to Stephen Langton, for instance, Bele Aaliz is said to be the Blessed Virgin, 'de qua sic dicitur "speciosa specialis, preciosa ut gema"'.[3] More striking is the story in the *Fioretti* of how St. Francis once gave a religious application to the following lover's couplet:

> Tanto è il bene ch'aspetto
> Ch'ogni pena m'è diletto.[4]

In England there is a parallel in the short sermon on the verse:

> Atte wrastlinge mi lemman i ches
> and atte ston kasting i him forles.

The preacher explains: 'Nu mon we understondin i þeise wordis to manere of folk. þe ton is þat bleþeliche and mid swet herte herin godis

---

[1] Thomas Wright, *The Nutbrowne Maid* (London, 1836), xii–xv.

[2] The texts, which are fragmentary, have been printed by Gaston Paris, 'Bele Aaliz', *Mélanges de littérature française du moyen âge* (Paris, 1912), 616–24.

[3] The sermon has been printed by T. Wright in M. Haupt, *Altdeutsche Blätter* (Leipzig, 1840), ii. 143–5; it is discussed by A. Lecoy de la Marche, *La Chaire française au moyen âge* (Paris, 1886), 91–94, who points out a sermon, by the same unknown author, in which another secular verse is similarly treated (pp. 197–8). In one of the *exempla* of Jacques de Vitry there is a short verse parody of the song: 'Quant Aeliz fu levee, et quant ele fu lavee, et la messe fu chantee, et deable l'en ont emportee', *The Exempla of Jacques de Vitry*, ed. T. F. Crane (London, 1890), no. cclxxiii, p. 114 and notes p. 253.

[4] P. Sabatier, *Life of St. Francis of Assisi*, trans. L. S. Houghton (Paris, 1894), 172. 'So great is the good that I expect that all pain is joy to me.'

word and mid bisinesse ben abutin to chesin Jhesu Christ here saule
lemman, þat dere had about here love mid blodi wondis and mid deth
on rode, and chesin him atte wrastlinge as i er seide.'[1] The wrestling,
the preacher continues, is the fight against the world, the flesh, and the
Devil, and the stone-throwing at which Christ is lost refers to the hard-
heartedness of people who are unmoved by sermons designed to stir
them to repentance. In a fourteenth-century sermon on the text *quia
amore langueo* a simple secular verse enumerating the signs of love-
languishing is ingeniously applied to Christ:

> He Iesus is myth and waxit wan,
> He syket as a sorful man.
> Alone he drawes fro compenye
> And ever he herkenes one ys drurie.
> Loneliche he spekis to his herte,
> For hym he suffrus peynis smert.[2]

The sermon then expounds in detail how Christ became discoloured
through the seven torments, sighed on account of seven humiliations,
was alone when abandoned by his disciples, etc.[3]

In both the English examples it is very clear that the original verse is
treated in the style of biblical glossing: from the literary point of view a
very elaborate allegory is erected upon a very small foundation. They
therefore provide a relevant context, but not an exact parallel, to the
kind of poem that we are about to discuss, in which the secular verse
provides not only the literal level of the allegory but also the verse
form, structure, and even some of the actual lines. In France this
happened occasionally: there is, for instance, a version of the *Bele
Aaliz* in this manner, in which a *beguine* gets up and prepares herself
to go, not into the garden, but to church,[4] and there is a *pastourelle*
which has been transformed into a poem about the Blessed Virgin.[5]
There is, however, no early example of this in England. It is notable
that in *The Red Book of Ossory*, whose methods obviously provided an
opportunity for this kind of parody, the verse forms are preserved only
for the sake of the tune: there seems to be no literary relationship
between secular model and religious substitute. The word *substitute*
should be emphasized here: the Bishop would have been pleased if the
secular songs had been quite forgotten, but the genuine parody thrives
only so long as the original continues to be known.

---

[1] Carleton Brown, 'Texts and the Man', *Modern Humanities Research Association*,
ii (1928), 106–7.

[2] MS. Balliol 149, 32ᵛ. *Index*, 1140. *Iesus*: loses; *ever he herkenes one ys drurie*: he
thinks of nothing but his love.

[3] ff. 31ʳ–38ᵛ.

[4] E. Järnström, *Recueil de chansons pieuses du xiiiᵉ siècle*, ii. cxxxi. 181–2.

[5] Ibid. cxxvii. 169–73.

This habit seems to have developed in England only in the late fifteenth and early sixteenth centuries. Certainly it is from this period that the two most striking parodies survive, those of 'The Nutbrowne Maid' and 'Come over the borne, Besse'. 'The Nutbrowne Maid'[1] seems to have been an exceedingly popular poem: it was copied in Richard Hill's commonplace book, printed in 1502 in R. Arnold's *Customs of London*, and in 1520 it was printed again as a penny chapbook. As late as 1558–9 it was printed illicitly by John King. The religious parody, 'The Newe Notbrowne Mayd', does not survive in manuscript form, but was printed by John Skot.[2] The adaptation matches the original perfectly in structure, i.e. in the number of stanzas and the timing of the narrative, and it is also metrically similar, preserving the recurring b-rhyme (a, c, d, etc., do not rhyme in either version) and also the repeated refrains 'a banished man' and 'alone'. Indeed it is probable that in this, as in earlier parodies, it was key phrases— here those of the refrains—that provided the starting-point for the allegory: we may compare 'bele' in *Bele Aaliz* and 'lemman' in *Atte wrastling*. It cannot have been any radical similarity of plot that suggested the adaptation, for the discrepancies are so strong that they in fact mar the poem despite considerable technical achievement. In 'The Nutbrowne Maid' a squire and maiden at first dispute the constancy of women, and then act out a situation, not unlike that of the Clerk's Tale, in which a woman asserts her love in the face of every proposed hardship and humiliation, until the man at last reveals that his part was no more than a test, and all will end happily. The initial discussion on the fickleness of women makes a convenient parallel with the discussion between Christ and the Blessed Virgin on the sinfulness of mankind. The Squire says that it is:

> A labour spent in vaine,
> To love them wele, for never a dele
> They love a man againe.[3]

Whilst Christ complains of mankind that it is:

> A laboure spent in vayne,
> To love hym well, for never a dell
> He wyll me love agayne.[4]

After this, however, the Blessed Virgin's part, which is that of admitting man's sin, though pleading for mercy, is as remote from the *Puella*'s

---

[1] E. K. Chambers and F. Sidgwick, *Early English Lyrics* (London, 1921), 34–48, and 334–6 for notes on the history of the text.

[2] See the colophon, *Remains of the Early Popular Poetry of England*, ed. W. C. Hazlitt, iii (London, 1866), 22. I have not been able to trace this work in either the *S.T.C.* or Dibdin-Ames.

[3] Chambers, op. cit. 34.   [4] *Remains*, ed. Hazlitt, iii. 2.

asseverations of devotion as is Christ's denunciation of man from the Squire's pretended tale of banishment; but there is here, as we said before, an isolated parallelism in the idea of banishment, and therefore some of the descriptions of banishment are appropriately transferred to Christ:

(*Squire*)

Yet take good hede, for ever I drede
That ye coude not sustein
The thorney wayes, the depe valeis,
The snowe, the frost, the rein,
The colde, the hete, for drie or wete,
We must lodge on the plain,
And, us above, noon other rove
But a brake bussh or twaine;
Which sone shuld greve you, I beleve,
And ye wolde gladly than
That I had to the grenewode go
Alone a banisshed man.[1]

(*Christ*)

Now, for mannes nede, sith I wolde blede,
And great anguysshe sustayne,
In stony wayes, both nyghtes and dayes,
Walkynge in frost and rayne.
In colde and hete, in drye and wete,
My fete were bare both twayne;
Though I for love to mannes behove
Endured all this payne,
That I therfore sholde spare the more,
No reason fynde ye can;
Rather I sholde more strayte him holde,
And as a banysshed man.[2]

The second half of this stanza is quite different from the original, but the first half is close, and some of the small verbal differences have no doubt arisen from accidents in textual transmission. It is difficult to know whether we should take this poem more as a display of technical skill than as a complaint in the old tradition.

No non-allegorical text of 'Come over the borne, Besse' has survived, though it is easy to infer that it was a very popular song from the number of its imitations and adaptations. Apart from the texts of the religious allegory, which we are about to discuss, there is the historical allegory,

---

[1] Chambers, op. cit. 41.   [2] *Remains*, ed. Hazlitt, iii. 11–12.

in which the speaker is England and Bess Queen Elizabeth;[1] the lyric lament of Pamphilus, spoken by Parrot in Skelton's *Speke Parrot*;[2] and, of course, the Fool's snatch in *King Lear*.[3] The religious version survives in four manuscripts: in three, MSS. B.M. Add. 5665 (Ritson's Manuscript with music),[4] Emmanuel 263, and Ashmole 176, as a short poem of one or two verses with refrain; and in one, MS. Trinity, Camb. 1157, in a long version of twelve stanzas.[5] Although the long text survives in the earliest manuscript, the short text may nevertheless have preceded it. Certainly in the Trinity version the adaptation of 'Come over the borne, Besse' serves only as a framework for a traditional complaint, and, throughout the Passion narrative that constitutes the main body of the poem, is recalled only by the refrain.[6] Nevertheless, the parallelism between the two situations (the lover appealing to Bess and Christ appealing to man) is much more pointed here than in 'The Newe Notbrowne Mayd' and its model, and the picture of Bess, pretty, vain, and absorbed in the pastimes of the world and heedless of Christ's calling, has an ironic sting missing in the latter. The first verse introduces this scene succinctly:

> The borne is this word blinde,
> And Besse ys mankynde,
> So praty can noon fynde
>   As she:
> She dauncyth, she lepyth,
> And Crist stondyth and clepith,
> Come over the borne, Besse.[7]

And the last three lines

> The water hit fallyth
> And Crist stondyth and callyth,
> Come over the borne, Besse.

provide an effective summing-up, particularly in the casual felicity of 'The water hit fallyth', which is descriptively pleasant and at the same

---

[1] *Harleian Miscellany*, x. 260.

[2] *Works*, ed. A. Dyce, ii (London, 1843), 12–13.

[3] III. vi. 26–29, ed. K. Muir (London, 1952), 132.

[4] John Stevens, *Music and Poetry in the Early Tudor Court* (London, 1961), 348. The secular version from MS. Harley 2252, referred to in his notes as 'a "Speke Parrotte" poem', is an incomplete text of the lament from Skelton's *Speke Parrot* mentioned above.

[5] The only printed text of this version is that of Thomas Wright, *The Nutbrowne Maid* (London, 1836), xii–xv: it contains many errors.

[6] It is important, however, that the refrain is part of the stanza, in contrast, for instance to *Carol*, 270, where the element of secular love-song is confined to the (no doubt) borrowed burden, 'Com home agayne, / Com home agayne, / Min owine swet hart, com home agayne'. For later religious adaptations of secular songs see Appendix J.

[7] Wright, op. cit. xii.

time suggests an irrevocable endlessness. If the poem was designed as a whole, however, it illustrates the characteristic medieval fault of indifference to proportion. Within such a slight framework only a short complaint could relevantly be contained, but the author through ten verses sets out all the traditional pains of the Passion, with Bess apparently forgotten, except for the refrain. For instance:

> On crosse myne arme spred is,
> My body forbled ys,
> Wit gall my mowth fed is,
>   Come se.
> Renewed are my paynes,
> And voyde are my veynes,
> Come over the borne, Besse.[1]

The stanza form, moreover, with its feminine rhymes and scampering pace, quite evidently requires music, and without this support is inadequate to the dignity of the subject-matter.

It would be over-rigorous to assert that the speaker of 'Come over the borne' must be imagined in the form of an *imago pietatis*, for at this late date there was no question of a meditative image, though, if there were one, tradition and propriety would suggest the *imago pietatis*. This iconographic form, however, was useful not only as an aid to the visualization of the speaker of love-complaints but also as the speaker of complaints which are largely narratives of the Passion. Since it was often required that the content of these complaints should extend to the death and burial, such a timeless image was obviously extremely suitable, for in the poems where the complaint is said to be spoken by Christ on the Cross there is nearly always inconsistency over tenses and detail. Wherever there is not direct textual evidence to the contrary, one may fairly assume the speaker to be an *imago pietatis*. The finest of these narrative complaints is that beginning 'Brother, abyde, I the desire and pray'. The poem relates Christ's activity for man from the moment of the Incarnation, but the first stanza, without reference to the very clear chronological outline, describes the speaker:

> Brother, a-byde, I the desire and pray;
> A-byde, a-byde, and here thy brother speke.
> Be-holde my body in this blody aray,
> Broysed and betyne wyth whippis that wold not breke.
> This ferefull force, this wo, this wrongfull wreke,
> ffor the I sufferd, what canst thou do, then, less agayne,
> But stonde a while and harke how I complayne?[2]

The Body, marked by wounds, but without the Cross, must be that of

---

[1] Ed. cit. xiv.   [2] Brown xv, 109, p. 169.

an *imago pietatis*. For various reasons the poem is exceptional in its
quality. One is the lucid and dramatic narrative, based upon detail drawn
from works such as the *Meditationes*: it can be well illustrated by the first
two and last three lines of the following stanza, which describes the
childhood of Christ:

> Borne in bedlem, lappyd and laide in strawe
> Ine a powur howse wher bestys ete ther mete,
> Brought to the temple after the Iues lawe
> And circumcysed—this ys not to fogette,—
> I lede my yought wyth children in the strette,
> Poorly a-rayed in clothes bare and thyne,
> Such as my mother for me dyde make and spyne.[1]

Another reason is the confident firmness of the verse, and in particular
the concluding of each stanza with some strong or even memorable line,
such as 'And I stode styll, seke and sore appalled'. The author has a
sense of dramatic speech and timing, and the last quotation can in fact
be better appreciated in its context:

> 'Speke, manne,' qd pylate, 'how ys thy lyf convayed?'
> And wyth that worde, wattur to whasche he callde,
> And I stode styll, seke and sore appalled.[2]

The author proceeds with the timing and control of a master poet:
unlike many others, this poem never gives the impression that tradition
has been followed without exercise of judgement, or that everything
has been included regardless of shapeliness or chronology. Even in the
last verses didacticism does not obscure the expressions of love. They
are, in fact, dominated by the statement of the old view of ecstatic love,
'Love dyde me lede, love dyde me thus constrayne'. This poem shows
fifteenth-century style at its best: it is far more dramatic, technically
accomplished, and severe than the earlier poetry; the lack of the earlier
grace and sweetness is compensated for by skill and dramatic force.

Another poem which would seem to be spoken by an *imago pietatis*
is that now preserved only in the fragments of a printed book of carols,
Douce Fragments, f. 48.[3] No description is given of the speaker, but the
span of time within the poem extends from the scourging to the Harrowing of Hell, and therefore no other meditative image would be
appropriate. The poem itself, 'Synfull man, thou art unkynde', is a
mediocre narrative of the Passion characterized by extreme flatness of
expression, as in the following line (describing the Virgin), 'Seyng my

---

[1] Ed. cit., p. 170. The last three lines derive from the passage in *Meditationes*
ascribed to Bonaventura, where the poverty of the Virgin and her Child and the
Virgin's task of spinning are beautifully imagined and described (*Meditations*, trans.
Ragusa and Green, 69–76).

[2] Op. cit., p. 173.   [3] *Carols*, 171.

travel, she fel downe ryght'. It is difficult to estimate whether the refrain
has value:

> Blow þe winde styl and blow nat so shyl;
> My blode, man, I shed for the al at wyl.
> Blow þe winde styl and blow nat so shyll;
> This paine to suffre is my Fathers wil.

In its apparently irrelevant allusion to natural phenomena it recalls the
striking use of such refrains in some of the horrific and violent ballads.
But unlike the refrains in the ballad parallels it here seems hardly to
succeed. This kind of refrain, however, was not always so ineffective.
Another carol, for instance, has the following verse prefixed:

> There blows a colde wynd todaye, todaye,
> The wynd blows cold todaye;
> Cryst sufferyd his passyon for manys salvacyon,
> To kype the cold wynd awaye.[1]

And the last line of this verse becomes the recurrent refrain. Despite the
unexciting allegorical explanation in the opening stanza that the 'colde
wynd' is temptation (an explanation which anyway does not fit the last
three verses), the refrain here is mysteriously evocative, and transforms
a pedestrian narrative into a poem that stirs the feelings by some indefinable stimulus to the imagination. The adaptation of poems into
carol form must often have led to the invention, or more often the borrowing, of refrains by fairly mechanical redactors. The *Vexilla regis*
refrain in the *Dollorus Complant* (which we shall consider shortly) is
probably an example of this,[2] and the refrain, 'Shall I moder, shall I/
Shall I do soo, etc.', in the carol, 'I was born in a stall' is obviously
borrowed from a 'cradle prophecy', being inappropriate in a complaint
addressed to man.[3] The refrain in the poem from the Douce Fragments
mentioned earlier is no doubt also an example of such work, an arbitrary
juxtaposition which does not spring to life through some lack of in-
cantatory or numinous quality in the refrain.

One of Lydgate's complaints is spoken by an *imago pietatis*, as the
first stanza makes clear:

> Erly on morwe, and toward nyght also,
>   First and last, looke on this ffygure;
> Was ever wight suffred so gret woo
>   For manhis sake suych passioun did endure?
>   My bloody woundis, set here in picture,
> Hath hem in mynde knelyng on your kne,
>   A goostly merour to every Cryature,
>   Callid of my passioun the dolerous pyte.[4]

---

[1] *Carols*, 170. Inc. 'Thys wynde be reson ys callyd tentacyon'. See below, p. 409.
[2] See pp. 202–5.   [3] *Carols*, 166 and note p. 387.
[4] E.E.T.S., E.S. 107, 250–2.

Indeed, the insistence in the poem on *looking*, and the indulgence promised in the last verse for those who say a paternoster, ave, and credo, 'In remembraunce of Crystys passioun / Knelyng before this dolorous pite', show that the poem cannot be obediently followed without such a representation. Like many of Lydgate's poems it would seem to demand an illustrated, devotional manuscript, though curiously enough, these poems all survive in poetical collections obviously made with a literary rather than a didactic intention. Possibly, however, the poem is primarily intended to supply the kind of devotional thoughts which should precede the liturgical exercise, which itself will be performed in church. The reference to kneeling in the above quotation, and the line 'Beth not rekles when ye forby passe', support this interpretation. The main content of this poem, however, is not a Passion narrative, but a learned unwinding of the traditional image of the grapes and winepress of the Passion. There was a key Biblical source for each of these, and both were from the time of the Fathers applied to the Passion.[1] One was the episode in Numbers xiii where the Israelite spies bring back a bunch of grapes from the Promised Land. Augustine, Isidore, Rabanus Maurus, Honorius of Autun, and many others commenting upon this, saw Christ in the grapes and the Cross in the staff. Behind this identification, of course, lay the eucharistic sacrament and other texts, such as Christ's 'Ego sum vitis vera'[2] and Canticles i. 13, 'Botrus cypri dilectus meus mihi in vineis Engaddi'.[3] In the Middle Ages the spies with the grapes became a common type of the Crucifixion: it occurs frequently in dogmatic hymns and in typological compendiums; it is listed in the early medieval English compilation of 'Pictor in carmine';[4] and in the later Middle Ages it would be widely known from the *Biblia pauperum* and the *Speculum humanae salvationis*.

The other was the first six verses of Isaiah lxiii, in which a dialogue takes place between unidentified speakers. The questions are, 'Quis est iste qui venit de Edom tinctis vestibus de Bosra' and 'Quare ergo rubrum est indumentum tuum, et vestimenta tua sicut calcantium in torculari', to which the other speaker—in the Middle Ages always taken to be Christ—replies '. . . propugnator sum ad salvandum' and 'Torcular calcavi solus . . .'.[5] The clothing was, of course, assumed to be red with

---

[1] For a fuller account see R. Tuve, *A Reading of George Herbert* (London, 1952), 115.

[2] John xv. 1. 'I am the true vine' (A.V.).

[3] 'My beloved is to me a cluster of Cyprus grapes in the vineyards of Engedi.' It was thus that the Middle Ages understood the text: *the botrus cypri* is more correctly 'a cluster of Cyprus blossom' (R.V. has 'henna-plant').

[4] M. R. James, 'Pictor in Carmine', *Archaeologia*, xciv (1951), 161 (no. ci).

[5] 'Who is this that cometh from Edom, with dyed garments from Bozrah?'; 'Wherefore art thou red in thine apparel, and thy garments like him that treadeth in the winefat?'; 'I am the champion who fights to save you', 'I have trodden the winepress alone' (A.V. except for the translation of *propugnator sum ad salvandum*).

the blood of the Passion, as in the following verse from MS. Harley 7322:

> Wat is he þis þat comet so brith
> Wit blodi cloþes al bedith?
> respondentes superiores dixerunt
> He is boþe god and man:
> swilc ne sawe nevere nan.
> for adamis sinne he suffrede ded.
> And þerfore is his robe so red.[1]

Friar William Herebert turned the whole passage into an English para-phrase with interpretation. It is a clumsy slow-moving verse, of which the only interest is that the phrase *propugnator sum* has suggested to the author the Christ-knight image:

> What ys he, þys lordling þat cometh vrom þe vyht
> Wyth blod-rede wede so grysliche ydyht,
> So vayre y-coyntised, so semlich in syht,
> So styflyche ȝongeþ, so douhti a knyht?[2]

This passage from Isaiah could be given various applications: in the Chester *Ascensio*,[3] for instance, it was interpreted as a dialogue between Christ and the angels, who are mystified by the blood-stained figure ascending into heaven; the author was here following the *Glossa ordinaria*.[4] But more commonly attention was given to its liturgical position (it was one of the lessons for the Wednesday in Holy Week),[5] and it is the crucified Christ who is the treader of the winepress.

These two images from Numbers xiii and Isaiah lxiii, though related allegorically, are distinct. In the one Christ is the bunch of grapes, affixed to the Cross, from whom came the redemptive blood and sacra-ment of wine: in the other Christ Himself is the grape-harvester and comes from His labours stained with the juice symbolical of His blood. But, though distinct, their common identity in fields of reference and allegorical meaning inevitably led to their association. As a result the grapes (from Numbers) are thought of as being pressed into wine by the weight of the Cross.[6] From this conflation sprang the grotesque Flemish and French illustrations of the winepress of the Passion, in which Christ Himself is squeezed beneath the winepress of the Cross (in contrast to

---

[1] E.E.T.S. 15, 259.

[2] Brown XIV, 25. *Y-coyntised*: apparelled; *so styfliche ȝongeþ*: so stoutly marching.

[3] E.E.T.S., E.S. 115, 367–9.   [4] *P.L.* 113, 1306.

[5] Durandus in his commentary on the liturgy discusses its allegorical significance, *Rationale de divinis officiis* (Naples, 1859), 508.

[6] L. Lindet, 'Les représentations allégoriques du moulin et du pressoir dans l'art chrétien', *Revue archéologique*, xxxvi (1900), 403–13; É. Mâle, *L'Art religieux de la fin du moyen âge en France*, 117–22; M. Vloberg, *L'Eucharistie dans l'art* (Grenoble and Paris, 1946), ii. 172–83.

the earlier iconographic form, found, for instance, in the *Hortus deli-ciarum* of Herrad of Landsberg, where Christ, surrounded by repre-sentatives of the Church, treads the grapes).[1]

In 'Erly on morwe' Lydgate very ingeniously links this already interwoven theme with the *imago pietatis*. The poem begins, as we have said, with an exhortation to meditate upon 'this dolerous pyte', but imperceptibly the *imago pietatis* acquires the role of the treader of the grapes, 'In Bosra steyned of purpil al my [weede]', and this figure in turn changes into the Christ of the winepress of the Passion:

> The vyne of Soreth railed in lengthe and brede,
>> The tendre clustris rent down in ther rage,
> The ripe grapis ther licour did out shede,
>> With bloody dropis bespreynt was my visage,—
> Man to socoure, I suffred gret damage,
>> I was maad thral for manhis lyberte,
> I bar the bront allone of this ventage,
>> Lyk as witnesseth this dolorous pite.[2]

In this stanza there is a very subtle progression in which one image fades into another, the progression being both logically and imaginatively fitting. The first three lines are a direct narrative statement of a type: the bunch of grapes, so often depicted in typological manuals,[3] is here described, but already they are torn down and beginning to shed their juice; in the fourth line they are superseded by the face of the suffering Christ with the drops of blood upon it. In the seventh line the whole figure of the suffering Christ is presented, bearing alone the full weight and pressure of the winepress,[4] and in the last line, which is a refrain, this figure returns to that of the *imago pietatis*.

The series of associations here are partly those explored by patristic exegesis and partly the visual associations made by fifteenth-century iconography. They would be readily followed by a monastic audience, except that the skill with which Lydgate returns the stanza to its refrain would perhaps not be appreciated in England. The link here is icono-graphic, for the Christ of the winepress is invariably the Man of Sor-rows. But, like other extravagant continental themes, the winepress of the Passion was not adopted in English devotional art. Lydgate himself could easily have come across it during the years he spent in Paris;

---

[1] Vloberg, op. cit. 174. Cf. Lydgate's *A Seying of the Nightingale*, ll. 155–6: 'Hit is I, quod he, þat trade it al allone. / Withouten felawe I gane þe wyn outpresse . . .', E.E.T.S. E.S. 107, 227.

[2] Ed. cit. 251. *Railed*: trained on rails; *I bar the bront allone of this ventage*: I bore alone the heavy force of the grape-pressing.

[3] e.g. *Speculum humanae salvationis*, ed. Lutz and Perdrizet, pl. 44. Cf. Tuve, *A Reading of George Herbert*, pl. vii.

[4] Cf. Vloberg, op. cit. 177 and 183.

but in England the theme would be known only from verbal descriptions such as that in the widely used prayer, the Fifteen Oes, in which the fifteenth apostrophe is to Jesus as the 'very and true plenteous vyne' whose 'blessyd body' was pressed 'as a rype clustre upon the pressour of the crosse'.[1] But without such a background the full significance of the last two lines is lost.

The compressed, allusive use of the complex of grape-harvest imagery in this stanza is very effective, but it is not enhanced by the image of the Christ-knight that encloses it. The use of the image in this context was no doubt suggested to Lydgate, as it had been to Friar William Herebert, by the phrase *propugnator sum* in the passage from Isaiah, and Lydgate develops it in a traditional way:

> My deth of deth hadde þe victorye,
> Fauht with Sathan a myhty strong batayl,
>
> .   .   .   .   .   .
>
> My platys severed, to-torn myn aventail,
> Lik as witnesseth this dolorous pite.[2]

But the Christ-knight and his armour were, as we have already said, a persuasive image that could not be visualized: therefore to bring it into sharp association with the *imago pietatis* was not happy: so irrelevant a conjunction can only diminish the poetic power of each part. If the tone of the poem had been passionate, discrepancies might have been sustained by strength of feeling. But the poem is cool, accomplished, and iconographically ornate: its success must be measured by the degree of cleverness shown in the manipulation of the imagery.

Though the form of the *imago pietatis* lent itself to various ingenious developments, its chief virtue was, as we have said before, that it provided a timeless image, in the forefront of which could pass all the many torments of the Passion sequence. Nevertheless, it did not totally supersede the old, well-established image of the crucified Christ. There are two very fine poems, 'The Dollorus complant of oure lorde Apoune þe croce Crucifyit'[3] and 'Wofully araide',[4] which are both manifestly spoken

---

[1] W. Maskell, *Monumenta ritualia ecclesiae anglicanae*, ii (London, 1846), 255–61. Lydgate himself was one of the various writers who made a vernacular verse paraphrase of this devotion, ed. cit. 238–50; another version is in *Devotional Pieces in Verse and Prose*, ed. J. A. W. Bennett (S.T.S. 1955), 170–81; cf. note on pp. vii–viii.

[2] Op. cit. 251. *Platys*: plate-armour; *aventail*: beaver.

[3] Brown xv, 102, inc. 'Now herkynnis wordis wunder gude'.

[4] Ibid., 103, inc. 'Beholde me, I pray þe, with all thyne hole reson'. Both this poem and 'The dollurus complant' have been attributed to Skelton, on the grounds of his reference in the *Garlande of Laurell* (ll. 1418–20) to two of his compositions as 'Wofully arayd, and shamefully betrayd' and 'Vexilla regis'. 'The dollurus complaynt', however, seems to have been current in mid fifteenth-century manuscripts about a decade before Skelton was born, and the refrain *Vexilla regis prodeunt*—the one tenuous link with Skelton—seems to be a late addition, being found only in Kele's *Christmas*

by Christ upon the Cross. Their form is, however, different from that of the earlier Crucifixion complaints. The meditator is no longer required to imagine himself present in the historical scene: if he did so, disturbing inconsistencies would arise. He would, for instance, find himself exhorted by the yet living Christ to see how He was slain. The speaker is in fact the crucified Christ made timeless by His portrayal in art: in other words the meditator must see before him or imagine a crucifix or a painting of the Crucifixion.

'The dollorus complant' was copied three times, printed once, and incorporated in the Towneley Play of the Resurrection. Two of the manuscripts that preserve it are the great religious collections, MSS. B.M. Add. 37049 and Arundel 285. In B.M. Add. MS. 37049 the devotional image, presupposed by the poem, is provided: beside the poem is a large representation of Christ on the Cross, which is here an actual tree bearing branches of love and charity; surrounding it are the instruments of the Passion:[1] this Crucifixion has the same qualities of affectiveness and timelessness as has the *imago pietatis*. The poem begins with an echo of the 'O vos omnes', 'Thow synfull man þat by me gais', but this traditional, though here not very appropriate, appeal is quickly forgotten as the poem proceeds in moving and accomplished stanzas through the various torments which preceded and succeeded the moment at which Christ actually hung on the Cross. The style of the poem may be illustrated from the following stanza, describing one of the commonest apocryphal episodes in the Passion narrative, that in which the executioners cruelly drag Christ's limbs to make them fit the holes already bored in the Cross:

> Behalde how, with þair rapis teuch,
> the Iowis fell my lymmes oute dreuch,
> ffor þat na lymme was meit aneuch
> > Unto þe bore.
> > This anger, þis wa,
> > þou seis me ta,
> > I tholit þe for.[2]

This stanza is typical of the best part of the poem: a suffering of Christ is vigorously described in the three long lines, whilst the personal and moral reference is brought home to the meditator in the concluding

---

Carolles printed between 1542 to 1546. The manuscript evidence also suggests that 'Wofully araide' is too early to be by Skelton, and this is confirmed by the absence in the poem of the phrase 'shamefully betrayd'. A discussion of the Skelton canon is given by F. Brie, 'Skelton-Studien', *Englische Studien*, xxxvii (1907), 1–86.

[1] See Plate 2.

[2] Brown xv, p. 152. *Teuch*: tough; *dreuch*: dragged; *bore*: hole (bored for the nails); *ta*: receive; *tholit*: endured. For the action see *Meditations*, ed. Ragusa and Greene, 334.

short lines. The Passion section of the poem is only marred once, by the following weak stanza:

> ffor þe, man, þou sall understande,
> In body, heid, fute and hande,
> ffyve hundreth woundis, and fyve thousande,
> And þairto sexty
> And fyftene,
> Was taulde and sene
> On my body.[1]

The content of this arithmetical stanza is scarcely poetical material: it draws upon a cult designed to bring the saying of the paternoster (the standard lay devotion) into relation with the Passion: a story repeated over and over again in fifteenth-century *horae* tells of the revelation to a woman recluse of this devotion, wherein the total number of Christ's wounds might be worshipped in the course of a year by the saying of fifteen aves and fifteen paternosters a day.[2] From the poetical point of view, however, the point is sufficiently made in the first line of the next stanza, 'Behalde, on me nocht hale was left'.

In the Arundel text of the poem (that printed by Carleton Brown) the Passion sequence is followed by a more didactic section in which Christ recalls the sinners towards whom He showed mercy, the penitent thief, Mary Magdalene, etc. This remedy for despair was embodied in a Latin prayer found in the *horae*.[3] But, though deriving from liturgical prayer, this is not unpromising material for poetry. Langland has a fine passage about Robert the robber, who prays to Christ because He had mercy on Dismas 'for *memento* sake'.[4] But in this poem the summary is prosaic, and succeeds only when keeping close to what is already moving in the New Testament, 'Thairfor with me / þe day Is he / In paradice'. Structurally this passage unbalances the poem, and, as it is omitted in two of the five texts (although not in the earliest), it may well be that it is an addition.[5]

---

[1] Brown xv, p. 153. Cf. notes to no. 92.

[2] The following are some of the manuscripts in which the story is told: C.U.L. Ii. 6. 43, 100ᵛ, B.M. Add. MS. 37787, 71ᵛ, Harley 2869, 204ʳ, Arundel 506, 28ʳ, Tanner 407, 82ʳ. The woman recluse is sometimes St. Bridget. An unprinted vernacular poem (*Index*, 1439) in MS. Trinity 601, 277ᵛ–8ᵛ, gives the story and a detailed account of the benefits that this devotion will produce. It is followed by a mnemonic jingle (*Index*, 3443) found also in other manuscripts; cf. *Carols*, p. 401.

[3] V. Leroquais, *Les livres d'heures manuscrits de la Bibliothèque Nationale*, ii (Paris, 1927), 345 (no. xxxv).

[4] *Piers Plowman*, B Text Passus V, 467–78, ed. Skeat, 172.

[5] The other manuscripts containing these verses are B.M. Add. MS. 37049 and the MacKulloch MS. (S.T.S. 65, 33–36), the former, however, presents them in two parts and in the reverse order (ff. 67ᵛ and 45ᵛ). The Kele and Towneley texts (which are closely related in their choice of stanzas) keep only the stanza beginning 'I was more wrother with Judas'. When so many manuscripts are missing, it cannot be assumed that the earliest surviving ones will necessarily conserve the best texts.

PLATE 2

Christ crucified
B. M. Add. MS. 37049

Popular poems tended to gain accretions. A clear example is the version of this poem in the Kele volume, where a refrain has been added, 'Now synge we as we were wont / Vexilla regis prodeunt', and an attempt has been made to integrate this to the lyric by a new opening stanza, beginning 'The kinges baner on felde is playd'.[1] The jubilant tone of the ancient hymn by Venantius Fortunatus, from which this refrain derives, suited well the patristic view of the Crucifixion as a scene of triumph, but is awkwardly unfitting to a Crucifixion lament.[2] No illuminating paradox springs to life from this juxtaposition. The two ways of looking at the Crucifixion are set out side by side, seemingly at random: neither rationally nor imaginatively do they meet.

The occurrence of 'The Dollorus complant' in the Towneley Play of the Resurrection[3] is interesting in the light it casts upon the timeless nature of the speaker, for in this part of the play Christ, though risen, must be in the form of an *imago pietatis*. There are many complaints of Christ in the mystery plays, particularly in the Crucifixion and the Last Judgement. But the Towneley Resurrection setting is unique in English drama, and historically inappropriate, in that, according to the New Testament, the marks of wounds in Christ's glorified body were symbols of past suffering, not painful signs of present agony. In the Towneley play the Easter antiphon 'Christus resurgens' is sung by the angels, and Christ then begins His complaint. In the York analogue the dialogue between the three Marys begins at this point.[4] The complaint was evidently inserted by the Towneley writer, an inference also borne out by an almost imperceptible change in the rhyme scheme.[5] The Towneley reviser was undoubtedly influenced by the form of the *imago pietatis* in which a half-length Christ as Man of Sorrows emerges from the tomb, perhaps supported by angels.[6] This episode in the play is exactly equivalent to the meditative lyric: the actor portraying Christ is in the same relationship to the audience as is an illumination of an *imago pietatis* to the reader of the accompanying lyric. It is interesting to see how what was ostensibly a Crucifixion complaint could be so simply translated into an acted *imago pietatis*.

[1] Greene 265. For the whole volume see *Christmas Carols*, ed. E. Bliss Reed (Cambridge Mass., 1932), 19–66.

[2] In 'Of alle the ioyus that in this worlde may be' (*Three Middle English Religious Poems*, ed. R. H. Bowers, University of Florida Monographs, Humanities no. 12, 1963, 33–43) the banner is successfully absorbed into the lament:

> There was the baner of lyf displayed
> His standard was py3 on an hey hil.
> There bod that kyng in the feld arayed
> With blody sydes and woundes gril. (ll. 169–73)

[3] E.E.T.S., E.S. 71, 313–16.

[4] Ed. L. Toulmin Smith (New York, 1963), 406.

[5] The preceding stanzas rhyme a a a b a b, the inserted poem a a a b c b.

[6] See Appendix E, p. 389 and n. 2.

Like 'The Dollorus complant', 'Wofully araide' has as its speaker an artistic representation of the crucified Christ. In its earliest manuscript, MS. Harley 4012 (a Carthusian manuscript designed for lay use), it is preceded by a small drawing of the Crucifixion, although (except for a few decorated initials) the manuscript is otherwise not illuminated. The poem demonstrates fifteenth-century style at its best: rhyme, alliteration, and vocabulary all contribute to an effect of force and movement:

> Of sharp thorne, I have worne a crowne, on my hed
> So rubbid, so bobbid, so rufulle, so red,
> Sore payned, sore strayned, and for þi love ded.
> Unfayned, not demed, my blod for þe shed,
> 　My fete and handis sore,
> 　With sturde naylis bore;
> 　What myght I suffer more
> þen I have sufferde, man, for þe?
> Com when þu wilt, and welcome to me.[1]

In this stanza the verbs, whose vigorous meaning is enhanced by rhyme and alliteration in the first two lines, form a striking prelude to the simplicity of the last three lines, and especially to the slow and moving quality of the last. The emphasis on the verbs in this stanza, as throughout the poem, is particularly noticeable. A series of verbs, bearing the rhyme, *fretid*, *thretid*, *defasid*, *rasid*, *chasid*, also bear the dominant feeling of the poem. The mystery plays perhaps contributed to the fifteenth-century tendency for scenes to be imagined in action rather than still, and painting at the same time became more naturalistic and filled with movement. A line such as 'The mowid, they spittid and dispisid me' suggests very well the grotesque and brutal faces, sometimes with streams of spittle proceeding from their mouths, which may be seen in paintings and alabasters depicting the mocking and scourging, and in representations of the Instruments of the Passion as isolated heads.[2]

'Wofully araide' was one of the fifteenth-century lyrics that continued to be known in the sixteenth century. There are three sixteenth-century texts of it as well as an allusion to it in *The Conversion of Swearers* by Stephen Hawes.[3] Two of these late texts are interesting because they occur in the famous musical manuscript of Robert Fayrfax and are set to music.[4] A recent discussion of the poem and its settings by Mr. Stevens is interesting for its implication that, even in such formal surroundings, the poem was still being thought of as a meditative work. He

---

[1] Brown xv, p. 157. *Rubbid*: despoiled by violence; *bobbid*: beaten.
[2] There is a particularly striking example in MS. Douce 1, 68ʳ. Fairly typical is that reproduced in E.E.T.S. 46, 189.
[3] *Englische Studien*, xxxvii. 25.
[4] John Stevens, *Music and Poetry in the Early Tudor Court*, 369–71.

says of the lyric that it 'is the clearest possible example of a poem being chosen for setting for non-musical qualities', and in his interesting remarks about the settings he stresses their uncommon naturalistic qualities, the way in which on the word *strained* 'long notes with pauses are introduced in every voice: the performer *sees* an elongated shape on the page in front of him; the listener *hears* a note stretched out'; the way also in which the setting of 'O man for thy sake' reinforces its emotional pleading, and the setting of the words 'Thus nakyd am I nailid' 'introduces the rare progression of a diminished fourth, F to C sharp, emphasizing the brutal act of the tormentors'.[1] With the exception of the carols, which form a group on their own, very few religious lyrics were set to music: it is very interesting to see that when they were thus set, the music was also exceptional in echoing the feeling of the words, a romantic style of writing that was quite uncharacteristic of the period.

Lydgate uses the form of the complaint of the crucified Christ as well as that of the *imago pietatis*. Two poems of this kind, Part V of the *Testament*,[2] which also circulated as an independent poem,[3] and 'Man, to refourme thyn exil and thy loos'[4] enumerate events from the scourging to the burial or the Harrowing of Hell (e.g. 'Beholde the sepulcre in which my bones lay'), and therefore must again be supposed to be spoken by timeless images. It is interesting that at the end of Part IV of the *Testament* Lydgate explicitly relates that it was a crucifix, seen in a monastery cloister, that was the starting-point of the succeeding meditation on the Passion. He describes how, as a boy,

> . . . holdyng my passage,
> Myd of a cloyster, depicte upon a wall,
> I saugh a crucifyx, whos woundes were not smalle,
> With this [word] 'Vide', wrete there besyde,
> 'Behold my mekenesse, O child, and leve thy pryde.'[5]

—and how in his later age he decided to write 'this litel dite' on the word *vide*. The complaint follows the standard fifteenth-century pattern: the major part is an enumeration of the events of the Passion, whilst the concluding part pleads for love, 'Beholde my love, and gyf me thyn ageyn' or 'Gyf me thyn herte and be no more unkynde', though it also gives didactic encouragement. The most curious and 'unpoetic' feature of the poem is that the recurrent exhortation 'Behold' is followed, not by sustained narrative description (as it is in 'The Dollorus complant'), but by mere enumeration of disjointed details. In many lines obedience to the injunction *behold* would lead to a visualization of the Instruments

---

[1] Ibid. 37 and 104. [2] E.E.T.S., E.S. 107, 357–62.
[3] See *Index*, 2464. On the paintings of the verses at Long Melford see J. B. Trapp, 'Verses by Lydgate at Long Melford', *R.E.S.*, N.S. vi (1955), 1–11.
[4] E.E.T.S. 107, 216–21. [5] Op. cit. 356.

of the Passion, 'Behold the cordes with whiche þat I was bounde', 'Behold the peler and the ropes stronge', 'Behold the spere most sharply grounde and whette', 'Beholde the reed spyre gall and eysel fett'; in other words, it would not lead to the mental visualization of a complete scene but of isolated objects. In many ways this poem is no more than mnemonic; it recalls each scene or object which may be fittingly meditated upon, but provides hardly any emotional stimulus to undertake or sustain a meditation, nor any guidance to the visual imagination. It is surely a poem entirely dependent upon current iconographic forms, one which, had they not existed, could neither have been written nor profitably read.

For a just understanding of this poem, and for others of Lydgate's complaints, some further comments upon the Instruments of the Passion is needed.[1] From the early Middle Ages in scenes of the Last Judgement angels are gathered behind Christ holding the Cross and some of the more important instruments of the Passion. During the fourteenth century angels holding these instruments were occasionally represented separately, but it was only in the fifteenth century that the instruments became isolated from the Last Judgement and from their angelic bearers, and they were then also greatly increased in number. In England, as in France, Germany, and the Netherlands, the instruments were represented in every artistic medium. In church they were convenient to carve on small areas, such as roof-bosses, bench-ends, misericords, and the capitals of pillars. Some of these, however, would not be easily visible, and to the literate layman, at least, they would be more readily known from the English verse prayer, 'O vernacule i honoure him and the',[2] with its copious illustrations, and from the representations in the frames surrounding a Pietà or *imago pietatis*. The extraordinarily wide currency of the English poem has been pointed out by Professor Robbins.[3] It survives now in fifteen manuscripts (and there are of course Latin analogues). These are either books of hours or short rolls, the latter being, as it were, the poor man's book of hours, though rolls may sometimes have been fixed on *tabulae* in churches, and nearly all the texts are accompanied by illustrations. There is obviously here a cult of looking, and Professor Robbins draws attention to the indulgences attached to mere gazing at the arms of the Passion. In the poems of Lydgate, not only the instruments referred to, but also the manner of description reflects these very common visual illustrations. This is very clear in the other Crucifixion complaint already referred to, 'Man to

[1] É. Mâle, *L'Art religieux de la fin du moyen âge en France*, 103–7; M. D. Anderson, *The Imagery of British Churches*, 59–61; C. Carter, 'The *Arma Christi* in Scotland', *Proceedings of the Society of Antiquaries of Scotland*, xc (1956–7), 116–29, pls. x–xv.

[2] E.E.T.S. 46, 170–93.

[3] R. H. Robbins, 'The "Arma Christi" Rolls', *M.L.R.* xxxiv (1939), 415–21.

refourme thyn exil and thy loos',[1] where each item derives from the *arma Christi*, the 'bloody fface', the reed and sponge, 'hatful spittyng', the face 'blyndfellid', the pellican, dice, ropes, lanterns, swords and staves, hammer and pincers, ladder, and crowing cock. The visual influence may be seen, for instance, in the 'xxxti pens rounde' of the *Testament*, for in every illustration their roundness is particularly apparent. Of the first half of 'Man to refourme' the same judgement must be made as of Part V of the *Testament*, that is that the emblematic treatment of the Passion has not the emotive force of continuous narrative: these instruments, isolated from the historical scene, though they might demand the honour of a pater noster or be reminders of guilt, could hardly stir to a responding love.

The second part of this poem turns into a narrative of the Passion interspersed with dogmatic teaching. It is preceded, however, by the following stanza:

> I ffought for the a fful greet batayll,
>   Ageyn Sathan the tort[u]ous serpent,
> Nakyd on the cros withoute plate or mayll,
>   Bood in the ffeld tyll al my blood was spent;
>   To wynne thy love this was myn Entent,
>   On to that ende I was thy Champioun;
>   To ffynde thy salve my flessh was al to-rent—
>   Whan thou art woundid, thynk on my passioun.[2]

There is here a bleak but complete statement of the theme of the lover-knight, an image to which Lydgate constantly recurs: we have already noticed it, for instance, in association with the image of the winepress. In the present context it may at first sight seem to be no more than another example of Lydgate's indiscriminate drawing upon the traditional themes of the Passion in order to fill out his complaints. The idea of the lover-knight, however, acquired in the fifteenth century an accretion, giving it a superficial relevance to visual descriptions of the Crucifixion that it had not possessed before. This accretion was the new iconographic form of a shield with the five wounds upon it arranged as an heraldic device.[3] Like the instruments of the Passion this is to be found frequently in small spaces, roof-bosses, bench-ends, etc., and in woodcuts and manuscript illumination. It was on the one hand the visual culmination of a long tradition of devotion to the five wounds in prayers, hymns, in the liturgy of the office and the mass, and in mystical and devotional treatises; on the other hand it drew from the traditional idea of Christ's noble birth and of Him as the true source of gentility.

---

[1] E.E.T.S. E.S. 107, 216–21.   [2] Ibid. 219.

[3] Anderson, op. cit. 61–62; D. Gray, 'The Five Wounds of Our Lord', *Notes and Queries*, N.S. x (March, 1963), pp. 88–89. I am very indebted to Mr. Gray for having let me read this article in typescript.

The latter aspect will be familiar from Langland's reference to the Crucifixion:

> And blody bretheren we bycome there of o body ywonne,
> As *quasi modo geniti* and gentil men uche one.[1]

But both aspects are interestingly combined in a verse accompanying a blazon of the five wounds in MS. Lansdowne 874:

> Why should earthes gentry make herself so good,
> Giving coate armes for all the World to Gaze on;
> Christs blood alone makes gentle men of blood,
>   his shameful passion yeelds ye fairest Blazon.
> For he is auncienst & of best behaviour
>   Whose auncestors & Armes are from his Saviour.[2]

In the first part of 'Man to refourme' the refrain is 'Looke on my woundis, thynk on my passioun' (though it later becomes simply '. . . thynk on my passioun'). If this injunction suggested, not a wounded Christ, but a shield with the wounds upon it, then the association with the Christ-knight would be much closer, and there can be little doubt, in view of Lydgate's constant preference for emblems, that it is the wounds, isolated from the body, to which he refers. Therefore, whilst the refrain of the poem at first suggests the simple appeal for love characteristic of the earlier lyric, in its content it rather draws upon the iconographic conceits of the fifteenth century.

There is within the group of complaints spoken by an *imago pietatis* or a crucified Christ a distinctive and curious form, that of the Charter of Christ,[3] which developed into a cross between the two. In origin the charter, like the lover-knight, is a persuasive image and, as in some descriptions of the Christ-knight's armour, its details were elaborated with the effect of a conceit: the charter, endowing man with the kingdom of heaven, is written on the parchment of Christ's skin, the pen is the lance and nails, the ink the blood, the letters the wounds, and the seal His wounded heart.[4] This kind of allegory is not suited to visual expression, though an attempt at it is made in B.M. Add. MS. 37049, in which there is portrayed a figure of the Man of Sorrows, with the

---

[1] B Text xi, 195–6, ed. Skeat, 342. This definition of gentility may be contrasted with that in the Wife of Bath's Tale, 'That he is gentil that dooth gentil dedis' (D 1170), ed. Robinson, 105.

[2] Quoted by Gray, op. cit., p. 89, footnote 57.

[3] For the poems see M. C. Spalding, *The Middle English Charters of Christ* (Bryn Mawr, 1914), who describes the manuscripts and prints all the texts.

[4] Conceits of this kind were already commonplaces of devotional literature: they occur, for instance, in the *Philomena* of John of Howden (verses 285–6, ed. C. Blume, 25), the *Meditations on the Passion*, Text ii, of Richard Rolle (*English Writings*, ed. H. E. Allen, 36), *A Meditacion of þe fyve woundes of Ihesu Crist*, also attributed to Rolle (*Yorkshire Writers*, ed. Horstman, ii. 440), and 'þou wommon boute vere' (Brown xiv, 16, p. 19).

instruments of the Passion behind Him, and holding a large sheet on which is inscribed the 'short' charter. The earliest Charter complaints, however, antedate this illustration by about fifty years and do not presuppose it. In so far as the poems themselves contain an unchanging meditative image, it is that of the crucified Christ: this is possible because speaker and image are not here identified in the way that they were in the Christ-knight allegory; in the one Christ is the speaker of an allegory about Himself, in the other Christ is only present in the poem under the allegory of the lover-knight. It is interesting, however, to notice that the figure of Christ is treated differently in the two versions of the 'long' charter. In Version A the speaker is a timeless figure, the Passion narrative is in the past tense, and the sequence of events extends to the Burial; in Version B an attempt has been made to fix the complaint in time, so that the pains of the Passion are narrated in the present tense and events later than the Crucifixion are related as a foretelling of the future. This version is less successful: it reads as the awkward reworking of a reviser who has not understood or has not liked the original meditative structure.

To the extent that the Charters of Christ are Passion complaints they need no further comment, but the legal image at their centre requires elucidation. The application of legal terminology to the doctrine of the Redemption begins with St. Paul and seems first to have been applied to historical events by St. Ambrose, who described the committing of the Virgin and St. John to one another as a part of Christ's *testamentum*.[1] Christ's promise to his disciples, 'Pacem relinquo vobis', also suggested by its form a testamentary disposition.[2] This may be illustrated from the *Pèlerinage de la vie humaine* of Guillaume de Guilleville, where in the earlier text Christ bequeaths only His peace,[3] whilst in the second the bequest is extended to include Christ's body to the sepulchre, and thereafter to all Christians, His mother to St. John, His blood to those who feel compassion for His sufferings, etc.[4] Similar lists may be found in a variety of works, both homiletic, such as the *Legenda aurea*,[5] and literary, such as the *Stanzaic Life of Christ*[6] and Lydgate's *A Seying of the Nightingale*.[7]

---

[1] *Comment. Lib. x in Evang. Luc.* xxii, P.L. 15, 1837; Spalding, op. cit. xli. Arnold of Bonneval also followed Ambrose in seeing the commission of the Blessed Virgin to St. John as part of a *testamentum*, *De septem verbis domini in cruce*, P.L. 189, 1696.

[2] On this see E. C. Perrow, 'The Last Will and Testament as a Form of Literature', *Transactions of the Wisconsin Academy of Sciences, Arts and Letters*, xvii (1913), 707–8.

[3] ll. 2459–512, ed. J. J. Stürzinger (Roxburghe Club, 1893), 77–79.

[4] *The Pilgrimage of the Life of Man*, trans. from the second recension by Lydgate, ll. 4752–5036, ed. F. J. Furnivall (London, 1905), 125–32.

[5] *The Golden Legend*, i. 66–67. Cf. Wycliffe, *De civili dominio*, ed. R. L. Poole and J. Loserth, iv (London, 1904), 626–8.

[6] E.E.T.S. 166, 183–4.   [7] E.E.T.S. E.S. 107, 230.

Though imagery is comparatively rare in medieval English literature, the law was one of its most popular and recurrent sources, providing not only isolated comparisons but whole structures: both religious and secular poems may be set in the form of bills, charters and, most commonly, wills. The Biblical and patristic image was therefore very easily adopted by the literary tradition and found in it a fertile context for amplification and variation. The most important variation was the transformation of a will into a charter, the Charter already belonging to the literary tradition as, for instance, the *Charter of the Abbey of the Holy Ghost*[1] or the better known (though later) Charter of Favel in *Piers Plowman*.[2] The fairly large step, however, between describing the Redemption as an endowment given by Christ and describing Christ's body as itself the Charter was no doubt effected by the image of Christ's body as a book,[3] and with its aid the diverse traditions were brought together in a strange but powerful way. The final stage was the assimilation of the content of the charter to the complaint form, so that within a few lines a simple transition could be made from the liturgical appeal, 'O vos omnes qui transitis per viam . . .', to the charter proclamation, 'Sciant presentes et futuri . . .'.[4]

The same question arises with the Charter image as with the armour of the Christ-knight: that is, granted that the image expresses lucidly and logically the doctrine that Christ died for the love of man and for his benefit, does this very detailed and often ingenious elaboration of it seem more curiously witty than affective? It is clear that strange and startling images of this kind can be expounded in a very moving way. The conclusion of Richard Rolle's second Meditation on the Passion illustrates this very beautifully: in it Christ's wounded body is compared to many diverse things, such as a net, a dove-house, and a honeycomb;[5] and, whilst some of the images such as the star-filled sky or the flower-covered field bear an aesthetic correspondence, the very unlikeliness of some of the comparisons, in particular that of the net, suggests the humility of Christ and the enormity of what He suffered. It is less certain to what extent the imagery in the Charter complaints is moving, and to what extent quaint or at best coldly ingenious. The passage of conceited comparisons begins as follows:

> Ne myght I fynd na perchemyne
> ffor to last with-outen fyne,
> Bot als luf bad me do
> Myne awen skyn I toke þer-to.[6]

---

[1] *Yorkshire Writers*, ed. Horstman, i. 337–62.
[2] B Text, Passus ii, ll. 74–113, ed. Skeat, 46–49.
[3] See below, p. 253, footnote 2.
[4] Spalding, op. cit. 28.
[5] *English Writings*, 34–36.
[6] Spalding, op. cit. 22–24.

In these lines the idea of Christ's skin as a parchment immune to the laws of decay and the reference to Christ's obedience to the command of Love soften and warm the image; but later the same image is developed with an aptness that is too precise to be moving:

> And waschen in myne awen blode,
> And strAytely strened on þe rode;
> Streyned to dry on þe rode tre
> Als perchemyne aw for to be.[1]

The precision of the comparison may be seen from the following fifteenth-century recipe for parchment-making: 'Forto make parche-myne gode and ffyne: Take þe a schepis skynne and caste hit inne lyme and water and late hit ligge ix dayes þer inne, þanne take hit up and streyne hit a brode on a harowe . . . þan set hout þyn skynne on þe harowe forto drye. . . .'[2] The soaking of the parchment (to provide supple-ness) is done by Christ's own blood; its stretching on the frame (for thinness) represents Christ's body pulled to fit the holes in the Cross, and its subsequent drying the hanging on the Cross.

These two quotations show different methods of using the same con-ceit. In the one the literal meaning is irradiated by the image, in the other it is confined. It would be possible, though tedious, to work through the whole poem, making the same distinctions, but the final impression is that the tone of loving lament predominates. It shines through the Charter image, despite passages of constricting cleverness, through direct paradoxes, such as 'ffor þou art ded and I am lyfe / I most dy to gyf þe lyfe', and through echoes of the *Improperia*, 'A luf-drink I ask of þe / Ayzell and gall þai gaf to me'. Whilst there are many faults in the poems, parts are clumsy, parts too narrowly ingenious, parts too dully didactic, the exploration of the Charter image, with the paradoxes gathered around it, succeeds in provoking a profound surprise at the munificence of love demonstrated and bestowed in the Passion.

The 'short' charter is quite different. In this the longer version has been greatly shortened and tidied up, so that the charter metaphor is exclusively present, and the emphasis is upon the legal forms, the seal, the witnesses, etc. There remains nothing of the Passion narrative, of the appeal for love, or of the conceits apart from the seal.[3] From the literary point of view this poem is scarcely more attractive than the dry legal

---

[1] Spalding, op. cit. 26.

[2] Quoted by G. S. Ivy, 'The Bibliography of the Manuscript-Book', in F. Wormald and C. E. Wright, *The English Library before 1700* (London, 1958), 35.

[3] With this treatment may be contrasted a very popular section from *The Pore Caitiff* —a section often copied separately from the whole treatise—where the charter is mentioned only briefly in the introduction and it is the conceits that are expanded at length. On *The Pore Caitiff* see M. Deanesly, *The Lollard Bible* (Cambridge, 1920), 346-7, and Sister Mary Teresa Brady, '*The Pore Caitif*: An Introductory Study', *Traditio*, x (1954), 529-48. For the text of this charter see Spalding, op. cit. 100-2.

document that it parodies. Though it is accompanied by the Man of Sorrows in B.M. Add. MS. 37049, this illustration seems only justified by a memory of the 'long' charter. In other manuscripts it is more appropriately illustrated by a realistic drawing of a seal with the wounded heart as its emblem.[1] The reference to the seal, 'The wounde in myn harte þe seale it is', provides the sole touch of moving imagery. In itself it is clever. There is an allusion to Psalm xxi. 15, 'Factum est cor meum tanquam cera', and also to the contemporary practice of using the wound or wounds as the emblazon for a seal. But the wound in Christ's side was so traditionally a symbol of Christ's love that no reference to it could be quite unmoving, however terse or ingenious. When also represented pictorially, it would be undeniably affective, though this would be a clear example of emotion being aroused by the illustration presupposed by the poem, rather than by the poem itself.

Beside the Passion poems so far described there is a second substantial group of complaints in the fifteenth century, of which the content is chiefly didactic. They inherit the manner of the Vernon lyrics, though not their vigour or idiosyncratic tone, sincerity, and irony. In these there is little visual meditative description, and the tone, minatory or reproachful, seems more appropriate to a judge or preacher than to a friend or lover. Three of these, however, may be singled out because they make use of the potentially moving image of Christ as a friend: they are 'Late as I wente one myne pleynge'[2] (one of the few complaints later to be printed),[3] 'This is goddis owne complaynt',[4] and a dialogue, 'Salvator mundi domine'.[5] The explicit portrayal of Christ as friend is a persuasive image and, in that *exempla* are sometimes alluded to, its use in the lyrics from time to time resembles that of the Christ-knight. It may even draw on the same kind of literary associations, for the ideal of friendship had become part of the chivalric tradition.

The references to friendship in these poems are sometimes brief, sometimes developed; but even when unexpanded they would not necessarily be unimportant, for the image of Christ as a friend was rooted in a store of evocative feeling.[6] It sprang from the medieval inheritance of the classical ideal of friendship, which was fostered by the use of the *Ethics* as a university textbook, and by the fairly wide diffusion of Cicero's *De amicitia* and of Aelred's Christian adaptation of it, the *De spirituali amicitia*. This body of thought was used to illumine the traditional gloss on John xv. 13, 'Maiorem hac dilectionem nemo habet, ut

---

[1] Spalding, op. cit. xix–xxix; the descriptions of manuscript illustrations are not always quite accurate.

[2] Brown xv, 105.　　　　　　　　　　[3] Douce Frag. f. 48.

[4] E.E.T.S. 15, 190–9.　　　　　　　　[5] Brown xv, 107.

[6] *R.E.S.*, N.S. xiii (1962), 15, and footnote 2 for bibliography.

animam suam ponat quis pro amicis suis',[1] in which the text was applied to the Crucifixion. In sermon literature the theme was common: the classical and romance stories of faithful friends, such as Damon and Pythias or Amis and Amiloun, were allegorized to signify the relationship of Christ to man. Two allegorical *exempla* are particularly important for the lyrics. One is the adaptation of the lover-knight *exemplum*, wherein one friend fights and dies for another;[2] the other is that of the four friends:[3] according to this, a man condemned to die for a crime that he had committed turned for help to his former friends; the first three (signifying the world, the flesh, and the Devil) offered no comfort, but the fourth friend, who had been until then poorly esteemed, ransomed the man. The fourth friend, of course, signified Christ. Echoes of *exempla* such as these allow the image of Christ as friend to be applied with particular appropriateness to the Crucifixion.

It can perhaps be seen, even from these sketchy references to what was a solid tradition, that by the fifteenth century the image of Christ as friend had an abundance of emotional associations which a poet could draw on. Unfortunately, however, these three poems only partially develop the potentialities of the idea. The main reason is that Christ is not shown solely as a courteous friend expecting no return ('Dilexit, inquam curialiter, nullam remunerationem expectando', as Pecham in a sermon movingly expresses it),[4] but is too often represented as a reproachful friend who recalls benefits conferred or ingratitude shown; and love and a guilty conscience can coincide only with difficulty.

'Late as I wente one myne pleynge' begins quite pleasantly with a *chanson d'aventure* opening, in which the poet feigns that in his 'pleynge' (a word difficult to translate, but suggesting a life of thoughtless diversion and delight) he came upon a crucifix, and the figure of Christ thereon addressed him. There follows in the next four stanzas a general complaint, of which the fourth stanza is particularly effective:

> My hondes for þe on þe crosse bene spredde,
> To shew þe mercy yf þou wilt crave.

---

[1] 'Greater love hath no man than this, that a man lay down his life for his friends' (A.V.). Cf. R. R. Purdy, 'The Friendship Motif in Middle English Literature', *Vanderbilt Studies in the Humanities*, i (1951), 113–41.

[2] *Summa praedicantium*, ii. 176ʳ, col. 2.

[3] The *exemplum* occurs in the collections of Odo of Cheriton (*Les fabulistes latins*, ed. L. Hervieux, iv (Paris, 1896), 317–18, 394), Jacques de Vitry (Crane, no. 120), and in the *Gesta romanorum* (E.E.T.S., E.S. 33, 127–32). It is used also in the *Middle English Sermons*, ed. W. O. Moss, E.E.T.S. 209, 86–89. This *exemplum* is elsewhere given the moralization familiar from *Everyman*. For a general account see K. Goedeke, *Everyman, Homulus und Hekastus* (Hanover, 1865).

[4] Quoted by D. Douie, 'Archbishop Pecham's Sermons and Collations', *Studies in Medieval History presented to F. M. Powicke*, ed. R. W. Hunt, etc. (Oxford, 1948), 278. 'I tell you that He loved courteously with no expectation of reward.' Cf. Julian of Norwich, *Revelations of Divine Love*, ed. Warrack, 49, 51, 81, and *passim*.

Me to offende þu shuldest be adrad,
ffor yf þu do wel I wol þe save.
Whane þu art dede and lefte in grave
[And all thy frendes from the flee,]
Yt þy sowle I seke to save,
    Quid ultra debui facere?[1]

There is here a deft combination of the theme of Christ as the one faithful friend with the recurrent idea of the poetry on death of the corpse forsaken by all its former companions.[2] But the effectiveness of this is diminished by the openly threatening tone of line 3. The rest of the poem consists of an enumeration of God's gifts, the creation of the world and the making of man in His likeness. A grateful awareness of the natural world had been a common theme of medieval devotional literature, and had been used in the form of a complaint as early as the *De arrha animae* of Hugh of St. Victor[3] and the *Ancrene Wisse*.[4] In both of these, however, Christ appealed in the tones of a bridegroom or lover. The list of gifts, when detached from this context, has an air of goading insistence, appropriate to a preacher but not to Christ. The refrain, *Quid ultra debui facere*, also sounds more recriminatory than lovingly generous when its foundation does not lie primarily in the figure of the suffering Christ.

In 'Late as I wente one myne pleynge' the image of friendship is introduced only fitfully, but in 'This is goddis owne complaynt' the refrain, 'Whi art þou to þi freend unkinde?', relates the image to the substance of each stanza. Sometimes this is effective:

Poore, naked, shamed, and shent,
    that Frendeshype myghttest þou nat fynde,
But me that on the Roode was Rente;
    why art þou to thy freende onkynde?

Man, I love the! whome Lovyst thowe?
    I am þy frende; why wolt þou feyne?
I for-yave, and þu me slewe:
    ho hath departyd oure love A tweyne?
Turne to me! by-thenke the howe
    thowe haste go mys! come home Agayne!
And thowe shalt be as welcome nowe
    As he that synne never ded steyne.[5]

The first line of this quotation perhaps contains an echo of the criminal of the *exemplum* led miserably to the gallows, whilst the last four lines

[1] Brown xv, p. 160.   [2] See above, pp. 83–84.
[3] *P.L.* 176, 951–70.   [4] E.E.T.S. 294, 203–4.
[5] Ibid. 15, 192. L. 12, *steyne*, MS. *fayne*.

derive their warmth from the welcome of the Prodigal Son. The paradoxical antithesis, 'I for-yave, and þu me slewe', is also moving, and
forms part of a pattern of antithesis that recurs throughout the poem:
though many of the antitheses derive from the *Improperia*, others, such
as 'I bounde my selffe, þe to onbynde', are less liturgical and more
subtle. There is, however, a very strong didactic strain in the poem that
does not fit the mourning reproach of the refrain. The most extravagant
example is the beginning of the last stanza, 'Man! by-thenk the what
þou Arte . . .', where the traditional preacher's injunction[1] comes very
strangely from Christ the friend of man.

The last poem, 'Salvator mundi domine', is a dialogue, a form rare in
the earlier period, but more common in the fifteenth century. It opens
with man's appeal for mercy, and in the alternate stanzas allotted to him
man continues to plead, to repent, and to grieve. Though much of this
is dull, lines here and there are touching: 'Ffor þat I have don wrong,
/ ryghte as þi chylde, þu schalte me bete.' As in 'This is goddis owne
complaynt' the speeches of Christ draw largely on the *Improperia* and on
variations on the theme of Christ as friend. This image is introduced
strongly in the first speech of Christ:

> Man, qwat have I done to þe?
> qwy art þu, man, to me unkynde?
> Qwy has þu, man, for-sake me?
> qwy flese þu, man? I am þi frynde.[2]

but it is then abandoned until the following lines:

> If þu can fynde a-noþur frynde,
> to do so mycul for þi foly,
> Leve now me and with hym wende,
> of me aske þu no more mercy.[3]

The substance of this recalls the refrain of the Anglo-Norman poem we
have already quoted:

> Si poez trover nul amant,
> Ke por vus face autretant,
> Lessez moi e amez lui;
> En joie vivez ambedui.[4]

However, the difference in tone illustrates well the more didactic cast
of the later period. The reference to 'foly' makes the second line of the
English more judicial than loving, whilst the last line suggests the rejection of the sinner rather than the joy and gaiety of love. In this poem the
image of friendship is intermixed with menacing implications of vengeance, in a way that is disturbing for those who have been pleased by

---

[1] See, for instance, p. 107.   [2] Brown xv, p. 164.
[3] Ibid. 167.   [4] See p. 61 above.

the earlier lyrics. Technically, however, the chief defect of the poem is
that, whilst the arrangement suggests a dialogue, for the main part of
the work neither speaker truly answers the other: it is only in the very
last stanza, beginning 'Now, swete sole, welcum to me', that Christ seems
to have heard the voice of the penitent, and the effect then is moving.
But the intimacy that one would expect in a meditative dialogue is quite
lacking in the rest of the poem.

The tendency for affective imagery to be swamped by didacticism
can be seen at its most extreme in the long dialogue 'Thus oure gracious
god prince of pitee'. In this there are agreeable echoes of the theme of
friendship. Man says to Christ:

> Whi woldist þou, lord, be slayn for me?
> þat am þin enemy moost unhende?
> Siþen no man haþ more charite,
> þan deeþ to suffre for his freende.[1]

And later Christ tells man: 'Whanne þou alle þi freendis hast asaied, /
þou schalt fynde no freend lijk me.'[2] But such touches are engulfed by
the great weight of didactic material. Christ reproaches man for the
seven deadly sins, particularly lust and avarice, for the sins of the five
wits, and for his omission of the seven works of mercy. He threatens the
inflexible justice of the Day of Doom and the horrors of the pains of hell.
All these subjects are resumed in man's contrite responses, where he
pleads his own frailty and Christ's mercy. In its subject-matter this
dialogue looks back to the penitential poems[3] (which provided a stimulus
and the framework for a confession) and to the Last Judgement complaints of the mystery plays;[4] for many details it is indebted to the lyrics
on death. Christ, for instance, denounces man in the *quid profuit* formula, 'What schal þanne profite þi gowne y-pleite . . .',[5] whilst man
laments his predicament in the image of the strife between body and
soul: 'Whan my soule woulde faynest þe paye, / My flesche is the fyrst
þat wole it lett.'[6] Indeed, though the dialogue is between Christ and
man, the tone is not unlike that of a Body and Soul debate, though a
debate in which the body admits the truth of the soul's accusations.

---

[1] E.E.T.S. 15, 222. This edition prints 'Oure gracious god prynce of pite' as though
it were a continuation of 'This is goddis owne complaynt', but they are distinct poems:
see *Index*, 3612 and 2714. It is only in the two Lambeth manuscripts from which the
texts are printed by Furnivall that these two poems occur adjoining one another.

[2] ll. 717–18, op. cit. 231.

[3] e.g. Patterson, op. cit., nos. 4, 5, etc.

[4] *The Towneley Plays*, E.E.T.S., E.S. 71, 379–80; *Chester Plays*, E.E.T.S., E.S. 115,
440–2. It may be noted that there is also a short vernacular Last Judgement complaint
in prose, which was obviously very popular. It occurs, for instance, in MSS. Bodl.
416, 106ᵛ; Bodl. 789, 146ᵛ–7ᵛ; and Harley 2339, 38ᵛ.

[5] l. 283, op. cit. 209.

[6] ll. 367–8, op. cit. 212.

The most extensive description of the Passion occurs in Section 8, a complaint against swearers, in which blasphemous oaths are seen as a renewal of the Crucifixion.[1] This traditional image is ingenious in a narrowly moral way, but far removed from a loving meditation on the Passion. It demonstrates in a small, clear way a point implicit in the whole poem, namely that thought on the Passion leads, not to love, but to amendment and contrition. From the beginning of the lyric form there had been a subordinate association between the Passion complaint and demand for virtue. The Latin tag which some manuscripts prefix to Lydgate's 'Upon the cros naylled I was ffor the' seems to be of early origin:

> In cruce sum pro te, qui peccas; desine pro me,
> Desine; do veniam; dic culpam retrabo penam.[2]

This verse had been translated into English in the *Fasciculus morum*[3] and in John of Grimestone's preaching-book,[4] and was paraphrased lengthily and elaborated in the mid fourteenth-century poem 'Man, þus on rode I hyng for þe'.[5] Moreover, didactic treatises had from the twelfth century recommended meditation on the Passion as an antidote to the stirrings of sin (particularly lust),[6] but these had been only byways in early meditative literature. But, as we can see from this dialogue, or from other poems of the period, such as that in MS. Harley 4012, where the meditator prays, 'And let thy passion be in my mynde / To put away tantacoun of the fende',[7] the penitential conception of the Passion became the dominant theme of much fifteenth-century Passion poetry; and however salutory it may have been morally, it provided far less fitting and agreeable material for the meditative lyric.

There is another group characteristic of the fifteenth century and having no ancestry among earlier vernacular poems, which may be called 'numbered poetry', for the structure and length are determined by a number deriving from a liturgical or meditative exercise. In this they resemble the poems on the joys of the Blessed Virgin. The subjects are the seven words from the Cross, the five or seven wounds, and the

---

[1] For an account of this form see Appendix G.

[2] E.E.T.S. E.S. 107, 252. 'I am on the Cross for your sake, you who are sinning; desist for my sake. Desist and I forgive; confess your guilt and I will withdraw the punishment.' For earlier occurrences of the Latin see E.E.T.S. 225, xxii–xxiii.

[3] MS. Rawl. C. 670, 45ʳ. Inc. 'I honge on cros for love of the'.

[4] Brown XIV, p. 261. Cf. MS. Magd. Camb. 13, 2ʳ (James, *Catalogue*, 26).

[5] Ibid. 47.

[6] The following are amongst the treatises that recommend it: *The Chastising of God's Children*, ed. J. Bazire and E. Colledge (Oxford, 1957), 213; *The Pore Caitiff*, MS. Bodl. 3, 97ʳ; *Disce mori*, MS. Laud Misc. 99, 66ᵛ: 'The seconde remedie not oonly ayenst this synne [lust] but ayenst all other is infallible, that is an herti remembrance of Cristes passyon.'

[7] f. 107ᵛ. Inc. 'Ihesu the sonne of Mare mylde'.

seven blood-sheddings. Sometimes these are made the foundation of a general petition, but more often they are opposed to the sins of the five senses or to the seven deadly sins. Most of these lyrics are didactic rather than meditative, in that the suffering is recalled as a reproach or anti-dote to sin rather than as an appeal for love. The poems may be set in the form of a complaint or of a first-person meditation: it is a mark of their didactic austerity that there is scarcely any difference of tone be-tween the two. The style of the poems varies, but often seems inhibited by the inevitably rigid adherence to number. An introduction or an epilogue may extend the poem beyond the five or seven stanzas strictly required by the theme, but in general the Passion narrative cannot be spread over as many verses as the poet requires, and each verse must contain a sharply isolated unit of description. It is difficult nowadays to appreciate the value of such numbers for their own sake. Appreciation of *The Pearl* is admittedly enhanced by its hundred stanzas symbolizing perfection, but this is exceptional, for the hundred here is both a test of the poet's skill and a brilliant sign of his success. A significant number wretchedly achieved will nowadays pass unnoticed or at best seem an irrelevant hindrance to a poetic development of the theme. But in the Middle Ages the simple achievement of the number may have seemed to confer weight and dignity.

There survive three poems on the theme of the Seven Words from the Cross: one, a fragment only, from MS. C.U.L. Dd. v. 76,[1] another which adjoins 'The Dollorus complant' in MS. Arundel 285,[2] and a third which is amongst the many liturgical poems of Audelay.[3] Though this subject was not adopted by the English lyric until the fifteenth century, it had a long Latin tradition behind it. Its earliest occurrence is in *De septem verbis domini in cruce*[4] by the twelfth-century writer Arnold of Bonneval, and then after a gap in time it was revived in important works such as the *Vitis mystica* of Bonaventura,[5] and became a regular part of meditative narratives of the Passion, such as the *Medi-tationes vitae christi*[6] and the more learned *Vita Jesu Christi* of Ludolf the Carthusian.[7] The form in which it received most widespread

---

[1] Person, op. cit. 4.

[2] Bennett, *Devotional Pieces*, 259–61.

[3] E.E.T.S. 184, 7.

[4] *P.L.* 189, 1677–1726. The history of this theme has been traced by A. Wilmart, 'Le grand poème bonaventurien sur les sept paroles du Christ en croix', *Revue Béné-dictine*, xlvii (1935), 235–78.

[5] *Decem Opuscula*, 436–47.

[6] Trans. Ragusa and Green, 336–7.

[7] Ed. L. M. Rigollot (Paris, 1878), iv. 112–29. In England it was one of the many devotional themes adopted by Wycliffe, who uses it in the *De civili dominio* (Bk. iii, ch. 26, ed. J. Loserth, iv. 625–6), and in a sermon for Good Friday, *Sermones* iv, ed. J. Loserth (London, 1890), 330–7.

currency, however, was the prayer *De septem verbis Christi in cruce* attributed to Bede,[1] which was one of the most recurrent items in books of hours.[2]

It is this compact prayer that is translated in the three English poems, though with minor variations, particularly in the nature of the petitions. The Latin prayer, however, was so economical in style that it was necessarily expanded in English verse translations, and the interesting question from the literary point of view is the extent to which the translators successfully drew on the meditative tradition for their amplifications. The Latin description of the word committing the Virgin of St. John is as follows:

> Et sicut tu dixisti matri tuae, *Mulier, ecce filius tuus*, deinde dixisti discipulo tuo, *Ecce mater tua*, fac ut matri tuae me societ amor tuus et charitas vera.[3]

In the Arundel text, 'O Lord God, O Crist Iesu', this becomes:

> And as þou said to þi moder deir,
> Quhilk dulit and murnit and maid gret beir,
> Said to hir þan: 'Woman, lo heir
> Sanct Iohnne thy sone to be,
> And þou his moder, Mary meik':
> To þame me follow I þe beseik,
> Throu verray lufe and cherite.[4]

The Latin has here been amplified in an accomplished but fairly conventional way: The Virgin's grief is stressed, and the adjectives 'deir' and 'meik' suggest a little warmth. But the effect is mechanical; one feels that these touches spring from the exigencies of the metre rather than from the poet's own feeling for the meditative tradition. With this may be contrasted Audelay's poem, 'O Ihesu Crist hongyng on cro[y]s', in which two stanzas are given to each word:

> O Ihesu, þi moder had gret pete
> When heo se þe turment on rod tre;
>   To here þus con þou say,
> 'Womon, lo, here þi sune,
> Take here to þi moder, Ion,
>   And kepe here now I þe pray.'
>
> O Ihesu, for þi moder love,
> þat is cround in heven with þe above,

---

[1] *P.L.* 94, 562; Leroquais, *Les Livres d'heures MSS.*, ii. 342.

[2] Leroquais has noted it in more than sixteen manuscripts in the Bibliothèque Nationale, *Livres d'heures*, ii. 400, s.v. 'Domine Ihesu Christe qui septem verba'. It occurs in nearly all the manuscript books of hours that I have consulted for their relevance to the lyric.   [3] *P.L.* 94, 562.

[4] *Devotional Pieces*, 260. *Dulit*: lamented; *maid gret beir*: cried out loudly.

and Ion, þi dere derlyng,
Ffore þe love þai hadyn to þe,
Uppon my soule þou have pete,
And graunt me good endyng.[1]

The amplifications here show a far less perfunctory treatment of the
theme. The Word has reminded Audelay not only of the traditional grief
of the Blessed Virgin but also of the love between Christ and St. John,
the 'beloved disciple' who, as Christ's friend, was also, according to
medieval thought, in a unique relationship to Him:[2] he was, in the
phrase of the much used prayer, the *O intemerata*,[3] *Christi familiaris
amicus*. Audelay's style has a tender lucidity that catches excellently the
force of so much love, whilst gently relating it to the meditator's prayer.

The Latin prayer *De septem verbis* and its English translations initially and briefly oppose the seven words from the Cross to the seven
deadly sins. But the more common antithesis was between the seven
deadly sins and the seven blood-sheddings or other closely related contrasts. The history of this theme cannot be traced without confusion,
for there were a number of closely related antitheses which influenced
one another and caused a mingling of originally distinct pairs. The
earliest Latin examples are based upon the sins of the five senses—one
of the headings for the examination of conscience—which are contrasted
with the five wounds or with Christ's sufferings in His senses. The former has been noted by Gougaud as early as the eleventh century, in the
work of Peter Damian: '. . . quinquepartito vulnere illius caro perfoditur,
ut nos a vitiorum, quae in nos per quinque sensus ingrediuntur, irrup-
tione curemur'.[4] When stated briefly, as here, the number five makes
the antithesis apt, but this theme obviously did not offer opportunity
for the pointed elaboration of each item. A slightly later variation was
that of the *Ancrene Wisse*, where in the section of the custody of the
senses there occurs a diffuse meditation on the Passion, in which the sins
of the senses are contrasted with Christ's sufferings in His five senses,
the stench of corpses in His nose, the jeering of the crowd in His ears,
etc.[5] Here, of course, the relationship is exact. An analysis of Christ's
sufferings in all five senses remained an invariable substantiation of the
theological point that Christ's sufferings could not have been greater.

---

[1] E.E.T.S. 184, 58.

[2] On this see R. Egenter, *Gottesfreundschaft* (Augsburg, 1928), 272–80, and p. 214,
footnote 6 above.

[3] A. Wilmart, *Auteurs spirituels et textes dévots*, 474–504.

[4] *P.L.* 145, 683; L. Gougaud, *Devotional and Ascetic Practices of the Middle Ages*
80. 'His flesh was pierced by a fivefold wound, so that we might be cured from the
attacks of sins that enter into us through the five senses.' A version of this prayer occurs
in the *Ancrene Wisse*, E.E.T.S. 249, 17.

[5] E.E.T.S. 249, 56–61.

It can be found, for instance, in the *Summa theologica* of St. Thomas, in answer to the question 'Utrum Christus omnes passiones sustinuerit'.[1] When related to man's sins, the point could be given a semi-intellectual, semi-devotional amplification, as in the *Summa praedicantium,* where Bromyard describes movingly how, since man had sinned in all his senses, it was necessary for Christ to suffer in all His senses:

Quod caput illud, cuius pulchritudo nullo termino metitur, spinis coronaretur. Et quod facies, quam Angeli desiderant prospicere, a Iudeis conspueretur. Quod etiam aures, quae angelorum cantum audire solebant, blasphemias audirent Iudaeorum. Et pedes et manus, quae illi coniuncta erant, qui mundum operabatur, cruci affigerentur. Quod in gustus aceto et oculi videndo matris dolorem affligerentur.[2]

It can be seen from this historical outline that the theme was quite firmly rooted in emotive meditation on the Passion, and was therefore potentially suitable for the meditative lyric. Unfortunately, however, only one independent lyric on this theme survives, an unprinted poem from B.M. Add. MS. 37049, of which the first verse is as follows:

> Take hede man how þe jewes dyd cry
> To put me to deth in hye
> And fyld my heryng wykkydly:
> To heryng of yl kepe þe for þi.[3]

This is typical of the structure and style of the whole. It can be seen that the sense of hearing is, as in the tradition, related precisely to one of the pains of the Passion, and that only one line is reserved for the contrasting sin. But in this poem literary development of the theme is restricted by a visual emphasis upon it as numbered verse. It is presented as part of a tree. The centre trunk consists of illustrations of the Passion with a related poem on the Hours of the Cross on the left.[4] On the right is the present poem, made up to the number seven by the addition of *consentyng* and *frenes of wille*.[5] The pleasure to be derived from the poem

---

[1] Pt. III, qu. xlvi, art. 5, *Opera omnia*, ed. Fratres ordinis praedicatorum, xi. 441. 'Whether Christ endured all sufferings.'

[2] Ed. cit. II, 171ʳ. 'That head, whose beauty is boundless is crowned with thorns, and the face that angels desire to see is spat upon by the Jews. His ears, accustomed to hear the song of the angels, now hear the blasphemies of the Jews. The feet and hands belonging to Him who made the world, are nailed to the Cross. He suffers in His sense of taste from the vinegar and in His sight from beholding His mother's grief.'

[3] f. 68ᵛ. *Index*, 251.

[4] The whole design is a late version of a form of tree that was much copied in the late thirteenth century and appended with other trees and tables to Bonaventura's *Lignum vitae* (F. Saxl, 'A Spiritual Encyclopaedia of the Later Middle Ages', *Warburg Journal* v, 1942, 82–142). It is to be found in quite a number of learned English manuscripts, including the De Lisle Psalter; Saxl, loc. cit., lists many others, p. 110, note 5.

[5] These derive from the Latin poem attached to the tree, inc. 'Audi clamantes in me mortemque minantes' (MS. Laud Misc. 156, 63ᵛ, Walther, 1693), in which *consensus* and *liber arbitrium* are added to the five senses. The English verse follows the Latin in

on the senses therefore does not lie in any individual literary quality, but springs from the enjoyment of it as part of an ingenious whole presenting a symmetrical and intellectual scheme directly to the eye. Indeed, a verse of any particular worth in such a context would be too self-assertive.

With the exception of a brief allusion to the theme in Lydgate's *A Seying of the Nightingale*,[1] this remains the only vernacular poetical presentation of the subject, for other forms were more popular. In penitential self-examination the category of the seven deadly sins was far more important than that of the sins of the five senses, whilst in devotion Christ's sufferings in the five senses were comparatively rarely alluded to, and it was the five wounds that became the focus of meditation,[2] providing the content of so many laudatory or petitionary Latin hymns and prayers and vernacular poems. But the very fact that the seven deadly sins and the five wounds developed and became popular in externally unrelated religious practices made the formulation of relevant antitheses between them more difficult. The most obvious discrepancies lie in the absence of concord in both idea and number. There was, for instance, no reason why the wound of the right hand should be opposed to wrath and that of the left to avarice (or indeed why either sin should be opposed to a wounded hand at all). Therefore in different texts of the same poem, 'Wiþ scharpe þornes þat weren ful kene', these pairs are interchanged,[3] and indeed in one manuscript of the text the right hand is by mistake repeated for both.[4] The more serious defect arising from lack of congruity in subject-matter was that it exposed flatness of style, for there was no ingenuity of content to sustain it. The following is a typical example:

> Thoruȝ my lifthond a nail was dryve—
> þenke þou þeron if þou wolt lyve,
> And helpe þe pore wiþ almesdede,
> If þou in hevene wolt have þi mede.[5]

A witty relationship can carry poetical force even when not expressed pointedly in style, but without this there is constant deflation, for the formal structure arouses an expectation that it does not satisfy, and the effect is like that of quatrains or couplets that invariably fail to rhyme.

outline only: the contrast between Christ's sufferings and man's sins seems to be the invention of the English writer, though there may well be some lost or unidentified Latin text in which this occurs.

[1] E.E.T.S., E.S. 107, 228.

[2] Gray, 'The Five Wounds of Our Lord', *Notes and Queries* (1963), Feb. 50–51, Mar. 82–89, Apr. 127–34, May 163–8.

[3] Person, *Middle English Lyrics*, 7, and Brown XIV, 127. The former appears to be a corrupt text of the latter: they coincide in four of the sins.

[4] Person, op. cit., no. 8.　　　　　　　　　　[5] Brown XIV, p. 227.

The less serious difficulty was the discrepancy in number, and various devices were found to bring the number of the five wounds up to seven. Sometimes a detail was borrowed from the earlier theme of the five senses. In three poems, for instance, an unprinted complaint from John of Grimestone's preaching-book beginning 'þe garlond þat of þorn is wroth',[1] the popular complaint already quoted above, 'Wiþ scharpe þornes þat weren ful kene', and in its corrupt variant, 'Thurwe my ryȝt hande a nayle was driven',[2] gluttony is opposed to Christ's thirst and the proffered drink of vinegar. Such borrowings invariably stand out in their context through the pointed propriety of the antitheses. The other common source of borrowings was the seven blood-sheddings, from which is drawn the crown of thorns contrasted with pride in 'þe garlond þat of þorn is wroth', and the scourging contrasted with lust in 'Thurwe my ryȝt hande'.[3]

The items of the seven blood-sheddings were originally the circumcision, the bloody sweat, the scourging, the imposition of the crown of thorns, the wounds in the hands, the wounds in the feet, and the spear thrust in the side.[4] There was here no difficulty over number, but, with the exception of the antithesis between Christ's sufferings in the circumcision and man's lust, there remained the same poetical problem of total lack of congruity between the pairs. Random variations in the pairs again illustrate their unconnectedness: the scourging, for instance, is once paired with lust in 'þe garlond þat of þorn is wroth',[5] whilst in another, 'Ihesu, for þi precious blod', it is joined to gluttony.[6] However, whilst this theme had no advantage in wit over that of the five wounds, it was potentially more moving as a meditative subject, for the five wounds

---

[1] MS. Adv. 18. 7. 21. 124ʳ. *Index*, 3356.   [2] Person, op. cit. 7.

[3] In prose works the seven deadly sins were sometimes contrasted with a more freely chosen list of sufferings and a more serious attempt was made to find a correlation. Some sermon notes in a thirteenth-century manuscript, Ashmole 360, 145ʳ, are an early example of this: 'O bone Ihesu capud tuum spinis coronatur contra luxuriam, inclinat contra superbiam; os tuum vino mirrato potatur contra gulam; manus perforantur contra avariciam; latus aperitur contra invidiam; pedes clavis affiguntur contra accidiam; omnia convicia et contumelias sustinuit contra iram.' A later example occurs in *A Treatise of Ghostly Battle* (*Yorkshire Writers*, ii. 426), where sloth is contrasted with the nailed feet, avarice with Christ's nakedness, gluttony with the drink of vinegar, etc.

[4] The items may vary a little but the series is always recognizable by the fact that it begins with the Circumcision. The seven blood-sheddings became a fairly popular theme of later meditation. A popular prose meditation occurs in a fifteenth-century Carthusian manuscript (F. Wormald, 'The Revelation of the Hundred Pater Nosters', *Laudate*, xiv, 1936, 165–82); its contemporary popularity is shown by the fact that it was printed with other devotional pieces by Wynkyn de Worde (*S.T.C.*, 14546); this version does not contain the exercise of the Hundred Pater Nosters, but Wormald's title stresses an element that is subordinate in the meditation.

[5] 'ȝif þu wilt wit herte / Of flesses lust ben purged, / þingc of þe knottes smerte / werwit I was scurged.' MS. Adv. 18. 7. 21, 124ʳ.

[6] Brown XIV, p. 218.

springs from the medieval liking for dissection and itemizing (a method not in itself affective), whereas the seven blood-sheddings was (with one exception) a list of separate events, and therefore allowed a meditative treatment of the most important moments of pain in the life of Christ.

This distinction between the themes is reflected in the meditative structure of the poems, for they fall into two groups. In one the poem is set in the first person, it is usually liturgical in form, and the framework is the seven blood-sheddings; in the other the form is usually a complaint, and the framework is that of the seven deadly sins. The most popular of the first kind was 'Ihesu, for þi precious blod',[1] which survives in four manuscripts, two of them liturgical. In one of these, MS. Rawl. liturg. g. 2, it is surrounded by Latin prayers, and each stanza is followed by a paternoster and ave. The poem itself can be best understood when judged within this context, for it is strictly liturgical in form: each stanza falls evenly into two halves, the first setting out the grounds for the petition, the second the petition itself:

> Ihesu, for þi blodi heved,
> þat wit thornes was beweved,
>   longe, scharp and kene,
> chast me þat am so wilde;
> Make my herte mek and mylde,
>   to be þi servaunt clene.[2]

The relationship between the two parts is liturgical, not witty: in liturgical prayer Christ's sufferings can be the grounds for any requests, and there are almost innumerable Latin prose prayers that have a pattern of this kind. There is nothing exciting in the style of this poem, but it is agreeable: the meditative description of the first part, with the emotive adjectives of line 3 (recalling visual representations of the crown of thorns), fits well with the contrite plea of the second half: though contrition is different from the earlier meditative response of compassion, it has sufficient affinities with love for it not to seem an emotion alien to meditative poetry.

The appropriateness of the seven blood-sheddings for meditative poetry can be better illustrated from another poem, 'Ihesu, that alle this worlde hast wroghte'.[3] In this the separate (and meditatively feeble) enumeration of the wounds in the hands and feet has been done away with, and the apocryphal incident of the tearing of Christ's robe from His body[4] has been inserted instead:

---

[1] Brown XIV, 123.

[2] Ibid. p. 218. *Beweved*: enveloped; *wilde*: self-willed.

[3] Brown XV, 92.

[4] This detail is very common in meditative literature, e.g. *Meditations* trans. Ragusa and Green, 333; *Vita*, ed. Rigollot, iv. 95; *A Hundred Meditations, Laudate*, xiv. 177; and an unprinted prose liturgical prayer in MS. Magd. Camb. 13, 203^r–209^r.

> Then, berynge þe Cros to calvarie,
>   Unto þe mounte þou cam at last;
> Thi bodyly wounde were woxe al drye,
>   The purpure þer-to was cleved ful fast.
>   They rente it of with a grete haste,
>   And þat was, good lord, more peyne to þe
>   Than al þe scourgynge þat was now past,
>   And þus þi blode þou sched for me.[1]

An eight-line stanza is given to each blood-shedding and, as can be seen from this example, there is sufficient space for meditative elaborations. The personal address to Christ at the beginning of each stanza, sometimes repeated towards the end, combined with the meditator's recollection of himself in the refrain, emphasizes a close and immediate relationship. In some stanzas this feeling is given further substance by references to love (e.g. 'I love þe, lord, with trewe affeccioun'), and even to the image of Christ as friend, 'So kynde a frende schal I noon fynde'. The spaciousness is achieved by delaying the petitions until the four concluding stanzas, where they are then set out more briefly. They are not based on the seven deadly sins, but are of a general kind. Two are striking: one is the plea that the nails which pierced Christ's hands and feet may 'Ioyne all oure hertis unto þat roode, / That we þi kyndenes never forgeet'; the other is:

> And for þe thornes þei dide the take,
>   Crounynge þin heed in-to þe brayne,
> Yeve us þat croune þat þou dide make
>   In heven for us, witht al þi payne.[2]

This sharp antithetical parallel is very intellectually and aesthetically satisfying; it is not here so tautly expressed as in Donne's line, 'By these his thornes give me his other Crowne',[3] but the looser vernacular style of the Middle Ages is not quite without advantages in the expression of paradox, for the loss in pointedness is recompensed by the gain of emotive references to suffering.

The most popular of the complaints based upon the seven deadly sins was 'Wiþ scharpe þornes þat weren ful kene',[4] surviving in ten manuscripts that are mainly collections of moral and devotional works. The defects of the poem have already been described. It is interesting, however, to notice the attempt that has been made in B.M. Add. MS. 37049 to give it meditative force. In this manuscript the verses are copied symmetrically on either side of a figure of the wounded Christ on the

---

[1] Brown XV, p. 135.
[2] ll. 77–80, Brown XV, p. 136.
[3] 'Hymne to God my God, in my sicknesse', *The Divine Poems*, ed. Gardner, 50.
[4] Brown XIV, 127.

Cross,[1] and thus visually the point is driven home that the poem is a
Crucifixion complaint. Nevertheless, there is little in it that is meditative, except for the injunction, twice repeated, to 'behold'; and the
didactic finality of the last line of each stanza quite overshadows the
description of suffering that precedes it. It would seem that only
the medieval liking for numbered poetry can account for the popularity
of this work.

Whilst 'Wiþ scharpe þornes þat weren ful kene' was by far the most
popular of this group of poems, others, from the literary point of view,
are more interesting. In a Cambridge manuscript of a miscellaneous
learned and devotional kind, there is a curious and corrupt text. The
usual symmetrical proportions are missing, and nine lines, for instance,
are given to avarice, seven to sloth, two to lechery, etc. Only the opening
lines on avarice leave room for the development of a true complaint, and
here there are echoes of genuine lament oddly concluded with what looks
like a colloquial saying:

> Thurwe my ryȝt hande a nayle was driven,
> þer on þou think ȝif þou wilt lyven,
> And helpe þe pour with almusdede
> for I xal ȝelde þe þi mede.
> Of al my ryche tresour golde and prescius ston,
> þis werld þat is so fikil wil leve me nouȝt on
> But a hayre or a schete to hile withal my bon.
> þerfor I ȝou sey with werdis few,
> Werldis welth þou hav goday þi leman lovis a schrewe.[2]

It is, however, the unprinted poem from the Passion section of John
of Grimestone's preaching-book, which alone catches the original style
of the complaint form, perhaps because it is the earliest surviving poem
on this theme. Its style may be illustrated from verses 1 and 6:

> þe garlond þat of þorn is wroth
> An stikid on my crune
> Wit prikking hat þe blod out brouth
> þat dot my fored frune.
> Myn her, my muth, is al bebled,
> Myn heved draut doun on side;
> Love hat me þus lowe led
> To don awey þi pride.
>
> .   .   .   .
>
> Ȝif þu wilt wit herte
> Of flesses lust ben purged,
> þingc of þe knottes smerte
> Werwit I was scurged.

[1] f. 30ʳ.   [2] Person, op. cit. 7; cf. pp. 224–5 above.

Mi skin was rent, my bak was toren
To peler was I bunde,
I stod naked as I was born,
þe blod ran doun to grunde.[1]

The most obvious points are the tone of lament and the meditative descriptions designed to arouse compassion. The action is amplified, not merely to fill out the verse, but in order to provide a meditative image. The tone is set by the use in the first stanza of the moving conceit of the compelling power of love. There is, however, one further point, which only a reading of the whole poem can reveal; it is that a successful attempt has here been made to relate the antitheses poetically: the angry man with his arm raised to strike must remember Christ's right hand nailed to the Cross; the covetous man as he snatches what he should not have must remember Christ's left hand; the slothful man, who will never persevere, must remember Christ's feet nailed to the Cross. Here one can see the activity of a poetic imagination: the deadly sins are half personified, and their characteristic gestures are contrasted with those of Christ in the Crucifixion. This is the style of the complaint against the dandy, rather than of the later poems on this subject. Though not outstanding, the poem reflects the agreeable and unpretentious tone of the earlier complaint: it is far removed from the hortatory or liturgical.

First-person meditations, that had earlier been complementary to the complaint form, are comparatively rare in the fifteenth century. The poems set in the first person in which Christ's pains are opposed to man's sins belong in their general characteristics to a large group of verse prayers of a kind that it would not here be relevant to discuss. Most of the material has been examined and classified by Professor Robbins.[2] On the borderline between these and genuine first-person meditations come such works as William Billyng's address to the five wounds, which has survived on a prayer roll. The form of the poem is liturgical: a salutation to each wound (which is illustrated) and a brief petition of a general nature. The following is the salutation to the wound in the right foot:

Hayle welle of pyte most dulce and delycate,
Dygged in thy ryght fote so pytefully;
In odure most fragrant and most mellyfluate,
Chefe refute and salve of alle our maledy.
Thy skarlet floode dystyllyth habundantly,
Most ioyouse in thought most helpyng at o nede,
Us to proferre in every goostly spede.[3]

---

[1] f. 124ʳ. *Index*, 3356. *Frune*: crease with pain (?); *draut*: drops.
[2] 'Private Prayers in Middle English Verse', *Studies in Philology*, xxxvi (1939), 466–75.
[3] William Billyng, *The Five Wounds of Christ*, ed. W. Bateman (Manchester, 1814), 3.

The style is so thickly aureate and the imagery so outlandishly ornate in this and all the verses that it is difficult, at least nowadays, to distinguish any effect of emotional conviction through the exotic adjectives and clogging diction.

There are, however, a small group of first-person meditations more interesting to discuss. Their most striking characteristic is unfortunately a negative one: the loss of the style of the Harley lyrics and of the poetry of the 'school' of Richard Rolle. The poems that show any sign of the emotional serenity of the first or of the imagery and intensity of the second are so small in number that they can be quickly enumerated. Of the first kind there is perhaps only one, 'Godys sone þat was so fre', which is entirely devotional in kind.[1] It is a poem with a light, swinging metre and with an O and I refrain.[2] It consists of a simple narrative of the Passion, quite uninfluenced in its amplifications by formulas, such as the lists of the wounds or of the instruments of the Passion that contribute so much to the substance of most fifteenth-century Passion poetry. It reiterates only the ancient points of Christ's love for us, 'And let hym naylyn upon a tre / Al for þe love of man' or 'He hadde us evere in mynde / In al his harde þrowe', and the need for us to love Him in return, 'Who-so wele love trewe, / Byhold Ihesu on þe croys'. The tone, as in the earlier poetry, is established by loving epithets, 'His fayre blod, þat was so fre', His 'mylde voys', and by emotive descriptions or comments, 'He heng pale of hewe', 'A dwelful syȝte it was to se', etc. Above all, the last verse, in which the poet promises his service to the Blessed Virgin, 'þe fend I forsake anon / ffor on lady so hende', unmistakably recalls the lyrics of the late thirteenth century. The poem achieves some of the indefinable freshness of the earlier tradition, and it is entirely free from the menace and bleak didacticism of the fifteenth century. But it is unique.

Two short verses recall the style and idea of love to be found in the poetry of Rolle. One occurs in a manuscript chiefly containing Rolle's work, MS. Trinity Coll., Dublin, 155, where it is inserted near the end of the *Ego dormio*. This is the first of the two verses:

> Ihesu, for þe mourne I may
> As turtel þat longeþ boþe nyȝt and day
>   for her love is gone hyr froo,
> For aftur þe, lorde, me longeþ ay;
> And þat is al my myrþe and pley,
>   where I sitte or goo.[3]

---

[1] Brown xv, 95.
[2] On this kind of refrain see R. L. Greene, 'A Middle English Love Poem and the "O-and-I" Refrain Phrase', *Medium Ævum*, xxx (1961), 170–5.
[3] Brown xv, 68.

The image of the dove as a symbol of true love (a bestiary allegorization more familiar from the *Parlement of Foules*) is here movingly developed, with a restrained simplicity of style. The same mystical conception of love is expressed, though less finely, in a small verse in B.M. Add. MS. 37049, where it occurs on the same folio as 'O man unkinde' and the representation of the Man of Sorrows pointing to His wounded heart. The illustration is typical of the fifteenth century, but the poem, though appropriate to the new iconography, is in itself quite traditional:

> Ihesu, my luf, my ioy, my reste,
> þi perfite luf close in my breste
> þat I þe luf and never reste;
> And mak me luf þe of al þinge best,
> And wounde my hert in þi luf fre,
> þat I may reyne in ioy ever-more with þe.[1]

The loving variations on the name of Jesus and the reference to the wound of love show the style and imagery of the 'school' of Rolle.

Of long Passion descriptions only a few are set in the first person, and only one describes the Passion in the tone of loving lament that was characteristic of Rolle. This poem, 'Of alle the ioyus that in this worlde may be',[2] derives its content from the brutal narratives of the Passion, which were encouraged in the fifteenth century by art and mystery plays. Typical of the fifteenth century are the details of the number of Christ's wounds, the wrenching off of His skin with His clothes, the pulling of His arms to reach the holes already bored in the wood, the violent dropping of the Cross into its socket, and the mourning of the Blessed Virgin. But the tone is that of Rolle. The poet begins with emphasis on the fact that he feels no pleasure save in the thought of Jesus, and continues:

> 3if I behold fram top to too
> Sey3tus of sorwe I may see þore:
> Hys swete body was wrappud alle in wo
> Wyth blode and bytter wondus sore.
>
> 3yf I beholde on Hys blyssed heved
> þat governuþ boþe heven and helle
> Wyth a wreþe of þornes y see it beweved,
> þe þornes þrullud þat blyssud felle.[3]

Throughout the poem there recur loving epithets such as 'dere', 'blessed', and 'swete', and phrases such as 'hys face so schene', his 'mouthe þat was so swete', and 'his body þat was so why3t as flour'. The tone of loving grief is so dominant that it is able to absorb the brutality

---

[1] Ibid. 67.
[2] *Three Middle English Religious Poems*, ed. R. H. Bowers, 33–43.
[3] Op. cit. 34.

of detail without shock or faltering. It seems, as it were, to cauterize the emotional effect, so that horror is instantly transformed into compassion, purified of sadism or morbidity. The tone also serves to give coherence to the narrative. The amassing of detail does not give the impression of springing from lack of selectiveness, but rather of resulting from a loving recollection, which cannot cease until it has remembered everything. The metre, incidentally, is the simple quatrain,[1] so often used in the earlier poetry, but rare in the fifteenth century.

Other poems set in the form of personal meditations on the Passion are almost entirely bare of warmth and tenderness, though some of them are striking in other ways. There are, for instance, two curious dream visions about the nightingale, both attributed to Lydgate. They are directly indebted to Pecham's *Philomena*, but turn that passionate and moving poem into an odd blend of ornateness, didacticism, and emotional intensity. Despite resemblances of tone and their debt to a common original, the two poems are in other ways unalike. One, 'Go, lityll quayere',[2] is far more didactic and coherently organized than the other. The dreamer is roused by the nightingale, seeks until he finds her on her laurel tree, and then listens as she sings of her approaching death. The episode is then moralized: the nightingale is Christ, the dreamer's sleep is sloth, the Hours sung by the bird symbolize the ages of the world as well as the Passion (indeed far more space is given to the former). It is only the introductory description that is interesting, and in it, in particular, the nightingale's repeated cry of 'Occi' carries with it some of the associations of warmth and feeling that it had had in Pecham's *Philomena*. The word 'occi' seems to have been onomatopoeic in origin, but in due course to have become associated with the Old French verb *occir*, to kill,[3] so that in Pecham's work, by an imaginative transformation that transcends grammar, it became the nightingale's ecstatic and melancholy plea for death.[4] It is used in the same way in 'Go, lityll quayere', where the bird sings 'Ocy, Ocy, o deth, well-come to me!'.

In '*A Seying of the Nightingale*[5] the cry of 'Occi' is less movingly used, for with better regard for grammatical correctness but far less emotional force, the word is treated as the imperative of *occir*, and becomes a command to slay all those indifferent to the love of Christ. But

[1] Bowers, op. cit., prints it continuously although it falls quite regularly into quatrains.

[2] E.E.T.S., E.S. 80, 1–28. MacCracken does not follow Glauning in attributing this poem to Lydgate. For the argument see E.E.T.S., E.S. 80, xxxiv–xxxvi, and ibid. 107, xxxiii–xxxiv; cf. W. Schirmer, *John Lydgate*, trans. A. Keep (London, 1961), 281.

[3] R. Köhler, '*Oci, Oci* als Nachtigallensang', *Zeitschrift für romanische Philologie*, viii (1884), 120–2; E.E.T.S., E.S. 80, 35–38.

[4] For this interpretation see F. J. E. Raby, 'Philomena praevia temporis amoeni', *Mélanges Joseph de Ghellinck*, ii (Gembloux, 1951), 435–48.

[5] E.E.T.S., E.S. 80, 16–28; E.E.T.S., E.S. 107, 221–34.

in other ways this poem is far more moving. There is no dichotomy here between the literal and allegorical levels, and the bird's song is entirely of the Passion, though it is mostly in the form of a complaint, not of a first-person meditation. Its substance is a series of themes, most of which we have already discussed: the rose of the five wounds,[1] the image of the winepress, the pains of the Passion contrasted with the sins of the senses and the seven deadly sins, Christ's testament, and, finally, a list of types of the Cross. Much of this is well done, and here and there can be heard a note of poetic confidence in the statement of a great and moving truth that is new and impressive: 'To paye þe raunsoun of our gret losse / He was in love so gentyle and so free . . .'[2] or 'Hit was a thing incomparable feyre / þe sone to dye to make his servaunt free'.[3] Statements such as these break the traditional meditative form, in that by creating wonder they distance Christ from the meditator, but, in a period of decline, they break the form in a way that is entirely profitable.

More sustainedly powerful than either of these is Dunbar's poem on the Passion.[4] It is set in the form of a dream, which Dunbar feigns to have had as he knelt before a Crucifix. The events of the Passion are described in vigorous and precise detail, with some of the more horrific additions which had become accepted as integral parts of the sequence through the authority of the *Meditationes*, the mystery plays, and iconography. Those used by Dunbar include the reopening of the wounds of the scourging by the brutal tearing of Christ's robe from His back, and the dropping of the Cross into its socket with Christ's body already attached to it. Interspersed with description such as this are paradoxical statements, of the kind we noticed in the mystical poetry, such as 'And lyk ane theif or ane tratour / Thay leid that hevinlie prince most hie', but, on account of the contexts in which these are used, they suggest the enormity of the action rather than the love of Christ:

> Ane croce that wes bayth large and lang
>   To beir thay gaif this blissit Lord;
> Syn fullelie, as theif to hang,
>   Thay harlit him furth with raip and corde;
>   With blude and sweit was all deflorde
> His face, the fude of angellis fre;

---

[1] This image recurs in Latin devotional literature, e.g. *Vitis mystica*, ch. xvii (*Decem Opuscula*, 454–5), but this seems a unique reference to it in the medieval English religious lyric; Charles Joret, *La Rose dans l'antiquité et au moyen âge* (Paris, 1892), 242, refers to a fifteenth-century German poem in which the five wounds are compared to roses. It is typical of Lydgate that he should introduce a learned image into vernacular poetry.

[2] ll. 99–100, E.E.T.S., e.s. 107, 225.

[3] ll. 276–7, ibid. 231.

[4] *Poems*, ed. W. Mackay Mackenzie (London, 1932), 155–9.

His feit with stanis was revin and scorde,
O mankynd, for the luif of the.[1]

The implications of personal emotion in the descriptions are tempered
by the hortatory address of the refrain: indeed, through it the poem has
imperceptibly passed from personal meditation to sermon invocation,
for the refrain is not an expression of love, but the moral statement
that you ought to love. As we have noticed before, the tone of a poem
can be substantially established by a refrain, and here the preacher's
comment at the end of each stanza gives the poem a didactic cast. In
the last verses Dunbar returns to his original structure of personal
meditation, and the proper responses of pity and compassion are fully
introduced and emphasized, but they appear as allegorical figures who
beset the dreamer, and the effect is therefore intellectual rather than
emotional. These negative comments are unjust if they suggest that the
poem is weak or tedious: on the contrary, it has the poise and power
one would expect in any poem of Dunbar's, and the story is told with
precision and speed, which demand a taut attentiveness from the reader.
In tone it resembles those parts of the mystery plays which are most
dramatic, and where it is intended that the audience shall be appalled
by what they see. The poem in fact succeeds like these harsher parts of
the mystery cycles, but it has also an impressive severity which they
do not achieve.

Another poem that is also dramatic but untender occurs in MS.
Arundel 285. The first stanza expresses compassion in language too
formal and ornate to evoke it:

Compatience persis, reuth and marcy stoundis
    In myddis my hert, and thirlis throw þe vanis.
Thy deid, Ihesu, þi petuous cruell woundis,
    Thy grym passion, gret tormentis, grevous panis,
    In-gravit sadlie in my spreit remanis.
    Sen me of noucht þou hes boucht with þi blude
My ene, for doloure, woful teris ranis,
    Quhen that I se the nalit on þe rude.[2]

Thereafter the poem, with taut syntax and many striking adjectives and
verbs, gives a compressed and vigorous description of the seven stages
of the Passion. The intention is evidently to provide a dramatic enumeration and commemoration of Christ's sufferings, and though in many
stanzas various events are unchronologically crammed together, the
basic design is clearly the Seven Hours of the Passion, which was a
devotion of ancient origin.

[1] *Poems*, ed. Mackenzie, 157. *Fullelie*: shamefully; *harlit*: dragged; *deflorde*: dis-
figured; *fre*: fair; *scorde*: cut.
[2] Brown xv, 91.

The monastic Office was already in the sixth century divided into seven in fulfilment of the psalmist's assurance, 'Septies in die laudem dixi tibi' (Ps. cxviii. 164), and at some later date an episode of the Passion was allegorically allotted to each hour. This association of the Office with the Passion was already made by Rabanus Maurus in his *De clericorum institutione*,[1] and from there it was imitated, for instance, in the Old English Benedictine Office.[2] From then onwards the idea appears recurrently. Goscelin advised Eve 'Omnes horas Christi passionibus consecra';[3] Pecham's nightingale sang her love song of the Passion at these hours;[4] a meditation on the Passion, thus divided, occurs in the *Speculum ecclesiae* of St. Edmund;[5] there was a much copied Latin meditation, the *De meditatione passionis Christi per septem diei horas libellus*;[6] and this division was followed in the Passion section of the *Meditationes*,[7] though its main structure is that of the days of the week,[8] and also in the Passion section of the *Vita* of Ludolf the Carthusian,[9] though in the remainder of this long work the author does not use any meditative or liturgical divisions.

Amongst English lyrics which follow this division into hours the largest group is formed by the many translations of the Latin 'Patris sapientia', an anonymous hymn of the fourteenth century, which in England became incorporated into the Little Office of the Virgin, and of which a translation therefore often occurs in vernacular primers.[10] English translations, however, are not restricted to these. There is an early version in John of Grimestone's preaching-book,[11] another was added to the miscellaneous material at the end of the *Cursor mundi*,[12]

---

[1] *P.L.* 107, 327–9.

[2] *The Benedictine Office*, ed. J. M. Ure (Edinburgh, 1957), 15–16.

[3] C. H. Talbot, 'The liber confortatorius of Goscelin of Saint Bertin', *Studia Anselmia*, xxxvii (1955), 83. 'Dedicate all the Hours to the sufferings of Christ.'

[4] *A.H.* l. 602–10.

[5] The Middle English translation is printed in *Yorkshire Writers*, i. 219–40. The original French text has been edited by H. W. Robbins, *Le Merure de Seinte Eglise* (Lewisburg, 1925); the latter has been translated by E. Colledge in *The Medieval Mystics of England*, 105–40, but with the meditative section omitted.

[6] *P.L.* 94, 562–8.

[7] This section circulated independently, and then the sole meditative structure was that of the hours; for the Latin see *Meditaciones de Passione Christi olim Sancto Bonaventurae attributae*, ed. M. Jordan Stallings (Washington, 1956). For an English verse translation see E.E.T.S. 60; amongst manuscripts containing a translation into English prose are, MSS. Bodl. 789, 1–51ʳ, Trinity, Camb. 223, 1–52ᵛ, and the Thornton MS. (*Yorkshire Writers*, i. 198–218).

[8] This division of meditative works into days of the week was also very popular, e.g. 'The Contemplacioun of Synnaris', ed. Bennett, *Devotional Pieces*, 64–119.

[9] Ed. Rigollot, iv. 12–156.

[10] E.E.T.S. 105, 15, etc. In E.E.T.S. 71, 82–87, an English version is conveniently set out side by side with the Latin. Cf. *A.H.* xxx. 13.

[11] Brown xiv, 55.   [12] Ibid. 30.

a French version occurs on the fourteenth-century prayer roll already described,[1] and versions were composed by William of Shoreham[2] and Audelay;[3] other anonymous texts are included in the Vernon and Thornton manuscripts, and in various miscellaneous collections.[4]

The literary merits of the Latin hymn lies chiefly in its concision, in the quantity of detail which is lucidly compressed into each verse. Its style is otherwise undistinguished, except for the occasional effective use of paradox, such as appears in 'Vultum Dei conspuunt, lumen caeli gratum' or 'Talem mortem subiit vitae medicina'. Both of these virtues, as we have so often said before, were difficult to imitate in Middle English. The English versions either use a longer stanza form or give two verses to the Latin's one, and they evade or reduce the paradoxes as, for instance, in Audelay's 'Seche a deþ He sofyrd þen, of our syn to be medysyn'. But, whilst the English texts never achieve the sustained accomplishment of the Latin, they do from time to time display the typical English virtues of vigour and gentleness. These qualities are particularly noticeable in the early version in John of Grimestone's preaching-book. The text is set in the form of a personal meditation, the paradoxes of the original are completely omitted, and the tone of affection and immediacy is established by epithets, 'þe felle Iewes', 'þi faire face', 'kene þornes', 'sarp spere', 'swete bodi', etc. There is also an exceptionally dramatic touch in the translation of the Latin 'In collo percutiunt'[5] by 'He smiten þe under þe ere and seiden "wo was tat?" ', an ironic application of the game of Blind Man's Buff, which, as Owst has pointed out, was fairly common in sermons and mystery plays.[6] The laconic colloquialism of the line is especially realistic and sinister. Though less striking than this, there are many examples of simple directness in the English texts: for instance, the Latin 'a suis discipulis cito derelictus'[7] is translated by 'Hys discipulis fled awaye, / And fast from hym they went',[8] or the rendering of *crucifige* by 'day on rode'[9] or 'Delyvere vs baraban, / And do þis on þe cros'.[10] Such dramatic effects are obviously not the result of contrived artistry, but the natural achievement of those writing in the English tradition and free from the literary pretensions of the fifteenth century. The gentleness is particularly noticeable in another early text, which is only loosely related to the *Patris sapientia*. The first verse illustrates this quality well:

[1] See p. 57, n. 3 above.   [2] E.E.T.S., E.S. 86, 79–85.
[3] E.E.T.S. 184, 101–4.   [4] See *Index* s.v. 'Hours of the Cross'.
[5] *A.H.* xxx. p. 32. 'They strike Him on the neck.'
[6] *Literature and Pulpit*, 510. Cf. also V. A. Kolve, *The Play called Corpus Christi* (London, 1966), 185–8, and *passim*.
[7] 'He was quickly abandoned by His disciples.'   [8] Brown XV, p. 137.
[9] Brown XIV, 34.
[10] E.E.T.S. 105, 22.

Iesus, þat wald efter mid-night
þi swete face, þat was sa bright,
  With Iuus spitting file;
And suffer siþen, for ur sin,
Boffetes on þi soft chin,
  In þat ilk quile.[1]

Throughout it there are echoes of the style of Rolle, and even a use of its imagery, as in 'þi pines in ur hertes write'. Though, as one would expect, this kind of tenderness is chiefly found in the fourteenth-century versions, even the later ones, which, for instance, draw attention to the Virgin's grief, have a gentleness unattempted by the Latin.

There is another kind of poem, in which the canonical divisions are used for the sake of breaking up a long narrative, and this is well typi-fied by Walter Kennedy's *Passioun of Crist*.[2] This is a long narrative, written in slightly aureate style, interspersed with hortatory injunctions to compassion. This poem, however, brings us to the unmarked border-line of the religious lyric. Though it shares with the lyric the same content and the same meditative visualization of each scene, it is too leisurely in style and too narrative in structure to be classified as a lyric. There are two possible tests of a Passion lyric, and it satisfies neither. One is that, though it may be narrative in form, i.e. the preacher address-ing the meditator, it should be easy and possible to transform it into a personal meditation or complaint. This could not be done with Walter Kennedy's *Passioun* without a radical rewriting. Secondly, there should normally be a single situation, which in the long Passion lyrics of the fifteenth century was provided by unchanging image of the *imago pietatis*. The difference can be seen if we compare *The Passioun* with Pecham's *Philomena*, which is also a long narrative divided by the canoni-cal hours. But here the single situation is provided by the nightingale who sings, and at last dies. There is nothing corresponding to this in *The Passioun*.

Though it is possible to exclude some poems in this way from the lyric genre, the lyrics themselves, discussed in this chapter, differ too widely in style and quality to be summed up satisfactorily in generaliza-tions. The critic of fifteenth-century literature, however, who wanted to study the Passion lyric within a convenient compass, could with some appropriateness confine himself to the lyrics of Lydgate. In these can be seen three of the most distinctive characteristics of the later lyric. Firstly, in his poems, themes, which could form the structure of indivi-dual lyrics, are reduced to a few stanzas, and packed tight, one after the

---

[1] Brown XIV, 30 (from the *Cursor mundi*).
[2] Bennett, *Devotional Pieces*, 7–63.

other, in a fairly long work. Secondly, there is a strong didactic colouring. Thirdly, there is a tone of fervour detached from either tenderness or love. Readers who find these characteristics less agreeable than those of the earlier lyric should probably not lay the blame for them on Lydgate himself. He was a far more accomplished poet than many of the earlier lyric writers, and there is no reason to suppose that he held the form of the lyric in any lesser esteem. It is much more likely that it is the disruption of the meditative tradition that we feel in Lydgate's work, rather than any defect in him as a writer.

VII

Lyrics on the Compassion of the Blessed Virgin

Poems on the Compassion of the Virgin are so rare in the earlier period of the Middle English lyric and so clearly dependent upon Latin hymns that they cannot be usefully isolated as a distinct branch of the lyric; for this reason they were not discussed in the first part of this book. It was not until the fifteenth century that the complaint of the Blessed Virgin emerged as a clear branch of the lyric, and at that time with the help of meditative and iconographic traditions—which we shall later trace in detail—it developed into an exact parallel to the Crucifixion complaint: in it we find a direct address and appeal to the meditator, the speaker fixed in a static visual image, and the enumeration of many scenes of dramatic action which successively pass in front of that of the speaker. The scattered earlier poems, however, are quite different in form and style, and cannot be put so uncompromisingly into a category paralleling that of the Passion lyric. But in themselves they are interesting and agreeable, and they may also be studied as an influence upon the later complaints and as a contrast to them.

Unlike the Passion lyrics the complaints of the Virgin leave on the reader an impression of aridity. The explanation of this may be merely one of time: that they are predominantly fifteenth-century, when, as we have seen, the ease and sweetness of the earlier lyric was completely lost. But it is possible to speculate that the cause lies rather in the fact that in the *planctus* of the Virgin there was never the perfect harmony between intellectual dogma and spiritual devotion which laid the foundation so securely for the Passion lyrics. For theologically the Virgin's role in the exposition of the nature of the Redemption was that epitomized in her early title of *Theotokos*, and therefore the earliest feasts in her honour and the earliest Western poetry in her praise celebrate her child-bearing, and in the great theological *Summae* of the Middle Ages the Virgin has a place only at the time of the birth of Christ. The stress, however, upon the Nativity as the moment of closest unity between Christ and the Virgin necessarily led to an emphasis incompatible with the spiritual tone of the period in which theology and devotion agreed in concentrating upon the Passion.

In the patristic period there had been only occasional references to the grief of the Virgin. From the time of Origen it had been explained in Biblical commentaries that Simeon's prophecy that a sword should pierce Mary's heart referred to her anguish at the Crucifixion, and the metaphorical sword was already associated with the spear which entered Christ's side.[1] But more often it was the Virgin's faith and her composed gravity that were emphasized. St. Ambrose in a *consolatio* quoted the example of Mary: 'Stantem illam lego, flentem non lego.'[2] At a time when all mourning for the dead was held to be pagan conduct, quite unfitting to the Christian, the Virgin could not be portrayed as a model of distraught and inconsolable lamentation. Moreover, the Virgin was a type of the Church, and indeed its only representative from the time of the Crucifixion until the Resurrection: 'Sola mater tenet fidem';[3] in her alone the faith of the Church at that time resided. In art she is represented solemn and unmoving: even in Eastern representations of the Crucifixion, where Christ was portrayed with a body curved in suffering, earlier than in the West, the Virgin remained for a time in some hieratic attitude, either with both hands extended in prayer or with one outstretched, witnessing to the Crucifixion.[4] There was here, however, an inconsistency which was to be corrected, for it was inevitable that the Virgin should make some gesture of distress once the representation of the crucified Christ ceased to be dogmatic in intention: the Virgin could remain impassive only whilst Christ reigned from the tree. Certainly in English art as soon as Christ is shown to suffer, the Virgin and St. John express their sorrow by the antique iconographic gesture of distress, that of the hand held beneath the cheek.[5]

When Christ's sufferings were emphasized in the earliest meditative literature, such as the two collections of meditations ascribed respectively to Augustine and Anselm, it was obviously not sufficient for the Virgin's response to be indicated solely by so restrained and stylized a gesture. Therefore her weeping and sobbing are described, but still in

[1] Yrjö Hirn, *The Sacred Shrine* (London, 1958), 268–9 and footnote 13.

[2] *De obitu Valentiniani consolatio*, xxxix, *P.L.* 16, 1371. 'It is written that she stood, not that she wept.' This point is made to support the common doctrine of early Christian consolatory elegies that weeping for the dead is unchristian (cf. the elegy of Paulinus of Nola, *Carmen* xxxv, *P.L.* 61, 676–90). The genre of the *consolatio* is described by C. Favez, *La consolation latine chrétienne* (Paris, 1937).

[3] *A.H.* xxiv. 39, p. 125. 'The mother alone retains her faith.'

[4] G. Millet, *Recherches sur l'iconographie de l'évangile* (Paris, 1960), 401. Chapter 7, 396–460, traces the development of attitudes of pain and sorrow in Christ and the Virgin respectively in the eastern tradition of iconography.

[5] For instance, the Crucifixion in the late tenth-century psalter, already referred to, p. 22, reproduced in M. Rickert, *Painting in Britain in the Middle Ages* (London, 1954), pl. 30.

a way that was both decorous and useful. It was useful because a description of the Virgin's distress enabled the meditator to be stirred through sympathy with the internal sufferings of Christ—Christ's pains had obviously to be described externally—and decorous because by the Middle Ages the Church had accepted that tears for the dead were morally fitting even for a Christian.[1] The mourning Virgin thus became in part the object of the meditator's sympathy, and she, like Christ, may be addressed in compassionate apostrophe:

Domina mea misericordissima, quos fontes dicam erupisse de pudicissimis oculis, cum attenderes unicum filium tuum innocentem coram te ligari, flagellari, mactari? Quos fletus credam perfudisse piissimum vultum, cum suspiceres eumdem et Deum et Dominum tuum in cruce sine culpa extendi, et carnem de carne tua ab impiis crudeliter dissecari?[2]

In such a passage the Virgin's grief is both an incentive to the meditator's and also a measure of what his should be. At this stage in the development of the theme of the Compassion of the Virgin there were two proprieties to be observed: firstly, the recollection that the Virgin's grief was chiefly important as a mirror of Christ's sufferings and a moving plea to the meditator for companionship in grief; secondly, the balancing of distress with faith and with modesty, so that the Virgin should not be shown abandoned to the kind of unrestrained lamentation that would have been considered morally reprehensible and socially indecorous in any Christian. These theological and devotional considerations necessarily had literary consequences. The tension between faith and grief could only be indicated by an imaginative and stylistic delicacy, whilst the fact that the Virgin's grief formed an intermediary between Christ and himself had the structural effect that the meditator must face the Virgin, whilst she herself faced the Cross: it followed, therefore, that the complaint form, in which the Virgin would face the meditator, was not a suitable structure for writers on this subject.

In the early period there are therefore no complaints of the Virgin addressed to the meditator, and the few thirteenth-century poems which treat of the Compassion of the Virgin are set in the form of third-person narrative or of the first-person address of the meditator. Though these

---

[1] The proof quoted for this was that Christ had wept for the death of Lazarus. An early, moving lament for the dead occurs in the twenty-sixth of St. Bernard's *Sermons on the Song of Songs* (P.L. 183, 903–12), where he mourns the death of his brother Gerard.

[2] *Meditationes*, xli, P.L. 40, 941. In the Middle Ages these meditations were attributed to St. Augustine, but they are now identified as the work of John of Fécamp (Wilmart, op. cit. 127–8). 'My most merciful lady, how shall I describe the fountains that burst forth from your most chaste eyes when you saw your innocent and only son bound, scourged and slaughtered before your eyes? How shall I imagine the tears that poured down your holy cheek, when you saw your God and your Lord stretched guiltless on the Cross and the flesh of your flesh cruelly torn to pieces by wicked men?'

structural classifications may imply a parallel with the Passion lyric, this implication is unhelpful, for it may obscure the radical difference between the two, which is that the dominant form of the early Passion lyric, namely the short and easily memorized meditation, is entirely lacking for the Compassion. The only possible exception to this generalization is the famous and beautiful quatrain:

> Nou goth sonne under wod,—
> me rweth, marie, þi faire Rode.
> Nou goþ sonne under tre,—
> me reweþ, marie, þi sone and þe.[1]

This verse is quoted in the meditation on the Passion for sext in the *Speculum ecclesiae*, and it therefore remains a possibility that it was originally part of an early poem on the Hours of the Cross or that it was part of a longer Passion poem. Nothing can be inferred from the manner of preservation about its original form. Admittedly the sad isolation of the figures in these lines seems to be reflected in the solitariness of the verse, but it is possible that it is mere chance that has conferred this emotive grace. In style it is quite unlike any other religious poetry of this period, unless one were to multiply unverifiable hypotheses and to guess that 'I Syng of a myden þat is makeles'[2] is also an early poem. There are stylistic affinities between the two, in that both combine the incremental repetition of the ballads, with verbal subtlety and an oblique, emotive, use of symbolism. The tact of the verse in its treatment of the Compassion, however, is characteristic of its period; for there is here a dignified treatment of the Virgin's grief, and the poet's delayed reference to Christ does not unduly emphasize the Virgin, but by a paradoxical timing most beautifully focuses the attention on her Son.

In this verse it is only by implication that we know that the Virgin is looking at the Cross. A clearer statement of this theme occurs in a long narrative poem of the Crucifixion from MS. Trinity 323, 'On leome is in þis world ilist':

> Hasse he biheuld þe rode,
> þe modir þat was of miste
> and þer I-sei al ablode
> Hir sone þat her wes briste,
> Hisse tuo swete honden
> Wid nailes al to-ronden,

---

[1] Brown XIII, 1, and notes pp. 165–6. *Rode*: face. This verse has received a great deal of commentary recently: John Cutler, 'Nou goth Sonne under wod', *Explicator*, iv (1945), no. 7; C. G. Thayer, 'Nou goth Sonne under wod', ibid. xi (1953), no. 25; S. Manning, 'Nou goth Sonne under wod', *Modern Language Notes*, lxxiv (1959), 578–81.

[2] Brown xv, 81.

Is fehit iþurlid bo,
Is swete softe side
I-þurlit depe and wyde —
Wey, þat hire was wo!

Ha isei þe rode stonden,
Hire sone þer-to ibunden
Hoe wroinc hire honden,
Bi-heild his swete þunden.
þe gyves to him leden
On him for-to greden
Asse þat hoe weren wod.
Hire þucte a miste aweden,
Hire herte bi-gon to bleden,
Teres hoe wep of blod.[1]

In these stanzas the Virgin's looking is emphasized: we are told four times that she gazes at the suffering body of Christ, and all the description, with the emotive epithets, is the object of what she sees and feels. The style and selection of detail, which in the Passion poems were intended to stir the feelings of the meditator, are here the justification of the Virgin's grief. Though there is no explicit association of the Virgin's grief with the meditator's, as, for instance, in the plea of the *Stabat mater*, 'Fac me tecum condolere',[2] the style compels this identification.

In contrast to this third-person narrative, an interesting attempt at first-person address may be seen in the two translations of the Latin hymn 'Stabat iuxta Christi crucem'.[3] These two translations are part of a small group of thirteenth-century lyrics, all in Latin stanza form, all accompanied by musical notation, and all translating or closely modelled upon Latin hymns. They seem to belong to a brief moment before 1300, in which Latin hymns were paraphrased or imitated in the vernacular —perhaps for extra-liturgical use in monasteries—and set in a simple polyphonic form.[4] Unlike the stilted work of Herebert fifty years later, these translations, though they lack the dignity and compactness which could only be achieved in Latin, are not lacking in feeling.

In contrast to the more emotional *Stabat mater dolorosa*, the *Stabat iuxta* is chiefly concerned to establish and correctly circumscribe a doctrinal statement of the Virgin's sufferings. It emphasizes the much-repeated point that what Christ suffered *foris* the Virgin suffered *intus*, and neatly stresses the intellectual parallels between the Nativity and the Crucifixion, that at the Crucifixion the Virgin endured *cum usura* the

---

[1] Brown XIII, 24. *Hasse he*: as she; *miste*: power; *briste*: glorious; *wroinc*: wrung; *greden*: shout at, revile; *aweden*: go mad.

[2] *A.H.* xxxix. 50 (textual variant to str. 13, p. 315). 'Make me to share your suffering.'

[3] Brown XIII, 4 and 47.

[4] On these see F. Ll. Harrison, *Music in Medieval Britain*, 153–5.

pains of childbirth, which against the laws of nature she had been spared when Christ was born, and that Christ rose from the tomb without breaking the seal, in the same way as He had been born of the Virgin. The Latin hymn succeeds by magnificent lucidity of expression, the unique thirteenth-century gift of expressing dogma in verse, as though it were its most natural medium. The merits of the two translations, 'þat leveli leor wid spald ischent' and 'Iesu cristes milde moder', are quite different from those of the Latin. As one would expect, where they are most concerned to preserve the paradoxes or doctrine of the Latin they are least good, and they are at their best in suggesting a tender sympathy for the Virgin's sorrow, at which the Latin does not aim. This is achieved partly by the insertion of emotive epithets, 'þat *leveli* leor' or 'þat *feire* fel', but chiefly by the striking fact that the third-person narrative of the Latin is transformed into a direct address to the Virgin. The effect of this can best be seen from a comparison of a stanza from the Latin with the respective translations of it:

> Os verendum litum sputis
> Et flagellis rupta cutis
>   Et tot rivi sanguinis,
> Probra, risus et quae restant,
> Orbitati tela praestant
>   Et dolori virginis.[1]

In 'þat leveli leor' this becomes:

> þat leveli leor wid spald ischent,
> þat feire fel wid s[cur]ges rend—
>   þe blod out stremed overal.
> Skoarn, upbraid, and schome speche,
> al hit was to sorhes eche—
>   i poa þu was biluken al.[2]

And in 'Iesu cristes milde moder':

> Nu his bodi with scurges beten,
> And his blud so wide hut-leten
>   maden þe þin herte sor.
> War-so þu castest thin eyen,
> Pine strong þu soie im dreien—
>   ne mithte noman þolie mor.[3]

The first of these is the closer to the Latin and the more taut. The last line, by means of which narrative description becomes an expression of

---

[1] *A.H.* viii. 58. 'The mouth so venerable is smeared with spittle, the skin broken by scourges, and all those rivers of blood: abuse, mocking and the rest are as spears of bereavement and pain to the Virgin.'

[2] Brown XIII, 4, p. 9. *Leor*: face; *spald*: spittle; *fel*: skin; *eche*: increase.

[3] Ibid. 47, p. 83. *Soie*: saw.

personal compassion, is movingly placed. The same emphasis on personal involvement—combined with a more explicit statement of the Virgin's looking at Christ—is found in the second translation. But the effect is weaker, for, by translating more freely, the author has become more diffuse.

There is one further point about these translations, which is interesting for its illustration of the changing feeling towards the Virgin. In the Latin hymn there is a stanza in which the Virgin's modesty is stressed, the *pudicos gestus foris*,[1] which her anguish could not deface, although it consumed her within. In 'Iesu cristes milde moder' this stanza is omitted completely, whilst in 'þat leveli leor' the author has struggled awkwardly to preserve it:

> Ah, lavedi, þah þu wonges wete,
> þah þe were wo at unimete,
>   þine loates weren lasteles;
> þi wep ne wemmede noht þin heaw
> þat made þi leor ful louk and lep—
>   swa sari wmmon never neas.[2]

The author has not accepted the implication of his original that the Virgin did not weep, and he therefore loses entirely the idea of virgin modesty and outward composure paradoxically contrasted with inward anguish. Without knowledge of the original the moral force of *wemmede* is not plain and is especially confused by the following line. The poet's lack of understanding damages the poem only to the extent that this particular stanza is weak, but it may also be seen as an ominous foreshadowing of later developments, when the virtue of modesty was forgotten at the cost of both devotional and literary decorum.

The two other poems belonging to this group, 'þe milde Lomb isprad o rode' and 'Stond wel, moder, ounder rode', have no known Latin originals, but by musical setting and stanza form they belong with the translations of the *Stabat iuxta*, and there is a fair probability that originals once existed that are now lost or unidentified. Like the two translations of the *Stabat iuxta*, however, they have a warmth not characteristic of Latin hymns, and therefore probably peculiar to them. 'þe milde Lomb' is an agreeable third-person narrative, embodying a speech of Christ addressed to the Virgin. Though there is no dialogue, the relationship described is mutual: the Virgin suffers to see Christ's wounds: Christ's own sufferings are increased by the sight of His mother's grief. The latter detail became a commonplace of Latin meditative literature, and could not derive from the early liturgical tradition.

---

[1] 'Modest outward gestures.'

[2] Brown XIII, 4, p. 9. *Wonges*: cheeks; *unimete*: measureless; *loates*: outward bearing; *lasteles*: blameless; *wemmede*: did not deface; *louk and lep*: pale and wan.

Though the content of Christ's speech is the paradox of the pains of childbirth, through its style and context it seems mournful rather than doctrinally clever:

> Ac nu þu must þi pine dreien,
> wan þu sicst me with þin eyen
> pine þole o rode, and deien
>   to helen man þat was forlorn.[1]

Though 'Stond wel, moder' is a dialogue, it does not have the tenderness which in 'þe milde Lomb' springs from the meeting of compassion with compassion. In it the Virgin describes the sufferings which she sees and laments them, whilst Christ amplifies His initial exhortation—

> Stond wel, moder, ounder rode,
> Bihold þi child wiþ glade mode,
> Moder bliþe miȝt þou be.[2]

—by expounding in sermon style the necessity for His death. This dialogue is set in Latin form, with half of each stanza allotted to each speaker: this symmetrical arrangement draws attention to the distinction, which was to be maintained throughout the Middle Ages in both narrative and mystery plays, that, whilst the Virgin laments with unrestrained human distress, Christ speaks dogmatically with an impassiveness befitting His divinity.

The small group of poems so far described are in a sense Passion lyrics, in which the Crucifixion is seen through the eyes of the Virgin. There are, of course, details—normally of a doctrinal kind—that refer exclusively to her, but to a large extent her part is that of the compassionate meditator. She is not involved historically in the action. However, in the next group of lyrics to be discussed, which may perhaps be later than these by fifty years or more, the Virgin's part becomes more distinctive and important, and the dramatic framework of the lyric is therefore different. The sources of this change may be found in some of the Latin meditations on the Compassion of the Virgin, and it is therefore necessary to make a preliminary consideration of these.

In the gospels very little is said of the part played by the Virgin during the events of the Passion: only that she stood by the Cross and that Christ committed her to the care of St. John. It was inevitable that the question of what the Virgin did from the time of the arrest until the burial should in due course be both asked and answered. Invented detail is found fairly early in the writings of the Eastern Church. These works have nowadays been enumerated repeatedly by writers on the

---

[1] Brown XIII, 45, p. 78.   [1] Ibid. 49, p. 87.

Marienklagen:[1] the Eastern redaction of the *Gesta Pilati*,[2] the sixth-century imitation Greek drama, the Χριστὸς πάσχων[3] in which the Virgin is the tragic heroine, and the much later, ninth- and tenth-century, sermons of George of Nicodemia[4] and Simeon Metaphrastes.[5] Between this tradition and that of later Western works there are so many coincidences of detail and treatment that a connexion is certain, though the link has not yet been traced.

The two most important Latin works of the Middle Ages are the *Dialogus Beatae Mariae et Anselmi de passione Domini*[6] and the *Liber de passione Christi*,[7] which may more conveniently be referred to by its opening words, *Quis dabit capiti meo*. In both, in reply to questioning, the Virgin gives an eye-witness account of the Passion sequence, with especial emphasis laid upon her actions and feelings. The *Quis dabit capiti meo* was quite exceptionally popular: it circulated in nearly every western European country, and translations of it into either prose or verse exist in nearly every vernacular. The inclusion of a large part of it in the *Stimulus amoris*[8] considerably increased its diffusion. Quite apart from transcriptions of the *Stimulus amoris* the *Quis dabit capiti meo* survives in England in at least twenty-three manuscripts—and probably in many more—beginning with MS. Bodley 750 of the thirteenth century.[9] A French translation occurs in a fourteenth-century Anglo-Norman devotional manuscript, MS. Emmanuel Coll. 106,[10] and a fifteenth-century

---

[1] H. Thien, *Über die englischen Marienklagen* (Kiel, 1906); E. Wechssler, *Die romanischen Marienklagen* (Halle, 1893); F. Ermini, *Lo Stabat Mater e i pianti della Vergine nella lirica del medio evo* (Città di Castello, 1916).

[2] C. Tischendorf, *Evangelia apocrypha* (Leipzig, 1876), 288–332. A convenient summary of its main points is given by Wechssler, loc. cit. 8–9. The earliest English work containing a *planctus* derived from the *Gesta Pilati* is the early narrative in couplets known as *The Assumption of Our Lady* (E.E.T.S. 14, 111–36). This poem belongs to the late thirteenth century. In it are six quite touching lines of appeal by the Blessed Virgin to Christ (ll. 36–42; cf. G. C. Taylor, 'The English *Planctus Mariae*', M.P. iv, 1906, 605–37). Behind the first part of this poem must lie a Latin text of the *Gesta* closely related to the Greek printed by Tischendorf as Recension B. What intermediary there may have been between such a text of the *Gesta* and *The Assumption* is, however, not known.   [3] *P.G.* 38, 138–338.

[4] *In SS. Mariam assistentem cruci*, P.G. 100, 1458–90.

[5] *Oratio in lugubrem lamentationem sanctissimae Deiparae pretiosum corpus domini nostri Jesu Christi amplexantis*, P.G. 114, 208–18.

[6] *P.L.* 159, 271–90.

[7] *P.L.* 182, 1133–42 (with a defective opening).

[8] For an account of this work see the Introduction to Walter Hilton, *The Goad of Love*, trans. C. Kirchberger (London, 1952).

[9] F. J. Tanquerey, *Plaintes de la Vierge en anglo-français* (Paris, 1921), p. 6, lists twelve manuscripts. To these may be added the following: MSS. Bodl. 555, 91 ff.; Bodl. 750, 120 ff.; Bodl. e Mus. 177, 54 ff.; Canon. Misc. 90, 4 ff.; Royal 7 A. vi, 77 ff.; Royal 8 B. viii, 76 ff.; Royal 8 C. vii, 81ᵛ ff.; Harley 1801, 88 ff., St. John's Camb. 127, 46 ff.; Trinity Coll., Dublin, 277.

[10] An Anglo-Norman translation occurs also in MSS. Egerton 2281, 131 ff. and Royal 20 B. v, 147 ff.

English translation—made from the French, according to the concluding rubric—occurs in a popular English devotional manuscript, MS. C.U.L. Kk. 1. 6.[1] It is very likely that vernacular prose versions were more current than these meagre references suggest. In the fourteenth century, too, there was an English paraphrase, 'Lewed men be not lered in lore', which was fairly current,[2] and a different version was incorporated into the *Cursor mundi*.[3] Two Anglo-Norman complaints of the early fourteenth century were also based upon it.[4]

The *Quis dabit capiti meo* undoubtedly had a strong and direct influence upon the English complaints of the Virgin belonging to the fifteenth century, which we shall be discussing later. They derive from it much of their detail and also the excessive emotionalism which colours both content and style. The earlier influence of the *Quis dabit*, however, was more limited and probably less direct. It is the dramatic situation that it seems to contribute, rather than detail or tone. Moreover, the fourteenth-century English poems are probably at least as much indebted to a group of Latin hymns as to the *Quis dabit* (though the hymns themselves must have been influenced by this or similar works). The hymns are those that Young indicates as possible sources for the Latin Passion play.[5] These, like the English poems that are structurally close to them, are fragments of dramatic scenes. Some, such as the *Planctus ante nescia* and *Flete, fideles animae*,[6] are monologues of the Virgin, but they are dramatic, in the sense that complaints of Christ are not, for they are addressed to figures within the historical scene, to Christ, the Jews, or St. John. Others, such as the *Qui per viam pergitis*, actually consist of a brief and loosely devised dramatic scene, in which the Virgin, St. John, and Christ all speak.[7]

---

[1] This manuscript is not mentioned by Tanquerey, but he lists five others, none of which, however, contains this text (loc. cit. 12, footnote 3A): MSS. Harley 2251, Harley 2255, and Laud Misc. 683, contain Lydgate's *planctus* (not based on the *Quis dabit*), 'Who shal yere unto myn hed' (E.E.T.S., E.S. 107, 324–9); MS. Cotton Cleo. D. viii, has 'When I Mary' (see p. 361, and footnote 3); and MS. Cotton Tib. E. vii, has the Dialogue between the Virgin and St. Bernard (*Yorkshire Writers*, ii. 274–82).

[2] E.E.T.S. 98, 298–328.   [3] Ibid. 68, 1368–417.

[4] One, beginning 'Pur ceus e celes ki n'entendent / Quant oient lire le latin, / Jeo ai commence icest livre' survives in two manuscripts, MSS. Greaves 51 with the *Manuel des pechiez* and C.U.L. Gg. i. 1, a miscellaneous collection largely of French material; this adaptation keeps closer to the Latin than does the other and may have been one of the sources of the English paraphrase. The other poem beginning, 'Reïne corounee, Flur de paraïs', occurs in three manuscripts, including the important Anglo-Norman collection (which also contains the lyrics of Friar William Herebert), B.M. Add. 46919 (*olim* Phillips 8336). The earliness of this version seems to be indicated by the fact that it ends with the Crucifixion, not the Entombment. Both these Anglo-Norman works probably ante-date the earliest English version by about fifty years. They are printed by Tanquerey, loc. cit. 63–135.

[5] Karl Young, *The Drama of the Medieval Church*, i. 492–539.

[6] Ibid. 496–500.   [7] Ibid. 500–3.

The earliest English laments of the Virgin are of this kind. Like the Latin hymns, and incidentally like some of the *laude* of Jacopone da Todi,[1] they are fragmentary or miniature plays, although in general they technically conform to the two lyric kinds of monologue and debate. They have, however, to be understood against the dramatic background of a continuous narrative, such as is found in the *Quis dabit*. Several of the English poems of this kind are contained in John of Grimestone's preaching-book. One of these is a complaint of the Virgin addressed to the Jews as she stands by the Cross. Curiously enough, it is found, not in the Passion section, but in that headed *de beate virgine*:

> Why have ȝe no reuthe on my child?
> Have reuthe on me ful of murn(n)g,
> Taket doun on rode my derworþi child,
> Or prek me on rode with my derling.
>
> More pine ne may me ben don
> þan laten me liven in sorwe and schame;
> Als love me bindet to my sone,
> So lat us deyȝen boþen i-same.[2]

The Jews, with death, the Cross, etc., were traditional objects of the Virgin's reproaches. In the *Quis dabit*, for instance, the Virgin turns from her lament to Christ on the Cross to an appeal to the Jews to crucify her with Him:

O Judaei, ipsi nolite mihi parcere, qui natum meum crucifixistis. Matrem crucifigite, aut alia quacunque me saeva morte perimite. Dum meo cum filio finiar simul, male solus moritur.[3]

Behind this much repeated theme there lies, of course, David's lament for Absalom (2 Sam. [2 Kings] xviii. 33), which in the preceding paragraph of the *Quis dabit* is quoted almost word for word: 'Fili mi, fili mi, quis mihi dabit ut ego moriar pro te?'[4] There was an obvious propriety in the supposition that, if David had wished to die for his son, the Blessed Virgin could not have done less. Although some words roughly related to the above quotation from the *Quis dabit* are copied in the manuscript as an inscription for the poem,[5] the chief source of the poem is more probably a verse from the *Planctus ante nescia*:

---

[1] For instance, 'Pianto de la Madonna de la passione del figliolo Iesú Cristo', *Le Laude*, ed. Caramella, 228–30.

[2] Brown XIV, 60. *Prek*: nail.

[3] *P.L.* 182, 1136. 'O Jews, do not spare me since you have crucified my son. Crucify the mother or slay me by any other brutal death. May I die together with my son, it is bad that He should die alone.'

[4] Ibid. 1135. 'My son, my son, who will grant it to me that I may die for thee.' The translation of the A.V. is here not close to the Latin.

[5] Brown XIV, p. 265.

> Nato, quaeso, parcite,
> Matrem crucifigite,
> Aut in crucis stipite
> Nos simul affigite,
> Male solus moritur.[1]

The two English stanzas, with their expressions of love, are obviously far more touching than the barer Latin, and have an innocent intensity, which excludes any strain of rhetorical melodrama from the Virgin's wish to die.

Another brief monologue from the Passion section of the same manuscript is a more moving poem, addressed directly to Christ. It has, however, partially the same theme, that of the Virgin's desire to die with her Son:

> Swete sone, reu one me and bring me out of þis live,
> for me þinket þat i se þi detȝ, it neyhit swiþe;
> þi feet ben nailed to þe tre—nou may i no more þrive,
> For al þis werd with-outen þe ne sal me maken bliþe.[2]

Deliberate abruptness of syntax and emotive description make this a convincing and touching lament; and there is also an interesting progression of feeling from the Virgin's first appeal, 'Swete sone, reu on me, and brest out of þi bondis', through the resigned acceptance of the second stanza, to the desire for death in the third. For the period there is an unusual freedom of invention here. There is no parallel to this progression in the *Quis dabit*, and the Latin meditation attributed to Bede, which is referred to in the manuscript rubric, is yet further from such a way of thought.[3] There is a brief dialogue in MS. Balliol 149, 'A Sone! tak hede to me whas sone þou was', which for its subject-matter should be grouped with these poems: the Virgin beseeches Christ that she may be set on the Cross with Him, whilst He replies, as in the *Quis dabit*, with a doctrinal statement of the need for His death.[4] It is, however, too dull to require further examination or quotation.

As an example of an embryonic drama, the most interesting of the poems in John of Grimestone's preaching-book is that beginning 'Maiden and moder, cum and se'.[5] The poem is apparently written in couplets, though, out of thirty-six lines, sixteen could equally well be in mono-rhyming quatrains. In fifteenth-century manuscripts it was turned into carol form through rearrangements and additions.[6] Like the *Qui per viam pergitis* it is drama in the sense that there is no narrative

---

[1] *A.H.* xx. 199; Young, loc. cit. 'Spare the son, I beseech you! crucify the mother! or fasten us both together to the stem of the cross, it is bad that He should die alone.'
[2] Brown XIV, 64.
[3] Ibid. p. 266.
[4] Ibid. 128.
[5] Ibid. 67.
[6] *Carols*, 157, A, B, and C.

and three people speak. The ascription of the first speech to *Ihesus* is undoubtedly a mistake: in two of the three later texts it is ascribed to St. John,[1] and in the third to an unnamed 'he',[2] who again must obviously be the apostle. St. John traditionally brought the evil news to the Virgin, either of the arrest as in the *Meditationes*, or of the actual Crucifixion, as in the *Gesta Pilati*,[3] and the York Plays.[4] The mistake presumably arose from a copyist's assumption that this was a dialogue between Christ and the Virgin. It is, however, an interesting mistake, in that it draws attention to the oddity of the structure: episodes in the action are omitted and there is even a change of scene; the speeches are thematically but not dramatically related to one another, the Blessed Virgin does not reply to St. John's message, and, although Christ at the beginning of His speech replies to the Virgin, He ends with a traditional complaint to man. In the later carol versions these awkwardnesses have disappeared: the final didactic address to man is gone, and a narrative quatrain fills in the gap in the sequence of action:

> Wan Johan this tal began to tell,
> Mary wyld not lenger dwell
> Thyl sche cam to that hyll
> Ther sche myth her owyn Son see.[5]

But, though the carol versions are smoother, they are less poetically effective, for the additions, made for the sake of the form and for steady progression of narrative, lead to diffuseness. The compression of the original, despite the abruptness inherent in it, is very effective, and the complaint of the Blessed Virgin, immediately adjoining St. John's urgent description of Christ's suffering, is especially touching:

> Mi swete sone þat art me dere,
> Wat hast þu don, qui art þu here?
> Þi swete bodi þat in me rest,
> þat loveli mouth þat i have kist,—
> Nou is on rode mad þi nest.
> Mi dere child, quat is me best.[6]

It would be tedious to describe at length other dramatic dialogues of this kind, though they may be briefly enumerated. There are three of them: two are dialogues between the Virgin and Christ, and one a dialogue between the Virgin and St. John after the death of Christ. The earliest of these, 'Behold, womman, a dolful sith', occurs in John of Grimestone's preaching book on the page before 'Maiden and moder,

---

[1] Ibid. 157, A (Kele, *Christmas Carolles*), B (MS. Eng. poet. e. i.).
[2] Ibid. 157, C (MS. Sloane 2593).
[3] Tischendorf, op. cit. 303. [4] Ed. L. T. Smith, 341.
[5] *Carols*, p. 118. [6] Brown xiv, p. 85.

cum and se'. Though it appears now to be a dialogue between Christ and the Virgin, the first two lines would more appropriately belong to St. John:

> Behold, womman, a dolful sith,
> þis is þi sone þat hanget here.[1]

These lines, however, are so metrically intertwined with a speech of Christ, that they cannot now be disentangled, though one may conjecture that the text has become corrupt. The poem itself is mediocre and it has not been printed. It is not, however, very different in either style or quality from many fifteenth-century carols. But, like the Nativity poems from the same manuscript, which we discussed earlier, it lacks the refrain, which Professor Greene has shown to be one of the chief characteristics of the carol. Had it been given a refrain, however, it could have been included quite suitably in a collection of carols: for it has the swift-moving narrative, the simple dialogue, unheightened style, and metrical lilt which are all typical of one stylistic branch of the carol.

There is a dialogue between the Virgin and St. John, 'Thys blessyd babe that thou hast born', very similar in style.[2] This is a true carol, for it has a refrain, though the refrain itself, 'Mary moder, cum and se / Thy swet Son nayled on a tre', is borrowed, and does not always come in appropriately. Another defect is the confusion of the time sequence: nevertheless, it expresses the traditional commonplaces of grief quite pleasantly, as in 'Alas, alas now may I crye. / Why mygh[t] i not with my Son dye?'. The best of the three dialogues, however, is that from the Ryman Manuscript, beginning 'O my dere Sonne'.[3] In this there is a sustained tone of measured tenderness, and a greater weight of feeling, made possible by the amplitude of the seven-line stanzas.

There is finally one late fourteenth-century poem (found first in the Vernon Manuscript), which, though entirely different in style, may nevertheless be loosely associated with this group. For, though in form it is, like the lover-knight allegory, a persuasive image, it still has affinities with a dialogue in an historical scene. It is the dialogue or debate between the Virgin and the Cross, 'Oure ladi freo, on Rode treo made hire mon', which is a variation upon the 'O crux de te volo conqueri' of Philip the Chancellor.[4] According to the tradition of the Eastern version of the *Gesta Pilati*, the Cross was one of the many people or objects reproachfully questioned by the Virgin. The Latin

---

[1] f. 120ᵛ. L. 2, þi, MS. þis. [2] *Carols*, 158.
[3] Ibid. 156.
[4] E.E.T.S. 117, 612–26; ibid. 46, 197–209. The text is set out in parallel columns with the Latin by F. Holthausen, 'Der mittelenglische Disput zwischen Maria und dem Kreuze', *Archiv*, cv (1900), 22–29. There is also an, as yet unprinted, Anglo-Norman adaptation of the Latin in MS. B.M. Add. 46919 (*olim* Phillips 8336), 79 ff.

poem is, however, removed from the historical scene, partly by the fiction that the Cross actually speaks, and partly by the style, which makes it more a debate than a dialogue.[1] The two speeches are, in fact, intellectually linked by a pattern of conceited parallels, whereby the roles of the Virgin and the Cross as bearers of Christ are reversed, so that the Virgin becomes the fruit-bearing tree and the Cross the mother or nurse.

The Latin poem is thus a neat and well-turned debate, and the possibility of visualizing the speakers does not arise. But the strength of the meditative tradition prevents such a convenient silence in the English imitation. The English poem preserves and amplifies the conceits of its Latin source, and in the second half, which is entirely free, it draws on other sources for its conceits, such as that of the Cross as the board for a book.[2] But intermingled with the conceits is traditional description of Christ's sufferings, and both tenses and style suggest that the Virgin is gazing at the Cross with Christ upon it:

> Tre unkinde, þou schalt be kud;
> Mi sone step-Moder, I þe calle.
> Mi fruit was born wiþ beestes on bed,
> And be my flesch my flour gan falle.
> Wiþ my brestes, my brid I fed;
> Cros! þou ȝevest him Eysel and Galle.
> Mi white Rose Red is spred,
> þat fostred was in a fodderes stalle.
> Ffeet and fayre hondes
> þat nou ben croised, I custe hem ofte;
> I lulled hem, I leid hem softe.
> Cros! þou holdest hem hiȝe on lofte,
> Bounden in bledyng bondes.[3]

The impression that the Virgin is speaking within the historical scene is, however, contradicted by the concluding part of the poem, in which the poet deals explicitly with the appearance of the speakers and the nature of the poem. The Virgin is said to be the crowned Empress of Heaven, and the Cross 'A Relyk þat shineþ shene', in other words a jewelled symbol. The poem, too, is described as a 'figour / of Maries

---

[1] There had been one earlier debate poem, in which the Virgin, taking the part of *Ecclesia*, disputes with *Synagoga* to prove the doctrine of her virginal childbirth, H. Walther, *Das Streitgedicht* (Munich, 1920), 102–3.

[2] The ultimate source was the *librum scriptum intus et foris* of Apoc. v. 1. In the *Vitis mystica* of Bonaventura the book is already taken to refer to Christ, *Decem Opuscula*, 466. The A B C poem on the Passion is entirely constructed on this image, E.E.T.S. 15, 270–8 (ll. 189 ff. are almost certainly an addition for they do not continue the image, and the text of MS. Adv. 18. 7. 21. ends at this point).

[3] E.E.T.S. 117, 613–14.

wo to wite som', and the poet stresses this to the point of *naïveté*, explaining that the Cross did not speak on Calvary, nor did the Virgin reproach it. It is interesting that the poet here expounds the idea of the persuasive image. Nevertheless, though the apotheosis of the Virgin and the Cross was no doubt designed to meet the difficulty of the Cross speaking, it fits incongruously with the expressions of grief and the descriptions of present suffering. There is left an impression of a dialogue within an historical scene, in which the Virgin laments and the Cross replies by taking the part of unyielding doctrinal instructor, the part which in the carols had been given to Christ or St. John.

It is worth noting how two quite different poems, which use the theme incidentally, deal with the problem. One is the *Pèlerinage de l'âme* of Guillaume de Guilleville, translated into English in the fifteenth century. In this the scene is made totally allegorical,[1] for it becomes a debate between two trees, the green tree, which is the Virgin, and the dry tree, which is the Cross. This transformation introduces fresh difficulties, but solves the particular one with which we are concerned. The other poem is Walter Kennedy's *The passioun of Christ*, which we have already briefly mentioned. This keeps the Virgin's reproach of the Cross and the latter's answer firmly within the historical scene.[2] It is perhaps the sheer length of the poem, and its mass of detail, which enable this fantasy to be included amongst so much meditative realism without its leading to a sense of incongruity.

The depiction in 'Our ladi freo' of the Virgin glorified, but nevertheless expressing the passion of grief, may be compared with that in the Latin prose treatises, already discussed, the *Quis dabit* and the *Dialogus*. In these the Virgin appears to St. Bernard and St. Anselm respectively as Queen of Heaven, and in reply to their questions, relates her sufferings in the past tense. The fact that she is now glorified is stressed and also its consequences: 'sed quia glorificata sum flere non possum'.[3] This would obviously not be satisfactory from the meditative point of view, since the image is not a visual symbol of the emotion; and indeed, though fifteenth-century poets constantly imitate the content of the *Quis dabit*, they never make use of this opening. At the same time the image of the Virgin standing beside the Cross was not adequate, for quite apart from the fact that this was a subsidiary position from which she could scarcely face the meditator, it was also too limited in time, for it could not contain the lamentation before the burial, which formed such an important part of the *Quis dabit*. There is in fact only one fifteenth-century poem, 'There stood besyde the crosse of Ihesu / Hys moder', that uses this earlier

---

[1] Ed. J. J. Stürzinger (Roxburghe Club, 1895), 194–220.
[2] *Devotional Pieces*, ed. Bennett, 42–45.
[3] 'But because I am glorified I cannot weep.'

form. In content this has many of the characteristics of the *planctus*, in particular the customary antitheses between the Virgin's joy at the Annunciation and her grief at the Crucifixion, and her delight in the Christ-Child and her misery at the sight of the crucified Christ:

> Somtyme I lappyd the in myne arme,
> And thought full kyndely the to kysse;
> I weryd the wyll fro all kyn harme,
> On the was all my ioy and blysse.
> But now methynke hit ys all amysse
> To se thy blood renne from thy hert.
> But I most take hit as hyt ys,
> And sofre sorow with peynes smert.[1]

But it is structurally less compact, diverging into narrative and petitionary prayer. It is a quite pleasant poem and more controlled in feeling than many: it illustrates well what fifteenth-century poetry on the Compassion would probably have been like had there not been available an iconographic form comparable in kind to the *imago pietatis*.

The iconographic form was that of the Virgin seated with the dead body of Christ in her lap, commonly called a Pietà. This scene is chiefly familiar nowadays from Italian Renaissance painting, but there is evidence that it was fairly common in England in the fifteenth century, though it was so inevitable an object of the iconoclasm of the reformers, that this evidence consists only of the assembling of scattered traces.[2] The use of the Pietà had evident advantages for a writer who wished to compose a meditative poem of which the central figure was the mourning Virgin. Its chief advantage was that, like the *imago pietatis*, it had the character of an *Andachtsbild*, which normally isolated from a realistic historical scene one or two figures as objects of devotion,[3] frozen at some moment of significant action. It also gave to the Virgin the prominence that was aesthetically fitting, once she, instead of Christ, became the central object of compassion: the Pietà, in which without impropriety she could occupy the centre, Christ being dead, and in which she appeared in an attitude epitomizing her role of grief, was the perfect form for her complaint.

---

[1] Brown xv, 97, p. 146. *I weryd the wylle*: I protected you well.

[2] A brief history of the Pietà form with particular reference to its currency in England will be found in Appendix F.

[3] Though Margery Kempe's response to affective images was no doubt more emotional and intense than that of the average medieval Christian, her description of herself before the Pietà in St. Stephen's, Norwich, is nevertheless worth quoting as an indication of the kind of response that a Pietà was designed to evoke: '. . . wher þis creatur sey a fayr ymage of owr Lady clepyd a pyte. And thorw þe beholdyng of þat pete hir mende was al holy ocupyed in þe Passyon of owr Lord Ihesu Crist and in þe compassyon of owr Lady, Seynt Mary, be whech sche was compellyd to cryyn ful lowde and wepyn ful sor, as þei sche xulde a deyd', E.E.T.S. 212, 148.

There is a clear example of the use of the Pietà in a short, moral, aureate complaint in MS. Ashmole 189. It opens with a line that echoes the text, *O vos omnes*, 'Thou synfull man of resoun þat walkest here up and downe',[1] and follows this with an injunction to him to look at the speaker's suffering appearance. That the speaker is the Virgin of the Pietà is made plain by a line in the next stanza, '. . . Yet wepe for my dere sone, which one my lap lieth ded'. As a poem it is quite undistinguished, over-didactic in tone, and inelegantly aureate in diction. But it is a simple and interesting example of the use of the Pietà form. The meditator is obviously to imagine himself present in a Pietà scene, and this gives compactness and coherence to the three long stanzas. At the same time the poem is dry, because, as in some fifteenth-century Passion poems, there is no description of the scene: the reader has to supply this for himself from outside the poem.

A much more interesting poem, which makes use of the same form, is that beginning 'Off alle women þat ever were borne', an appeal, as was traditional, from the Virgin to other mothers who may feel a particular compassion for her. The first stanza makes the scene plain:

> Off alle women þat ever were borne
> þat berys childur, abyde and se
> How my son liggus me beforne
> Upon my kne, takyn fro tre.
> Your childur ȝe dawnse upon your kne
> With laȝyng, kyssyng and mery chere;
> Beholde my childe, beholde now me,
> ffor now liggus ded my dere son, dere.[2]

In the second half of this stanza there begins the series of contrasts which form the substance of this poem: contrasts, of which many recall by their ingenious precision those in Christ's address to the dandy; mothers pick their children's hair for lice, the Virgin pulls out thorns; mothers dandle their children's hands and feet, the Virgin can feel her Child's limbs pierced through and through. The success of this poem lies in fact in the realistic observation of maternal fondness and caresses, and the contrast of this with the Virgin's actions of grief as she holds the crucified body of her Son. No doubt the invention of these antitheses was helped by the traditional series of contrasts made between the Nativity and the Crucifixion,[3] and also possibly by the related

---

[1] Brown xv, 8.

[2] Ibid. 7, p. 13. For other texts see Sandison, op. cit. 104–9.

[3] Cf. for instance, the loosely rhymed prose passage from MSS. Worcester F 10, and Balliol 149, 12ᵛ: 'O blessful mayden and moder þys his a wondirful chaunge. þe angel bihete þe þat Crist sculde be þi sonne and dwelle wiþ þe, and now he takeþ þe a newe sone and goþ fram þe. þe angel said to þe þat þe fruit of þi wombe schulde be blessid, and now þe dome of þe Iewis hit haþ cursid. At his burþ þow hurdist angell syng, ande

iconographic form in which a grieving Virgin holds a child-sized, crucified figure in her lap.[1] It seems likely that this invention was not the poet's own, though no source has been found for the poem. There is no doubt, however, that, whatever the nature of the poet's indebtedness to a learned source, he has amplified and expressed the antitheses with considerable assurance. Any dissatisfaction that may be felt with the poem perhaps arises from a defect of content—that the grounds for the Compassion do not here rest upon the doctrine of the Redemption, but on a conceit only loosely related to it. In the poem, too, can be seen the combination of overt didacticism with strident emotionalism, which is so disagreeable a characteristic of much fifteenth-century religious poetry.

'Off alle women þat ever were borne' survives in five manuscripts, of which four are notable poetical collections, MSS. C.U.L. Ff. v. 48 and Ff. ii. 38, Ashmole 61, and Rawl. C. 86. The text in the last two is peculiar in that an additional three stanzas are prefixed to the poem. The first is as follows:

> In a chirche as I gan knele,
> This enders daye to here a masse,
> I sawe a sighte me liked wele,
> I shal you tell what it was.
> I saw a pite in a place,
> Owre lady and her sone in feere;
> Ofte she wepte and sayde, 'Alas.
> Now lith here dede my dere sone dere!'[2]

The second stanza is addressed to 'all women' and the third to 'al man-kynde'. It seems a fair inference from these inconsistencies that the three stanzas are not original, but show an attempt to adapt the poem to a slightly strange variation of the Pietà convention. According to this, the meditator is not to imagine himself in the historical scene, but in a chapel where there is a Pietà statue. A secondary image has intruded between the original and its literary re-creation. No doubt the idea of a statue speaking was encouraged by the many miracle stories in which a statue came to life and spoke to the beholder, but from the point of view of the history of meditation there is here another unmistakable sign of the decay of the tradition.

now seest his frendist wepyng. At his burþe kyngis and schephurdis dede hym homage and worchip, and now al maner men doþ spit and schenship. At his burþe þu wantid womans wo, but as we felis now hit is not so. Some tyme þow hadest cause to syng lullay, but þi song is alle walouway. Some time þu fedist hyme wiþe þi milke at his hese, and now þe Iewis fedeth hyme wiþe bittir galle at his diseise. Somme tyme þu fondist hym sittyng in þe middelle of doctours in þe temple, and now þu fondist hym in midill of þe Iewis on the Crosse.' In both manuscripts this passage is followed by 'A Sone! tak hede to me whas sone þou was', Brown xiv, 128.

[1] Mâle, *L'Art religieux de la fin du moyen âge en France*, 128 and fig. 68.
[2] Sandison, loc. cit. 104. *This enders daye*: one day not long ago; *pite*: Pietà.

A striking poem with a statue opening is that described as 'a tretys to lerne to wepe', which survives in two manuscripts, both of a devotional kind. In this the opening manipulation of the meditative image is tortuous but unsubtle. The speaker kneels before 'an image of pite', but it is within his imagination; and then, as he gazes at the pitiful image, his soul is transported from his body (as is the dreamer's in *The Pearl*):

> Purtreyd and peyntid piteously
> This ymage was with terys of blode,
> As for a meroure veryly
> Of oure lady I understode.
> Hir sone uppon hir kne did ly,
> All rent and revyn brought fro þe rode.
> And thrught this sight full sodenly
> I ravished was with mayn and mode;
> My spiryte from my body yoode,
> My minde was on that lady fre,
> Me thought she seide these wordis goode:
> Who can not wepe come lerne att me.[1]

The poet seems here to have combined pretentiously a number of possible, but quite distinct, openings.

The poem is very long—the manuscript text that has been printed has seventy-two stanzas—and it falls into three parts, covering events from the childhood of the Virgin to the Assumption. Much of this, of course, is unsuitable material for a *planctus*, and the refrain, 'Who can not wepe, come lerne att me' is often not appropriate, for many of the events could not reasonably provoke tears, and indeed these often have to be described as tears of joy. The middle section, however, is a genuine Passion complaint, and the events from Holy Thursday to the burial are narrated with an exceptional number of interventions from the Virgin. In the first scene, where Christ tells her that He must die, the Virgin begs Him to retract or else that they may die together; at the trial she takes no part, but later presses forward to help Christ carry the heavy Cross, only to be thrown to the ground by the Jews; when the robe is torn off Christ at Calvary, the Virgin would embrace Him, but fears that her touch may pain Him the more; nevertheless, she bends to kiss Him as He lies stretched on the Cross. After a long complaint, in which the Virgin begs that she too may die, she stretches up to embrace the Cross, but is again cast down by the Jews, who are always maliciously intent on tormenting her as well. At Christ's death she swoons, and continues in a sad alternation of sighing and fainting, being deprived of the

---

[1] R. M. Garrett, 'De arte lacrimandi', *Anglia Zeitschrift*, xxxii (1909), 269–94. Ll. 1–2: 'This statue had tears of blood painted upon the face in a way that was pitiful to see' (statues, whether wooden or stone, were usually painted in the Middle Ages). The title, 'a tretys to lerne to wepe', occurs in MS. Bodl. 423, 292ᵛ.

comfort of the Holy Ghost. At the deposition the Virgin begs to receive the body in her lap, and at this point there is another long complaint, which ends in further distress when Joseph of Arimathea insists that the burial can no longer be delayed.

It is perhaps impossible to summarize this poem decorously: to do so with the reverence which the subject-matter itself requires would be to suggest a dignity which the poem lacks, whilst to do so with the emphasis upon the more hysterical parts would be objectionable on other grounds. It is unlikely that anybody who admires the quality of the earlier meditative lyric could find this poem agreeable. Technically, of course, it is immensely more accomplished. The tight rhyme scheme and refrain of the twelve-line stanzas are adequately maintained and the number of padding phrases is reasonably small. But the technical achievement makes the tone of enclosed, unrestrained emotion the more distasteful. The impression of the poem is that of a whipping up of emotion for its own sake rather than as an understanding response to Christ's work in the Redemption. There could, perhaps, be no clearer example of how the decay of the meditative theory led to a decline of poetic sensitivity. Amongst so much strident emphasis on pain and sobbing the stanza based on the Bernardine 'arms outstretched' motif stands out as startlingly moving:

> Beholde my sone on crosse displayed
> With armes on broode the to enbrace;
> His hed uppon his schuldyre leyde,
> The fore to here and graunt the grace;
> His syde openyd redy arayed,
> His herte to yelde to thi solace;
> His feet faste to the crosse forsayde,
> With the to abyde in every place.
> Beholde how he bowes doun his face
> The cusse of pite to offyr the.
> Have mende, whiles that thou haste space,
> And for to wepe come lerne att me.[1]

In the rest of the poem so much excess leaves one aesthetically repelled, emotionally alienated rather than moved to compassion. The impression is left that the author has ransacked Latin meditative literature for painful detail, and has built a poem out of this accumulation. It is as though the author assumed the insensitive conclusion that the degree of compassionate response is exactly commensurate with quantity of painful description.

A *planctus*, where an original Pietà opening seems to have been lost, is that beginning 'Listyns, lordyngus, to my tale'. The confusion of the

---

[1] Ed. cit. 285–6.

first stanza, with which all three manuscripts now begin, is unmistakable, as is also its impropriety:

> Listyns, lordyngus, to my tale
> And ȝe shall here of on story,
> Is bettur then ouþer wyne or ale
> þat ever was made in this cuntry,
> How iewys demyd my son to dye.
> ychan a deth to hym þei drest.
> 'Alas!' seyd Mary þat is so fre,
> 'þat chylde is ded þat soke my brest.'[1]

The first four lines read as a minstrel opening: *Sir Beves of Hamtoun*,
for instance, begins 'Lordynges lystniþ to my tale'. It is only the phrase
'my son', in line 5, which reveals that it is the Virgin who speaks, and
this seems to be contradicted by the words 'seyd Mary' in line 7. It is
highly incongruous that the Virgin should address a company of seated
and convivial nobility, and line 8 of this stanza, which is repeated as a
refrain, suggests very strongly that the speaker should be a Pietà Virgin.
But only the discovery of a better text could now clear away the layers
of mistake. The content of the poem is of a fairly traditional kind for a
Pietà complaint: partly a narrative beginning with the betrayal, and partly
a dramatic apostrophe of Judas, the Jews, and the carpenter who made the
Cross (more commonly it is the smith who provided the nails).[2] All the
description and dramatic reproaches are effectively brought back by
the refrain to the single moment in time when the Virgin holds the dead
body of Christ. Though the four stanzas describing the Harrowing of
Hell, in which the refrain is turned to the joyful form 'The childe is
risen þat soke my brest', might seem to disrupt this structure, this
is not necessarily so, for they could be suitably spoken by a Pietà statue.
The real disruption, in fact, comes only with the last verse, in which the
poet as preacher intervenes with an exhortation to the audience to pray
to 'That prince þat soke oure lady brest'.

A variation of the Pietà opening is that in which it is combined with
the form of the *chanson d'aventure*. As we have seen earlier, this was a
secular convention, already used in the fourteenth century for Nativity
scenes. Its suitability as a stylized opening to a meditative poem has
already been stressed (in that the meditator is actually present in a scene
outside the historical sequence of events), and the fact that the secular
content was usually that of a maiden lamenting a loss made its transference to a religious *planctus* particularly simple and superficially apt.
A carol amongst those printed by Richard Kele (*c.* 1550), but presumably

---

[1] Brown xv, 10, pp. 18–19. *A deth to hym þei drest*: arranged his death.

[2] A carpenter is shown boring holes in the Cross in the *Holkham Bible Picture Book*,
f. 31ʳ. Cf. p. 66, footnote 2.

composed much earlier, illustrates very well this combination of Pietà and *chanson d'aventure*. The first verse is of a neutral and conventional kind:

> As I went this enders day,
> Alone walkyng on my play,
> I harde a lady syng and say,
> 'Woo is me and all alone'.[1]

The second verse describes how the lady was seated and lamented, whilst the third verse, with its exhortation to look at the wounded body, at last makes plain that it is a Pietà scene. Of the five verses, two are in fact given to the *chanson d'aventure* convention, which would be very disproportionate were this merely a convenient and decorative opening; but it is probable that here—and indeed elsewhere—it has an additional allegorical force; that the speaker's wandering in his 'play' represents man's journey through life, heedless of religious devotion. We cannot abandon our view that the style of this poem is quite undistinguished, but attention to its content may show it to be not quite so feeble as it appears on casual reading.

There is a far more impressive poem, 'As Reson Rywlyde my Rechyles mynde',[2] which uses a *chanson d'aventure* opening, but not combined with a Pietà. In the opening of this lyric the poet feigns that, on his journey 'by wayes and wyldernes' (in other words the journey through life in the wilderness of this world),[3] he found himself outside a 'solempne cite', and there he met a maiden who wept and tore her hair and clothes, and whose name, as in the French convention, is not revealed. The rest of the poem consists of a monologue, in which the Virgin narrates the events of the Passion, each of the twelve-line stanzas ending with a refrain drawn from 2 Samuel xviii. 20, 'Filius regis mortuus est', words which in their original context referred to Absalom, but which were traditionally applied to Christ, as they are, for instance, in the Passion section of the *Summa praedicantium*.[4] The traditional mixture of descriptive detail and the rhetorical reproaches of the executioners is here expressed highly dramatically. Sometimes the immediate realism, hysterically conceived, seems to pass the bounds of good taste:

> Alas! y sawe my dere chylde blede;
> He may not speke to modur his.
> I lullyd hym, y lapped him, y wolde him fede—
> so cruelly wes nevyr childe slayn y-wys.[5]

---

[1] *Carols*, 164.
[2] Brown xv, 6.
[3] Cf. *Ancrene Wisse*, E.E.T.S. 249, 108.
[4] Ed. cit. ii. 181ʳ.
[5] Brown xv, p. 9.

But at other times it is powerfully effective, as in the following image:

> Throwe Ierusalem stretis a man myȝte trace
> þe blode of my childe like a beeste.[1]

This image is rare in regard to both source and function: that is it seems to be an original image drawn from hunting (cf. *The Pearl*, 345–6), and its primary intention is to present the scene vividly to the imagination and emotions, whilst its intellectual content is slight.

It was probably the author's feeling for the dramatic that led him to ignore the usual Pietà opening, and to imagine instead the figure of the distracted Virgin, roaming in mental anguish outside the walls of Jerusalem after the burial of Christ. This invention, of course, contradicts the Gospel statement—normally retained and amplified in meditative literature—that St. John after the Crucifixion took the Virgin home to his own house. Moreover, by removing the lament from its formal elegiac setting, this invention has the further disadvantage of emphasizing the already existing tension between the Virgin's faith and her immoderate grief. The latter difficulty led to an addition to the poem in MS. Douce 78, in which a voice from heaven at the end promises the Virgin that she shall see her Son at the Resurrection.[2] Poetically this is dull and an anticlimax.

Of the four manuscript texts of this poem there is one, MS. Harley 3954, which in meditative structure is quite different from the rest.[3] In this text the unity of place and speaker, normally imposed by the Pietà form, and preserved in the other versions, has been altogether lost. The meditator is entirely engaged in the action. When the Virgin swoons, he bathes her face and breast; when she pauses in her narrative, he prompts her with a question, 'Why deyed þi sone, þou maydyn cha[s]t?'. When she has finished her lament, the meditator goes to the blood-stained Cross and watches by it for three days. He is at the sepulchre when angels announce the Resurrection to the mourning women, and he in turn tells the Blessed Virgin of the Resurrection, and witnesses Christ's appearance to His mother with the famous salutation from the *Carmen paschale* of Sedulius, 'Salve sancta parens'.[4] In structure this resembles the many Latin works in which the meditator goes everywhere with the historical figures, at each stage reverently aiding them. In a short poem, however, it gives an effect of disorder, and it was

---

[1] Brown xv, p. 9.   [2] Ibid. p. 13.
[3] E.E.T.S. 15, 238–42.
[4] G. G. Meerseman, *Der Hymnos Akathistos im Abendland*, i (Freiburg Switzerland, 1958), 133. This was the introit for the mass of the Virgin from the Purification to Septuagesima, and also the words traditionally ascribed to Christ in this scene, cf. *Meditationes*, ed. cit. 359–60, and *Carols*, 200. For a fuller account of the scene see above, pp. 138–9.

surely the absence of the controlling framework of the Pietà which led
to this unsuccessful deviation from the traditional structure of lyric
meditation.

With these lyrics may be grouped the long Pietà complaint of the
Virgin in the Digby play of the Burial of Christ.[1] The inclusion of a
complaint from what is usually called a play, of course, needs justification in a work on the lyric. The fact that it is a speech addressed to an
audience outside the historical scene, though relevant, would not in
itself be a full justification, for if it were, some of Christ's complaints
from the Cross in the mystery cycles, which have only been alluded to
in passing, would have to be given a similar prominence. The explanation
is that *The Burial* is not properly a play, but rather a meditation to be
read. This can be inferred from the manuscript. In contrast to the manuscripts of the mystery cycles, which normally seem to have been registers
of plays kept by the corporations, the manuscript of *The Burial*, Bodl.
MS. e Mus. 160, is a devotional compilation, containing also a long set of
prayers to patriarchs and saints and a set of a hundred meditations on
the Passion. The manuscript is thus manifestly intended for private
reading. It is, however, hardly necessary to proceed by inferences, for
the fact that *The Burial* was a meditation intended for private reading is
made plain by the initial rubric and by narrative links within the work.
The rubric describes it as a 'treyte or meditatione off the buryalle of
Criste and mowrnynge þerat', and there follows a prologue beginning:

> A Soule that list to singe of love
> Of Crist, that com till us so lawe,
> Rede this treyte, it may hymm move,
> And may hym teche lightly with awe,
> Off the sorow of Mary sumwhat to knawe,
> Opon gudfriday after-none.[2]

Moreover, scattered through the text are narrative links such as 'saide
Mawdeleyne' or 'This hard holy Joseph'. A corrector, however, has
worked through the text, crossing out the passages of narrative, and
where necessary adding words to fill out the metre; and he has also
added a note in the bottom margin of the verso of the first page, in
which he describes the work as 'a play' to be acted half on Good Friday
and half on Easter Sunday.[3]

That the author of *The Burial* had in mind a meditation rather than

---

[1] *The Digby Mysteries*, ed. F. J. Furnivall (London, 1882), 171–200.

[2] Ed. cit. 171.

[3] Furnivall's text is at first sight misleading in that he prefixes this note to the play,
although admittedly in brackets. This arrangement seems to have misled Hardin Craig,
English Religious Drama (Oxford, 1955), since on p. 318 he quotes this passage without
indicating that it is the note of an adaptor.

a play also seems clear from the style, which has the leisurely expansiveness endurable in a work read, rather than the dramatic tautness of a work designed for acting. Neither part of the play shows the speed, vigour, or colloquialism characteristic of the surviving mystery cycles. It seems much more likely that its qualities belong to the tradition of meditative rather than of dramatic literature, though set in a more exclusively dramatic form: the occasional exhortations of a preacher to a meditator, such as 'Man, harkyn how maudleyn with the maris þre / Wepis and wringes thair handes os thay goo' have an immediately recognizable derivation.

The substance of this meditative play is still that of the *Quis dabit*, indeed the opening lines of this are quoted:

> Who shall gife me water sufficient,
> And of distillinge teris habundance,
> That I may wepe my fill with hart relent
> After the whantite of sorofull remembrance.[1]

The structure itself is ingeniously designed to throw emphasis on to the Virgin—unsuitably so if it were indeed a Good Friday liturgical play. The events of the Crucifixion, the swooning of the Virgin, her attempts to reach her Son upon the high Cross are related only through the laments of Joseph of Aramathea and Mary Magdalene: a device well suited to meditation but very undramatic. The Virgin on her appearance speaks two long complaints, which are yet more obviously poems (as opposed to dramatic speeches) than the complaints of Christ in the mystery cycles. The first one[2] is addressed to the meditator with the refrain, which we have already seen in the 'tretys to lerne to wepe', 'Who can not wepe, com lern at me', though here the refrain is used less regularly, being sometimes omitted, and sometimes moved to the penultimate line, so that it provides the *b*-rhyme instead of the *c*. The second[3] is chiefly addressed to the dead Christ with the refrain, 'Yit suffer me to hold yow her on my lape, / Which sumtym gafe you mylk of my pape', which recalls of course 'The childe is ded þat soke my brest'. The content of these *planctus* is wordily expressed, but their main outlines are the familiar ones, the reproaches to the Jews and the Cross, the antitheses between Christ's birth and death, the appeals to man to weep with her, the wish to die. As she speaks the Virgin is seated beneath the Cross (line 604) and holds Christ's body in her lap. The scene is referred to as a *crucifixe* and an *ymage of pitee*. It is difficult to estimate the quality of this work. It is possible to pick out many individual lines, which by the nature of the subject and the directness of expression move to compassion, 'Was never child to moder so lovinge' (636), 'Thus to be slayn

---

[1] Ed. cit. 192. [2] Ed. cit. 192–5. [3] Ed. cit. 195–7.

in all giltlesse' (661), 'All is but blude, so bett was he' (684), 'O derest childe! What falt haf ye done?' (726), 'Your face, most graciose to behold' (697), etc. But the total effect is one of monotonous excess. We recoil from the indiscriminate copiousness of lamentation. Admittedly, the complaint of the Virgin is made less tolerable by its context. If, like the complaints of Christ in the mystery plays, it stood as a set piece in the middle of brisk, colloquial dialogue, it would be more moving by contrast; if it were an independent lyric, the absence of framework would throw it into relief. But the curious form of the work, a series of lyrics strung together by scraps of narrative and dialogue, makes inevitable this effect of an unmodulated battering upon the emotions.

Alongside the complaints of the Virgin there are in the fifteenth century a small number of first-person meditations upon the Compassion. The two most pleasing of these are set in a dream form. In these the dreamer and meditator are not to merge together, for the dreamer addresses the meditator, reliving as it were the experience of his dream as he relates it: by the intensity of feeling expressed, the reader comes to share in the experience of the dream. It may be worth briefly distinguishing here between the dream form and the vision form when used in lyric meditation. The vision form, as we shall see later, was occasionally used for subjects such as the Coronation of the Virgin, but in the lyrics of the Compassion there is only one trace of it, and that is in the confused opening of the 'tretys to lerne to wepe'. It is less apt for subjects arousing love and pity, for in it the experience is outward and objective (the speaker is transported out of himself to some visionary place), whilst in the dream form the experience is inward and existent only within the mind: it is thus more private and personal.

The sense of an inwardly and intensely apprehended experience is very strong in both the poems on the Compassion that use the dream form. The first of these to be discussed is that beginning 'With favoure in hir face ferr passyng my Reason', which is preserved in two manuscripts, MS. Rylands Lat. 395 and MS. Trinity 1450. In the first of these the refrain, copied as an initial quatrain, makes it clear that the setting is that of a dream:

> Sodenly afraide,
>   Half wakyng, half slepyng,
> And gretly dismayde,
>   A wooman sate weepyng.[1]

The verse is elliptical, and common sense must be trusted rather than syntax, so that the first two lines, and probably the first three, are understood to refer to the speaker. It would be hard to imagine how the Virgin

---

[1] Brown xv, 9.

could be suddenly afraid or caught between sleeping and waking. Moreover, the last line of the poem, 'And with that word she vanysht away',
bears out this interpretation, for here there is a touch of the realistic use
of the dream form in which the surprise and abruptness of actual
dreams is suggested. Within the dream form there is a Pietà scene which
the dreamer recounts to the reader:

> With favoure in hir face ferr passyng my Reason,
> And of hir sore weepyng this was the enchesone:
> Hir soon in hir lap lay, she seid, slayne by treason.
> Yif wepyng myght ripe bee it seemyd þan in season.
>> Ihesu, so she sobbid,
>> So hir soone was bobbid
>> and of his lif robbid,
> Saying þies wordis as I say þee,
> 'Who cannot wepe come lerne at me'.[1]

The poem consists partly of the dreamer's affective narrative, partly of
the Virgin's direct complaint. Throughout there is the typical fifteenth-
century mingling of didacticism—the Virgin addresses the dreamer with a
sharp rebuke—emotionalism—for the Virgin cries and swoons—and of
a sense of the dramatic: there is dramatic interest in the manner in which
the Virgin turns from lamenting her Son to instructing the dreamer, and
in the language, which echoes the colloquial vigour of the mystery plays,
as in the repeated rhyme words, 'bobbid': 'robbid': 'sobbid'.

The other dream poem, 'To Calvery he bare his cross', however, is
yet more successful. It is preserved with music in the famous Tudor
song-book, B.M. Add. MS. 5465, which is commonly given the name
of Robert Fayrfax, the Tudor composer, who was organist of St. Albans
and a Gentleman of the Chapel Royal. Again, the fact that the poem is
in the form of a dream is chiefly conveyed by the burden:

> My feerfull dreme nevyr forgete can I:
> Me thoug[h]t a maydynys childe causless shulde dye.[2]

The burden here has exceptional power in its reiterated implication that
the content is so horrifying that it could only have happened in a dream.
The same poetic force can be felt in the last stanza with its final lines
which catch up the theme of the refrain:

> Unto the cross, handes and feete, nailid he was;
> Full boystusly in the mortess he was downe cast;
> His vaynys all and synowis to-raff and brast;
> The erth quakyd, the son was dark, whos lyght was past,

---

[1] Brown xv, 9. *Enchesone*: cause; *ripe*: suitable; *bobbid*: beaten.
[2] *Carols*, 165.

> When he lamentable
> Cried, 'Hely, hely, hely!'
> His moder rufully
> Wepyng and wrang her handes fast.
> Uppon her he cast his dedly loke,
> Wherwith sodenly anon I awoke,
> And of my dreme was sore agast.[1]

There is here a remarkable sense of timing and the familiar story is made to seem strange and new by the abrupt refusal to complete it. The way in which the dream ends as Christ casts His last dying look on the Virgin has a haunting quality of unlimited evocative power. Within this brilliantly manipulated form the content of the dreamer's narrative is of the earlier dramatic kind: the Virgin, standing by the Cross, addresses the dreamer, there is a dialogue between her and St. John, and Christ speaks a Word from the Cross. A prose summary suggests traditional, familiar material, but the effect of the poem is of a dramatic narrative, horrifying and strange.

There are two other first-person meditations, the one, another short lyric from the Fayrfax Manuscript, the other, a long poem, undistinguished in style and as yet unprinted. The Fayrfax lyric, 'Sith it concludid was in the Trinite', consists of four stanzas of consolation: the meditator has the role earlier and traditionally given to St. John. The appearance of the Virgin is not described: the only indications are that the time is after the death of Christ and that she is weeping. It is possible, therefore, to imagine a Pietà figure, but it is also possible that in such a late poem the poet had no clear visual image in mind at all. In the second stanza the poet describes the sufferings of Christ, but having already stated the Redemption, he is able to add a direct consolation to the Virgin:

> But blessid be that oure,
> That he suffird that sharpe shoure!
> Therefore though deth be never so sore,
> Now, blessid Lady, wepe no more.[2]

And the next stanza begins:

> Glorius Lady, of hevyn hie quene,
> Lay downe all thi wepyng, let no more be sene!

The attribution to the Virgin of a title, 'of hevyn hie quene', which she had not as yet chronologically or symbolically received, introduces at this point a gentle paradox, charming in effect. Through such devices

---

[1] Ibid. p. 124. *Boystusly*: violently; *mortess*, i.e. the hole dug to receive the cross; *to-raff*: burst asunder.

[2] John Stevens, *Music and Poetry in the Early Tudor Court*, 369. *Shoure*: suffering.

as this, the poem becomes an agreeable variation on the theme of the Compassion.

The other poem, 'Who can the sorow conceyve allas',[1] is in structure an act of devotion to the glorified Virgin: it is an enumeration of her sufferings in order to arouse compassion and to do her honour. The poet, however, is very skilful in holding in balance the two ideas of the impassive Queen of Heaven and the suffering mother; he achieves this by mingling throughout the poem eulogistic titles with appellations of compassion: 'Gloriouse mayde and moder moste soverayne', 'Gloriouse quene in heven moste renowned', but also, 'lady full of hevynes', 'O paynful lady'. The poet also exploits the absence of a consistent meditative image and the indefiniteness of time. The main substance is a narrative of the Passion, set in the past tense, but directly addressed to the Virgin, emphasizing over and over again the grief that she must have felt: 'O, ladi, howe grete was þi disease . . .', 'And for the sorowe þou had whan þou by him stode', 'I cannot utterly þat drede and sorow expres / Whan þou saw Ioseph of aramathy . . .', etc. There is hardly a stanza that is not coloured by some expression of this kind. The narrative stress falls on all the moments of particular anguish: St. John bringing the news of Christ's arrest, the Virgin watching the trial and scourging, her interception of Christ as He bore the Cross, her endurance beside the Cross, the Body laid in the Virgin's lap, and the burial. The poem thus covers much of the same ground as the 'tretys to lerne to wepe', but is far quieter in tone; though it lacks the accomplishment of the long complaint, in its restraint and modesty of feeling it is much more pleasing.

Just as the sufferings of Christ, described in the gospels, and emphasized in meditative literature, were isolated and numbered in various devotional forms, such as the Hours of the Cross, so also were numbered the sufferings of Mary.[2] The earliest example of this occurs in the Office of the Compassion, attributed perhaps erroneously to Bonaventura, but certainly dating from the thirteenth century. Later there were quite a large number of Latin hymns which versified the theme. In the Office of the Compassion, the one form of the subject that must have been generally known, every hour contains a meditation with a prayer based upon it for each of the seven pains, the arrest, the scourging, the condemnation, Crucifixion, death, deposition, and burial. As one would expect in liturgical texts, there is little trace of apocryphal invention in

---

[1] MS. Lambeth 560, 118ʳ–124ᵛ, *Index*, 4089, where it is incorrectly compared with Lydgate's poem on the fifteen sorrows of the Virgin. W. F. Schirmer, *John Lydgate* (trans. A. E. Keep), 194, note 1, repeats this mistake.

[2] On this see A. Wilmart, *Auteurs spirituels et textes dévots*, 505–22, and Stephen Beissel, *Geschichte der Verehrung Marias in Deutschland* (Freiburg im Breisgau, 1909), 404–15.

this or, indeed, in any of the other versions. The sorrows of the Virgin are all events described in the gospels—often corresponding exactly to those of the Hours of the Cross—but related with reference to the Virgin's feelings. Deviations from this treatment are obtrusive through their rareness: for instance, the iconographic reference in the meditation for Vespers in the Office, '. . . quando, ut pie creditur, in amplexus ruebas exanimi corporis filii tui dulcis Ihesu de cruce depositi',[1] or the mention in one of the hymns of the news being given to Mary, '. . . Dum Jesus apprehensus / Nuntiatur virgini'.[2] But the normal rule is austere adherence to the gospel narrative.

In contrast, the only extant English verse narrative of the Hours of the Compassion[3] (which survives in a series of meditations for the whole week preserved in MS. Arundel 285) draws closely on the meditative tradition in order to emphasize the Virgin's part. 'At prime scho followit him to Pilotis place / With sobing, siching, lik to fall in swone'; at terce, 'Thai scurgit him; and our Lady, þat stude by, / Saw him beir þe croce and crownit with thorne'; at sext, during the Crucifixion, 'The blud droppit doun on his moder Mary', and at evensong the body of Christ was laid 'in our Ladyis bosum'. This emphasis upon emotive apocryphal detail is not the only way in which the English is different from its Latin analogues: the differences in style and structure are almost equally important. In the Latin Office there are petitions appropriate to each pain (often worked out through ingenious allegorization), in the English a general prayer concludes the poem; whereas the Latin is formal and stylized, the English Hours are expressed in colloquial simplicity. It is in fact a mediocre poem, but as a mnemonic enumeration of the pains described more elaborately in poems such as 'Who can the sorow conceyve allas' it is obviously adequate, and in its naïvely direct statements of suffering it is not completely without power to move the reader.

The only other English poem containing an enumeration of the Virgin's sorrows is an elaborate poem by Lydgate.[4] This is devotionally different in that it follows a tradition of numbering the sorrows based, not upon the Hours of the Cross, but upon the joys of the Virgin. An enumeration of the sorrows which is modelled upon that of the joys differs from that modelled upon the hours since the number is variable—five is as common as seven—and because the sorrows are drawn from the Virgin's whole life instead of being restricted to the Passion. Two versions of seven have been printed by Wilmart, one

---

[1] Wilmart, *Auteurs spirituels*, 525. '. . . When, according to pious belief, you rushed to take into your arms the lifeless body of your sweet son, Jesus, after it had been taken down from the Cross.'

[2] *A.H.* xxiv. 41, p. 130. 'When the news was brought to the Virgin that Jesus had been arrested.'   [3] Bennett, *Devotional Pieces*, 234–6.

[4] E.E.T.S., E.S. 107, 274–9. For the first half of the poem see below, p. 298.

under the title of *Les sept glaives*, the other of *Les tristesses*.[1] The first list consists of Simeon's prophecy, the Massacre of the Innocents, the losing of Jesus in the temple, the scourging, Crucifixion, deposition, and burial. The second list is similar, the only difference being that the fourth is the betrayal and the seventh the Virgin's remaining in the world after the Ascension. The latter list must have been fairly widely known, as it was incorporated as an epilogue in the *Speculum humanae salvationis*[2] (a work similar in design to the *Biblia pauperum*, but more learned and elaborate).

Lydgate's enumeration is exceptional in that it includes fifteen sorrows, though the printed text has only fourteen. It forms the second half of a poem, of which the first part consists of the fifteen joys, so that the symmetrical need for fifteen is obvious. The list of sorrows, being so long, necessarily includes apocryphal incidents: of these the two most striking are the Virgin's distress when ordered to marry (the marriage of the Virgin was a common part of the many apocryphal accounts of her early life), and the trial of the Virgin by the water of proof. The latter, deriving from the *Protevangelium*, was very rarely referred to in either medieval art[3] or literature, an exception being the very interesting play on this subject in the *Ludus Coventriae*.[4] The more apocryphal matter is used, the more attention is focused on the Virgin. In Lydgate's poem the emphasis on the Virgin in content is matched by the structure of the individual stanzas, in which a brief summary of each sorrow is enclosed in a dominating framework of compassionate or eulogistic apostrophe and closing petition. The formal style, in which praise and compassion are elegantly blended, may be illustrated by two stanzas, one in which St. John brings the news of Christ's arrest, the other a Pietà scene:

> Off mortal pite myn herte waxith coold
>   To remembre, thynken or expresse
> The sorwe thu haddist, whan Seyn Iohn hath the toold,
>   Iesu was taken, by the gret felnesse

---

[1] Wilmart, op. cit. 528–36. Cf. also 'La Vierge aux sept glaives', *Analecta Bollandiana*, xii (1893), 333–52; É. Mâle, *L'Art religieux de la fin du moyen âge*, 122–6. M. D. Anderson, *The Imagery of British Churches*, 149, notes the occurrence of this form in foreign glass at St. Mary's Church, Shrewsbury.

[2] This work was very popular, particularly in France and Germany: 200 copies have been enumerated by Lutz and Perdrizet in their edition (vol. I. ix–xvii), and this list according to M. R. James is not complete (*Speculum humanae salvationis*, Oxford, 1926, 6). Twenty-six manuscripts of English origin are included in the list, but, like the *Biblia pauperum*, it was never printed in England. Not all the manuscripts contain the epilogue after the Last Judgement, in which the sorrows are described, but they are contained in sufficient number to show a moderately wide diffusion in English learned circles. For the English text see *The Miroure of Mans Salvacionne*, ed. A. H. Huth (Roxburghe Club, 1888), 154–9.

[3] Louis Réau, *L'Iconographie de l'art chrétien*, II, ii (Paris, 1957), 208–10.

[4] E.E.T.S., E.S. 120, 124–35.

> Of the Iewys hatful cursydnesse;
>> And as that takyng was to the gret greeff,
>> Releeve alle tho that calle the in myscheef.
>
> . . . . . .
>
> Was evir woo that myhte be comparyd
>> To thy distresse, pryncesse of goodliheede,
> Whan thu sauh Iesu how he was nat sparyd,
>> Crucified, take down whan he was deede,
> Lay in thy lappe, and al his body reede
>> Of pitous bledyng, for whoos meek suffraunce,
>> O queen of mercy! sauf us fro myschaunce.[1]

Unlike the poem on the Hours of the Cross, this poem is a first-person meditation, and though in part it is a liturgical exercise (as the instruction to say a paternoster and ten aves after each stanza makes very plain), it is also designed to arouse and express compassion: 'With our lady, hir sorwes to complayne'. And though the Virgin is addressed by royal titles, 'Prynces', 'Emperesse', etc. the initial meditative image is a Pietà, 'an ymage ful notable, / Lyke a pyte depeynt', a figure which Lydgate, following the Chaucerian tradition, feigns to have come across in a book one sleepless night, the book being presumably a book of hours. It is interesting to notice that the intrusive secondary image is here, not a statue, but an illumination.

There is one other version of the sorrows of the Virgin, that was widely current because a form of it was included in a late collection of the Miracles of the Virgin, John Herolt's *Promptuarium*.[2] In this St. John hears the promises which Christ makes to the Blessed Virgin for those who meditate on any of her five sorrows, which are then described. This version survives only in vernacular prose, but it has relevance to the lyric because the context of its occurrence in one manuscript is of interest. The manuscript is B.M. Add. MS. 37787, a monastic collection probably from Bordesley Abbey. In this it is preceded by a fragment of a *planctus*, six lines of which are evidently the conclusion of a narrative of the Crucifixion spoken by the Virgin, probably with the body of Christ in her lap:

> They leyde hym dede me before,
> Me thouth for sorw my lyfe was lore.
> Loke what sorw and what rede
> Was like mi sorw to se hym dede.
> More sorw hed never none,
> That berith witness marie and Ion.[3]

---

[1] Ibid. 107, 276 and 278.

[2] Johannes Herolt, *Miracles of the Blessed Virgin Mary*, trans. C. C. Swinton Bland (London, 1928), 29–30.

[3] N. S. Baugh, *A Worcestershire Miscellany* (Philadelphia, 1956), 151.

In literary terms this deserves little consideration: the versification is perfunctory and there are unsuitable jingling rhythms, padding phrases, and clichés, such as 'marie and Ion' which is ludicrously inappropriate in its context. Many lyrics, however, are very uneven in quality, and it is possible that this is a poor, ill-copied fragment from what in its entirety had been a passable poem. Historically it is of interest in that its combination with the five sorrows reflects so well the literary forms and manner of devotion to the Blessed Virgin in the period.

The poems on the Compassion are not only far fewer than those on the Passion, but also, as we said at the beginning, they are far less poetically pleasing. The reason for this does not seem to lie in the manner of writing, but rather in the devotion itself, with its lack of a substantial theological frame of reference, which could control invention and feeling. That a feeling of distaste for the devotion does not spring solely from modern prejudice is shown by the fact that the theme of the extravagant grief of the Virgin was repudiated not only by Protestant writers (as one would expect), but also by writers of the Counter-Reformation. Molanus, the Catholic scholar, who composed an iconographic handbook, rejected the whole medieval theme of the extravagant grief of the Virgin, with its accompanying inventions, and returned to the tradition of the fathers:

Eam [the Virgin] quidam sub cruce pingunt deliquium patientem, aut in terram corruentem, iuxta illud Revelationum Sanctae Birgittae: Tunc ego exinanita corrui in terram. Sed plerique alii improbant hanc picturam, cum Ioannes dicat: Stabat iuxta crucem Iesu mater eius. Stabat, inquit pater Guardianus Petrus Montanus, corpore, quae stabat corde per fidem (quae non vacillavit in ei, sicut in Apostolis) et per virilem constantiam firmato: stabat, nihil impotentis animi prae se ferens, nec in terram labens, nec capillos lacerans, neque pectus tundens: stabat, etiam pro salute humani generis, ait Ambrosius, mori parata. Et Iudocus Clichthoveus in homilia de statione Virginis iuxta crucem: Verum stabas optima mater iuxta crucem filii tui, non solum corpore, sed et mentis constantia: neque ullum immodestiae signum vultu prodebas: dolor plane tuus animo contectus, exterius non innotuit gestibus, aut motu, nisi pallentis vultus tristitia, et uberrimis lacrymis. . . . Pulcre denique S. Anselmus: Inter tot pressuras filii sui, constanter ipsa sola stabat, in fide firma, et pulcre stabat, ut decet pudicitiam virginalem; non se laniabat in tanta amaritudine, non maledicebat, non murmurabat, nec vindictam hostium a Deo petebat, sed stabat disciplinata, verecunda, Virgo patientissima, lacrymis plena, doloribus immersa.[1]

[1] *De historia SS. imaginum*, iv. 8 (Louvain, 1594), 176–7. 'Some represent her in a swoon beneath the Cross or collapsing to the ground, according to the passage in the *Revelations* of St. Bridget: "Then I fell lifeless to the ground". But most others disapprove of this representation, since St. John says: "By the Cross of Christ stood His Mother". Father Guardianus Petrus Montanus says that she stood firm physically because she stood firm in her heart through faith, which did not waver in her, as it did in the apostles, and was made firm in manly steadfastness: she stood, not giving any sign of faint-heartedness, not falling to the ground, nor tearing her hair, nor beating her

Jeremy Taylor's beautiful description of the Virgin by the Cross in his *Life of Christ* may be quoted as an example of the Anglican return to the same tradition:

By the cross of Christ stood the holy Virgin-mother, upon whom old Simeon's prophecy was now verified: for now she felt a sword passing through her very soul: she stood without clamour and womanish noises; sad, silent, and with a modest grief, deep as the waters of the abyss, but smooth as the face of a pool; full of love and patience, and sorrow, and hope. . . . But her hope drew a veil before her sorrow; and though her grief was great enough to swallow her up, yet her love was greater, and did swallow up her grief.[1]

These lines from Jeremy Taylor show the stronger literary potentiality of the patristic treatment of the subject. Restraint in grief is more moving than hysteria. But in the Middle Ages, unfortunately, the devotional understanding of the Virgin's grief became superficial and melodramatic, and the spiritual meagreness of the devotion seems to have become matched by triteness of convention and style. There is an ingenious little parody of the *planctus* in Skelton's *Philip Sparrow*:

> I sighed and I sobbed,
> For that I was robbed
> Of my sparowes lyfe.
> O mayden, wydow, and wyfe,
> Of what estate ye be,
> Of hye or lowe degre,
> Great sorowe than ye myght se,
> And lerne to wepe at me![2]

This is a satiric pastiche of the diction and formulas of the *planctus*. In literary terms perhaps the fifteenth-century complaint deserved such mocking treatment.

---

breast: she stood, says St. Ambrose, prepared even to die for the salvation of mankind. Josse Clichtove writes in his homily on the Virgin standing by the Cross: Truly, best of mothers, you stood by the Cross of your Son: you stood not only in body but in constancy of mind: nor did you show in your face any sign of lack of restraint: your grief was entirely concealed in your heart, it could not be seen externally in gesture or movement, but only in the sadness of your pale face and your abundant tears . . . and, to end with, St. Anselm says finely: amongst the many afflictions of her Son, she alone stood firm, resolute in faith, and she stood with beauty, as befitted her maidenly virtue: in all the bitterness of her loss she did not lacerate herself, she spoke no abuse or complaint, nor did she seek from God vengeance on her enemies, but she stood controlled and modest, the Virgin, all-enduring, filled with tears, plunged in grief.'

[1] *The Life of Our Lord and Saviour Jesus Christ, Works*, ii (London, 1850), 710.

[2] *The Poetical Works of John Skelton*, ed. Dyce, i. 52.

T

VIII

Lyrics on the Virgin and her Joys

THE body of poems in honour of the Virgin probably form both the largest and also the most ornate and rhetorical section of the religious lyric in the fifteenth century. By this time there were no longer lacking secular models, literary self-consciousness, and artifices of diction and metre. All the characteristics of Marian poetry which, in the verse of the earlier period had to be searched for, could now be illustrated with innumerable examples. In this period the influence of secular poetry on the lyrics to the Virgin is everywhere discernible, but they can nevertheless still be divided into those that ostentatiously imitate the conventions of secular love poetry and those that take their form from Latin liturgical sources, though, of course, in diction and metre there is substantial overlapping between the two.

In the earlier poetry, secular influence could be seen chiefly in isolated phrases: in the fifteenth-century lyric it appears in long passages and whole poems. Complete imitations of this kind are first found in the Vernon Manuscript, a volume which, like John of Grimestone's preaching-book, in its contents both reflects the older style and, in part, inaugurates the new. An interesting example of the new style is the second half of the poem beginning 'Mayden, Modur, and comely Qween'[1] in which every part of the body of the Blessed Virgin is enumerated and called blessed. The description of the Virgin's forehead may be quoted as a typical illustration of the style:

> Blessed beo, ladi, þat holy frount,
> þat holy is holden and sount,
>   þe cheef of al þi face;
> þer-in is set a bond of wit,
> Undur þe croune comly knit
>   Wiþ a lovely lace.   Ave.[2]

In its design the poem recalls secular models, such as 'Mosti ryden by Rybbesdale',[3] for both conform to the rhetoricians' prescription for the

[1] E.E.T.S. 98, 121–31.

[2] Ibid. 126. *Frount*: forehead; *sount*: perfect; *cheef*: top or dominating part; *wit*: intelligence; *bond*: circlet; *lace*: thread.

[3] *Harley Lyrics*, ed. Brook, 37–39.

delineation of physical beauty, which is to enumerate the excellencies of different bodily parts, observing a regular order downwards from head to feet. This secular style had been imitated closely and elegantly by Richard Rolle in his *Canticum amoris de beata virgine*, a long poem in praise of the Virgin, which survives in two manuscripts, with a rhymed signature in the last stanza.[1] The passage of physical description begins as follows:

> Puella pulcher rima prostravit ludentem.
> Fronsque serenissima facit hunc languentem;
> Crines auro similes carpunt conquerentem;
> Gene preamabiles solantur sedentem.[2]

The Vernon poem, however, has a more openly religious reference than does the *Canticum amoris*, for behind it probably also lie the Latin hymns in which Christ's wounded hands and feet were praised individually, and perhaps also the Biblical text, 'Beatus venter qui te portavit, et ubera quae suxisti' (Luke xi. 27). A quite ingenious balance is preserved between the purely conventional physical description of beauty, such as 'þi ffeire Neose, þat comely sittes / Amidde þi frount bi-neþen' or 'þi þhommes and þi ffyngres alle / þat genteliche are Maket', and the blessing of these parts in doctrinal terms according to their relationship to Christ: the right ear through which passed the Holy Ghost, the hands which swaddled the Christ-Child, the knees which still kneel in intercession, etc. The liturgical emphasis obscures the element in this kind of secular poetry, so disconcerting nowadays, namely that in it there is 'no attempt to fuse these independently perfect *disjecta membra* into a visualizable whole'.[3]

With this may be compared the later poem beginning 'With humble hert I praye iche creature'[4] which survives in two fifteenth-century poetical manuscripts. In its design it is the same, but it is less agreeable in that the secular and religious elements are more independently emphasized. Each verse again begins 'Blessed be', but, apart from this, most of the stanzas could be a description of the beauties of the poet's ideal mistress, with the traditional comparisons to flowers and precious stones. The cheeks, for instance, are thus described:

[1] A. Wilmart, 'Le Cantique d'amour de Richard Rolle', *Revue d'ascétique et de mystique*, xxi (1940), 131–48; G. M. Liegey, 'The "Canticum amoris" of Richard Rolle', *Traditio*, xii (1956), 369–91.

[2] Wilmart, op. cit. 143. 'The most beautiful maiden has brought the care-free lover to his knees and her serene forehead makes him languish for love; her hair like gold has captured him as he laments, and her love-inspiring cheeks comfort him in his dejection.'

[3] Leo Spitzer, '*Explication de Texte* applied to three great Middle English Poems', *Archivum Linguisticum*, iii (1951), 7.

[4] H. N. MacCracken, 'Lydgatiana' no. 14, *Archiv*, cxxxi (1913), 40–63.

Blissede ben þi chekes, frescheste of coloure,
They likenede bene unto þe lely white,
þe whilke weddede hath þe rose to paramour
Thaym tweyn depaynttede þi vesage of delyte,
þe merounte Ruby with the margaryte
With þam in blysse myghte hafe no partie
Bewte hath luste to belde in siche a sete,
O Florum flos, O Flos pu[l]cherime![1]

The turn at the end, therefore, when the defacing of the Virgin's beauty at the Crucifixion is described, and the last stanza on the theme of the *Scala salutis* come both unexpectedly and inappropriately. In contrast to 'Mayden, Modur, and comely Qween' the poem does not always seem to be quite decorous in tone. Whilst in theory there was no reason why a convention developed to praise the perfect beauty of an ideal woman should not be used of the Virgin, one suspects in practice that here the appearance of the Virgin has been reduced to the modishly pretty. A French religious pastourelle, in which the detailed description of its secular model has been reduced,[2] suggests that this distrust is not due solely to modern taste.

In the Vernon Manuscript there is also a poem beginning, 'Of alle floures feirest fall on',[3] which again reflects the same transitional combination of secular and religious. The poet speaks of the 'love-likyng' that has befallen him, complains that 'Love me haþ in Bales brouȝt', and praises the Virgin's beauty and virtue in terms also appropriate to an earthly mistress. But intermixed with the ideas and vocabulary of romantic love are prayers of repentance and intercessions for the Virgin's help against the Devil at the hour of death. There is here the same mingling of themes, already noticed in the earlier poems, and, though the secular references are more overt, the poem gives no impression of incongruity. The penultimate verse is an especially agreeable example of this successful combination:

þe love þat I have ȝeorned ȝore,
þe kyng of love graunt hit me!
In eorþly love is luytel store,
ffor al þat is but vanyte.
Wher I schal ever þat day I-se,
To plese my ladi ones to pay?
Heo is of colour and beaute
As fresch as is þe Rose In May.[4]

---

[1] MacCracken, op. cit. 61. For a discussion of the phrase *florum flos* see Peter Dronke, *Medieval Latin and the Rise of the European Love-Lyric*, i (Oxford, 1965), 181–92.
[2] Järnström, op. cit. ii. 33–34. [3] E.E.T.S. 117, 708–11.
[4] Ibid. 710–11.

This poem, like many secular ones, is a New Year's poem—the poet offers the Virgin five Aves as a New Year's gift—and, in form, therefore, it anticipates Lydgate's Valentine poem to the Blessed Virgin.

The exercise of composing Valentine poems, perhaps in form of a love debate, was a French aristocratic habit, and on St. Valentine's Day there might also be held a court of love.[1] There is no actual evidence of Valentine ceremonies in England, unless they may be inferred from the poems themselves. But the French literary fashion, begun by Otes de Graunson, and much practised by Charles of Orleans, was at least transplanted, to some degree.[2] Apart from the *Parlement of Foules*,[3] there is in England also Chaucer's *Complaint of Mars*,[4] and *Complaynt d'amours*,[5] two of Gower's *Cinkante Ballades*,[6] and the *Flour of Curteysie*.[7] St. Valentine's Day (like New Year's Day) undoubtedly became the traditional setting for a love poem, and may also have been the historical occasion for its recitation. Lydgate's Valentine to the Blessed Virgin, 'Saynt Valentyne, of custume yeere by yeere',[8] begins by describing the custom of lovers choosing their mistresses on this day, but explains, in the line that becomes the refrain, 'But I love oon whiche excelliþe alle'. He then proceeds to praise the Virgin's pre-eminence over the heroines of Biblical and classical literature:

> Tesbe þe mayde borne in Babyloun
> þat loved so weel þe yonge Pyramus,
> And Cl[e]opatre of wilful mocyoun
> List for to dye with hir Antonyus.
> Sette al on syde oone is so vertuous
> Whiche þat I do my soverein lady calle,
> Wham I love best for she excelleþ alle.[9]

The most famous example of this secular convention in English is of course, the ballade from the *Prologue* to *The Legend of Good Women*, 'Hyd, Absalon, thy gilte tresses clere',[10] but it was a common device of French ballades and virelais,[11] and, of course, like the proper names of the *ubi sunt* convention, was designed to draw upon the evocative power of other work, particularly of romances. Lydgate himself makes use of the

---

[1] Stevenson, *Music and Poetry in the Early Tudor Court*, 184–6.

[2] On this and for the following list see J. M. Manly, 'What is the Parlement of Foules?', *Festschrift für Lorenz Morsbach* (Halle, 1913), 279–90.

[3] Ed. D. S. Brewer (London, 1960), and see pp. 4–7 of the introduction.

[4] *Poetical Works*, ed. Robinson, 623–7.

[5] Ed. cit. 636–7.

[6] Nos. xxxiv and xxxv, *The French Works*, ed. G. C. Macaulay (Oxford, 1899), 365–6.

[7] *Chaucerian and Other Pieces*, ed. W. W. Skeat (Oxford, 1897), 266–74.

[8] E.E.T.S., E.S. 107, 304–10.   [9] Ibid. 307.

[10] Ed. cit. 574.

[11] H. L. Cohen, *The Ballade* (New York, 1915), 247–50.

same device in his secular New Year's poem.[1] In the lyric to the Virgin (as can be seen from the stanza quoted) Lydgate does not pause to make any of the comparisons moving or pointed. The enumeration seems to be a matter of hit or miss, and it seems mere chance that Lucrece, earlier praised for her 'clennesse', is, perhaps, just slightly less irrelevant than Cleopatra who died for love of Anthony. But the morality of the martyrs of love bears so little Christian examination that the list must be accepted whole as a decorative fantasy. The latter part of the poem, by contrast, praises the Virgin in conventional religious manner as the Woman of the Apocalypse and of Octavian's vision, and as the saviour of Theophilus. This poem is an extreme example of the type of verse common in the fifteenth century, in which the poet makes something in honour of the Virgin, which, unlike the praise in the Vernon lyric, does not also aim to stir devotion in the reader.

There is another poem which may be a Valentine to the Blessed Virgin, though this is a matter of controversy. It is Chaucerian in style and begins 'I have non English convenient and digne'.[2] It was printed by Thynne as part of Lydgate's address to the Virgin, 'A thousand stories coude I mo reherce', and though either he or the manuscript which he followed was clearly wrong in joining the two poems, this early sixteenth-century judgement that the poem was addressed to the Virgin must carry some weight. Though there are only two points that confirm this view, the invocation to the lady, 'To help my making bothe florisshe and floure'[3] and the later salutation to her, *Salve regina*, these are both important as they have no alternative explanation that is fully satisfying.[4] There are also many passages, such as the following fine stanza, that grow in meaning if addressed to the Virgin:

> All our love is but ydelnesse
> Save your aloon; who might therto attayne?
> Who-so wol have a name of gentillesse,
> I counsayle him in love that he not fayne.
> Thou swete lady! refut in every payne,
> Whos [pitous] mercy most to me avayleth
> To gye by grace, whan that fortune fayleth.[5]

---

[1] E.E.T.S. 192, 424–7.   [2] *Chaucerian Pieces*, 281–4.
[3] On the invocation to the Virgin to act as muse see below, p. 281.
[4] Skeat's view (op. cit. xlviii) that an historical queen (Katherine, wife of Henry V) could be addressed in this form cannot be accepted for the religious reference is inescapable. The suggestion that the salutation is to Venus (E. Seaton, *Sir Richard Roos*, London, 1961, 287) is more plausible, but involves a change of address awkward in a short poem, and one that is without parallel unless we accept Dr. Seaton's suggestion that the perplexing phrase, 'thow Herenus quene' in 'The Complaint unto Pity' (Chaucer, *Poetical Works*, 621) refers to Venus (op. cit. 166). Each is only convincing if the other is true, and the argument therefore seems irremediably circular.
[5] Op. cit. 283.

Trite phrases can become fresh when set in a new context. The references to the lady's 'eyen clere', her 'goodly fresshe face', her 'womanhede', etc., acquire a resonance if they refer to the Virgin, whilst some lines that anyway have a direct, colloquial reality, e.g. 'To live wel mery, two lovers were y-fere', have a gay audacity when interpreted in religious terms. The poem undoubtedly gains in warmth and originality if the poet's mistress is the Virgin.

It cannot be proved beyond all doubt that this plea for mercy is addressed to the Virgin, any more than it could be proved that 'Trewlove trewe, on you I truste' was correctly described as 'Querimonia Cristi languentis pro amore';[1] but if there were religious poems so entirely written in the style and conventions of secular love poetry that there was no inescapable religious reference, then by definition they would be difficult to identify. There seems, however, no reason to reject the occasional testimony of the later Middle Ages that poems of this kind were written, and, if we accept the evidence of Thynne (or more probably of the manuscript that he followed), we may read 'I have non English convenient and digne' as a very supple and delicate handling of secular conventions for religious purposes.

There are a number of short poems that consist less of praise and more of eloquent professions of constancy and devotion, accompanied by prayers for mercy. These are very similar to almost innumerable secular models both in French and English, and share with them the effects both of skilled craftsmanship and of a grey and over-fluent style. A more interesting poem is that beginning 'Awey, ffeyntt lufe, full of varyaunce',[2] which is again a highly ingenious adaptation of secular conventions. The poet's justification, for instance, of his choice of so exalted a lady is engagingly expressed in terms of secular narrative:

> Percase sche be off hygh degre
>   And [I] off lowe and pover estate,
> 3yit if fortune my frend wyll be,
>   I may her wyn other erly or late.
>   I have knowyn sum so ffortunate
> Wych, though they wer ful lowe off kyn,
> Kynggys doghtyrs by grace dyd wyn.[3]

He continues by feigning to conceal his lady's name in a series of types. In the arbour of his heart he will plant a five-leaved flower (*pentafiloun*), upon which are the five letters of her name. Each of these letters is said to stand for a Biblical figure and a precious stone, e.g. I is for Judith and jasper. Those who wish to understand his meaning are instructed to seek

---

[1] See above, p. 187.   [2] 'Lydgatiana', no. 11.
[3] *Archiv*, cxxxi. 52. L. 4, *erly*, MS. *erthly*.

it in the Bible and in lapidaries. This is an agreeable imitation of the poetical convention of concealing the lady's name, whilst at the same time identifying her by some acrostic or similar device. A twist is given to the convention by the poet's pseudo-naïve pretence that his meaning is obscure. The poem is concluded by an envoy beginning 'Go lytell balett', a forumla popularized in England by the epilogue to Chaucer's *Troilus and Criseyde*.

This formula has been traced back to Ovid, and to later Italian poets, Dante, Petrarch, and Boccaccio.[1] In French and Provençal lyrics it was especially used in the context of love. Lydgate concludes his address to the Virgin, 'Qween of hevene, of helle eeke emperesse'[2] with an envoy of this kind, and in MS. Douce 326 there is a poem which, according to the fifteenth-century custom, begins in this way, 'Goe, lytyll byll, and doe me recommende / Unto my lady'.[3]

Here we see an example of the deliberate borrowing of conventional, and often rhetorical, formulas from poetry of secular subject-matter to embellish lyrics to the Virgin. There are many other examples. A poem by Walter Kennedy, for instance, uses a series of conventionally fantastic hypotheses to emphasize the inexpressibility of the Virgin's beauty:

> The moder' se, fludis, lochis, and wellis
> War' all þir' ynke, and quyk and deid couth wryte,
> The hevyne stellat, montanis, planetis and fellis
> War' faire parchiament, and all as virgillis dyte,
> And plesand pennis for to report perfyte
> War' woddis, forestis, treis, gardingis and grawis,
> Couth nocht discryve þi honouris Infinit!
> Speciosa facta es et suavis.[4]

The 'inexpressibility topos' was also embodied in the other rhetorical formulae, enumerated by Curtius.[5] Its basis, according to him, is 'emphasis upon inability to cope with the subject'. Its proper context is the panegyric, and it was therefore simple to transpose it to Marian poetry. Examples may be found in Lydgate's work: 'Or halfe the joie who cowde wryte or telle, / When the Holy Goost to the was obumbrid . . .'[6] is a clear example of the *pauca e multis* formula; 'No clerk hath

---

[1] J. S. P. Tatlock, 'The Epilog of Chaucer's Troilus', *M.P.* xviii (1920), 625–30.

[2] E.E.T.S., E.S. 107, 284–7.

[3] Brown xv, 46.

[4] *The Asloan Manuscript*, ed. W. A. Craigie, ii (S.T.S., 1924), 273. *Stellat*: starry; *fellis*: fields.

[5] E. R. Curtius, *European Literature and the Latin Middle Ages*, trans. W. R. Trask (London, 1953), 159–62.

[6] E.E.T.S., E.S. 107, 258. *To the was obumbrid*: overshadowed thee.

konnyng thy bountes to descryve'[1] is a brief statement of the formula in which the name of famous authors, who would have been unequal to the subject, are enumerated. Another topos is that of 'affected modesty', which has been traced back by Curtius to classical and early Christian origins.[2] Lydgate uses it several times: 'Allas! unworthi I am bothe and unable, / To loffe suche on . . .'[3] or 'I am to Rude, O lady! for texpresse / Howe gloryous thinges beon song and sayde of þee'.[4] A further embellishment is the opening of a poem by an invocation to the muse or to a Christian substitute. Chaucer's invocations at the beginning of each book of *Troilus and Criseyde* had no doubt contributed to the acceptance and authority of this ancient convention. Lydgate in his poems to the Virgin uses this opening frequently: once he invokes Cleo,[5] but more often it is God the Father or the Holy Ghost,[6] and once, by a medieval innovation, it is the Virgin herself.[7] The significance of these invocations is the same as that of the 'inexpressibility topos'. It is the dignity of the subject-matter that makes the invocation necessary.

This kind of opening matches the style and intention of the love poems to the Virgin and of many others addressed to her. In them there is an exact reversal of the theory of style and language implicit in the early lyric. There a simple style was appropriate because its point of reference was not the subject-matter of the poem but the reader: not the dignity of God but the simplicity of man's emotional responses. A tendency to heighten the style to fit the subject-matter is, of course, visible in nearly all fifteenth-century religious poetry, but in the poems on the Passion this was modified by the strength of the earlier tradition. In the lyrics to the Virgin, however, poets were untrammelled in their borrowing of aureate diction and rhetorical devices, and the inevitable exclusion of the reader from sympathetic involvement did not appear a blemish. There are two reasons for this. One is the tradition (which we have already noticed in earlier French poetry) in which the poet's aim was to exercise his art in honour of the Virgin: festivals, such as that of the *puys*, had encouraged this. The other is less certain, but it is possible that there is here a symptom of the decline of medieval devotion: that is, to put it in a crudely simplified form, that a man was no longer expected to meditate on the Crucifixion, but to say a number of paternosters in honour of it. In other words, he was no longer expected to have a feeling of tender love for the Virgin, but to show his reverence for her by reciting a poem that glorified her, in which case of course the more ornate the glorification the better.

---

[1] Ibid. 286. Cf. Brown xv, 46, p. 76.
[2] Op. cit. 83–85.   [3] E.E.T.S., E.S. 107, 255.
[4] Ibid. 318.   [5] Ibid. 255.
[6] For instance, 'þou first moever', ll. 8–21, ibid. 131. Cf. Curtius, op. cit. 239.
[7] E.E.T.S., E.S. 107, 311.

The poems so far discussed form a small group, distinctive through their structural dependence upon secular models. Unlike the majority of religious lyrics, they can be most satisfactorily classified according to the rhetorical devices of secular poetry which they imitate: the enjoyment of them depends upon the appreciation of how skilfully the poet has transplanted the adornments of secular style to a religious subject-matter. These courtly poems to the Virgin, however, are far outnumbered by those that are in the form of prayers or which praise in liturgical manner. These, for which a knowledge of the devotional background is once again relevant, make up a much larger collection. As in France at this time, there are many which are translations, paraphrases, or farced versions of much-used Latin hymns and prayers: the *Obsecro te* and *O intemerata*, the *Salve regina* and *Ave maris stella* are some of the most recurrently used.[1] Oddly enough, these are not particularly to be found in books of hours but are common in poetical manuscripts. There is only one of these that raises any point of interest, the hymn *Stella caeli exstirpavit*,[2] of which there are three paraphrases, two by Lydgate[3] and one by Ryman.[4] There is here an indication of the cult of the Virgin as protectress against the plague,[5] one that was very common on the Continent, but which, like that of St. Sebastian, seems to have been fairly rare in England. The Latin hymn itself occurs in books of hours and in collections such as the famous Eton College choir-book:[6] in the *Ludus Coventriae* it is sung by the shepherds on their way to Bethlehem.[7] Ryman's translation, 'The hevenly sterre so bright and clere', is approximately close, but Lydgate in both poems makes substantial additions. One of Lydgate's additions is the plea that the bright rays of the Virgin may dispel the pestilential mists—which were then thought to carry the plague—and this conceit is expressed fairly elegantly in Lydgate's elaborate style:

> Thu same sterre, of sterrys noon so briht,
> Celestial sterre of beute moost sovereyne,
> To the we pray, on us cast doun thy siht,
> Oonly of mercy, that thu nat disdeyne,

---

[1] For English versions see the index to Brown's *Index*. This type of vernacular religious poetry was much commoner in France. For examples see Sonet, 472, 910, 2231 (*Obsecro te*); 561, 568, 1437, 1537, 1600, 2143 (*O intemerata*); 430, 431, 1877, 1880, 2093 (*Salve regina*); 424, 866 (*Ave maris stella*).

[2] *A.H.* xxxi. 207. Only verses 1 and 2 were used in the liturgy (the remainder being an addition), and it is therefore only these two that are paraphrased in the English versions.   [3] E.E.T.S., E.S. 107, 294–6.

[4] J. Zupitza, 'Die Gedichte des Franciskaners Jakob Ryman', *Archiv*, lxxxix (1892), 248.

[5] P. Perdrizet, *La Vierge de miséricorde* (Paris, 1908), and for St. Sebastian, pp. 109–15.

[6] U. Chevalier, *Repertorium hymnologicum* (Louvain, 1892–1921), 19438.

[7] E.E.T.S., E.S. 120, 148.

> Off infect heyr the mystis to restreyne,
>   That be thy gracious moost holsom influence
> We have no cause on hasty deth to pleyne,
>   Which sleeth the peeple by swerd of pestilence.[1]

In another poem Lydgate includes a reference to the *Schutzmantel* Madonna, 'Thy merciful mantel lete cloth al in the shade',[2] an image relating to the plague, in that the Virgin was imagined to interpose her mantle between mankind and the arrows of pestilence hurled by Christ.[3] This allegory was a very common iconographic theme in votive pictures on the Continent, but apparently was not adopted in England. The allusion to it in 'Haile blissed lady, the moder of Crist Iesu' is a further example of a characteristic of Lydgate's work, already noticed in his choice of Passion themes, namely, the introduction of references to foreign iconographic forms, which are otherwise hardly found in art or literature in England.

The most important liturgical poems, however, are the carols to the Virgin, of which there are a large number.[4] They are liturgical, not in the sense that they were intended solely or primarily for liturgical use, but because in style and content they resemble the Latin hymns and sequences that formed part of the church's liturgy. In their reiteration of clear doctrine and in their enumeration of types, they resemble no vernacular lyric genre, but recall unmistakably the typological sequences of writers such as Adam of St. Victor. These English equivalents of Latin hymns demand intelligence and learning in the hearer if they are to be fully understood, and it is therefore unlikely that they can have been primarily intended for popular singing.

In style the carols appear to have a naïve lucidity, and it is this perhaps that has deceptively suggested that, like many of the meditative lyrics, they were designed for a simple audience. But in the carols to the Virgin the stylistic and syntactical simplicity are not matched by a correspondingly simple content; on the contrary, they consist largely of an enumeration of types, and these are in fact easier to understand and respond to when developed in a more literary manner, as they are in non-liturgical fifteenth-century poetry. The bare presentation of them in the carols reflects the manner of typological hymns, where the type is set out with unembellished clarity so that its logical appropriateness may shine out to the intellect:

> Rubus quondam exardebat,
> Et hunc ardor non urebat
>   Nec virori nocuit:

---

[1] Ibid. 294–5. [2] Ibid. 300.
[3] Perdrizet, op. cit. 115–24. [4] On carols in general see Appendix D.

Sic ardore spiritali,
Nec attactu conjugali,
Virgo Deum genuit.[1]

It is this style that the carols are surely imitating, and the simplicity, which enhances the difficulty of content for a popular audience, cannot be intended for their aid, but is rather the chance result of turning the Latin style into English: it is a fair hypothesis that if the authors had been able to reproduce the poise and precision of their originals, they would have chosen to do so. In support of the interpretation it may be noted that the most austerely typological carols, such as 'Lo, Moises bush shynynge unbrent' or 'Thow holy doughter of Syon', are found only in liturgical manuscripts.

It is difficult to judge the carols as literature, for the discrepancy between style and content appears a radical defect when they are read, but largely disappears when they are sung.[2] In appraising them individually it is therefore necessary to disregard the style and to examine only the organization of content.

In many of them the value lies in the effect of a triumphant procession of types: the Virgin is praised by the amassing together of the people or objects in the Old Testament that prefigured her. Sometimes, however, there is greater theological and literary subtlety, and the types, which on the surface may seem a random grouping, are in fact held together by an unexpressed unifying theme. A good example of this method is a carol from the Ryman collection, 'O fayre Rachel semely in syght', which has as its subject the glorification of the Immaculate Conception.[3] The following are the first four verses:

O fayre Rachel semely in syght,
    Ther is no spotte of syn in the;
Therfore of ryght thy name shall hight
    Mater misericordie.

As Holy Writte thus concludith,
    For cause oure helthe is wone by the
Thou art bothe Ester and Judith,
    Mater misericordie.

---

[1] *The Liturgical Poetry of Adam of St. Victor*, ed. D. S. Wrangham (London, 1881), ii. 228. 'Once upon a time the bush was ablaze and the flame neither consumed nor hurt its verdure: so by spiritual flame and not by conjugal embrace did the Virgin become the mother of God.'

[2] Three carols (*Carols*, 30, 103 A, and 426) are included in the recording of Medieval English Lyrics [Argo (Z) RG (5) 443]. The record issued by Columbia University Press to accompany *Early English Christmas Carols*, ed. R. H. Robbins, is unfortunately not available in England.

[3] The expression of this doctrine in art has been discussed by M. Levi D'Ancona, *The Iconography of the Immaculate Conception in the Middle Ages and Early Renaissance* (New York, 1957).

> Holofernes, the fende, is hede
> With his owne swerde, O lady fre,
> Thou hast smytte of and made hym dede,
> Mater misericordie.
>
> Aman alsoo, the fende, oure foo,
> Thou hast hangyd uppon a tre;
> Thus thou hast brought mankynd fro woo,
> Mater misericordie.[1]

That the subject is the Immaculate Conception is indicated by the quotation in the second line from Canticles iv. 7, 'et macula non est in te', and the two types that follow, Esther[2] and Judith, are amongst those that suddenly increased in currency in the later Middle Ages through their application to the Immaculate Conception (in the carols they rival the older Nativity types, Gideon's fleece, Aaron's rod, etc., in frequency). Their logical point of comparison lies in the destruction of a powerful enemy by a woman: as Esther and Judith, respectively, caused the death of Holofernes and Hamon, so the Virgin conquered the Devil, thus fulfilling, as it was thought, God's promise in Genesis iii. 15, 'ipsa conteret caput tuum'.[3] In another carol these ideas are explicitly fused; 'O stronge Judith, O Hester meke, / That the serpentes hede of did streke . . .'.[4] By these types the Virgin is especially glorified in that the time of victory is moved back from the Annunciation to the very moment at which the Virgin was conceived. It will be seen from this brief explanation that behind the slack style of this carol there lies taut and coherent thought.

Whilst in many carols that have an 'O' or 'Hail' anaphora and that confine each type to one line, the point of the comparison is similarly not made explicit, in others it may be developed and explained. The carol beginning 'Lo, Moises bush shynynge unbrent' contains a series of types for the conception and birth of Christ, but each one is explained, as in the following example:

> Aronnys rodde, withoute licoure,
> By merveyl bare bothe fruyte and floure;
> So God and man, oure Savyoure,
> A clene mayde hath borne this day.[5]

---

[1] *Carols*, 210.

[2] Elsewhere, e.g. the *Speculum humanae salvationis*, Esther appears as a type of the Virgin interceding at the Last Judgement, in that she pleaded for her people to King Ahasuerus.

[3] '. . . and she shall bruise thy head'. The idea of the Virgin's conquest of the Devil was an ancient one, being based on this text, but it only became typologically emphasized when it referred especially to the Immaculate Conception.

[4] *Carols*, 194, p. 144.

[5] Ibid. 182, p. 136.

Whereas an unexplained series of types gives an effect of something at once mysterious and sumptuous, types that are expounded have a logical clarity that delights the intellect: as in the Latin hymns that they imitate, these carols show the use of exposition, not for didactic, but for aesthetic purposes, and the imagination is pleased by the symmetrical relationship of ideas. But in all the Marian carols, whether the type is developed or not, there is one common characteristic, namely that the typology is treated in a strictly theological way and is never developed into emotionally evocative imagery.

This distinction may be illustrated by a comparison between the treatment of some common types in the carols and in later lyrics of another kind. The burning bush, a type of the virgin birth, is often described in the carols in a single line, 'O ardent busshe that did not wast'[1] or 'O flamed busshe withoute leasure':[2] with these brief statements may be compared a stanza from Chaucer's ABC:

> Moises, that saugh the bush with flawmes rede
> Brenninge, of which ther never a stikke brende,
> Was signe of thin unwemmed maidenhede.
> Thou art the bush on which ther gan descende
> the Holi Gost, the which that Moyses wende
> had ben a-fyr; and this was in figure.[3]

Chaucer here catches some of the wonder inherent in the type, and the beauty and marvel of the flaming bush appropriately illuminates the quality of the Virgin's 'unwemmed maidenhede'. This literary development of the aesthetic potentiality of the type can be compared with the painting of Nicholas Froment,[4] where the Virgin and Child appear at the top of a burning rose-bush: in this, similarly, the effect produced by the abundance of rich and precise detail is that the two ideas match each other in beauty rather than in theological correspondence.

The same kind of extreme antithesis can be seen in the treatment of the type of Gideon's fleece. The type is common in the carols as it had been before in Latin hymns: 'This is Gedeonys wulle-felle, / On whom the dewe of heven dyde dwelle'[5] or 'Thow ert eke the flees of Gedeon, / Ydewed with the Holi Goste'.[6] The miracle of the fleece which became filled with dew, though the ground around it was dry, demonstrated well the fecund virginity of Mary, but it was an image neither poetically nor visually beautiful as can be seen in its many illustrations. At the opposite

---

[1] *Carols*, 199, p. 147.

[2] Ibid. 193, p. 143.

[3] *Poetical Works*, 618.

[4] E. Harris, 'Nicolas Froment's "Moses and the Burning Bush" ', *Essays presented to F. Saxl* (London, 1957), 88–95.

[5] *Carols*, 182, p. 136.

[6] Ibid. 190, p. 141.

extreme is the much-praised lyric 'I Syng of a myden' where, perhaps through the influence of associated texts,[1] the fleece is forgotten:

> I Syng of a myden   þat is makeles,
> kyng of alle kynges   to here sone che ches.
>
> he cam also stylle   þer his moder was
> as dew in aprylle,   þat fallyt on þe gras.
>
> he cam also stylle   to his moderes bowr
> as dew in aprylle,   þat fallyt on þe flour.
>
> he cam also stylle   þer his moder lay
> as dew in aprille,   þat fallyt on þe spray.
>
> moder and mayden   was never non but che—
> wel may swych a lady   godes moder be.[2]

The important point here is the development of the dew in an especially poetical way: for the dew is the dew of April, which carries with it the associations of the spring convention; it falls not on the fleece but on grass, flower, and spray, the latter a specifically 'poetical' phrase. This poem has been praised for its wit,[3] but it should rather be praised for its exquisite imagination, whereby an originally logical image has been transformed into one conveying the mystery, simplicity, and beauty of the manner of Mary's conception. In aesthetic effect it is comparable to such iconographic subjects as Mary in the rose-garden.

The poet in this obviously draws upon the flower imagery tradition-ally applied to the Blessed Virgin, imagery that, even in its origins, sug-gested her beauty as well as her humility or chastity. Biblical authority for this imagery lay in the Song of Songs, and in the interpretation of the tree of Jesse, according to which the Virgin was the stem or branch on which grew the flower, Jesus, though occasionally she was herself the flower. A charming poem by Audelay, 'þis Flour is fayre and fresche of heue', elaborates the more standard tradition.[4] The idea of the Virgin as the 'rose of Jericho'[5] of course drew upon and fused with the long tradition of the rose as a symbol of feminine beauty and the flower appropriate to love.[6] In classical legend it had been said that the rose

---

[1] All the relevant texts with their liturgical references are assembled by Barbara Raw, 'As Dew in Aprille', *M.L.R.* lv (1960), 411–14. The association of Ps. lxxi. 6 ('Descen-det sicut pluvia in vellus et sicut stillicidia stillantia super terram'), with Gideon's fleece may be seen in the *Biblia pauperum*, ed. Henrik Cornell (Stockholm, 1925), pl. 1. Leo Spitzer in his discussion of the poem (*Archivum Linguisticum*, iii. 157–8) has mistaken the typological reference in his equation of the dew with manna.

[2] Brown xv, 81.

[3] Stephen Manning, *Wisdom and Number* (University of Nebraska, 1962), 158–67.

[4] E.E.T.S. 184, 202–3.

[5] 'Plantatio rosae in Iericho', Ecclus. xxiv. 18.

[6] On the history of the rose see C. Joret, *La Rose dans l'antiquité et au moyen âge*

first blossomed when Venus rose from the waves or that it had sprung from the blood of Adonis. Lyric poets, such as Catullus, compared the modest blush of their mistress to the colour of the rose. In the early Christian tradition the rose became the symbol of the blood of martyrs or of Christ Himself, whilst at the same time there developed the fancy that in Eden the rose was not only unfading but also grew without thorn.[1] In the Middle Ages the Christian association of the rose with martyrdom and the Passion survived, but the pressure of the secular tradition was stronger, and far more often the rose was related to the Virgin. Attempts were made in this to find a close allegorical equation, as in the analysis by Hugh of St. Victor: 'Rosa natura frigida per vitiorum exstinctionem, forma lata per charitatem: colore alba aut rubra per puritatem et passionem, vel certe compassionem, odore grata per bonam opinionem.'[2] Beside dissective allegory, however, may be found explanations, such as the following from a sermon of Helinand, in which the rose stands unexpounded as a symbol of beauty, '. . . rosa, quia sicut rosa pulcherrima florum, sic Maria pulcherrima mulierum'.[3] Behind the English fifteenth-century use there extends, on the one hand, a long line of Latin hymns in which the Virgin is saluted as 'rosa sine spinis', and on the other, the long tradition of French secular poetry in which the classical simile had become a commonplace. In English references to the rose are too frequent and repetitive to require individual comment, but there are one or two curious or fine examples which cannot be passed over. Sometimes the image of the rose was used paradoxically: in a carol from the Ryman collection, 'To this roose Aungell Gabriell/Seide',[4] the rose stands for the Virgin throughout a narrative stretching from the Annunciation to the Crucifixion, but the effect is disquieting: unsuccessful paradoxes are merely odd. Far superior to this mechanical substitution are the famous

(Paris, 1892). There are some relevant comments and quotations in D. C. Allen, *Image and Meaning* (Baltimore, 1960), 67–79; the mystical meanings of the rose are discussed by P. Dronke, op. cit. i. 186–8.

[1] Ambrose, *Hexaemeron*, III. xi, *P.L.* 14, 175; Basil, *De peccato, Sermones viginti quatuor de moribus*, no. vii, *P.G.* 32, 1211.

[2] *Sermo* lxv, *In nativitate B.V.M.* quoted from J. J. Bourassé, *Summa aurea de laudibus Beatissimae Virginis Mariae*, x (Paris, 1862), where on pp. 221–9 are collected many examples of the rose as a symbol of the Virgin. 'The rose is by nature cold to signify the quenching of sin, and of a shape that opens outwards to signify charity; it is white or red in colour for chastity and suffering or indeed compassion, and has a pleasing smell for good reputation.' Cf. *P.L.* 177, 1104.

[3] *Sermo* xix, *In assumptione*, Bourassé, op. cit. 222. '. . . a rose, because just as the rose is the most beautiful of flowers, so is Mary the most beautiful of women.' Cf. *P.L.* 213, 644. Leo Spitzer, ' "Fleur et rose" synonymes par position hiérarchique', *Estudios dedicados a Menendez Pidal* (Madrid, 1950), i. 135–55, gives many quotations from French, Spanish, Italian, German, and Latin literature, in which the point of the comparison of the simile or metaphor is that the rose is the most beautiful of all flowers.

[4] *Carols*, 174. No. 175, in which the five joys are said to be five branches of a rose-tree, is discussed by Leo Spitzer in *Archivum Linguisticum*, iii. 137–52.

lines from the poem which borrows its short Latin lines from the
Laetabundus[1] ascribed to St. Bernard:

> Ther is no ro[se of] swych vertu
> As is the rose that bar Jhesu;
> Alleluya.
>
> For in this rose *con*teynyd was
> Heven *and* erthe i*n* lytyl space,
> Res miranda.[2]

If this is compared with Dante's line, 'Quivi è la Rosa, in che il Verbo
divino / carne si fece',[3] its imaginative brilliance is particularly evident:
for here the symbol of the rose has been combined with the traditional
paradox of the Virgin's womb containing Him whom the heavens and
earth could not contain,[4] and the result is indefinably stirring and beautiful.

More often, however, the rose is part of a list of flowers to which the
Virgin is compared, and the effect can often be that of a secular praise
of beauty rather than religious. A very agreeable, though untypical,
example occurs in the translation of the *Philomena*:

> Lady, þou art so bryȝt of ble
> Nothyng likeneþ þi beute.
> Primerole to þe is not of pris;
> þou art rodier þan rose on rys.
> þe violet ne lilies clere
> Of beaute is not þi pere;
> þe medwes grene and blosmes on tre
> Ben in no reward un-to þe;
> Ne flour in feld on someres-day
> Ne lef on tre, ne spryng on spray,
> May ben lich þi swete face
> þat is so fayr and ful of grace.
> ffairnesse of flour is sone agon,
> þi beute lesteþ evere in on.[5]

More representative is the following stanza from a poem of Lydgate,
where the rose is listed with other types, but throughout which adjectives draw attention to visual beauty:

> Glad Aurora, kalendis of cleer day,
> Of Phebus uprist, massageer most enteer,
> Rose of Iherico, groweth noon so freissh in May,
> Gracious Lucifer, dirk morwenynges for to cleer,

---

[1] *P.L.* 184, 1327.   [2] *Carols*, 173, pp. 130–1.
[3] *Paradiso*, xxiii. 73–75. 'There is the rose in which the Divine Word was made
flesh.'
[4] For this ancient paradox, incorporated in the Office of the Virgin, see Hirn, *The
Sacred Shrine*, 313–14.   [5] E.E.T.S. 158, 56.

And silver deuh, which that did Appeer
Uppon the flees shynyng of Gedeoun,
  Shew upon all thy liht, thyn hevenly cheer,
To thy .v. Ioies þat have devocioun.[1]

Very common is the kind of poem—often with a hail anaphora—in which
types are heaped up in order to convey by cumulative effect an impression of incomparable fairness and precious value. Stanzas six to eight
of Lydgate's 'A thowsand storiis kowde I mo reherse' is a good example
of a deliberate selection of types drawn indirectly from nature in order to
convey this effect:

O closid gardeyn al void of weedes wicke,
  Cristallyn welle of clennesse cler consigned,
Fructifying olyve of foilys faire and thicke,
  And redolent cedyr most derworthly ydyned.[2]

Jewel imagery may, as in this poem, also be used for the same purpose,
though behind this lies the equation of the Blessed Virgin with the City
of New Jerusalem, as well as the material of the traditional lapidary
allegories. This may be seen in the 'Ave, Iesse virgula' of Lydgate,
where the Virgin is saluted in the list of precious stones that formed the
foundation of the New Jerusalem (Apocalypse xxi. 19–20).[3] There is
here again a coincidence between secular and religious poetry. Lists of
flowers and jewels are common in French love poetry, and occur in
English as early as the Harley Lyrics.[4]

    It is curious to notice that, whilst the typological praise of the Virgin
is extensive in the fifteenth century, little attention is paid to the paradoxes, and these remain quite rare. The only paradox to become popular
was a new one, the *O felix culpa*, now well known from the famous
'Adam lay I-bowndyn', but repeated over and over again in the poems of
Lydgate and elsewhere: 'Wele I wate if synne ne were / Goddes moder
were þou noght'[5] or 'O felix culpa! thus may we syng'.[6] This paradox
had from an early date formed part of the Easter liturgy but it seems to
have passed from there into poetry only in the later Middle Ages. It was,
of course, also given a Marian twist: in the liturgy the fortunate consequence of man's sin is that he received such a redeemer, not that
Mary was crowned Queen of Heaven. The recurrence of this paradox,
when others were neglected, can probably be explained by its value as

---

[1] E.E.T.S., E.S. 107, 285.

[2] Ibid. 256. Cf. John Lydgate, *Poems*, ed. J. Norton-Smith (Oxford, 1966), 143–4,
where it is pointed out that this list of types derives from the *Anticlaudianus* of Alan of
Lille.

[3] E.E.T.S., E.S. 107, 301.   [4] Ed. Brook, pp. 31–32.   [5] Brown XV, 15, p. 30.

[6] E.E.T.S., E.S. 107, 293; cf. p. 298. There are eight lines of Latin verse on this
subject on the last page of a fifteenth-century book of hours, St. John's Camb. 129;
they begin: 'Si pro peccato vetus Adam non cecidisset / Mater pro nato non exaltata
fuisset .'

a brief and neat denial of the controversial doctrine of Duns Scotus that the Incarnation was predestined whether or not man fell. Normally this paradox is stated in mediocre style: it is only in the little ballad-like verse, 'Adam lay I-bowndyn' that the element of paradox is poetically exploited:

> Adam lay I-bowndyn, bowndyn in a bond,
> fowre þowsand wynter þowt he not to long;
> And al was for an appil, an appil þat he tok,
> As clerkis fyndyn wretyn in here book.
>
> Ne hadde þe appil take ben, þe appil taken ben,
> ne hadde never our lady a ben hevene qwen;
> Blyssid be þe tyme þat appil take was,
> þer-fore we mown syngyn, 'deo gracias!'[1]

It is very rarely that the structure of a medieval lyric deserves praise: the modern reader has to accustom himself to the absence of shapeliness, and learn not to look for the kind of lyric in which there is a single well-turned thought. But 'Adam lay I-bowndyn' is an exception, for in this the paradox is made pointed by the deftness of structure. The middle four lines, forming the heart of the poem, describe the taking of the apple, and the apparently simple triviality of the action is suggested by the rollicking style. Encasing this is a statement of the Fall and of the glorification of the Virgin. The paradox is heightened by the deliberately naïve statements of momentous facts: 'Blyssid be þe tyme þat appil take was' is very different from its original in the *Exultet*, 'O felix culpa, O necessarium peccatum ade'. This assumption of *naïveté* show the imaginative skill of a sophisticated poet.

A rather dull and mechanical way of glorifying the Virgin was the fifteenth-century device of forming acrostics with her name. The devotional praise and insistence on the Name of Mary obviously sprang by analogy from the devotion to the Holy Name. But stylistically it did not normally show itself in ecstatic repetition of the Name nor in moving descriptions of the delights that it conferred. The approach to it was more formal and technical. In his section on Maria in the *Summa praedicantium* Bromyard uses the letters of the Virgin's Name to define her qualities and prerogatives: she is *Misericordiae mater, Adiutrix, Reconciliatrix, Illuminatrix,* and *Amabilis.*[2] Verse was a particularly suitable form for the setting out in an acrostic of alliterative titles. A poem by Jean Molinet begins:

> Marie, mere merveilleuse,
> Marguerite mundifiie,
> Mere misericordieuse,
> Mansion moult magnifiie,

---

[1] Brown xv, 83.   [2] Ed. cit. ii. 7ʳ–8ʳ.

> Ma maistresse mirifiie,
> Mon mesfait maculeux me matte,
> M'ame mordant mortifiie;
> Mercy m'envoye m'advocate![1]

There are another four stanzas for the four other letters. No English verses on the Name of Mary are as stylized and polished as this. But they follow the same principle. In the play of Mary in the Temple in the *Ludus Coventriae*, the angel thus addresses the Virgin:

> In ʒour name Maria ffyve letterys we han
> M. Mayde most mercyfull and mekest in mende
> A. Averte of þe Anguysch þat Adam began
> R. Regina of regyon Reyneng with-owtyn ende
> I. Innocent be Influens of Jesses kende
> A. Advocat most Autentyk ʒour Antecer Anna
> hefne and helle here kneys down bende
> Whan þis holy name of ʒow is seyd Maria.[2]

Lydgate's 'Ave, Iesse virgula' contains three stanzas on the Name, of which the following is the second:

> M. in Maria betokenyth Eek meknesse,
>   A. next in Ordre, tokne of attemperaunce,
> R. remedye, our surffectys to redresse,
>   I. betoknyth Iesus, helpe for al our grevaunce,
>   A. is Amor, moost sovereyn of pleasaunce,
> Al set in Oon tu sola puerpera,
>   This name shall nevir out of our remembraunce
> Callyd fflos campi, O Ave Iesse virgula.[3]

Alliterative statements in aureate diction are characteristic of the acrostic style, though this is more evident in the Coventry stanza than in 'Ave, Iesse virgula'. The choice of titles and eulogistic phrases is entirely subordinated to the exigencies of the acrostic and alliterative pattern. In the Middle Ages it was perhaps possible to take delight in the pattern itself, but nowadays the achievement in itself does not seem worth the technical effort taken to accomplish it. The acceptance of it as something valuable depends upon the medieval belief, expressed, for instance, in the *Summa praedicantium*: '. . . quinque literae eius nomen (de quo Luc. i. Nomen Virginis Maria) componentes, pulcherrime eiusdem non solum videntur significare, sed etiam ostendere proprietates, et conditiones.'[4] The acrostic verse was obviously very suitable for giving literary

---

[1] *Les Faictz et dictz de Jean Molinet*, ed. Noël Dupire (S.A.T.F., 1937), ii. 455.
[2] E.E.T.S., e.s. 120, 80.   [3] Ibid. 107, 303.
[4] *Summa praedicantium*, ii. 6ᵛ. 'The five letters of which her name is composed (on which see Luke i, "the Virgin's name was Mary"), very beautifully not only seem to signify but also reveal her nature and qualities.' Cf. also B.M. Add. MS. 37049, 21ᵛ and 25ᵛ.

form to this principle, and from the medieval point of view it may have seemed that fashionable literary practice and religious need here fitted each other with quite exciting precision.

There is a short carol, 'Of thes iiii letters purpose I',[1] in which the Name of Mary is used in a different, though related, way. The subject is partially the compassion of Mary at the Crucifixion, but this is expressed through the refrain-like use of the letters of her Name, and the Name itself by implication has further meaning. In one of the two manuscripts in which the carol survives, MS. Sloane 2593, the four letters of the Name are described as 'letterys of purposy',[2] *purposy* (presumably a nonce form of 'purpose' required by the rhyme-scheme), meaning of riddling significance. These letters, however, are not interpreted but repeated mysteriously in an internal refrain in which they seem to be lingered over with lovingness, and which, like many refrains, is without syntactic relationship to the rest. The Virgin's sorrowful involvement in the scourging is thus expressed:

> Upon the mounte of Calvery,
> M and A, R and I,
> Ther thei betyn hys bar body
> With schorges that war sharp and long.[3]

Professor Green has pointed out parallels in other carols and lyrics to this use of letters, comparing it especially with those that have an O and I refrain.[4] But the strange evocativeness of the refrain, partly induced by its placing, can be better understood if it is related to the devotion to the Name of Mary. Though the virtues and privileges traditionally indicated by the letters are not expounded as in acrostic poetry, these are not therefore without significance: the implication is rather that the meaning is too holy and too exalted for it to be treated with common explicitness. This allusive suppression is extremely effective.

There was one further innovation in the vernacular lyric praise of the Virgin in the fifteenth century: her glorification through the apparently oblique method of praising her mother. However, just as poems to the Virgin could serve to honour Christ, so too could poems addressed to St. Anne reflect a glory on the Virgin. The lyrics to St. Anne, however, not only glorify the Virgin by celebrating her parentage, but also imply the Virgin's unique privilege of the Immaculate Conception. Emphasis upon this doctrine by theologians was invariably accompanied by a devotion to St. Anne in literary forms and by the appearance in art of the iconographic forms (such as the meeting of Joachim and Anne at the

---

[1] *Carols*, 180. P. Vinc. van Wijk, *De Naam Maria* (Leiden, 1936), 112–14, prints and comments on this carol.

[2] Ibid. 180 B.   [3] Ibid., p. 135.

[4] Ibid., p. 390.

Golden Gate) that portrayed her parents and symbolically indicated the moment of her conception.

This association between the doctrine of the Immaculate Conception and a devotion to St. Anne can be first seen in England in the twelfth century, when one of the chief defenders of the disputed doctrine, Osbert of Clare, composed hymns and lections in her honour.[1] In the same period, Wace, in the *Conception Nostre Dame*,[2] drew in his narrative upon the apocryphal material that was later to become so popular. Thereafter there was a lull in the treatment of this subject in both theology and devotion, and in England, with the important exception of the carving of the legendary material in the Lady Chapel at Ely,[3] it did not again become emphasized in literary and artistic forms until the fifteenth century, when it was expressed in pictorial form in the stained glass at Malvern[4] and in literature in the *Ludus Coventriae*[5] and various narrative poems.[6] By this time, however, literary and iconographic forms rested upon a solid foundation in the liturgy. The feast of the Conception was fully established in the West[7] (it was of ancient origin in the East), and the apocryphal story of St. Anne's conception of a daughter in her old age, based upon the *Protevangelium*, had become the official exposition of the older feast of the Nativity of the Virgin. It is included, for instance, in the *Legenda aurea*[8] and in Mirk's *Festial*.[9] Knowledge of the story illuminates occasional references in the lyrics to the miraculous conception of the Virgin and, yet more importantly, it generally enhances an appreciation of their meaning.

Four poems in honour of St. Anne survive, two by Lydgate and two by Audelay, and in their approach all four show the immediate influence

[1] Wilmart, op. cit. 261–86.
[2] W. R. Ashford, *The Conception Nostre Dame of Wace* (Chicago, 1933).
[3] M. R. James, *The Sculptures in the Lady Chapel at Ely* (London, 1895).
[4] G. McN. Rushforth, *Medieval Christian Imagery*, 271–4, and figs. 138, 139.
[5] E.E.T.S., E.S. 96, 62–71.
[6] *The Middle English Stanzaic Versions of the Life of St. Anne*, E.E.T.S. 174.
[7] The history of the feast is discussed by Wilmart, op. cit. 261–7. A full account of the medieval devotion to St. Anne is provided by B. Kleinschmidt, *Die heilige Anna: ihre Verehrung in Geschichte, Kunst und Volkstum* (Forschungen zur Volkskunde, 1930).
[8] *The Golden Legend*, v. 95–111.
[9] E.E.T.S., E.S. 96, 15–16. Versions of the story varied, particularly in the crucial point of the tense used in the angel's announcement to Joachim (Hirn, op. cit. 167), but in general they are largely a paraphrase of the *Protevangelium*. English writers seem to have ignored the extravagant fantasies related in the French *Roman de Fanuel* (*Le Romanz de Saint Fanuel et de Sainte Anne*, ed. C. Chabaneau, Paris, 1889), although an interest was shown in the curious legend of Anna's three husbands. This had already been set out by Wace, and Latin mnemonic verses, summing up the intricate genealogy, are found in some twelfth-century monastic manuscripts (Walther, 1062). A far less compact vernacular account is copied in the fifteenth-century commonplace book, MS. Tanner 407 (*Index*, 1560), and the manuscript of the *Ludus Coventriae* contains Latin notes on the subject before the play of the Immaculate Conception (E.E.T.S., E.S. 120, 62). Cf. *Suppl.* 2153. 5.

of Latin hymns to St. Anne, of which a large number survive from the twelfth century onwards.[1] It follows from the doctrine of the Immaculate Conception that the work of Redemption can be said to begin at the moment of Anne's child-bearing rather than that of Mary: therefore, from the literary point of view, the formulas and commonplaces appropriate to the latter can be transferred backwards to the former. There are some striking examples of this in the Latin hymns: 'Quod Eva tristis abstulit / Redditur partu filiae',[2] or even, '. . . In partu Mariae / Mutans Evae nomen'.[3] St. Anne could also be saluted with a *gaude*,[4] and she could be entreated to intercede, either directly to Christ, 'Ad nepotem tuum clama'[5] or 'Funde preces ad filium / Tuae prolis, Jesum pium',[6] or to the Virgin (as though she had been given the bottom rung in the *scala salutis*), 'Ora pro me filiam quae est mundi domina'.[7] Like the Virgin's, her intercession was especially sought for at the hour of death.[8] These points recur in the English poems.

Of the two poems by Lydgate one, 'He that intendeth in his herte to seke',[9] is a short verse prologue, designed to introduce a prayer ('Lo, here a devoute oreyson'), though no prayer follows it in the manuscripts. It praises the devotion to St. Anne, for whoever loves '. . . the doughter of any womman fre, / He must of gentilles, love the moder eke', and recommends the prayer by the story of a holy man, who, having a devout love for the prayer, '. . . at his dyeng, he saugh hem both appere, / This blessid mayden and her moder fre'. The other poem, 'þou first moever, þat causest every thing',[10] is a long and ornate address to St. Anne. In the first part it is adorned with some of the rhetorical conventions which we have already described, the modesty formula and the invocation to the Holy Ghost:

> Ffor but þou help, my wit is to bareyne,
> My mynde derk and dul is my memorye
> But yif þey beo emoysted with þe reyne
>   þat doun descenden frome þy see of glorye
>   Whos golde dewe dropes fro þy reclynatorye
> In-to my soule, awhaped and amaate,
> Shed from aboven þy licour aureate.[11]

---

[1] A large group are printed in *A.H.* iv. 122–41.

[2] Ibid. 131. 'What Eve took away to our sorrow was regained at the birth of your daughter.'

[3] Ibid. 126. 'In the birth of Mary reversing the name of Eve.' Other examples of this kind of transference may be seen in 'Monstra te esse matrem' (iv. 126) and, more typically, in 'Beata mater munere, / Quae pavit sacro ubere' (iv. 122).

[4] Wilmart, op. cit. 54.   [5] Ibid. 278. 'Cry aloud to your grandson.'

[6] *A.H.* iv. 128. 'Pour out prayers to your daughter's son, the holy Jesus.'

[7] Wilmart, op. cit. 279. 'Pray for me to your daughter who is the queen of the world.'

[8] e.g. *A.H.* iv. 134.   [9] E.E.T.S., E.S. 107, 130.   [10] Ibid. 130–3.

[11] Op. cit. 131. *See*: throne; *reclynatorye*: couch; *awhaped and amaate*: dismayed and confounded.

The longer part of the poem, however, follows the manner of the Latin hymns: St. Anne is said to have brought forth the 'lodesterre' which guides those in distress, the 'tryacle and medecyne' for the serpent's poisonous bite, and 'þe halowed ark þat bare þe holy manna', the last title specifically recalling a line from a twelfth-century Latin hymn, 'Urnam continentem manna parturisti clemens Anna'.[1] Here the praise of the mother is rooted in the eulogistic typology for the daughter: just as the Virgin had been honoured through praise of Christ, so St. Anne is honoured through praise of the Virgin. The poem ends with a plea that St. Anne may, before the Judgement, 'þe wrathe of þe Iuge queeme', the dignity of her role in the Redemption being the ground of her intercessory power. This poem never comes alight but it shows Lydgate's characteristic skill in fusing different traditions into a smooth and accomplished whole.

Audelay's two poems are simpler and more exclusively in the liturgical style. One, 'Gaude! felix Anna, þe moder of Mari',[2] is, as the first line indicates, a gaude poem, each line beginning with this word. One stanza praises the marvellous nature of the conception:

> Gaude! felix Anna, þe moder of Mari,
> Gaude! þou consayvyst clene be Ioachym þat hole man,
> Gaude! þat long tyme before baren þou hadist be;
> Gaude! þou broȝtist furþ þat burþ was our salvacion.[3]

The precise meaning of 'clene' is not plain: it could refer either to the legend that St. Anne miraculously conceived at the moment when she and Joachim embraced at the Golden Gate or, more probably, to the less fanciful belief, that Mary, being begotten at God's command in the passionless quiet of old age, was born without any taint of lust. Whatever the interpretation, the verse shows the purity of the Virgin reflected in the chaste circumstances of her conception and her pre-eminence emphasized by supernatural intervention in the natural course of procreation. Though this quotation does not show Audelay's style at its best, it is a pleasing example of how well limpid simplicity of style can carry complexities of story or thought.

The best of these four poems is Audelay's 'Swete saynt Anne, we þe beseche',[4] for it is written in a more attractive metre and shows more of Audelay's characteristic sweetness of imagination and feeling. Its structure has the fitting and traditional combination of eulogy and

---

[1] Wilmart, op. cit. 276. 'O merciful Anne thou didst bring forth the pot which contained the manna.'

[2] E.E.T.S. 184, 178–9.

[3] Ibid. 179.

[4] Ibid. 184, 200–1; Carols, 311.

prayer: St. Anne is besought to intercede with the Virgin and is praised in a narrative of her conception, the story being coloured by echoes of the Annunciation such as '. . . þen God he se to þi mekenes'. At its centre is a description of a common iconographic form symbolizing the Immaculate Conception:

> þen God hem grawntid graciously,
>   Betwene ȝoue two a floure schul spryng,
> þe rote þer-of is clepid Iesse,
>   þat ioye and blis to þe word schal breyng.
>   Here-fore I say.
> The moder of Mary, þat merceful may,
> Pray fore us boþ nyȝt and day.[1]

This is a Marian variation of the Tree of Jesse. Whereas earlier the Virgin had been the stem and Christ the flower, now the Virgin herself becomes the flower, and Joachim and Anne the stalks. But, though the reference of the imagery is doctrinal, it retains in Audelay's style some of the associations of natural imagery, the beauty of flowers and perhaps even of the joy in their growth. There is a sense of delight in the poem that was lacking in the more formal and ornate style of Lydgate.

The Virgin also continued to be celebrated in the narration of her joys, whether in the ornate manner of Lydgate or in the simple recording of the carol. Most of the carols are straightforward lists of the five joys, quite undistinguished in style. The only poem in carol form which is poetically pleasing is that attributed to Audelay, 'Gaude Maria, Cristes moder'. This has the sweetness and gentle feeling typical of Audelay's poetry. The second stanza, for instance, contains a touching Nativity scene:

> Gaude Maria, yglent with grace,
>   Whan Jhesus thi Son on the was bore,
> Full nygh thy brest thou gan him brace;
>   He sowked, he sighhed, he wepte full sore.
>   Thou fedest the flowr that never shall fade
>   With maydons mylke and songe therto,
>   'Lulley, my swet, I bare the, babe,
>   Cum pudoris lilio.'[2]

Audelay is the only fifteenth-century writer on the five joys, who, encouraged by the theme, is able to break through ornateness and formality to the affective meditation of the earlier poetry.

---

[1] Op. cit. 201.

[2] *Carols*, 230, p. 163. The text without emendation is printed in E.E.T.S. 184, 202–4. *Cum pudoris lilio*: with the lily of chastity; cf. Brown XIII, 22, l. 6, where the same phrase is thus translated.

Amongst lyrics that are not carols may be noticed a poem on the five joys which contains an acrostic of the Name of Mary. Each of the five eight-line stanzas of this lyric, 'Myldyste of moode, and mekyst of may-dyns alle',[1] begins with a letter of the Name, but the author has taken no trouble to choose a word of weight, and only the first one, 'Myldyste', even refers to the Virgin. The first A, for instance, is the indefinite article, and the second A is provided by 'And'; I is furnished by 'In'. This verbal acrostic could hardly be weaker. Were it not that the letters are obtrusively ornamented in the manuscript, the acrostic might easily be missed. Unlike the carol on the Compassion, which became transformed by the use of the Name of Mary, this remains a poem on the five joys, for which the acrostic provides an attempt at adornment.

Apart from the poems on the five joys, there are two descriptions of the fifteen joys by Lydgate. One of these, 'Blessed lady, O Pryncesse of mercy',[2] is said by an initial rubric to have been translated from French. This is plausible, in that the fifteen joys seem to have been a theme liked by French poets, though none of the French poems that are extant and printed correspond exactly to Lydgate's. Lydgate's second enumeration occurs in the first half of the poem already referred to on the fifteen joys and sorrows of the Virgin.[3] Like the fifteen sorrows, and unlike the other poem on the fifteen joys, this draws on the apocryphal life of the Virgin. The first joy, for instance, is the offering of the Virgin to the temple by Joachim and Anne:

> Blissed braunche that sprong out of Iesse
>   Which were allone, as clerkys telle can,
> Ground and gynnyng of our felicite,
>   For thilke ioye which thu haddist than
>   Whan thu were offryd by Ioachim and Anne
>   In-to the temple, by scripture as I fynde,
>   Pray for thy servauntis and have upon hem mynde.[4]

The fifth joy is the water of proof, this time not a humiliation, but a glory in its demonstration of the Virgin's chastity.[5] This poem, like all Lydgate's work, is highly accomplished but, unlike Audelay's poem, it conveys neither tenderness nor delight.

A fifteenth-century development in the treatment of the joys of the Virgin was that the Coronation and Assumption became the subjects of individual poems. Their treatment derives from the antiphons of the Office of the Assumption, which are chiefly taken from the Song of Songs, and in which the Virgin is summoned by Christ as His beloved.

---

[1] Brown xv, 31. Cf. 'Away ffeynt lufe full of varyaunce', *Archiv*, cxxxi. 51–53, and pp. 279–80 above.

[2] E.E.T.S., E.S. 107, 260–7.   [3] See above, pp. 269–71.

[4] Op. cit. 269.   [5] Op. cit. 270–1. See above, p. 270.

In the lyrics, as in art, the Assumption and the Coronation are sometimes combined, and the splendour of the occasion is emphasized by the surrounding hosts. Again both in lyric and in art the Coronation is sometimes performed by Christ alone, sometimes by the Trinity.[1] There are altogether six poems on this subject, of which three are monologues addressed by Christ to the Virgin. The shortest and simplest of these consists of two verses incorporated by Mirk in his sermon for the feast of the Assumption, of which the first is as follows:

> Com, my swete, com my flour,
> Com my culver, myn owne boure,
> Com my modyr, now wyth me;
> For Hevyn qwene I make þe![2]

This verse is charming in its combination of exact doctrinal imagery ('myn owne boure') with the sensuous endearments of the Song of Songs. It is also illuminating in that its prose context (which describes the descent of Christ with the angelic hosts to fetch the Soul of His mother, and their re-ascent culminating in the Coronation) has also to be understood for two other monologues. Both these monologues, like the verse from Mirk, open with the invitation from the Song of Songs, 'Surge mea sponsa, so swete in syʒte'[3] and 'Come, my dere spowse and lady free',[4] and both have an identical refrain from the same source, 'Veni coronaberis'. The first of these proceeds by mingling the titles from the Song of Songs with recollections of Christ's humanity and the Virgin's maternity. The following quotation is typical:

> Veni de libano, þu lylye in launche,
>   that lapped me lovely wyth loulynge songe!
> Thow shalte a-byde wyth þy blessed braunche
>   That so solemply of þe spronge.
> Ego, flos campy, þy flowre, was fonge,
>   That on Calverye cryede to þe ywisse.
> Moder, ʒe knowe hyt ys no wronge,
>   Veni coronaberis.[5]

The other poem, one of Ryman's carols, is less doctrinally ambitious, and reserves to the end the reference to the Virgin's motherhood. The main part keeps close to the Song of Songs and preserves the tone of its exotic and eulogistic imagery:

---

[1] For the iconography of the Coronation of the Virgin see Marion Lawrence, 'Maria regina', *Art Bulletin*, vii (1924–5), 150–61; P. Wilhelm, *Die Marienkrönung der Kathedrale von Senlis* (Hamburg, 1941); and, for the Coronation by the Trinity, Margaret Rickert, *The Reconstructed Carmelite Missal* (London, 1952), 48–49.

[2] E.E.T.S., E.S. 96, 224, where it is printed continuously as prose. *Culver*: dove.

[3] Brown XV, 37.   [4] *Carols*, 262.

[5] Brown XV, 66–67. *Lapped*, MS. lappes. *Launche*: stalk; *flos campy*: flower of the field.

> Come, my myelde dove, into thy cage,
>   With joye and blis replete whiche is,
> For why it is thyne heritage;
>   Iam veni, coronaberis.[1]

There is another carol, 'The most worthye she is in towne',[2] that is associated with this group through its use of the same refrain. It is, however, not an address of Christ, but a song in praise of the Virgin, who is riddlingly concealed beneath the traditional image of the ivy. Far more important are the two poems set in vision form, in which the whole scene of the Assumption and Coronation is revealed to the meditator. In one, 'The infinite power essenciall',[3] the vision setting is indicated briefly and without attention, 'Me thoght I sawe', the poet says; but in the other, 'Undir a park ful prudently pyght',[4] it is elaborately introduced. The poet feigns that (like the dreamer in *The Pearl*) his soul was transported to heaven, 'So was I enspyred froom the speculat splendure [angelic singing], / That my spirit was ravysshed, my boody abood': an ingenious device for enabling the meditator to be present in the heavenly scene. Both poems are written in highly ornate diction, whose richness is no doubt intended to match the precious and luxurious detail of visual representations of the scene. The splendour of the angelic hosts is, for instance, thus described:

> A melodious myrthe it was to me,
> fful pure and precious by poyntes passaunt,
> So shynyng upward the excelcite,
> With obediaunt beemys bryghtly abundaunt.
> Angellys, Archangellys, froom vicis advertaunt,
> Moore gloryous than evere was gleem or glas,
> Thronys, Dominaciouns, thus Crist collaudaunt,
> With 'Benedicta sit sancta Trinitas'.[5]

It is difficult to estimate the quality of this. As the reading of sixteenth- or seventeenth-century lists of neologisms so clearly shows, a modern ear alone cannot separate standard vocabulary from the exotic and outlandish, though possibly the natural selection effected by speakers and writers is not without relationship to the value and necessity of the original coinage. Certainly there now seems little to be said for lines

---

[1] *Carols*, p. 187.

[2] *English Carols*, ed. R. L. Greene (Oxford, 1962), 35, and for a note on the allegorical use of the ivy see pp. 33–34. This carol is also printed by Robbins, *Secular Lyrics*, 52, but the refrain makes the religious reference inescapable, and there is no reason to assume with Professor Robbins (p. 242) that the poem is a religious parody.

[3] Brown xv, 38.   [4] Ibid. 39.

[5] Ibid. p. 70. *Poyntes passaunt*: surpassing qualities; *excelcite*: heights; *advertaunt*: turning away from; *collaudaunt*: greatly praise; *Benedicta sit sancta Trinitas*: blessed be the holy Trinity.

loaded clumsily with polysyllabic Latinisms (many of them nonce words), such as 'Phebus persplendent made his abdominacioun . . .'[1] or '. . . of the luciant corruscall resplendent'.[2] The effect of the two poems is that of an ugly, indiscriminate verbosity, which excludes the precision at which they aim.

In this group should perhaps also be included two dramatic complaints in which the Virgin pleads with man, not through the Passion as in the *planctus*, but in her own right as Queen of Heaven: in the one she is the Virgin of the Coronation, in the other, of the Assumption. The first is the well-known lyric, 'In a tabernacle of a toree', with the refrain *Quia amore langueo*, in which the meditator sees 'A crowned Queene . . . sittyng on a trone'.[3] In stanza form and refrain it resembles the complaint of Christ already described, and on account of its poetic inferiority to the latter and the eccentricity of attributing the text from the Song of Songs to the Virgin, it is tempting to see in it an imitation. The curiosity of this, as of the other poem, 'Regina celi, quene of thy sowth',[4] is the application of the terms of love-longing to the Virgin. In allegorical interpretations of the Song of Songs, if the bride was the Virgin, then the bridegroom was necessarily Christ, and in the second poem, which is closely dependent on the Song of Songs, this is largely remembered. But there are passages such as 'With my hony my combis I ete, / With my swetnese man is fedde', in which the allegory seems to refer to the relationship between the Virgin and man. The tone of both poems in fact suggests this, though it was perhaps not the authors' conscious intention, but rather the unintended result of a not very happy transference: the bride of the Song of Songs and the Virgin of Pity could not be satisfactorily identified. The retention of most of the sensuous and exotic imagery of the Song of Songs in 'Regina celi, quene of thy sowth' combined with the Virgin's invitation to man, makes the poem little more than a hybrid curiosity.

'In a tabernacle of a toure', however, cannot be so briefly dismissed: it was evidently popular in the Middle Ages (it survives in eight manuscripts), and nowadays it is included in most anthologies. There are undoubtedly moving verses in it, such as the following:

> I byd, I byde in grete longyng,
> I love, I loke when man woll crave,
> I pleyne for pyte of peynyng;
> wolde he aske mercy, he shuld hit have.
> Say to me, soule, and I shall save,

---

[1] Ibid. 38, l. 21. *Persplendent*: resplendent (not in the *O.E.D.*); *made his abdominacioun*: surrendered his rule (*abdominacioun* not in the *O.E.D.* or *M.E.D.*).

[2] Brown xv, 38, l. 44. *Corruscall*: radiant (not in the *O.E.D.* or *M.E.D.*).

[3] *Quia amore langueo*, ed. H. S. Bennett (London, 1937), 13.

[4] *Archiv.* cxxxi. 50–51.

> Byd me, my chylde, and I shall go;
> Thow prayde me never but my son forgave,
>   *Quia amore langueo.*[1]

Moreover, with its moral emphasis, its remembrance of the Passion and expressions of mercy, it is much more satisfactory in content and much more dignified in style than 'Regina celi, quene of thy sowth'. Nevertheless the discrepancy remains: the language of love-longing is not fitting to a loving mother. The use of other images for the relationship, that of sister, recurrently, and, in the last line, that of wife, adds to the confusion. The mixture, of course, derives from the Song of Songs and is paralleled in the complaint of Christ with the same refrain. But whereas in the latter the contradictory images were held together by one satisfactory dominating theme, in the present poem they remain separate and disparate. It was customary in both devotion and literature to transfer to the Virgin what was said of Christ: this poem is an example of such a transference not succeeding.

In the fifteenth century, however, the joy most commonly celebrated independently was the Nativity, and carols on this subject are particularly abundant. These carols which celebrate the Christmas season in narrative, undogmatic, and often lively fashion are of a different kind from the liturgical carol, and they usually occur in different collections: in Richard Hill's commonplace book, for instance, or in the printed volumes of the sixteenth century. Of all the religious verse we have discussed, these carols alone could perhaps be called popular without qualification: that is they are not merely popular by destination, but in their emphasis and treatment of material they may also reflect popular taste. Many of them deal with the adoration of the Magi and with the annunciation to the shepherds and their adoration of the Child. The first of these requires no particular comment, but the second needs elaboration. The popularity of the subject was no doubt stimulated by the mystery plays, in whose Latin origins the *Officium pastorum* was one of the earliest elements.[2] In the vernacular drama of England and France it was the story most commonly given charming or boisterous elaboration. It seems to have developed with distant echoes of the pastoral form. The idea of the shepherd-musician, originally of eastern origin,[3] was almost invariably adopted: in the De Lisle Psalter[4] and Queen Mary's Psalter[5]—some decades before the extant English plays—a shepherd

---

[1] Brown xiv, 132 (the folio reference to MS. Douce 322 should be 12ᵛ not 8ᵛ).
[2] Young, *The Drama of the Medieval Church*, ii. 3–28.
[3] G. Millet, *Recherches sur l'iconographie de l'évangile*, 114–35.
[4] MS. Arundel 83, 124ʳ, E. G. Millar, *English Illuminated Manuscripts of the XIVth and XVth Centuries*, pl. 8.
[5] Ed. G. Warner, pl. 162.

is playing his pipe when the angels appear, and in the *Holkham Bible Picture Book* the shepherds already ignorantly stumble as they try to repeat the Latin of the angels' song.[1] One carol, 'Abowt the fyld thei pyped full right', makes the music of the shepherds its recurrent theme by embodying it in the refrain: 'Tyrle, tyrlo, / So merylye the shepperdes began to blowe'.[2] The other recurrent element is that of the shepherds' homely gifts, now so well known from the *Secunda pastorum*,[3] but found in the earlier *Shrewsbury Fragments*[4] and in all the later cycles, and exploited over and over again with comic sweetness in the French *Noëls*.[5] A comparison with the *Noëls* throws into relief the straitness of the carols. It is not, for instance, merely that in them there are no shepherdesses[6] (this was largely a sixteenth-century development which could not take place in countries of the Reformation), but that there is no concern even for the shepherds with their gifts, except in the carol from Richard Hill's book, 'The sheperd upon a hill he satt':

> The sheperd upon a hill he satt;
> He had on hym his tabard and his hat,
> Hys tarbox, hys pype, and hys flagat;
> Hys name was called Joly, Joly Wat,
> > For he was a gud herdes boy.
> > With hoy!
> For in hys pype he made so mych joy.[7]

In this poem there is the emphasis upon musical instruments, the contemporary proper names, and the simple realism of the shepherd who leaves his dog to guard his sheep, who sweats after his run to Bethlehem, and who advises the Virgin, 'Lull well Jhesu in thy lape'. This poem is a very accomplished example of a kind common in France, and it is difficult not to believe that there were others like it in England. The only other elaboration in the Nativity carols is that of the ox and the ass, who, in the tradition of the *Meditationes*, warm the Christ-Child with their breath:

---

[1] Ed. W. O. Hassall, fol. 13ʳ, and notes p. 90.

[2] *Carols*, 79; this carol was incorporated in a Nativity play from Coventry, *Two Coventry Corpus Christi Plays*, E.E.T.S., E.S. 87, pp. 12 and 31.

[3] E.E.T.S., E.S. 71, 139.

[4] Young, op. cit. ii. 516.

[5] On these see M. Vloberg, *Les Noëls de France* (Grenoble, 1934), 115–42. For the texts see, for instance, *Vieux Noëls*, ed. H. Lemeignen, i (Nantes, 1876), 41–44, 45–47, 57–60, 61–64, 76–79, 106–11, etc. Some of these, however, are later than the fifteenth century. The theme is equally common in French mystery plays, for instance, *Nativités et moralités liégeoises du moyen-âge*, ed. Gustave Cohen (Brussels, 1953), 172–3. Analogous scenes in Italian drama are cited by N. de Robeck, *The Christmas Crib* (London, 1938), 69–70.

[6] e.g. Lemeignen, op. cit. 125 ff.; Cohen, op. cit. 173.

[7] *Carols*, 78, p. 49. *Tabard*: a loose upper garment of coarse material; *tarbox*: box containing tar as a remedy for sheep; *flagat*: flask.

> A babe was born
> Erly by the morn
>   And layd betwen the ox and the asse;
> The child they knew
> That was born new;
> On hym thei blew.
>   Deo gracias.[1]

Even this, however, is found only occasionally. In general, these carols are simple undecorated narratives of the Redemption, sometimes extending in reference from the Nativity to the Passion. Those concerned with the Epiphany are equally plain, though there are minor dramatic interchanges in the carols of the Three Kings.

In contrast to the *Noël*, but like the German *Wiegenlied*, the English carol is often in the form of a lullaby. The earliest examples of this in John of Grimestone's preaching-book have already been noted, and those which followed them are very similar. Of the Christmas festive carols these are the only ones that appear in manuscripts for the Court. The well-known carol beginning 'This endurs nyght' survives, for instance, in the Fayrfax Manuscript: it is a poem in which paradox is admirably turned to pathos in the lines:

> Nothyng, my spowse,
> Is in this howse
>   Unto my pay;
> My Son, a Kyng
> That made all thyng,
>   Lyth in hay.[2]

In all these poems there is emphasized poverty, tenderness, and the shadow of future suffering. The complete absence of ornate diction and the emphasis on lullaby words contribute to the effect. There are over twenty carols of this kind, some in monologue form, but chiefly dialogues between the Virgin and Child. Like the poems in John of Grimestone's preaching book, they often have a *chanson d'aventure* opening. These are amongst the most agreeable of the carols, and, with their roots in the traditional emphasis upon the poverty of the Christ-Child, they are more strictly in the meditative tradition than any of the others. Moreover, the description in them of the Virgin with her Child, often not in the crib or cradle but at her breast, provides a meditative image, which must have recalled innumerable paintings and statues. This image had the advantage that, like the earlier subjects of meditation, and unlike inventions such as the shepherds' gifts, it had precise doctrinal significance. Professor Millard Meiss has pointed out how the Virgin and Child was a

---

[1] *Carols*, 45, p. 30. Cf. *Meditations*, trans. Ragusa and Green, 33–34.
[2] *Carols*, 146, p. 99. Cf. Stevens, op. cit. 366–7. *To my pay*: to my contentment.

precise counterpart to the Pietà, a devotional image in which was isolated a moment of time, and in which was expressed the relationship between Virgin and Child, a relationship significant for the Redemption of man and the hope of salvation for each individual. In their controlled feeling these carols stand out from the rest, and the explanation surely lies in their meditative-doctrinal ancestry.

There is one further development amongst the carols which must finally be noted. It is perhaps only from the point of view of the modern reader—who, sitting alone by himself, reads the carol printed upon the page—that the lullaby carols are the most pleasing, for they continue the tradition of meditative poetry, which was probably unique amongst medieval literature in being primarily intended for solitary study. The lullaby carols are private in feeling and scarcely suitable for choral singing on public occasions. But the conditions of performance encouraged in the carol a return to the liturgical tradition, which emphasized the theological significance of the event, and there are other carols that are successful in a more public way. The difference may be summed up by the contrasting of two refrains: 'To syng, "By, by, lully, lulley" ',[2] as against 'Verbum caro factum est'.[3] From the theological point of view the Nativity was a time of triumph, and therefore the tone of these carols is different from that of the lullabies. There are two distinct ways of achieving this tone of triumph.

In one kind of carol the traditional narrative of the Nativity continues, but there is deliberately no attempt at tender feeling. The public, liturgical associations are made pointed by a frequent use of Latin lines and also of the paradoxes which were so strikingly lacking in the meditative tradition. The following quotation is typical of the style:

> When he was borne that made all thyng,
>   Pastor creator omnium,
> Angellis thei began to syng,
>   'Veni, redemptor gencium.'[4]

The same approach to the Nativity is shown in the lyric, 'I Passud þoru a garden grene',[5] which is in structure a meditative poem with a *chanson d'aventure* opening. The poet comes upon a maiden in a garden (the Virgin of the Nativity), and, after questioning her he passes on, meeting the shepherds and the three kings on his way. But although much traditional narrative detail is used, all suggestion of the suffering

[1] Millard Meiss, *Painting in Florence and Siena after the Black Death* (Princeton, 1951), 145–56.
[2] *Carols*, 150 C.   [3] Ibid. 35 B.
[4] Ibid. 23, p. 17. L. 2: 'The shepherd and creator of all things'; l. 4: 'Come, Redeemer of mankind'.
[5] Brown xv, 78.

Christ Child is excluded. The Virgin, for instance, describes the Nativity scene as follows:

> Sche said, 'a prynce withouten pere
> Ys borne and layd betwene to best;
> Therefore I synge as ӡe mey here
> Verbum caro factum est.'[1]

The poem seems an unsuccessful compromise. It has eschewed the compassionate interpretation, which was the poetic strength of the meditative tradition, but at the same time it is prevented by its structure from conveying resoundingly the glory of the Word made flesh: for this the refrain in itself is insufficient.

There is another small group of carols, about four in all, which celebrate the Nativity by means of the *Te Deum*. There are a large number of carols which paraphrase the *Te Deum*, and Professor Greene has included them all in a section entitled 'Carols to the Trinity'. But amongst them are a few, which are not addressed to God, praising Him because He is worthy to be praised, but which—like the middle section of the *Te Deum*—are addressed to Christ and praise Him for His incarnation.[2] These carols consist of a brief description of the Nativity followed by the angelic song of praise: the *Sanctus, sanctus, sanctus* of the *Te Deum* sung by the angels in heaven has suggested the *Gloria in excelsis* sung by the angels on earth. The carols are quite effective in catching the majestic tone of the title-roll of the angelic hosts. One carol, 'The Faders Sonne of Heven Blis', describes how when Christ was born:

> Cherybyn and seraphyn alsoo,
> Tronis, potestates, and many moo
> Fulle sweetly sunge to that Lorde tho,
> 'Te Deum laudamus.'[3]

These carols are not only interesting in themselves but also because they provide a relevant background for Dunbar's fine poem on the Nativity. In this lyric the whole universe is summoned to do honour and rejoice at the birth of Christ. There is obviously a direct echo here of the *Te Deum*: amongst those summoned, the angelic hosts, the martyrs, and the clergy particularly recall this. But it may be right to guess that the turning of narrative into hortatory invocation derived from the *Benedicite*; from this too would come the enumeration of planets, elements, birds, and animals. The identifying of these sources in no way detracts from the poem: the combination and transformation of them could have been achieved only by a poet of powerful and individual

---

[1] Brown xv, p. 115.   [2] *Carols*, 295, 297, 300, 301.
[3] Ibid. 300, p. 208. *Potestates*: powers.

imagination. It is a magnificent poem, difficult to quote from, for each verse is as strong, confident, and resounding as every other. It is, however, perhaps a further achievement of the poem that, despite this sustained strength, the last stanza is able to sum up the rest without anticlimax:

> Syng hevin imperiall, most of hicht,
> Regions of air mak armony;
> All fishe in flud and foull of flicht
> Be myrthfull and mak melody:
> All *Gloria in excelsis* cry,
> Hevin, erd, se, man, bird, and best,
> He that is crownit abone the sky
> *Pro nobis Puer natus est.*[1]

With this may be compared another poem of Dunbar's, his lyric on the Resurrection. For this no analogues or antecedents can be found in the carols, although it would have been a very suitable subject for public, liturgical poetry.[2] Only a strong liturgical link with Christmas can explain this. There are, however, two fifteenth-century poems on the subject in MS. Arundel 285. One of the latter, 'O Mothir of God, Involat virgin mary', is a song of triumph in aureate diction. In one stanza, in which the angelic hosts are exhorted to meet the victorious conqueror, it recalls the *Te Deum* Nativity carols:

> Be glaid, ye angellis and ye archangellis cleir!
> ȝoure wailȝeand prince, victorius in battall,
> Met with all hevinlie melody and cheir;
> And to ȝoure king ȝe sing, 'haill, victour, haill!'[3]

The other, 'Thow that in prayeris hes bene lent',[4] is addressed to the penitent, inviting him to share in the triumph of Easter. But the influence of Passion meditation is still strong on this poem, and the author passes soon from exhorting the penitent to rise with Christ in His glory to urging the hard-hearted: 'Behald þi meik, sweit Salviour, / The to enbrace, how þat he bowis'. Dunbar's poem, 'Done is a battell on the dragon blak',[5] is far finer and more consistent than either of these. It is made up largely of a triumphal series of definitions and consequences of the redemptive victory and rising of Christ. These are expressed in a language which is a most successful combination of the colloquial, 'Dungin is the deidly dragon', or 'The auld kene tegir with his teith on char', with a more decorative diction and manner, 'Sprungin is Aurora radius and bricht, / On loft is gone the glorius Apollo'. So skilfully are

---

[1] *Poems*, ed. Mackenzie, 155.   [2] See Appendix D, p. 385.
[3] Brown xv, 112, p. 177. *Wailgeand*: valiant.
[4] Ibid. 113.   [5] *Poems*, 159–60.

these interwoven that the one does not seem too casual nor the other too coldly elevated.

Both the Nativity and the Resurrection were amongst the five joys of the Virgin. In the triumphal poems, however, these events are not interpreted from the human and maternal point of view, but are seen as great events in the history of the Redemption, celebrated in public style. The reader is moved, not to sympathetic delight, but to stupefied amazement and a sense of awe. In that they are designed to express the glory of the subject, these poems are in style more like those that praise the Virgin herself than like the traditional poems on the joys. Strictly they do not belong in a history of medieval meditative poetry. But, quite apart from the fact that Dunbar's poems have a claim of literary merit which can override neatness of classification, they are also useful in showing, still within a medieval framework, the kind of religious poetry that was not normally written in the Middle Ages. They illustrate too the distinction between anonymous and named poetry, which was made in the first chapter. As we have said before, Dunbar's poem on the Passion is frigid, and even those who disagree with this and can take a cordial pleasure in it must admit that it is surpassed by the best Passion poems that preceded it. The inference is that these subjects were treated better by writers with less distinctive gifts, who quite naturally accepted a genuinely anonymous style of writing and a willing subservience to tradition. But the triumphal celebration of the Nativity and the Resurrection requires the tone of self-assertion and personal confidence, which only a talented and self-conscious poet can possess. Therefore, Dunbar's poems on these subjects tower over the few lyrics that preceded them.

IX

Lyrics on Death

LYRICS on the subject of death continued to be abundantly produced in the later Middle Ages. In this period there are many warnings from the dead—often in the form of epitaphs or *exemplum* verses —warnings from the old and from the dying, and also—a new development—warnings from the proud. Moreover, it is not only the dead who warn, but also death itself personified, and many poems too are angry or fearful apostrophes of death. Lyrics on death that are set in the form of sermon exhortation are particularly numerous, no doubt on account of the particular affiliation of the death-lyric to the sermon, which we noticed before. In addition, two continental themes, the Three Living and the Three Dead and the Dance of Death—both closely related to iconography—were transplanted into English verse.

There are two points of interest that arise from a comparison of the historical development of the death lyric with that of the Passion lyric. First, for the death lyric there are no new substantial Latin sources. The literary preference of the fifteenth century for longer and more elaborate poems was matched in the Passion lyric by the choice of different Latin sources, which could give body to the poem by their copious incident and detail. But, in the later death lyric, length and elaboration seem sometimes to have been achieved merely by the spreading of earlier material more thinly, so that the style is far less compressed and taut, and is therefore less readily turned to irony. Indeed, though passages of ironic taunting continue, this ceases to be the characteristic style of the death lyric. The writers seem to have adopted a different principle of propriety and to have assumed that decorum of tone and style should consist of heavy-footed gravity: both poetically and morally this is less effective than the satirical agility of the earlier poetry.

The second point emerges from the relationship of the lyric to iconography. It has already been emphasized how the late lyrics of the Passion and Compassion were dependent upon iconographic forms; and this was also true of the earlier Passion lyric, where, for instance, the *Candet nudatum pectus* with its disjointed detail, required the recollection of a carved or painted Crucifixion to hold it together. But, in that the visual image was so central, the poetic dependency upon it was much less noticeable. In the thirteenth century, however, there was as yet no iconographic portrayal of death or the dead: the visual reference was manifestly not to art but to personal experience. But very often in the later lyric either visual description is avoided or the reference is to funerary monuments, double tombs or cadaver tombs, or to iconographic inventions such as the Three Living and the Three Dead. There are only two or three poems which develop the old theme of the decomposing corpse, and generally the whole complex of the humiliations of burial and the grave is ignored.

Whilst the explanation of this may be the straightforward one of the influence of the Passion lyric, it may also be possible that the content of the death lyric was influenced by the recurrent outbreaks of plague in the fourteenth and fifteenth centuries,[1] influenced in the sense that when the immediate probability of death and the inescapability of its sights were so unnaturally intensified, verse descriptions could only seem ironically irrelevant. There is no description of the plague in medieval England[2] comparable to the powerful and detailed description by Boccaccio in the Prologue to the *Decameron*[3] nor by Petrarch in the much-quoted letter to his brother at Avignon.[4] Nor is there anything to compare with the descriptions by later English writers, such as Dekker and Defoe, who drew from it also the traditional moral applications, imagining the body of a rich man 'bruisde and prest with threescore dead men' at the bottom of a trench,[5] or, after the emptying of the dead-cart into a pit, the bodies of rich and poor 'huddled together into the common grave of mankind'.[6] It is, however, certain that in England in the Middle Ages a high proportion of the population died, and that methods of burial were necessarily humiliating and inadequate. The chronicler, Robert of Avesbury, refers to the practice of burial in a common pit;[7] and at times corpses were left unburied in houses,

---

[1] For accounts of the plague see G. G. Coulton, *The Black Death* (London, 1929), and F. A. Gasquet, *The Great Pestilence* (London, 1893), though both are unreliable and tendentious; also C. Creighton, *A History of Epidemics in Britain*, i (Cambridge, 1891), 114–236.

[2] References to the plague in English literature are rare, and chronicles often contain nothing but the much-repeated phrase *magna mortalitas*. The following is a little more elaborate: 'Tunc villae, olim hominibus refertissimae, suis destitutae sunt colonis; et adeo crebro pestis invaluit, ut vix vivi potuerunt mortuos sepelire', *Chronicon Angliae 1328–88 auctore monacho quodam Sancti Albani*, ed. E. M. Thompson, Rolls Series, 1874, p. 27.

[3] Trans. J. M. Rigg (London, 1941), 4–11.

[4] Passages in translation are quoted by Gasquet, op. cit. 29–30; the full text is in *Epistolae familiares* (London, 1601), 290–303.

[5] Thomas Dekker, *Plague Pamphlets*, ed. F. P. Wilson (Oxford, 1925), 29.

[6] *History of the Plague in London 1665*, *Works*, v (London, 1855), 47.

[7] *De gestis Edwardi tertii* (Rolls Series, 1889), ed. E. M. Thompson, 406–7: 'Eodem die mortis xx, xl, lx, et multotiens multo plura corpora defunctorum simul in eadem

streets, or fields: Boccaccio describes how often it was the stench alone which drew attention to the dead.[1] The irreverent treatment of a corpse was thus no longer a poetic idea, springing from the desire to probe beneath the superficial, conventional decencies, but must have been widely evident on account of the necessity of organizing burials on such a vast scale.

The widely held view that as the occurrences and appearances of death became more terrifying so did its aesthetic representation become more gruesome and distasteful is not in general true of the English lyric. On the contrary, a comparison with the thirteenth-century lyric suggests that the more stridently life itself supplied the warning of the inevitability and repulsiveness of the grave, the less articulate was its expression in literature. In many ways fifteenth-century poetry is reticent and discreetly evasive about the horrors of death. In so far as some of it may seem more macabre than earlier poetry, this springs, not from the presentation of horrific and realistic detail, but from the dependency on iconographic forms.

The habit of representing skeletons and larvae in art developed so quickly in all western European countries that it is difficult to find its place of origin. In particular, there seems no way of distinguishing to what extent the new visual forms received both content and authority from late classical art,[2] and to what extent they sprang from the supposedly coarsened sensibility of the plague survivors. Moreover, not even a combination of both of these influences can provide a complete explanation, for the willingness to paint or carve a decomposing body cannot be dissociated from the production, abroad at least, of iconographic themes such as the winepress of the Passion: in all of these can be seen a loss of a sense of decorum which would indicate that not all subjects suitable for expression in words could with no less fitness be depicted visually. Some of the lyrics, notably those in B.M. Add. MS. 37049, are accompanied by illuminations of tombs, skeletons, and corpses. But the far larger number, unillustrated though they have iconographic analogues, share with these a particular quality of repulsiveness that properly belongs to the visual representations of death. These lyrics are both more formal and more macabre than their predecessors, acquiring both qualities from the visual forms which they describe or imply.

fovea tradebantur ecclesiasticae sepulturae.' Information about the difficulties—both practical and religious—of dealing with such large numbers of dead may be found in A. Hamilton Thompson, 'Registers of John Gynewell, Bishop of Lincoln, for the years 1347–1350', *Archaeological Journal*, lxviii (1911), 301–60, and 'The Pestilences of the Fourteenth Century in the Diocese of York', ibid. lxxi (1914), 97–154.

[1] *Decameron*, 10.

[2] F. P. Weber, *Aspects of Death in Art Epigram and Poetry*, 1–63.

There is a large group of poems, of widely varying styles, that are in the form of warnings from the dead. They illustrate both tendencies described: some are closely associated with visual representations, others are visually imprecise and written in a narrative, didactic style; many poems of course fall between these two extremes. In discussing them it seems best to begin with those that are manifestly iconographic since they are accompanied by illustrations, and then to continue by a gradual progression to reach those that are quite removed from any warning meditative image.

There are two verses in B.M. Add. MS. 37049,[1] which are illustrated by the painting of a double tomb.[2] This kind of tomb, which became current in England from the late fourteenth century onwards, consists of two layers: on the top lies a statue clothed in the full dignity of royal, aristocratic, or ecclesiastical robes, whilst underneath is carved a skeleton or naked body, partly decomposed, and sometimes with worms crawling upon it. There were quite a number of tombs of this kind in England, such as that of John Fitzalan (d. 1434) at Arundel[3] or that of Thomas Beckington (d. 1465) at Wells.[4] The best known is perhaps that of Henry Chichele at Canterbury: on the top of his tomb there lies an image of him in cope and mitre, with a line of writing giving his identity, whilst underneath is a swathed and wasted corpse with the following words:

> Quisquis eris qui transieris rogo memoreris
> Tu quod eris mihi consimilis qui post morieris,
> Omnibus horribilis, pulvis, vermis, caro vilis.[5]

Here is put into words the significance of the iconographic form, and the tomb is particularly interesting for that reason. But words are hardly necessary to demonstrate that this kind of tomb was a most striking physical embodiment of one half of the corpse's traditional contrast between *quod eram* and *quod sum*.

One of the illustrations of the double tomb in B.M. Add. MS. 37049 shows a tomb, on the top of which lies a crowned king, holding an orb

---

[1] 'Ffader sum tyme what was þu', *Index*, 789, f. 86ᵛ, and 'In þe ceson of huge mortalite', Karl Brunner, 'Mittelenglische Todesgedichte', *Archiv*, clxvii (1957), 30–35.

[2] Double tombs have been discussed by E. H. Kantorowicz, *The King's Two Bodies* (Princeton, 1957), 431–6. The use in B.M. Add. MS. 37049, however, shows that his ingenious interpretation of their significance (that they illustrate the principle 'Dignitas non moritur') is not correct. Of similar moralizing significance are the skulls, which in the fifteenth century in northern Europe appear on the back of portrait panels (H. W. Janson, 'The Putto with the Death's Head', *Art Bulletin*, xix, 1937, 436).

[3] Richard Gough, *Sepulchral Monuments*, ii (London, 1796), 359 and pl. cxxv.

[4] Ibid. 209 and pl. lxxx.

[5] Ibid. 129 and pl. xliii; Weber, op. cit. 106–7. 'Whosoever you are who will pass by I beg you remember this: you who will die after me will be like me, horrifying to all, dust, worm-ridden, worthless flesh.'

and sceptre, whilst underneath a corpse, half-skeleton, is covered with
long worms. It accompanies a version of the *exemplum* of the emperor's
son who visits his father's tomb.[1] It is obviously a more elaborate variant
of the story (described in Appendix H), to which the names of Simon
de Crépy and the Comte of Pontoise were sometimes attached. This
exemplum, in which a son is converted by looking into his father's grave,
was exceptionally popular throughout the Middle Ages, and was included
in many English preaching-manuscripts, such as MSS. Harley 7322
and Harley 2316, and in the *Summa praedicantium* of John Bromyard.
This exceptional version, however, actually contains a dialogue between
the living and the dead. The prose narrative tells how a wicked emperor
dies, and is succeeded by a yet more wicked son, whose career of evil is
ended by his prudent steward, who says to him: 'Syr, behald unto ʒour
fader, which þat was so worthy a knyght, and so nobyll a conqueror.
Take hede how he lyges in his grave, wormes and snakes etyng opon
hym.' The emperor is angry until he sees the tomb open, and holds the
following dialogue:

> Ffader, sum tyme what was þou?
> Swylk, son, as I was, art þu nowe.
> A fowle stynke I fele of þe.
> Son, wele fowler sone sal cum of þe.
> Horrybyll bestes restes wit þe.
> Thow sal cum and rest wit me.
> þi fayr flesche falles and fades away.
> Son, so þine do þat is now so gay.[2]

The emperor then returns home penitent, and has a painting made to
remind him of this moral lesson: 'And in hys bed chawmer he gart
paynt þe lyknes of his fader as he lay in his grave. And when he was
styrred to any syn he beheld þe ymage of his fader, knawing wele þat
he come fro þe erthe and suld turne to þe erthe.'

This verse seems almost naïve in its laboured retorts and its clumsy
efforts to find new forms of irony by which the dead can jeeringly
rebuke the living. The writer's intention undoubtedly exceeded his
powers of execution, but the intention itself was clever: for this is an
attempt at stichomythia, which with its antitheses and ironical repetition
of the opponent's words, was very well suited to the context. It is a pity
that the fumbling style almost obscures the pointed fittingness of the
rhetorical pattern.

The other representation of a double tomb in the same manuscript
shows a dead queen or lady, in all her former finery, with a row of
heraldic shields upon her tomb, whilst beneath this magnificence lies

---

[1] The story is on ff. 86ᵛ–87ʳ. See above pp. 88–89.
[2] f. 86ᵛ.

a putrifying body. The accompanying stanza consists partly of commentary on this and partly of introduction to a debate between a corpse and worms, which has its own illustrations (this debate will be discussed later). The relevant part of the stanza is as follows:

> Take hede unto my fygure here abowne
> And se how sumtyme I was fresche and gay,
> Now turned to wormes mete and corrupcoun.
> Bot fowle erth and stynkyng slyme and clay.[1]

These lines, which concentrate solely on the *quod eram, quod sum* antithesis are a perfect match to the iconographic form. But, although in diction and stylistic smoothness they have far more poetic pretension than the previous dialogue, structurally they are less important, being no more than *titulus* verses: whereas the first-mentioned double tomb is an illustration of the *exemplum*, the second is a self-contained picture, and it is the words that are dependent upon it.

Double tombs were necessarily an expensive way of conveying the moral and warning of the grave: normally they would only be found in cathedral and abbey churches, unless a village church was also the burial place of a noble family, as with the tomb of Alice de la Pole at Ewelme. Therefore, though their message was powerful, many people would have no opportunity of seeing such a tomb; no doubt their reproduction in B.M. Add. MS. 37049 was in part a device for making a wider use of so pregnant but costly an image. Usually, however, the epitaphial warning was inscribed on a memorial brass, or possibly on some kind of scroll,[2] without sculptural illustration. Fourteenth-century Latin epitaphs of this kind have already been mentioned. The first surviving vernacular expression of this theme seems to be an epitaph, dated 1425, from Higham-Ferrars, Northants, and with it is combined the favourite injunction, *Disce mori*, and a statement of Death the Leveller:

> Such as ye be, such wer we,
> Such as we be, such shall ye be.
> Lerneth to deye, that is the lawe
> That this lif yow to wol drawe.
> Sorwe or gladnesse nought letten age
> But on he cometh to lord and page. . . .[3]

These lines are of course weak in style. Medieval verse epitaphs, locally composed, show the same amateurish and primitive style of writing, as do country epitaphs at all other periods. Their content, however,

---

[1] *Archiv*, clxvii, 30. The second part of the stanza introduces the debate between the body and the worms, see below, pp. 328–30.

[2] On scrolls used for this purpose see R. H. Robbins, 'An Epitaph for Duke Humphrey (1447)', *Neuphilologische Mitteilungen*, lvi (1955), 241–9.

[3] T. F. Ravenshaw, *Antiente Epitaphes* (London, 1878), 8.

prevents them from being merely ludicrous, for strength of style is not needed to give it point; indeed, the gaucheness of the writing often curiously heightens the personal reference of the warning.

It would be tedious to enumerate the many fifteenth- and sixteenth-century verse epitaphs employing traditional death themes. The one that has just been quoted is typical in regard to both content and quality of the epitaphial verses that seem to have been composed for the occasion. The better epitaphs are short verses or quotations from longer poems, which were originally composed as poetry on the theme of death. 'If man him biðocte' was, for instance, used in this way,[1] and so were stanzas from the later and expanded versions of 'Erþe toc of erþe'.[2] The most effective epitaph is the final stanza of the long poem, 'Ffare well, this world' (which we shall be discussing later):

> Farewell my friendes the tide abydeth no man
> I am departed hence, and so shall ye.
> But in this passage the best song that I can
> Is requiem eternam, now Iesu grant it me,
> When I have ended all mine adversitie,
> Grant me in Paradise to have a mansion,
> That shedst th[y] blood for my redemption.[3]

This stanza occurs as a fitting climax to the whole poem, but, with its mixture of warning and faith, it is also moving as an independent epitaph.

Of course, not all medieval epitaphs are warnings or quotations from the lyrics on death. Many record no more than the name of the person there buried and a brief prayer, but it obviously became a pious custom for a person to desire that his dead body should, as it were, preach a warning to the living, as for so long the dead had fictionally done in *exempla*. For the theme 'quod tu es ego fui' the wheel thus came full circle, and the warning from the tombs of the Appian Way[4] passed, perhaps by means of *exempla*, back into sepulchral inscriptions.

Fictional warnings from the dead continued in sermons and *exempla*. In MS. Harley 2316, a manuscript not much later than John of Grimestone's preaching-book, occurs a collection of *exempla*, of which four contain verses.[5] Though all of these are written in the direct style and obvious rhythms, which would make them easy to memorize, they are more accomplished than the epitaphs. The best is the following verse,

---

[1] *Index*, 4129.

[2] Ravenshaw, op. cit. 35.

[3] For this, and the subject in general, see D. Gray, 'A Middle English Epitaph', *Notes and Queries*, ccvi (Apr. 1961), 132–5.

[4] See pp. 402–4 below.

[5] Three of these have been printed, Brown xiv, 53, 54, and T. Wright, *Latin Stories*, Percy Society, viii. 107; the fourth is quoted below.

addressed by a dead merchant to a colleague whom he had made his executor:

> Weilawey what me is wo,
> now rote ilc in molde.
> My frendes love is al ago,
> þe deede has fewe holde.
> He ben now mi meest foon
> þat me meest loven shoelde;
> He drawen to hem and fro me don,
> þat i spenden ne woelde.[1]

There is no reason to think that story and verse were composed together or for each other, and, indeed, the narrative context here constricts the feeling of the poem. The falseness of executors was a topical medieval subject[2] (related to the ancient satirical theme of legacy hunting),[3] and had in the Body and Soul poems become an element in the exploration of death, for the executors' appropriation of a dead man's wealth for their own pleasure was seen as yet another symptom of the futility of accumulating riches. It is in this way that the subject is used in the Harley verse, for it is only one idea (in line 7) in a sequence of traditional thoughts: the putrefaction of the grave, the friendlessness of the dead, and, in the last two lines, the moral paradox, expressed frequently in epitaphs, 'quod donavi habeo . . . quod servavi perdidi'.[4] The last four lines are perhaps stylistically unremarkable, but the first four, culminating in the climax of the understatement 'þe deede has fewe holde', have a jingly strength in their communication of sad irony.

Similar in style is a verse embodied in a Latin sermon, in which the preacher apostrophizes a dead noble woman and imagines that she speaks:

Tell us, O lady *de blacworth*, what worth have worldly glory and the aforesaid vanities, of which men are wont to make boast. Once you were fair in body, gentle of blood, privileged with honours, abounding in houses and wealth. All these things you possessed, and now of all you can say thus:

> Now all men mowe sen be me,
> that wordys Joye is vanyte.
> I was a lady; now am I non.
> I hadde worchepes; now it ys begon.
> I was fayr and gentil both.
> Now ich man wyle my body loth.
> My frendys, my godes me hav forsake.
> To wyrmes mete now am I take.

---

[1] f. 2ʳ. *Þe deede has few holde*: 'few are faithful to the dead', or, more probably, by understatement, 'none is faithful to the dead'.

[2] For independent lyrics on the subject see the index to the *Index* s.v. executors.

[3] David S. Wiesen, *St. Jerome as a Satirist* (Cornell, 1964), 26.

[4] Ravenshaw, op. cit. 5. 'What I gave I have . . . what I kept I lost.'

Of al the wor[l]d now haf I no3th
bitt gode dedes that I wrogth.
Only tho schuln abyde wit me.
Al other thynges arn vanyte.[1]

The contents of this verse are familiar: all worldly privileges now gone, the repulsiveness of the dead, 'wyrmes mete', and finally the Last Judgement theme (based on Apocalypse xiv. 13, and well known from *Everyman*) of good deeds as a dead person's sole companion. In kind it is a cross between an *exemplum* verse and an epitaph. On the one hand it is a preacher's invention used in a sermon, on the other hand the lesson is drawn from one prosperous, well known, and recently dead. The whole unit of verse plus sermon context resembles a homiletic poem, which will be discussed later, in which a rhetorical and homiletic disquisition on death is given precision by reference to what was no doubt the local tomb of Ralph, Lord Cromwell. It is a fifteenth-century development that the minatory dead are not solely great men of the past, such as Alexander, but also contemporary figures known to the audience. The effectiveness of such topical reference is unfortunately nowadays quite lost.

Though the warning from the dead is particularly characteristic of *exempla* verses and epitaphs, there are also a number of long fifteenth-century poems set in this form. One of these shows exceptionally a return to the theme of the Signs of Corruption. It is preserved in MS. Bodley 789, a manuscript of the first half of the fifteenth century, containing the typical assembly of miscellaneous devotional treatises of the kind which came to be privately owned during this period. It is preceded by the rubric 'Here is a good counseil for synful men to take heede to while þei ben in þis liif', and is as follows:

Mi leeve liif þat lyvest in welþe,
In mete and drinke and fayr schroud,
In richesse, honour and in bodili helþe,
Loke þerfore þou be nou3t proud.

But whanne þu art in þi beste lekinge,
Have mynde sum tyme I þe rede,
How foule þou schalt be and stynkinge,
A litil after þat þou art deed.

I was ful fair, now am I foul,
My faire fleisch bigynneþ forto stynke;
Wormis fynden at me greet prow,
I am hire mete, I am hire drinke.

[1] Owst, *Literature and Pulpit*, 530 (Owst has translated the Latin prose into English).

I ligge wounden in a clout,
In boordis narwe I am nailid:
Allas þat evre I was proud,
Now alle mi freendis ben to me failid.

In mi riggeboon brediþ an addir kene,
Min eiȝen dasewyn swiþe dymme:
Mi guttis rotin, myn heer is grene,
Mi teeþ grennen swiþe grymme.

Mi bodi þat sumtyme was so gay,
Now lieþ and rotiþ in þe grounde.
Mi fairhed is al now goon awai,
And I stynke foulere þan an hounde.

Mi faire feet, mi fingris longe,
Myn eiȝen, myn eeren and mi lymes alle,
Noon wil now wiþ oþer honge,
But everech wole from oþer falle.

I rede every man þat wiis wil be,
Take kepe herof þat I have seid,
þanne may he sikir of heven be,
Whanne he schal in erþe be laid.[1]

This poem has never been printed, and it is perhaps too repellent in content and too inadequate in style to deserve inclusion in any anthology. The simple style is hardly sufficient to clothe the deliberately repulsive meditative image or the nakedly didactic advice. Nevertheless its emphasis on the decay of feminine beauty is worth noticing. With its repeated reference to former beauty, and details such as 'fingris longe', the poem is obviously spoken by a woman, and it was evidently thought that the rotting of feminine beauty gave a turn of the screw to the theme of putrefaction.[2] The feeling in this is that epitomized in the common *exemplum* of the hermit, who was cured of lustful thoughts by opening the grave of his dead mistress.[3] In the fifteenth century there was certainly a preference for the warning from the female dead, but there is nothing in England comparable to the most unnecessary and most repellent exploitation of the idea, namely the French adaptation of the *Danse macabre* in female form.

With 'Mi leeve liif' it is interesting to compare the speech of the risen Lazarus in the Towneley Cycle, for in it the same themes of decay

[1] f. 149ʳ. L. 7, *Stynkinge*, MS. *stynke*. *Scroud*: clothes; *prow*: profit; *dasewyn*: grow dark.

[2] This poem may be contrasted with a French one, quoted by Debruyne (op. cit. ii. 193–4), which is far more decorous and formal in that its structural outline is the rhetorical list of the parts of feminine beauty, not the signs of corruption.

[3] For references see Herbert, *Catalogue of Romances*, iii. 20, 463, 501, and 530.

are used, but with such eloquence that nausea is dissipated in awe. Correctly, of course, this speech is not a lyric, except in the sense that many of the formal monologues in the mystery plays are only distinguishable from lyrics by their dramatic contexts. Nevertheless, the proper place for a discussion of them would normally be in a work on medieval drama. But the play of Lazarus is exceptional in that it consists of little but the monologue, and the subject here seems to have been used simply as an occasion for a dramatic warning on the horrors of death. Moreover it is such an outstanding example of the organization of the traditional death themes that a digression about it seems relevant.

The starting-point for the play seems to be the idea of physical decay hinted at in the New Testament narrative: in all the mystery plays alarm is expressed at the remembrance of Lazarus's body, four days dead, just as in many medieval pictures the bystanders realistically hold their noses. But it is only the Towneley writer who, with imaginative invention, perceives the opportunity to show a character who is alive as he speaks and yet has undergone the decay of death. The speech is composed of the early and familiar themes, the gnawing of worms, the roof touching the nose, the bareness of the winding sheet, the falseness of executors, etc., and it is set out in sermon style as a warning of the future, yet, because of the strength of the style and the rhythms of the verse, the tone suggests the agony of recollected experience and the passionate feeling of personal knowledge:

> Your dede is Wormes coke,
> youre myrroure here ye loke,
> And let me be youre boke,
>   youre sampill take by me;
> ffro dede you cleke in cloke,
>   sich shall ye all be.
>
> . . . . . .
>
> Youre rud that was so red / your lyre the lylly lyke,
> Then shall be wan as led / and stynke as dog in dyke;
> Wormes shall in you brede / as bees dos in the byke,
> And ees out of youre hede / Thus-gate shall paddokys pyke;
>   To pike you ar preste
>   Many uncomly beest,
>   Thus thai shall make a feste
>   Of youre flesh and of youre blode.
>   ffor you then sorows leste
>   The moste has of youre goode.[1]

In most warnings from the dead there is a deliberate flatness of style:

---

[1] E.E.T.S., E.S. 71, 390–1. *Coke*: food; *rud*: cheek; *lyre*: complexion; *byke*: nest of bees; *paddokys*: toads; *pyke*: bite, pick at; *ffor you then sorows . . . goode*: For he who has now inherited the most of your possessions is the one who grieves for you least.

the full emotional response is to be supplied by the reader outside the poem. But the style here suggests a speaker who is appalled by what he must say. It is therefore far more effective poetically and is at the same time an especially frightening *Memento mori*.

A yet more literary version of the theme may be seen in *The Thre Deid Pollis*, a poem printed amongst the works of Henryson by Harvey Wood, though ascribed in the manuscript to Patrick Johnston. In it three skulls, thrown up perhaps like Yorick's in a graveyard (and three in number no doubt through the influence of the Three Living and the Three Dead), apostrophize the passers-by, the 'wantone yowth' and 'ladeis quhyt'. Their present finery, evocatively described, is contrasted with their future state, so poor and hideous:

> O wantone yowth, als fresche as lusty may,
> farest of flowris, renewit quhyt and reid,
> Behald our heidis: O lusty gallandis gay,
> full laichly thus sall ly thy lusty heid,
> holkit and how, and wallowit as the weid,
> Thy crampand hair, and elk thy cristall ene;
> full cairfully conclud sall dulefull deid;
> Thy example heir be us it may be sene.[1]

The contrast is summed up by the ancient and unanswerable riddle:

> Quha was farest, or fowlest, of us thre?
> or quhilk of us of kin was gentillar?

The poem uses the diction and conventional description of courtly poetry: the ladies have 'hals [so] elegant' and 'finyearis small, quhyt as quhailis bane', and death's ravages are expressed in the same elevated style, '. . . full cairfully conclud sall dulefull deid'. Little is made of the possibility of harsh ironic contrast, of the kind found in the monologue of Lazarus, where worldly values are described in conventional diction and imagery, 'Your rud that was so red / your lyre the lyyly like', but its fate in deliberately low vocabulary and realistically repulsive imagery, '. . . and stynke as dog in dyke'. The sharpness of the message in *The Thre Deid Pollis* is to some extent taken off by this sustained pleasantness of style, and also by diffuse moralization: nevertheless the work succeeds both in warning like an epitaph and pleasing like a poem.

The typical fifteenth-century tendency to overwhelm the warning meditative image beneath a weight of moralization can, however, be seen far more clearly in another poem from B.M. Add. MS. 37049. It

---

[1] *Poems and Fables*, ed. Harvey Wood (Edinburgh, 1933), 205–7. *Renewit*: grown fresh; *lusty*: joyful; *holkit and how*: pitted and hollow; *wallowit*: discoloured; *crampand*: curly; *conclud*: bring to an end. With the number three may be compared the three skulls against a ruined wall in the engraving by Barthel Beham (*Art Bulletin*, xix, 439 and pl. 27).

begins well with a macabre and ironic transference of the *O vos omnes* text, 'O ȝe al whylk þat by me cummes and gothe', followed by the warning that all these passers-by shall come 'to lyke symylitude'; and the same idea is reiterated in the last stanza, which is written in the epitaph tradition:

> Who sum ever it be þat by þis cummes and gothe,
> Stande and behold þis litterall scripture,
> And it se and over rede, be þou lefe or lothe,
> þi wepyng teres fast sched in gode ure;
> þat art now as I was in warldly fygure,
> I was as þou art sum tyme be dayes olde:
> O pray ȝe al for me, I pray ȝow, a þowsand folde.[1]

But the eleven intervening stanzas could equally well be spoken by a preacher. The material is a series of rhetorical questions: Why are you so bent upon the seven deadly sins? Where are Samson, Solomon, Cicero, Aristotle, etc.? Why is your heart so set on worldly prosperity, etc.? Such questions when asked by the dead should be coloured by horror and melancholy, but in this poem they are presented in an impersonal, hortatory style. There is no suggestion in the poem that the questions spring, not from rational reflection, but from personal experience. The framework of the warning from the dead is used only mechanically and ineffectively.

Another warning from the dead, which has an *O vos omnes* opening, is that beginning, 'All crysten men þat walke by me, / Be-hold and se þis dulfull syȝht'.[2] Unfortunately one of the two texts most easily available nowadays, and indeed the one which at many places preserves the better readings, is that in E.E.T.S. 15, but it is based on MS. Ashmole 61, where, by the addition of three lines near the beginning (lines 4–7), which disturb the metre, it has been turned into a prologue for the story of the Falmouth Squire damned for his adultery, but this is evidently a rather inappropriate adaptation in that the speaker confesses most of the seven deadly sins, whilst the story is closely designed to emphasize the need for faithfulness in marriage.[3] There seems to be a further confusion in the last two lines, in which the speaker bids farewell on the blowing of a horn, as though this were a return from the dead made to a specific person as in so many *exempla*.

---

[1] *Archiv*, clxvii, 28. In the manuscript the poem is inappropriately illustrated by a figure of death.

[2] E.E.T.S .15, 123–6; cf. ibid 26 (revised ed. 1914), 115–16.

[3] It is only in the Ashmole MS. that this poem and the story of the Falmouth Squire are combined. Apart from this, 'All crysten men' occurs in five manuscripts and the Falmouth Squire in eight, all different. The poem should therefore not be referred to, with Furnivall and the *Index*, as the Prologue to the Adulterous Falmouth Squire.

The main part of the poem, however, bears out the opening and is quite clearly a warning from the dead. In its first lines and general design it resembles a Latin poem beginning:

> O vos omnes qui transitis
> Et figuram hanc inspicite,
> Memores mei semper estis
> Et mundum hunc despicite.[1]

Both poems are highly didactic warnings from a dead person, who is at the same time in the grave ('Nunc a vermibus corrosus', 'With todys and snaks, as ȝe may se, / I ame gnawyne my body a-boute') and in hell (e.g. 'Voraci flammae sic sum datus', 'Ever to bryne in þe pytte of helle'). In both poems the speaker died in the midst of life, absorbed in the pleasures of the world, and careless of repentance, and in both he insists on the deadly sins that he committed, which are characteristically those of the rich:

> In lechery I lede my lyfe,
> Ffore I hade gode and gold at wylle;
> I scleuȝe my selve with-outene knyffe,
> And of glotony I hade my fylle;
> In sleuth I ley, and slepyd stylle.[2]

In both poems too the speaker emphasizes himself as an example for others, 'Relictum vobis sum exemplum', 'Wo be þei, who ... wyll not be-wer be me'. Moreover, both poems are similar in structure, in that they are alike in their lack of steady progression of thought: the ideas of sin and of its disastrous consequences weave in and out with no discernible pattern. Whilst this lack of steady direction is quite common in the English lyric, it is rarer in Latin poetry. In both poems this ill-organized reversion to the same themes blunts their sharpness of outline. It is thus conceivable that the English poem derived from the Latin, but there is no close verbal echo to prove this, except in the first two lines, and the resemblance there could derive from a common tradition, which formed both poems, but which only at one point became verbally chrystallized. Nevertheless it is worth considering that the English might be a native adaptation of the Latin, and, whether it is or not, certainly the Latin casts light on the genre of the English.

All the poems, which have been discussed so far, have been, at least to a limited extent, meditative: in them there has always been some explicit

---

[1] K. Künstle, *Die Legende der drei Lebenden und der drei Toten und der Totentanz* (Freiburg im Breisgau, 1908), 35–36, where the first stanzas are printed. 'O all ye who pass by look at this form; ever remember me and despise this world.' The whole poem is in *A.H.* xlvi. 307, but with a poor text of the first stanza. The poem survives in one manuscript of English origin, MS. Douce 54, with 'Noctis sub silencio' and 'Mortales Dominus cunctos' (see below, p. 349, footnote 1).

[2] E.E.T.S. 15, 124.

reference to the worm-devoured body in the grave. There remain to be
discussed a small number of poems, which, though they are dramatic
and didactic warnings from the dead, contain no reference whatsoever to
a warning meditative image. The best of these is that beginning, 'Ffare
well this world! I take my leve for ever.'[1] The dramatic and effective
abruptness of its opening seems to have been influenced by the earlier
French genre of *congé* poem, in which the poet bade farewell to a town
or country. The individual quality of the poem springs, however, partly
from the use in it of literary metaphors for death. The first, 'I am arested
to apere at goddes face', is now well known from Shakespeare's 'this
fell sergeant, death',[2] but it seems to have developed in the late fourteenth
century—it is used for instance in the famous sermon of Thomas
Wimbledon preached at St. Paul's Cross[3]—and no doubt became current through the widespread tendency to personify death. The idea of
death knocking upon the door is probably an extension of this, though
it might alternatively be an instance of the bitter parody by which death
uses the forms appropriate to Christ (e.g. the *O vos omnes* text), in which
case this line would echo the *ecce sto* theme.[4] The image of the game of
chess again is not new, though it is now better known from the *Book of
the Duchess*, where the hostile and infallible opponent is not death but
fortune. Even more important than these metaphors, however, is the
poem's lack of blunt clarity:

> Speke softe, ye folk, for I am leyd aslepe!
> I have my dreme, in trust is moche treson.
> ffram dethes hold feyne wold I make a lepe,
> But my wysdom is turnyd into feble resoun;
> [I see this worldis joye lastith but a season].
> Wold to god, I had remembyrd me be-forne!
> I sey no more but be ware of ane horne![5]

Evasion of a full and explicit statement can be seen in the last line, with
its enigmatic reference to death's summoning trumpet,[6] as though it
were referring to some mysterious event too frightening or too esoteric
to be fit for explicit statement; or the line, 'Speke softe, ye folk, for I am
leyd aslepe', with its compressed and elusive irony, since the dead cannot

---

[1] Brown xv, 149.

[2] For other sixteenth-century references see Samuel Chew, *The Pilgrimage of Life*
(New Haven and London, 1962), 245–6.

[3] *A famous Middle English Sermon preached at St. Paul's Cross, 1388*, ed. K. F.
Sundén (Göteborg, 1925), 23–24. In the same context is a description of the Signs of
Death. This passage is referred to by Owst, *Literature and Pulpit*, 532, where he quotes
another example from a sermon of John Waldeby.

[4] An echo, perhaps indirectly, of Horace (see below, p. 401) can also be considered
a possibility.

[5] Brown xv, 236–7.

[6] For Death's trumpet see below, p. 354 and footnote 4.

wake, and, if the living should speak softly, it is for a more compelling
and alarming reason. The middle stanza is in fact strikingly unlike typical
medieval style, for it gains its effect, not by startling lucidity, but by the
romantically half-concealed, which forces the reader's imagination to
complete or disentwine the meaning, a co-operation which leads the
content to be apprehended in a particularly personal way. There are in
fact hints of this style in all the stanzas, save the last, as, for instance, in
the superficially irrelevant aside, 'Som be this day that shall not be to-
morow'. The very last stanza, however, has no subtlety, but, combined
with a prayer, returns to the familiar warning, 'I moste departe hens and
so shall ye'. This directness is worth observing, in that it led to the
stanza becoming dissociated from the rest and used as an epitaph: at
least seven instances of this are known and no doubt there were more.[1]

This poem seems to have been the first to make use of the farewell
address of the dead man, but thereafter it was used again, no doubt
encouraged by the many late medieval secular love poems, which make
use of the *congé* structure. In the early sixteenth-century collection of
poetry, MS. Rawl. C. 813,[2] the form is made use of in two poems. One is
the lament of Sir Gruffydd ab Rhys, a knight who had been present at the
field of the Cloth of Gold, and who died of some unknown cause, perhaps
at Calais. The author of the poem imagines that he was musing at sunset,
when a griffith (griffin) flew over head, coming from the mountains of
Wales and saying a 'hevy and lamentable epytaphye':

> Farewell! England, farewell! Walys;
> I take my leve now att thys tyde.
> Farewell! Cales and Englyshe pales.
> Farewell! Kyng Henry, I may nott abyde,
> dethe hathe me lancyde into þe syde.
> Farewell! knyghthode, farewell! chyvalrye!
> of the curteys courte, farewell! good cumpanye.[3]

After this opening, the main part of the poem is concerned with sympathy for the knight's widow (the next poem in the manuscript is an
elegy spoken by her), but the last verse with its warning of death's
'soden darte' and invitation to take warning from his example, returns
the poem to the older tradition. The other poem is spoken by the dead
Edward Stafford,[4] who at the age of forty-three had been executed at the
order of Henry VIII. Although supposedly spoken from the grave, like
the last poem, it contains no uncourtly reference to putrefaction, and in
fact it may more properly be called a moral wheel of fortune tragedy,

---

[1] See above, p. 315 and footnote 3.

[2] The contents of the manuscript have been printed by F. M. Padelford, 'The
Songs in Manuscript Rawlinson C. 813', *Anglia*, xxxi. 309–97.

[3] No. 19, *Anglia*, xxxi. 348.   [4] Ibid. 364–5.

for the speaker sees in his own fall from high estate a punishment for pride ('through my greate pride I have a soden fall'). The double nature of this poem—in form deriving from the warning from the grave, in content from *The Fall of Princes*—is reflected in the contents of the manuscript, in which there is copied, on the one hand, 'All crysten men that walke by me', and, on the other, a moral poem summarizing the wheel of fortune stories of Eleanor Cobham and Duke Humphrey of Gloucester, stories later to be incorporated and told at length in the *Mirror for Magistrates*.[1]

There is one other poem which demonstrates this ambiguity, the lament spoken from the grave by Edward IV.[2] Despite a discrepancy of dates the poem was originally ascribed to Lydgate, and was copied in two manuscripts, containing some of his work. Later it was ascribed to Skelton, but, if Lydgate is too early, Skelton is too late, for the poem depends for part of its effect on topicality, such as a knowledge of Edward's sumptuous building works or his exaction of taxes for the French wars. The poem is written in an elaborate stanza form, with the grey, edgy style of much fifteenth-century verse, with a preference for obtrusive and inharmonious three- or four-syllable words. Even the *ubi sunt* passage is too dry and hortatory to be evocative, and the poem is chiefly moving through the effect of the refrain from the Office for the Dead, 'Ecce nunc in pulvere dormio' (Job vii. 21). In ancestry the poem is indebted to the traditional idea that the omnipotence of death is most powerfully displayed in the death of a king: some of the most popular *exempla*, for instance, were those associated with the Alexander legend, thus stressing how even the magnificence and virtues of so great a conqueror ended in the grave. At the same time, the idea of inventing a lament for a recently dead king was perhaps influenced by the funeral tradition of the Black Prince's epitaph or the tomb of Henry Chichele. Nevertheless, the emphasis on fortune, who smiled upon the king with 'sewger lyppus', and then banished him in death long before the end of his natural span, clearly relates the poem to the *De Casibus* tradition, and it is easy to see why it was later included among the tragic tales of the *Mirror for Magistrates*,[3] even though formally it is out of place there. In the *Mirror for Magistrates*—as with some of Boccaccio's stories—it is the ghost of each historical character who appears in the poet's study and speaks: a ghost whose appearance is not clearly visualized, but who is probably identical with the figure in his lifetime.[4] It is certainly not a decaying corpse. But it is not this distinction in the nature of the

---

[1] Ed. L. B. Campbell (Cambridge, 1938), 432–59.

[2] Brown xv, 159.   [3] Op. cit. 236–9.

[4] On Boccaccio's framework in the *De casibus* see W. Farnham, *The Medieval Heritage of Elizabethan Tragedy* (Oxford, 1956), 73–74. The *Mirror for Magistrates* is discussed in ch. 7.

speaker which most importantly distinguishes the *De Casibus* tradition from that of the warning from the dead. It is rather that in the latter the speaker and the auditor are equal and interchangeable, *quod fui, tu es*, whilst the wheel of fortune tragedy is rather a moral comment upon the great and rich. The reaction of an ordinary man might well be that he was appalled and stirred by the thought of such calamities, and yet at the same time felt a satisfaction that 'He that is down needs fear no fall.'

The warning from the dead had been rare in the earlier lyric; indeed, it occurred only in *exemplum* verses. The chief developments in it of the later period were, on the one hand, its widespread use in epitaphs, and, on the other, its expansion into long, and often ornate, poems. The influence of analogous long Latin poems, such as the 'O vos omnes qui transitis / Et figuram hanc inspicite', may be suspected, but this influence cannot be proved, nor is its hypothesis urgently demanded. The history of the Body and Soul debate contrasts with this development in that, whereas in the earlier period it had been a striking expression of death themes, by the fifteenth century its use had declined. The latest and finest of the early debates, 'Als I lay in a winteris night',[1] had been written in the second half of the fourteenth century, but its manuscript transcription seems to have been restricted to the succeeding fifty years, though the six manuscripts are a testimony to its popularity within that period. The Latin analogue, 'Noctis sub silencio', continued to be copied: a fair but not remarkable proportion of its almost innumerable manuscripts are of English origin,[2] and it was printed once for English readers at Louvain in 1488.[3] Oddly enough it reappeared again at the beginning of the seventeenth century, when it was printed in a small volume with an English translation on the opposite page made by William Crashaw, the father of Richard Crashaw.[4] No medieval English version of the Body and Soul debate was ever printed, unlike the French *Débat du corps et de l'âme*, which was printed in nearly all of the many editions of the *Danse macabre*.

Despite the fact that the Body and Soul debate ceased to be a dominant form of death literature in England in the fifteenth century, there was one new translation of 'Noctis sub silencio':[5] it is preserved with two other death poems in MS. Porkington 10.[6] This translation has both the rhetorical adornments and the homiletic moralizing typical of its period.

---

[1] See above, pp. 98–102.

[2] Walther, *Das Streitgedicht*, 211–14.

[3] E. Ph. Goldschmidt, *Medieval Texts and their first Appearance in Print* (London, 1943), 33–4.

[4] See below, p. 365, footnote 3.

[5] Inc. 'The fadyr of pytte and most of myserycorde'. J. O. Halliwell, *Early English Miscellanies* (Warton Club, ii), 12–39.

[6] The contents of the manuscript have been enumerated by Auvo Kurvinen, 'MS. Porkington 10', *Neuphilologische Mitteilungen*, liv (1953), 33–67.

It is presented with a flourish as a translation from the Latin: in the first eight stanzas there occur an invocation to the Virgin for guidance in the work, and a translator's plea to the reader for correction and forbearance combined with an apology for his lack of skill, his 'sympul connyng and bestyal rudenysse'. This prolonged introduction now reads oddly: the conventional modest apology sounds decorous before, for example, Gavin Douglas's translation of the *Aeneid*, but out of place before a translation of a medieval Latin homiletic poem, however excellent the latter may be. Moreover, the attempted elevation of the opening is matched by the smooth style of the translation itself in its rhyme royal stanzas. A comparison with earlier versions suggests that poetically it was in a sense more rather than less *rudenysse* that was required.

The translation keeps closer to the Latin than does any of the other medieval versions. The general, though not invariable, method is to transpose one Latin quatrain into one English stanza of rhyme royal. Since, even then, some of the Latin content is often omitted, the English achieves its metrical pretensions at the cost of diffuseness. It would not be fair to imply that the English is everywhere inferior to the Latin and to its English predecessors. There are occasional colloquial touches, necessarily absent in the Latin, and dramatically effective: for instance, the Soul's recalling of the Body's former insistence on the pleasures of the world, '. . . of deth I take no hede: / I wylle dance whylle the world wylle pype'. There are also occasional inventions of ironic detail, as in the comparison of the shroud to a sheet, 'Al thi bede-schettes beth all rowȝe'. Above all, the well-established use of the language for poetic descriptions of aristocratic and luxurious living enables the poet to amplify the descriptions of the delights and elegances now lost and to make them particularly effective:

> Thy ryche vesture, thi beddys of collors dyverse,
> Thi wennesone, thi wyld foulle, spycus of delyte,
> Vesselle, nappre, mettus, I cannot reyhers,
> Sawsis, subdelytys to thine appetyte;
> Thy lusty pellois, thi schettus fayre and whyte;
> Where ys this now? one this was alle thi thouȝte:
> Her mayst thou se worldis joy is noȝte.[1]

But despite passages such as this, the translation in general lacks force and inventiveness, and any immediacy of effect is finally dispersed in the long moralizing conclusion, in which eight lines of the Latin are expanded into thirteen stanzas about Fulbert, who was a king's son, but after his vision adopted a life of poverty, etc., and which ends with a moralizing address to the reader. Whereas the Latin *Visio* and its

---

[1] *E. E. Misc.* 17-18. *Nappre*: table-linen; *subdelytys*: ornamental devices made of sugar.

earlier vernacular analogues are in the first person, so that the reader can identify himself with the speaker, in this version the hermit-visionary has been built up into an exemplary character, described in the third person, so that there is an increase of distance between the reader and the content of the poem. This distancing is of course matched by the effect of the formal opening and the style. This translation, which draws upon the devices and techniques of the fifteenth-century literary style, is interesting as showing the limitations of these for meditative poetry and therefore the superiority of the earlier direct and unself-conscious style.

In B.M. Add. MS. 37049 there are two works which show an interesting bifurcation in the decaying tradition of the Body and Soul debate. It has already been seen how the debate consisted partly in philosophical argument about the relative moral responsibilities of body and soul and partly in reproach and abuse which embodied all the important meditative death themes. In B.M. Add. MS. 37049 these interrelated parts have split in two. The manuscript contains no traditional debate, but has two other dialogues respectively emphasizing the two elements which had formerly been held together in one work. The moral-philosophical arguments concerning the degree of responsibility for sinful conduct borne respectively by Body and Soul are here isolated from any meditative description (though the illustrations show the corpse ugly and repellent) and presented in a prose translation of a passage from Guillaume de Guilleville's long narrative poem, the *Pèlerinage de l'âme*.[1] These arguments, when divided from horrific abuse, lose their dramatic force. We have the impression that the participants have become convenient mouthpieces for the analysis of an intellectual problem, not that intellectual argument has been put to the service of a literary depiction of the state of the damned.

The impoverishment caused by the bifurcation in the tradition of the Body and Soul debate is, however, of more concern to us in the other work. This poem, 'In þe ceson of huge mortalite',[2] is a debate from the grave between a body and the worms that devour it: it is illustrated by an erect corpse and worms of monstrous size. The nature of the debaters provides an ingenious and disturbing framework to contain the themes of putrefaction used earlier in the Body and Soul debate. But, though much of the poem is meditatively effective, it suffers from the lack of firm intellectual outlines, that could serve to contain the horrifying and disgusting descriptions within them, making them at the same time more intense but less squalid.

The poet feigns that during an epidemic of the plague he set out on a

---

[1] Ed. J. J. Stürzinger (Roxburghe Club, 1895), 135–44. For an account of the prose passage in BM. Add. MS. 37049 see Appendix I, and for the illustration see pl. 3 (*b*).
[2] *Archiv*, clxvii. 30–35.

PLATE 3

a. Figure of Death
Bodley MS. Douce 322

b. Body and Soul with angel
B. M. Add. MS. 37049

pilgrimage, and entered a lonely church, where he knelt before an 'ymage' (a crucifix as illustrated), and then saw a new tomb with 'sondre armes' upon it and the statue of a woman 'wele atyred in þe moste newe gyse', and thereupon fell into a sleep, during which he heard a dialogue proceeding beneath the tomb. The dead woman begins by recalling her former estate in contrast with the worms' present foulness:

> Of bewte I was a lady precious
> Of gentil blode descendyng of right lyne,
> Of ewe and of trewe begyning generous,
> All hertes glad my plesaunce to dyvyne.
> Men of honour and of gret worschip al dyd declyne.
> And nowe here in erth mortal deth come me to,
> Emang ȝow wormes, nakyd lyg I loo.

> Most unkynde neghbours þat ever war wroght,
> Dynner mete and sowper al to lyte,
> Now fretyng and etyng ȝe hafe me þorow soght
> With ane insaciabyll and gredy appetyte;
> No rest bot alway ȝe synk, sowke and byte,
> Day tyme ne houre with ȝow is no abstynence,
> Bot ay redy agayne me with vyolence.[1]

The worms in reply use the ancient and recurrent theme of the corpse hated by all (the theme summed up in the verse of the *Fasciculus morum*, 'Was ter never careyn so loþ . . .'),[2] explaining with physiological explicitness that it is only they, wretched creatures, lacking the senses of smell and taste, who can endure to be near a corpse. The lady then recalls and apostrophizes the knights and squires who had formerly vowed her service ('Now where be ȝe knyghtes . . .') and the worms reply with the familiar commonplace of the great (here the nine worthies) and the beautiful who have all entered the dominion of the worm. From here onwards, there is a change of tone in the poem since the worms preach as a moralist, whilst the lady becomes reconciled to the loss of worldly pride, symbolized by the worms. The worms first point out that messengers of the grave, 'lyce or neytes', accompany the body from its birth—a detail made popular by its inclusion in the *De contemptu mundi*

---

[1] Ibid. 31. *Ewe*: appearance; *generous*: noble; *dyd declyne*: bowed to me; *fretyng*: gnawing.

[2] The full verse is:

> Was þer never caren so lothe
> As mon when he put goth
> And dethe has layde so lawe;
> For when deth drawes man from oþur
> þe suster nul not se þe brother,
> Ne fader þe sone iknawe.
>
> (MS. Rawl. C. 670, 20ᵛ.)

of Innocent III[1]—and then, after a meek reply, develop the liturgical message of death repeated on every Ash Wednesday, 'Memento homo quia cinis es . . .': at this the body becomes entirely penitent for its former pride, and in a last speech interprets literally the text of Job xvii. 14, in the plea 'Let us kys and dwell togedyr evermore', and thus awaits the Resurrection with hope, charity, and resignation.

This dialogue may be seen as a curious byway leading from the Body and Soul debate. The worms are partly a vehicle for expressing the contempt and moralizations normally spoken by the soul but are also in part an evocative symbol of the end of vanity. A yet more subtle innovation, however, is the gradual psychological change in the dead woman. Normally in the debate form the opponents, as in a scholastic exercise, have taken up fixed positions from which they do not move: at most, if the theme requires it, one may yield spectacularly and without warning at the end, and the other will have an intellectual victory. It would not perhaps be an entirely anachronistic interpretation to see in the Body and Soul debates a suggestion of the psychological fixity of damnation, for the only reasonable alternative to recrimination would be resignation, a quality beyond the reach of the damned. The present poem, however, has, in common with the prose dialogue from the *Pèlerinage*, the fact that the dead person is not damned but (though in this work only by implication) in purgatory. In its concern with gradual reform, it shows a new moral and literary awareness. In the early Middle Ages, examples of repentance were always sudden and striking, and no interest was shown in the slow movements of reason and feeling. But in this poem, as in *The Pearl*, the author traces the psychological development of resignation with the kind of realistic observation that arose in the last quarter of the fourteenth century. This is the merit of the poem, but the fancifulness of making the worms speak both in their own character and as preacher is perhaps not wholly satisfactory, and the poem also necessarily lacks the tension of wit that was made possible by the rational foundations of the Body and Soul debate.

The warnings given by the dying and the old also continued to be the subject of fifteenth-century poetry. The signs of death, as we have already seen, remained a fifteenth-century theme, and the idea was also embodied in *exemplum*-type verses. From the early thirteenth century onwards there had been *exempla* which drew attention to the unrepentant deathbed, such as those of Jacques de Vitry concerning the dying usurer, who angrily commends his soul to the Devil because it will not stay with him,[2] or the dying lawyer who quibbles over his friends'

[1] Ed. Maccarrone, 14. See above, p. 108.
[2] *The Exempla of Jacques de Vitry*, ed. T. F. Crane (London, 1890), no. clxx, pp. 72–73.

right to advise, when they urge him to receive the sacrament.[1] There is
a rather dull poem of this kind, as yet unprinted, in MS. Sloane 1313,[2]
and also a neat little verse (preserved on the flyleaves of a copy of the *Pars
oculi*) in which a rich man bids farewell to his wealth:

> Worldys blys, have good day!
> No lengur habbe ych þe ne may,
> þe more for þe lasse y have for-lore;
> y-cursyd be þe tyme þat ych was bore!
> y have lore for-ever hevun blys,
> and go now þeras ever sorow and car ys.[3]

The scrap of Latin narrative that follows stresses that the rich man has
acquired his money through false dealing. The effect of this is therefore
more didactic and less subtle than had been the verses on the Signs of
Death. The Signs turned every dying man, whether good or bad, into
an image of death, and therefore conveyed a general truth that transcended the narrowly moral, but this verse, despite a dramatic touch of
bravado, remains a didactic demonstration of the fearfulness of the
death of a sinner.

There is a long account of the deathbed of a sinner in Hoccleve's *Ars
utilissima sciendi mori*,[4] a poem based on an episode in the *Horologium
sapientiae* of Henry Suso.[5] Suso's treatise, written in the first half of the
fourteenth century, was by the fifteenth century common in English
manuscripts, and, in particular, Chapter V, the section on death, was
both copied separately and also translated into English.[6] Its main
substance is a vision, given to the disciple by Eternal Wisdom, of an
unrepentant sinner about to die. In a set of long speeches the dying man
laments his fear, his irremediable state of unrepentance, and, in reply
to the disciple, delivers a long moral warning of how others may avoid
a similar plight. The image of the dying man is made precise towards
the end in a description echoing the signs of death.[7] In Hoccleve's poem
this appears as follows:

---

[1] Crane, op. cit. no. xxxix, p. 15. [2] f. 134ʳ, *Index*, 2307.
[3] Brown xv, 160. [4] E.E.T.S., E.S. 61, 178–212.
[5] An account of this work is given in the introduction to Henry Suso, *Little Book of
Eternal Wisdom*, trans. J. M. Clark (London, 1953). A fourteenth-century English
translation was fairly current in manuscripts and was printed by Caxton (*S.T.C.* 3305).
A text of the translation is printed in *Anglia*, x. 323–89. For the manuscripts see
W. Wichgraf, 'Susos Horologium Sapientiae in England nach Handschriften des 15.
Jahrhunderts', *Anglia*, liii (1929), 123–33.
[6] It occurs, for instance, in a group of *Ars moriendi* texts in MSS. Douce 322 and
Harley 1706, and in a slightly different translation and context in MS. Bodley 789. For
an account of the *Ars moriendi* see M. C. O'Connor, *The Art of Dying Well* (New York,
1942), and for its illustrations, Mâle, *L'Art religieux de la fin du moyen âge en France*,
380–9. In MS. Arch. Selden Supra 53, f. 118ʳ, Hoccleve's poem is accompanied by
an illustration of this kind.
[7] Trans. Clarke, 132.

> Ther is noon othir y see wel ynow
> The tyme is come as blyve y shal be deed;
> See how my face wexith pale now,
> And my look ful dym and hevy as leed;
> Myn yen synke eeke deepe in-to myn heed,
> And torne up so doun and myn hondes two
> Wexen al stif and starke and may nat do.[1]

The poem thus contains the traditional meditative image, which the *exemplum* verses had ignored. The point is driven home in Hoccleve's version by the constant reference to 'Thimage of deeth', where the Latin (in Clark's translation) has the 'unprepared dying man'. In general, Hoccleve preserves the moralizing advice and generalizations about death found in his original, but there are recurrent touches that make the whole more personal and immediate, 'Let me be your ensaumple and your mirour', 'Every day have of me deep remembrance', 'Myn yen been al dymme and dirke also', etc.

The same movement away from a precise meditative image to generalized homiletic and reflective statements can be seen in the poems on old age. There are only two which draw substantially on the earlier tradition. One is set in sermon form:[2] it is not self-description but a warning of what will happen, but the precision of its content derives directly from the tradition of the elegies of Maximian. Some of it is written in the style of a list, one or more distressing details to each line:

> Oure body wol yche, oure bonys wol ake,
> Owre owne flesshe wol be oure foo,
> Oure hede, oure handys, þan wol schake,
> Owre legges wol trymble whan we goo.[3]

There is also compression in the enumeration of other afflictions, such as the faithlessness of friends:

> Oure feynte frendes han us forsake.
> And also we schullen goo unkyste,
> Boþ at þe dore and at þe gate,
> ffor al þe chere þat we can make.[4]

The poem is not as lively and ironic as its predecessors, and the change of form makes its warning less dramatic, and its precision slightly unnatural; nevertheless, its directness of expression, 'And sume wold sey we lyve to longe', and its adherence to the literary tradition of base realism, 'And sumtyme clawe for scabbe and icche', are refreshing in contrast to the remote, ornate style of so much fifteenth-century poetry.

---

[1] E.E.T.S., E.S. 61, 202–3.   [2] Brown XV, 148.
[3] Ibid. p. 234.   [4] Ibid.

The other poem is the 'Ressoning betwix Aige and Yowth' by Henryson.[1] In this there is a series of alternate stanzas. Youth describes himself with thoughtless and arrogant delight, 'Waddin I am, quod he, and woundir wicht . . . My face is fair, my fegour will not faid';[2] whilst Age, overtly describing to Youth what he will be, at the same time describes himself:

> The bevar hoir said to this berly berne:
> 'This breif thow sall obey, sone be thow bald;
> Thy stait, thy strenth, Thocht it be stark and sterne,
> The feveris fell and eild sall gar the fald;
> Thy corps sall clyng, thy curage sall wax cald,
> Thy helth sall hynk, and take a hurt but hone,
> Thy wittis fyve sall vaneis, Thoct thow not wald:
> O yowth, thy flowris fadis fellone sone.'[3]

In Youth's pleasure and imprudent confidence in his own attributes there is perhaps an echo of Satan's biblically based praise of himself in the mystery plays. If this were so, it would give an additional twist to Age's warning. But Henryson's concluding lines, in which he allows truth to both speakers, suggest that he intended no more than an elegant series of contrasts between two extremes.

The other poems in this group of warnings nearly all have the refrain from the Office for the Dead, 'Timor mortis conturbat me':[4] some are spoken by an old man, though there is rarely any physical description, others by a man at some unspecified point in his life; one, a carol, is actually spoken by a child, who foretells the future. At least in this poem, 'I am a chyld and born ful bare',[5] there is a simple contrast between youth and death, even though it is not nearly so powerful as was the earlier concordance between warning and meditative image. But in two other carols the use of a meditative image has been quite forgotten: both of these are set in the *chanson d'aventure* convention, and the speaker, in accordance with one elaboration of this form, is a bird! One of these, 'As I went in a mery mornyng',[6] is mechanical: the commonplaces about the certainty and uncertainties of death, which had earlier been pithily summarized in 'Wanne ich þenche þinges þre', are here expressed weakly and diffusely. The fact that the speaker is a bird seems merely a quaint abuse of an artificial convention. In the other carol, 'As I me

---

[1] *Poems*, ed. Harvey Wood, 179–81.
[2] Ibid. 179. *Waddin . . . and . . . wicht*: supple and agile.
[3] Ibid. 181. *Bevar hoir*: feeble, grey-haired man; *berly berne*: handsome man; *breif*: summons; *clyng*: shrivel; *curage*: spirits; *hynk*: falter; *but hone*: without delay.
[4] This quotation is very common in the literature of death: it is, for instance, embodied by Bromyard in the long section on death in the *Summa praedicantium*, ii (Venice, 1586), 59ᵛ; later it continued to be used in epitaphs (*Notes and Queries*, N.S. xi. 403–4).
[5] *Carols*, 368.   [6] Ibid. 370.

rode in a Mey mornyng', however, something is made of the bird speaker
and a slight but quite effective allegory is developed:

> Sum tyme I went in purpull pall;
>   In soro and care now is my nest;
> My fedurs so fast now fro me fall,
>   Quod omnis caro fenum est.[1]

The inconsistency of the allegory is here oddly effective.

The same *Timor mortis* idea is expressed in more elaborate poems,
which draw upon medieval themes not necessarily associated with
warnings of death. One, for instance, draws its substance from the
Seven Ages of Man.[2] The speaker, overheard by the poet, is ultimately
related to Maximian: he is 'an ould mane houre' and walks upon a stick;
but his lament is not an ironic description of his present state, but a
summary of his misuse of his life, one stanza being allotted to each age.
In another poem the passage from youth to age is expressed in terms of
the turning of fortune's wheel:

> 'Timor mortis conturbat me',
>   þys is my song in my old age;
> Wyle Y was ʒonge Y myght nat see
>   þe strayte waye to my last age.
> Fortune, wit, and unstabilte
>   Disseyvyd me with hir bryght visage;
> Sche set me on hyr gret ryolte,
>   Uppon hir whele, on hire hie stag;
> But sodenli all þys gan swage,
>   And deth is com; lo, Y hym see!
> þerfore to sey is myne usage,
>   'Timor mortis conturbat me'.[3]

This use of the wheel of fortune is different from that in the *De casibus*
tradition. The turning of the wheel here does not symbolize the falling
from a high estate, but only the decay and death natural to everybody.
Everybody at birth mounts the wheel. The point is elsewhere made
iconographically plain in an illumination of the *Rota vite alias fortune*,
in which Fortune, blindfold, turns the wheel of the seven ages, whilst
at the bottom there is on the one side a cradle with an infant and on the
other a dead man in his coffin.[4]

---

[1] *Carols*, 378, p. 253. L. 4, 'For all flesh is grass' (Isa. xl. 6).

[2] Brown xv, 147.

[3] R. L. Greene, 'A Middle English "Timor Mortis" poem', *M.L.R.* xxviii (1933),
234–8. The variant for l. 5 that Greene quotes from MS. Porkington 10 'With mutabi-
litie' is to be preferred. *Ryolte*: regal splendour; *stag*: 'a recognised term for a step or
station on the rim of Fortune's wheel' (Greene).

[4] F. Saxl, 'A Spiritual Encyclopaedia of the later Middle Ages', *Journal of the
Warburg and Courtauld Institutes*, v (1942), 97–98.

There are two other poems with the *Timor mortis* refrain in which the
poet actually speaks in the assumed convention of personal narrative.
In one, Lydgate uses the device of feigning to relate the thoughts which
preoccupied him one night before he slept, and muses on all the Old
Testament figures long since dead, the nine worthies and heroines of
romances.[1] The *Timor mortis* theme has here combined with the enumeration of evocative names so common in the *ubi sunt* motif, and which
survived in many forms, including the early but continuously popular
Latin poem, *Cur mundus militat*.[2]

The second, and better known poem, is Dunbar's 'Lament for the
Makaris'.[3] The first and stronger part of this is based on the Dance of
Death: everybody from princes and bishops to the unweaned child are
carried off by death:

> He takis the campion in the stour,
> The capitane closit in the tour,
> The lady in bour full of bewte;
> *Timor mortis conturbat me*.[4]

The second half is encumbered poetically by the need to include so many
proper names, but it is interesting in the awareness that it shows of the
poet as an individual different from other people. Before the end of the
fourteenth century the very words *poet* or *maker* normally seem to have
been used only of classical writers. In Dunbar's lament for dead poets,
there is, of course, as yet no idea of the special poignancy of a poet's
death, of the kind, for instance, summed up in Pope's well-known line,
'Poets themselves must fall, like those they sung', but there is perhaps
some suggestion that death's power is seen at its most intense in the
fact that a poet dies, though his work continues to be read. The point
is not made explicit, but surely even in the fifteenth century the effect
of the poem would have been different if Dunbar had been, for instance,
a lawyer, and enumerated the names of other dead lawyers.

Of the many *Timor mortis* poems by far the most moving is that by
Audelay beginning, 'Dred of deþ, sorow of syn'.[5] In this, for perhaps
the first time in an English lyric poem, the poet truly speaks in his own
voice. The poems of Lydgate and Dunbar were personal since in the
former the very structure confined it to the poet in his minstrel personality, whilst in the other Dunbar's preoccupation with poets who
had died made his poem a warning from a poet to others: neither adheres

---

[1] E.E.T.S. 192, 828–32.

[2] Two Middle English translations of this survive: one (which was very popular) is
printed in Brown XIV, 134, the other in *Cambridge Middle English Lyrics*, 18–19. It was
also translated several times in the sixteenth and seventeenth centuries, *The Paradise of
Dainty Devices* (1576–1606), ed. H. E. Rollins (Cambridge, Mass., 1927), no. 1, and
notes pp. 180–2.   [3] *Poems*, ed. Mackenzie, 20–23.

[4] Ibid. 21.   [5] E.E.T.S. 184, 211–12.

exclusively to the intense but unindividualized statements of emotion which had enabled the 'I' of the earlier lyric to be personal to each who used it. But this is yet more true of Audelay's poem, where the poet quite clearly describes his own state in order that it may serve as an example to others of painful resignation and Christian trust. The success of the poem lies in the way the distressing signs of old age are expressed with a depth of emotion and individuality of syntax that strongly convey the impression of personal feeling:

> Fore blyndness is a heve þyng,
> And to be def þer-with only,
> To lese my lyʒt and my heryng;
> *Passio Christi conforta me.*
>
> And to lese my tast and my smellyng,
> And to be seke in my body,
> Here have I lost al my lykyng;
> *Passio Christi conforta me.*[1]

The deep distress of each stanza is balanced by the refrain, *Passio Christi conforta me*, a line from the beautiful fourteenth-century eucharistic prayer, *Anima Christi*, which was later incorporated in the Roman missal as the work of St. Ignatius. Audelay's use of this was no doubt a deliberate and intentionally noticeable variation of the traditional *Timor mortis*, which he relegated to the two-line burden, 'Lade, helpe! Ihesu merce! / *Timor mortis conturbat me*'. Again in this poem we see an ancient medieval theme treated with an emphasis which is un-medieval: the 'I' is no longer Everyman, but the poet with his individual experience and sensibility.

A fifteenth-century development in the poetry of death is that warnings are delivered not only by the dead, the dying, and the old, but also by death itself personified. The authoritative source for this personification was the fourth rider of Apocalypse vi. 8,[2] who from the fourteenth century onwards appears in manuscripts as a skeleton astride a horse,[3]

---

[1] E.E.T.S. 184, 211.

[2] 'Et ecce equus pallidus, et qui sedebat super eum; nomen illi mors, et infernus sequebatur eum.'

[3] H. W. Janson (*Art Bulletin*, xix. 43) notes that the fourth horseman is shown as a skeleton from the early fourteenth century onwards. R. Helm, *Skelett- und Todesdarstellungen* (Strasburg, 1928), on p. 63 refers to and reproduces in fig. 28, a carving from the west door of Notre Dame of Amiens, where the rider is followed by a corpse on horseback. Before the fourteenth century, when there had been no impulse to personify death, illuminated manuscripts of the Apocalypse either suppose that the fourth rider, like the other three, was Christ (e.g. *The Apocalypse in Latin and French*, ed. M. R. James, Roxburghe Club, 1922, pl. 16), or they make the figure evil and identify him with the Devil (plausibly since hell follows him), but they avoid what would seem to be the plain meaning of the text; cf. Kozaky, op. cit. i. 152–6; on thirteenth-century iconography see G. Bing, 'The Apocalypse Block-Books and their Manuscript Models', *Journal of the Warburg and Courtauld Institutes*, v (1942), 143–58.

whilst at the same time in some early versions of the Triumph of Death,
the skeleton is not, as later, borne in triumph on a chariot, but pursues
mankind as an armed warrior on horseback.[1] One of the earliest allusions
to this kind of subject occurs in *Piers Plowman*, Passus xx, where Old
Age carries Death's banner in the vanguard, and then:

> Deth cam dryvende after   and al to doust passhed
> Kynges and knyʒtes   kayseres and popes;
> Lered ne lewed   he let no man stonde,
> That he hitte evene   that evere stired after.
> Many a lovely lady   and lemmanes of knyghtes
> Swouned and swelted   for sorwe of Dethes dyntes.[2]

Death personified is an important figure in other fourteenth-century
texts: Chaucer's brilliant amplification of the *exemplum* of the hermit and
the gold in *The Pardoner's Tale* depends upon the idea of death as a
real person, who slew the rioters' former comrades 'with his spere'; in
the early morality play, *The Pride of Life*, Death must actually have
appeared upon the stage, carrying a fighting weapon.[3]

There is, however, only one fourteenth-century lyric in which death
personified speaks; it is a brief verse in the section on *Mors* in John of
Grimestone's preaching-book:

> Be war, man, i come as þef,
> To preven þi life þat is þe lef.
> þat is bitter to mannis mende,
> þat is siker to mannis kende,
> þat is deler of al oure ende.[4]

This verse is so early that the issue of whether a precise visualization of
death was intended may be questioned. But the main body of verse in
this manuscript is so strictly in the meditative tradition, and the tone

---

[1] Alberto Tenenti, *La vie et la mort à travers l'art du xvᵉ siècle* (Paris, 1952), 23. This
book is very useful in discussing the illustrations of *horae*, the *Ars moriendi* and subjects
such as the Triumph of Death.

[2] Passus xx (B Text), 99–104, ed. Skeat, i. 584. For comment see *Essays in Criticism*,
xii (1962), 117.

[3] Ed. F. Holthausen, *Archiv*, cviii (1902), 32–59. Death also appears in *Everyman*,
but there is no visual description of him in the play, though the two editions of John
Skot, containing a woodcut of a skeleton deriving from the *Kalender of Shepherds*,
show how the figure was understood in the sixteenth century (see frontispiece to *Everyman*, ed. A. C. Cawley, Manchester, 1961). In the Play of the Death of Herod in the
Ludus Coventriae Death appears and, according to his self-description, he is a decaying
corpse (E.E.T.S., E.S. 120, 177):

> Thow I be nakyd and pore of array
> and wurmys knawe me al a-bowte,
> ʒit loke ʒe drede me nyth and day
> ffor whan deth comyth ʒe stande in dowte:
> even lyke to me as I ʒow say
> shull all ʒe be here in þis rowte.

[4] f. 86ᵛ. The first two lines are quoted (slightly inaccurately) in Owst, op. cit. 532.

of the verse is so direct and personal that it seems unlikely that the writer intended no more than the voice of an abstract personification.

With the two fifteenth-century warnings there is no difficulty of this kind. One, 'Syth that ye lyste to be my costes',[1] is an oddly composite poem. Of its eight stanzas the three that contain Death's description of himself (nos. 1, 2, and 4) seem to belong to the poem, whilst the other five are borrowed from the account of the Fall of Adam and Eve in Lydgate's version of Boccaccio's *De casibus virorum illustrium*.[2] These five are part of the narrator's commentary on the action and most of them are necessarily of a general, moralizing character. In their new context they lose the force of their original application but gain a new grimness from the nature of the speaker. Only one, however, has fully taken root after its transplantation:

> Remembre your yeres almost past be,
>   Of flowryng age lasteth but a seasoun,
> By procese at ey[e] men may see
>   Beaute declyneth, hys blossom falleth doune,
>   And lytyll and lytyll, by successioun
> Cometh croked elde, unwarly [in] crepyng,
> With hys patent purely than manysshyng.[3]

In the *Fall of Princes* these generalizations arise from the sad ageing of Adam and Eve, who appear to Boccaccio in his study 'quakyng for age', but, with the introduction of the imperative in the first line,[4] they become extremely appropriate to Death, who was, as we have already seen, often associated with old age.

In the three stanzas proper to the poem there is a general description of Death, who refers in particular to his bell and 'dredefull spere [that ys] full sharpe ygrounde'. The description, however, is too undetailed to be fearful, but in two of the three manuscripts of the poem the menace and meditative warning are supplied by an accompanying illustration.[5] In the better of these, MS. Douce 322,[6] the picture consists of a skeleton standing on brightly coloured grass that covers about a quarter of the space, whilst the rest of the background is filled by a delicate red design. Written eighteen times, and clustered thickly round the bell, is the word 'dethe', whilst the spear extends in a menacing way beyond the blue

---

[1] E.E.T.S. 192, 655–7. For authorship see E.E.T.S., E.S. 107, xv. *Costes* is meaningless and cannot be satisfactorily emended. MS. C.U.L. Ff. v. 45 has *hostes*; Wager (*P.Q.* xv. 378) suggests *cosines*: 'intimate'. This gives better sense, but both words are, awkwardly, feminine.

[2] W. Schirmer, *John Lydgate*, 198, footnote 5; *Suppl.* 3143.

[3] E.E.T.S. 192, 656. *At ey(e)*: clearly; *patent*: authority conferred upon him. Cf. *Fall of Princes*, i. 764–70, E.E.T.S., E.S. 121, 21–22.

[4] In the *Fall of Princes* the first line of this stanza reads, 'For whan the yeris fulli passid be'.

[5] MSS. Douce 322, 19ᵛ, and Harley 1706, 19ᵛ.   [6] See pl. 3 (a).

frame. Together, text and illustration make an effective meditative warning: separated, the poem is too vague to convey the horrifying warning
characteristic of earlier poetry. This severance of text and image is, as
we have already seen, entirely typical of fifteenth-century style and
methods.

The other poem, 'Maist thou now be glade, with all thi fresshe aray',
though it is not any more visually precise, is far more taut and threatening in style:

> Maist thou now be glade, with all thi fresshe aray,
> One me to loke that wyll dystene thi face.
> Rew one thy-self and all thi synne uprace!
> Sone shalte þu flytte and seche anoþer place,
> Shorte is thy sesoun here, thogh thou go gay.[1]

The second stanza turns the reference to looking at Death into a command, 'Lyfte up thy ieye, be-holde now, and assay! / Yche loke one me
aught to put þe in affray'. This insistence on gazing at the figure of
Death is taken up in the description of the poem in the French rubric,
preceding it in the manuscript: 'Cest le myrroure pur lez Iofenes Dames
a regardir aud maytyne pour lour testes bealment adressere'.[2] From the
poem itself one would assume the image to be the already traditional
skeleton with weapon. The word 'myrroure', however, suggests a slightly
different, though closely related, idea. The concept of death as a mirror
of the living was developed in the later Middle Ages. Professor Panofsky,
with reference to this, quotes an epitaph of the *Sum quod eris* type from
the Jakobskirche in Straubing, which begins, 'Sum speculum vitae'.[3]
A more striking example is the painting of Hans Burgkmair and his wife
(1529, Vienna), in which the aged couple gaze into a mirror, which
reflects their faces as skulls.[4] This idea had also been embodied in
exempla: in one, a lady looking at herself in a glass sees a skull; in another, a maidservant brings her mistress a skull, after two looking-glasses
have been arrogantly rejected.[5] This slight discrepancy between rubric
and poem draws attention to the difficulty of distinguishing the almost
indistinguishable borderline between representations of Death itself
and visions of living persons' future appearance when dead. The attributes of Death—lance, bell, etc.—are emblematic, but a skeleton itself
is only an appropriate symbol of death because it is a likeness of the
dead. In this poem the auditors addressed, who are in 'fresshe aray'
and live in prosperity and delight, are obviously exhorted to look on the
figure of Death as a reflection of themselves. In this sense rubric and

[1] Brown xv, 152, p. 241.   [2] Ibid.
[3] E. Panofsky, 'Father Time', *Studies in Iconology* (New York, 1962), 82, footnote 50.
[4] L. Réau, *L'Iconographie de l'art chrétien*, ii. ii. 658.
[5] Herbert, *Catalogue*, iii. 446.

poem coincide. Though there is no physical description in the poem, it draws so skilfully on familiar iconographic tradition that the threatening image does not seem any the less powerful for being left unexpressed.

There are also a number of poems set in the form of an apostrophe of death. It of course does not follow that when death is apostrophized it must also be visualized. Biblical ejaculatory address, such as, 'Ubi est, mors, victoria tua? ubi est, mors, stimulus tuus?' (1 Cor. xv. 55), would provide sufficient precedent for the invocation of death as an abstraction. Moreover the poems are written mostly in a rhetorical style, which would accord with the address of an abstract personification, limited in its potentialities of realism. Nevertheless, there are in these poems touches that suggest the meditative tradition, and it is noteworthy that chronologically they accompany the prevalence of iconographic forms and the speeches of Death within the lyric and drama.

One of these, 'O Deth, hough better ys the mynde of the',[1] not only owes its first line to the text, 'O mors, quam amara est memoria tua',[2] but also its progress of thought, consisting of variations on the recollection of death, in particular its dominion over the rich and the great. The memory of death, however, turns into the image of the mirror: death is a 'myndly myrrour', and when the poem turns from apostrophe of death to sermon address, the audience is twice exhorted to look in this mirror, 'Beholde this myrroure in thy mynde' and 'Muse in this mirrour of mortalite'. There is a difficulty in the text of this poem, however, because in one version (that of MS. Harley 116) there occurs a stanza describing how Lord Ralph Cromwell provided a tomb for himself and his wife, and the opening line of the last stanza, 'Muse in this mirrour of mortalite', refers, not to death but to the tomb, to which the speaker, points (it was, incidentally, not a double tomb). The stanza on Lord Cromwell's tomb, however, is probably an insertion: a discrepancy in sense between it and the following stanza[3] and the interruption by it of a fairly consistent sequence of thought are both points suggesting that this stanza was not part of the original work.

This poem is sometimes described as an elegy,[4] but, even if the reference to Lord Cromwell were original, this would not be an appropriate description: for Lord Cromwell is not mourned, but rather cited as a particular example of the poem's general theme. It is an instance of topical reference, which was, as we have already seen, characteristic of

[1] Brown xv, 154.

[2] Ecclus. xli. 1. 'O death, how bitter is the thought of thee.'

[3] See Brown's note to ll. 55–56, p. 340, and introductory comments to the poem, p. 339. Brown, however, supposes the Cotton text to be the amended one. MacCracken (M.L.N. xxvi [1911], 243–4) also assumes the Harley text to be the earlier, and suggests that the poem was written to hang by the tomb.

[4] e.g. Index, 2411, '. . . an elegy for the tomb of Lord Cromwell'.

fifteenth-century poetry. There is, however, another poem, 'Ha! cruell deeth, contrarious to creatures in kynde', of which the first part is an apostrophe of death, but which becomes towards the end an elegy for the poet's mistress. This lyric in its first four verses rails upon death as a tyrant and murderer, whose malice is insatiable. One line of abuse, however, 'Thu art to alle creatures hidous to be-holde', indicates at least a temporary pictorial imagining of death. The most interesting of the denunciations, however, is the conceit that death is a cruel tyrant, whom kingdoms should rise up against and overthrow:

> Ffor þi malice, me semeth reames sholde arise
> To destruye cruell deeth and do hym of dawe.[1]

This recalls the blasphemous presumption of the young men in *The Pardoner's Tale*, though here the solution is different; whereas verbal echoes in *The Pardoner's Tale* recall the fact that the only slayer of Death is Christ, in this poem Death is credited with a legal right deriving from Adam. The recognition of Death's power as just leads into the last three verses, consisting of praise and prayer for the poet's dead mistress, conventional in content, but movingly expressed.

The last apostrophe of death to be discussed contains within it a speech of Death itself. It is a poem by Ryman beginning 'O cruell deth paynfull and smert', and it is the only one of the apostrophes that is straightforwardly in the meditative tradition. The image described, however, is not that of death but of the signs of death in the dying man:

> Why art thou so cruell to man
> Of hym no man grisly to make,
> His nose sharpe and his lippes wan,
> His chekes pale and his tethe blake,
> His handes and his fete to shake
> And alle his body quake for colde
> And returne hym ayene to molde?[2]

The speech of Death is brief and unintroduced, but it has the directness of approach, which suggests one person talking to another, and the dramatic intimacy which had been characteristic of the meditative style:

> I sende sekenesse you to ataste
> And to meke you in every place,
> But, whenne that I come at the last,
> I make an ende within shorte space.
> I sette no lawe day in the case,
> For, whenne that I sey: 'Make an ende',
> Withouten delay ye shall hense wende.[3]

---

[1] Brown XV, 153, p. 242.
[2] J. Zupitza, 'Die Gedichte des Franziskaners Jakob Ryman', *Archiv*, lxxxix (1892), 266.   [3] Ibid. 266–7. *Ataste*: test.

The last three lines are interesting as an example of the use of an ironic persuasive image. Legal imagery was fairly often used for both death and the Last Judgement. The commonplace of death as a sergeant linked the two together, since a sergeant was an officer whose duty it was to arrest offenders and bring them to court. Sometimes, however, this kind of imagery was used ironically, with the implications that the day of death or of the Last Judgement were legal occasions, on which none could escape by the just or unjust manipulations of the processes of law. There is a fine passage in the *Confessio amantis*, in which the potential satiric reference is made explicit:

> That dai mai no consail availe,
> The pledour and the plee schal faile,
> The sentence of that ilke day
> Mai non appell sette in delay;
> Ther mai no gold the Jugge plie,
> That he ne schal the sothe trie
> And setten every man upriht,
> Als well the plowman as the kniht.[1]

In Ryman's poem, however, the image is not that of a criminal trial, but that of a debtor called upon to pay his debt (the image of death as a debt is of course Pauline). There is a trace of irony in the warning that this is not the kind of debt in which the debtor can receive protection or a right to delay repayment from the law:[2] death can demand payment at any moment. The irony consists in the postulation of an image, only to deny its likeness.

The tendency in many of these poems was towards homiletic address. No matter who the speaker, and what the fictional situation, the style, rhetorical and hortatory, was primarily appropriate to a preacher, and the content, with its abstract generalizations, was suited to a public and formal occasion. As one would therefore expect, there are also poems, which do not attempt a meditative form, but are composed openly in sermon style. Some of these are very dull, and make use of the warning of death only mechanically. An extreme example is the unpublished lyric, 'O mortall man, mased with pompe and pride', which is almost totally didactic in content.[3] Were it not for the refrain, 'Remember man thow art but wormes mete', it would be solely a sermon on the seven deadly sins. The poem consists of eight verses, one for each sin, and one for a summing up: very little relationship is made between the stanza-long discussion of the sin and the refrain.

---

[1] Ed. Macaulay, i. 222.
[2] *O.E.D.* s.v. law day.
[3] B.M. Add. MS. 29729, 7^r–8^r. *Index*, 2523.

The two most lively of the sermon addresses are those keeping nearest to the earlier tradition. One, 'Man, hef in mynd and mend þi mys', has, like 'O mortall man', a warning refrain, 'Memor esto novissima', but in this poem the refrain comes relevantly and effectively at the end of each stanza, clinching the points preceding it. The poem contains many of the generalizations and commonplaces characteristic of the later style, fortune's wheel, for instance, though here referring to mutability not death, and the list of the famous, long since dead, Hector, Achilles, and Alexander. But the style has a slightly mocking verve:

> Quhen þow art ded and laid in layme,
>   and þi ribbis ar þi ruf tre,
> þow art þan brocht to þi lang hayme—
>   adew al warldis dignite!
> than is to lait forswcht, think me,
>   quhen wormys g[n]awys þe to and fra,
> now mynd þi mys in al degre.
>   memor esto novissima.[1]

The second line is a quite ingenious variation of the old ironic commonplace of the dead man's roof lying upon his nose. The roof has here become the actual skeleton, the breastbone and ribs suggesting the main beam and rafters of a ceiling. This touch of ironic inventiveness recalls the witty spiritedness of some of the earlier lyrics on death.

The other poem of this kind, worth singling out, is the carol, 'This word is falce, I dare wyll say'. In this the commonplaces are those of the earlier tradition, the falseness of executors, the indifference of the living towards the dead, 'dede man have no frond', and the levelling power of death. Moreover, they are expressed in a terse and forceful way, with a colloquial directness that drives home the folly of the pretensions and ambitions of the rich:

> Tell me sothe qwoso canne:
> Qwan he hys dede, qwat has he wan?
> Qw[e]re se ye ony rych dede man?
> Revela mihi hodie.[2]

The equality of the grave was, as we have seen, an ancient theme, but it comes over freshly in the ingeniously ironic conjunction of adjectives in the phrase 'rych dede man'. These two poems, however, stand out from the rest in such touches of verbal felicity. In the others the horror and irony inherent in the subject are suffocated by the unmodulated elevation of style.

All the forms of the later death lyric so far discussed, with the exception of those containing a personification of death, had their ancestry

---

[1] Brown xv, 156, 247–8.   [2] *Carols*, 366.

directly in the earlier lyric. There remain to be discussed two fifteenth-century themes which were borrowed directly from the vernacular litera-ture of the Continent, the legend of the Three Living and the Three Dead and the Dance of Death. The chief characteristic of these was that traditional commonplaces were expressed in elaborate and related literary and iconographic forms. The Three Living and the Three Dead, in which was fused the warning from the tomb and the *exemplum* story of the Simon de Crépy type,[1] had at its heart the ancient warning *Sum quod eris*,[2] whilst the Dance of Death, in which a representative of every rank and profession in society dances with his own skeleton, isolated and powerfully expressed the universality and levelling power of death. In England, though the iconographic portrayal of these themes was fairly widespread, they were not fully made at home in the native tradi-tion of poetry. The Dance of Death, with the exception of some late *titulus* verses, exists only in Lydgate's version, which is very competent but very dependent upon its French original: it can only be considered as a translation (in contrast to many other medieval works, which, though they profess to be translations, are at most free paraphrases of their model). The Three Living and the Three Dead was made the subject of one independent English poem, but only one (again apart from *titulus* verses), in contrast to the many versions on the Continent; and also it was late, being written about two centuries after the earliest French texts, and indeed almost two centuries after its first appearance in England as an iconographic theme.

The story of the Three Living and the Three Dead[3] differs from the *exempla*, already discussed, in two important ways. The first difference is that the initiative comes from the dead. The living do not chance to pass through a churchyard or even seek out a tomb: instead they are bent on pleasure—sometimes the typical pastime of hunting—when the dead suddenly stand in their path. The dead are thus apparitions; not ghosts or devils, as the Three Living sometimes take them to be, but

---

[1] It is tempting to see an intermediary stage between these two sermon themes and their dramatic formulization in a Latin poem of Italian origin, 'Cum apertam sepul-turam / Viri tres aspicerent' (K. Künstle, *Die Legende der drei Lebenden und der drei Toten und der Totentanz*, Freiburg im Breisgau, 1908, 33–35). In this poem three men, on looking into an open tomb, draw a lesson from its decomposing corpses, and express their dismay in the traditional stylistic forms, 'Quod nos sumus, hi fuere', 'Ubi vestra pulchritudo', etc. The poem has been dated at various points between the twelfth and fifteenth centuries, but the treatment of the subject suggests that it is an early work or a direct derivative of one.

[2] On this see R. Köhler, 'Der Spruch der Toten an die Lebenden', *Kleinere Schrif-ten*, ed. J. Bolte, ii (1900), 27–37; S. Glixelli, *Les cinq poèmes des trois morts et des trois vifs* (Paris, 1914), 20–25.

[3] W. Rotzler, *Die Begegnung der drei Lebenden und der drei Toten* (Winterthur, 1961), provides a useful summary of the occurrences of this theme throughout the literature and art of western Europe.

skeletons or decaying corpses who, by an extension of the Body and Soul convention, are able to speak and move. In this way the story becomes both more dramatic and more moral. The second difference is that the dead stand up.[1] In terms of plot this is of course part of the first, but its effect, in iconography at least, is quite distinct and very striking. The force of the warning from the tomb lay in the anonymity of death: the living, confronted with a decaying corpse, sees in it a likeness of what he must inevitably become. When the dead stood up, however, the scene became yet more horrible and the reflection more exact. In the earliest illustration of the theme, that in the English De Lisle Psalter,[2] this point is very marked: the two groups of living and dead approach each other from opposite margins, and the dead gruesomely mimic the attitudes and gestures of the living. This illustration accompanies an Anglo-Norman text of a French poem written in the second half of the thirteenth century:[3] in this three arrogant and vain young ladies are confronted by the decaying corpses of a bishop, a count, and a king. The point of this choice is self-evidently a demonstration of the futility of earthly rank, but it obscures the idea of a prophetic mirror. But in the illustration, which is to some extent independent of the poem, three young gallants appear to encounter their dead selves, and the illustration is therefore more appropriate to the English *titulus* verse, that is inscribed above it:

Ich am afert	Lo whet ich se,
Me þinkeþ hit	Beþ develes þre.
Ich wes wel fair	Such scheltou be,
For Godes love	Be wer by me.[4]

---

[1] It is not quite clear in the two earliest French poems on this subject (Glixelli, op. cit. nos. 1 and 2) whether the dead are imagined erect or prone in their coffins, though admittedly the illuminators of the earliest manuscripts understood the dead to stand. Certainly the idea of the dead in their coffins remained a possible variant in the handling of the subject, as in the well-known fresco at Pisa (Künstle, op. cit., pl. vi) in which three men on horseback look down at three coffins stretched before them. M. Meiss, 'The Problem of Francesco Traini', *Art Bulletin*, xv (1933), 168–71, argues that the form with recumbent corpses is characteristic of Italian art. G. Servières, 'Les formes artistiques du "dict des trois morts et des trois vifs" ', *Gazette des beaux arts*, lxviii (1926), 26–27, notes the recumbent form at Pisa, Cremona, and Subiaco.

[2] The De Lisle Psalter (MS. Arundel 83) is of East Anglian provenance and was given by Robert de Lisle to his daughter in 1339. The illumination in it of The Three Living and the Three Dead has now been shown to have influenced the French parallel in MS. Arsénal 3142, and not vice versa as once supposed (R. Freyhan, 'English Influences on Parisian Painting of about 1300', *Burlington Magazine*, liv, 1929, 320–30). This illumination, together with the panels of the Three Living and the Three Dead known to have been bought in England by the Count of Savoy in 1303–4, suggests that there was a very early iconographic tradition of this theme in England.

[3] Glixelli, op. cit. no. 2.

[4] Gray, *Notes and Queries*, N.S. x. 167; S. Chew, *The Pilgrimage of Life*, 231 (with modernized spelling).

It can be inferred from this that the most powerful medium for the theme of the Three Living and the Three Dead was visual representation, perhaps accompanied, as it so often was, by a *titulus* verse to supply the epigrammatic warning.[1] In England this was its usual form. From the middle of the fourteenth century it became widely diffused in wall-paintings: thirty examples of these, in village churches all over England, either still exist or were still to be seen in the last century.[2] At the end of the fifteenth century it appears from time to time in early printed books, being used in didactic treatises[3] and in *horae* to accompany the Office for the Dead.[4]

The only English poem to survive on this subject is 'An a byrchyn bonke þer bous arne bry3t', which is copied in MS. Douce 302 of which the whole contents is normally attributed to Audelay.[5] The poem is written in the conventions of the alliterative romance: metre, diction, and style all unmistakably show its kind. The author follows the tradition, found in two German poems, which stresses the narrative setting in order to make the interruption of the dead the more dramatic. But, whilst the hunting scene as a plot element is related to the German tradition, perhaps through some common French source, the style is that of *Sir Gawain*. The poem is designed with a clear but mechanical sense of proportion. Four stanzas describe the hunt and the separation in the fog of the kings from their retinue; in a stanza apiece they then express fear and dismay at the grisly apparitions, and these are matched by the three stanzas in which each of the Dead expresses his warning; a concluding stanza then drives home the moral for the reader. Each stanza is tightly held together by both rhyme and alliteration, and each is linked to the next by verbal repetition. The vocabulary has much of

---

[1] Chew, op. cit. 230–1.

[2] W. F. Storck, 'Aspects of Death in English Art and Poetry', *Burlington Magazine*, xxi (1912), 249–56, 314–19; E. Carleton Williams, 'Mural Paintings of the Three Living and the Three Dead in England', *Journal of the British Archaeological Association*, 3rd series, vii (1942), 31–40.

[3] *Ars moriendi* (*S.T.C.* 787); *Cordiale* (*S.T.C.* 5759; cf. O'Connor, *The Art of Dying Well*, 4, footnote 26); *Doctrinal of Death* (*S.T.C.* 6931, cf. O'Connor, op. cit. 188); and the *Contemplations of the Dread and Love of God* (ascribed to Richard Rolle), printed by Wynkyn de Worde (*S.T.C.* 21259). This theme was far more common in French illuminated manuscripts and books; for a list see W. Storck, *Die Legende von den drei Lebenden und von den drei Toten* (Tübingen, 1910), 18–23.

[4] *S.T.C.* 15875, 15898. For *horae* printed abroad for the English market see pp. 366–7 below. On this theme as an illustration for the Office for the Dead see Abbé V. Leroquais, *Les Livres d'heures manuscrits de la Bibliothèque Nationale*, i (Paris, 1927), xlviii. According to Leroquais's analysis, the Three Living and the Three Dead was one of the four most common illustrations of the Office for the Dead in the fifteenth century. There is no comparable survey of English liturgical manuscripts, but a sample suggests that the only regular illustration for this Office was a burial scene, and that the Three Living and the Three Dead, Lazarus, and Job were not common alternatives as they were in France.

[5] E.E.T.S. 184, 217–23. It is most unlikely that this poem is by Audelay.

the elaboration of the poetic diction of the north-western alliterative
school. The setting of the hunt no doubt suggested the propriety of the
style, but the grim simplicity of the warning almost vanishes in the
knotted ornateness of metre and style. Occasional lines in the warnings
from the Dead have the necessary punch, 'Lo here þe wormus in my
wome þai wallon and wyndon' or 'Makis ȝour merour be me, my myrþus
bene mene', but in general the starkness of the subject is softened by
so much literary artifice. In the French poems the blunt confrontation
of living and dead, described in direct style and crisp couplets, is
extremely effective. The early fourteenth-century English style would
have been yet better suited to the subject, and it is a pity that either no
poem on this theme was then written or at least that none survives.

Whilst in France the later history of the Three Living and the Three
Dead and the Dance of Death was almost exactly parallel, both printed
together, both painted together in churches, and both used as illustrations of liturgical manuscripts, in England their history was distinct.
The earliest representation of the Dance of Death[1] was probably that
painted round the walls of the Churchyard of the Innocents in Paris,
and from there it was imitated in St. Paul's churchyard, with verses
translated from the French by Lydgate who had seen the original at
the Innocents. This at least is an early manuscript tradition about the
transition from France to England, though it may well be an over-
simplified one.

The Dance of Death is a more complex literary form than the Three
Living and the Three Dead, and its relationship to earlier themes of
death can therefore not be indicated in so brief and straightforward a
way. Its ultimate starting-point is clearly the sermon commonplace of
the levelling power of death, and, as has often been pointed out, an
intermediate stage between such a generalization and the Dance of
Death itself, was the Latin poem, *Vado mori*,[2] in which persons of
various ranks, lay and ecclesiastical, introduce themselves, and with
resignation announce that they must die, each verse beginning *Vado
mori*. Nevertheless, though a cross between this and the Three Living
and the Three Dead might seem sufficient antecedent for the Dance of
Death, the latter has a subtle literary character, suggesting that a common tradition has become modified by the intervention of a powerful

---

[1] For the Dance of Death see J. M. Clark, *The Dance of Death* (Glasgow, 1950),
and for further reading its bibliography. To the latter may be added: R. Eisler, 'Danse
Macabre', *Traditio*, vi (1948), 187–225, and H. Rosenfeld, *Der mittelalterliche Totentanz* (Münster/Cologne, 1954), which includes a most comprehensive bibliography.

[2] On the *Vado mori* see W. F. Storck, 'Das "Vado Mori" ', *Zeitschrift für deutsche
Philologie*, xlii (1910), 422–8, and E. P. Hammond, 'Latin Texts of the Dance of Death',
M.P. viii (1911), 399–410. A short English version (Brown xv, 158) is copied in B.M.
Add. MS. 37049 and two related manuscripts.

and literary imagination. This impression is borne out by the fact that there are not, as with the Three Living and the Three Dead, various treatments of the same theme, but one poem only, occasionally added to or imitated, as in the *Danse des femmes*.

The Dance of Death was undoubtedly painted in places other than St. Paul's churchyard, but from the mural fragments that remain it seems that in England one episode only was commonly represented. At Salisbury, for instance, there was a wall-painting of a young man confronted by a skeleton, accompanied by the following verses:

> Alasse, Dethe, alasse, a blesful thyng þu were
> Yf thow wolldyst spare us yn our lustynesse
> And cum to wretches þat bethe of hevy chere
> Whene they þe clepe to slake there dystresse.
> But owte alasse thyne owne sely selfewyldnesse
> Crewelly werieth them þat seyghe wayle and wepe
> To close there yen þat after þe doth clepe.

> Grasles gallante in all thy luste and pride
> Remember þat thow ones schalte dye.
> Deth shalt from thy body thy sowle devyde
> Thow mayst him not ascape certaynly.
> To þe dede bodyes cast downe thyne eye,
> Beholde thaym well, consydere and see
> For such as thay ar, such shalt þow be.[1]

The picture and verse combined form a curious hybrid. The picture appears to be a scene isolated from the Dance of Death, and we would therefore interpret it as a symbolic representation of the moment of death; the verse, with its elaborate diction and stanza form (both far removed from the style of the *titulus* verses that accompany the Three Living and the Three Dead) also recalls Lydgate's 'Dance of Death'. In content, however, they are nearer to the theme of the Three Living and the Three Dead, for Death only warns and does not seize: indeed, he speaks more like a preacher, basing the ancient warning in the last line, not upon himself, but upon the token coffin within the picture or perhaps upon the tombs beneath it in the cathedral. This hybrid form is not very satisfactory: though the verses are smoothly written, they lack the punch peculiar to each of the forms from which they derive.

The whole cycle of the Dance with Lydgate's verses was fairly rare. It was in manuscripts that the poem was chiefly copied and here there is a curious point. There was no widespread printing of the Dance of Death in England as there was in France, and, though it circulated fairly widely in manuscripts—fourteen survive—they are poetic collections of

---

[1] Gough, op. cit. 187 and pl. lxxi. No entirely trustworthy text survives.

the works of known poets, of Lydgate and Hoccleve or Lydgate and Chaucer, and the Dance of Death is included, without illustration, as part of the canon of Lydgate's work, and not primarily for a didactic or meditative purpose. There are only two manuscripts, MSS. Trinity Camb. 601 and Bodl. 686, where the Dance is followed, not by other poems by Lydgate, but by verses connected to it by theme. They are short Latin poems on the subject of death, and had already become accreted to the Dance in the French editions of the *Danse des morts*, which were compendiums of the poetry and iconography of death.[1] There is, however, only a very small and infrequent echo in England of the French custom of presenting the *Danse des morts* as a frightening meditation.

The strength of the French poem and the translation[2] lies in accumulation, in the successive pairs of stanzas in which Death satirically and harshly warns his victim, and the replies in which each—in the convention of the warning speech of the man about to die—laments the treasures he must lose and moralizes on the futility of trusting in them. The English is a very capable translation of the French: whilst some stanzas exhibit the typical fifteenth-century English fault of assembling line after line of pompous ill-sounding words, where the French had a vigorous directness, others could equally well be chosen to illustrate the force and precision of the English, where the French was grey and flaccid. There are very few passages in which the translator has been guided by the native tradition: perhaps the only unmistakable one is an addition in the emperor's lament, 'A simple shete ther is no more to seyne / To wrappe yn my bodi and visage'. Moreover, though irony was an important part of the native style, the translator sometimes loses the point of Death's ironic parody of the dying man's occupation or habits: he keeps, for instance, the reference to the knight's former dancing, 'Sommetyme ȝowre custome and entencioun / Was with ladies to daunce yn the shade', but omits the following line with its ironic contrast, 'A autre danse fault veillier'; and when he does preserve the irony, as in

---

[1] In MS. Trinity Camb. 601, The Dance of Death is followed by 'Mortales dominus cunctos in luce creavit' by Bruno the Carthusian; 'In cinerem rediit cinis et nequit hic remanere', otherwise found only in MS. Caius 223; and 'Sunt tria que vere faciunt me sepe dolere', a verse widely current in western European manuscripts (it was also translated into Low German, A. Freybe, *Das memento mori*, Gotha, 1909, 156), and closely related to 'Wanne ich þenche þinges þre' (see p. 86 above). English manuscripts to include it are MSS. Ashmole 1393, 51ᵛ, Trinity Camb. 1157, 73ʳ, etc. In MS. Bodl. 686 two verses are incorporated into the Dance of Death, being assigned to speakers (an angel and the 'doctor') and followed by the *explicit*. They are the poem mentioned above by Bruno and a four-line stanza, 'Discite vos choream cuncti, qui cernitis istam': both of these are found in the French printed editions of the *Danse des morts*.

[2] The editions are: *The Dance of Death*, E.E.T.S. 181, and *La danse macabré*, ed. E. F. Chaney (Manchester, 1945).

Death's arrest of the bailiff, he does not in any way improve on the French. There is, however, another kind of irony in the poem, which consists of satirical description of the appearance or pleasures of those summoned by Death, so that often brief sketches are provided in which typical faults of the representative characters are ironically insisted upon. In some of these, the translator, with the help of Chaucer's *Prologue*, adds a great deal of effective detail that is lacking in the original. The Abbot, for instance, is not described in the French, though there is a simple implication about his physical appearance in the reference to the monastery 'Qui gros et gras vous a nourry'; in the English this becomes:

> Come forthe Sire Abbot with ȝowre brode hatte,
> [B]e[e]th not abasshed though ȝe have right,
> Grete is ȝowre hede, ȝowr beli large and fatte,
> Ȝe mote come daunce thowȝ ȝe be nothing light.[1]

This has surely been achieved through a recollection of the Monk and perhaps even of the heavily bantering tone of the Host. In the same way the Squire, who in the French was merely described as *gent*, in the English is 'right fressh of ȝowre arai', and the 'amorous squire', who in the French was only 'gay et frique', is addressed as follows in the English:

> Ȝe that be Jentel so fresshe and amerous,
> Of ȝeres ȝonge flowryng in ȝowre grene age,
> Lusti, fre of herte, and eke desyrous,
> Ful of devyses and chaunge yn ȝowre corage,
> Plesaunt of porte of loke and [of] visage.[2]

The general resemblance between the figures in the Dance of Death and the characters in the *Prologue* has been noted before, and, were it chronologically possible, some critics would like to assume that Chaucer was in fact influenced by it. Whilst difficulties of dating are for this almost insuperable, there can be no doubt that the reverse is true and that the *Prologue* influenced Lydgate's translation.

There are two passages in the English, which are not in the French, though almost certainly derived from other French sources. One consists of the insertion of a number of women characters, who are placed at their proper points in the social hierarchy, the empress, the lady of great estate, the abbess, and the amorous gentlewoman. A year after his successful publication of the *Danse des morts*, Guyot Marchand published a feminine adaptation, the *Danse des femmes*,[3] (a work also circulating

---

[1] E.E.T.S. 181, 30.   [2] Ibid. 54.

[3] A convenient account of this may be found in Mâle, *L'Art religieux de la fin du moyen âge en France*, 376–8.

in some manuscripts with the *Danse des morts*)[1] but the English verses are not a translation from this, though they most probably derive from some lost French analogue: there is nothing in them that is typically English. Indeed, the lament of the empress, with its variation on the motif, 'Que vaut biautez', strongly suggests a French original:

> What availeth gold richesse o[r] perre,
> Or what availeth hih blood or Ientylnesse,
> Or what availeth freshnesse or beaute,
> Or what is worth hih porte o[r] strangenesse?
> Deth seith chek-mat to al sich veyn noblesse;
> All worldly power now may me not availe,
> Raunsoun, kyndrede, frenship nor worthynesse,
> Syn deth is come myn hih estate tassaile.[2]

It is usually thought nowadays that it was a taste for sensationalism that was pleased by the *Danse des femmes*. But there is no suggestion of this in the additions to the English Dance of Death. Indeed, they are far more abstract and austere than some of the other descriptions of the decay of feminine beauty, in which the erotic associations, though not exploited for sensationalism, were hinted at deftly and discreetly.

The other addition occurs in only one manuscript, MS. Trinity 601, and consists of a dialogue between Death and Adam. This recalls another, less popular French poem, the *Mors de la pomme*,[3] much of which emphasizes the legal *mandement* given to Death after the Fall, a document which Death grotesquely reads. This idea is echoed in these stanzas, in which Death reminds Adam of 'Thy makers chartre morieris'. It is obvious from this that the English Dance of Death gathered accretions, as the French had already done, for the French text was normally preceded by four stanzas of warning from four skeletons, and towards the end included a warning from the tomb. The latter was imitated in some but not all of the manuscripts of the English Dance.[4] It is historically interesting because it became associated with the tradition of sculptural warning, which we discussed before. The only complete and surviving English printed text of the Dance of Death (that of Tottel in 1554 at the end of *The Fall of Princes*) contains only two illustrations. The first shows the Dance of Death as a procession, led by Pope and Emperor with their accompanying skeletons, and all the other characters

---

[1] L. P. Kurtz, *The Dance of Death and the Macabre Spirit in European Literature* (New York, 1934), 25–69, lists manuscripts of the *Danse macabre* of which six also contain the *Danse des femmes*.

[2] E.E.T.S. 181, 13. The two verses of the Empress and Death are copied separately in MS. Arch. Selden Supra 53, 158ᵛ. In the *Index* they are entered as a separate poem (1867). The *What availeth* formula derives from the *Vers de la mort* of Helinand, S.A.T.F. 1905, 27; see above, p. 111, n. 1.

[3] Ed. L. P. Kurtz (New York, 1937).

[4] Op. cit. xxv–xxvii. The dead king does not occur in manuscripts of Group B.

crowded in the rear. The second is inserted before the stanza spoken by
the dead king: in it a carved emaciated figure lies on a tomb, a crown
upon his head, and long worms wreathed about the torso and limbs;
behind stand three noblemen, making gestures of admonition or dismay. The noblemen are no doubt an echo of the Three Living and the
Three Dead: without them the illustration recalls the kind of cadaver
tomb to which we have already referred. Whilst the illustration is clear
evidence of the influence of funerary sculpture, the stanza itself is in the
tradition of the dead speaking from the grave:

> 3e folken that loken upon this purtrature,
> Beholdyng here alle the estates daunce,
> Seeth what 3e ben, what is 3owre nature,
> Mete unto wormes, not elles yn substaunce,
> And have this myrroure ever yn remembraunce,
> [H]ow I lye here, som-tyme crowned kynge,
> To al estates a trewe resemblaunce
> That wormes fode is fyne of owre lyvynge.[1]

This stanza does not fit the structure of the poem, but it was useful in
correcting the balance in a poem which has a double character, part
satire, part warning from the dead. This double character is particularly
evident in the difference of effect between poem and painting. The poem
with its particularization of the typical faults of the individual ranks of
society is more purely satire: in it the summoning of death becomes
largely a standard by which to measure the vanity and frivolity of all the
material concerns of man. The average, decent reader, aware of himself
as a private individual, will not necessarily recognize in it a likeness of
himself. The warning of death, however, is clearer in the painting, for
the figures there are not satirically represented, and their fellow skeletons
are necessarily a likeness of everybody. The stanza of warning from the
dead king brings the element supplied in visual representation more
forcibly into the text. From the point of view of literary consistency its
insertion was a blemish, but didactically it was essential if the poem was
to be the *myrroure* that the epilogue to the English translation stresses it
to be. But of course it does not transform the poem, which by itself
stands as a satire, and it was probably at least partly for this reason that
English copyists were so often satisfied to transcribe the work in poetical
anthologies without illustration.

The English death lyric in the fifteenth century was surprisingly
unmeditative and, though this at first sight may not seem true, surprisingly limited in quantity and diffusion. Judgements of size and quantity
vary according to implicit measures of comparison and the death lyric

[1] Op. cit. 74.

of the fifteenth century may, from the modern point of view, seem copious and gruesome. But if it is measured against the contemporary French production, then its scarcity is plain. The poem on the Dance of Death, for instance, was, as we have already seen, not printed until 1553, whereas in the last decades of the fifteenth century the *Danse macabre*, with other poems of a similar kind, came for about twenty years almost annually from the French printing-houses.[1] The difference here is that there is no evidence in England of an actual popular taste for literature on the subject of death. The speed with which Guyot Marchand produced editions of the *Danse macabre* and variations upon it suggests the commercial judgement of a businessman rather than the didactic concern of a preacher. Caxton and Wynkyn de Worde were no doubt likewise shrewdly sensitive to the demands of popular taste, but ignored the poetry of death. There is no suggestion in England, as there is in France and Germany, that a perverse enjoyment was derived from the fear of death and from death's distressing physical signs. The generalizations about morbidity made by Huizinga[2] would have no basis whatsoever in English literature.

There is, however, one exception to the ignoring of the death lyric in printed works, and that is the translation of the *Kalendrier des bergers*, which was published seventeen times in English between 1503 and 1625.[3] This work contains a large amount of miscellaneous medieval information, largely of an astrological, medical, and didactic kind, with a number of death poems scattered through it, and the whole dressed in a superficial pastoral disguise. Though the content of this work varies slightly from edition to edition, there are usually four poems on death in it, two spoken by death personified and two by the dead. The first two are fairly dull. One is a warning from Death, as the fourth rider of the Apocalypse (a woodcut illustrates this).[4] The English here is a rather halting translation of the French,[5] and its opening line, 'Above this horse blacke and hydeous',[6] is curious in its unhistorical translation of the

---

[1] J. C. Brunet, *Manuel du libraire* (Paris, 1860–4), ii. 490–5. For a description of the manuscripts as well as the incunabula see L. P. Kurtz, *The Dance of Death and the Macabre Spirit in European Literature*, 25–69.

[2] *The Waning of the Middle Ages* (London, 1950), ch. xi, 124–35.

[3] For an account of the printed editions see H. O. Sommer, *The Kalender of Shepherdes* (London, 1892), 27–57.

[4] The woodcut shows a skeleton on horseback hurling a dart, with the jaws of death behind him. A similar illustration occurs in the *Boke named the Royal* and in the *Pastyme of Pleasure* by Stephen Hawes. With this poem may be compared the speech of death from the *Danse des aveugles*, 'Je suis la mort de nature enemye', which was frequently printed separately in French editions of the *Danse des morts*.

[5] Inc. 'Sur ce cheval hydeux et palle', *Le compost et kalendrier des bergers* (printed Guyot Marchand, 1499), G, vi.

[6] *Kalender of Shepherdes*, ch. xix (printed Wynkyn de Worde, 1528, *S.T.C.* 22411), L.vii–viii.

A a

'cheval . . . palle' into the traditional colour of evil. The other warning of Death, 'Ho, ho you blynde folke, derked in the cloude',[1] is iconographically interesting in that it is illustrated by the figure of a black man blowing a trumpet. This unusual portrayal of Death presumably derives from hagiographical stories in which the Devil appeared as a black man.[2] Nothing is made of Death's appearance in the poem, but the summoning trumpet is extensively elaborated.[3] In the French this is done by the intricate repetition of the word *cor* with its formations and compounds, and the effect is clever but unmoving. The English, though it too has a high proportion of homiletic didacticism, does achieve by its opening 'Ho, ho', and by its direct and peremptory style, something of the effect of a summoning blast.

Far more interesting are the two warnings from the dead, both of which are accompanied by figures of skeletons or decaying corpses.[4] One, 'Thoughe my pycture be not to youre pleasaunce', follows the French closely, but retains an independent vigour:

> Alas worldely people beholde my manere,
> Somtyme I lyved with beauteous vysage;
> Myne eyen ben gone, I have two holes here,
> I am meet for wormes in this passage.
> Take hede of welthe whyle ye have the usage,
> For as I am thou shalte come to duste,
> Holed as a thymble, what shall the avaunce,
> Noughte but thy good dedes, thou mayste me well truste
> And with my lykenesse ye muste all daunce.[5]

The main part of the poem consists of the dead man's laments for lost opportunities for repentance, and his warning to the living to learn by him and know themselves. But the hideous self-description in the passage quoted is very effective meditatively, and in particular the image 'holed as a thymble' (also in the French), with its unusualness and horrifying visual appropriateness, is very striking in a 'modern' style. The

[1] *Kalender of Shepherdes*, ch. li, pp. U, iv^v–X, i; cf. *Kalendrier*, N. vi.

[2] Cf. 'The blake-faced ethiopiens' in Hoccleve's *Ars utillissima sciendi mori*, E.E.T.S., E.S. 61, 203. On the connexion of the black man with the Dance of Death see E.E.T.S. 181. xix–xx.

[3] The idea of death's trumpet recurs in late medieval literature: 'Ffare well, this world! I take my leve for evere' (Brown xv, 149, see above, p. 323); *Everyman*, 843 (ed. A. Cawley, 25); *The Castell of Perseverance*, 2806 (E.E.T.S., E.S. 91, 160), etc. Cf. Jan Vanderheijden, *Het Thema en de Uitbeelding van den Dood in de Poëzie der Late Middeleeuwen en der vroege Renaissance in de Nederlanden* (Ledeburg/Ghent, 1930), 258–9, who also notes it in Helinand's *Vers de la mort*.

[4] In some of the French editions, one of these, 'Se mon regart ne vous vient a plaisir' (from which 'Thoughe my pycture' is translated), is inappropriately illustrated by a cut of the Three Living and the Three Dead; but the English printers followed the better tradition, and prefaced the poem with either a cut of a skeleton seated on his coffin or of one standing in a cemetery with a coffin lid in his hand. Cf. *Kalendrier*, ed. cit. G. v.

[5] Ch. xvii, ed. cit. L. v.

second poem of this kind seems to be independent of the French. All editions, English and French, have towards the end a cut of a skeleton, but, whereas the French puts with it a harsh little didactic reproach of the rich, 'O mauvais riche enfle diniquite', the English editions have the following poem:

Man loke and se,	The tyme hath bene,
Take hede of me,	In my youthe grene,
How thou shall be	That I was clene
Whan thou arte deed:	Of body as ye are.
Drye as a tre,	But for myne eyen
Wormes shall ete the,	Now two holes bene,
Thy greate beaute	Of me is sene
Shall be lyke leed.	But bones all bare.[1]

The metre of this poem, typical of the new forms and rhythms of the sixteenth century, has a tolling quality, which confers on the whole an effect of melancholy. Moreover, in content the poem does not present the decay of the grave as the just punishment for sin, but as the sad fate of all that can arouse nothing but a sense of loss. These moving verses thus give a nostalgic twist to traditional meditative material: the intense clear-cut thought of the Middle Ages is here becoming submerged in the broader, warmer, and didactically less well-defined sympathies of the Renaissance.

The verses in the *Kalender of Shepherdes* represent an interesting byway at the end of the lyric tradition. The volume has no direct bearing on the native tradition, except in so far as the latter must have prepared the way for the public acceptance of these lyrics, providing a natural home for them. They are the only works, fully conceived as poems, and fully in a medieval style, which survived throughout the sixteenth century. It is perhaps a sign of the decline of the native lyric that they are translations from the French.

[1] Ch. xlix, ed. cit. U, i.

X

Conclusion

THE date at which the medieval lyric began can be inferred with reasonable certainty. The poems first appear in quantity in manuscripts of about 1240–50, and there is no reason to suspect that many were written before this decade. There are grounds for associating them with the preaching work of the friars,[1] and for the lyric movement this would therefore give a *terminus ante quem* of 1223, and since some time would necessarily have to elapse between the friars' first coming and their actual composition of verses in English, the hypothesis that the lyric began about twenty years later is very satisfactory. The date, however, at which the lyric ended cannot be determined so neatly. The authors of the *Index of Middle English Verse* drew a line at 1500, and in a work of reference this was a practicable solution, but to the student of literary history there obviously cannot be so sharp a dividing line.[2] On the one hand, it seems likely that the lyric was already declining before 1500; on the other hand, some poems, such as 'The borne is this word blinde', survive only in sixteenth-century manuscripts, but are unmistakably medieval in thought and style. There is also a further problem. Though the thirteenth-century death lyric came trailing antecedents in the preceding century and even in the Anglo-Saxon period, the material here was very limited in quantity, and the Passion lyric sprang to life fully grown, with its ancestry only in the Latin theological and devotional literature of the twelfth century. But the late medieval lyric had many collateral descendants. The meditative tradition reverberated from time to time in the literature and iconography of the sixteenth century, and re-emerged strongly in the metaphysical poetry of the seventeenth century. The latter is self-evidently a different subject, but the relevance of some of the sixteenth-century echoes is not easily to be decided.

In examining the end of the lyric there are two important points to

---

[1] See Appendix B, 377–8.

[2] The *Supplement* uses a more flexible approach (see pp. xv–xix). But the flexibility inevitably leads to some arbitrariness. As the editors point out the only solution would be an index of Tudor and early Elizabethan verse.

consider; firstly, the question of when lyrics ceased to be composed, and
secondly, when lyrics ceased to be known. The two points are interrelated, for it would obviously be very dubious to classify a poem as a
medieval lyric—however clear the resemblances might be—if it was
written at a time when the poems, which we have been describing, ceased
to be current. There is a danger here of producing an unbreakable circle
of argument, and the problem can therefore most safely be discussed
from an actual instance.

The example is that of *The Gude and Godlie Ballatis*,[1] first published
at Edinburgh in 1567, and thereafter reprinted four times in the space
of fifty years. Many of the poems in this work are Scottish paraphrases
of the Psalms, but a few have the Nativity as their subject, and one is a
debate between Flesh and Spirit during life. The feeling in these poems
and the treatment of the subject-matter are undoubtedly medieval, but
the explanation of this most probably lies in their sources: for these are
translations of vernacular hymns used in the German Reformed Church,
and these in turn were either translations of medieval Latin works or
were actually pre-Reformation German hymns. Medieval sentiment can
most clearly be seen in the Christmas carols: vernacular lullabies, pathetic to the point of excess, were current in Germany for almost a century
before the Reformation. *The Gude and Godlie Ballatis* contains, for
instance, the first translation into English of *In dulci jubilo*,[2] now very
popular as a Christmas carol though in a later version, and also a very
agreeable carol, beginning 'I come from hevin to tell', which catches
very well the medieval controlled tenderness for the Christ-Child, the
compassion for His poverty, and the touchingness of the traditional
paradoxes:

> O God that made all Creature,
> How art thow now becumit sa pure,
> That on the hay and stray will ly,
> Amang the Assis, Oxin and Ky.
>
> .   .   .   .   .   .
>
> The Sylk and Sandell the to eis,
> Ar hay, and sempill sweilling clais.[3]

But this is a translation of a hymn by Luther,[4] and the sweetness of the
sentiment and composed simplicity of the language may both equally
derive from the original, for German in the sixteenth century possessed
the qualities of literary unselfconsciousness and lack of artifice, which
had been so advantageously exploited in the English thirteenth-century

---

[1] Ed. A. F. Mitchell (S.T.S. 39).

[2] Ed. cit. 53. The later version is in *The Oxford Book of Carols*, ed. Percy Dearmer
(Oxford, 1964), 94–95; it is accompanied by the original German, pp. 95–96.

[3] Ed. cit. 50.

[4] Martin Luther's *Geistliche Lieder*, ed. P. Wackernagel (Stuttgart, 1848), 63–64.

lyric. The dialogue between Flesh and Spirit is free of gruesome meditative detail since it takes place during life, but it has colloquial and
dramatic vitality, as in the following stanza in which the Flesh with self-
satisfaction describes itself and its pleasures:

> The flesche said I am stark and wycht,
> To wacht gude wyne, fresche, cold and brycht,
> And tak my plesour day and nycht,
> With singing, playing, and to dance,
> And set on sax and sevin the chance.[1]

Though very different from the Nativity poems, this is again typically
medieval. It has been suggested that the author of the *Godlie Ballatis*
was influenced by Henryson and Dunbar. But the tenderness of the
Nativity poems is not that of Henryson, nor the vigour of the Flesh
and Spirit debate that of Dunbar. The author could have learnt these
varieties of medieval style only from a large body of English medieval
poetry, which almost certainly was not available to him, or directly
from his German sources, which he usually translated line by line. The
latter explanation seems inescapable. Admittedly the poems will be best
enjoyed by those familiar with the qualities of the medieval lyric, but
from the point of view of literary history they cannot be classified without
reservation under this heading.

The questions of when lyrics ceased to be written and when they
ceased to be known are, however, interrelated in a second and more
important way: it is not merely that both have to be borne in mind in
the critical discussion of later poems, but also that historically the one
affected the other, for, of the many forces which were destructive of the
meditative lyric, it was the blow to their diffusion which, coming the
earliest, was probably the most fatal. There were in all probably four
causes for the decline of the lyric. The ultimate ones were those that
spring first to mind, the Reformation and the Renaissance, whilst the
more immediate ones were the printed book and, associated with this
and with earlier production of manuscripts on a commercial scale, the
use of prose for meditations, which would earlier have been expressed
in verse.

The effect of printing on the diffusion of the lyric can be seen from
a comparison of the principles of selection by which the contents of
fifteenth-century manuscripts were determined with those that may be
inferred from the productions of Caxton, and his successors Robert
Pynson and Wynkyn de Worde.[2] The manuscripts in which lyrics were

---

[1] Ed. cit. 26.

[2] The following remarks about printed lyrics are necessarily based on first impres-
sions. A thorough search through all early printed books would probably reveal some

chiefly copied in the fifteenth century were roughly of three kinds:[1] firstly, poetical collections, the work (or poems thought to be the work) of poets known and esteemed, Chaucer, Lydgate, and Hoccleve; secondly, manuscripts designed for the person who would own only one volume, and which therefore included a miscellany of romances, lyrics, didactic treatises, etc. (the Thornton Manuscript is a well-known example of this kind); thirdly, manuscripts which were produced by religious orders, particularly the Carthusians. As an appendix to these should be included the manuscripts of any kind which might contain one or two lyrics as a 'fill-up', to prevent the waste of leaving expensive parchment blank. The economics of manuscript production led to large volumes with as much as possible included within one cover, but the economics of printing led to small volumes containing only one work: according to Duff, Caxton had by 1478 printed about twenty-one books, of which sixteen were short, containing less than fifty leaves.[2] Large works were a burden on the printer, and, when they were made, it was because one of the many massive medieval works, such as the *Legenda aurea*, was in demand.

Therefore even lyrics by known poets, such as Lydgate, did not survive the transition from manuscript to print. Many of Lydgate's poems were printed over and over again, the *Fables*, the *Temple of Glass*, etc., but only one of his religious lyrics was printed, the *Testament*, and it was only printed once.[3] The fifteenth-century principle of collecting together all the works of one poet in a manuscript was for a very long time not imitated in the printed book. The two other kinds of manuscript had even less chance of being transferred to print, for the criteria of selection in these were not those of a scholarly and rational assessment of the material, but the needs of those who would use them. This approach disappeared entirely with the more self-conscious book production of the printing-houses: at that time began in England the modern notion of one work to one volume. Romances, for instance, were printed over and over again in the sixteenth century; but no devotional works were included with them: the readers who, in the traditional way, wished both entertainment and edification bought them in separate covers. The whole character of the religious lyric, however, had

printed texts of lyrics. W. A. Ringler, 'A Bibliography and First-Line Index of English Verse Printed through 1500', *Papers of the Bibliographical Society of America*, xlix (1955), 153–80, made such a search for the year 1500: it is noteworthy that his catalogue contains no meditative lyric except for a farced version of the *Salve regina* (E.E.T.S., E.S. 101, 60–61), which, with some miscellaneous didactic verses, is included at the end of Lydgate's *Stans puer ad mensam* (S.T.C. 17030).

[1] For a fuller account, see Appendix A.

[2] E. G. Duff, *The Printers, Stationers and Bookbinders of London and Westminster in the Fifteenth Century* (Aberdeen, 1899), 7.

[3] S.T.C. 17035. At the beginning and end there is a cut of the Man of Sorrows seated on a rock, with the Cross behind Him.

depended upon its being an anonymous and unpretentious work which could be slipped into manuscripts containing works of greater literary importance or religious works, whether didactic or devotional, in the grave form of Latin (and later, sometimes English) prose. The works of Richard Rolle, for instance, were printed often, but no lyric was ever associated with them, as 'Crist makiþ to man a fair present' had been in MS. Hunterian v. 8. 15. More strikingly, though printers made use of 'fill-ups' of many kinds, they did not normally use lyrics, despite their convenient length. An exception to this is a small volume of homilies, attributed to Origen, printed by Fakes,[1] which has on the recto of the last leaf a late and abbreviated version of the *Iesu dulcis memoria*, 'A Ihesu thy swetnesse who myȝt hit se'. But this stands out as a late and isolated example.

The copying of lyrics, however, did not end immediately with the establishment of the printing-house, for, though the production of the traditional kind of manuscript declined, there emerged two new types of manuscripts, which helped to preserve some of the lyrics at the end of the fifteenth century and the beginning of the sixteenth. Towards the end of the fifteenth century there developed the custom of keeping commonplace books, and these provided exactly the informal surroundings in which lyrics might survive, for here, once more, the contents were not determined by rational theory, but simply by the taste and interests of the compiler: examples are MS. Tanner 407, kept by a Norfolk merchant, and the more famous commonplace book of the London grocer Richard Hill, now MS. Balliol 354. The other new kind of manuscript was the song-book, such as the Fayrfax Manuscript: these reflect the musical customs and interests of the early Tudor court. The song-books, of course totally, and the commonplace books to a large extent, show that the late interest in the medieval lyric was in those that had been intended for singing, such as the carol, or that were at least suitable for setting to music: a large number of carols, for instance, were copied by Richard Hill. The same phenomenon can be seen in the printed book; though no collection of meditative lyrics was ever published, small collections of carols came regularly from the printing-houses throughout the sixteenth and the seventeenth centuries:[2] the day-book of the Oxford bookseller John Dorne contains no less than fifteen entries for

---

[1] T. F. Dibdin, *Typographical Antiquities*, begun by Joseph Ames, augmented by William Herbert, iii (London, 1816), 11.

[2] For sixteenth-century collections see Greene, *Carols*, 349–50. There are at least three seventeenth-century collections: *Good and True, Fresh and New Christmas Carols*, printed at London by E. P. for Francis Coles, 1642; *New Christmas Carols*, printed by J. M. to be sold by W. Thackeray and T. Passinger, 1662(?); *A Cabinet of Choice Jewels: or the Christian's Joy and Gladness, set forth in sundry new Christmas Carols*, printed by J. M. for J. Deacon, 1688.

Christmas carols:[1] they were issued simply and cheaply, like later broadside ballads, one sheet for one penny, two for twopence.

These carols were obviously not printed as a contribution towards the preservation of meditative literature, but to serve as a liturgical and also as a social and convivial celebration of the Christmas season. Clearly when the printers thought in terms of satisfying the need for meditative literature, they thought in terms of prose. The fifteenth-century tendency to use prose for short meditations where verse would earlier have been the natural medium, has already been noticed. So long as it had been necessary for the meditation to be memorized, a verse form was necessary, but once literacy became more common and manuscripts more cheap, meditations could be permanently owned, and committal to memory became superfluous. This tendency therefore, which began with the commercial production of manuscripts, was inevitably increased by printing. There was also a second reason for the printers' invariable preference for meditative prose: they chose, on the whole, works of prestige, but the works of prestige in the meditative tradition were not the vernacular lyrics, but the Latin sources on which they were modelled; therefore, whilst lyrics on the Passion were not printed, Nicholas Love's translation of the *Meditationes vitae Christi*, ascribed to Bonaventura, was printed nine times in a few decades, twice by Caxton in 1488 and 1490, and six times thereafter by Pynson and Wynkyn de Worde.[2]

The general acceptance of prose as the normal medium for meditation can be illustrated from a variety of examples. Though no verse *planctus* was printed, the prose text, 'Whan that I, Mary, ihesus moder', was printed twice, prefixed by a woodcut of a Pietà.[3] A group of meditative prose texts were printed together in a volume published by Wynkyn de Worde before 1500:[4] it contains a meditation on the seven blood-sheddings and the seven sorrows of the Virgin, a complaint to the Jews based on the *Improperia*, and a Pietà complaint, in which the Jews, the Cross, the other instruments of the Passion, etc., are reproached. A collection of lyrics on these subjects could equally well have been made. Similarly there were many metrical versions of the Fifteen Oes, including one by Lydgate, but it was a prose text that Caxton printed in 1491.[5] Moreover, it was this version which became included in printed *horae*. Indeed, the same preference for prose is everywhere evident in the

---

[1] F. Madan, 'The Day-Book of John Dorne', *Collectanea*, First Series (Oxford Historical Society, 1885), 152.

[2] *S.T.C.* 3259–67.

[3] *The Lamentacyon of our Lady*, *S.T.C.* 17535 and 17537. See below, p. 393.

[4] *S.T.C.* 14546; see above, p. 225, footnote 4.

[5] *S.T.C.* 20195. Cf. Helen White, *The Tudor Books of Private Devotion* (Wisconsin, 1951), 216–29.

horae. Manuscript *horae* had often included vernacular lyrics amongst the basic Latin contents, but, though printed *horae* might admit a few subsidiary prayers in English, they were again always in prose. It was not until the extensive production of *horae* on the Continent for the English market, from about 1525 onwards, that verse was once again used. In these, the work of Thielman Kerver and Francis Regnault, metrical versions of the Hours of the Passion and Hours of the Compassion are found,[1] just as they had been in the fifteenth century. But the translations are not medieval ones, and rather dull: the inference here is that this does not represent any direct continuity with English medieval practice, but rather a reintroduction of the latter through the influence of the French.

Despite the printers' general indifference to the meditative lyrics, they did not, of course, disappear totally and at once. A poem on the wounds of Christ was, for instance, included in a small devotional collection;[2] the short verse 'O man unkinde', with a woodcut of an image of pity, appeared at the end of the *Treatise* of William Bonde,[3] to which we have already referred, and also at the end of the 1530 edition of John Becon's *Pomander of Prayer*;[4] the same verse and a version of the Signs of Death are copied in Robert Reynis's commonplace book (MS. Tanner 407). Moreover, poets such as Skelton, show unmistakably that they were quite well acquainted with the medieval lyric tradition. It was the Reformation and the new Renaissance styles of writing that completed the unintentional destruction of the lyric, which had been so substantially begun by the printers.

The effect of the Reformation was to make disreputable the traditional forms of Passion meditation and to destroy their foundation. It was a cardinal Protestant doctrine that man was incapable of loving God: instead of the perfect movement of love being, as medieval theologians had taught, from God to man to God, it was held to be, from God to man to his neighbour. But the medieval theory of meditation on Christ in His humanity had been built upon the earlier theory of love. The result of this change in doctrine was that, whilst meditation on the Passion did not disappear from sixteenth-century devotional works at one blow, it became modified, and in particular the fifteenth-century tendency to show its proper issue, not as love, but as moral reform, became predominant. For example, in the Byddell-Marshall primer of 1535,[5] in the section 'A frutefull remembraunce of Christes passion', the fruit is said to be the awakening of the conscience and remorse; the value of a

[1] White, op. cit. 83.

[2] 'Gracyous lorde for thy gret passyon' in *A Gloryous Medytacyon of Jhesus Crystes Passyon* (*S.T.C.* 14550), cf. Gray, *Notes and Queries*, Feb. 1963, 50–51.

[3] See above, p. 185.

[4] Printed Copland; Dibdin-Ames, iii. 115.

[5] *S.T.C.* 15988.

compassion for Christ in His sufferings is denied by reference to the text, which long before the Lollard denouncer of mystery plays had used for the same purpose, 'Daughters of Jerusalem, weep not for me, but weep for yourselves and for your children'.[1] In the same polemical passage the writer also rejects the helpfulness of all images and paintings.[2] These, which had formed such an important part in the medieval meditative tradition, had become suspect for a variety of reasons: partly perhaps because they had tended to become objects of an external cult, rather than to be used as exterior aids to interior meditation; and partly also because they contained so much non-Biblical incident, for which the original meditative purpose and justification had been forgotten.

Not all works that dealt with meditation were as extreme as this primer. Typical of the more moderate approach is the *Disce vivere* of Christopher Sutton, written towards the end of the sixteenth century. This makes use of all the traditional methods, the detailed visualization, the presence of the meditator in the scene, the emotive and associative force of the compassion of the Virgin.[3] But the value of this is never explicitly said to be the stirring of love: it is the willingness to suffer oneself, contrition, admiration, and the resolution to devote one's life to Christ. In this period traditional meditation with the traditional purpose stated plainly can be found only in the work of Recusant writers,[4] and these are often not writing immediately in the medieval tradition, but imitating or translating the work of sixteenth-century continental Catholic writers. Many of the devotional treatises discussed by A. C. Southern are translations from the Spanish. The following, for instance, is a quotation from a Rosary meditation translated from the Spanish of Gaspar Loarte:

The meditation of the thirde point wil furnish thee of fitt matter to move compassion, if thou consider, howe this moste mightie monarche, this King of al kinges, he whom neither the heavens nor earth can holde and comprehende, hath in such wise debased, humbled, and throwen himselfe downe in a harde manger upon a litle haye; he, whom the Angels doo adore, and in whose presence the powers of heaven doo quake againe, lieth quaking himselfe for colde betwixt two brute beastes. O divine darling, what meaneth this geere?[5]

---

[1] Ibid. E. iv. Cf. 'A tretise of miraclis pleyinge', *Altenglische Sprachproben*, ed. E. Mätzner, i (Berlin, 1869), 232.

[2] Ibid. F. iv^v. 'But they that fall to theyr meditations, thinkyng therby to get, I can not tell howe moche merites, and beholde this passion eyther in paynted tables, or in printed papyrs . . . take greate labours . . . but all aboute nought.'

[3] The following is typical of the meditative description: 'Stand, and behold a little with the devout women, the body of thy Savior upon the crosse, see him afflicted from top to toe, see him wounded in the head, to heale our vaine imaginations . . .', ch. xxvii (London, 1602), 509.

[4] *Elizabethan Recusant Prose 1559–1582* (London, 1950), 181–262.

[5] Op. cit. 217–18.

With this may be compared a Nativity description from another Rosary meditation:

And therefore was the Mother of God enforced to turne into an Oxe stall that stoode by the high way, no better then an hovel or cotage, and there brought foorth that blessed babe her deare Sonne, betweene an Oxe and an Asse, lapping him in suche poore cloutes as she had, and layde him in the maunger. Where ye may beholde our Lady borowing a little hay from the sely Asse, to lay her child uppon.[1]

The interest of these passages lies in the style: to some extent in the first and fully in the second, there is an immediacy and simplicity of effect, which recalls medieval meditation, and contrasts with the literary formality of Protestant devotional works at the time. They are a good example of the relationship between the theory of meditation and the style. A style which drives home the tender homeliness of description will not be relevant to the arousing of remorse or admiration, but, as we have often said, it is an important aid to the stirring of love.

These prose passages, so reminiscent of the style and feeling of the medieval meditative lyric, raise the question of whether the lyric, so nearly destroyed by the indifference of the printers, might not, nevertheless, have been revived, had spiritual circumstances been favourable. This question leads to the last of the causes of the end of the lyric, the new sixteenth-century style. Were it not for the change of style, one could rightly have expected that a continuation of the medieval tradition would be seen in the Passion poetry of some Recusant poets, and also in the poems on death of any writer, for mortality meditation, because of its penitential value, continued to be praised by all.

The sixteenth-century religious lyric, however, cannot be usefully discussed against the background of medieval vernacular poetry, for, as we said earlier, the religious lyric tends to imitate contemporary secular fashions, whenever this is possible. It had been an advantage of the early medieval lyric that there were no English love poems to influence it, whilst in the fifteenth-century religious lyric the style, metre, and adornments of secular verse became increasingly evident. Therefore, when in the sixteenth century a Recusant poet, such as Southwell, resumed the versifying of medieval themes, he did so in the style of Sidney and Spenser. Even a poem such as 'Upon the image of death', which is stylistically neutral and very traditional in content, has a poise and nostalgic rhythm which mark it out as sixteenth-century:

> I often looke upon a face
>   Most ugly, grisly, bare and thinne;
> I often view the hollow place,
>   Where eyes and nose, had sometimes bin:

[1] Op. cit. 215.

> I see the bones acrosse that lie,
> Yet little think that I must die.[1]

Moreover his Nativity and Passion meditations are filled with paradoxes and conceits, which distinguish them completely from the Medieval lyric. Southwell, however, may seem too extreme an example, for his poems are unmedieval, not only in their style, but also in their technique of meditation, of which the most important part is an ingenious exercise of the intellect, and in this way the poems of Southwell foreshadow those of Donne. But even in works where the content is totally medieval, the medieval heritage is stylistically irrelevant. Translations, for instance, of such popular medieval works as the *Cur mundus militat*[2] or the *Noctis sub silencio* can only usefully be discussed as works of their own period. The question at issue concerning William Crashaw's version of the *Noctis sub silencio*[3] is to what extent the diction and conventions of contemporary poetry were helpful to the work of translation, just as this had been the question concerning the fifteenth-century version in the Porkington Manuscript.[4] In the work too of lesser Recusant poets, such as Thomas Vaux or Swithin Wells, whose thought is traditional and whose style is less assertively Elizabethan than that of Southwell, there is still no true continuation of the medieval lyric. Many of their themes are strikingly the same: for instance the aged man's description of himself:

> The harbinger of death,
> To me I see him ride:
> The cough, the colde, the gaspyng breath,
> Dothe bid me to provide.
>
> .   .   .   .   .   .
>
> Loe here the bared scull,
> By whose balde signe I know:
> That stoupyng age away shall pull,
> Which youthfull yeres did sowe.[5]

or the meditation on the Passion:

> O Angelles (looke) is this your kinge
> O queene of Heaven: is this thy childe
> Is this the maker of eche thinge,
> Alas who hath him thus defilde?
>
> .   .   .   .   .   .

[1] *Poems*, ed. A. B. Grosart (London, 1872), 155.

[2] *The Paradise of Dainty Devices* (*1576–1606*), ed. H. E. Rollins (Cambridge, Mass., 1927), no. 1 and notes, pp. 180–2.

[3] *The Complaint or Dialogue betwixt the Soule and the Bodie of a damned man … Supposed to be written by St. Bernard from a nightly vision of his*, London, 1616 (*S.T.C.* 1909). There were two reprints of this (*S.T.C.* 6025–6).

[4] See above, pp. 362–8.

[5] 'The aged lover renounceth love', *Tottel's Miscellany*, ed. H. E. Rollins, i (Cambridge, Mass., 1928), 166, and notes in vol. ii. 285–6.

> My pride of harte hath peerst his braine
> my garments gay hath strypt him so
> my envy opened all his vaines
> my sinnes alas did him this woe.[1]

But there is a strong, though almost indefinable difference of effect. In the first quotation the metre and syntax, and above all the tone of nostalgia, mark it out from the ironic tradition of the elegies of Maximian. The second is more self-dramatizing than a medieval lyric would have been: the paradoxes and rhetorical questions are traditional, but in the Middle Ages they would normally have been spoken by Christ or the Virgin; there is a suggestion here of melodramatic penitence quite foreign to medieval feeling. But even passages, which have as close an affinity to the medieval lyric as these, have to be searched for, and a search for what is uncharacteristic is not likely to be profitable. A consideration of the work of the lesser Recusant poets, which did not begin from a study of the medieval lyric, would scarcely mention these rare and minor echoes of it.

Though the pressures of contemporary style made continuity with the medieval tradition impossible in any poetry of literary pretensions in the sixteenth century, in sub-literary forms there did remain some direct influence from it. This may be seen, for instance, in the *titulus* verses still embodied in *horae* and other devotional works. The *horae* produced by Thielman Kerver for the English market contain a large number of woodcuts with explanatory verses. An example is the cut preceding the Office for the Dead, which, in accordance with continental custom, shows the Three Living and the Three Dead. Beneath the picture are the following verses:

> We have somtyme abyden our chaunce
> In this worlde, passyng tyme lustely,
> But now ye must come trace on our daunce
> All Adams kynde be ordeyned to dye.
>
> We ben in glory and worldly favour,
> Full of all welth, rychesse, and substaunce,
> But now we perceyve that come is the houre
> That we must leve all lust and pleasaunce.[2]

This is translated from the French verses used by Kerver in his *Heures* of 1525,[3] and though it has no literary merit it does show the continuity

---

[1] Louise Guiney, *Recusant Poets with a Selection from their Work*, i (New York, 1939), 174.

[2] *Horae*, 1531 (*S.T.C.* 15974), 89[v]–90[r].

[3] The verse has been printed by W. Storck, 'Der Spruch der Toten an die Lebenden', *Zeitschrift des Vereins für Volkskunde*, xxi (1911), 55.

of a low, unadorned style in contexts where the verse was unobtrusive because subordinated to a picture.

A better and more interesting example of the same type of *titulus* verse are the couplets which accompany the Dance of Death depicted in the margins of *A Book of Christian Prayer*, printed by John Daye in 1569 and 1578. In his discussion of the iconography of this volume, Samuel Chew suggested that, whilst the woodcuts derived from the French *horae*, the couplets might well have been borrowed from some English wall-painting of the Dance of Death now lost.[1] The parallel with the verse of the Three Living and the Three Dead, however, suggests that they may have been borrowed with the Dance and be translations from the French; as against this their colloquial and ironic vitality may indicate a native origin. Though entirely lacking in metrical and stylistic poise, they often have the ironic tautness, which was so noticeably lacking in Lydgate's translation. The following couplets are some of the neatest:

> Plead as thou lust: With me thou must.
> (to the attorney)
> Sir Justice arise: come to my assise.
> Come Baylife, no bayle: with me shal prevayl.
> By thy water, I do see: thou must away with me.
> (to the physician)[2]

In all of these there is a crude but satirically effective playing with the character's profession, either by the statement that his former habits or wiles will no longer avail him, or by Death metaphorically assuming his profession: the address to the physician in particular is marked by a half-farcical, half-savage fantasy.

Whilst these *titulus* verses are probably not directly of English origin, actual Medieval lyrics were often preserved as epitaphs. Though there was a growing tendency for epitaphs to become commemorative and eulogistic (and thus to reflect the more formal style of the time), texts of common medieval verses, such as 'Erþe toc of erþe', 'Ffare well, this world', 'If man him biocte', 'Such as ye be, such wer we', etc., continued to be used. But there is little trace of invention here, and many of the epitaphs are merely weakened versions of their originals. As an example of an attempt at variation within the tradition, the following verse may be quoted:

> From Earth wee came, to Earth wee must returne,
> Witness this EARTH that Lyes within this URNE.

---

[1] 'The Iconography of *A Book of Christian Prayers (1578)*', *Huntingdon Library Quarterly*, viii (1945), 293–305.

[2] John Daye, *A Booke of Christian Prayers* (1578), 86ʳ, 85ᵛ, 87ʳ, 87ᵛ.

> Begott by EARTH: Borne also of Earth's WOMBE,
> 74 yeares Lived EARTH, Now Earth's his TOMBE.
> In Earth EARTH's Body Lyes Under this STONE,
> But from this Earth to Heaven EARTH's soule is gone.[1]

This is an epitaph for Roger Earth, who died in 1634. The attempt to combine the traditional theme with a rebus is clumsily ineffective, and the fact that no better example of invention within the tradition can be found strongly suggests that these epitaphs were fossilized relics of medieval verse. Elsewhere, however, there remain hints of vitality. A large earthenware dish of 1660 had the following inscription on it:

> Earth I am et is most true
> Desdan me not for soo ar you.[2]

The couplet itself, of course, has no merit, but in its relationship to its context can be seen a flicker of the ironic invention, which was characteristic of the best medieval treatment of the themes of death: the confident are once again caught off guard by the unexpected but pointed jeer.

More important amongst sub-literary forms than *titulus* verses or epitaphs are the broadside ballads. Though many of these were composed by the learned rather than by ballad-mongers (and those which imitate medieval religious themes are almost certainly in this class), they are written in a style remote from the educated poetry of the day. Indeed, they have in common with the lyric that the style is not chosen primarily to suit the subject but to match the sensibilities of the audience: the broadside ballads were in the late sixteenth and seventeenth centuries the literature of the unlearned, and they were sold cheaply at a penny a sheet. It is not on the whole profitable to look amongst the broadside ballads for Passion meditations, though a few were written; but they are generally didactic in tone and flat in style. The following is a quotation from a complaint of Christ, which forms part of a longer poem:

> I thee pursude with hartes desire,
>   I ranne with faintinge breath;
> Wilt thou unkinde from me retyre,
>   and frustrate soe my death?
> My enemies they did not payne
>   my bodie halfe so sore,
> As thy unkyndness doth constraine
>   my sorrowes tennes more.[3]

---

[1] Ravenshaw, *Antiente Epitaphes*, 79.

[2] Weber, *Aspects of Death*, 664.

[3] Inc. 'Behould our saviour crucifide', H. E. Rollins, *Old English Ballads* (Cambridge, 1920), no. 17, p. 123.

The thought is medieval but the feeling is drab and unloving. In this and similar poems the effect of the interruption of Passion meditation by the Reformers' doctrine is plainly seen.

In the ballads on death, however, both the medieval forms and the medieval spirit continue. There are ballads on death in sermon form, warnings from Death, dialogues between Death and man, a Dance of Death and even a translation of *Noctis sub silencio*.[1] The latter is the only one that is dull: it adds nothing to its source and loses most of the force and irony. But in general these ballads are lively and ironic, though the irony is more satiric than personal. This may be seen in the Dance of Death: in this the dance is no longer a procession; a folio page is filled by representatives in the centre, and by four static scenes in the corners which are particularly emphasized; in one, for instance, a pair of richly dressed lovers are caressing one another beside a table laden with food, and Death addresses them as follows:

> Ye dallying fyne lovers,
>   In mydst of your chere:
> To daunce here be partners,
>   And to grave draw ye nere.[2]

The element of social satire is even plainer in the sermon ballad, 'Yf death would come and shew his face'. In this there is a series of pictures of places filled with people, corrupt and unthinking of death (the Court at Westminster, the harbour where merchants meet, ale-houses, etc.), where Death, by showing himself, would cause amazement and dismay:

> Yf death would make a step to dance,
>   where lusty gallants bee,
> And take the dice and throw a chance
>   where he doth gamsters see,
> And say, 'my masters, have at all,
>   I warrant it will be mine!'
> I am sure it would amaze them all
>   To set him any coyne.[3]

Those that are less satirical and more concerned to emphasize the universality of death are less good. There is one, for instance, beginning 'I am that champion, greate of power, / one barbed horse, with coulor pale' that contains a list of the famous dead and an *ubi sunt* passage:[4] it is quite competent but dull. More lively is another warning

---

[1] 'Saint Bernard's Vision', *Roxburghe Ballads*, ed. J. W. Ebsworth, ii (Hertford, 1874), 491–7.

[2] *The Daunce and Song of Death*, B.M. Huth 50 (32). The complete text, but with an inaccurate reading in the first line of this quotation, is printed in E.E.T.S. 181, 100–1.

[3] D. Gray, 'Two Songs of Death', *Neuphilologische Mitteilungen*, lxiv (1963), 68.

[4] Rollins, *Old English Ballads*, no. 46.

from Death, recently reprinted, 'Canne yea dance the shakinge of the sheetes',[1] in which the tone is set by this first line, with its colloquial directness and grim pun. Finally, in the dialogue between Death and the young man, which is one of the few religious broadside ballads written in medieval ballad style, irony is achieved by the jolly, nonsense refrain, 'hey ho, hey ho', as in:

> My name is Death, I come for thee,
> hey ho, hey ho, thy Glass is run.[2]

Whilst the broadside ballads on death are so seemingly medieval, they lack the complexity and depth of medieval poetry. Indeed, if the two are compared, it can be clearly seen how deceptive was the medieval appearance of simplicity and weightlessness. In medieval poetry the simplicity is on the surface, and beneath is a strong foundation of serious and subtle thought. But there is no such foundation to the broadside ballads, and they therefore are lightweight, mere shades of what their originals had been.

It is perhaps not fair to criticize the religious broadside ballads in this way, for, whilst in one sense they are in their period akin to the medieval lyrics since they are written by the learned for the moral benefit of the unlearned, in another sense the equivalent of the medieval lyric in this period are the poems of the metaphysical school. But in this poetry the change in meditative tradition, already referred to, is well established: the work of the intellect is an essential part of each meditation. The resemblance between the medieval lyrics and some of the poems of Herbert, for instance, has been pointed out in detail by Rosamund Tuve,[3] and, as she so strongly argued in her book, criticism of metaphysical poetry, which does not recognize this resemblance, is likely to go astray. But the acknowledgement of this resemblance should be the foundation of the criticism of seventeenth-century poetry, not its goal. For, once the resemblance is seen, the most interesting point becomes, not the likenesses between the two, but the differences. A final contrast may be made between two poems on the subject of shedding tears for the Passion. The first of these we have already quoted in the introduction to the medieval Passion lyric:

> Loverd þi passion,
> Who þe þenchet arist þaron,
> teres hit tollet,
> and eyen hit bollet,

---

[1] Gray, loc. cit. 64–67.
[2] 'Death's Uncontrollable Summons', *Roxburghe Ballads*, iv (1883), 28.
[3] *A Reading of George Herbert* (London, 1952).

nebbes hit wetet,
and hertes hit swetet.[1]

The second is a sonnet by the Catholic poet, William Alabaster:

> When without tears I looke on Christ, I see
> Only a story of some passion,
> Which any common eye may wonder on;
> But if I look through tears Christ smiles on me.
> Yea, there I see myself and from that tree
> He bendeth down to my devotion,
> And from his side the blood doth spin, wheron
> My heart, my mouth, mine eyes still sucking be;
> Like as in optick works, one thing appears
> In open gaze, in closer otherwise.
> Then since tears see the best, I ask in tears,
> Lord, either thaw mine eyes to tears, or freeze
> My tears to eyes, or let my heart tears bleed,
> Or bring, where eyes, nor tears, nor blood shall need.[2]

Both these poems have the same meaning: the Passion, when rightly meditated upon, moves to tears and love. But in the medieval poem this is stated in a simple style to reflect a great general truth, and with a lowly description of physical symptoms, which will bring it home to the heart. But in metaphysical poetry there are no great general truths and the way to the heart is through the head. The proposition is therefore analysed with ingenuity and unravelled through a series of tightly worked conceits and paradoxes: the poem was conceived through wit and must be understood through intellectual attentiveness. With metaphysical poetry, therefore, the medieval lyric was superseded by something alike but different, and thus, with the minor exception of its continuing influence from time to time on sub-literary forms, it was truly ended.

---

[1] Brown XIII, 56 B. Cf. p. 20 above.
[2] *The Sonnets of William Alabaster*, ed. G. M. Story and Helen Gardner (Oxford, 1959), 39.

APPENDIX A

The Manuscripts

SOME of the earliest known texts of the lyrics are written in the margins of learned monastic manuscripts. Among the treatises in MS. Laud Misc. 112 is Defensor's *Liber scintillarum*: on f. 275ᵛ, which contains part of the chapter *De dilectione Dei et proximi*,[1] there is a verse in the bottom margin beginning 'Lovert þe mincginge of þe it is so swete'. It is a version of 'Þe minde of þi passiun, swete ihesu' (Brown XIII. 56A).[2] In MS. Digby 45 two verses are written in the margins of a Latin sermon on the Passion: on ff. 21ᵛ–22ʳ the *Homo vide* is written in a top margin and a rather corrupt text of an English translation in a bottom margin;[3] on f. 25ʳ a verse translation of the *Candet nudatum pectus* appears in the bottom margin, though here the Latin is given in neither text nor margin. The inferences from evidence such as this[4] are that from about 1240 onwards Latin meditative commonplaces were versified in English and that they were often associated with preaching.

Lyrics first appear in quantity, and in the body of the text not in the margins, in manuscripts that were preaching-notebooks of the friars.[5] The earliest are MSS. Trinity Camb. 323 and MS. Jesus Oxf. 29. MS. Trinity 323 contains a substantial number of lyrics on death, three Body and Soul poems, one on the Signs of Death, and 'Wen þe turuf is þi tuur'; a surprisingly large collection of lyrics addressed to the Virgin, including 'Seinte mari, moder milde' and 'For on þat is so feir ant brist', a poem on the five joys (Brown XIII. 18); and the much-copied Passion lyric, 'Wose seþe on rode'. These verses form part of a collection of preaching-notes, mainly in Latin. Later volumes of roughly the same kind are MSS. Harley 913 (the Kildare MS.), Harley 2316, and Harley 7322. Fully organized preaching-books are the *Fasciculus morum* and the alphabetical preaching-book of John of Grimestone.

---

[1] Defensor, *Liber scintillarum*, P.L. 88, 605–8.

[2]   Lovert þe mincginge of þe it is so swete,
      þat min einen it to-bolneþ,
      and min teres in tollet,
      minne leres it weteþ,
      and min erte it sweteþ.

The first line has been influenced by the *Dulcis Iesu memoria*. The verse is followed by its equivalent in Latin prose, and then by the following scrap of English (also with Latin translation): 'þe name Ihesu honiit is in muþe, murie drem in ere, michel blisse in herte.'

[3] Inc. 'Mon þu bihode þat hic thole *for þe*'. The writing is very faded.

[4] I am very indebted to Dr. Hunt for pointing out to me that texts of the lyrics occurred in these manuscripts.

[5] R. H. Robbins, 'The Authors of the Middle English Religious Lyrics', *J.E.G.Ph.* xxxix (1940), 230–8. Professor Robbins also gives a very clear historical account of the manuscripts in the Introduction to *Secular Lyrics of the xivth and xvth Centuries* (Oxford, 1952).

Different in kind are the big collections of English and French poetry, MSS. Harley 2253, Digby 86, and B.M. Add. MS. 46919 (*olim* Phillipps 8336).[1] All of these are mixed in contents, containing work both religious and secular. Though they include prose texts, the proportion of verse to prose is very much higher than in the preaching books. MS. Harley 2253,[2] which may have belonged to Leominster Priory, Hereford, contains religious and love lyrics in English, saints' lives, a romance (King Horn), and many French secular poems, including the only collection of fabliaux found in an English manuscript:[3] the latter are, incidentally, exceptionally obscene, even by the standards of the genre. MS. Digby 86 is less wide-ranging in its contents,[4] but, apart from English and French religious poems, it includes various French secular poems of an uncourtly kind, and *Dame Sirith*,[5] the only surviving English fabliau before *The Canterbury Tales*. This kind of manuscript seems to have been made by members of religious orders, who wished to preserve in them anything of interest. Whilst there is an overlap between the religious lyrics in these manuscripts and those in the more obviously didactic volumes, this overlap in itself emphasizes the difference: for the religious lyrics chosen are the more elaborate ones and those that most obviously have literary pretensions.

Though these large poetical collections are very important for the works that they preserve, they are, as far as we can tell, far less characteristic of the period than are the preaching manuscripts. The latter are far more numerous, and the texts in them seem to have had far wider currency, some surviving in many manuscripts and over the space of nearly three hundred years. 'Wanne ich þenche þinges þre', for instance, was recorded first in MS. Jesus Coll. Oxf. 29, and finally in MS. Balliol 354 at the beginning of the sixteenth century. Manuscripts such as MS. Harley 2253 seem to have provided a final resting-place for lyrics, whereas the preaching manuscripts were points of dissemination.

In the fifteenth century there is a far wider variety in kinds of manuscripts, and the chief form then ceased to be the manuscript compiled by a religious order for the purpose of religious instruction. There remained some important manuscripts of this kind; the *Fasciculus morum*, for instance, continued to be copied widely in the fifteenth century,[6] and one of the most valuable

---

[1] For a list of contents see P. Meyer, 'Notice et extraits du MS. 8336 de la bibliothèque de Sir Thomas Phillipps à Cheltenham', *Romania*, xiii (1884), 497–541.

[2] The contents are listed by K. Böddeker, *Altenglische Dichtungen des MS Harl. 2253* (Berlin, 1878), ix–xiii.

[3] They are nos. 24, 28, 55, and 73 in the list of fabliaux given by Per Nykrog, *Les fabliaux* (Copenhagen, 1957), 310–24. The texts may be found in A. de Montaiglon and G. Raynaud, *Recueil général et complet des fabliaux du xiiie et xive siècles* (Paris, 1872–90), ii. 47, vi. 147, iv. 99, ii. 48.

[4] A description of the contents is given by E. Stengel, *Codex manuscriptus Digby 86* (Halle, 1871).

[5] *Early Middle English Verse and Prose*, ed. J. A. W. Bennett and G. V. Smithers (Oxford, 1966), 80–95. MS. Digby 86 also contains a French fabliau, Nykrog, op. cit. no. 136.

[6] See A. G. Little, *Studies in English Franciscan History* (Manchester, 1917), 139–57; F. Foster, 'A Note on the *Fasciculus Morum*', *Franciscan Studies*, viii (1948), 202–4.

collections of later lyrics is B.M. Add. MS. 37049.[1] It differs, however, from its predecessors in that its lyrics cannot have been communicated orally, for the accompanying illustrations are an essential part of the meditations. Like the *Holkham Bible Picture Book* it was probably shown to rich laymen privately and individually.[2]

Religious manuscripts of the fifteenth century are more often of other kinds. There are, for instance, *horae* and other collections of prayers that contain vernacular lyrics. They are often of the formally liturgical kind: MS. Rawl. lit. g. 2, for instance, contains a poem contrasting the seven blood-sheddings with the seven deadly sins (Brown XIV. 123), and MS. Douce 1, a poem on the five wounds;[3] MS. Camb. Un. Ii. 6. 43 ends with 'O vernacule i honoure him and the'.[4] Sometimes, however, the concluding piece of these volumes would be a less formal meditation: MS. Lambeth 560, for instance, ends with 'Who can the sorow conceyve allas'.[5] There were also many other less clearly classifiable kinds of devotional manuscripts, such as the collections of meditations and prayers (preponderantly in verse) in MS. Arundel 285.[6]

As manuscripts came to be owned by the laity, lyrics were often included as appendages to vernacular prose texts. In two manuscripts, for instance, 'Crist makiþ to man a fair present' follows Richard Rolle's *Form of Perfect Living*;[7] in MS. Douce 322 'Syth þat ye list to be my costes' immediately precedes the fifth chapter of the *Horologium sapientiae* and the *Boke of the Craft of Dying*. Some manuscripts are made up largely of meditative prose texts, some as yet unidentified. MS. C.U.L. Kk. 1. 6 contains amongst other texts meditations on the Name of Jesus and the Name of Mary, meditations for the seven days of the week, a set of twenty-one meditations on the Passion, and a translation of the *Quis dabit capiti meo* (beginning 'A God hoo shall 3eve me so grett habaundance of teyerys').[8] Following these are two of Lydgate's complaints, 'Man to refourme thyn exil and thy loos' and 'Upon the cros naylled I was ffor the'.

The most striking fifteenth-century innovation in manuscripts, however, was that purely poetical collections were made. Meditative lyrics by Lydgate or Hoccleve were copied in manuscripts with other poems on quite different subjects by them or thought to be by them.[9] In these the unifying principle is no longer that of subject-matter but that of the assembly of all the known work of one author (the principle of compilation nowadays so much taken for

---

[1] Some account of the manuscript will be found in T. W. Ross, 'Five fifteenth-century "Emblem Verses" from B.M. Addit. 37049', *Speculum*, xxxii (1957), 275.

[2] *The Holkham Bible Picture Book*, Introduction and Commentary by W. O. Hassall, 30–33.

[3] D. Gray, 'The Five Wounds of Our Lord', *Notes and Queries*, N.S. x (1963), 50–51.

[4] E.E.T.S. 46, 170–93.

[5] *Index*, 4089.

[6] *Devotional Pieces in Verse and Prose*, ed. J. A. W. Bennett, S.T.S. 1955.

[7] See Brown XIV, p. 273.

[8] The Catalogue description of this manuscript is inadequate: the five texts here enumerated and two others (Meditations from Augustine, etc., and 'Veni domine Ihesu'), are presented in the Catalogue as Items 2 and 3.

[9] e.g. MSS. Harley 2251, Laud Misc. 683, and Trinity Camb. 600 (Lydgate and Chaucer).

granted). A related kind of manuscript is the privately owned anthology: in a volume of this kind texts are collected that in the days of printing would have been issued in separate volumes. Romances, religious lyrics, secular poems by known authors, etc., are assembled as a large collection of verse.[1] This kind of manuscript may be seen as related to those that contain, for instance, the works of Lydgate, because in them the religious lyrics are copied again primarily as poetry: their manuscript context is not other devotional material in prose but other poems on secular themes.

Inevitably, in manuscripts such as these, it was usually substantial and elaborate poems that were included, but in determining their influence it is difficult to distinguish between cause and effect. Clearly, religious lyrics would not have been copied in them had they not already had sufficient poetic pretensions to be associated with work of literary prestige; but the effect may well have been to depress the short unpretentious verse, whose literary merit might be genuine but of a less objectively definable kind. Certainly, comparatively few short lyrics were written and earlier lyrics gradually ceased to be copied. But towards the end of the period there arose a new kind of manuscript that was quite unpretentious in design, namely private commonplace books. Richard Hill's commonplace book (MS. Balliol 354) contains various short moralistic verses, including texts of 'Erþe toc of erþe' and 'Wanne ich þenche þinges þre'. MS. Tanner 407, which belonged to a Norfolk merchant, contains, amongst miscellaneous didactic scraps, a Latin farced version of the Signs of Death and a text of 'O man unkinde'.

This attempt at classification of medieval manuscripts in terms of content may suggest that the manuscripts fall more readily into formal groups than in fact they do. An emphasis upon important kinds necessarily excludes those that are less important and quite different, such as medical manuscripts which sometimes contain lyrics.[2] It also necessarily excludes the many manuscripts that fall somewhere between the groups that can be clearly defined. The reading of lyrics in their manuscripts, however, is a valuable exercise for they often then give an impression very different from that which they give in modern anthologies. The manuscript context of the lyrics is one of the clearest indications of how they were regarded in the Middle Ages.

[1] e.g. MSS. Lincoln Cath. 91 (Thornton MS.), C.U.L. Ff. ii. 38, and Ashmole 61.
[2] e.g. MS. Sloane 1313.

Authorship

NEARLY all the lyrics written in the earlier period are anonymous. But, though the authors are not known by name, it is known what kinds of men they were by profession. It is certain that they were learned clerics, and there is strong evidence that most of them were friars who composed the lyrics for use in their pastoral work. Professor Robbins has shown that nearly all the early preaching manuscripts are of Franciscan or Dominican origin,[1] and this evidence of the manuscripts is supported by general probability.

The movement for the instruction of the laity in the vernacular, which developed strongly in the thirteenth century, was a dual one, and from it two types of literature emerged. One strain is that marked by the Lateran Decrees of 1215;[2] from these came the rhymed versions of the Paternoster, Ave, and Creed,[3] penitential poems, versified expositions of the Seven Deadly Sins, the Ten Commandments, the Seven Sacraments, and other works summarizing doctrinal or didactic information.[4] Such literature was composed by both secular and religious orders. The friars in their preaching missions, however, were free of this fixed pattern of teaching, and were therefore able to concentrate on the kind of spirituality that evaded the precise and careful prescriptions of the Lateran Council. The friars sought to transmit to the laity in simple forms the essentials of the meditations which emanated in the twelfth century from Cistercian spirituality, and which in the thirteenth century were fostered and increased by the Franciscans. Both lyrics and mystery plays seem to have been the media used by the friars for bringing the piety of the learned to the laity.

The latest evidence of a close connexion between the friars and meditative poetry is John of Grimestone's preaching-book, which gives its date as 1372. In the fifteenth century there is nothing to connect the lyrics specifically with the friars. Amongst the known authors of lyrics in this period only Ryman was a friar: Lydgate, for instance, was a Benedictine and Audelay a chaplain

---

[1] 'The Authors of the Middle English Religious Lyrics', *J.E.G.Ph.* xxxix. 230–8.

[2] For the text of the canons see J. D. Mansi, *Sacrorum conciliorum nova et amplissima collectio*, xxii (Venice, 1778), 981–1067. For the diocesan constitutions in England, which followed upon this Council, see M. Gibbs and J. Lang, *Bishops and Reform 1215–1272* (Oxford, 1934). Their effect upon vernacular literature is discussed by E. J. Arnould, *Le Manuel des péchés* (Paris, 1940), 1–59.

[3] See above, p. 3.

[4] Apart from compendiums such as the *Manuel des péchés* itself, there are many shorter poems on these subjects. Typical are the three poems by William of Shoreham on the seven sacraments, the ten commandments, and the seven deadly sins (E.E.T.S., E.S. 86, 1–78, 86–97, 98–114).

or chantry priest. In so far as there is a noticeable connexion between the lyrics and a religious order in this period, the order is the Carthusians.[1] B.M. Add. MS. 37049, which is the most striking of later meditative manuscripts, is of Carthusian origin, and so also is MS. Harley 4012, which contains three Passion meditations, including 'Wofully araide'. The Carthusian interest in affective piety at this time is well known; the English prose translation of the *Meditationes vitae Christi* was, for instance, made by a Carthusian, Nicholas Love,[2] and the copying, and perhaps writing, of meditative lyrics should be included in their contribution to the propagation of lay spirituality.

For the early period only four names of authors survive, three of these being friars. One of these (Thomas of Hales) is given in an initial rubric, the other three in colophons, which are either in the form of Latin prose notes (William Herebert and William of Shoreham) or embodied in the concluding stanza of a poem[3] (Michael Kildare). There are two very noticeable points about the manuscript preservation of the lyrics of these three writers: firstly, that a revelation of authorship usually accompanies a series of lyrics by one writer (if we accept the probable hypothesis that most of the poems in MS. Harley 913 are by Michael Kildare, then this is true of three out of the four known authors); secondly, that the poems now accompanied by a colophon did not circulate (those of William Herebert and William of Shoreham occur only in one manuscript each, and so also do the poems in the Kildare Manuscript that have a distinctive character, though this manuscript also contains texts of the more popular pieces, such as a long version of 'Erþe toc of erþe' and a paraphrase of the *Homo vide*). The reasonable inference from these two points is that all three collections of verse are close to the authors' autographs.[4] All three men can at best have had a local reputation: in contrast, Thomas of Hales had general fame as a theologian, and his name may well have been preserved in order to enhance the authority of his poem: this is certainly the way that Richard Rolle's name was later used.[5]

The conjecture that in the early period a name would be valued for its authority (and not for purely literary reasons) is supported by the fact that the names associated with many of the short meditative verses are those of the authors, or supposed authors, of the sources on which they are based. Sometimes the lyrics are preceded by their Latin sources ascribed to famous theologians, such as Augustine, Anselm, and Bernard. The *Candet nudatum pectus*, for instance, is quoted as the work of Augustine,[6] and the *Homo vide* as the work of Bernard.[7] Sometimes the lyrics themselves are ascribed to such authors: 'A Sone! take hede' is said to be by John Chrysostom,[8] one of the

---

[1] For the Carthusians see E. M. Thompson, *The Carthusian Order in England* (London, 1930), and in particular pp. 313–53.

[2] *The Mirrour of the Blessed Lyf of Jesu Christ*, translated by Nicholas Love (Roxburghe Club, 1908). A prose work (later printed) which consisted of a hundred meditations on the Passion was also of Carthusian origin (see p. 255, footnote 4).

[3] 'Swet Iesus, hend and fre', *Die Kildare-Gedichte*, 85.

[4] Had the poems become widely dispersed the Latin colophons would most probably have not been copied, and 'Swet Iesus, hend and fre' would then inevitably have become separated from its companions.　　　　　　　　　　　　　[5] See Appendix C.

[6] Brown XIV, p. 241.　　　　　[7] Brown XV, p. 326.　　　　　[8] Brown XIV, 128.

poems based on the *Meditationes piissimae* is called 'Les diz de seint Bernard',[1] and one of the laments of an aged man, 'Le regret de Maximian'.[2] It is clear from these examples and many others that it was the authorship of the originals that interested the manuscript compilers and not the authorship of the lyrics themselves, even when the vernacular writers, as in the last two examples, were by no means mere translators.

It was not until the fifteenth century that manuscripts recorded the names of authors of the lyrics because this information was in itself of literary interest. This occurs in the manuscripts (already referred to in Appendix A) which assemble together the work of one or two poets of reputation. These attributions are not necessarily correct: just as earlier attributions of Latin meditations to Anselm or Bernard were often without historical foundation so also were some of the later ascriptions of lyrics to native poets. The canon of the work of many fifteenth-century poets, such as Audelay, still requires investigation. But from the literary-historical point of view the value of these attributions lies not in the precise information that they convey but in the attitude that they express.

Though there are many lyrics by known writers in the fifteenth century, Lydgate, Hoccleve, Audelay, Ryman, Dunbar, Walter Kennedy, etc., the majority still remain anonymous. The authors will still have been largely clerics, and, unless like Richard of Caister or William Lichfield they had contemporary fame for their sermons or other prose works,[3] their names would either have not been known or have been ignored by manuscript copyists. In Carleton Brown's collection of fifteenth-century lyrics, which contains many of the most important meditative poems of the period, there are hardly any lyrics for which the author is given, for in all devotional manuscripts of the fifteenth century the authorship of individual pieces had continued to seem irrelevant.

Our ignorance of the authorship of the lyrics is not a serious loss. It is only rarely that, starting from modern critical principles, we are tempted to assign a group of poems to one author. The poems in the Kildare Manuscript present this temptation and there we have an indication of authorship. But nothing is known of the authorship of the Vernon lyrics, and they are so powerful and idiosyncratic in style that this lack of knowledge is frustrating. But, apart from the purely historical interest, we could dispense with our knowledge of William Herebert, William of Shoreham, Ryman, and perhaps even of Lydgate, as writers of lyrics, for their work has the genuine anonymity of style described in the Introduction. In none of these is it an advantage to read one poem in the light of another.

---

[1] E.E.T.S. 117, 757.   [2] Brown XIII, 51.

[3] Richard of Caister, to whom the popular poem 'Ihesu lorde, þat madest me' is ascribed in four manuscripts, was Vicar of St. Stephen's, Norwich, and, according to Bale, he was the author of a substantial number of didactic treatises, including works on the Ten Commandments and Eight Beatitudes (D. Harford, 'Richard of Caister and his Metrical Prayer', *Papers of the Norfolk and Norwich Archaeological Society*, xvii, 1908, 221–44). William Lichfield was Rector of All Hallows the Great, London, and seems to have composed a large body of sermons (Owst, op. cit., *passim*, refers to the sermons in MS. Roy. 8. C. i, as his work).

APPENDIX C

The Canon of Richard Rolle's Poetry

IN terms of the question of authorship, the poems that have been considered the work of Richard Rolle fall into two groups: those incorporated in his vernacular prose works and those ascribed to him in MSS. C.U.L. Dd. 5. 64 and Longleat 29. The first group, as Hope Emily Allen pointed out, occur regularly in all the manuscripts of the *Ego dormio* and *The Form of Living* and they must therefore be part of the original texts.[1] In constructing his works in such a way that the prose is interspersed with poetry Rolle may have been influenced by the use of verse in vernacular sermons or perhaps by the more serious and learned tradition that goes back to the *De consolatione philosophiae* of Boethius. The question of which model he followed is relevant in that the preaching tradition would encourage quotation from the work of others, whereas the Boethian tradition would lead an author to compose his own poems as an integral part of the work.

With two exceptions these lyrics occur nowhere else. One of these, 'Whils I satt in a chapel in my prayere',[2] from B.M. Add. MS. 37049 is a curious amalgam of verses, largely from 'My keyng, þat water grette', with introductory lines based on ch. 15 of the *Incendium amoris*. The poem is preceded by extracts from Rolle's vernacular prose works and accompanied by a portrait of him:[3] it is therefore certain that the poem is presented as a work of Rolle's. The other exception is the short lyric in *The Form of Living*, 'Loved be þou, keyng',[4] introduced there as a meal-time grace, but reappearing as a Levation prayer in *The Lay Folks Mass Book*.[5] The anonymous presentation of this verse in a different context may suggest that both Rolle and the author of *The Lay Folks Mass Book* were independently quoting an already existing verse, and, if so, some of Rolle's other poems might also be quotations. But the possibility that Rolle was working in the Boethian style, combined with the fact that all the poems in the prose works contain echoes or translated

---

[1] H. E. Allen, *Writings Ascribed to Richard Rolle* (New York and London, 1927), 287–8. Her conclusion that for this reason they must also have been written by Rolle does not follow.

[2] F. M. Comper, *The Life and Lyrics of Richard Rolle* (London, 1928), 315–16.

[3] Beside the poem is the representation of a seated and bearded figure, wearing a religious habit; in his lap he holds a book on which is inscribed the words, *Ego dormio*. Extracts from the *Ego dormio* precede the poem.

[4] *English Writings of Richard Rolle*, ed. H. E. Allen (Oxford, 1931), 104.

[5] E.E.T.S. 71, 40. On Levation prayers see R. H. Robbins, 'Levation Prayers in Middle English Verse', *Modern Philology*, xl (1942–3), 131–46. The best account of medieval piety at the Elevation is in E. Dumoutet, *Le Désir de voir l'hostie et les origines de la dévotion au saint-sacrement*, 1926.

passages from the *Melos amoris* and *Incendium amoris*, suggest very strongly that Rolle wrote the poems as an inseparable part of his works. So very strong a probability can withstand the faint doubt cast by the later quotation of 'Loved be þou, keyng'.

The main group of poems traditionally ascribed to Richard Rolle occur as a series in MS. C.U.L. Dd. 5. 64,[1] a few of them occurring also in later manuscripts.[2] They are preceded by a neutral incipit, 'Hic incipiunt cantus compassionis Christi', but followed by an explicit attributing an unstated number of the preceding poems to Rolle. The first two poems are short complaints, one on the Christ-knight theme and the other a translation of the *Homo vide*.[3] These are evidently covered by the opening rubric alone and there is no reason to consider them as Rolle's work: they are quite unlike any other poems attributed to him. All the remaining eight poems are more elaborate, and only one of them, 'When adam delf',[4] seems on grounds of style unlikely to be Rolle's. It is a forceful exposition of traditional death themes, but necessarily has no marks of Rolle's style for in ecstatic thought death is not to be feared but intensely welcomed.[5] It is difficult to know what inference to draw from the copyist's inclusion of it in this group: on the one hand, it could be argued that the copyist would not have included a poem so untypical of Rolle's work unless he had external information that it was in fact by him; on the other hand, a compiler, strongly influenced by the common meditative tradition, might well have felt that the lack of a poem on death in a collection of Rolle's work was a blemish impossible to accept.

All the remaining poems show to a greater or lesser extent the characteristic language and thought of Rolle and many echo his known works, the *Incendium amoris* and the vernacular prose texts including their lyrics.[6] This resemblance, however, may well be an argument duplicating that of the copyist's attribution, for it was this kind of reasoning that evidently led to many other manuscript attributions now known to be wrong. Moreover, the name of Rolle, at least by the fifteenth century (MS. C.U.L. Dd. 5. 64 is late fourteenth-century), was used with the same indiscriminate reverence as that of St. Bernard had been, and a credulous attentiveness to the attributions of fifteenth-century manuscripts would lead one to suppose that nearly all devotional prose had been written by Rolle and nearly all didactic prose by Wycliffe.

It would be agreeable if the fear of falling into excessive credulity or excessive scepticism could be eliminated by some further piece of evidence.

---

[1] Brown xiv, 77–86.

[2] The two in MS. Longleat 29, 'Ihesu, god sone' (Brown xiv, 83) and 'All vanitese forsake' (*English Writings*, ed. Allen, 49–51), are there also ascribed to Rolle.

[3] Brown xiv, 77 and 78.

[4] Ibid. 81.

[5] In his vernacular treatises Rolle allows the usefulness of fear as a specific remedy: in a passage in *The Commandment* he replies to those who say, 'I may noght despyse þe worlde', with a warning that echoes the Bernardine *ubi sunt* (*English Works*, 80–81; cf. p. 108 above). It would, however, be unlike Rolle to compose a poem that did not move from fear of death and hell to desire for heaven and Christ.

[6] For a detailed account see H. E. Allen, *Writings ascribed to Richard Rolle*, 295–301.

Unfortunately, there is only one detail that can give any help: it is that a stanza from 'My trewest tresowre' is quoted in the first of the *Meditations on the Passion*.[1] The weight to be given to this is very uncertain: it is likely but not incontrovertible that the *Meditations* are by Rolle,[2] and, even if they are by him, he could on this occasion have been quoting from somebody else's work. But, if the latter suggestion is true, we have to assume an unknown author, whose work was known to Rolle and who wrote in his style. This supposition is credible but perhaps unnecessary.

The question that emerges from this survey is plainly whether Rolle wrote all the lyrics attributed to him or whether he had some colleague or disciple who shared his literary talents and wrote in a manner strongly influenced by him. If we wished to consider the literary achievement of Rolle himself, this would be an important question; but, from the point of view of the general history of meditative literature, it matters very little whether it was one man or two men in some association who composed the mid fourteenth-century collection of ecstatic lyrics.

[1] *English Works*, 24.
[2] H. E. Allen, *Writings ascribed to Richard Rolle*, 278–85; cf. also Margery Morgan, 'Versions of the Meditations on the Passion ascribed to Richard Rolle', *Medium Aevum*, xxii (1953), 93–103. That the *Meditations* do not show Rolle's characteristic mysticism is not an argument against his authorship of them, nor does it need to be explained in terms of his spiritual development (Morgan, loc. cit. 101). Rolle frequently recommends meditation on the Passion, and, when he wrote in the vernacular, the treatment of his material would be primarily determined by the needs and capacity of the person for whom he was writing.

APPENDIX D

The Carol

CAROLS written in the meditative tradition have been discussed amongst the lyrics in this book, but the proportion of carols that could be relevantly included is less than a quarter of the total surviving, and of these (approximately a hundred) only a very few are meditative in a strict sense. The carol, in fact, through its form and function, is not normally a meditative poem. It is difficult to make generalizations about the nature and purpose of the carol, for the evidence is to some extent contradictory, or at least open to different emphases in interpretation, and only limited agreement is shown in the various learned investigations of the subject. Fortunately, one of the main points in dispute, that of the origins of the carol, though important in itself, is not urgently relevant here: for whether the carol's ancestry lies in the dance-song,[1] its content being transformed for doctrinal and devotional reasons by the religious orders, or whether it has a direct religious and liturgical descent,[2] is primarily of historical interest. It cannot alter the plain fact that, whilst a few of the carols are secular, whether in content or spirit, the majority are religious, showing a very exact care and understanding of theological doctrine, and that amongst these, whilst many are evidently written by the learned for a popular audience, others are strictly liturgical, and would almost certainly only be understood amongst the theologically educated.[3]

Fortunately, however, there is agreement concerning many aspects of the

[1] *Carols*, xxix–lix; *A Selection of English Carols*, ed. R. L. Greene (Oxford, 1962), 1–12.

[2] R. H. Robbins, 'The Earliest Carols and the Franciscans' *M.L.N.* liii (1938), 239–45; 'Friar Herebert and the Carol', *Anglia*, lxxv (1957), 194–8; 'Middle English Carols as Processional Hymns', *Studies in Philology*, lvi (1959), 559–82; *Early English Christmas Carols*, ed. R. H. Robbins (New York and London, 1961), 1–6.

[3] Professor Greene has described the carol as being 'popular by destination', and in this he has been followed by most scholars with the exception of Professor Robbins. A comparison of the carol with the lyric, however, throws into relief the learned and unpopular character of a substantial group of them, particularly those in the Ryman Manuscript and MS. Eng. poet. e. 1. In four manuscripts, MSS. Trinity Camb. 1230, Arch. Seld. B. 26, B.M. Add. 5665, and Egerton 3307, the carols are accompanied by parts of the liturgy, the mass, antiphons, hymns, etc. (*S.P.* lvi. 559–82; cf. also B. Schofield, 'A Newly Discovered 15th-Century Manuscript of the English Chapel Royal', *Musical Quarterly*, xxxii (1946), 509–36). Whilst the literary point here made casts no light on the more precise arguments of Robbins and Schofield (for arguments against the latter see *Journal of the American Musicological Society*, vii (1954), 1–34), it does suggest that an approach to the carols from the point of view of manuscript context rather than from the lexicographical one of the development of the word 'carol' is more likely to be illuminating and just in emphasis.

carol that are relevant to a comparison of it with the meditative lyric. The carol is a poem designed for singing—musicologists identify in it a distinctive musical shape[1]—with regular stanzas (most often quatrains), and a burden which recurs after each. They were written by men in religious orders[2] for use on festive or liturgical celebrations: there are, of course, many stages between conviviality and the performance of the liturgy, though the two can be connected by a firm series of steps: whereabouts on this ladder, as it were, the carol stands is an issue dividing scholars. From the point of view of content it is impossible to imagine one single setting in which all surviving carols could fittingly be sung, and it is likely that they should be freely scattered between purely liturgical and purely convivial assemblies and all grades of occasion between these two.

The connecting link seems to be an association with the Christmas season. It is quite certain that, in the sixteenth century, poems called Christmas Carols, identical with some of those in fifteenth-century manuscripts, were published: Richard Kele's volume, printed *c.* 1550, is an interesting example of the mixture which could be given this title, for, apart from carols for the Christmas season (which includes the twelve days of Christmas), there are carols on the Passion, Compassion, death and the Last Judgement, and amongst these two bawdy songs. The word 'Christmas' in the title evidently signifies poems to be sung at Christmas, but not necessarily about Christmas, though the liturgical inattentiveness of this volume perhaps suggests the decay of the tradition and the work of secular hands. Professor Greene's contention, however, that the word 'carol' was still used loosely in the sixteenth century and that 'for a late medieval writer or singer the carol was distinguished from other lyrics by its form rather than by its subject'[3] does not take sufficient account of the somewhat earlier currency of the alliterative collocation 'Christmas carol', as in the title of the volume published by Wynkyn de Worde in 1521[4] (of which unfortunately only the last leaf survives) and the fifteen entries in John Dorne's day-book in 1520.[5] It is far more likely that the printers were satisfying a well-established need rather than trying to initiate a new social custom, and the date of the 'Christmas carol' could then not be later than the end of the fifteenth century.

Less than a hundred of the carols printed by Professor Greene seem to be unsuitable for the Christmas season, either because they have some other strong liturgical connexion (e.g. a saint's day occurring later in the year), or

---

[1] M. F. Bukofzer, *Studies in Medieval and Renaissance Music* (New York, 1950), 113–75; F. Ll. Harrison, *Music in Medieval Britain*, 416–23.

[2] Two authors of carols are known, Ryman and Audelay, both in religious orders. That the authors were learned clerics rather than minstrels seems generally agreed. That the music is the composition of trained, ecclesiastical musicians is stressed by all musicologists. For references see previous footnote and also the brief but important preface of John Stevens, *Medieval Carols*, Musica Britannica, iv (2nd ed. 1958), xiii–xv.

[3] *Carols*, p. xx.

[4] See Dibdin-Ames, ii. 250–2, 394. Greene, loc. cit., refers to this and to Audelay's instruction, 'I pray you syrus, boothe moore and las, / Syng these caroles in Cristemas', but attaches great weight to the glossing of 'carol' as 'song' in some sixteenth-century vocabularies (op. cit. xx, footnote 6).

[5] *Collectanea*, First Series, 1885, p. 152.

because they are unfitted by tone, as, for instance, the warnings of death or the Last Judgement. The Christmas associations are, however, plain in about half of them, and in far more, if one assumes that carols to the Virgin and secular carols might, for divergent reasons, normally be sung at Christmas. The negative evidence, that there are no carols of the Resurrection, is especially striking.

If the carols were intended for singing at Christmas amongst religious and secular communities, one would expect them to be partly liturgical, partly convivial, and indeed in content the carol extends from the purely convivial and festive, such as the Boar's Head carols,[1] to the austerely liturgical, such as the typological carols in praise of the Virgin[2] or the paraphrases of two of the Advent O's.[3] But, no matter what the degree of affinity with church services or with domestic festivities, it will remain true that all the carols are public, celebratory poems, designed for singing, in contrast to the religious lyric, which was private poetry, intimate in feeling, and with the complexity and sensitivity possible in poetry intended for private reading or memorizing. One would expect carols, therefore, to be remote from the meditative tradition, and in general this expectation is borne out by a consideration of their style and content.

Many of the carols are narratives, short in length, but compendious in the events they cover: very often these will stretch from the Nativity to the Epiphany, but also from the Nativity to the Crucifixion, and even from the Fall to the Crucifixion. Obviously there would be no room for meditative detail in such poems, and in fact the events are not put in a meditative framework, but within the theological context of the Redemption. There is a concern for explicit doctrine in the carols, which is not found in the lyric, and the authors seem to intend, not the stirring of emotion, but the imparting of knowledge in a doctrinally accurate way. The festive and personal reference is usually confined to the refrain, in which the audience may be invited, 'Now let us syng, both more and lesse, / Of Cristes commyng, "Dei gracias" ',[4] or 'Make we joye nowe in this fest, / In quo Christus natus est'.[5] Narrative structure with public, communal refrain is typical of the carol: the meditative structure, which consisted of Christ speaking to man or man speaking to Christ, is very rarely found, and, when it is, it is most commonly within a *chanson d'aventure* opening. Dialogue may occur in the carols without introduction, the narrative slipping into direct speech; but its purpose—and probably its ancestry—is dramatic rather than meditative. There are exceptions, such as the brief complaint of Christ in 'This babe to us now is bore', where a brief history extending from the Nativity to the Crucifixion finally breaks into a complaint, 'Man, why art thow unkynd to me? . . .'[6] But far more often, as in the carols of Herod and the Massacre of the Innocents, the dialogue is unmeditative: it occurs between characters within the poem, and there is no poet-eavesdropper. Here the influence would seem to be the mystery plays rather than the meditative lyric.

[1] *Carols*, 132–5.
[2] *Carols*, 182, 189, 190, etc. See above, pp. 283–6.
[3] *Carols*, 1–2.   [4] *Carols*, 45.   [5] *Carols*, 31.   [6] *Carols*, 20.

The carols that have been discussed under appropriate headings in this book have been chiefly poems on the Nativity or those addressed to the Virgin. The first of these two groups contain the only carols which are truly meditative: indeed, the versified Nativity meditation is found almost exclusively amongst the carols. The earliest Nativity poems are those in John of Grimestone's preaching-book, of which several are carols,[1] and this tradition is continued in the carols of the fifteenth century. Nearly all of these are set in the *chanson d'aventure* convention, though occasionally the author introduces a reference more casually to his overhearing 'I hard a mayd lulley and synge'[2] or to his seeing 'So blessid a syght it was to see, / How Mary rokked her Son so free'.[3] The only carols in which the onlooker plays a substantial part are the early ones in John of Grimestone's preaching-book. Granted that the carol was especially connected with Christmas, it could scarcely have escaped the influence of the Nativity meditation, current not only in meditative literature but also in sermons for Christmas. Perhaps even more important was the influence of the mystery plays: contact between the two is shown by the carols sung respectively by the shepherds and the mothers of the Innocents in the two Coventry plays.[4] The second of these two carols, 'O sisters too', is an elegiac lullaby for the babies about to be slain, and is especially touching in a traditional meditative way. Apart from these influences, the lullaby meditation might seem by its very roots to be more external than the Passion meditation, and therefore more fitted for public performance. Though a devotion to the Christ-Child formed part of the religious experience of many contemplatives, it was far more readily adaptable to public worship than was a devotion to the Passion.

Carols to the Virgin were included amongst the lyrics, although they are in general only on the border of the meditative tradition. There are two ways of celebrating and addressing the Virgin, one, the style of a lover speaking to his mistress, the other that of a court doing honour to their queen. Only one carol, 'Upon a lady fayre and bright',[5] belongs clearly to the first kind, though quite a number, which are set in direct address, speak with the familiarity of the meditative tradition, despite the formality of the content. Nevertheless, there are many in which the language is ornate, the content an enumeration of types, and the petitions of a formal and liturgical kind. It is, however, impossible to draw a clear dividing line between the two styles, for so many poems, whether lyrics or carols, fall between them. There is, however, a difference of proportion between the lyric and the carol, in that whilst the lyric provides nearly all the addresses to the Virgin which are most informal and personal, the carol provides most of those which are objective and liturgical.

The carols that are meditations on the Passion are few in number, and nearly

---

[1] See above, pp. 149–52.

[2] *Carols*, 152; cf. *Carols*, 146 B.

[3] *Carols*, 153; cf. *Carols*, 143, 146 A, etc.

[4] *Carols*, 79 and 112; E.E.T.S. 87, 31–32.

[5] *Carols*, 183. In the notes (p. 391) Greene plausibly suggests the influence of secular love-song.

all exceptional for one reason or another. Whereas the meditative Nativity carols are simple in thought and written in typical metre and style, simple quatrains with the burden usually integrated to the sense of the stanzas, most of the carols on the Passion are carols only in the limited and technical sense that they have a burden: for in them the stanzas are often long, and the thought is correspondingly more intricate and the language more emotive. Examples are some of the best poems, which we have already discussed, 'With favoure in hir face',[1] 'To Calvery he bare his cross',[2] and 'The Kinges baner on felde is playd'.[3] None of these occur in the characteristic carol manuscripts (though the last was printed by Kele), and it is not even certain that all of them are carols in the technical sense, for a burden can well be an addition: Lydgate's complaint of Christ, 'Uppon the cross nailid I was for the', was, for instance, turned into a carol by the addition of a burden.[4] This kind of technical transformation was extremely easy, and when a carol is written in uncharacteristic style and uncharacteristic metre, and is not preserved with other carols, then it is a fair guess that a redactor has been at work, making a carol out of a meditative lyric.

There are, however, a few carols on the Passion and the Compassion written in quatrains in a simple narrative style, and amongst these there are even one or two which are actually meditative in structure. There is, for instance, one very beautiful address to Christ, 'Thou sikest sore', filled with meditative detail, and with a moving refrain which turns it into a love lament, 'Lu[v]eli ter of loveli eyghe, / Qui dostu me so wo? . . .',[5] but this is early and uncharacteristic in that it comes from John of Grimestone's preaching-book. There are also three complaints of Christ by Ryman,[6] but these are again distinctive in that this collection gives the impression that Ryman systematically expressed all traditional meditative themes in carol form. The only direct address amongst the carols, about which no reservation should be made, is a complaint of the Virgin, 'Whan that my swete Son was thirti wynter old':[7] this is untypical only in the sense that a dramatic monologue of this kind cannot have the ballad-like briskness and fluidity which marks most of the carol narratives; the refrain, however, which refers to the Virgin in the third person, '. . . Mary, she sayd so . . .', interrupts the meditative confrontation of Virgin and listener.

The remaining small group of carols that have affinities with the lyric are those on the theme of death. Several of these are set in the *chanson d'aventure* convention: the author overhears someone complaining, 'Timor mortis conturbat me'. The one which is most distinctively meditative is a warning from the tomb by Ryman, 'I hadde richesse, I had my helthe',[8] and the one most personal and moving is by Audelay, 'Dred of deth, sorow of syn',[9] who, like Ryman, but with far greater feeling and delicacy, adapted traditional themes

---

[1] *Carols*, 161.   [2] *Carols*, 165.

[3] *Carols*, 265; cf. Brown xv, 102, and p. 205 above.

[4] *Carols*, 263; cf. E.E.T.S., E.S. 107, 252–4.

[5] *Carols*, 271.

[6] *Carols*, 267–9. For *Carols*, 270, see p. 193, n. 6, above.

[7] *Carols*, 163.   [8] *Carols*, 353.

[9] *Carols*, 369; see above, pp. 335–6.

to the carol form. A number of carols on death are set in sermon style, a mode in which the carol sometimes overlaps with the lyric. It is difficult to imagine any season of the year in which the singing of fear-inspiring carols would be appropriate, since presumably in the penitential seasons of Lent and Advent carol singing would not be appropriate at all.

History of the Imago pietatis

THE early history of the *imago pietatis* as an iconographic form is unclear, and the issues are more ravelled than those relating to the Pietà, in that, though one form of the *imago pietatis* eventually predominated, it was preceded and even chronologically accompanied by a number of differing, though closely connected, forms. It seems to begin in twelfth-century Byzantine art, in which there occurs a strange cross between the Crucifixion and the Entombment: a half-length Christ is depicted with the Cross at His back, but His arms are folded over one another as though He lay in the tomb.[1] As this form developed in Italian painting, it became modified by historically associated themes:[2] sometimes the presence of the Virgin and St. John supporting the body from either side seems an echo of the Deposition scene, sometimes the sole figure of the Virgin behind the body suggests the Pietà. Later the supporting figure becomes an angel or occasionally God the Father (the figure of the suffering Christ thus replacing the crucifix in the traditional *Gnadenstuhl*[3]). The doctrinal significance of the *Gnadenstuhl* is that of God the Father offering the Son, but the *imago pietatis* also became associated with a theme of reverse significance, the *scala salutis*, in which Christ shows His wounds and offers His sufferings to the Father.[4] A full visual depiction of the *scala salutis* does not occur until the fifteenth century, but in the fourteenth century the same idea was sometimes expressed on the panels of diptychs, one of which would show a Byzantine-style Man of Sorrows, the other the Virgin and Child[5] (it is interesting to notice that B.M. Add. MS. 37049 opens in this way).

Though the origins of the *imago pietatis* are a matter of controversy, the means by which it acquired its final and popular form is known with certainty: it became associated with a eucharistic miracle attributed to Gregory the Great. According to an early life of St. Gregory by Paul the Deacon, a sceptical communicant was restored to faith by the vision of the host as a little finger bleeding.[6] This story is repeated exactly in the *Golden Legend*;[7] nevertheless,

---

[1] Gabriel Millet, *Recherches sur l'iconographie de l'évangile*, 483–6.

[2] The best account of this development is that of E. Panofsky, 'Imago Pietatis', *Festschrift für Max J. Friedländer* (Leipzig, 1927), 261–308.

[3] E. Mâle, *L'Art religieux du xiie siècle*, 182–3.

[4] See pp. 34–35 above.

[5] Millard Meiss, 'An Early Altarpiece from the Cathedral of Florence', *Bulletin of the Metropolitan Museum of Art*, xii (1954), 302–17.

[6] *P.L.* 75, 52–53.

[7] Ed. cit. iii. 69.

the supposition arose that St. Gregory saw in his mass, not a little finger, but Christ under the appearance of the Man of Sorrows.[1] A representation of this version of the legend was painted in S. Croce in Rome, and was copied over and over again.[2] From the story of the Mass of St. Gregory there developed two popular iconographic forms: the one, in which Christ appears above the altar, whilst the celebrant pope kneels before it, and the other (and yet more widespread one), in which Christ appears alone, whilst the surrounding frame is filled with the arms of the Passion. In both of these a most important change has taken place: we are no longer shown a lifeless body supported by the Virgin or some other figure, but an alive and self-supporting, though suffering, Christ.

The *imago pietatis* is now most familiar from Italian art, and general works on iconography usually refer to it as a continental theme, but the evidence that it was widely current in fifteenth-century England is astonishingly copious. In B.M. Add. MS. 37049 it occurs, for instance, no less than five times.[3] In illuminated books of hours it occurs before the Hours of the Cross, the Psalms of the Passion, and various prayers to the suffering Christ.[4] In the late fifteenth century sheets were printed to be sold separately, probably to be incorporated into unillustrated *horae*. Campbell Dodgson has shown that amongst these devotional woodcuts the *imago pietatis* was by far the most common: out of twenty-one woodcuts that he enumerates, eleven are of this subject.[5] Some manuscript *horae*, such as MS. Bodl. 939, have these inserted. Many printed *horae* contain a cut of the *imago pietatis*, most commonly before the Psalms of the Passion.[6] Although there were not many decades of printing before the Reformation, more than twenty cuts of the *imago pietatis* are listed by Hodnett, many of these being used in more than one religious work.[7]

The popularity of the *imago pietatis* was enhanced by the superstitious promises and fantastic indulgences attached to it. Anything between twenty

---

[1] A typical narrative of this later version is given by Audelay in his poem 'Apon a day Saynt Gregore' (E.E.T.S. 184, 79–81).

[2] J. A. Endres, 'Die Darstellung der Gregoriusmesse im Mittelalter', *Zeitschrift für christliche Kunst*, xxx (1917), 146–56. See also p. 391, n. 4.

[3] ff. 2^r, 20^r, 23^r, 24^r, and 62^v. For f. 20^r see pl. 2.

[4] Leroquais, op. cit. i. lv, notes the customary contexts for it in French books of hours (it seems to be rarer in France than in England). Some of the English manuscripts are as follows: Trinity Coll. Camb. 257, 100^r (with the Psalms of the passion); Trinity Coll. Camb. 1247, ix^r; Pepys 1576, 146^v (with the Seven Requests of St. Gregory); Emmanuel 41, 39^v (with the Seven Requests) and 52^v (before the Psalms of the Passion); Bodl. 850, 99^v (with the story of the Mass of St. Gregory); Gough Liturg. 7, 59^v (with the Seven Requests); Douce 1, 70^r (preceding the vernacular prayer by the five wounds, printed by Douglas Gray, 'The Five Wounds of Our Lord', *Notes and Queries*, N.S. x. 50–51).

[5] Campbell Dodgson, 'English Devotional Woodcuts of the Late Fifteenth Century', *Walpole Society*, xvii (1928–9), 95–108. Cf. also Henry Bradshaw, 'On the Earliest English Engravings of the Indulgence known as the "Image of Pity"', *Collected Papers* (Cambridge, 1889), 84–100.

[6] Edward Hodnett, *English Woodcuts, 1480–1535* (London, 1935), 568, 390, 391, 1434, 350, 1348.

[7] Ibid., 390, 391, 2380, 1374, 2039, 1434, 2024, 2062, 1343, 2065, 1347, 1348, 793, 442, 446, 448, 2061, and 2279.

and forty thousand years of pardon were often promised to anyone who recited five paternosters and five aves, 'pytously beholdyng these armes of Christes passyon'.[1] For those who could not afford their own manuscript or print there were representations in churches with similar indulgences attached. On painted rood screens, in stained glass, wall-paintings, and carvings the *imago pietatis* was to be found. Its position was often a prominent one, for instance, a painting over the chancel arch as at Great Hockham.[2] The *imago pietatis* was also a favourite subject for tombs, memorial brasses, and chantry chapels because the indulgences gained by the beholder would avail for the person there buried or commemorated. Miss Anderson has noted it on brasses at Macclesfield, Hellesdon (Norfolk), and Hurstmonceux (Sussex).[3]

It would be tedious even to attempt to enumerate all the surviving representations of the *imago pietatis* in England. The total sum would probably be of the order of a hundred. This may not now seem a very large number, but the unbiblical Man of Sorrows, like the Pietà, would have especially provoked the hostility of the Reformers. When it is remembered that innumerable manuscripts were destroyed, that nearly all stained glass was smashed, and that every painted wall was whitewashed over, then a hundred may fairly be taken to indicate that there were originally many thousands of such representations all over England.[4]

[1] Bradshaw, loc. cit. 89.

[2] A. Caiger-Smith, *English Medieval Mural Paintings* (Oxford, 1963), 158; cf. also pp. 136, 138, 142, and 146. For other references to the *imago pietatis* in English art see G. McN. Rushforth, *The Kirkham Monument in Paignton Church, Devon* (Exeter, 1927); C. Woodforde, *The Norwich School of Glass-Painting in the Fifteenth Century* (London, 1950), 23, 121, 175, and 177.

[3] *The Imagery of British Churches*, 57–59.

[4] Whilst this book was in proof, an important essay appeared, Carlo Bertelli, 'The *Image of Pity* in Santa Croce in Gerusalemme', *Essays in the History of Art presented to Rudolf Wittkower* (London, 1967), 40–55. Particularly of interest for the present argument is the author's emphasis on the English connexions of the *imago pietatis* and on its associations with the Carthusian order. (For the connexion between the Carthusians and the lyrics see p. 378 above.)

APPENDIX F

The History of the Pietà

THE source of the Pietà as an iconographic form cannot be plainly identified. Whilst eastern art emphasized a stage of lamentation between the Crucifixion and the burial, its form is either that of a group of figures surrounding the dead body, which lies on the stone of unction or in a sarcophagus, or else the head and shoulders lie in the lap of the Blessed Virgin, and the disciples are again grouped around the remainder of the body.[1] These eastern themes were borrowed into western art and remained the dominant form of the Italian Renaissance: Giotto's 'Lamentation over the Dead Christ' in the Arena Chapel in Padua is an early and well-known example of this kind of dramatic grouping.

This eastern sequence of events is reflected, not only in the earliest Italian Renaissance art, but also in the various Latin meditations. In the *Meditationes vitae Christi*, for instance, the head and shoulders are laid in the Virgin's lap, whilst the disciples encompass the rest of the body, and it is in this position that the Virgin speaks her last complaint.[2] Similarly, in the later *Vita* of Ludolf the Carthusian, the Body lies on the unction stone, with the Virgin at the head and Mary Magdalene at the feet.[3] The scene had been similarly imagined by the author of 'Anselm's' *Dialogus*.[4] Vernacular tradition either imitates this scene or, as in the early English vernacular narratives, the *Cursor Mundi*[5] or the *Northern Passion*[6] completely omits this stage of the Burial. Even the mystery cycles, composed in the late fourteenth century, and to some extent reworked in the fifteenth, indicate that a Pietà was not part of the traditional narrative meditation. In all cycles, save the *Ludus Coventriae*, the Virgin's complaints cease with the death of Christ, and the burial is performed briefly by Joseph of Aramathea and Nicodemus. Only in the *Ludus Coventriae* is there a Latin rubric directing that the dead body shall be placed in the Virgin's lap,[7] and this is no doubt a later fifteenth-century addition. In all of these it can be seen most clearly that the Pietà grouping and complaint were not part of the common Passion amplifications, and the majority of works ignore it, though they may contain such details as the Virgin's wish to carry the Cross, her many faintings, her attempt to reach

---

[1] See G. Millet, *Recherches sur l'iconographie de l'évangile*, 489–516.
[2] Trans. Ragusa and Green, 342; cf. *P.L.* 182, 1139.
[3] Ed. cit. iv. 144.
[4] *Dialogus B.M. et Anselmi de passione domini*, ch. xvi, *P.L.* 159, 233, 286–7.
[5] E.E.T.S. 66, ll. 16869–80. These ten lines briskly describe the preparations for the burial.
[6] E.E.T.S. 145, 225–7.   [7] E.E.T.S., E.S. 120, 311.

to her Son on the high Cross, or her resistance to His burial. It is only in the late meditation beginning 'Whan that I, Mary . . .'[1] that there occurs a Pietà scene: the Virgin says '. . . and þanne I cleppyd al þe body in myn armes', and in the printed edition of Wynkyn de Worde the text is preceded by a woodcut of a Pietà.[2] Even here, however, there would appear to be a late variant of another tradition, for a poem of similar content, 'Who can the sorow conceyve allas',[3] describes the earlier grouping, 'His hede lay in þi lappe with gret lamentacioun'.

In tracing the history of the Pietà in literary narrative there is considerable difficulty in that the phrases used to describe the Virgin's holding of the body, *in armis* or *in gremio*, are ambiguous, and do not necessarily distinguish between the eastern pose of the head and shoulders in the Virgin's lap and the genuine Pietà group. Though the reference, for instance, in the Office of the Passion to the body being placed *in tuae matris manibus, ut pie creditur*, has been assumed to refer to a Pietà,[4] it is far more likely, on account of its early date, that it alludes to the eastern convention; the phrase *in gremio* in some texts of the *Quis dabit*, and *en mun devant* of the French translation are completely ambiguous. In the *Speculum humanae salvationis* the Latin text refers to the body placed *in brachiis tuis*,[5] whilst the manuscript reproduced by Perdrizet shows the body of Christ laid on a pedestal slab with the head and shoulders supported by the Virgin.[6]

It is evident from this that the meaning of such phrases can be established only by reference to the visual tradition which lies behind them. The earliest representations of the Virgin with the dead Christ in her lap occur in Germany in the fourteenth century.[7] They are, however, distinct from the later forms in that the Virgin is young, smiling, and composed and the figure of Christ— as in some later instances—is far smaller than life-size. It has been conjectured that here the artist had in mind, not the Virgin of the Crucifixion recalling the infancy of her Son, but the Virgin of the Nativity foreseeing the Passion.[8] But, whether or not this is so, there can be no doubt that this scene is a true *Andachtsbild* and not one properly belonging to a continuous Passion narrative.

Germany is exceptional in its development of this iconographic form at an early date. In England, as in France and Italy,[9] the Pietà is typical of the fifteenth century, and there is no trace of it before this period. The exact diffusion of the Pietà in England is difficult to estimate, for by definition the reformers would have been especially outraged by such a non-Biblical

---

[1] This text survives in two manuscripts, Bodl. 596 (C. Horstmann, 'Nachträge zu den Legenden', *Archiv*, lxxix, 1887, 454–9), and Longleat 29; cf. p. 361, n. 3 above.

[2] *S.T.C.* 17537.

[3] See above, pp. 268–9.

[4] E. Gilson, 'Saint Bonaventure et l'iconographie de la Passion', *Revue d'histoire franciscaine*, i (1924), 405–24.

[5] Ed. J. Lutz and P. Perdrizet (Mulhouse, 1907), i. 95 (l. 161).

[6] Op. cit. ii (1909), pl. 92.

[7] See W. Passarge, *Das deutsche Vesperbild im Mittelalter* (Cologne, 1924).

[8] E. Reiners-Ernst, *Das freudvolle Vesperbild* (Munich, 1939).

[9] For the Pietà in France and Italy see J. B. Ford and G. S. Vickers, 'The Relation of Nuno Gonçalves to the Pietà from Avignon, with a Consideration of the Iconography of the Pietà in France', *Art Bulletin*, xxi (1939), 5–43.

iconographic form and one so associated with Marian piety. For this reason very few carvings or murals of a Pietà survive. Only one is recorded by A. Caiger-Smith in his Catalogue of wall-paintings;[1] a wooden version is noted by Joan Evans at the church of Battlefield in Shropshire,[2] and a carving by M. D. Anderson on a font at Orford, Suffolk.[3] Many references have, however, been collected to Pietà images no longer surviving: it is known, for instance, that Pipewell Abbey, Northants, had an alabaster Pietà, and that there were *images of pity* in Blackfriars, London;[4] St. Stephen's, Norwich,[5] and in various Norfolk villages.[6] Many churches, such as those at Durham, Melford, Peterborough, and Hull, had altars of 'Our Ladie of Pittie',[7] and it is almost certain that there would have been statues on them. It seems likely, in fact, that the Pietà in the fifteenth century supplanted the Virgin and Child as the normal iconographic form for the Virgin. Father Waterton's supposition that in this century there was hardly a Lady Chapel in England without a Pietà[8] has the ring of probability, though it cannot be proven.

More copious evidence is to be found in books of hours. According to Leroquais, a Pietà was a fairly common illustration in French *horae* for the *Obsecro te* and the *O intemerata*,[9] and even a tentative investigation of English *horae* suggests that the same is true of them. These two famous prayers to the Virgin were not so frequently illustrated in English manuscripts as they were in French, but when these prayers are accompanied by an illumination, as they are, for instance, in MSS. Pepys 1576 and Bodl. Liturg. 98, it is of a Pietà. The rubric in MS. Magdalen Camb. 13, which directs the *Obsecro te* to be recited before a picture of a *lady of pite*, is yet stronger evidence for the currency of the form, and important too is Lydgate's preface to his poem on the Fifteen Joys and Fifteen Sorrows of the Virgin, in which he feigns that he opened a book containing an image of the Virgin 'Lyke a pyte'.[10] Only in MS. Trinity Camb. 601 is the poem accompanied by a Pietà.

Many printed *horae* also contain a cut of the Pietà, and it was used also in other printed devotional works, such as the *Meditationes vitae Christi* and *The Imitation of Christ* by Thomas à Kempis. Hodnett lists eight different cuts, each of them occurring in from two to five works.[11]

The evidence for the Pietà in England is less abundant, and, in part, of a more circumstantial kind than it is for the *imago pietatis*. But it is quite sufficient to show that authors of religious lyrics in the fifteenth century could reasonably expect their readers or audience to recognize an iconographic form from their often brief verbal descriptions.

---

[1] A. Caiger-Smith, *English Medieval Mural Paintings*, 146 (Hemel Hempstead).
[2] Joan Evans, *English Art, 1307–1461* (Oxford, 1949), 88.
[3] Anderson, op. cit. 125.   [4] Evans, op. cit. 88.
[5] See above, p. 255, n. 3.
[6] Daniel Rock, *The Church of our Fathers*, iii (London, 1852), 271.
[7] E. Waterton, *Pietas Mariana Britannica* (London, 1879), 238–42.
[8] Op. cit. 240.   [9] *Les livres d'heures*, I. xliv.
[10] E.E.T.S., E.S. 107, 268. Waterton, op. cit. 241, refers to an indulgence in the Sarum Primer of 1534 for those who say the 'Obsecro te' 'before our blessed ladye of pitie'.
[11] Hodnett, op. cit., 550, 394, 351, 666, 1465, 455, 461, and 462. Cf. Dodgson, op. cit. 97, 100.

Complaints against Swearers

THE medieval habit of swearing by parts of Christ's body, so often reproved at the time by preachers, is now most familiar from the Pardoner's sermon and tale. The Pardoner stresses the viciousness of blasphemous oaths, and the revellers of his tale resort to them every few lines as they vow their undertaking:

> 'Ye, Goddes armes!' quod this riotour,
> 'Is it swich peril with hym for to meete?
> I shal hym seke by wey and eek by strete
> I make avow to Goddes digne bones!'
>
> . . . .
>
> And many a grisly ooth thanne han they sworn,
> And Cristes blessed body al torente—
> Deeth shal be deed, if that they may hym hente![1]

In this passage Chaucer uses the blasphemy of swearing to suggest the far greater blasphemy of their attempted usurpation of Christ's powers as conqueror of death. In his very skilful use of the theme Chaucer shows his knowledge of the sermon tradition, and, in particular (in the last line but one of the quotation), of the recurrent image of the swearing by Christ's body as a fresh Crucifixion.

A denunciation of blasphemous swearing was common in medieval sermons, as Owst has shown,[2] and many, though not all writers, make use of the image which was to become the foundation of the complaints against swearers. A typical example is the following passage from Bromyard's *Summa Praedicantium* under the heading of *iuramentum*:

Primo Iudaeorum, qui ipsum Christum Deum ignorantes, et mortalem blasphemaverunt, et deriserunt, Christiani vero scientes ipsum esse Deum, glorioso et regnanti hoc faciunt, illi dimiserunt corpus Christi integrum, isti membratim et per frustra gladio diaboli (id est) lingua sua illud dividunt.[3]

Later, Bromyard makes the parallel, not with the mocking, but with the Crucifixion itself: '. . . non peccant minus, qui blasphemant Christum

[1] *Poetical Works*, ed. Robinson, 183–4.

[2] *Literature and Pulpit*, 414–25.

[3] *Summa praedicantium*, i. 419ʳ. 'The Jews did not know Christ to be God; they blasphemed against Him and mocked Him when a mortal man, but the Christians, knowing Him to be God, do this to Him when He is reigning in glory. The Jews gave up Christ's body unmaimed, but the Christians cut it up in pieces, limb by limb, with the devil's sword, i.e. their tongue.'

regnantem in caelis, quam qui crucifixerunt ambulantem in terris'.[1] The earlier passage, however, is interesting because it sets out the paradox, which was repeated in many medieval complaints, but never expressed with the force of Donne's succinct lines:

> They kill'd once an inglorious man, but I
> Crucifie him daily, being now glorified.[2]

The theme of a fresh wounding or crucifying of Christ seems to have occurred very early in a spectacular and popular form, that of the *exemplum* of the Bloody Child. Its first appearance is in the *Handling Synne* of Robert Manning of Brunne under the heading of the second commandment.[3] In the description of the sin, Robert Manning keeps close to his source, the *Manuel des pechiez*, but the *exemplum* is one of the many that he added to the work. In this version of the story the Blessed Virgin shows to the sinful swearer her child wounded and torn, at which he becomes penitent, and the Virgin agrees to intercede for him. The same *exemplum* in slightly different form occurs in later and notable preaching works, such as the *Summa praedicantium*, Mirk's *Festial*, and the *Gesta romanorum*.[4] The interest of Robert Manning's version, however, is that unlike the others, it provides not the bare bones of a story, but a full literary development of it, and in it we see the address of the Virgin to the sinner, which could so easily turn into a Pietà complaint:

> 'þou', she seyd, 'hast hym so shent,
> And with þy oþys al to-rent.
> þus hast þou drawen my dere chylde,
> with þy oþys wykked and wylde;
> And þou makest me sore to grete,
> þat þou þyn oþys wylt nat lete.
> hys manhede, þat he toke for þe,
> þou pynyst hyt, as þou mayst se;
> þyn oþys done hym more grevesnesse
> þan alle þe Iewys wykkednesse.
> þey pyned hym onys, and passed a-way,
> But, þou, pynest hym every day.
> þe pyne, he suffred for þy gode,
> And þou upbreydyst hym of þe rode;
> Alle hys flessh, þan þou teryst,
> whan þou falsly by hym swerest.'[5]

All that was needed for a Pietà complaint was a difference of setting and this may almost certainly be seen in the version of the English *Gesta romanorum*, where the Blessed Virgin describes herself and her Son as follows:

'Why come ye hidder?' 'For to shew the my sone. lo!' she saide, 'here is my sone, lyeng in my lappe, with his hede all to-broke, and his eyen drawen oute of

---

[1] 'They do not sin less who now blaspheme Christ reigning in heaven than did those who crucified Him when He walked the earth.'

[2] *Divine Poems*, ed. Gardner, 9.

[3] E.E.T.S. 119, 25–28.

[4] For references see Owst, op. cit. 424.

[5] Ed. cit. 26–27.

his body and layde on breste, his armes broken a-twoo, his legges and his fete also.' . . . Then oure lorde putte his hande in his side, and toke oute blode. . . .[1]

There is here no reference to Christ as a child or *parvulum puerum*, and it would seem that this is a Pietà scene. This interpretation is supported by the fact that this version has been contaminated by another *exemplum* in which Christ, as Man of Sorrows, flings His blood in the face of the recalcitrantly unrepentant sinner. This seems an unlikely gesture for the Christ-Child. That the Virgin with a lacerated baby should, in the fifteenth century, turn into a Virgin holding her dead and wounded Son in her lap is so likely a transition that it requires no very strong proof to support it.

The most interesting analogy, however, lies in the visual illustrations of the subject, and particularly in the stained glass which was formerly at Heydon Church, Norwich, and that which is still at Broughton, Bucks.[2] At Broughton there is a Pietà scene, in which parts of Christ's body are missing: the right leg ends at the ankle, the arm at the elbow. Around are a group of fashionably dressed young men, grotesquely holding the missing limbs. At Corby, Lincs., there is a similar scene,[3] except that here scrolls, on which the actual oaths (now illegible) were inscribed, extend from the mouths of the youths or float above their heads. The most complete and relevant instance of this iconographic theme, however, is that which was once in the north window of Heydon Church. Knowledge of this depends upon the descriptions of two nineteenth-century antiquarians, of whom one gives no information about the central figure, whilst the other puzzlingly describes it as Christ. But the verses above are a complaint of the Blessed Virgin. Dr. Woodforde has reconstructed them as follows:

> Alas my chyld qwy have ȝe þus dyth,
> Ȝe cursyd swererys al bedene;
> Hys lemys be rent asundyr ryth,
> Alas my mone how may I mene.
> þe Jewys þat on þe cros hym pyte
> þei wyst nowt qwat þei ded inded.[4]

Around this again was a group of profligate dandies with oaths on scrolls, and a scene of hell with similar people therein. This window is obviously very closely related to a poem entitled in the manuscript, 'A lamentacioun of our lady for sweryng', which has been printed by Brotanek in his edition of MS. Trinity College, Dublin, 432, the commonplace book of a fifteenth-century Northampton merchant (the Book of Brome).[5] The first four lines are identical in each. But the poem, after the complaint, proceeds with couplet oaths, and then with parallel lamentations of the blasphemers now in hell. The window illustrates this poem exactly and was quite obviously based upon it.

[1] E.E.T.S., E.S. 33, 410–11.

[2] Christopher Woodforde, *The Norwich School of Glass-Painting in the Fifteenth Century*, 183–92.

[3] E. C. Rouse, 'Wall Paintings in the Church of St. John the Evangelist, Corby, Lincolnshire', *Archaeological Journal*, c (1943), 150–76.

[4] Woodforde, loc. cit. 184.

[5] *Mittelenglische Dichtungen*, ed. R. Brotanek (Halle, 1940), 99–115.

One further window of this kind is known, that which was formerly at Walsham-le-Willows, Suffolk.[1] Here, however, the central figure was not a Pietà group, but a Man of Sorrows, probably demonstrating His wounds, as He does in the related iconographic theme, sometimes called the 'Christ of the Trades', in which the figure is a reproach and a warning to those who break the sabbath by labour or gaming.[2] This iconographic variation between the Pietà and the Man of Sorrows is not paralleled in literature, where the complaint against swearers seems to belong more properly to Christ than to the Virgin, if one excepts the rudimentary elements of it in the *exemplum*. An early example seems to be a few lines in Mirk's sermon *De Dominica in Passione Domini Nostri*, which follow immediately upon the antitheses between the crucified Christ and the dandy, and are in turn succeeded by the *exemplum*. The lines are as follows: 'And over þys þat grevyth me most, þou settyst noȝt by me passyon that I suffryd for þe; but by me horrybull swerus all day, umbraydys me sweryng by my face, by myn een, by myn armes, by myn nayles, by myn hert, by my blod, and soo forth, by all my body.'[3] This short passage from the *Festial* is of importance chiefly in suggesting some earlier origin: that Mirk either knew some Latin dramatic commonplace or some English lyrics already written in this form. But whilst the beginnings of the complaint against swearers may be fourteenth century, it is in the fifteenth century that it becomes a recurrent element of the complaint form. One example, interesting for its place of survival, is in a poem carved round the roof-plate of the nave in the church at Almondbury, Yorkshire. The poem itself could hardly be flatter or more clumsy. It begins with an echo of 'O man unkind', and then for four verses enumerates the pains of the Passion, in a manner, which in content, though not in quality, recalls the earlier lyric. The sixth verse is as follows:

> Thou doys me mor dire
> When thou doth swer
>   Be me here of my body
> Then the Jwyss did
> That speyld my blod
>   On the mont of Cavere.[4]

It would not be possible to quote all the many other examples. Some are to be found in poems referred to in other contexts, such as 'The Newe Not-broune Mayd' and 'The borne is this word blinde', and the dialogue, 'Salvator mundi domine', others in poems outside the scope of this work, such as Barclay's translation of *The Ship of Fools*. Another context is the Last Judgement complaint of the Chester cycle.

There are, however, two works which treat this theme so extensively that they may be noted individually. The earlier is Section 8 of 'Thus oure gracious

---

[1] Woodforde, loc. cit. 185–6.
[2] Anderson, loc. cit. 172.
[3] E.E.T.S., E.S. 96, 113.
[4] Described and quoted in J. E. Morris, *The West Riding of Yorkshire* (2nd, ed. 1923), 82; cf. *Journal Brit. Arch. Assoc.* xxx. 231.

god, prince of pitee', which shows the traditional elements manipulated with
some skill:

> Man, if þou wolt my mercy gete
>   þoruȝ my passioun of myche vertu,
> Whi levest þou not of me to bete?
>   Eche day on crosse þou doist me newe
> With deedli synne, at morn, at meete,
>   As a turmentour to me untrewe,
> And nameli, with þin oþis greete,
>   To swere þou wolt not eschewe.
>
> No lyme on me, man, þou forbeerist:
>   Whi doist þou yvel aȝens good?
> By my soule þou ofte tyme sweerist,
>   Bi my body, and bi my blood.
> With þi tunge þou me al to-teerist
>   Whanne þou art wrooþ, as wiȝt moost wood.
> Man with þin unkindenes þou more me deerist
>   þan þei þat diden me on þe roode.
>
> .   .   .   .   .   .
>
> Sweete ihesu, how schulde y aȝen say,
>   But þat y caitife am, more curst
> þan þo þat doon þee on þe crosse eche day
>   With greet ooþis and werkis wurst,
> And myche more þee greeveþ þan þei
>   þat on calveri slowen þee firste;
> For hadde þei knowe þee for god verray,
>   þee to deeþ þei hadde not durst.[1]

The complaint of Christ sets out the main points of the theme, but with some
slackness in that the image is used as a term of comparison rather than a
metaphor; and in the one attempt to unite moral statement and image the
description of the tongue as a sharp weapon seems too odd to be successful,
though the representation of the wrathful man as knife-thrower in the *Ancrene
Wisse* suggests that when skilfully developed it could be effective. In poems
where the image is more tensely stated it is usually also more metaphorical:
for instance, 'With athys my flessh torne ys' from 'The borne is this worde
blinde', or 'With þi grete oþus þat þu swerus ay, / my body þu wonduste
evur-more newe' from 'Salvator mundi domine'. The reply from man, containing the paradox already noted, is more effective. Though the diffuseness of
style softens the potential pungency of the image, it is not unfitting to the
tone of contrition.

The only complete poem on this subject, however, is also the latest, *The
Conversyon of Swerers* by Stephen Hawes, first printed in 1509 by Wynkyn de
Worde,[2] and accompanied by illustrations. The first, at the opening of the
work, is a Judgement scene, in which Christ shows His wounds, whilst
the Blessed Virgin and St. John intercede, and below St. Michael weighs
a soul. This is in keeping with the usual tone of such complaints. The
second is an *imago pietatis* of the traditional kind, the half-length

---

[1] E.E.T.S. 15, 222–5.   [2] Ed. David Laing (Edinburgh, 1865).

Christ, surrounded by a frame filled with the instruments of the Passion.
This accompanies the more emotive lyric that at one point interrupts the
rhyme royal stanzas.

The main part of the poem feigns to be in the form of a letter sent by
Christ to the earthly princes (perhaps through some recollection of the
'Sunday letter'),[1] a letter which, like the charters of Christ, is sealed with the
imprint of the Passion:

> With my blody woundes I dyde your chartre seale,
> Why do you tere it, why do ye breke it so,
> Syth it to you is the eternall heale
> And the releace of everlastyng wo.
> Beholde this lettre with the prynte also
> Of myn owne seale by perfyte portrature,
> Prynte it in mynde and ye shall helthe recure.[2]

Its general tone is moralistic and threatening, though some verses at the
beginning are of a more devotional kind. The lyric, however, is a genuine
planctus, set in ingenious patterned metrical form, beginning in lines of
monosyllables (See / Me / Be / Kynde), increasing to two, three, four, five, and
six syllables, and then diminishing symmetrically again. The middle part is as
follows:

> Beholde thou my syde,
> Wounded so ryght wyde,
> Bledynge sore that tyde,
>   All for thyn owne sake.
> Thus for the I smerted,
> Why arte þu harde herted?
> Be by me converted
>   And thy swerynge aslake.
>
> Tere me nowe no more,
> My woundes are sore,
> Leve swerynge therfore,
>   And come to my grace.
> I am redy
> To graunte mercy
> To the truely
>   For thy trespace.[3]

There is here a devotional note exceptional for the form and the period. The
moral has been fully integrated with the image, and the image itself effectively
visualized in the traditional way, the wounds seeming more a proof of Christ's
love than a demonstration of the sinner's wickedness. The complaint against
swearers had been normally part of the didactic complaint of the fifteenth
century: it is remarkable that at this late date it should have been so successfully assimilated to the love complaint.

---

[1] On this see the article by E. Renoir, *Dictionnaire d'archéologie chrétienne et de
liturgie*, iii. 1534 ff.   [2] Ed. cit.
[3] Ed. cit. A iii^v. The lyric is printed independently by R. T. Davies, *Medieval English
Lyrics* (London, 1963), 259.

The History of the Warning from the Dead

THE warning from the dead first appears in the sermon injunction to visit the tomb, an early and striking form that was much used to provide an epitome of the physical horrors of death. Its first known occurrence is in the *Necrosima* (funeral hymns) of Ephraem of Syria. These hymns are eloquent in the moral application of the revoltingness of death: over and over again Ephraem urges the proud, the powerful, the rich, and the lovers of luxury and adornment, not simply to imagine a corpse, but to look into a grave, and from the body therein, immobile and disintegrating, to infer the futility of the world. In Canon xxviii the speaker looks into the adjoining graves of a king and a pauper: in the latter he sees cobwebs upon the skull, the trunk motionless, the teeth fallen from the gums, the mouth full of ashes, the bones reduced to dust; then by looking into the royal grave and seeing the same wretched sight, he learns the levelling power of death.[1] In an equally powerful hymn, Ephraem actually begins with the injunction to look into the tomb:

> . . . Iterum oro vos, fratres, subire sepulcra non pigeat, multum juvat videre dehiscentes in frustra marcidas carnes, et inde scatentem vermium colluviem, et cadaverum acervos.[2]

and he continues with a rhetorical description of the values of this world, only to deflate them by an insistence upon the identity of rich and poor in the grave. There is here, of course, the substance of a meditation, long before the formulation of a meditative theory. The idea of Death the Leveller, expressed as a great commonplace in the well-known lines of Horace, *Pallida mors aequo pulsat pede pauperum tabernas / Regumque turres*,[3] is here given a frightening and personal realism through the detailed description of the dead, and through the fiction of the dramatic involvement of the listener.

The injunction to visit the tomb occurs in the sermons of other eastern writers. The very popular and effective preacher, St. John Chrysostom, emphasizes in one of his sermons the equality of the grave with its three cubits of earth, and urges his listeners to look into a grave and comments upon

---

[1] *Opera omnia, Syriace et Latine*, iii, ed. S. A. Assemani (Rome, 1743), 277–8.

[2] Op. cit. 295. I quote from the Latin translation. 'Brothers, I beseech you again: be not reluctant to go down to the tombs, for it is very beneficial for you to see the decaying flesh falling to pieces, the mess teeming with worms and piles of corpses there.'

[3] *Carm.* i. iv. 'Pale death with equal force knocks on the hovels of the poor and the halls of kings.' Cf. Weber, op. cit. 283–301.

what they will see there in a series of *ubi sunt* questions[1] (a usage of the *ubi sunt* form that later led into the Soul's harsh questioning of the Body in the debates of Body and Soul). However, this injunction, together with other of Ephraem's death themes, seems to have passed, by some as yet untraced path, directly into the Latin sermons of the post-patristic Church. In a sermon of Caesarius of Arles, which was known to Anglo-Saxon sermon-writers,[2] Caesarius urges his audience to look into the graves of the rich, and then, rather than commenting himself as preacher, as Ephraem and John Chrysostom had done, he imagines that the dead themselves preach to the living:

> Adtende ad me, et agnosce te; considera ossa mea, et vel sic tibi horreat luxuria vel avaritia tua. Quod tu es, ego fui; quod ego sum, tu eris. . . . Vide pulverem meum, et relinque desiderium malum.[3]

The fiction of the corpse actually speaking is, of course, highly effective, and the words *Quod tu es, ego fui* are perhaps a clue to the source of this development.

In Roman times the dead were not buried in cemeteries, but in tombs which lined the highways outside the cities.[4] This geographical situation led to the kind of epitaph in which the traveller or passer-by was exhorted to pause and think of or grieve for the dead. Amongst many epitaphs of this general kind there are a number which are a clear *Memento mori*, such as *Carissime viator, quod tu es et ego, quod ego et omnes*,[5] or *Quod tu es ego fui, quod nunc sum et tu eris*.[6] However, many verses of this kind are but fictional epitaphs, surviving only in the *Anthologia latina*, and probably never inscribed. This form of epitaph is important, not merely for its possible influence on the sermon injunction to visit the tomb, but also because it seems to have extended directly into medieval Christian epitaphs. The Life of Alcuin, written about 830, contains an epitaph embodying the *quod tu es ego fui* formula,[7] and later Peter Damian and Peter Comestor composed epitaphs of this kind for themselves.[8] It seems to have been an act of piety for the living to make provision for their dead selves to serve as sermon *exempla*. Later such epitaphs ceased to be purely literary and became tomb inscriptions: one of the earliest of these in England is that which the Black Prince had inscribed on his tomb at Canterbury, which includes the words *Tiel come tu es ie au tiel fu*.[9]

---

[1] *P.G.* 47, 288. This passage, though with an incorrect reference, is quoted by R. Ortiz, *Fortuna labilis, Storia di un motivo medievale* (Bucarest, 1927), 61.

[2] On this sermon and its imitations in Old English see J. E. Cross, 'The Dry Bones Speak—A Theme in some Old English Homilies', *J.E.G.Ph.* lvi (1957), 434–9.

[3] *Sermones*, ed. D. G. Morin, Corpus Christianorum, Series Latina, ciii (Turnhout, 1953), 135; Cross, loc. cit. 434–5. 'Look at me and know yourself; consider my bones, and lust and avarice will become abhorrent to you. What you are, I was; what I am, you will be. . . . Gaze at this dust and desist from your evil desires.'

[4] For a general account see R. Lattimore, *Themes in Greek and Latin Epitaphs* (Urbana, 1962).

[5] Lattimore, op. cit. 257. 'Dear wayfarer, what you are I was also, what I am now all will be.'

[6] Ibid. 'What you are I was, what I am now you too will be.'

[7] 'Quod nunc es, fueram, famosus in orbe viator: / Et quod nunc ego sum, tuque futurus eris', *Beati Flacci Alcuini Vita, P.L.* 100, 106.

[8] W. Storck, 'Der Spruch der Toten an die Lebenden', *Zeitschrift des Vereins für Volkskunde*, xxi (1911), 59.   [9] Ibid.

There are also many English vernacular epitaphs in this tradition, but they belong to the fifteenth century when memorial brasses became more common and the uses of the vernacular were extended.[1]

Alongside the literary epitaphs the sermon injunction to visit the tomb—including the address of the dead—continued to be widely used. Two Old English homilies and one in early Middle English all make use of it, and it has been shown that all three were probably directly modelled upon that of Caesarius.[2] It was also embodied in one of the Pseudo-Augustinian *Sermones ad fratres in eremo*[3] and in the *Meditationes püissimae*, though in the latter it is the beholder who addresses the dead, not vice versa: *Quod ego sum, ipsi fuerunt*, etc.[4] A further modification of the theme was that it was turned into an *exemplum*, so that it was no longer the preacher's audience who were instructed to look into a grave, but some person within the story himself opened a tomb, and the audience learnt by the example of what he then did. Such a story occurs in the early collection of *exempla*, the twelfth-century *Disciplina Clericalis* of Peter Alphonsus, which contributed a great deal to later collections of *exempla*: in this a philosopher, walking through a cemetery, sees words from the dead carved upon a marble tombstone:

> Tu prope qui transis nec dicis 'aveto!', resiste,
> Auribus et cordis hec mea dicta tene:
> Sum quod eris; quod es, ipse fui, derisor amare
> Mortis, dum licuit pace iuvante frui.[5]

Thereafter, having settled his affairs, the philosopher became a hermit. This rather bare statement of Peter Alphonsus was much amplified in the French paraphrase, the *Chastoiement d'un père à son fils*.[6] Versions of this *exemplum* occur over and over again in medieval preaching. Two instances at random are Myrk's sermon for Quadragesima Sunday[7] and the *Summa praedicantium*, where, in accordance with another minor development, the hero is a young man who looks into his father's grave:

> Priori, lapide amoto, invenit bufones horribiles in puteo, seu tumba, cum patris corpore, qui magno percussus horrore, et timore . . . omnes vanitates mundi contemnens: in habitu pauperis, Romam ignotus adiit.[8]

This heightened version of the story had been told, not only in *exemplum* form, but had also become attributed to historical people in their semi-

---

[1] Vernacular epitaphs are discussed in Chapter IX, pp. 314–15.

[2] Cross, loc. cit. 435–7.

[3] *P.L.* 40, 1352–3.

[4] *P.L.* 184, 487.

[5] Ed. A. Hilka and W. Söderhjelm (Heidelberg, 1911), 48. 'O you who pass by me, and do not say "farewell", stay, and keep my words in your ears and hearts: I am what you will be; what you are, I myself was, one who scoffed at bitter death so long as he was permitted to enjoy peaceful delights.'

[6] Ll. 3535–54, *Disciplina clericalis*, ed. Hilka and Söderhjelm, iii (1922), 136.

[7] E.E.T.S., E.S. 96, 85. This sermon also contains a description of the signs of death.

[8] *Summa praedicantium*, ii. 79. 'When the stone had been moved he found horrifying toads with his father's body in the pit or tomb, and by these he was struck with great horror and fear . . . and despising all the vanities of the world he returned to Rome in private, dressed as a poor man.'

legendary lives now collected in the *Acta sanctorum*. The Anglo-Norman poet Thibaud de Marly wrote two poems based upon the account of this incident in the life of Simon de Crépy,[1] who was said to have been converted by looking into his father's grave, and whose life thereafter was guided by *l'ymage | de la mort peint en sa pensee*.

The final stage of this theme was its passage into *exemplum* verses, a development described above in Chapters III and IX.

---

[1] *Deux anciens poèmes inédits sur saint Simon de Crépy*, ed. E. Walberg (Lund, 1909). The Life of Simon de Crépy in the *Acta sanctorum*, 30 Sept. 730, contains the same story. A similar story is told of the Count of Pontoise by Alexander Neckham, *De naturis rerum*, ii. 188 (ed. T. Wright, Rolls Series, 1863, 334–5). The story also circulated independently in collections of *exempla*, as for instance, in the *Liber de dono timoris*, see *Catalogue of Romances in the British Museum*, iii, ed. Herbert, 99.

The Prose Dialogue between Body and Soul in Guillaume de Guilleville's Pèlerinage de l'âme

A TRANSLATION of this dialogue occurs in B.M. Add. MS. 37049 on ff. 82^r–84^r. A translation of the whole French poem into English prose had been made in 1413, according to the colophon in MS. Egerton 615,[1] and this passage, although it shows some small verbal differences and the northern forms characteristic of the manuscript, is closely dependent upon it.

The *Pèlerinage de l'âme*,[2] like its companion the *Pèlerinage de la vie humaine*, was very popular in England, being known not only in its original couplet form, but also in a French prose paraphrase made by Jean Gallopes[3] and in the English prose translation referred to above. The latter was printed by Caxton in 1483.[4] The *Pèlerinage de l'âme* derives its main theme from the vision literature stemming from the *Apocalypse of St. Paul*, and includes many popular motifs of medieval literature, the psychostasis, the debate of the Four Daughters of God, the Green Tree and the Dry Tree, and the argument between Body and Soul.

The poem recounts how, after the psychostasis, the soul of the dreamer is taken by its attendant angel on a journey in which it may see all parts of the universe, including purgatory and hell. At one point on this journey, the soul sees its own corpse, and immediately joins in argument with it concerning their respective responsibility for their past sins. The speeches consist largely of a continuous rational argument concerning the relationship of the soul to the body: the body argues that it is as blameless as ashes once the fire is out, or as the evil-smelling wick of a torch once the flame is gone; whilst the soul retorts that it was encumbered by the body, helpless as a man tied up in a sack. At last, however, the angel intervenes, proclaiming that such uncharitable disputation is fitting for the damned, not for a body and soul that will be saved. Whilst this dialogue is entirely suitable in its original context, and well illustrates the recurrent philosophical preoccupations of Guillaume de Guilleville, it is quite unlike the traditional kind of debate, of which the main point was to provide an all-embracing form for the various *topoi* of death, the *ubi sunt* motif, the faithless executors, the devouring worm, and the

---

[1] H. L. D. Ward, *Catalogue of Romances in the British Museum*, ii. 580–4.

[2] Ed. J. J. Stürzinger (Roxburghe Club, 1895). The debate is on pp. 135–44.

[3] Rosemond Tuve, *Allegorical Imagery* (Princeton, 1966), 148 and 150.

[4] *S.T.C.* 6473. There is no modern edition except for the tendentiously abbreviated version of K. I. Cust (London, 1859). It contains, however, the whole of the Body and Soul debate on pp. 55–59.

loathsomeness of the decaying body. In this dialogue a subsidiary theme of the earlier debates has become the sole content.

The compiler of the manuscript, unless it was some intermediary writer, has also emphasized the psychological moral of the work by appending to it the story of the blind and lame man in the orchard. This fable had been used in Rabbinic tradition[1] to demonstrate the relationship of mutual responsibility between body and soul, but it acquired authority in western Europe through its inclusion by Vincent of Beauvais in his *Speculum morale*.[2] His version of the *exemplum* was repeated by Étienne de Bourbon in his *Tractatus*,[3] and occasionally elsewhere. It was not, however, a popular *exemplum* and was obviously less didactically illuminating than the usual Body and Soul debate, in which the body's abasement symbolized the vanity of worldly pleasure, and the soul's failure to control it provided an urgent instance of the need for the moral will to control all movements of sin, whether physical or spiritual. It is difficult to believe that the compiler of this manuscript would have chosen such an *exemplum* or such a philosophical debate, had he found at hand a traditional poem on the Body and Soul; for the prose debate does not illustrate the plight of the damned, a theme which would far better have served the meditative purpose of this manuscript collection.

[1] J. Perles, 'Rabbinische Agada's in 1001 Nacht, Ein Beitrag zur Geschichte der Wanderung orientalischer Märchen', *Monatschrift für Geschichte und Wissenschaft des Judenthums*, xxii (1873), 75–77.

[2] *Speculum maius*, III. xix. 3 (Venice, 1591), 173^v.

[3] B.M. Add. MS. 28682, 223^v, B.M. Add. MS. 24641, 211^r. Herbert, *Catalogue* 84 and 537.

Some Sixteenth-Century Parodies

THE custom of writing religious poems to the metre and tunes of popular songs seems to have become especially popular after the Reformation. It was a common practice not only in England and Scotland but also in France, Germany, and the Netherlands. About twenty of *The Gude and Godlie Ballatis* are of this kind, and it is these in particular that may be usefully discussed in relationship to earlier medieval practice. In general the perfunctory nature of these later adaptations throws into relief the skill of earlier writers, who did not simply borrow verse structures and refrains, but also exploited the emotional qualities of the original for religious purposes.

Often the only verbal resemblance between the *godlie ballat* and its secular model is the first line: poems may begin with attractive openings about spring or day-break, 'In till ane myrthfull Maij morning'[1] or 'Hay now the day dallis',[2] and continue with a penitential prayer or an abusive attack on the Roman Catholic Church. In these instances, and in many others, the opening line seems to do no more than indicate the tune, as the prefaced lines of English song had done in *The Red Book of Ossory*. More instructive is the group of poems in which the secular song has been allegorized, as it had been in 'The borne is this word blinde'. In this category belong adaptations of some of the most popular Elizabethan songs, 'Iohne, cum kis me now',[3] 'With huntis up',[4] and 'Quho is at my windo, quho, quho'.[5] In the first of these one might expect that the personal quality of the original appeal would be of service to the adaptor. The symbol of a kiss recalls the mystical kiss of the Song of Songs, 'Let him kiss me with the kisses of his mouth', or its more familiar and re-strained expression in 'Man, folwe seintt Bernardes trace'. But devotional potentialities of this kind were unacceptable to Calvinist writers, and there-fore the kiss that John (i.e. mankind) must give is the disposition of faith which brings justification.

'With huntis up' is similarly disappointing. Memories of *Quia amore langueo* and even of 'The hound of heaven' lead one to expect that the divine hunts-man's quarry will be man's soul. But in the version of *The Gude and Godlie*

---

[1] *The Gude and Godlie Ballatis*, ed. A. F. Mitchell (S.T.S. 39), 137–8; cf. notes, p. 270.

[2] Op. cit. 192–5; cf. notes, pp. 288–9, and T. Spencer's essay on the dawn-song in English, *Eos*, ed. A. T. Hatto (The Hague, 1965), 508–10.

[3] *Godlie Ballatis*, 158–61; cf. W. Chappell, *Old English Popular Music*, revised by H. E. Wooldridge, i (London, 1893), 268–9.

[4] Op. cit. 174–7; cf. Chappell, op. cit. 86–89.

[5] Op. cit. 132–6; cf. Chappell, op. cit. 146–7.

Ballatis the hunt is bent on destruction, and the fox which it pursues is the Pope. There is, however, another adaptation of this song, which is not satirical.[1] In this poem, attributed in the manuscript to John Thorne, Christ the huntsman pursues the deer which have strayed from the Garden of Eden and by the Redemption builds a new park for them. Though the allegory is sometimes farfetched, often too moralistic to be poetically agreeable, and occasionally ineptly appropriate (sin, for instance, is 'the rot' from which the deer suffer), the author has obviously respected the devotional possibilities of his original image in a way that other writers did not.

A particularly interesting example in this group is 'The wind blawis cauld, furius and bauld',[2] in which there are hints of an original refrain in the line, 'Or keep the cauld wind away',[3] a refrain with the evocative imprecision characteristic of some folksongs. This refrain is obviously the same as that used in the earlier carol, 'Thys wynde be reson ys callid tentacyon',[4] which we have already discussed.[4] The allegorization of a beating wind as some aspect of sin was traditional. In *Piers Plowman* the winds that rock the tree of charity are the world, the flesh, and the devil, and behind this lie patristic sources.[5] In the post-Reformation poem the wind becomes the heresies of the Catholic Church throughout the Middle Ages. But whereas the author of the carol had allowed his refrain to retain an emotional resonance unjustified by the narrowly allegorical introduction, the later writer remains severely within the didactic frame of his allegory.

There remain three poems to be discussed (one of them not in the *Godlie Ballatis*), in which the sixteenth-century authors seem to have remained within the medieval tradition and perhaps even to have learnt from it. One is the poem which C. S. Lewis singled out from *The Gude and Godlie Ballatis* as an 'excellent lyric',[6] 'All my lufe leif me not'. Unfortunately the secular original is not known, but it is clear that it is echoed in the second, fourth, and eighth lines of the stanza with their pattern of repetition:

> All my lufe, leif me not,
> Leif me not, leif me not,
> All my lufe, leif me not,
>   This myne allone:
> With ane burding on my bak,
> I may not beir it, I am so waik;
> Lufe, this burding fra me tak,
>   Or ellis I am gone.

---

[1] *Wit and Science and Early Poetic Miscellanies*, ed. J. O. Halliwell (London, 1848), 65–68.

[2] Op. cit. 189–92.

[3] W. Chappell, *Popular Music of the Olden Time* (London, 1855–7), i. 193.

[4] See above, p. 198; cf. also Greene, *A Selection of English Carols*, 217–18, who notes this parallel.

[5] Gregory I provides this allegory in his exposition of Job xiii. 25, *Moralium Lib.* xi, ch. xliv, *P.L.* 75, 980. D. Robertson and B. Huppé, *Piers Plowman and the Scriptural Tradition* (Princeton, 1951), 193, n. 37, give this reference.

[6] *English Literature in the Sixteenth Century excluding Drama* (Oxford, 1954), 112.

With Sinnis I am laidnit soir,
Leif me not, leif me not,
With Sinnis I am laidnit soir
   Leif me not allone:
I pray the, Lord, thairfor,
Keip nocht my Sinnis in stoir,
Louse me, or I be forloir,
   And heir my mone.[1]

In this poem a plea to Christ for help and forgiveness has happily combined with the plea of a lover who fears that he (or she) may be forsaken, and the emotional intensity is equally fitting to both. The relating of religious to secular is therefore not a trick to catch the interest of the worldly, but is shown by the poet to stem from an illuminating likeness between the situations.

In that 'All my lufe, leif me not' is the plea of a sinner for help and not an expression of compassion, it may seem unmedieval in its emphasis though not in its feeling. A poem that is entirely medieval in design is the complaint of Christ beginning, 'Grevous is my sorrow'. It is modelled upon a late fifteenth-century poem, fortunately preserved in MS. Sloane 1584, which is the lament of an abandoned lover, killed by *unkyndnes*.[2] Both poems have in common the second half of each eight-line stanza, which is invariably a variation upon:

For unkyndnes haith kylled me
   And putt me to thys payne;
Alas, what Remedy
   That I cannott refrayne![3]

In the secular song the first half of each stanza is given to reflections upon the lover's plight, in the religious adaptation to an incident of the Passion:

Than to ane Croce on hie,
Thay nalit my bodie,
And syne betwen twa thevis,
   Thay did me mony grevis,
Till unkyndnes did keill me,
And put me to greit paine:
Allace! quhat remedie,
   I thocht nocht to refraine.[4]

Not only is this structural parallelism very satisfactory but also the religious poet has whenever possible precisely adapted the sense of his original. The lady's bequest of her heart, 'O harte, I the bequyeth / To hyme that is my deth' turns into Christ's committal of His soul into the hands of God, 'My Saule in thy handis fre, / My last will sall be'. This poem is quite as good as 'The borne is this word blinde' or 'The Newe Notbrowne Mayd', and, as in most good parodies, a keyword, in this instance *unkindnes*, has provided the inspiration for the successful adaptation.

---

[1] Op. cit. 220.   [2] Robbins, *Secular Lyrics*, 206.
[3] Ibid., p. 215.   [4] *Godlie Ballatis*, 153.

Another text of 'Grevous is my sorrow' survives separately from the *Godlie Ballatis* in MS. Dyce 45, a manuscript which contains another interesting parody, unknown until it was recently identified by Professor Greene,[1] and hitherto unprinted. It is as follows:

> Swete harte, be trwe,
> Chaunge for [no] newe,
> Come home to me agene;
> I shall full swetely
> Take the to mercye
> And delyver the owte of payne.

> When thou arte synfull
> My harte ys paynefull
> And bledyng for thy sake;
> Yete onece remember
> Howe my harte tender
> Will the to mercy take.

> Then love be trwe,
> Come and renewe
> Thyselfe yet wonse agayne;
> I shall full swetely
> Take the to mercye
> And delyver the owte of payne.

> A wownde full wyde,
> Deape in my syde,
> Was pearsed for þi sake;
> To grawnte þe grace
> For thy trespace,
> Thou mayste þi sorow slake.

> My dear harte trwe,
> Come and renewe
> Thyselfe yete onse agayne;
> Sometyme remember
> Howe my harte tender
> Thus for þi sake was slayne.

> Thys lover trwe,
> Whoo wolde renewe
> Mans soule to vertuouse lyfe,
> Ys Chryste Jesu
> Wythe hys vertu,
> Mans soule to be hys wyfe.

[1] *A Selection of English Carols*, 225.

Then love be trwe,
Come and renewe
Thyselfe yete onse agayne;
And I shall full swetly,
Take the to mercye
And delyver the owte of payne.[1]

The love-song upon which this is based seems not to have survived, but it was probably of fifteenth-century origin, since, as Professor Greene has pointed out,[2] the religious carol, 'Mankend I cale, wich lyith in frale', may well have borrowed its refrain from the same source. Though the element of Passion description in it is slight, it resembles 'The borne is this word blinde' in its emphasis upon the appeal to *come*, and, even more than the latter poem, it taps the same well of feeling as did some of the versions of the lover-knight theme with their associations with the parable of the prodigal Son.[3] The appeal to *come home* carries its full weight of loving forgiveness. There is, however, too much repetition in it for the poem to be fully successful, though the arrangement suggests that this was deliberate and it is of a kind that can be pleasant in song. Like 'All my lufe', however, it has an intimacy of tone unsuited to choral singing. The *Godlie Ballatis* were written as hymns and therefore the lack of a private tone in them is suited to their function though it makes them less good as poems. Intensity and intimacy are embarrassing in works designed for public choral singing, as they are in some of the hymns of Cowper. But, as with some of the *Olney Hymns*, the sixteenth-century parodies which exploit this tone make the best poems.

[1] MS. Dyce 45, 21ᵛ–22ʳ. In the manuscript the first two lines of the last stanza are in the reverse order.

[2] Op. cit. 225.   [3] See above, p. 46.

Index of First Lines of Religious Lyrics

Each lyric is entered under the form of the first line given in the edition or manuscript referred to in the text. Since this is often different from that of the *Index*, it is followed by the number of the *Index* or *Supplement* (a reference to the latter is always identifiable by the decimal point). Varieties of spelling are ignored in the arrangement and for convenience of the reference the spelling norm (as in the *Index*) is taken to be that of modern English.

Index of First Lines of Latin Poems, Hymns, and Antiphons

Poems invariably referred to by a title (for instance, the *Philomena* of John of Howden) are not included and will be found in the Index of Titles and Proper Names.

Index of Titles and Proper Names

Index of Themes and Subject-Matter

The aim of this index is to list alphabetically the identifiable themes of the lyrics. Some, such as the Crucifixion, recur so constantly, however, that it would be impracticable to include them.

PRINTED IN GREAT BRITAIN
AT THE UNIVERSITY PRESS, OXFORD
BY VIVIAN RIDLER
PRINTER TO THE UNIVERSITY